THE EXECUTIVE BRANCH OF STATE GOVERNMENT

People, Process, and Politics

Other Titles in ABC-CLIO's
ABOUT
STATE GOVERNMENT
Set

THE EXECUTIVE BRANCH OF STATE GOVERNMENT

People, Process, and Politics

Edited by
Margaret R. Ferguson

A B C ⬤ C L I O

Santa Barbara, California   Denver, Colorado   Oxford, England

Library of Congress Cataloging-in-Publication Data

The executive branch of state government : people, process, and politics / edited by Margaret R. Ferguson.
       p. cm. — (ABC-CLIO's about state government)
 Includes bibliographical references and index.
 ISBN 1-85109-771-6 (hardcover : alk. paper) — ISBN 1-85109-776-7 (ebook) 1. Executive departments--United States--States. 2. Administrative agencies—United States—States. 3. State governments--United States. 4. Governors—United States. I. Ferguson, Margaret Robertson. II. Series.
 JK2446.5.E94 2006
 352.3'2130973--dc22

                                                    2006001696

09 08 07 06   10 9 8 7 6 5 4 3 2 1
This book is also available on the World Wide Web as an eBook. Visit abc-clio.com for details.

ABC-CLIO, Inc.
130 Cremona Drive, P.O. Box 1911
Santa Barbara, California 93116–1911

Production Team
     Acquisitions Editor: Alicia Merritt
     Media Editor: Karen Koppel
     Media Resources Manager: Caroline Price
     Production Editor: Martha Ripley Gray
     Editorial Assistant: Alisha Martinez
     Production Manager: Don Schmidt
     Manufacturing Coordinator: George Smyser

Text Design: Darice Zimmermann, ZimmServices LLC

This book is printed on acid-free paper ∞ .
Manufactured in the United States of America

To my family

CONTENTS

FOREWORD

Most Americans have some familiarity with the role and structure of the federal government. At an early age, we are taught in school about the president of the United States and the roles performed by the three branches of the federal government: the legislative, the executive, and the judicial. In civics classes, we are often given a skeletal picture of how the nation's government works; we are told that Congress writes the laws, the president executes them, and the Supreme Court acts as the interpreter of the U.S. Constitution. Outside of the classroom, the media repeatedly remind us of the important duties that all three branches play in the nation's political system. Through television news, radio talk shows, newspapers, magazines, and web blogs, the media draw our attention to the major political battles in Washington, D.C., building our knowledge of the president, Congress, and the U.S. Supreme Court.

While most Americans have some knowledge of the federal government, they tend to know far less about their state governments. Our schools frequently teach us about the governments in our own states, yet what we learn about state government does not become as deeply ingrained as what we learn about the federal government. The media do little to improve our knowledge about the states. With their attention primarily drawn to conflict in the nation's Capitol, the media tend to devote little attention to the politics in our state capitols.

The lack of knowledge about state government is unfortunate because state governments today play a major role in American politics. Certainly, one cannot dismiss the importance of the federal government. The president, Congress, and the Supreme Court routinely address some of the most vital political issues confronting the nation today, from the health of the economy to the advancement of civil rights to whether the nation will go to war or seek peace. Yet on a day-to-day basis, the state governments may have an even greater effect on our lives, for they tend to be directly responsible for establishing most of the laws under which we live and for providing the everyday services that we need to survive. The importance of state governments can be seen by simply noting three facts.

- State legislatures produce more laws than the U.S. Congress. Combined, more than 20,000 new laws are passed each year across the states, with an average of more than 400 new laws per state. Congress tends to adopt fewer than 300 laws in a given year. State laws are essential because they constitute most of the rules governing criminal behavior in the nation and help shape such things as the character of our schools, the strength of the states' economies, the type of help that is provided to the needy, the quality of our roads, and the health of the environment.

- State governments are large and growing. Their growth has been outpacing that of the federal government for the past several decades. In fact, the expansion of government bureaucracy over the past three decades has come primarily at the state and local level, while the number of federal employees has seen little change. As of 2004, more than 5 million people were working for state governments compared with 2.7 million for the federal government. Another 11 million people are employed by local governments, many of whom handle responsibilities determined by the state government.
- Far more cases are heard in state courts each year than in the federal courts. In an average year, more than 93 million cases are filed in state courts. This compares with approximately 2.6 million cases filed in the federal courts.

Not only does state politics matter, but state governments are in many ways different from the federal government. The three branches of government are common to both the national and the fifty state governments, yet beyond this rather cosmetic similarity, significant differences exist. One of the most central is that while the executive branch of the national government is led by one individual—the president—the executive branch of state governments is led by several executives. Beyond the governor, who is the state's chief executive, the fifty states have other elected executives who have their own independent responsibilities and sources of power, including such figures as the lieutenant governor, the secretary of state, the attorney general, the treasurer, and the superintendent of public instruction.

The state legislatures also vary considerably from Congress. Some of them, most notably the California and New York legislatures, look a lot like Congress, meeting year-round, with full-time staff and well-paid members. Yet other legislatures, such as those in Wyoming and South Dakota, meet only briefly every year or every other year, have minimal staff support, and pay members very little. The legislature in Nebraska, unlike Congress or any other state, has only one chamber and is the only nonpartisan legislature in the nation. With 400 representatives, the house of representatives in the state of New Hampshire has almost as many members as the 435-seat U.S. House. The boundaries for all state senate districts in the nation are based on population so that each district in a given state has approximately the same number of residents, whereas population does not affect the number of members each state elects to the U.S. Senate. All states elect two U.S. senators, even though the states vary widely in population.

The state courts are similarly distinctive. One of the most significant differences between the state and federal courts is that all state court judges are selected through some type of election, whereas federal judges are appointed by the president with senate approval. Thus, state court judges are more directly beholden to the public. State courts are also affected by variations in state constitutions, some of which grant more extensive rights and liberties than what is set forth in the U.S. Constitution. Thus, important differences may exist across the states in what the state supreme courts will consider constitutional and unconstitutional.

These differences across the states and between the states and federal government affect how politics is practiced, who wins and who loses, the substance of state laws, the extent to which government pays attention to voters, the ability of government to fulfill its responsibilities, the types of rights and liberties we enjoy, and the type of people who are elected to public office. Learning about state government provides a means for understanding different ways in which democratic government can be structured and how those differences affect us.

Part of the reason that Americans know so little about state government is likely a result of the strong emphasis placed on the federal government by the media and the schools, but some of it also reflects the lack of available resources on state governments. Numerous books are devoted to the national government generally and to each of the three branches of the national government, yet there are very few places where you can turn to find information about the structure and character of state governments. If you want to understand how government and politics works in the states, it is just not easy to do so. The few scholarly books available on state governments can be difficult to locate, narrow in scope, or hard for someone unfamiliar with government studies to understand. A few general reference books on American politics touch on topics related to state government, but these often provide only a bit of the picture of how state government works. You can also find books on the governments of individual states, but these tell you little as to how the structure of government and character of politics in those states compare with the government and politics in other states. Simply put, there is no reference work available that focuses solely on explaining the workings of state government across the nation.

About State Government is designed to help fill this gap by providing a comprehensive source of information on state government for high school students, college undergraduates, and the general public. The *About State Government* reference set consists of three volumes, with each volume devoted to a different branch of state government: the legislative, the executive, and the judiciary. All three volumes provide general information about the states, explaining major trends found across the states, while also pointing out important differences that make some states unique or unusual. The books explain how each branch of state government has changed over time, what roles the three branches play in state politics, how the three branches are structured, who serves in them, and how these individuals are selected. The books also describe the character of politics in the states today, the relationship among the different branches of government, some of the major problems confronting state government, and modern proposals for political reform. Each volume also includes a lengthy chapter providing information on the governments state by state, including a description of how each state government is structured, an overview of how the elected officials are selected, and some insights into the character of politics in each state. All three books include a glossary of terms, a comprehensive index, and an annotated bibliography to provide direction for further study.

This set will not make everyone in the nation as familiar with state government as they are with the federal government. But it should provide a good starting place for those who have questions about government in the nation's fifty states and are looking for a book to provide them with answers.

Richard A. Clucas
Portland State University

PREFACE AND ACKNOWLEDGMENTS

This volume looks closely at the governors, the other key statewide actors, and the many offices of the state bureaucracy that together comprise the executive branch of state government. It traces the historical development of the governorship and the changing features of the office over time, while also focusing on the personal and professional characteristics of the individuals who have occupied that office. It attempts to place the governors in the larger political context of the states so that the reader can understand their true function in state politics. This volume also devotes attention to the multitude of other elective and appointive offices and principal actors in state bureaucracies who have been introduced over the years to accomplish the work of administering the growing number of state government programs.

Like state governments in general, the executive branch has undergone a remarkable transformation since the early days of limited powers and few responsibilities. Today, governors are the most prominent actors at the state level. They receive the lion's share of media coverage in their states and represent those states in interactions with citizens and leaders in other states as well as with the national government in Washington and even the governments of other countries. All of these factors have contributed to the central role that modern governors play in the politics and policymaking of their states. However, their authority, while great, is not unlimited. The separation-of-powers system in the United States requires that multiple actors work together to achieve their political goals. Governors must share power with many other players in the state and national political arenas.

The challenges for governors, however, go beyond those traditionally associated with the separation of governmental power into three branches. The states typically have "plural executives." Unlike the national government, in which only the president and vice-president are elected, these states elect multiple statewide officials, most commonly including lieutenant governors, secretaries of state, attorneys general, auditors, and treasurers. The fact that governors share executive branch responsibilities with other elected officials who have their own reservoirs of public support affects their ability to dominate in the executive arena, despite holding the title of chief executive granted by most state constitutions. Similarly, while governors carry the informal title of chief legislator, they must work with many other important actors in their quests to influence state lawmaking. The governors' priorities often define the states' legislative agendas, but they do not dictate the final outcomes. Successful governors are those who manage to maneuver within the complicated state policy process, making use of formal and informal powers, forging coalitions with other like-minded officials.

The governor, other statewide elected officials, and the bureaucracy make up the executive branch. However, in practice, the governor stands apart. Though the chief executive is officially the head of the state bureaucracy, he or she and the bureaucracy act independently enough of one another that it is easier analytically to treat them as separate entities. Accordingly, for ease of discussion, this volume does just that, conceptually dividing the executive branch between the governors, on one side, and the bureaucracy (including other statewide elected officers), on the other.

Chapter 1 gives a broad overview of the state executive branch, both as it exists today and as it was throughout the nation's history.

Chapter 2 provides a detailed look at the many roles fulfilled by governors across the country and the powers they use to carry out these roles.

Chapter 3 examines the makeup of the rest of the executive branch and discusses the many actors other than the governor who do the work of executing the laws of the states.

Chapter 4 offers a closer look at the people who hold the office of governor. It investigates the paths that governors typically follow to get to the office and where they go on leaving it. It also discusses the growth of staffs surrounding the governorship, for as their responsibilities have expanded, governors have required more assistance to get their job done. This chapter also presents a discussion of gubernatorial campaigns and elections.

Chapter 5 addresses the complicated politics surrounding the executive branch. State legislatures are vital components in the work of state governments, and governors must interact with them in the pursuit of their legislative goals. This chapter also describes the various actors outside of state government who will have an impact on the work of the governor. Finally, the chapter considers the question of who controls the executive branch. It examines the struggle between making the executive branch independent and efficient and yet also responsive to the needs of the governor and other state officials.

Chapter 6 presents a description of the executive branch in each of the fifty states. It describes the essential workings of the institutions in every state and points out characteristics that make each state unique.

A volume of this sort could never have been produced by a single individual. Richard Clucas, the series editor, provided a wealth of editorial advice that improved the manuscript immensely. His eye for detail and his mastery of the subject matter continually impressed me. My student Thomas Schlatter performed a great deal of the research for the early phase of the book. I am indebted to the Office for Women at Indiana University at Indianapolis for providing financial resources to support his contribution. Cynthia Bowling, my colleague at Auburn University, undertook an enormous research task in preparing Chapter 3. She willingly prepared a much larger contribution than she had signed on for, and as usual, it was a pleasure to work with her. Professor Deil

Wright of the University of North Carolina, who has been my mentor since my first days as a graduate student there, encouraged my interest in executive leadership. More than anything, he believed I had something to contribute, and that fact encouraged and sustained me through the many challenges of graduate school and continues to do so today.

I would like to thank the many people at ABC-CLIO who did the hard work of taking what my co-authors and I wrote and finally bringing the project to fruition. In particular I thank Alicia Merritt, who has since retired, for her support in the early phase of this work, and Martha Gray, our production editor, for her tireless work under occasionally trying conditions. They were both very supportive of me as a new author and both a pleasure to work with. Thanks also to Darice Zimmermann, who created the beautiful design, and to media editor Karen Koppel, who gathered the photos.

Finally, as in all things, I owe thanks to my family. My father, a political scientist and onetime state elected official, sparked an interest in state politics in me at an early age, and he continues to be a sounding board for me. My mother gave of her time and attention very generously so that I could complete the final work on this book. My husband and my son are a constant source of happiness when I complete my work each day. I owe them my thanks for their support as well.

Margaret R. Ferguson
Indianapolis, Indiana
February 2006

CONTRIBUTORS

J. Michael Bitzer, assistant professor of political science at Catawba College in North Carolina, received his Ph.D. from the University of Georgia. He teaches courses in the fields of American politics, public administration, and policy, as well as constitutional law, administrative law, and judicial politics. Professor Bitzer's research areas include American politics, public law, and public administration. His research has been published in *Law and Society, Review of Public Personnel Administration,* the *Encyclopedia of Public Administration and Public Policy,* the *Encyclopedia of Civil Liberties in America,* the *Encyclopedia of American Federalism,* and the *Encyclopedia of American Parties and Elections.*

Jeffrey M. Blankenship is a Ph.D. candidate in public administration and public policy at Auburn University. He received a bachelor's degree in political science from the University of Alabama in Huntsville, his J.D. from the University of Alabama School of Law, and his MPA from the University of Alabama at Birmingham. His primary academic interests include public finance and budgeting; personnel administration; state and local politics; and campaign management.

Cynthia J. Bowling, associate professor of political science at Auburn University, received her Ph.D. from the University of North Carolina at Chapel Hill. She is currently the codirector of the American State Administrators Project, a large, multiyear research project surveying chief administrators in the states. She formerly served as director of the Master in Public Administration program at Auburn University. Her research has appeared in the *Journal of Politics, Public Administration Review,* and *State and Local Government Review.* Professor Bowling teaches courses on public administration and methods.

Brendan Burke, associate professor of political science at Bridgewater State University, received his Ph.D. from the University of North Carolina at Chapel Hill. He teaches courses on state and local government, organization theory, public finance, and program evaluation. He served as a senior budget analyst and assistant to chief executives in Prince William County, Virginia, and Wake County, North Carolina, prior to his academic career. His research interests include state and local bureaucratic performance, power and influence in organizations, and financial management strategies and techniques. He has published in *State and Local Government Review* and in the *Encyclopedia of Public Administration and Public Policy.*

Margaret R. Ferguson, associate professor of political science at Indiana University at Indianapolis, received her Ph.D. from the University of North Carolina at Chapel Hill. Her research interests include governors, legislatures, and lawmaking in the states;

executive branch politics; leadership and personality; and social capital and the quality of government. Her research has been published in the *Journal of Politics, Women and Politics, Political Psychology,* and *State Politics and Policy Quarterly.* Professor Ferguson teaches courses on state politics, southern politics, Congress, and the presidency.

Joseph J. Foy is an assistant professor of political science at the University of Wisconsin at Waukesha and earned a Ph.D. from the University of Notre Dame. A Manatt Fellow for Democracy Studies at the International Foundation for Election Systems in 2002, he was also a recipient of the Kaneb Center Award for Outstanding Teaching as a Graduate Student from the University of Notre Dame. He is currently completing a project that explores the relationship between traditional measures of gubernatorial power and the effects such measures have on policy outcomes and implementation across the states.

Jennifer J. Hora, assistant professor of public policy and political science at Roanoke College, earned a Ph.D. at the University of North Carolina at Chapel Hill. She teaches classes on American politics, public policy, public administration, and state and local politics. Her research interests include legislatures and executives, with a particular emphasis on presidential persuasion. Professor Hora's research has been published in *Presidential Studies Quarterly.*

Christine A. Kelleher is an assistant professor of political science at the University of Michigan at Dearborn. Her research and teaching interests include state and urban politics, women in politics, the policy process, and welfare policy. She has published articles in *Urban Affairs Review, Political Research Quarterly,* the *Journal of Public Administration Research and Theory (J-PART), Policy Studies Journal,* and *Public Administration Review.* She received her Ph.D. from the University of North Carolina at Chapel Hill. In 2004, Professor Kelleher received an award for the best dissertation defended that year, presented by the Urban Politics Section of the American Political Science Association.

James McDowell, professor of political science at Indiana State University, earned his doctorate in political science and communications from the University of Illinois at Urbana-Champaign. Professor McDowell teaches classes in American government, state and local government, political parties, the legislative process, and the presidency. His recent publications have appeared in the *Illinois Political Science Review, Southeastern Political Review, Spectrum: The Journal of State Government,* and *Comparative State Politics.* Other recent publications include chapters in *Money, Politics and Campaign Finance Reform Law in the States* (ed. David A. Schultz), and *Indiana Politics and Public Policy* (ed. Maurice M. Eisenstein).

Kristina K. Sheeler is an assistant professor of communication studies at Indiana University at Indianapolis. Her research focuses on rhetorical theory and criticism, women's public discourse, political communication, and public address. Her teaching interests include rhetorical theory and criticism, American public discourse, gender studies, persuasion, political communication, interpersonal communication, public speaking, and business communication. She received her Ph.D. from Indiana University. Recent publications include a book entitled *Governing Codes: Gender, Metaphor, and Political Identity* (co-edited with Karrin Vasby Anderson) and chapters in *American Voices: An Encyclopedia of Contemporary American Oratory* (ed. Bernard K. Duffy and Richard W. Leeman) and *Navigating Boundaries: The Rhetoric of Women Governors* (ed. Brenda DeVore Marshall and Molly A. Mayhead).

Neal Woods received his doctoral education at the University of Kentucky, where he specialized in public policy and administration and American politics. His research and teaching interests are in public administration, public policy, and American politics. His research focus lies at the nexus of political institutions and public policy, with an emphasis on how differing institutional arrangements affect policy outcomes. To date, his research has primarily involved the relationship of bureaucratic actors to their external political environments, including elected officials and interest groups. Other current research projects look at joint federal-state policy implementation and the policy role of state governors. His work has been published in the *Journal of Public Administration Research and Theory* and *Policy Studies Journal*.

1

INTRODUCTION TO STATE EXECUTIVES

Margaret R. Ferguson

The executive branch in the American states, like the states themselves, has undergone many dramatic changes in the course of the nation's history. Governors have evolved from overbearing representatives of the British monarchy to mere figureheads with the power to do neither good nor bad for the states and then to vital policy leaders both within the states and in the country as a whole. In part, their fortunes are tied to the fortunes of the states. Simply put, governors in the twenty-first century are important in part because their states are important.

Yet governors are not the only leaders in the states. Consequently, understanding governors and their multiple functions requires understanding the broader political system in which they serve. The American system makes sure that a single actor can rarely get too much done on his or her own. Accordingly, governors must work with their state legislatures, with other executive branch officials, and even with actors outside their states to accomplish their goals. The governors' role is often controversial, for Americans have always been uncomfortable with executive power. On the one hand, history tells us that power corrupts and absolute power corrupts absolutely. But on the other hand, history tells us that executive power is necessary if governments are to function with anything approaching efficiency and effectiveness. Because of this historical ambivalence, the official characteristics of the governorship have often prevented governors from rising to the challenges facing their states. This situation sometimes led to frustration and disillusionment among the citizenry, who asked why their governments could not solve their problems. In other instances, governors handicapped by limited legal powers exercised extralegal (or illegal) powers to attempt to meet the needs of the people (and sometimes to satisfy their own selfish desires). As American society has become more complicated and the expectations of the citizens for their governments have grown, states have moved to bring their governmental actors in line with citizen expectations. States have empowered their governments. Governors have surely benefited from these reforms and now can truly act as leaders in their states.

Parallel developments have occurred in other parts of the executive branch. Though governors are the most visible individuals in this branch, they are surely not the only important officials. Just as governors have gained greater powers, state bureaucracies have grown larger and more professional. While many state bureaucrats were once chosen by a political spoils system, most of the positions in the executive branch today are filled by a merit system. Bureaucrats now have greater knowledge and expertise regarding their areas of responsibility, and they are less hampered by the political expectations of the governors. This professionalization, which is necessary for the effective planning and carrying out of law, can also cause governors difficulty as they try to direct the work of state administrators, resulting in a core conflict in the executive branch. Other conflicts exist as well. In addition to the large portion of bureaucrats who are hired, many other top-level officials in the states are either appointed by the governor or elected by the public in their own right. Key examples of these important executive actors are the lieutenant governors, attorneys general, secretaries of state, and treasurers. Though the responsibilities of each of these officials vary somewhat from state to state, their underlying roles and duties are quite similar across the country. Due to the sharing of governmental responsibility, governors frequently need the help of these officials to achieve their goals. Such support may or may not be forthcoming, for many reasons that will be examined in this volume.

FUNDAMENTALS OF THE EXECUTIVE BRANCH

While one could spend a career studying the ins and outs of the state executive branch, certain fundamentals clearly need to be appreciated by anyone seeking a general understanding of the topic. This section will identify and discuss four primary features of the governorship and the state bureaucracy. The first point is that the entire topic varies significantly over time. Second, governors today are central figures, and so, it is important to understand the powers and responsibilities of the governorship and the characteristics of the people seeking and serving in the office. Third, the rest of the state executive branch, the state bureaucracy, has undergone a transformation equivalent to that of the governor. These agencies also carry out vital tasks of state government. Fourth, the governor and the executive branch must share power with many other actors in the overall quest to implement the laws of the states.

The Constancy of Change

The first fundamental feature of the state executive branch is that it seems to be constantly evolving. In short, the story of the executive branch is a story of change in the role of the states in the American political system, the place of the executive branch in the states, the features of the various executive offices, and the characteristics of the people who pursue and serve in these offices. The tale will certainly continue, but as the story stands today, the states and the governors are central to the narrative.

The power of the states in American federalism has changed dramatically through the years. The national government has generally gained power over time. However, since the 1980s, states have also come to occupy a particularly significant place in American policymaking. Responsibilities once carried out by the national government have been handed over, or devolved, to the states. In turning these responsibilities over to the states, the national government sometimes sends the money to pay for the services they entail—but sometimes it does not. Under an assortment of labels, the shifting of the focus to the states has been ongoing for many years. Though efforts to increase state power have traditionally been associated with conservatives, the ideological divide between conservatives and liberals in this regard is no longer really relevant. Conservative Republican president Ronald Reagan was a main proponent of shifting responsibility to the states in the 1980s, but the trend has continued under presidents in the 1990s and early 2000s—both Democrats and Republicans.

The current place of the states in the American federal system bolsters the position of the governors because they are such central figures in those states. The prominence of governors has grown due to the political climate since the 1990s, in which state governments are assumed to be invigorated, capable, and willing to address the problems of their constituents. The argument goes like this. The state governments are closest to the people. They know their needs and their desires, and they can best serve them in welfare, health care, and a variety of other critical areas. It is clear that the so-called devolution revolution has given the states more work to do and increased the visibility of governors. What is somewhat less clear is whether these changes have actually altered the essential power structure. Some scholars assert that laws passed by the national government in recent years, such as the No Child Left Behind legislation and the Homeland Security Act, actually pull greater power to the central government. But whether or not the fundamental power relationships have changed, states are prominent features of the American political system.

Governors generally have embraced this new position of prominence. Though complaining loudly about "unfunded mandates" from the federal government (those laws passed by Congress that require the states to provide services but without federal funding), governors assert that the states can and will carry out the necessary work. They believe that they best know the needs and desires of "their people" and are most likely to do what it takes to care for them. They also believe that the citizens will hold them accountable for the state's condition when they go to the polls to vote, and research about voting behavior tends to bear this out.

Governors: Central Figures in the States

The second fundamental feature of the state executive branch is that the governors are the key actors. Part of the explanation for their prominence lies in the changes that have been made in the office itself. The governorship has been granted new powers, and the people seeking and winning the office are different now as well. They are younger, better educated, and more diverse than ever before. All of these changes produce more ambitious and active governors, which in turn leads to their current high profile.

Formal Powers of the Governorship

The power of the governorship has varied dramatically since the office was created during colonial times. In fact, the governorship has undergone a metamorphosis on more than one occasion. Despite the controversy surrounding colonial governors and the weakness of the governors that followed, modern governors are the states' central figures, the symbolic heads of the states. They are the chief executive officers (CEOs), to borrow a term from industry—the economic development managers and the legislative leaders. They are the primary focus of the state news media as well. The governors' transformation has occurred simultaneously with the ascendance of the states in the U.S. federal system. So both governors and the states they lead have taken on a new importance.

Modern governors have a direct connection to the voters. They are among a very few elected officials who can legitimately claim to serve all of the people in the state, since they are elected by the entire voting public, not just the voters in any one district. They capture the public's attention more than any other government official at the state level, and they have greater access to the media than any other political actor. Though media attention sometimes has negative consequences (such as when governors become involved in scandals), coverage generally enhances the governors' position in the states and the nation, highlighting their activities and reinforcing the public's sense that they are in charge. And governors are surely a primary focal point of governmental action in the states. Former North Carolina governor Terry Sanford (1967, 185–188) summarized the chief executive's significance in this way: "The governor, by his very office embodies his state. He stands alone at his inauguration as the spokesman for all the people. . . . Few major undertakings ever get off the ground without his support and leadership. The governor sets the agenda for public debate; frames the issues; decides on the timing; and can blanket the state with good ideas by using his access to the mass media. . . . The governor is the most potent political power in the state." Governor Sanford wrote those words in 1967. The role of the governor has become even more prominent since that time.

The features of the governorship have undergone many changes over the years, and nearly all of these changes have served to make the office more significant. Joseph Schlesinger (1965) identified four categories of power: tenure potential (length of term and chances for reelection), the veto, budget power, and appointment power. He then classified each of the states as to how much power the governor had in each category. Political scientists have continued to employ Schlesinger's index to examine and compare the formal power of governors. Each of these elements is believed to strengthen governors in some way. Longer tenure means governors are in office long enough to develop skills and expertise and build relationships they can draw on in the future. The veto and budget power both give the governor a direct influence on lawmaking. These powers assure that the legislature must work with the governor in crafting state law. Finally, the appointment power assists the governor in the administrative arena. It means the governor gets to choose who will hold the highest-level positions in the bureaucracy. Administrators who are appointed by the governor are more likely to follow his or her lead.

In each of these categories, most governors tended to be very weak in the early part of the nation's history. But in the twenty-first century, governors are far more powerful as judged by these indicators. So the general national trend has been toward a strengthened governorship. However, governors across the country still vary significantly in the powers that the office provides to them. Later in this book, each of these powers—and the ways in which they differ both across states and over time—will be examined more closely. In addition, Chapter 6 provides detailed descriptions of the executive branch, including the governorship, on a state-by-state basis.

It is also important to remember that governors do not hold—or exercise—their powers in a vacuum. No matter how much the formal powers of governors have grown, other actors in the states continue to pursue their own goals as well, and these actors have powers, too. As it happens, state legislatures have also changed greatly during the period when governors have been granted enhanced formal powers. So at times, the powers of state legislatures may limit the ability of the governors to achieve their goals.

Because of the separation-of-powers system, governors and legislators have to work together to at least some degree, and they do so quite well on occasion, in pursuit of a shared goal. Yet people commonly discuss the governor as if he or she is in a constant battle with the legislature, and to be sure, they often do come into conflict. Their conflicts are sometimes driven by political party differences; sometimes they are caused by the fact that governors and legislators tend to view the world differently. Given the ongoing potential for conflict, people tend to think of a governor's power as something that can be used in opposition to the legislature. Put another way, they ask what tools the governor possesses that he or she can use against the legislators.

Personal Characteristics of the Governors

The changing features of the institutions of the executive branch are surely a major part of the story. However, it is also important to understand that the people who seek the governor's office today are, by and large, better qualified and more capable than ever before. Though the formal qualifications for office have not changed, governors today typically are better prepared than their predecessors were. They are more highly educated and professional. Thus, nearly all governors serving in 2004 had earned university degrees, and twenty-two held law degrees. Most governors also had served in other public offices prior to being elected to the governorship, and some had significant professional experience outside of government. (Members of Congress now sometimes leave Washington to run for the governorship of their home states.) Other governors held state legislative seats before seeking the governorship. Still others served in different statewide elected offices before becoming governor. Though individuals occasionally run for this position without having held a prior elective office, this is rather rare; only eleven of the current governors came to the governorship never having held office before.

Furthermore, governors today are younger on average than their predecessors—the current average age is five years lower than that in the 1940s—and younger governors are generally more energetic and more ambitious. The people holding the offices today are also more diverse than their predecessors. Like most governmental figures, governors were overwhelmingly white men throughout the nation's history. While a majority of governors even now fit that characterization, significant changes have occurred in terms of the diversity of governors in recent years. Douglas Wilder, elected to the Virginia governor's office in 1990, was the first (and, to date, the only) African American to be elected governor. Several Asian American governors have served in the office in Hawaii and Washington, and several Hispanics have attained the office as well. In addition, twenty-seven women have held governorships, though early female governors were more often stand-ins for their husbands than leaders in their own right. This is certainly not the case in the modern period. In 2004, nine of the nation's governors were women.

All of these changes indicate that the people who are elected governor today are more reflective of the diversity of their states' citizenry. They are therefore arguably more aware of and better able to meet the needs of their states. They are also anxious to really do something with the office. They have policy goals and ideas about how they would like to see their states grow and change.

Roles and Responsibilities of the Governorship

Another reason for the centrality of the governorship is the many key responsibilities of the office. The office of governor carries with it various roles or sets of jobs and responsibilities. Though the governorship varies from state to state and different events facing a state bring particular roles to the forefront, each of these roles is undertaken to at least some degree by governors in all fifty states. Further, the formal powers granted to the governor are important for carrying out each of these roles. Informal powers (those not associated with the office) will also assist governors in fulfilling these roles. Some of these powers grow from the personal features of those holding the office. But though all powers are important, not all of the powers of the governor are useful in pursuing all of the roles he or she is assigned. For example, the appointment power is most useful for a governor working in the role of chief executive, whereas the veto power is especially important for a governor acting as chief legislator. The discussion that follows identifies the many roles governors play and points out the powers that they use most often in the pursuit of these roles.

Chief Legislator.   One primary role of the governor in the modern period is that of the chief legislator. Most observers assert that governors have a great deal of influence in the legislative arena. They are perceived as the major policy initiators and the "change masters." The media clearly view the governors as holding this important position. So, too, do state legislators.

The political system is set up to include the governor in lawmaking. Formal powers such as the veto and the executive budget, in addition to the presentation of the state of the state address that is required of all governors, assure that the governor is a legitimate player in the legislative arena. In fact, the constitutional system of separation of powers means that legislatures must depend on the governor to serve as their partner in the formulation of public policy.

While one might suspect that legislators would resent the governor intruding into lawmaking, that does not seem to be the case. In fact, to the extent there is concern on the part of the legislators about the policy role of the governor, it is often that the governor is *not active enough*. Legislators as a whole seem to follow the old adage "the governor proposes, the legislature disposes."

State governments are set up in such a way that the governor and the legislature both have a great deal of power and responsibility for making the laws. In some cases, governors and legislators may work closely together almost like a team, each helping the other to achieve common goals. In other cases, though, the governor and some legislators may not agree on what policies would be best for the state. This situation is especially likely to occur under divided government (when the governor and a majority of legislators do not share a party attachment), but it can also happen under unified government.

Chief Executive.   Another important role for the governor is that of the state's chief executive. Governors are charged by their state constitutions with responsibility to "see that the laws are faithfully executed" by the many people and organizations that comprise the executive branch (the state bureaucracy). Needless to say, this job is quite complicated.

After laws are passed by the state legislature (and even sometimes by the U.S. Congress), they must be put into action by the state executive branch. Bureaucracies are large and complicated and notoriously difficult to manage. State bureaucracies are made up of individuals who come to their jobs by many different paths—some are simply hired, some are appointed by boards or commissions, some are elected, and some are appointed by the governor. Governors are expected to oversee these bureaucracies to make sure the laws are carried out in an effective and efficient manner. They also may want the laws to be carried out in a particular fashion, based on their opinions about good policy. While bureaucracies are insulated from political influences in many ways, governors certainly hope to influence their direction.

Typically, individuals working within the executive branch exercise at least some discretion as they write the rules and regulations that will put laws into effect. At times at least, governors attempt to influence how that discretion is used. The job of chief executive offers the governor some opportunity in this area, but as in the other arenas, the governor's freedom to direct the administration of the state is limited by various factors.

The chief executive role is a critical part of the governor's job, but it is not the subject of much public attention, and there are few political rewards for fulfilling this role well. Nevertheless, a governor ignores this role at his or her peril. The key to effective management for the governor seems to lie in concentrating on building other bases of support to free up resources for the necessary (but sometimes thankless) job of management.

Chief of State.   The chief of state is a largely symbolic role played by the governor. In this capacity, he or she serves as a symbol of the state, embodying the state to those outside its boundaries. The governor is the most visible state governmental actor. At home, the citizenry most often looks to the governor as the designated leader to set the direction the state will go and to bring the state together in times of crisis or disaster. The governor is the face of the state. This symbolic role as the embodiment of the state works to the benefit of both the governor and the citizenry. It keeps the governor connected to the public to some degree. As he or she travels the state holding town meetings or reaching out to citizens in various other ways, the governor is better able to stay in touch with the needs and desires of the public. This role also reinforces the idea that it is the governor who sits at the top of the state government, which further encourages the citizens to look to that individual for leadership.

Chief of Party.   As the highest elected officials in the states, governors also typically serve as the heads of their party organizations, attending party functions and often helping to raise money for the party's candidates. Governors may also serve an internal leadership role, working to iron out disputes among factions within the party that might weaken it if not addressed. While governors are not as dependent on their parties for support as they used to be, they must still pay attention to them and work to serve party needs in addition to their own. Cohesive support from one's party is also the best predictor of success in the legislative arena, so attention to party building is often a key priority for governors.

Intergovernmental Liaison.   Much of the work of the governor involves offering leadership within the home state. However, since the United States has a federal system, decisions that are made in Washington, D.C., will often have a significant impact on the state government. National government decisions may affect state government's access to resources. Further, programs developed by the national government must often be administered at the state level, which may create new burdens on the state government, responsibilities that it may or may not view as welcome changes. Because of the interwoven nature of the American federal system, every state government needs to have a presence in Washington, D.C.

Given the multilayered but overlapping powers of governments in the American system, governors must be concerned with the issues, problems, and governmental activities that take place in Washington and even perhaps in state capitals across the country. If anything, the many layers of government are more interrelated than ever before, and governors must pay attention to this fact.

Military Chief.   Though defense and security issues are most often associated with the president and the national government, governors do serve a military role within their states. Governors are the commanders-in-chief of the state militias, with the responsibility to protect the safety of the states' citizens. The National Guard has served multiple roles in the history of the states. Since World War II, Guard units have often served in rescue and relief missions in the wake of tornadoes, hurricanes, and floods. The governors' military role continues to evolve with the times. For example, governors have become key leaders on the issue of homeland security following the terrorist attacks of September 2001.

Chief Judge.   Like the president of the United States, governors also have the ability to grant pardons to convicted offenders. This power was occasionally the subject of controversy in the past, as some corrupt governors were found to be selling pardons. Generally, this power was used to right egregious wrongs in the judicial system. Today, many states employ clemency boards to assist the governors in making decisions, especially in death penalty cases. Further, governors typically participate in the decision to grant paroles for offenders in the state. This function has become increasingly important as many states' prisons are critically overcrowded.

The State Bureaucracy

The previous sections have examined the growing power and current preeminence of the governors in the American states. However, governors are not the only important actors in the state executive branches. The transformation of the state bureaucracies is the third fundamental development regarding the executive branch in the modern period. The earliest state governments were poorly organized. They were filled with people who got their jobs because of who they knew rather than what they knew. The role of the states has surely changed. Revitalized states with great and growing responsibilities now require better governmental structures to carry out their responsibilities. State bureaucracies have grown in size and in the scope of their activities, and they have also professionalized. They are now quite capable of doing the work of state government, and they play a very significant role in governing the United States.

One of the primary jobs of the governors is to take care that the laws are faithfully executed. However, governors cannot do the work of carrying out state laws on their own. Instead, in each of the states, thousands of officials—some elected, some hired, and others appointed—comprise the executive branch. It is the job of these public officials to assist the governors in implementing state law. The executive branch is typically referred to as the bureaucracy. Though the word *bureaucracy* is often associated with inefficiency and incompetence in the minds of outside observers, the reality is that state bureaucracies typically do a remarkable job of putting the laws passed by the legislatures and governors into action. The general term *bureaucracy* signifies a method of organizing complex institutions. It has two features: a hierarchical organization and a division of labor. While many entities, both public and private, are bureaucratic in nature, the term *bureaucracy* typically refers to the branch of government in charge of implementing or executing the laws.

There are more than 16.7 million employees of states and localities. The vast majority of these people work in the executive branch. State bureaucracies have grown steadily in the last 100 years even while the size of the federal bureaucracy has remained rather stable. The size and rate of the growth of state bureaucracies roughly matches the growth in state government responsibility. As the states undertook greater and more varied responsibilities, capacity had to be built in the executive branch to carry the work forward and actually put into action the laws passed by the legislature and the governor.

The Separation of Powers: Placing the Executive Branch in the American System

While it is certainly true that the governor is a major actor today, the fourth fundamental factor to keep in mind is that the governor and the bureaucracy must share power with many other actors both within and outside the state. Since the United States has a federal system of government, the national government in Washington, D.C., has a continual impact on what state governments can and must do. Above all, the U.S. government is a government of divisions and limitations. First, the system has a separation of powers, which means that governmental responsibility is divided into three branches, each with its own set of responsibilities. The legislative branch principally makes the law, the executive branch has the main responsibility of carrying out or executing the law, and the judicial branch is charged with interpreting the law. Each of the branches possesses certain responsibilities, and each of these institutions must also share power with many other institutions. This sharing and overlapping of powers was the founders' way of limiting the power of government and making sure that no particular element of government could overpower any other.

While governors are most often thought of as executives—meaning they are responsible for executing or carrying out the laws of the state—they also have legislative responsibilities. They have the power to sign or veto legislation and to participate in the budget-making process. Governors and legislatures therefore share the lawmaking power. Governors must work with or through their states' legislatures to accomplish nearly all of their lawmaking goals. Such overlapping of powers exists outside the legislative arena, too.

Even within the executive arena, governors are rarely autonomous actors. While they theoretically sit at the top of the state bureaucracy, they share the job of executing the laws with hundreds of other executive officials in the state. Understanding American government in general and the states in particular therefore requires that we always keep in mind the limitations that accompany the office of governor in addition to the powers.

The government of the United States is a federal system, made up of a central (or national) government in Washington, D.C., and multiple sub-national governments in the fifty states. Both the national government and the states have the power to make law. Federalism is further evidence that the men who wrote the U.S. Constitution in 1787 did not really trust those who would serve in government. The founders wanted to form a government that would have enough power to successfully run the country (especially to oversee interstate commerce), but they also wanted to ensure that this government could never have so much power that the rights of the people would be violated.

The many divisions within the U.S. government have led to conflict over the years. The relationship between the national government and the states and among the states themselves has shifted dramatically through history. At times, the states were clearly the dominant actors in the American government. At other times, the states seemed to recede into the background. Though the overall trend in recent history has been toward greater and broader power for the national government, even in the year 2005 the appropriate power of the states and the national government is still debated and discussed among citizens, political actors, and the courts. Governors have often been involved in working to gain autonomy for the states. Such autonomy leads to greater gubernatorial influence. Other times, governors have sought help from the national government to address challenges facing the states. This help often comes in the form of federal money, a welcome contribution during times of financial distress. But such funds are controlled by the national government, and governors often struggle to influence how the funds are distributed and for what purposes. Whether governors influence the shifts or not, the fact remains that their place in the American political system is intimately related to the position of the states in the federal system.

Modern governors are better situated than ever before to act as true leaders in the states. Their office provides them with more resources than in the past. The people who seek and win the office also bring with them better skills and experience. All of these things have led to the heightened prominence of governors in the states and the nation. In addition to this, the larger executive branch that the governor oversees is more professional and better able to implement the laws passed by the legislature. This positive scenario has not always prevailed. To understand the true significance of the role of the executive branch today, one must look to the very different situation found earlier in American history.

THE PROBLEM OF GUBERNATORIAL POWER: A HISTORICAL OVERVIEW

At all levels of government, one of the primary concerns expressed has been what to do about the executive branch. Effective government requires at least a moderately powerful executive. But placing authority in the hands of a central figure such as a governor is potentially dangerous. For a host of reasons (some of which will be discussed

Women in State Government

Since the 1970s women have made significant strides in terms of their representation in the executive branch of state governments—as governors and as state administrative agency leaders (both elected and appointed). Although they have yet to achieve full equality with their male counterparts, they have made notable progress, and their presence continues to expand.

We have used three sources of data to discuss current and historical trends with respect to the representation of women in state government: (1) documentation of women in statewide offices from the Center for American Women in Politics, (2) a 50 percent sample of individual names of persons (women and men) heading 125 types of state administrative agencies from listings by the Council of State Governments, be-

tween 1970 and 2004 (the Agency Name Sample, or ANS), and (3) responses to mail questionnaires sent to state agency heads twice each decade by the American State Administrators Project (ASAP) (Bowling and Wright 1998; Brudney and Wright 2002; Bowling and Wright 2004).

CURRENT TRENDS

Currently, women occupy 25 percent of all statewide elected offices. They serve as governors, lieutenant governors, attorneys general, secretaries of state, treasurers, comptrollers, and auditors, in addition to numerous other positions. In nine states, women have assumed the top post—the governorship (in Arizona, Connecticut, Delaware, Hawaii, Kansas, Louisiana, Michigan, Texas, and Washington)—and in

Michigan governor Jennifer Granholm emphasized the importance of economic success for improving the quality of life in her state of the state address on January 27, 2004. (Office of Governor Jennifer Granholm)

an additional sixteen states, women serve as lieutenant governors. Historically, however, out of approximately 1,051 governors in all fifty states, only twenty-seven women—barely 3 percent—have been elected.

On average, although women occupied approximately 28 percent of the leadership positions in state administrative agencies in 2004, there is much variation across the states. Arkansas and Nebraska have the smallest percentage of women (at 10 and 12 percent, respectively), while New Mexico had the most significant share (46 percent). In 2005, 22.5 percent of all state legislators were female, although as in the administrative agencies, there was great variation between states. The gains of women are notable and significant, but women have yet to achieve full equality, as evidenced by the fact that they have not yet achieved 50 percent representation in any branch of state government.

One dimension, however, deviates from this trend—salary equity. The salaries of women and men agency executives tell a quite different story about the status of women in state government administration. Since the 1970, the salaries of male and female agency heads have moved toward equality, which is especially notable considering salary gaps reported in other employment sectors. In the 1970s, the average salary for women executives was roughly 89 percent of that for men in comparable positions. By the 1980s, this number rose to approximately 94 percent. In the 1990s, the difference was almost nonexistent; in the 1994 and 1998 ASAP surveys, women administrators reported earning 96 percent and 98 percent of the salaries of men, respectively.

TRENDS IN AGENCY LEADERSHIP ACROSS THE DECADES

How has the representation of women in state governments changed over time? As evidenced in Figure 1.1, a clear upward trend exists for state agencies from the 1970s through the present. Additionally, in this figure we plotted and compared growth in state agencies with that in state legisla-

tures. While women accounted for less than 5 percent of state legislators and state agency leadership positions in 1970, the percentage of women in state legislatures and in administrative posts increased at a similar rate through the 1980s. In the 1990s, though it appeared that women made slightly more notable gains in administrative agencies, a similar upward progress on a par with state legislatures continued.

Are women more likely to lead different agencies than men? Since the 1970s, women have become quite diversified in terms of the types of agencies they head. Table 1.1 classifies approximately 100 state agencies into thirteen broad categories. The numbers in each cell represent the percent of women (out of all administrators) within each category.

Clearly, certain types of agencies are more likely to have women agency heads. In the 1970s through the 1990s, the percent of women was uniformly highest for agencies dealing with income security and social services, moving from 14 percent to 30 percent to 39 percent across the three decades. And the largest gains by women appear in agencies in which one might expect to see greater numbers of females. But women in other categories have also made substantial advances. For example, in the 1970s, women accounted for only 3 percent of the leadership for agencies dealing with fiscal staff. By the 1990s, however, this proportion had increased to 26 percent. The functional category for agencies in which women seem to be most severely lagging behind men is in natural resources and, to some extent, environment/energy, criminal justice, and transportation. The once-high walls constituting barriers to female access for top agency posts have been lowered. The relatively slow rates of change, however, indicate that it is not a simple or easy matter for women to leap over the declining heights of what have previously been institutionalized agency barriers. It appears that newer agencies may start out with lower walls.

continues

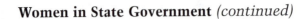

Women in State Government *(continued)*

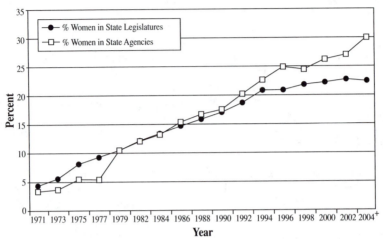

Source: Based on data from forthcoming *The Book of the States, 2006.* Lexington, KY: The Council of State Governments. (anticipated publication date May 2006)

Figure 1.1   Trends in female representation in legislatures and administrative agencies in the fifty American states, 1971–2004.

Do significant differences exist between men and women state administrators with respect to their opinions and, in particular, their partisanship and ideology? The simple answer is yes. According to the ASAP survey, a majority of women agency heads (54 percent) identified themselves as Democrats in the 1970s, whereas only 42 percent of men were Democrats. Additionally, the partisan gender gap among state administrators continued into the 1980s. The 1990s revealed a slightly different pattern, as the percentage of both women and men administrators identifying as Democrats declined.

Nonetheless, the gender gap shrank only slightly to 10 percentage points, with 46 percent of females and 36 percent of males identifying as Democrats.

Women administrators also revealed a more liberal ideology than their male counterparts, at least in 1998 (the first year this question was asked). Women were less likely to take a conservative stance on taxing and spending issues than men, although not overwhelmingly so. The gender differences were substantially larger for social and moral issues. Less than one-fourth of the female agency heads self-identified on

later), Americans have always had a love/hate relationship with executive power. In the twenty-first century, the American people are more likely than in the past to look to executives for leadership, yet even now, placing a lot of power in the hands of a single individual is controversial. A look at history will help to explain Americans' ambivalence toward executive power.

The office of governor actually preceded the adoption of the Constitution. Though the American colonies had officials called governors, these individuals did not really represent the residents of the colonies. Placed in their offices by the British king, these

TABLE 1.1   PERCENT OF WOMEN IN THIRTEEN
FUNCTIONS OF STATE ADMINISTRATIVE
AGENCIES, 1970S–1990S

Functional category	1970s	1980s	1990s
Elected officials	10	16	22
Fiscal staff	3	15	26
Nonfiscal staff	5	23	24
Income security and social services	14	30	39
Education	4	15	31
Health	6	16	33
Natural resources	3	6	7
Environment and energy	2	7	14
Economic development	4	17	21
Criminal justice	3	5	14
Regulatory	7	16	21
Transportation	2	9	16
Other	14	22	28

Source: Compiled by the authors with data from the American State Administrators Project (ASAP), 1974–1998.

the conservative side of social/moral issues, while nearly half (45 percent) of the men placed themselves at this end of the ideological continuum.

The presence of women in state government clearly increased in the last few decades, but we have yet to see complete gender equality. Since the nation's creation, only twenty-seven women have served as governor. The percent of women state legislators peaked in 2002 at 22.7 percent. In administrative agencies, women have made more notable gains, yet they are still more likely to be active in specific policy areas, often working on issues related to health, welfare, and education. Furthermore, men and women in positions of leadership in the state bureaucracy tend to have differing trends for partisanship and their ideologies. While arguably women have experienced their greatest advancement in the leadership positions of administrative agencies, we are still a far cry from a truly and equally representative democracy.

Christine A. Kelleher and Cynthia J. Bowling

colonial governors were often very powerful. The Crown granted them the authority to veto legislative acts and even dissolve the legislature completely if the governor felt the legislature was getting out of hand. In the years leading up to the Revolutionary War, as colonial legislatures were more and more critical of British control, colonial governors sometimes used their powers to quiet growing calls for independence among legislators. On occasion, they even exercised their powers to dissolve legislatures in order to silence critics of the Crown. Due to all of these experiences, the overall message that early American leaders took away from the colonial experience was that powerful governments—particularly powerful executives—could not be trusted. American experience said that both the king and the colonial governors were more likely to stand in the way of proper representation than to provide it. This heritage meant that those who created the American governmental systems distrusted centralized authority and limited the powers of executives as much as possible. They tended to view legislatures as the only governmental actors that could be trusted.

The distrust of executives can be seen at the national level. The Articles of Confederation, the first American constitution, gave scant authority to the central (national) government. The state governments held nearly all the power, and the national government did not even have a president or any single executive figure.

Just a few years later, the U.S. Constitution was written to replace the Articles of Confederation. This new document did create the office of the president, a single executive, but vested it with limited power. The vast majority of the power of the national government was located in the Congress. Nevertheless, the national government remained very small, and the states held most of the power of the American system. State governmental dominance persisted into the late 1800s.

Early state governments looked a lot like that under the Articles of Confederation. When the states adopted their own constitutions in the period following the Revolutionary War, many established "plural executives." Plural executives were basically committees in charge of carrying out state law, with the governor acting as the committee chair. The few states that did designate a single executive gave that individual only minimal power. They were mostly symbolic figureheads.

Post–Revolutionary War Period

Though the state constitutions drafted just after the Revolution varied, the typical constitution gave substantial power to the legislature and very little to the governor. Governors were extremely weak figures. For example, at that time, only two of the states, Massachusetts and New York, allowed their governors veto authority. Most states also created short terms for their governors: a typical governor was chosen for a one-year term and could serve a maximum of two terms. Thus, the governor in most states served two years in office at most. For even this short span in office, governors had little autonomy. Some were even chosen by the state legislatures rather than being elected by the people. Further, many of them lacked the other powers that are necessary to be a chief executive. They had no real authority over the budget (the allocation of money) and only a modest ability to appoint and remove key executive officials. Virginia offers a good example. The legislature elected the governor annually, and no person could serve more than three years in a row. The governor had no power to convene or dissolve the legislature, and he could neither recommend bills nor veto legislation. The governor even had to submit his administrative decisions to an eight-member council for approval. Though each state created its own government, the governors across these early states were by and large quite weak.

The weakness of the governor's office was often associated with poor performance of state governments. Reformers over the years have viewed weak governors as a problem for state government and have worked to give governors more authority to act as chief executives. These advocates have attempted to make governors more powerful in order to make state governments better able to rise to the challenges facing them. Various reform movements have tried to bring about changes in state governments. Some have tried to make state government more responsive to the citizenry. Others have been more concerned with the efficiency and effectiveness of state government activities.

The Nineteenth Century

Concerns about the quality of government and the need to empower the governors were first raised in the early 1800s, a turbulent time in American history. The very powerful legislatures in many states had become corrupt and overly responsive to special interests. Reformers believed the governors needed to be strengthened to counteract legislative power. The colonial idea that legislatures were to be trusted and executives feared began to fade away.

Appointments to jobs in the executive branch in the states were primarily made by the legislature or by the governor with legislative consent. This situation resulted in people seeking patronage jobs from government. In many states, these jobs were extremely numerous, and control of handing them out came to rest with party bosses in the major cities. These party bosses drew strength from having the "spoils" to distribute to former or prospective supporters.

The election of Andrew Jackson to the presidency in 1828 marked a significant change. Jackson and his followers argued for the inherent worth of the common people (in contrast to the country's history of government by aristocratic elites). Jackson's presidency connected the chief executive to the public for the first time and encouraged a rethinking of the role of the executives in American government. The impact of Jacksonian democracy on the strength of the office of governor was mixed. Many states changed the method of choosing their governors, from election by the legislature to election by the people directly. This change was intended to give governors greater autonomy, establishing their independence from overbearing legislatures. To further enhance the independence of the executive, some states made it harder for legislatures to impeach governors. Veto powers were also enhanced in some states. Other developments, however, worked in the opposite direction. The ideals of Jacksonian democracy also *weakened* governors by dividing the executive power among many elected state officials and boards. States moved to elect multiple statewide executive officials. This so-called long ballot gave the public a greater voice in choosing state officials (decreasing the patronage of the powerful party bosses), but it also meant the governor had to share power even in his own executive branch. As noted political scientist Leslie Lipson (1939, 23–24) wrote, "It was claimed that multiplying the number of elective officers made government more truly responsible to the people. In actual fact, the result was to cripple it. The chief executive was unable to harm the people. He was also unable to serve them."

The states firmly remained the dominant governments in the American system leading into the Civil War. However, the Civil War and the Reconstruction period that followed it fundamentally changed the political system. The aftermath of this period ultimately strengthened the national government at the expense of the states. The years following the Civil War were a period of tremendous economic development. In the United States, the Industrial Revolution marked a shift from a largely agricultural society to an industrial nation. Such a vast shift in the economic structure of the nation, not surprisingly, challenged governmental structures to manage the change, but the states were not really prepared to do so. State legislatures adopted laws in attempts to grapple with the changing times. These laws required executive agencies to execute them—to put them into force. Rather than give existing executive branch agencies the power to execute these new laws, legislatures often created new agencies to fulfill these new functions of state government. As a consequence, the number of state agencies grew significantly. For example, the state of New York had 10 agencies in 1800, 20 in 1850, 81 in 1900, and more than 170 by 1925. These new agencies were often outside the influence of the governor.

The governor's power was severely limited by the long ballot because other executive branch officials elected by a statewide electorate felt a responsibility only to the public (not the governor) and were therefore both legally and philosophically independent of the governor. To complicate matters further, those who held these other statewide elected offices often had their eyes on the governor's office and thus acted to set themselves apart from the governor at every opportunity.

The Twentieth Century and Beyond

So as the twentieth century approached, many governors had gained greater strength and independence due to the shift to popular election and the new access to the veto. Nevertheless, many of the offices involved with the execution of the law—presumably a primary job of the governor—remained beyond the reach of the governor's power. The continued impotence of the governor left a power void. Political parties and especially party bosses moved in to fill that void in many states. Not only were these bosses in charge of handing out patronage jobs, they also often handpicked people who would run for state offices, including the governors. Since governors in most states still had short, limited terms, governors came and went from public life, but the party—that is, the boss—exercised continuous influence. No governor could really rise up to challenge the power of bosses. Though bosses occasionally did choose impressive men to seek the office, they usually installed weak men in the governorship to ensure that their own authority would not be challenged. As the American economy continued to develop and American cities experienced mass immigration, party bosses increasingly held sway. City governments were often corrupt and much more likely to serve large business interests than the citizenry. Citizens and activists became more and more concerned with the alliance between big business and government officials. Economic interests that dominated government decision making (charging extreme rates for shipping goods on railroads, for example) could not be controlled without the overthrow of the political system that supported their corrupt practices. Reformers turned to the governor's office as a potential way of supplanting the party bosses. The governors became advocates for changing the laws surrounding government regulation, which required exerting influence over the making of law rather than simply over its execution. Reformers focused on legislative rather than executive power. And so, governors came to be important legislative leaders.

In part, governors came to occupy this chief legislator position because of their connection to the public. The governor was elected by the entire state, so, unlike members of the legislature who served only small segments of the state, he could claim to speak for the whole population. Though the formal powers of the governor remained relatively weak, a certain prestige was still attached to the office. Governors who chose to do so (and not all made this choice) could use their office to champion policy goals among the citizenry. In addition to the prestige of the office, most governors also had two important constitutional powers—the power to recommend and the power of the veto. Though they continued to lack control over the executive branch (despite their constitutional responsibility to see that the laws were faithfully executed), they at least exercised influence over lawmaking. The growing prominence of governors in the public and legislative arenas eventually led to attempts at reorganizing the executive branch to give the governors greater control in that arena as well.

A major drive for reform took hold in the states in the early 1900s. Reform efforts focused on achieving greater efficiency in government and greater responsiveness. Lipson (1939, 72) summarized the challenge this way: "If the official is weak, he is incapable of doing harm; but he is equally incapable of doing good. The less checks there are, the more efficient he can be; but also, the less checks, the less control over him."

The state reorganization movement took a cue from the scientific management movement, which attempted to use organizational principles of managerial efficiency to organize industries for maximum profit. State government reformers similarly hoped to promote efficiency in government through a centralization of authority (concentrating power in the chief executive and loyal agency heads). Reform proposals associated with this movement included restructuring the executive branch into a departmental hierarchy, with the governor at the top and a director to head each department; merit employment instead of patronage; executive budgeting; and a shortened ballot (giving the governor appointment power in regard to officials who were formerly elected by the public). In 1917, the state of Illinois implemented an executive reorganization plan, and thirty-seven more states reorganized at least some aspects of their executive branches over the next twenty-five years. The rate of reorganization picked up substantially after World War II. And the number of agencies was indeed reduced in many states. While the movement was less successful in its goal of electing fewer officials (shortening the ballots) in the states, it did succeed to some degree in giving the governor the power to make more high-level executive appointments. The length of governors' terms was increased in many states during this period. By 1955, nearly one-third of the governors had four-year (rather than one- or two-year) terms. More important, perhaps, governors were granted more power over the state budgets. The responsibility of preparing the budget for submission to the legislature was placed in the governor's office in most states, as was the power to implement the budget once it was passed. The legislature retained the power to make any changes it chose to the governor's budget, so the governor clearly had to share the budget-making power with the legislature. Nevertheless, this was a very significant development that gave the governor a much greater say in state government activities. Professionalization of state employees took place very slowly, lagging behind the federal bureaucracy.

The election of Franklin Roosevelt to the presidency and the dramatic expansion of the federal government during the Depression and World War II brought many changes to the country. The national government took on responsibilities that had previously been carried out by the states or by private institutions. President Roosevelt used national government spending to try to raise people up and lift the country out of the Depression. The national government was clearly in the lead, and the states were not well placed to offer much help. Poor apportionment of state legislatures meant that states continued to be more likely to serve rural interests while largely ignoring the growing urban areas. Apportionment is the process of drawing lines for districts; in this case, the term refers to distributing voters among state legislative districts. States historically drew these lines in ways that resulted in discrimination against African Americans and urban areas to the benefit of whites and rural areas. Cities increasingly looked to their U.S. House members, bypassing the state governments in search of solutions for their problems. As a result, federal money was funneled from the national government straight to the cities. The states receded into the background, and the national government was clearly dominant. Though the states and the country faced dramatic challenges in the mid-1900s, the governor still competed with multiple other statewide elected officials, and the legislatures often met only 120 days every two years. State governments had improved and empowered their institutions over the years, but they remained ill prepared to grapple with the challenges of modern society. The people who held the governorships during this time were a particularly unimpressive group. Since the office's responsibilities had dwindled, it often did not attract very qualified individuals. The governorship truly hit a low point.

Dramatic changes occurred once again beginning in the 1960s. For one thing, states finally began to tackle the poor apportionment of their state legislatures. Due to decisions rendered in a series of U.S. Supreme Court cases, states were required to draw their state district lines in a way that distributed voters more equally across the state. Fairer apportionment resulted in greater attention to the growing urban centers of states, which in turn aided the policy goals of the governors. Since statewide electorates chose the governors, they were typically more sensitive to the needs of urban areas, and governors therefore benefited from better-apportioned legislatures. The improved relationships between legislators and governors also made the legislatures more sympathetic to calls for constitutional amendments to carry out some of the leftover goals of the state reform movement. Nearly all of the states that still had two-year terms for their governors expanded them to four years by 1990. Veto powers, particularly the item veto, and the governor's role in overseeing the budget were also enhanced to a great degree in the mid-1990s. Some states even granted their governors a more potent veto—the amendatory veto. This veto allows a governor to revise the language and expenditure amounts in an appropriations bill before returning it to the legislature with his or her veto message.

Though most states still elect quite a few statewide offices, legislatures have tended to give governors the power to appoint the heads of new agencies as they are created. As a result, the newer agencies (which also have responsibility for some of the states' most important activities) are headed by governor appointees.

And this brings us back full circle to the place of the states in the American federal system. Though the states declined in importance quite significantly in the early twentieth century, they (and their governors) were rising again to positions of great importance as the century drew to a close. The renewed emphasis on the role of the states, coupled with changes in the personal and political makeup of the governorships, have combined to make the states' governors key actors in the American political system today.

As discussed in the previous section, history has brought myriad changes to the relationship among the many elements of American government. It has also brought numerous changes to the governmental actors themselves. The first few years of the twenty-first century have seen both governors and their states serving critical roles in the United States and even in the world.

THE STATE BUREAUCRACY: A HISTORICAL OVERVIEW

The development of the large bureaucratic structure required to manage the work of government has also spawned controversy. Moreover, creating such a structure and choosing people to fill it poses an ongoing challenge. Four historical trends define the development of the state bureaucracy, with major changes over time focusing on membership, organization, size, and the role and significance of the executive branch.

Executive Branch Officials

In the country's first years, state governments typically hired well-educated workers from the wealthy upper class. They were presumably also hired on the basis of their fitness for office. However, with the presidency of Andrew Jackson (1829–1837), the nation and the states shifted toward opening public employment up to all segments of white male society (rather than just the wealthy elite).

As a result of this Jacksonian influence, most states moved toward the patronage system, a more political or partisan means of filling executive positions, in the early 1800s. The patronage system (sometimes referred to as the spoils system) allowed chief executives (both U.S. presidents and state governors) to choose political allies for government positions. Consequently, after the election of a new governor, many state workers would be fired, to be replaced by friends and political supporters of the newly elected governor. This situation became an important source of power for governors, who could use the promise of jobs (the spoils of office) to build support for their candidacies. However, it also often led to unqualified individuals being appointed to public jobs for purely political reasons. The quality of the executive branch suffered as a result.

By the late 1800s, the patronage system was falling into disrepute. Following the end of the Civil War, civil service reformers advocated for the end of political patronage and argued for the hiring and retention of public employees based on merit. They contended that effective administration required that employees have appropriate education and experience and that employees should be judged on their job performance. Another feature of the merit system protected political activities. Under these reformed systems, once employees were chosen, they typically could not be fired for purely political reasons. The U.S. Congress passed the Pendleton Act of 1883, which set up the independent, bipartisan Civil Service Commission to employ objective, merit-based standards for filling executive branch offices in the national government. At the same time, states began the slow process of instituting merit systems for their state bureaucracies. In the years immediately following the federal reforms, a few states quickly moved to make similar changes. States such as Illinois and New York, which had been key in other administrative reforms, and progressive reform states such as California and Wisconsin were among the first to do so. However, the pace soon slowed.

By 1930, only nine states had adopted this reform, and eight years later, less than one-third of the states had a merit-based personnel system. In 1949, about half of the states had enacted merit-based civil service systems, and by 1960, roughly half of state employees were covered by some sort of civil service system. In 2004, nearly 70 percent of states (thirty-four) had developed comprehensive civil service systems that included almost all state employees. Though not all states have fully moved away from the earlier idea of using political considerations for filling government jobs, the general trend is clearly toward assuring that public employees are well qualified for their jobs and chosen based on an objective measurement of their skills and expertise.

As a result of changes in how they are chosen, bureaucrats now constitute a more diverse group than ever before. Bureaucracies are no longer the white male bastions they once were. Many states have embraced the idea of "representative bureaucracy," which asserts that major groups in society should participate proportionately in government work. Such diversity in the executive branch is believed to make state government more responsive to the needs of all people. In recent years, groups formerly unrepresented (or underrepresented) in state bureaucracy have experienced significant growth. The overall share of state government jobs held by women and minorities has increased. More specifically, from 1973 to 1989, the number of African Americans as a proportion of all full-time state employees grew from 10 to 18 percent, though other ethnic minorities experienced smaller growth (from 3 to 7 percent). In addition, the percentage of women grew from 43 to 49 percent. These changing numbers do not tell the entire story, however. For instance, significant changes also occurred in job stratification, which involves the types of jobs held by different groups. In this regard, women and minorities again have faired better than in the past. They now hold a larger share of higher-level (higher-paying) jobs with more responsibility. The proportion of African American agency heads increased from 1 to 7 percent between 1964 and 1997, while the percent of women agency heads grew from 2 to 24 percent. Nonetheless, these figures still fall well below the proportions of women and minorities in the population as a whole.

Organization of the Bureaucracies

The executive branch is a bureaucracy, meaning it is organized in a hierarchy and duties are divided among different officials (division of labor). The governor sits at the top of the pyramid, holding the responsibility of managing the entire bureaucracy. The bureaucracy in each state is divided into many units of differing size, composition, and title. The largest units are typically called departments. These departments are headed by individuals who often (but not always) carry the title of secretary. Unlike in the national government, where the president appoints all high-ranking officials in the executive branch, governors do not get to appoint all of their fellow executive branch officials. Instead, states have tended to choose the highest-ranking officials in the bureaucracy through elections.

As a result, and again unlike at the national level, the top level of bureaucrats in the states often do not owe any allegiance to the governor. The method of choosing executive branch officials through elections took hold during the mid- to late 1800s, the period of Jacksonian democracy. As noted earlier, Jacksonian democracy emphasized the worth of the common people and advocated frequent elections of many officials. The period produced the direct election of the governor (a move that empowered governors), but it also divided executive power among multiple elected state officials and boards and commissions. Throughout the nineteenth century, this philosophy persisted. New governmental activities were managed by new independent executive agencies—beyond the control and influence of the governor. As the twentieth century approached, reformers sought to reverse the trend of creating so many separately elected and independent boards and commissions, because they had resulted in managerial inefficiency and sometimes corruption. Meanwhile, individuals associated with the scientific management movement advocated improving the governor's legal powers. These reformers successfully sought to centralize administrative responsibility by creating fewer agencies and placing them under the control of the governor. They also emphasized the appointment power. Short-ballot reformers of the same time period encouraged the states to elect fewer public officials and put the power to appoint high-level executive branch officials in the hands of the governor. The trend toward granting these appointments to the governor continues today, but the attachment to electing state executive officials remains. In just two states—Maine and New Jersey—is the governor the only statewide elected official. Elected officials, such as the governor, feel an allegiance to the voters who placed them into office. States continue to fall on the side of such public accountability, even though many observers worry it results in inefficiency by forcing the governors to share administrative responsibility with many other officials who have independent sources of power.

The most important statewide officers (aside from the governor) are the attorney general, the lieutenant governor, the treasurer, and the secretary of state. In the vast majority of the states, these officers are elected by the public at the same time that the governor is chosen. In some cases, these officials can actually serve in their offices longer than the governor, since they are not bound by term limits. Each of these officers is examined in greater detail in Chapter 3.

In most states, the office of lieutenant governor is similar to the vice-presidency. Thus, this official has two primary responsibilities: to become governor in the event the sitting governor leaves office and to serve as president of the state senate. In some states, the legislative role of the lieutenant governor has real power and influence. In other states, this role is more symbolic. Lieutenant governors are typically elected. Some are elected on a ticket with the governor, but others run for office separately. Attorneys general are the states' legal counsels. They also provide formal legal opinions to the governor and other state officials, giving advice about the legality of actions these individuals may be considering. The secretary of state does not typically possess many formal responsibilities; they are the chief custodians of state records, and in several states, they are the keepers of the great seal of the state or commonwealth. The most visible jobs performed by the secretary of state's office are storing state documents and supervising state elections. The state treasurers are custodians of state funds. They collect taxes, administer the investment of state funds, and make payments on behalf of the state to employees and those who have provided the state with goods and services.

A large majority of states choose each of these officials by statewide election. This system enhances accountability to the citizenry, but it sometimes hamstrings governors attempting to serve in their chief executive role. Even the lieutenant governor, who stands in line to the governorship, is elected separately from the governor in many states and may therefore not even share the governor's party affiliation.

Size of Bureaucracies

The size of the bureaucracies has grown at a remarkable pace. This growth is reflected in the number of agencies instituted in the states and in the number of workers they employ.

The number of agencies has mounted steadily over the years (Jenks and Wright 1993). This growing number of agencies represents a significant expansion in the areas of bureaucratic responsibility, which in turn is a direct result of changing state government responsibility. As new public problems arise or capture the people's attention, state responsibilities increase. These added responsibilities lead to the creation of new bureaucratic entities to administer the new state programs. Though different states have different combinations of agencies, state bureaucracies have generally evolved along similar paths. Political scientists Stephen Jenks and Deil S. Wright (1993) characterize the process of new agency growth by "generations." They count "four-plus" generations between 1959 and 1989 and define a generation as agencies present in at least thirty-eight states. The "first generation" included fifty-one agencies present in more than thirty-eight states in 1959. Many of these agencies had been in place for years, and they represented the core work of state government. A sample of these agencies included: corrections, education, health, higher education, highways, mental health care, tax collection, unemployment insurance, welfare, and worker's compensation. Other first-generation agencies were agriculture, banking, fish and wildlife management, insurance regulation, parks and parole, in addition to the units headed by elected officials such as the secretary of state, attorney general, and treasurer.

Changing policy concerns in the 1960s gave rise to a second generation of new agencies, covering issues of air quality, economic development, juvenile rehabilitation, and natural resources. Interestingly, to a large degree, the focus on these particular agencies came from initiatives of the federal government, which made federal money available, encouraging states to take certain actions in these areas.

The 1970s were a time when the states reasserted themselves following the policy-making dominance by the national government in the 1960s. During this decade, twenty-nine new types of administrative entities (representing a third generation) were created in many states. Most notable were those concerned with alcohol and drug abuse, civil rights, consumer affairs/consumer protection, energy, the environment, mass transit, occupational health and safety, vocational rehabilitation, and women's commissions.

States faced budget difficulties in the 1980s, so this decade was not a time of much agency growth. Nevertheless, fourth-generation agencies were added, such as those dealing with emergency medical services, equal employment opportunity, groundwater management, hazardous waste, and small and minority business. The end of the 1980s, however, also pointed to other trends that were still developing. New agencies involved with coastal zone management, lotteries, ombudsman functions, public broadcasting systems, public defender functions, and victim compensation were present in twenty-five states and poised to spread to others.

Not surprisingly, the growth in the number of agencies was accompanied by growth in state government employment. In 1995, the fifty state governments added together employed 3,971,000 workers. This number was up from 3,177,000 ten years earlier. In both of these time points, the number of state government employees was greater than the number of workers employed by the national government. State employment increased by one-third between 1985 and 1995, though the growth was uneven across the states.

In addition to employment growth associated with the advent of new agencies, existing agencies also added to their workforces. This employment growth was uneven, however, across executive functions. In most functional areas, rates of employment remained relatively steady. But in some areas—notably corrections—employment exploded due to policy changes that resulted in a steep increase in the prisoner population and a need to build and staff more prison facilities. Another major employment growth area was higher education. Increasing numbers of instructors and other staff members at state colleges and universities resulted in a growth of nearly 50 percent from 1985 to 1995 in state higher education staff. The substantial growth seen in corrections and higher education is not the norm, though, as most agencies, once created, retain steady levels of employees or experience gradual increases and sometimes decreases in staffing.

Recently, attention has been focused on changing the way the bureaucracy does business. Various reforms have been advanced over the years. The earliest modern reform technique was reorganization, which involves consolidating the responsibilities of many separate agencies into a smaller number of broadly functional ones. Such reorganization is thought to reduce wasteful duplication and coordinate the delivery of services by state agencies. Reorganization also typically brings the heads of these consolidated agencies under the managerial authority of the governor.

Some observers dismiss such reorganization as too timid to have much real effect. A more aggressive approach was espoused by David Osborne and Ted Gaebler in *Reinventing Government: How the Entrepreneurial Spirit Is Transforming the Public Sector.* This book influenced American government at the state and national level and became required reading for American leaders including President Bill Clinton. A major element of their call for reinvention is the idea of catalytic governments, defined as governments that "steer but do not row." The idea here is that governments should determine what is needed, what services should be provided, and how they are to be funded but that the actual implementation of these services need not be done by government employees. A closely related idea is called competitive government. This concept advocates bringing competition into the arena of service delivery—using economic principles to assure that services are delivered efficiently and effectively. Many states have adopted the ideas of reinvention into their administration of services. Privatization is another common approach. Under this technique, states contract with private or nonprofit organizations for the provision of certain services. States have employed private contractors for services such as highway construction for a long time. Building maintenance services, food delivery, clerical services, and security services are other examples of service areas for which states often hire private contractors. In recent decades, the use of privatization has moved into other arenas, such as managing day care, adoption, and foster services; Medicaid claims management; and employee training and placement. A few states have even experimented with privately run correctional facilities (with some rather dire consequences in certain instances). The most common reason states offer for "contracting out" is that private providers can deliver services of equal or better quality at a lower cost than a government agency can. Privatizing also makes sense when the need for a particular service is short-lived—hiring someone else to provide them rather than building a state apparatus would be a quicker and cheaper solution. Privatization has not been uniformly successful. In certain cases, costs have declined, but sometimes, that is because services have declined in either quantity or quality. The fact that the outside contractors need to make a profit to stay in business may encourage them to cut corners, which may result in a poor-quality product. Another criticism of contracting out is that it lowers accountability to the public. Citizens who wish to complain about the provision of a service may have a difficult time knowing who is actually responsible, since there are so many levels of people involved.

Though none of the current reforms have been fully successful in achieving all they set out to do, states still experiment with these and other means of improving the work of government. Meanwhile, the state bureaucracies continue to be scrutinized and often unfavorably evaluated. As a result, there will always be an impetus to try to alter "business as usual" so that public officials—especially governors—can claim to be addressing the concerns of the public.

The Significance of the Bureaucracy

The ongoing changes in the composition, organization, and size of the state bureaucracies have all contributed to the current significance of the executive branch. States administer the vast majority of governmental programs in this country, both those created by the national government and those instituted by the states. Governmental programs have an influence on the lives of the citizenry only to the extent that they are actually put into force. It is the executive branch that carries this administrative burden.

The executive branch executes the law by interpreting the laws passed by the state legislatures and governors and writing rules and regulations to carry the laws into practice. Some level of discretion is therefore built into the process of carrying out the law. Bureaucrats apply their knowledge, expertise, and judgment to the often vaguely written laws to fill in the details and implement the laws. This opportunity for discretion on the part of executive branch officials (a necessity in carrying out laws) also opens the possibility of outside (or inside) political influences over how laws are implemented. Outside groups that will be affected by the new laws (sometimes called clientele groups) attempt to influence how the laws are carried out. Elected officials (legislators and the governor) hope to exert influence as well. Further, there is an inherent difficulty in unelected bureaucrats exercising such discretion in a democratic society, as the public has no means of holding these bureaucrats accountable for their actions. For this reason, both legislators and governors assert a legitimate role in overseeing executive branch activities. The challenge lies in holding executive branch officials accountable to the public good while minimizing outside political influences that might get in the way of the laws being executed in a neutrally competent way. Such interference might corrupt the implementation process. A tension therefore persists in allowing bureaucrats the freedom to implement the law as they see fit and compelling them to respond to the desires of elected officials (and presumably the people who elected them).

Even in the modern period, therefore, the appropriate role of the bureaucracy in the states is not always clear. The shift from patronage to merit systems illustrates an essential philosophical question. Should the bureaucracy be responsive to politics, following the lead of the governor and other elected officials, or should it be insulated from political influences, making its decisions based strictly on the neutral expertise of the bureaucrats? This tension remains significant in the states today. Despite apparent attempts at insulating the executive branch from politics, politics routinely finds its way in. Outside actors persist in attempting to influence how laws are implemented. And bureaucrats often involve themselves in the formulation of laws.

Governors are expected to offer leadership in many different arenas. Though they might be viewed first and foremost as executive leaders, in reality they perform duties in lawmaking, overseeing the safety of the state citizens, and representing the state in Washington, D.C., and in other countries around the world. Much is expected of the modern governors, but are they up to the task? Does the office provide state chief executives the tools necessary for fulfilling all that is expected of them? Do the executive branch officials who surround the governor work with or against the governors as they pursue their responsibilities? Do these officials perform their duties effectively? And do the governors bring with them the personal and professional qualities that are likely to result in success? All of these questions and many more are significant for assessing the place of the American governorship in the early years of the twenty-first century and beyond.

REFERENCES AND FURTHER READING

Bowling, Cynthia J., and Deil S. Wright. 1998. Change and continuity in state administration: Administrative leadership across four decades. *Public Administration Review* 58 (5):429–445.

———. 2004. American state administrators project. Unpublished data, Auburn University, Auburn, Alabama.

Bowman, Ann O'M., and Richard C. Kearney. 1986. *The resurgence of the states.* Englewood Cliffs, NJ: Prentice-Hall.

———. 2002. *State and local government.* Boston: Houghton Mifflin.

Brown, Brent W., and Eric B. Herzik. 1991. *Gubernatorial leadership and state policy.* New York: Greenwood.

Brudney, Jeffrey L., and Deil S. Wright. 2002. Revisiting administrative reform in the American states: Trends and emerging issues. *Public Administration Review* 62:353–361.

Buck, A. E. 1938. *The reorganization of state governments in the United States.* New York: Columbia University Press.

Durning, Dan. 1987. Change masters for states. *State Government* 60 (3):145–149.

———. 1991. Education reform in Arkansas: The governor's role in policymaking. In *Gubernatorial leadership and state policy,* ed. Eric B. Herzik and Brent W. Brown, 121–140. New York: Greenwood.

Gross, Donald. 1991. The policy role of governors. In *Gubernatorial leadership and state policy*, ed. Eric B. Herzik and Brent W. Brown, 1–24. New York: Greenwood.

Herzik, Eric. 1991. Policy agendas and gubernatorial leadership. In *Gubernatorial leadership and state policy*, ed. Eric B. Herzik and Brent W. Brown, 25–38. New York: Greenwood.

Herzik, Eric, and Brent W. Brown. 1989. Introduction: Symposium on governors and public policy. *Policy Studies Journal* 17 (4):841–862.

Jenks, Stephen, and Deil Wright. 1993. An agency level approach to change in the administrative functions of American state governments. *State and Local Government Review* 25:78–86.

Lipson, Leslie. 1939. *The American governor.* Chicago: University of Chicago Press.

Muchmore, Lynn R. 1983. The governor as manager. In *Being governor, the view from the office,* ed. Thad L. Beyle and Lynn R. Muchmore, 78–84. Durham, NC: Duke Press Policy Studies.

Osborne, David, and Ted Gaebler. 1992. *Reinventing government: How the entrepreneurial spirit is transforming the public sector.* Reading, MA: Addison-Wesley.

Press, Charles, and Kenneth VerBurg. 1991. *State and community governments in a dynamic federal system.* New York: HarperCollins.

Ransone, Coleman B. 1956. *The office of governor in the United States.* University, AL: University of Alabama Press.

———. 1982. *The American governorship.* Westport, CT: Greenwood.

Sabato, Larry. 1983. *Goodbye to good-time Charlie: The American governorship transformed.* Washington, DC: Congressional Quarterly Press.

Sanford, Terry. 1967. *Storm over the states.* New York: McGraw-Hill.

Schlesinger, Joseph A. 1965. The politics of the executive. In *Politics in the American states.* Henry Jacob and Kenneth N. Vines, eds. Boston: Little, Brown.

———. 1966. *Ambition and politics: Political careers in the United States.* Chicago: Rand McNally.

Van Horn, Carl E. 1996. *The state of the states.* Washington, DC: Congressional Quarterly Press.

2

ROLES, FUNCTIONS, AND POWERS OF THE GOVERNORS

Margaret R. Ferguson

Modern governors can be true leaders in their states and the nation. The challenge to incumbents is to employ the many resources available to them in the proper combination in pursuit of the many responsibilities their office entails today.

Early governors suffered from the historical American aversion to executive power. Though some individual governors did manage to exert power by virtue of their personal strength, charisma, or, in a few cases, corruption, the office itself typically granted the occupant few tools. Due to Americans' resentment of the overwhelming power of colonial governors appointed by the king, early state constitutions (much like the national one) created an executive of limited power. A delegate to the North Carolina Constitutional Convention approvingly described how much power had been given that state's governor as "just enough power to sign the receipt for his salary" (Lipson 1939,14). Governors in other states did not fare much better.

Over time, states began to sense a need for change. Since 1985, all of the states have made statutory changes (acts of the legislatures) and/or constitutional changes to grant their governors more formal powers. Though this has been a slow process and has been more pronounced in some states than in others, most governors now have the formal tools necessary to perform the duties of a true executive. States have made other changes as well. Most have developed more extensive support structures for their governors. Staff support for the chief executives (sometimes referred to as enabling resources) is much more generous and professional than ever before. This support means the governors no longer work alone. They can draw on the help of others around them to accomplish their work.

New formal powers and institutional support are not, however, the full explanation for the current prominence of the governorship. In addition to legal changes, the modern office has been transformed by changes in society. Greater access to the public via new types of media offers governors a new and formidable power source that their predecessors could scarcely have imagined. It is worth noting here that the idea of an executive drawing power straight from the public was exactly the sort of thing the founders of the country hoped to avoid. They understood the potential danger of a particularly charismatic governor mobilizing the public for his own selfish purposes at the expense of others, especially minority groups.

Governors bring to the office other informal (or personal) powers. Informal powers are resources related to the person holding the office rather than the office itself. Though formal powers do not vary much from one governor in a state to the next, incumbents differ greatly in the informal powers they possess. Such informal powers are nearly limitless, but a sample of the important ones would include the governor's skill, personality, and popularity. Each of these features can be employed by governors in their pursuit of leadership in their home states and abroad. However, it is up to the individual governor to mobilize these resources.

The challenge for modern governors, therefore, lies in exercising their formal, informal, and enabling powers effectively and in the appropriate combination, which is not a simple task. Not surprisingly, governors have taken on (or had forced on them) many new responsibilities. While they have more tools, much more is expected of them as well. Governors must wear many different hats. They must act as chief executive and chief legislator, head of state and intergovernmental liaison, chief judge and chief of party. The responsibilities are significant and growing. The challenge is great, but the office and the people who seek it are, on the whole, finally up to the job.

To understand the governors, it is important to place them into the larger political context. The growing prominence of the states and the increasing complexity of the state governments both empower and limit the governors. On the one hand, governors have more and better-qualified people and offices around them to help them carry out their responsibilities. On the other hand, the state government is far bigger, harder to manage, and more carefully scrutinized by national political actors. This chapter will examine the many roles that modern governors are expected to play and the array of tools they may employ as they carry out the various duties of their office.

ROLES OF THE GOVERNORS

As noted, modern governors must step into myriad roles. Some of them are constantly expected of the governor, others arise sporadically. Some roles are highly important, others perhaps less so. Finally, all incumbents will prefer some roles while disliking others, and such preferences will surely affect the choices they make in how they use their limited time in office.

The primary roles of the governor are those of chief legislator and chief executive. This combination suggests the overlapping powers of the political systems in the states. In addition, the governor must also serve the largely symbolic role of chief of state on an ongoing basis. The remaining roles—crisis manager, chief judge, chief of party, intergovernmental liaison, and military chief—while certainly significant features of the governorship, are not as time consuming or as constant. When they do arise, however, they will likely take center stage until the task at hand is complete.

Chief Legislator

Probably the most important role of the governors in the modern period is that of chief legislator. Given their status and stature, governors take the lead in lawmaking endeavors. They typically involve themselves very directly in the laws considered and passed by the state legislative body. They are not members of the legislative branch, of course, but the tools of the office of governor and the political environment in the states all encourage governors to assume an active role in lawmaking. State constitutions and laws offer governors some formal tools that they can use in their legislative leader roles, including the veto (package, line-item, and amendatory), the power to present a state of the state address, and the power to prepare and administer the budget. Informal and enabling resources are also important for the role of legislative leader. Informal resources such as their own popularity, their skill or charisma, and a popular mandate assist governors in legislative leadership, as do enabling resources such as having a strong professional staff.

The role of chief legislator is not a simple one to play. The environment in which the governor and the legislators function is sometimes marked by conflict. In fact, the media, the citizenry, and state officials themselves often characterize the relationship between the governor and the legislature as one of constant divisiveness. Yet there are other instances when the governor and legislators manage to work together in relative harmony.

The governor's place as the highest elected official in his or her party may help to bring the governor and the legislature together—which is especially helpful when the governor's party holds a majority of seats in the legislature. The role of the governor in the state party organization is also important, and some governors are more successful at uniting the party than others (Morehouse and Jewell 2003). When a party is divided into different camps (or factions), having a large number of seats in the legislature may not really help the governor's goals in the legislative arena much. Though party strength is important, it does not assure that partisans will follow the governor's lead.

Further, conflict is not only or not necessarily a matter of disagreement among public officials. Governors and legislators may simply view the world of their states differently, perhaps because of the different constituencies they serve. Legislators are elected by and represent a district—only a small part of a state, whereas the governor represents the entire state. Because of this, a legislator may believe that what is good for his or her district is good for the state, whereas a governor may try to convince the legislator that what is good for the state will ultimately be good for the legislator's district.

Differences between legislators and the governors may also arise due to varying lengths of terms. Governors in most states serve a four-year term, while legislators often must seek reelection every two years. In addition, though governors are often limited to a maximum of eight years in office, legislators may serve multiple terms, sometimes spanning the administrations of multiple governors. As a consequence, governors and state legislators (even members of the same party) may form competing opinions about the correct answers to the problems facing the state.

On top of all of these sources of conflict, the making of law is a long and complicated process in every state. Each state except for Nebraska has a bicameral legislature, meaning that actors in two separate chambers must process proposed legislation before it can be delivered to the governor for signature or veto. A proposed law must pass through multiple phases in its journey toward adoption. In a simplified form, the policy process can be divided into four phases: agenda setting, policy formulation, adoption or legitimation, and evaluation. The chief legislator role of the governors encompasses the first two phases of the policy process. To fulfill this role successfully, governors must use their powers (formal, informal, and enabling) in the first phase, the agenda-setting phase, to raise topics to be considered by the legislature. Governors also work in the second phase, the policy formulation phase, to influence the types of solutions adopted to address those problems. They may be more successful at asking legislatures to look at a particular problem (agenda setting) than they are at convincing legislatures to adopt a particular solution (policy formulation). Agenda setting is perhaps easier for the governors, and it is in this phase that they have unique powers. But governors are not as uniquely qualified to lead in the policy formulation phase, though they still are significant actors during this second stage. These two phases of policymaking are considered separately here. The contributions that the governors make to the final two phases of the policy process fall under the chief executive role, and these are considered elsewhere.

Agenda Setting

Agenda setting is the first step in the policymaking process. At this stage, problems requiring governmental action are identified. They are brought forward by multiple actors, including the governor, legislative leaders, interest groups, and the media. But the governor is better able than any of the other actors to place items on the agenda for governmental action. Major problems that affect the lives of large numbers of people are usually the issues that actually make it onto the public agenda to be considered for state government action. The governor's role as agenda setter arises from several sources.

First, it grows partially from the formal powers and responsibilities laid out in the state constitution. Each governor possesses veto powers, which give him or her a legitimate place at the table of lawmaking in the states and helps to assure that legislators are willing to consider the agenda items that the governor has brought forward. The governor is also required by law to present state of the state addresses to lay out legislative priorities and to prepare and present to the legislature a budget plan. Legislators often look to these statements of the governor's priorities to set the broad agenda that the legislature will follow that year. The governor's agenda also tends to represent the major issues facing the state. For all of these reasons, the governor is the key agenda setter in the state.

Calling Special Sessions.   One power that a governor can use to focus the legislature on key agenda items is the ability to call special sessions. Unlike the U.S. Congress, most state legislatures even in the twenty-first century do not meet year-round. In seven states, the legislatures do not even hold sessions every year. Instead, they meet biennially (every other year). Since regular legislative sessions are limited in most states, the power to call the legislature back into session is significant. In twenty states, only the governor can call a special session. The legislatures cannot call themselves back to session in these states. In the other thirty states, either the governor or the legislature by a majority vote (or a supermajority, depending on the state) can call a special session. In some states, the legislature can only take up issues identified by the governor. In most states, legislators are free to add to the agenda once a special session is called. This power provides the governor the opportunity to focus attention on the specific policy questions that he or she believes are most important. The governor may use such sessions to make the public aware of pressing issues, in addition to getting the undivided attention of legislators. If he or she succeeds in convincing the public of the importance of the issues, the governor may be able to elicit their help in swaying the legislature. Such direct attention to particular topics may put a negative spotlight on legislators if they seem out of step with public opinion.

Even when the governor has the power to define the topic for the session, however, he or she lacks complete control over the work of the legislature. Legislators may refuse to support the governor's wishes and may adopt a completely different proposal than the governor intended. Thus, calling a special session can be a risky strategy. In at least one instance (in Oklahoma in 1989), though the governor called a special session, no member of the legislature was willing to introduce the governor's desired legislation. So calling for a special session is a useful power for the governor, but it is far from absolute. Further, calling special sessions is often unpopular (with the public and with legislators), since the sessions represent added expense for the state and pull the legislators away from their other responsibilities.

Media Attention.   Other, less formal factors also help governors influence the agendas pursued in their legislatures. Governors are visible actors, with ready access to the media. They hold press conferences, town hall meetings, and other public events that attract media coverage. Such events offer a platform from which to address key gubernatorial priorities. Governors are often able to reach lawmakers through media outlets (in addition to direct communication). When governors employ the media, they often hope to reach another audience as well—the public. Drawing favorable attention from the public on gubernatorial priorities often translates into legislators adding such issues to their agendas.

State of the State Address.   Governors are required to report to the state legislature on the condition of their states. The state of the state speech is very useful for governors in their agenda-setting role. Most governors choose to offer this speech to the legislature at the beginning of a new legislative session. In the speech, they spend time commending themselves and the legislature for previous accomplishments and praising their states' beauty, perseverance, and success. Once they put these niceties behind them, governors use the state of the state address to lay out their vision of the problems facing their states as well as their proposed solutions. They often also use this opportunity to request new funding from the legislature for existing programs. Given the limited amount of time available and the limited attention span of the audience, governors usually choose to focus on the items they believe most important for their states.

In addition to offering the governors a chance to communicate directly with the legislatures, the state of the state address helps them reach the public and the media to advertise their policy goals. Governors can be very significant actors in the formation of the public policy agendas in their states.

Policy Formulation

Policy formulation is the second phase of the policy process. After a policy question is placed on the agenda, the work of understanding state problems, gathering information, and researching and drafting potential solutions is done. While this phase is primarily the domain of legislators, governors have at least a secondary role to play in this stage as well.

In all states except for Nebraska, the legislature is composed of two chambers that are equally involved in making law. Legislative committees (or subgroups within the legislature) typically do much of the work on potential laws. Legislative leaders have a good deal of influence over which bills make it out of committee, which make it to the floor of the chamber for consideration, and which finally pass. The governor has no official place in this process. The governor often relies on others, such a party leaders and other legislative allies within the legislature, to act on his or her behalf. Governors may also mobilize department heads to present information to the legislature and lobby on behalf of the governor's initiatives.

The governor is not a member of the legislature and only rarely participates in legislative hearings. Though legislative leaders or other legislators may choose to advocate for the governor's position, they are not really required to do so. Members of the governor's party are the most likely source of support, but even these members are not guaranteed to be much help. The governor must convince them—and many other legislators—that they ought to follow his or her lead. A governor who chooses to dedicate time and resources to this process often can achieve notable success.

Coalition Building and the Power to Persuade.   Executive power in the American system is often described as the power to persuade (Neustadt 1980). Though some legislators may start out agreeing with the governor, many do not. Some will be indifferent, and some will be opposed to the governor's goals. The governor must bargain with legislators to try to persuade them to move toward his or her position.

To win adoption of a preferred piece of legislation, one must forge a coalition of supporters. This is where bargaining clearly comes into play. Bargaining requires having something of value to offer to someone else. The governor certainly has things of value to offer to legislators in negotiating for their support. Though the governor, like everyone else who hopes to pass legislation, must engage in this time-consuming bargaining process, he or she (with the governor's many tools) is especially well placed to win. In this way, the governor is an important actor in policy formulation.

Bargaining can take many forms. For example, the governor can offer support on a member's pet legislation in exchange for that member's support for the governor's initiatives. This practice is sometimes called logrolling or reciprocity. A governor can offer to make a trade by indicating a willingness to withdraw opposition to another piece of legislation in exchange for a legislator's support. Similarly, a governor may offer to really throw the support of the office behind a legislator's pet legislation if that legislator will work with the governor.

Like the president, a governor also might benefit from the symbolic importance of the office he or she occupies (sometimes called the aura or trappings of office) in the bargaining with legislators. If a governor chooses to do so, he or she can invoke the symbolism of the office to convince certain legislators to change their minds. The governor is a well-known figure in the state, with a statewide electorate. No one else has the same high profile that the governor has. Some governors are able to translate respect and awe for the office into support among legislators. In short, if the governor calls a member in to the executive office, looks across the desk marked by the great seal of the state, and asks for his or her support, it may be hard for that member to say no.

Governors can build support in other more concrete ways. For example, they can perform "constituency service" for members, by helping their constituents with problems. The executive branch is a large and unwieldy mix of hundreds of offices. Constituents sometimes have problems with the bureaucracy that they cannot solve on their own. They often write or call their legislator's office seeking help. A legislator may, in turn, look to the governor's office for help. A legislator who has sought and received help from the governor's office for a constituent may be more willing to cast a vote in favor of the governor's legislative goals later on. It is smart, therefore, for governors to instruct their staffs to provide such support for legislators when they ask for it. Such positive interactions add to a store of good feelings that the governor can call upon when it is needed.

Governors also have numerous jobs they must fill through appointment. Legislators sometimes want to win jobs for citizens in their districts, and these jobs might be used as bargaining chips as well. Governors can offer a key appointment in exchange for a member's support on proposed legislation. Finally, governors may offer legislators their political support. They frequently help to raise money for elections and often make campaign appearances on behalf of their supporters.

The Role of Chief Legislator in Perspective

This bargaining process by which governors attempt to influence lawmaking is not necessarily ideal. Governors would undoubtedly prefer their legislatures to automatically line up behind their legislative goals. After all, the governors believe that the goals they have laid out are right and necessary for the good of the state. It is surely frustrating for them but nevertheless a fact of life that legislators have their own ideas. It is not impossible for governors to convince the required numbers of legislators to support their plans. But it is not a simple task. It is definitely much more difficult than simply convincing the legislature to take up a particular agenda item for consideration. Influencing policy formulation is much more of a challenge for the governors than is agenda setting. No matter the difficulty, due to the governors' role in both agenda setting and policy formulation, the chief legislator role is among the most important jobs of modern governors. At the same time, this role is a reminder of the limitations of power in the American political system. Even officials as prominent and powerful as governors are not able to make law single-handedly. They must work with others through an established and complicated process to achieve their policy goals.

Bob Riley and the Limits of Gubernatorial Power

Alabama governor Bob Riley (Office of Governor Bob Riley)

In November 2002, Republican member of Congress Bob Riley was elected governor of Alabama in a very close election. Riley had campaigned against the Democratic incumbent Don Siegelman and presented himself as a fiscal conservative opposed to new taxes. In fact, at one time, Riley was voted the most conservative member of the House of Representatives. After taking office in January 2003, however, Governor Riley faced a large state budget deficit for the coming year. After much consideration about how to resolve the budget shortfall, Riley announced that his solution to the $650 million deficit included an intricate plan calling for $1.2 billion in tax increases.

WHAT WOULD JESUS TAX?

To the surprise of many in the state, the governor vigorously set out to promote the seemingly unpopular tax plan, and in fact, it came to define and overshadow his new administration. Riley maintained that his Christian beliefs called for a more just tax system. In explaining his support for the largest tax increase in state history, he said that he was led by his faith to reform the state's tax system. He argued that Alabama's current tax system, which taxes a family of four when they make $4,600 per year, was

Chief Executive

The second key role of the governor is that of chief executive. Most state constitutions contain language indicating that the governor must take care that the laws are "faithfully executed," perhaps the most obvious of the governor's jobs. The role of chief executive is an extremely difficult one that offers few political rewards. While the governor must actively pursue this job, he or she will no doubt find it more time consuming and often less successful than the other key role, that of chief legislator.

No matter the inherent difficulties, governors must oversee the execution of the laws. Given the enormity of the challenge, they cannot do this job on their own. They must work with the state bureaucracy to carry out the laws. Consequently, governors are responsible for managing the bureaucracy. This managerial role is another truly massive undertaking. Governors may be tempted to ignore this job and focus instead on the more politically rewarding roles, but this is a critical job for the state. Bad administration of the laws equals bad laws.

---

immoral. He felt the existing tax structure was unfair, since it placed a huge tax burden on those least able to pay and a relatively light burden on individuals with high incomes, large corporations, and landowners.

WHAT WAS THE PLAN?

Governor Riley's various tax proposals were introduced in the state legislature and passed in June 2003. The tax package was scheduled to be voted on as a constitutional amendment in a special election to be held on September 9, 2003. The overall plan, known as Amendment One, called for a number of government accountability measures, but the most controversial aspects related to the proposed tax increases.

Under the plan, there would have been a number of changes to the state's tax laws. The proposal would have: almost doubled taxes on cigarettes and other tobacco products; changed the way property taxes would be calculated, resulting in an increase in taxes for many homeowners; increased mortgage and deed-recording fees; increased the sales and use taxes on cars, as well as a lease tax; and imposed a sales tax on repair and installation services. While the plan would have cut taxes for low-income residents by increasing the minimum amount of income subject to state tax and increasing the child tax exemption, it would have eliminated the federal tax deduction for all residents and increased the tax rate for higher-income residents. Provisions of the plan would specifically have affected businesses by: increasing the gross receipt taxes on utility companies, changing tax credits for insurance companies, raising taxes on financial institutions, and eliminating the federal income tax deduction and increasing the tax rate for corporations.

CHOOSING SIDES ON THE ISSUE

Once Governor Riley was able to get his proposed tax plan passed by the legislature and set for a statewide vote, the various special interests, as well as average citizens, quickly began taking sides. Though it was highly unusual for a conservative Republican such as Riley to back such a plan, the list of others who favored the plan was less surprising. The governor's plan was supported by the powerful teachers' union (the Alabama Education Association), the state employees' union, and the National Christian Coalition. Among those opposing the

(continues)

Bob Riley and the Limits of Gubernatorial Power *(continued)*

plan were Republican Party leaders and activists, the Alabama Farmers Federation, and the state chapter of the Christian Coalition, the Alabama Christian Coalition.

The campaigns for and against Amendment One took on the appearance of a traditional Alabama political race. Although many believed he started too late, Governor Riley held a series of town meetings throughout the state, as well as a number of last-minute airport press conferences as he flew around Alabama in the days before the vote. Both those who supported and those who opposed the tax plan campaigned with bumper stickers, brochures, Internet sites, and rallies across the state.

The backers of Amendment One enlisted the help of public employees other than Governor Riley by having public schools post yard signs on their lawns encouraging a yes vote and recommending passage of Amendment One on marquee signs. University presidents flooded the E-mail boxes of faculty, staff, and students with supporting statements. The head football coaches for both the University of Alabama and Auburn University appeared in political commercials urging passage of the proposal.

Not to be outdone, the opponents of the amendment held several strategy meetings around the state and bused their faithful to large "no vote" rallies in Birmingham and Montgomery. Those fighting passage of the governor's plan emphasized the complexity of the tax package and its most unpopular provisions.

National attention focused on the campaign, with the national office of the Christian Coalition supporting the plan while their own state office was one of the leading opponents. Former U.S. House majority leader Dick Armey traveled to the state to rail against increasing taxes, even as Birmingham's own, newly elected American Idol, Ruben Studdard, sang the praises of the governor's plan.

Throughout the summer of 2003, both sides increased their efforts to sway public opinion relating to Amendment One. The campaigns became somewhat nasty, with each side portraying the other as being deceptive. Riley's chief policy adviser was widely quoted as saying the reason the tax plan was not doing well in polls was because Alabama voters were "too stupid to know better."

WHAT WENT WRONG/RIGHT?

On September 9, Alabama voters strongly rejected Governor Riley's tax plan, by a two-to-one margin. The constitutional amendment was defeated, with only 33 percent voting in favor and 67 percent voting against it. The margin of defeat on Amend-

Managing the Bureaucracy

Governors do have certain powers to help them do this job. Formal powers of appointment (naming people to the offices in the executive branch) and the ability to reorganize bureaucratic structures to make them more responsive to the governor are the most noteworthy. However, formal power is not always sufficient to overcome the fragmented nature of the executive branches in the states. Bureaucracies are notoriously difficult to manage. They are made up of hundreds or thousands of people and many departments, divisions, and independent boards and commissions. Though we talk of an executive branch, this entity is not nearly as compact and well defined as the name might imply. Members of the executive branch, quite separate from the governor, possess their own ideas about the appropriate policy direction to follow. This

ment One clearly showed that Alabama voters were not ready to buy Governor Riley's tax increase proposals. However, whether one views the defeat of Amendment One as good or bad depends on one's opinion on a number of issues. Voters gave various reasons for why they voted for or against the proposed amendment.

A survey conducted by the Auburn University Center for Governmental Services found that of those who voted against the tax plan: 68 percent strongly objected to increasing the tax rate on automobiles and light trucks, 63 percent strongly opposed assessing real property at full market value, 61 percent disagreed with the governor's attempt to raise nearly twice as much revenue as was needed to meet the existing budget deficit, and 56 percent had concerns about trusting the legislature to allocate any new revenues.

The survey further noted that of those who voted for the tax plan: 66 percent were influenced by the threat of teacher layoffs, 52 percent were concerned about the threat of senior citizen centers being shut down, 59 percent were swayed by their perception of the unfairness of the current tax system, and 59 percent noted their support for the idea of a college scholarship fund.

CONCLUSION

While many people debated the merits of Amendment One, it was evident from the overwhelming vote against the proposal that citizens of Alabama were not persuaded by Governor Riley's all-out campaign for its passage. Many lessons may be learned from the defeat of Amendment One, not the least of which is the fact that governors have many limits on their power to advance a chosen agenda.

Jeff Blankenship
Auburn University

References

Alabama Partnership for Progress. Summary of legislation. www.abetteralabama.org.

Alabama Tax Watch. Wall of shame. http://www.alabamataxwatch. homestead.com/WallOfShame.html.

Mercurio, John. George W. Bush giveth, Bob Riley taketh away. CNN.com, September 9, 2003. http://www.cnn.com/2003/ALLPOLITICS/09/09/mgrind.day.riley.

Seroka, Jim. Alabama's tax reform: What went wrong and why? December 2003. www.auburn.edu/cgs.

Smietana, Bob. Alabama governor says faith drives tax hike. Beliefnet.com, July 17, 2003. http://www.beliefnet.com/story/129/story_12980_1.html.

Additional Resources

For text of amendment and legislative bills, see: http://www.sos.state.al.us/election/2003/scae/index.cfm.

For vote total of the special election, see: http://www.sos.state.al.us/election/index.cfm.

situation guarantees that administrators and governors will rarely operate as a close-knit unit. Governors must attempt to create a degree of coherence in order to pursue their policy goals.

One way that governors can handle this challenge is to reorganize the executive branch to give them more direct control. However, strong opposition will almost invariably meet gubernatorial attempts at reorganization, both from inside the government (the legislative and the executive branches) and from outside forces such as political interest groups. Though reorganization might strengthen the governor's hand at leading the executive branch, the price of reorganization or dramatic government reinvention may be very high.

And in their chief legislator role, governors must interact with many other actors in pursuit of the chief executive role. Numerous important actors, both inside and outside government, must be recognized and sometimes attended to. Bureaucrats, legislators, and interest groups (or clientele groups) are all important at times in determining how the laws will be carried out.

Many different actors are keenly interested in how laws are carried out. The lawmakers themselves presumably have ideas about how the laws are implemented, since they are the ones who drafted and passed the legislation. The bureaucrats with the responsibility to carry them out have their own opinions, since they have skills and expertise in the policy area. Finally, the groups outside of government that will be affected by the new laws want to make their opinions heard as well. Sometimes, these actors form a sort of network among themselves. Since they are concerned about questions in a common policy area, they regularly work together and often accommodate one another's needs. Sometimes, they form a rather exclusive group. The governors struggle to figure out how to fit in. If a single element of this powerful network opposes the governors' ideas, they can be quickly sidetracked. Governors need an inside person, which is why the appointment power is critically important for governors serving in the chief executive role.

In the network described here, the bureaucrats at the relevant agency occupy the governor's place at the table. The appointment power gives the governor the chance to decide who those persons will be. The ability to choose key bureaucrats (administrators) improves the chances that they will share the governor's outlook and goals. This connection should help the governor be more successful in the administration of government. Appointment is certainly not a perfect solution, however, because the executive branch functions separately from the governor to a large extent. The bureaucracy is discussed in more detail in Chapter 3.

Chief of State

The chief of state role is the third key role of the modern governor. Though this role is more symbolic than the chief legislator and chief executive roles, it is nevertheless a primary feature of the modern governorship. As chief of state, the governor represents and embodies the state. He or she is the focal point for internal and external observers of the state.

In many political systems, two different people exercise the roles of the chief of state and the chief executive. In the United Kingdom, for example, the queen serves as the symbolic chief of state, while the prime minister acts as the chief executive, laying out and pursuing the plan for the "queen's government." Lacking royalty, the American tradition is to require the chief executive to serve in both positions.

American chief executives (presidents and governors alike) therefore serve a symbolic role as the central figure of the government in addition to their more substantive responsibilities. In early American history, governors were actually not much more than symbolic leaders or figureheads. Though this is no longer the case, ceremonial and symbolic roles are still significant aspects of the modern governorship.

The governorship is surrounded by many symbols, both large and small. For example, most of the governors and their families live in stately mansions. These grand residences testify to both the prestige of the office and the civic pride of the state as a whole. Such residences are the location of formal state dinners and other official occasions.

Governors spend much of their time on ceremonial duties. They themselves report that after working with the legislature, performing ceremonial functions takes up the second-largest amount of their time. Governors appear at state fairs, cut ribbons at the

The Symbolic Role of the Governor

Arkansas governor Mike Huckabee with employees of the state department of health following a news conference announcing the governor's antismoking initiatives. (Kirk Jordan/Office of Governor Mike Huckabee)

Governors can use this symbolic position to help them pursue their policy goals. For example, Governor Mike Huckabee of Arkansas embarked on a statewide crusade against obesity. By undertaking a program of diet and exercise, he himself lost over 100 pounds. He decided to share his personal story to highlight the concerns regarding obesity in the children of his state. He invited the media to the governor's mansion to observe his morning jog and his healthy breakfast. Such gestures enabled him to gain the attention of the public and bring attention to the health problems associated with obesity.

opening of new businesses in the state, welcome foreign businesspeople, and even crown state pageant winners.

Though some of the governor's other ceremonial activities are purely symbolic, they are nevertheless important because they keep him or her in the public eye and because the people expect such actions. Citizens seem to want their governor to be a frequent presence at public events in the state. Further, turning down groups that request the governor's attendance is fraught with political difficulties, since this decision will surely lead to disappointment or irritation.

Though some governors attempt to limit these symbolic appearances, others seem to genuinely enjoy the opportunity to mingle with the people of the state in a more informal and less stressful environment than that created by other duties of the office. Further, the personalities of some governors lead them to thrive in these setting and perhaps even encourage these symbolic activities. Other governors find them uncomfortable and a waste of time. Such personal considerations undoubtedly affect how often governors pursue these functions and the enthusiasm that they bring to them.

Crisis Management

In 1981, the state of California was infested by the Mediterranean fruit fly. Since the state is heavily dependent on agriculture for its wealth, this infestation demanded governmental attention. Governor Jerry Brown's handling of the infestation was widely viewed as ineffective, and it failed to prevent enormous damage to California crops. The governor was concerned about the negative effects of spraying pesticide to kill the flies, and municipal officials in the area urged him not to allow spraying. Other state actors, especially in the agriculture community, were in favor of massive spraying. At first, the governor decided to employ nonpesticide treatments that he believed would be safer for the environment. But the U.S. secretary of agriculture threatened to quarantine California produce, and over twenty members of California's congressional delegation petitioned the Department of Agriculture to override the governor's decision. Brown ultimately did allow spraying of the pesticide malathion to kill the flies but only after farmers in the state incurred enormous economic losses. The governor did not appear to be on top of the situation, and he did not behave decisively in the face of a significant state crisis. In

Governor Jerry Brown of California (California State Archives)

other words, he failed in the symbolic role of the governorship as well as in his job as crisis manager. When Governor Brown left the governor's office and ran for the U.S. Senate, he was defeated. Many asserted that his han-

While some governors worry that ceremonial duties take too much time away from more substantive duties, the chief of state role is nevertheless an important one for the governorship. This role brings with it prestige. It focuses the attention of the media and the public on the governor—and the governor alone—at key moments. This attention, especially when managed well by the governor, can be translated into the authority to lead, which may prove useful to the governor as he or she performs other duties.

Crisis Manager

The role of crisis manager is not a constant job for the governor. However, when this role is called for, it will most likely dominate his or her time and attention until the crisis at hand is settled.

At certain moments, governors are called on to protect the public or to work to heal their wounds. Governors must respond to crises, both natural and man-made. The governor as crisis manager is filling both a managerial and a symbolic role. A governor's

---

dling of the "Med fly" crisis was a major reason for his massive loss in popularity.

In late August 2005, the Gulf Coast states were hit by the most destructive and costliest natural disaster in the history of the United States. Mississippi and Louisiana bore the brunt of the storm, though Alabama and Florida also incurred significant damage. Governors Haley Barbour of Mississippi and Kathleen Blanco of Louisiana, both in their first terms, faced a crisis-management challenge of enormous proportions. Huge segments of their states were devastated when a Category 4 hurricane named Katrina came aground. The damage in Mississippi and Louisiana was massive. Coastal towns in Mississippi experienced storm surges of greater than twenty feet and whole towns were wiped off the map. In addition to damage from wind, rain, and blowing debris, Louisiana experienced unique challenges. New Orleans, Louisiana—a large metropolitan area partially below sea level and surrounded by water on three sides—was hit especially hard. The huge pump systems that normally would have quickly emptied the city of floodwaters were overwhelmed when the levee system was breached. The city was deluged.

Millions of people in both states evacuated ahead of the impending storm, but many stayed behind. Hundreds and perhaps thousands of people were killed across the area (an accurate count is unlikely to ever be made). Countless more were stranded on their rooftops for days, especially in New Orleans. Families were separated by rising floodwaters and lost touch with one another during the chaotic rescue missions. Bodies were seen floating in New Orleans streets. The images of the destruction caused by the storm and the suffering that followed— seemingly untouched by governmental intervention—shocked the entire country. The president first indicated that no one could have expected the vast devastation that occurred, while critics responded that scientists had warned of such a catastrophic storm for decades. As late as November, thousands of people were still unaccounted for. The true toll of the hurricane will probably not be known for many months.

Such was the unprecedented challenge facing these Gulf state governors. Not only did they have to convince their state's citizens to evacuate in advance of the hurricane and then manage the state rescue and recovery response to this horrible disaster; they were also called upon to reassure devastated citizens that their safety was being addressed and normalcy would eventually

(continues)

Crisis Management *(continued)*

return. The governors had to act simultaneously as the symbolic and unifying heads of state and as crisis managers, finding stranded citizens and providing the daily necessities for the thousands huddled in evacuation centers. These vast challenges were made more difficult by what is widely agreed to have been a very ineffective federal response. Governors struggled on their own for days in the midst of devastated communities along their coasts. Adding to the dire situation was the fact that many thousands of National Guard troops who would otherwise have responded in such disasters had been called up by the national government and were serving in the wars in Iraq and Afghanistan. The governors were left without the resources necessary to launch a quick and effective response. While they would normally have been able to draw upon the assistance of neighboring states, the vast size of the area of destruction made this unworkable.

In New Orleans thousands of people were stranded at the Superdome, the city's largest evacuation center of last resort, and at the city's Ernest Morial Convention Center. When the levee system broke, 80 percent of the city became flooded with tons of water and sewage. Rescue workers struggled to gain access to those who had not evacuated and were now stranded. It took days to position the necessary resources to evacuate the thousands of people from the Superdome and the convention center. During this interval, the evacuees—most of whom had already lost their homes and jobs—suffered under the terrible conditions at the evacuation centers. Food and water were scarce, the temperature was unbearably hot, and the lack of working toilets resulted in unsanitary and unhealthy conditions. Some people turned to violence and other evacuees feared for their lives.

The government response to Katrina was widely viewed as ineffective. Many critics asserted that the poor government response actually added to the suffering of people already experiencing unimaginable losses. While much of the criticism has been directed at the national government, it is not yet clear how popular opinion (and the next

---

handling of a crisis in the state can surely make or break an administration. Ineffective or seemingly uncaring responses to problems experienced by the citizenry may raise doubts about a governor and create problems for him or her in other arenas.

Another reason that crisis response is a significant component of a governor's job is that crises demand attention. The ability to plan a response to unknown crises is limited, and the advent of crisis events demands the governor's attention no matter what else he or she had been hoping to focus on. Governors who fail to give adequate attention to such crises run the risk of seeming out of touch with or unsympathetic to the people. Neither of these perceptions is good for a governor's role as chief of state (nor for his or her reelection aspirations). Governor Jerry Brown learned this very hard lesson.

Many other types of crises may strike a state. When a hurricane devastates a coastal community, for example, the governor often shows up to survey the damage and offer support and sympathy to victims of the storm. Droughts, gypsy moths, and forest fires have all at various times required governors to take action and make it clear that they were "doing something" to address the problem.

election) will treat the governors' responses. Mayor Ray Nagin of New Orleans repeatedly criticized both President Bush and Governor Blanco for what he termed inadequate responses. Other criticisms revolved around Governor Blanco's refusal to allow the Red Cross to enter the city to assist victims of the storm who stayed behind and became stranded. State and local officials, intending to evacuate those left behind as soon as possible, chose to put resources into that effort rather than helping the Red Cross operations to hand out food and other supplies. Governor Barbour of Mississippi also received criticism for downplaying the seriousness of Katrina before it hit the Mississippi coast. Some fear the governor's attitude discouraged some residents of the area from taking the threat seriously. In the aftermath of the storm, however, his leadership was generally viewed in a more positive light than that of Governor Blanco. Since the Mississippi Gulf Coast does not have a major urban center comparable to New Orleans, Mississippi was spared the spectacle of thousands of people stranded, hungry, dehydrated, and sick. Governor Barbour could instead direct most of his attention to rescue and recovery rather than massive evacuation efforts. Governors Barbour and Blanco also differ in their partisan attachments. Barbour, former Republican national party chair, was lauded by conservative observers and he in turn praised rather than criticized the federal response. Blanco, a Democrat, repeatedly called for additional federal assistance and, with Mayor Nagin, complained bitterly about the effectiveness of the federal response.

Investigations into what went wrong at all levels of government will continue. Time and the results of these investigations will tell what the future holds for these two governors. Early speculation has compared Governor Barbour's performance favorably with Mayor Rudy Giuliani's leadership following the World Trade Center attacks in New York. Governor Blanco seems less likely to emerge from Katrina with such a positive reputation. Whether her perceived failures are the result of poor choices, a lack of leadership on her part, or instead the result of an unbearable, unmanageable situation made worse by a poor federal response remains unclear in the months following Katrina.

Other crisis events are the result of the actions of people rather than nature. Southern governors during the civil rights movement were most noteworthy for symbolic gestures meant to represent their continued opposition to changes in the racial status quo. Governors such as Orval Faubus of Arkansas and George Wallace of Alabama are two examples. Rather than offering leadership to move their states forward in the midst of crisis, these governors used the symbolic power of the office to divide the people of their states. They drew political power from these symbolic acts of defiance, though their actions did nothing to improve the conditions of their states.

The terrorist attacks of September 11, 2001, represent another example of governors placed in the position of responding to an unprecedented disaster. Though the entire country was, in a sense, attacked on that day, the reality is that the attacks themselves took place within the borders of three states, the World Trade Center (WTC) towers in New York, the Pentagon in northern Virginia, and a field in Pennsylvania where one plane crashed without reaching its target. Governors James Gilmore of Virginia, George Pataki of New York, and Tom Ridge of Pennsylvania all faced enormous challenges as

Three Mile Island

Crises are often temporary, their consequences mostly economic. Others are more long-lasting and even potentially lethal. One dramatic example of a crisis that spanned both these categories was the accident that occurred at the Three Mile Island nuclear power plant in Pennsylvania in 1979. Governor Richard Thornburgh had been in office only seventy-two days when the accident occurred, the first such accident in an American nuclear power plant. No governor in American history had ever had to respond to such a crisis, so the governor's role was somewhat ill defined. Though much of his response had to do with actually managing the situation, assuring the safety of the workers and the residents of the community, a significant part of his role was to assure the people that things were okay.

Throughout the crisis, the governor received contradictory information. He was unsure what to do and seemed to vacillate

(L–R) Harold Denton, director of the division of nuclear reactor regulation at the Nuclear Regulatory Commission; Pennsylvania governor Richard Thornburgh; President Jimmy Carter; Rosalynn Carter; and an unidentified plant official tour the control room of the Three Mile Island nuclear plant in Middletown, Pennsylvania, on April 1, 1979, four days after the nuclear accident that closed the plant. (Dirck Halstead/Time Life Pictures/Getty Images)

state, federal, and local officials attempted to grapple with the enormous destruction of property, loss of life, and uncertainty that the attacks and their aftermath created. Though the massive scale of the attacks focused much of the public attention on the national government for leadership, the governors of these states nevertheless bore a large responsibility to reassure the citizenry that their states were responding aggressively to the attacks.

over whether an evacuation was actually needed. He ultimately did order an evacuation of children and pregnant women in a 5-mile radius of the plant, and hundreds more citizens evacuated in a panic. He also advised people in the surrounding area to remain inside, with their doors and windows closed. In his most definitive act, Governor Thornburgh joined with President Jimmy Carter to tour the plant in the full view of network television cameras. Due to this public display, citizens of the state and the media became reassured that things had to be safe for anyone if the governor and the president would go inside. This disaster illustrates the critical role governors play in reassuring the public and its fears. When people feel uncertain and afraid, they need to believe that someone is taking steps to make (or keep) them safe and to tell them the truth about what is happening.

This particular disaster was accompanied by tremendous uncertainty. Unlike a hurricane or a fire, the people continued to be unsure of just how (if at all) their health or the health of their children would be affected. Thus, citizens of the state naturally looked to the governor's office for reassurance and for help in understanding what had actually occurred.

Chief Judge

Governors also serve a judicial role. Much like the president, American governors have traditionally possessed the power of executive clemency, which gives governors and pardon boards the ability to show leniency to criminals by granting pardons or commuting sentences. Pardons typically erase a criminal record and restore civil rights (such as the right to vote), while commutations make punishments less harsh. Some governors, for example, can commute death sentences, choosing instead to give a prisoner life imprisonment rather than execution. The idea of American chief executives possessing such power derives from the British monarch's power.

Until the beginning of the twentieth century, gubernatorial pardons were often the only way for prisoners to be released before the end of their sentences. Before states created pardon and parole systems, the governor pardoned nearly half of all prisoners before their sentences expired.

Though governors exercised this power fairly often in the past, the political climate since the late 1990s has not encouraged them to exercise their clemency powers. Governors have recently shied away from using them due to fears of appearing too soft on crime and insensitive to the victims. Because of these political challenges, governors often employ the pardon mainly in the last days of their terms, and some governors simply avoid the process altogether. Advocates for executive clemency argue it is an essential safeguard against failures in the overworked court systems. Others argue that the governors should show mercy to offenders when the courts have been too harsh. Though the powers are used sparingly, they are widely available to governors.

Thirty-three states give governors the exclusive and unconditional power to grant pardons or reduce prison sentences. Four states (Alabama, Connecticut, Georgia, and Idaho) have taken the pardoning power away from the governor and given it to clemency boards made up of members appointed by the governor. In nine states, the

Clemency

While it is generally true that governors now use the clemency power quite sparingly, there are some significant exceptions. The actions of outgoing governor George Ryan of Illinois are the most dramatic. He commuted the sentences of all 167 death row inmates in his state and pardoned three of the four of them. Those prisoners who had their sentences commuted will still serve life in prison, but the four who were pardoned were immediately released. Ryan's actions arose from his deep concerns about the application of the death penalty in Illinois. In a highly publicized case, a group of Northwestern University journalism students uncovered evidence that cleared Anthony Porter, a death row inmate in Illinois. After this, the governor declared a moratorium on executions during which officials investigated the death penalty in the state. During the moratorium period, a commission looked into the convictions of all Illinois death row inmates. Thirteen of these inmates were exonerated of their crimes. At the end of the study, the governor issued the blanket clemency. He explained the decision this way: "Our capital system is haunted by the demon of error: error in determining guilt and error in determining who among the guilty deserves to die. What effect was race having? What effect was poverty having?

Former Illinois governor George Ryan sparked controversy in January 2003 by granting clemency to four inmates and reducing the sentences of all death row prisoners to life without parole. (Office of Governor George H. Ryan)

Because of all these reasons, today I am commuting the sentences of all death row inmates."

No other governor has ever taken such dramatic steps. However, the issue of the death penalty does remain controversial in nearly all states where it is on the books.

governor remains involved but can only consider clemency recommendations made by state clemency boards. These states are Arizona, Delaware, Florida, Indiana, Louisiana, Montana, Oklahoma, Pennsylvania, and Texas. California law requires a recommendation by the state supreme court for the pardon of any person convicted of two felonies. Finally, governors in Nebraska, Nevada, and Utah sit as members of pardon boards and thus share the power to pardon with several other board members.

Some governors in the past abused the pardon power. Indeed, there are some spectacular examples of questionable behavior. Governor Jack Walton of Oklahoma freed nearly 700 prisoners in eleven months and was impeached and convicted for taking bribes in exchange for granting pardons. Similarly, Governor Miriam "Ma" Ferguson of

Governor George Pataki of New York has been a staunch advocate of the death penalty. In fact, reinstating the death penalty was a central issue in the 1994 governor's race between the challenger Pataki and the incumbent Mario Cuomo. Cuomo had long been an opponent of capital punishment, and during his time in office, New York in essence did not have a death penalty. One of Pataki's first legislative accomplishments after defeating Governor Cuomo was the passage of the New York death penalty statute. The statute was challenged, and the State Court of Appeals of New York (the state's highest court) ruled in June 2004 that New York's death penalty statute was unconstitutional. Advocates vow to amend the law so that it can be revived.

Governors receive hundreds of petitions for clemency each year. They reject the vast majority. Such requests are typically filed individually by prisoners and their families. However, in some instances, group challenges have been organized. The Michigan Battered Women's Clemency Project (MBWCP), for example, assists women who were convicted of murdering their abusive husbands but were not allowed the opportunity to introduce information about their abuse. In October 2003, the MBWCP petitioned Governor Jennifer Granholm for clemency for twenty women convicted of murdering their abusive husbands. Most of these women were convicted before the 1992 Michigan Court of Appeals decision that ruled that expert testimony regarding battered spouse syndrome is permissible evidence in court. The group had previously submitted clemency petitions to Governor John Engler, who declined all of the requests. As of May 2004, the group had succeeded in obtaining clemency for two of the women.

Similar groups have formed in Illinois, Ohio, and Maryland. In each of these states, the governors granted clemency in some cases. According to the National Clearinghouse for the Defense of Battered Women, at least 124 women from twenty-three states have been freed since 1978. Many were released in the early 1990s as part of mass clemency actions across the country. Governor Richard Celeste of Ohio, for example, freed twenty-five battered women on leaving office in 1990. Governors William Weld of Massachusetts, William Donald Schaefer of Maryland, and Pete Wilson of California also granted some clemency requests from battered women.

Associated Press. Excerpts from Ryan's speech. FOXNews.com, January 11, 2003. http://www.foxnews.com/story /0,2933,75270,00.html.

Texas pardoned 3,700 prisoners in two years. Pardons were apparently available for purchase, with the price keyed to the severity of the offense. Perhaps not surprisingly, Texas is among the states that have removed this power from its governor. More recently, Governor Ray Blanton of Tennessee raised significant questions when he planned to pardon fifty-two prisoners on his way out of the governor's office. His successor was sworn in three days early to undo these corrupt pardons. Such actions are, however, exceptions to the norm. Most governors seem to dislike holding responsibility for such life-and-death decisions.

The examples provided here have often generated a great deal of publicity, but clemency requests and the governors' responses are typically more mundane. However, as DNA testing is increasingly effective and available for convicted criminals, governors may have to weigh such evidence in more petitions in the future.

Chief of Party

Another primary role of governors is that of chief of party. This role is not an official job of the office; it grows naturally from the governor's position as the state's (and the party's) highest elective officer.

Particularly in states where the two parties are competitive with one another (rather than one party dominating), this role is very significant for both the power of the governor and the role of the party in the state. Governors who are strong party leaders can be more successful than those who lack strong party support. However, merely carrying the party label does not guarantee a governor strong support from the party. Party leadership is developed over time, the result of working to build coalitions of supporters.

In nearly every case, the major candidates for governor in all fifty states are running under the label of either the Democratic or Republican Party. Consequently, in addition to the personal organization that they build, gubernatorial candidates also inherit state party organizations. Some of these organizations are very helpful to the candidate while seeking the office, and they continue to be important for providing an organization to assist in governing the state after the election.

In many states, the governor plays a significant role in choosing the state party chair. Governors may also participate in fund-raising for the party in order to preserve party strength in the state. When the party organization is strong, the governor can draw on its help in the reelection campaign and in pursuing legislative goals. Researchers have found that governors who head strong state parties (which they define as parties that have greater control over the choice of nominees for the office) are able to draw on party support for their legislative goals. Governors who head weak party organizations cannot count on partisan loyalty from their legislators (Morehouse and Jewell 2003).

Certain governors pay very little attention to the state party. Some have been elected without the help of party leaders and may even have been chosen despite the opposition of party organizational leaders. Such governors may view working with party leaders or trying to reorganize the party as wasted energy.

Nevertheless, there is a significant connection between the role of the party in the election process and the role in governing. As Morehouse and Jewell (2003, 167) asserted: "If their parties were united behind them in the nominating and election process, they would be behind them in the governing process. A united party can provide the votes the governor needs when he or she proposes measures to the legislature for passage. A governor hamstrung by factions cannot hope to govern effectively."

Governors normally benefit from their parties' strength in the state legislature. When the governor's party has the majority in the legislature, legislative leaders may work for the governor: sharing the governor's party attachment, they may also share the governor's goals. When the party in the legislature gets very large, it is possible that the party will be divided into factions. If that happens, the governor may have a harder time depending on the party for support.

Intergovernmental Liaison

Some of the responsibilities of the governorship are exercised outside the state. Since the United States has a federal system, multiple governments have the power to make decisions. The decisions made by one level of government often have a substantial impact on the other levels, which means it is vital to pay attention to what other levels of government (especially the national government) are doing. Thus, in addition to being key leaders within their states, governors are important actors outside their states as well. They represent the interests of the state to the national government in Washington, D.C., and sometimes enter into agreements with other states to address common problems.

Governors are obviously not the only actors in Washington speaking for their home states. Members of Congress also view their job (at least in part) as serving the needs of their states and districts. But governors and members of Congress may not always see eye to eye. Members of the U.S. House of Representatives typically serve a district made up of only a portion of a state, so they tend to view their job as principally serving their local district. Senators are elected to serve the entire state, but as members of the national legislature, they must act in the interest of the entire country as well. Governors serve only the state. As a result, they do not depend exclusively on the state's congressional delegations to speak on behalf of the home state.

Sometimes, governors (and their staffs) work independently, lobbying to convince the national government of the positions they feel are best for their states. To facilitate this effort, many states have established offices in Washington, D.C. Other support structures have been created as well to help make sure the governors are able to protect their states' interests in Washington. Many governors have hired intergovernmental coordinators to gather information for them about what other governments are doing, to provide a central coordinating point for intergovernmental activities, and to introduce their perspectives into federal and state agency discussions. Each of these examples involves individual states and their governors taking steps to protect their own interests in Washington.

In other cases, governors may join together to make their voices heard in Washington. For example, the National Governors Association (NGA) is a professional organization of the nation's governors that advises them on policy concerns and brings them together to identify needs that cross state boundaries. This organization offers a way for the governors to speak together on issues that affect many states. The NGA lobbies Congress, arguing on behalf of the interests of the chief executives in the fifty states. There are also regional organizations of governors, such as the Western Governors' Association, and partisan groups.

Given all of these developments, the governors have become significant leaders on the national level. The governor-brokered solution to the 1995–1996 budget standoff between President Bill Clinton and the Republican-controlled Congress is illustrative. In that instance, governors worked out a budget deal that both the president and Congress could accept. This deal avoided a third federal government shutdown and sent federal employees back to their jobs. Since many governors have thoughts of running for the White House, their profile as national actors is likely to continue to rise. Such positive contributions are good publicity for individual governors and for the governors as a group.

Military Chief

Governors also serve a military role. As chief executives, they are responsible for the health and safety of the citizens of their states. Further, they are designated the commanders-in-chief of their state National Guards. Under certain circumstances, such as during a declared emergency, some states' governors can exert extraordinary powers to suspend authority, seize personal property, direct evacuations, and authorize the release of emergency funds. Governors are also critically important as the voice of the states in communicating with the public, requesting federal disaster assistance, and assisting residents in coping with the disaster.

The National Guard is often called out to keep peace and order during natural disasters and civil disturbances. Guard members work as emergency relief providers and assist with search-and-rescue operations at the will of the governor. Events requiring the governor to call out the Guard are obviously rather sporadic. However, Guard units have moved into other responsibilities as well. For example, since the late 1980s, they have sometimes engaged in missions outside their own states, such as patrolling the U.S.-Mexico border. Though there has been a traditional separation between military and law enforcement activities, National Guard troops are increasingly putting their skills and equipment to use in nontraditional ways. While on these missions, even outside its own state borders, the Guard remains under the control of the governor.

Since the attacks on the United States in 2001 and the heightened concerns about terrorism, much of the governors' commander-in-chief activities has been directed toward protecting against future terrorist attacks. National Guard troops have served many roles in the post-9/11 United States under the authority of both the governors and the president. State and local law enforcement and health workers will be the first to respond to any future attack on the United States. It is up to the governors, in coordination with other local, state, and national officials, to make sure that the systems are in place to respond quickly and effectively. After September 2001, Guard troops (under authority of the president) provided security at the nation's airports for a period of time until regular security forces could be put into place.

Since the control over the Guard is shared between the states and the national government, the relative power of each has often generated conflict between the governors and the national government. In the 1980s, several governors who opposed President Ronald Reagan's policies in Central America threatened to prevent their Guard units from participating in training there. The Pentagon asserted that it had the power to send National Guard units abroad for training as well as for fighting in conflicts. Some governors argued that the U.S. Constitution, which grants states "the authority of training the militia," gives the governors control over where National Guard units are trained. The question was ultimately pursued in federal court, where the U.S. Supreme Court disagreed with the governors and upheld the president's power to send Guard troops abroad for training without federalizing them.

Questions of presidential authority arose in the wake of the 2001 terrorist attacks as well. It is clear that the president has the authority to take charge of the National Guard when it is called to duty to deal with war and national crises. But the governors assert that when the Guard is performing domestic missions, it should do so under the authority of the governor. Various laws of the U.S. Congress support the governors' assertion. The National Governors Association issued a position statement attempting to clarify the governors' position on the roles of the National Guard in the post-9/11 landscape:

> The National Guard, historically a critical resource in emergencies, can be an effective force multiplier to civil authorities in responding to terrorism at the state, local, and federal levels. In the wake of the September 11, 2001, attacks, the National Guard has expanded its traditional role in homeland defense and security. National Guard activities include securing strategic facilities, such as airports, pharmaceutical labs, nuclear power plants, communications towers, and border crossings, and have been a cornerstone in protecting our citizens from domestic terrorism. Source: National Governors Association, Policy Position, February 27, 2004, http://www.nga.org..

The U.S. military increasingly depends on National Guard units to augment the active forces. Thousands of these "citizen-soldiers" have been called up for service in the Persian Gulf, for example, during both Gulf Wars. In May 2004, the national government undertook the largest National Guard deployment in U.S. history (144,000 troops, or 42 percent of the states' combined Army National Guard troops). The activation of so many Guard troops by the national government leaves states struggling to decide how to respond to challenges at home. In some states, more than 50 percent of Guard troops were deployed. In one state, the figure was as high as 85 percent. Governors must figure out ways to adjust to the temporary absence of Guard members in preparation for challenges that may arise within their states. The role of the National Guard and of the governors as commanders-in-chief will surely continue to evolve as the country faces new and unpredictable challenges.

POWERS OF THE GOVERNORS

The preceding sections examined the pivotal roles that governors must play when occupying the office today. To fulfill these many roles, governors must have a variety of tools, resources, and powers at their disposal. These assets come in a variety of forms. Some powers come from the office of the governorship itself. These are called formal, or institutional, powers. Enabling powers also derive from the office. Enabling powers are the staff and other support that the state provides to work for and with the governor. Other powers come from the situation at the time of the governor's term. Still other powers are inherent in the person who holds the office. These powers related to the particular incumbent are called informal powers. Of course, many different powers may come into play as governors pursue all of their varied roles. Some powers are important in only one of the roles; others are significant across multiple roles. The powers of the governors are discussed in the next sections.

Formal Powers

Reformers and researchers have directed quite a good deal of attention to the formal powers of the governor's office, perhaps because such powers are the easiest to identify and define. When the office provides few formal powers, a governor has to turn to other resources to have a chance at success in his or her official endeavors. These other powers are less concrete and more variable from one governor to the next and are decidedly hard for researchers to systematically measure. Over time, states have made significant changes in the powers bestowed on the governors.

Joseph Schlesinger (1965) first developed an index of gubernatorial powers that rated the states' governors in terms of types of powers, allowing observers to compare the powers possessed by governors across the states. This index measured four aspects of formal powers of the governor: tenure potential (length of terms eligible to serve and successive terms allowed); budget power (degree of gubernatorial control in preparing the budget); appointment power (degree of gubernatorial control over appointment of key state administrators); and finally, veto power (determined by the item veto power of the governor combined with the size of legislative majority required for override).

This index has been widely employed (and criticized) in the literature. Studies have used it to examine the relationship between formal powers and a variety of other conditions in the states. These studies have examined the association of formal powers with many areas, including: gubernatorial support of agency budget requests (Sharkansky 1968), managing the bureaucracy (Hebert, Brudney, and Wright 1983; Brudney and Hebert 1987), and legislative leadership (Dilger, Krause, and Moffett 1995; Ferguson 2003).

Though the index is widely used by researchers, some have complained that it does not accurately reflect the full range of resources governors have. This complaint has greater relevance today, as the governorships now possess resources that were not initially included in Schlesinger's design. These new resources include, for example, the joint election of governors and lieutenant governors, the amendatory veto, and the development of gubernatorial staffs (Dometrius 1987). Formal powers of the governors and the four features of the formal power index described here should not be viewed as the full explanation of the power of the governor: as noted throughout this discussion, formal powers are only one component of the resources governors can use. But even if they are not the whole story, they are a good place to begin because they provide a systematic means to look at power across the governor's offices in the fifty states.

The Veto

The veto is the governors' power to say no to legislation that they oppose. It is the single most important power governors have for affecting the making of law in the states. Again, this power varies from state to state. There are several types of vetoes: the package veto, item veto, amendatory veto, and pocket veto. Each state offers its governor some combination of these. Some governors have strong vetoes; other governors have weaker vetoes. The strength of the veto arises from several variables. For instance, states vary in the length of time allowed for the governor to sign or veto a bill. States also require different numbers of votes for legislative override of a veto. When the governor only has a few days to veto a bill before it becomes law, the veto is weaker. Similarly, in states where only a simple majority of the legislature is required to override the governor's veto, the veto has little force. Since it took a majority of legislators to pass the bill in the first place, it would typically be rather easy for the bill's advocates to come up with a majority again to override the veto.

The package veto is the most basic veto. It gives the governor (and the president) the power to reject entire pieces of legislation that have reached his or her desk. All fifty governors have this type of veto. Though this is an important tool, it is also limited. When a governor chooses to veto a bill, the whole bill is rejected, even if he or she took issue with only a portion.

An item veto goes a step further. This veto allows the governor to accept the parts of a bill he or she supports and veto other parts deemed objectionable. Governors in forty-three states have access to this type of veto. Item vetoes offer governors more flexibility for dealing with legislation once it reaches their desks.

The specific features of these vetoes vary from state to state. In some states, the item veto can only be used on appropriations bills; in others, it can be employed on all types of bills. In some states, the item veto can only be used to remove or reduce expenditure items; in others, it can be used to change language. Even in states where the item veto applies only to appropriations bills, language can at times be affected by the governor because state legislatures often place narrative language in appropriations bills, defining how the funds are to be spent. In some states, the item veto allows the governor to veto this narrative language, and such a veto would amount to a change in policy. As with the package veto, state legislatures can override item vetoes if they can garner enough votes. Thirty-seven states require an extraordinary vote (depending on the state, two-thirds or three-fifths of legislators elected, or two-thirds of those present) to override an item veto.

In theory, having the item veto encourages a governor to remove unnecessary spending from legislation and thereby hold down state spending. In practice, it seems that the item veto is used most often in the same way as the package veto is: as a bargaining tool to encourage the legislature to add or remove items from proposed legislation (Wiggins 1980). When a governor has only a package veto, legislators can purposefully combine elements of bills they know the governor dislikes with bills the governor supports. Such a practice sometimes forces the governor to accept the objectionable parts of a bill in order to enact into law the desired elements. The item veto helps the governor to counteract such tactics.

Fifteen states allow their governors the executive amendment, also known as the amendatory veto. This device gives the governor the power to veto a bill and send it back to the legislature with recommended amendments. If the legislature agrees to the changes, the governor signs the bill into law. Governors sometimes use this veto to bring together different parts of multiple bills and formulate a single, unified law. If the legislature accepts the governor's proposed amendments, then the governor has effectively shaped the legislation after the legislature had completed the lawmaking process. Though not much research has been conducted on the use of these vetoes, there is some evidence that these are useful tools for governors attempting to influence the actions of the legislature. Critics of such strong vetoes worry that they may result in a blurring of the lines of the separation between the branches. They may also encourage conflict between the legislative and executive offices. Governors might use this veto to make policy on their own, bypassing legislative intent altogether. This tact would appear to violate the spirit of shared powers set out in state constitutions, though the behavior has been upheld in some state courts.

The pocket veto is a passive way of vetoing bills. This power, allowed in fifteen states in 2002, permits the governor to reject a bill by refusing to sign it after the legislature has adjourned. In all but three states (Hawaii, Utah, and Virginia), the state legislatures lack the opportunity to reconvene to vote on a pocket veto. In the vast majority of states that allow the pocket veto, then, it cannot be overridden, which makes the pocket veto a particularly powerful tool. But it can only be used effectively at the end of the legislative term.

Like most powers of the office, the veto power has been fortified in the majority of states in recent history. In the earliest years, only two states provided the package veto to their governors. By 1812, nearly half of the states had adopted it. As more states joined the Union, they typically gave their governors veto powers from the outset. By 1860, the veto power was firmly established, with twenty-five of the thirty-three states' governors having the veto. The item veto was first established by Georgia and Texas in 1868, and it quickly spread to other states. In 1889, forty-two of the forty-five states gave their governor some type of veto. By 1949, all but one of the forty-nine states granted at least some veto power to the governor. North Carolina, the single holdout state, did not grant its governor any veto power until 1995.

Strong versus Weak Vetoes

Once the governor wields a veto (of any type except the pocket veto), the legislature may try to override it. The percent of votes required in the legislature to override ranges from a simple majority to a two-thirds majority of both chambers of the legislature. The number of votes required to override is important because it affects how frequently overrides take place and how useful the veto really is for the governor. If merely a simple majority (50 percent plus one vote) is required to override the veto (as is the case in six states), the veto carries minimal weight. If a supermajority is required to override the governor's veto (as is the case in forty-four states), the veto is much more powerful, and the override attempt is more likely to fail. Among the forty-four states that require a supermajority to override, the votes required range from three-fifths of the legislators present to two-thirds of the total number of legislators in the chamber. In the absence of an override, the veto is sustained, meaning the legislation does not become law.

The force of the veto powers held by each governor varies. To fully understand how weak or strong a governor's veto powers are, scholars examine a combination of factors. The strongest veto power, for example, would give the governor the greatest power in all categories. It would require a supermajority to override, would provide the governor with the item veto, and would also allow the governor the pocket veto. Such strong veto powers were initially the exception in the states. By 1899, nineteen of the forty-two states that had the veto gave their governors the strongest veto power. By 1949, that number had grown to twenty-nine of the forty-seven states with the veto. It has climbed steadily since then. In 2002, thirty-nine of the states' governors had very strong veto powers by this definition.

The veto is important for two reasons. First, it offers the governors a legitimate place at the legislative table. It means they have a role in making the laws of the state. Second, since vetoes are rarely overridden, the veto generally means the vetoed bill will die. This near guarantee that governors will have the "final word" on legislation gives them leverage as they bargain to achieve their goals.

While the veto is typically viewed as a negative power—a way to keep something from happening rather than causing something to happen—governors can employ this "threat" to entice legislators to their positions. Legislators do not wish to go to the immense work of formulating legislation only to have it end up dead on arrival at the governor's desk. Legislators also do not wish the embarrassment of having their ideas met with the public disdain of the governor. The threat of the veto is often enough to change legislative behavior toward the governor's desired goals.

Governors are wise to use the veto sparingly. A governor who vetoes a great deal of legislation is one who did not prevail earlier in the process. The frequent use of the veto might be interpreted by potential opponents of the governor as evidence of weakness rather than strength.

Governors rarely employ the veto power. Between 1945 and 1973, the average percent of measures vetoed across the states was around 5 percent. In the most recent year for which data are available (2002), governors vetoed somewhat fewer bills. The nationwide average was only 4 percent. Governors vetoed just over 1,000 bills and resolutions of the nearly 19,000 passed across the states in that year.

These national averages, however, mask quite a lot of state variation In 1973, for example, New York's governor vetoed nearly 30 percent of the bills passed by the legislature, whereas neither Vermont's nor Wyoming's governors used the veto at all. In 2002, California's governor Gray Davis used the veto more than any other governor. He vetoed 17 percent of measures passed by the legislature (432 vetoes). By contrast, five governors did not use the veto at all in 2002. Eight more governors vetoed less than 1 percent of the bills presented by their legislatures.

Governors of some states consistently cast more than an average number of vetoes. New York and California governors, for instance, have regularly vetoed a lot of bills. The largest number of vetoes is typically used in states with divided party control (sometimes called divided government), which means that the governor and a majority of the legislature do not share the same party (Wiggins 1980).

Overrides are even rarer than vetoes. In the middle of the twentieth century, it was very uncommon for a governor's veto to be overridden by the legislature. Less than 2 percent of vetoes were overridden in 1945 and 1947. Before that, overrides were almost nonexistent: a veto by the governor was nearly always the final word on a bill. However, legislatures seem to have become somewhat more aggressive and more willing to go against their governors. In the 1970s, the percent of veto overrides rose to 6 percent. Override numbers fluctuated in the 1980s and 1990s between 2 and 8 percent. The percent of vetoes overridden across the states was approximately 5 percent in 2002.

Appointment Powers

The executive branch is charged with administering the laws of the states, and as chief executive, the governor has the responsibility to oversee this process. As a political actor, the governor also hopes for the laws to be carried out in a certain way, in a direction that coincides with his or her policy positions. If the governors are going to be able to influence how the laws are administered, they need to have a say in appointing officers who are in charge of administering the laws.

Today, as the state bureaucracies have grown so large, the vast majority of the offices in the executive branch are held by people who are simply hired for their jobs through a merit hiring process. They are chosen due to their credentials rather than their political loyalty, and they often hold their jobs through the administrations of multiple governors. Consequently, career bureaucrats may not be particularly responsive to the political goals of the governor. The jobs of career bureaucrats, however, typically do not have much discretion associated with them, and their actions have little political significance. These offices are appropriately relegated to the status of career bureaucrat rather than political appointee.

There are, however, many officials in the state bureaucracy who do have policy-relevant authority. These officials also possess a significant amount of discretion, which makes their political beliefs relevant to the outcomes of state government. They are in charge of writing the rules and regulations that carry out the laws passed by the legislatures. These are the sorts of officials that advocates for executive authority believe the governor should have the power to appoint.

The appointment power is a vital tool for governors. Research shows that administrators who are appointed by the governor are more likely to respond to his or her political preferences. When agency heads are appointed by the governor, they are more likely to share the goals and ideals of the chief executive. Since many actors (both inside and outside of government) are able to influence the choices made by the executive branch and many of these have their own motivations and policy goals, it is necessary for the governor to have the chance to make sure his or her people will be part of the process.

The presence of state officials who are not dependent on the governor for their jobs limits the ability of the governor to perform the chief executive role. Though reformers continually try to shorten the long ballot (and thus give the governor the power to appoint more high-level state positions), states still elect a good number of executive officials. In 2000, the fifty states combined still elected over 300 officials to their executive branches (in addition to the 50 governors).

The number of gubernatorial appointees is different from state to state, but in general, states have given the governors the chance to appoint more of the people they will be working with in the executive branch. One way to examine the appointment power of the governor is to count the number of key officials he or she is allowed to choose. These officials can be defined as those in charge of the six major functions of the states: corrections, kindergarten through twelfth-grade education, health, highways, public utilities, and welfare. By this reckoning, governors are moderately powerful. In most states, someone other than the governor appoints these officials but with the approval of the governor, the legislature, or both. Another way of assessing the importance of the governor's appointment power is to look at how many executive officials besides the governor are elected. The best-case scenario for the governor would be election for only the governor and the lieutenant governor. But this arrangement exists in only five states. The average number of executive branch elected officials across the states is about eight. North Dakota has the highest number—twelve.

Without the appointment power, the governor's goals for the bureaucracy might essentially be ignored despite the chief executive role. Nevertheless, unlike the national government, no state gives its governor the power to appoint an entire executive team. Instead, governors must work with (and perhaps sometimes compete with) a host of elected, appointed, and hired individuals who also have their own goals and sources of power in the state. Again, this lack of unanimity in the executive branch has both positive and negative features. It hampers the governor's unilateral power, but it may ultimately be beneficial to the public because elected officials are not as indebted to the governor. Officials such as the attorney general and the auditor probably should be elected (as they are in most states) so that they can have the independence necessary to perform their jobs effectively.

As governors make choices regarding executive branch appointments, they may feel pulled by two competing goals. They may be torn between placing the best-qualified people in the position and choosing people on whose loyalty they can depend— people that they believe that they can control. This tension may create a dilemma for the governor. As Governor Dan Walker of Illinois observed, "The better the people you get, the more distance they place between themselves and you. They tend to adopt much more of that 'we/them' syndrome that can be disaster to government" (Dalton 1983, 94). This governor seems to assume that members of the executive branch do not share the goals of the governor, even when the governor placed them there. Such a situation makes for difficulty in working together and in simply communicating the needs of government, though information flow to the governor is of crucial importance.

This sentiment illustrates that simply appointing an official may not guarantee loyalty to a governor's goals. The power to remove officials is an important resource that facilitates the positive effects of the appointment power. However, in most states, the governor's power of removal is quite limited, unless the appointee in question has committed serious legal or ethical violations. Interested outside actors such as clientele groups who are supporters of agencies, legislators, and other bureaucrats often protest when governors attempt to remove key administrators. Further difficulties in the removal of officials derive from court decisions that protect public employees from being removed for "political reasons." While the courts have provided governors leeway by allowing a balance between governmental effectiveness and individual rights (of employees), this lack of total control over the appointment of public administrators can dilute support of the governor's ideals in the executive branch. It also illustrates a key difference between governors and the American president. The president has nearly total control over the removal of executive branch officials.

Tenure Potential

Another element that has historically been an important power of the governor and which is included in Schlesinger's index of formal powers is called tenure potential. Tenure potential is not a power in the traditional sense—it is not a tool the governor can directly employ. However, Schlesinger's idea was that power grows from the length of time the governor can hold the office. Governors who must leave office quickly will not fare as well in the legislature because legislators who disagree with the chief executive need not really take the governor seriously. They can just wait two years for a new governor with new ideas to come along.

TABLE 2.1   TENURE POTENTIAL

State	Length of term (in years)		Consecutive years allowed	
	1975	2003	1975	2003
Alabama	4	4	8	8
Alaska	4	4	8	8
Arizona	4	4	n/a	8
Arkansas	2	4	n/a	8
California	4	4	n/a	8
Colorado	4	4	n/a	8
Connecticut	4	4	n/a	n/a
Delaware	4	4	8	8
Florida	4	4	8	8
Georgia	4	4	4	8
Hawaii	4	4	n/a	8
Idaho	4	4	n/a	8
Illinois	4	4	n/a	n/a
Indiana	4	4	8	8
Iowa	4	4	n/a	n/a
Kansas	4	4	8	8
Kentucky	4	4	4	8
Louisiana	4	4	8	8
Maine	4	4	8	8
Maryland	4	4	8	8
Massachusetts	4	4	n/a	8
Michigan	4	4	n/a	8
Minnesota	4	4	n/a	n/a
Mississippi	4	4	4	8
Missouri	4	4	8	8
Montana	4	4	n/a	8
Nebraska	4	4	8	8
Nevada	4	4	8	8
New Hampshire	2	2	n/a	n/a
New Jersey	4	4	8	8
New Mexico	4	4	4	8
New York	4	4	n/a	n/a
North Carolina	4	4	4	8
North Dakota	4	4	n/a	n/a
Ohio	4	4	8	8
Oklahoma	4	4	8	8
Oregon	4	4	8	8
Pennsylvania	4	4	8	8
Rhode Island	2	4	n/a	8
South Carolina	4	4	4	8
South Dakota	4	4	8	8
Tennessee	4	4	4	8
Texas	4	4	n/a	n/a
Utah	4	4	n/a	n/a
Vermont	2	2	n/a	n/a
Virginia	4	4	4	4
Washington	4	4	n/a	8
West Virginia	4	4	8	8
Wisconsin	4	4	n/a	n/a
Wyoming	4	4	n/a	8

n/a = not applicable

Source: Data derived from multiple editions of the *Book of the States,* Council of State Governments.

Governors vary in how long their terms are and in how many times they are allowed (by law) to run for reelection. In the early years of the country, ten of the original thirteen states allowed their governors terms of only a single year (Beyle 1990), one state allowed a two-year term, and the other two set the term at three years. The constitutions often allowed these governors to seek reelection a number of times. As time passed, the length of time a governor might be allowed to serve in the office grew. Nevertheless, states have not completely relaxed their concerns about executives staying in office for too long. There was a general trend toward longer terms and greater opportunity to seek reelection for governors, but that trend seems to have hit a high point in the 1970s (see Table 2.1). Some states had actually shortened the potential years that governors could serve by the 1990s.

By the end of the 1980s, only three governors were limited to two-year terms. All of these governors could seek an unlimited number of future terms. However, a new change began to occur in a few states. In 1989, eighteen states allowed their governors a four-year term with no restraint on reelection (down one state from 1974). Twenty-six states set their governors' tenure at two four-year terms, and three states set theirs at one four-year term with no consecutive reelection. Over the next few years, a significant shift toward somewhat shorter tenure continued.

This change occurred not because the states shortened the length of the term but because some states placed new limits on the number of terms a governor could serve. In 2003, the number of states allowing their governors to serve an unlimited number of four-year terms had declined again, down to only eight states. The largest group of states (thirty-eight) allowed two consecutive four-year terms. One allowed three consecutive four-year terms (Utah). One state continues to limit its governor to a single four-year term (Virginia). The New England states of Vermont and New Hampshire continue to restrict their governors to two-year terms but allow them the unlimited opportunity to seek reelection.

Unlike the U.S. president, governors in some states are allowed to serve additional terms after being out of office for a designated period of time. Various governors have taken advantage of this option, sitting out for the required time and running for the office again. Perhaps not surprisingly, many of the governors who have returned to office after leaving due to term limits are controversial figures with very strong personalities. Big Jim Folsom of Alabama (1947–1951; 1955–1959), Theodore Bilbo of Mississippi (1916–1920; 1928–1932), and Earl Long of Louisiana (1939–1940; 1948–1952; 1956–1960) surely fit this description.

Tenure potential is most important for the governor's role as chief legislator. The possibility of holding the office for a longer period strengthens the governors in various ways. Being in office longer makes governors more knowledgeable and better able to exercise the power of persuasion. It frees them up from the "perpetual campaign," meaning that if the terms are longer, they can spend more time doing the job and less time seeking reelection. It also allows governors the opportunity to spend time gaining expertise while still having time left in office to put this expertise to work. Longer tenure should also increase the gov-

Returning to Office

Some states allow governors to return to office after sitting out for a defined period of time. Edwin Edwards of Louisiana served from 1972 to 1980, 1984 to 1988, and 1992 to 1996. Governor Edwards's success is especially remarkable in that he was indicted on multiple occasions throughout his career. He was finally convicted of fraud and racketeering charges and began serving a ten-year sentence in 2003. As another interesting side note, his opponent in the 1991 race, former head of the Ku Klux Klan David Duke, was also convicted of wrongdoing. He served a fifteen-month prison sentence for mail fraud and filing false tax returns.

Other less controversial figures also have served multiple terms, spread across many years. Walter Hickel served as governor of Alaska from 1966 to 1969 and again from 1990 to 1994. James B. Hunt served as governor of North Carolina from 1977 to 1985 and 1993 to 2001. These governors are certainly exceptions to what are usually rather limited gubernatorial tenures.

James Hunt Jr. served four terms as governor of North Carolina. (Office of Governor James Hunt Jr.)

ernors' bargaining power by strengthening their position relative to state legislatures and their leaders, who are not so limited in their tenure potential in most states.

Budget Power

The power to craft the budget is critically important for the role of chief legislator. Influence over the budget can translate into significant influence over the policy direction of the state, since spending priorities ultimately equal policy priorities.

The budget is the spending plan for a state. Like most things in state government, it requires the governor and the legislature to work together. Governors in most states are in charge of preparing the budget and submitting it to the legislature. This "executive budget" gives governors the chance to identify where they would like to see increases or decreases in spending. It also centralizes all agency requests for funds under the governor's control, which helps the governor because without the executive budget, agencies might go straight to the legislature to ask for funds and thereby circumvent the governor's input as to state priorities. It is certainly possible that such end runs will occur even with the executive budget, but this would most certainly result in the absence of an executive budget.

Having an executive budget definitely gives the governor a significant opportunity to influence state spending. Nevertheless, it is important to point out that legislatures typically have unlimited power to change the budget the governor proposes. So while this power is very important for governors, it does not at all guarantee that their policy goals will be achieved or pursued at the level they desired. Research indicates that the budget remains an area in which both the governors and the legislatures exert a great deal of influence when they choose to do so. Once the budget is adopted, governors can wield unique influence. They have considerable authority for administering the budget. They are in charge of spending the money that puts the legislative programs into force, and this gives them additional influence even when the budgetary process did not go their way.

Other Formal Resources

In addition to the four powers identified by Schlesinger and included in his formal powers index, the modern governor's office provides other tools to the chief executive. These other formal tools are the state of the state address and the power to reorganize the executive branch. They are important instruments for governors as they carry out their chief legislator and chief executive roles.

State of the State Addresses

State of the state addresses are most helpful to governors as chief legislators, especially in agenda setting. All governors are required to report on the state of their states. These speeches have come to be valued platforms for the governors, who use them to lay out their legislative goals.

Some issues are on the agenda of the states (and the governors) all of the time. Among these permanent agenda items are education, highways, health care, welfare, and law enforcement. In fact, these five issue areas account for nearly three-quarters of the budget of an average state. It is no surprise, then, that governors must always pay attention to problems in these areas. Other issues come and go from the agenda, almost in a cycle (Herzik 1991). For instance, tax reform seems to arise as a key issue in the states periodically, and then it recedes from public view. Finally, sometimes completely new problems arise. They burst onto the state scene and demand attention. Some will come along and remain on the agenda for years afterward, while others arise, are addressed, and then disappear. Newly discovered communicable diseases affecting the health of a state's citizens might fit this category. Severe acute respiratory syndrome (SARS) and acquired immune deficiency syndrome (AIDS) are two examples. While concern about SARS seems to ebb and flow, AIDS has unfortunately been on the agenda of the states since the early 1980s. Advances in treatments for AIDS may cause the disease to receive somewhat less attention for a time. However, if the rates of infection begin to rise again, governors, especially in certain states, will again turn their attention to placing the control and eradication of AIDS on the state agendas.

In some ways, governors' state of the state addresses are very individualized. In them, the governors often recognize family members and public officials to publicly express their gratitude. They reflect on and describe the positive accomplishments of their time as governor. They describe the state of the state, that is, the condition of its economy and industry. They also honor individuals who have made important contributions to the state. In addition to such reflection on the current conditions of the state, governors typically identify remaining problems and outline proposed solutions in hopes the legislatures will take them on. Governors normally limit their agendas to a few key items. But some governors do not follow this pattern. They instead offer a laundry list of issues for the legislature to consider. Usually, it seems that governors are better off to limit the number of items on their wish list because the attention span of legislatures is rather short and because legislators also have their own priorities to pursue (Ferguson and Barth 2002).

Topics addressed by governors are also predictable in certain regards. For example, states with common regional attachments share common problems. Because of these common problems, the priorities of governors within a region will be similar. Western governors often must focus attention on their states' water supplies. Southern state governors might focus on the regionwide problems in public education.

Party or ideological attachments also influence which issues governors choose to address. For instance, Republican governors may be more likely to address problems of crime and punishment. Other issues might span party and ideology divides, such as economic development. Yet even among the issues that cross party lines, party and ideological differences might arise in terms of the answers advocated by the governors.

Not only do governors often address similar public problems, they also tend to offer similar solutions to these problems. An examination of state of the state addresses in 1994 found that all but nine of the fifty governors discussed crime in them. Eleven of these governors advocated mandatory sentencing laws (often called "three strikes and you're out" laws). Nineteen governors pointed to guns as a primary cause for crime and proposed some sort of restriction on the possession or sale of these weapons to try to address the dangers. Thirty-eight of the fifty governors discussed the state education system in their state of the state address. Governors across the states identified similar problems in education and remarkably similar solutions. Several governors talked about giving local schools more control. Thirty-two governors discussed the need to reform health care, especially health care programs for the poor and elderly. Similarities can be observed across the other major policy areas addressed by the governors (Ferguson 2003).

State of the state addresses, therefore, offer a critical opportunity for governors to set the legislative agenda for the states. Legislators look to these speeches for indications of the governors' goals. However, governors hope to do more through these speeches. They attempt to use them to convince the legislature not only that a certain problem needs to be addressed but also that their own solution is the best alternative. The state of the state speech seems somewhat less successful for governors in regard to this more specific goal of policy formation (Ferguson 2003).

Executive Branch Reorganization

The power to reorganize the bureaucracy, a power possessed by governors in half of the states, is most useful in terms of the chief executive role. This power allows governors to organize the people and offices of the executive branch in such a way that the bureaucracy is more responsive to political control. Organizational structures definitely can affect the flow of information, the choices that are offered to decision makers, and the decisions ultimately made by those responsible.

State bureaucracies typically developed in a rather haphazard manner. The executive branch in most states has grown gradually as agencies were created to address new problems. As a result, the responsibilities of agencies are often poorly defined, and multiple agencies sometimes share overlapping responsibilities. In addition, agencies that probably should be grouped together because of shared functional responsibilities often refuse to merge or cooperate with other related agencies. Because of all of these concerns, governors often hope to organize the bureaucracies so that they are more manageable.

However, reorganizing state executive agencies is not merely an administrative task. The choices involved are very politically charged. Administrative agencies affect many different groups, and each agency invariably favors some of the participants over others. Rearranging the structure may therefore increase the power of some groups over others. This outcome is precisely the goal of governors attempting to rearrange such agencies. Governors hope to appoint those favorable to their programs to head the departments in charge of administering those programs. Placing such supporters in these positions is critical for governors, who cannot possibly exercise constant supervision over these administrators.

Reformers long sought to give the governors this power so as to place them at the top of the state bureaucracy. When governors organize the state bureaucracy to suit their goals and preferences, they should also have greater influence over the decisions and actions of these bureaucracies. Since 1965, more than twenty states have significantly reorganized their bureaucracies. In more than half of the states, governors can initiate organizational changes that will take effect unless the legislature objects in a specified period of time. However, this power is not unlimited. Legislatures do have the ability to object, and they often decide to do so. Administrators and clientele groups outside of government that will be directly affected by the reorganization may also lobby the legislature to overturn the governor's decisions. Even in the twenty-three states that have given their governors power to reorganize by executive order (subject to veto by one or both chambers of the legislature), the governors have rarely used this power. Instead, they tend to seek legislative approval for such dramatic changes, which means that governors must work very closely with legislators to succeed in the hard work of building coalitions to get their reorganization proposals passed.

Governors often hope to reorganize the state bureaucracy at the outset of their administrations. They believe that such organization can help them to get a handle on the apparatus of government and lead it in the desired direction. Moving early is smart because the beginning of a term is often when the governor is most successful with the legislature. Moving quickly might also minimize the ability of opponents to organize against the governor's plan.

A quote from President Dwight Eisenhower sums up the importance of this role: "Organization cannot make a genius out of an incompetent . . . on the other hand, disorganization can scarcely fail to result in inefficiency and can easily lead to disaster" (quoted in Greenstein 1988, 83).

Informal Powers

When talking about the power of the governor, it is natural to speak of the formal powers. These are powers that come with the office itself, either because the constitution provides them to the governor or because the state has passed laws giving the governor such powers. Accordingly, observers have long talked about strong and weak governors and compared one state's governors to others based on these powers. However, a host of other factors affect how powerful a governor will be. Many governors have managed to exert quite a lot of power even though they were serving in an office with very limited formal powers. How did they succeed in being powerful when the office was weak? They pulled power from sources outside the office itself. Since such resources do not come with the office, they are referred to as informal powers. Informal powers differ substantially from one governor to another, rather than from one state to the next. Some informal powers have to do with the person who holds the office. Each man or woman who becomes governor has certain knowledge, skills, and personality traits that will help in the performance of the job. These ideas about informal powers are sometimes harder for researchers to discuss because they are less concrete than formal powers. One cannot read the law or the constitution to determine how powerful the governor will be in an informal sense. Instead, one has to know more about the person in the office and the context or situation he or she is in to understand why some governors succeed without significant formal powers and, conversely, why some governors with substantial formal powers nevertheless fail.

Personal and Professional Characteristics of the Governor

Obviously, the people who hold the office of governor are individuals with strengths and weaknesses, goals and aspirations. They have knowledge and skills and experiences that they can put to use in the governor's office. Each of these factors may also affect which parts of the job the governor most enjoys and spends the most time on. They may also influence how successful the governor manages to be in his or her many endeavors.

Some governors truly love the legislative role. They enjoy the game of politics, the maneuvering, and negotiating with the legislatures. Others dislike this aspect of the job, preferring instead the managerial role or even the role as head of state. Governors who crave the excitement or the give-and-take of the legislative arena will spend more time and effort on that and probably achieve greater success. They may spend less time on other elements of the job. Having a particularly good personal relationship with the legislature might actually help the governor to succeed at being chief legislator. Being well liked, admired, and respected by state legislators might help a governor to succeed in the legislative arena. Similarly, some governors are more interested in being a manager of the state. This interest may lead to greater attention to this role and a willingness to invest the time and energy necessary to succeed in what is often the hardest part of the job. This dedication may lead to greater achievements for the governor.

For some politicians, arriving at the governor's mansion is their ultimate goal. They may hope to serve a single term in the governor's office or, more likely, to serve as many terms as the law allows. Others may hope to run for the U.S. Senate or for the presidency down the road. Such ambitions will have an effect on how a governor behaves in office. Governors with goals of seeking reelection or higher elective office might have reason to be more active in the pursuit of policy they believe important to their electorates. This attitude might also result in greater success for governors. Conversely, the ambition for seeking higher office may make governors wary of failure in the legislative arena, which could result in a lesser emphasis on policy formulation activities (though it may result in a greater emphasis on agenda setting).

Choices that governors make before or during their time in office might also help or hurt their chances for success. For example, when a governor is involved in scandals, he or she will probably not do as well in any of the roles of the office. His or her bargaining position with members of the legislature will likely be compromised. And members of legislatures might feel free to oppose scandal-ridden governors or even want to avoid being associated with them (Ferguson 2003).

Skill and Experience

Doing a good job across the many roles of the governorship is a difficult assignment, requiring a great deal of knowledge, skill, and perseverance. Nearly every governor approaching the job for the first time feels under-prepared. Governors must know a lot about a lot of things, and they have very little time to learn on the job. A governor who assumes office with a bigger bank of skills will be able to move into the job more quickly and easily.

For some, the governorship is the first elected position. That is not true for most governors, however. Instead, the majority have served in other elective offices and perhaps in private positions as well. This prior experience teaches them myriad different skills that will be of help in the governor's office. Thus, being a legislator would help to develop knowledge about how government in the state works. So governors who were formerly in the state legislature probably know more about the workings of the lawmaking systems. Legislative experience may also mean that the governor still has some friends in the legislature, which would also help in the role as chief legislator. Some governors already have experience in the executive branch, perhaps having served previously as lieutenant governor or attorney general.

This experience does not mean that these governors know all there is to know when they are first elected, but it most likely does give them a leg up over those who go straight to the governor's mansion. The skills and experience a governor brings to the office will surely impact his or her ability to do the job.

Personal traits may also be important. Some governors are exceptionally persuasive. Some are charismatic and likable. Some have very forceful personalities. All of these facets of a governor's personality can be used in doing the many jobs of the office.

Popularity

Governors draw some sources of power from outside themselves and their office. Many observers think that being well liked by the public helps a governor in the many roles he or she plays. Popularity is especially important for the chief legislator and head of state roles because of the importance of the public (and the public's desires) to these roles.

The popularity of governors always varies over time. A state's citizens will feel more positive about their governor in certain periods and less so in others. Generally, popularity is highest just after election, and then it declines over time. Certain events or actions may encourage the public to be more supportive of the governor, but many events also diminish a governor's popularity. Unfortunately for the governors, they do not have much control over how popular they are: there are very few things they can do to influence how the public views them. However, they can certainly try to use their popularity to their advantage. It is not entirely clear what leads some governors to be more popular than others. Personality may have something to do with it. The state of the economy may as well. Social upheaval, such as events that occurred during the civil rights movement, probably leads to lower levels of popular support, while decisive action on the part of the governor probably improves his or her standing.

Having the support of the public is important for governors as they work in the legislative arena. Being unpopular can surely hurt a governor who is trying to negotiate with the legislature. This may be because legislators do not want to be associated with the policies of an unpopular governor. Low public approval of a governor gives legislators who want to oppose the governor a greater opening to do so. Even more serious for the governor, being unpopular may actually cause legislators to oppose his or her goals because they do not want to be associated with an unpopular governor. By contrast, popularity might rally the public in favor of a governor's proposals. The people may be encouraged to contact their legislators on behalf of the governor, and this might in turn convince a legislator to support a governor's goals.

Popular Mandate

Another way of looking at the importance of the relationship between the governor and the people is to ask whether the governor can claim a mandate from the public. Unlike popularity, which remains important throughout a governor's term, mandates are only valid immediately after an election. Governors claim that they campaigned to and were elected by the people in the entire state. Since the voters elected the governor, they are behind his or her goals. Further, if the election shows that the people are behind the governor, then the legislature should be, too—at least, this is the claim governors make. They often assert that they have a mandate from the people to pursue their priorities and that the legislature should follow suit.

None of the members of the legislature were elected by the whole state, so none of them can claim that the whole state is behind them. This fact of political life can be a potent source of informal power. However, there are many reasons to be skeptical about such a claim. When people vote for a candidate for governor (or for any official), they have many reasons for doing so. They may simply strongly dislike one candidate and wish to vote against that person. They may really like one or two of the ideas of the chosen candidate but dislike many others. Because of such factors, strictly speaking, there is no way to know whether the fact that a majority of voters chose one candidate means that they are also behind all of the ideas of that candidate. Nevertheless, governors attempt to convince the legislature and other state officials that such a statement of support for the governor is exactly the message the voters were sending in the election.

Governors who win their positions by large margins at the polls are more likely to convince members of the legislature they have a mandate from the people to go after their goals. Under these circumstances, legislators may feel that the public is in support of the governor's agenda, a perception that might encourage the legislature to support the governor's proposals as well.

Members of the legislature, of course, represent only a single district of typically a few thousand people, while the governor can claim the whole state as his or her "district." This difference of constituency may make legislators vulnerable to governors' claims of mandates.

A governor who was not actually elected cannot claim a mandate. If a sitting governor dies in office, someone else must take over. In most states, the lieutenant governor steps into the post. Governors who succeed to the office after some particularly divisive event, such as the indictment or impeachment of the incumbent governor, will likely have a more difficult time than those succeeding due to the death of the incumbent. Governors in this latter situation may actually benefit from the goodwill of the people who are grieving over the loss of the elected governor.

The Governor and the Media

It goes without saying that the invention of new types of media has changed American life. The development of radio and then television and now the Internet (and who knows what tomorrow?) has had a very powerful effect on politics and government. The media, especially visual media such as television, tend to focus on stories that are easy to convey in short periods of time. Television news tends to shy away from covering legislatures, since the lawmaking process is so complicated. But a single figure, such as the president or the governor, is easier to examine and discuss.

The growth in television media has helped the chief executives (both the president and the governors) to rise to the center of public attention. For the governor, this is helpful in many different ways, especially within the chief legislator role. Media coverage gives the governor a way of communicating with the public and with other governmental actors. It also sends other less concrete messages to these observers. The media reinforce the idea that the governor is the state's leader. This reinforcement feeds into the governor's future attempts to lead. Looking like a leader on television helps the governor to be a leader in the state.

The media seem particularly preoccupied with the governor because he or she is a single actor who is easy to follow around and report about. Governors are also the topic of media attention because they serve an entire state. Though there are other officials in the states who are also elected statewide by the voters, these figures do not carry as much responsibility as the governor, and their jobs are less clearly related to the lives of most people in the state. So the voters tend to think of the governor as a pivotal leader, and the media in turn focus on the governor more than on any other state official.

Governors are very aware of the opportunity the media offer them in their efforts to reach the public and other government officials. In addition to reinforcing the image of the governor as a leader, the media may help them to send more specific messages. The message might be that some problem, such as poor educational performance in the public schools, is a major dilemma facing the state. Governors can use public speeches, press conferences, and interviews with specific reporters to get the word out about their key concerns. When a governor makes a speech or gives an interview, the public gets to hear directly from that individual. Also, the governor has the stage, so there are no other actors competing at that moment to get their ideas heard. In addition, no other actor has the access to the media that the governor has, and this gives the governor a great opportunity to put issues on the agenda.

Next, having directed the attention of the public (and other public officials) to a problem in the state, the governor will typically move to a specific proposal. The governor mentioned in the last paragraph who used the media to attract attention to students failing in the public schools may now want to convince the public that the way to fix that problem is to set stricter standards for teacher education. This step moves the process beyond merely identifying a problem: the governor is trying to define the solution as well. The media provide the governor with an outlet for these efforts.

When governors use the media, they are most likely to be targeting their message to the public. The governors hope that if the public is on their side, then the state legislature will be, too. If the governor can reach out to the voters and convince them, then the voters will (hopefully) contact and convince their legislators that the governor's goals are right for the state and should be pursued. Clearly, the governor has the attention of the public more than any other state official, and this is largely due to media coverage. It is also quite likely that using the media helps the governor to set the agenda—to encourage other state actors to look into problems that the governor identifies. But it is less likely that the media will stimulate the public to head to their phones (or their computers) to contact their legislators. Relatively few voters contact their legislators in any case, and they are not all that likely to do so at the governor's request. However, there may be times when the governor does succeed in motivating the public to assist in this way. If any state actor can encourage such a movement among the citizens, it would be the governor, given the unique access he or she has to the media.

Media exposure has broad implications for the governor. It helps the governor to exercise many of the other informal powers he or she possesses. For instance, media coverage is the mechanism that helps the governor to generate popular support, to get the attention of the legislature, and to remind other governmental actors of the governor's goals. In fact, access to the media helps the governor pursue nearly all of the roles of the office.

Modern governors possess many formal powers, and they come to office with a variety of informal resources that they may also put to use in performing the multiple roles they play. A governor who skillfully employs the right combination of these resources can succeed in the office, but not all governors manage to do so. The powers of the office and the skills of the person holding it do not fully explain why some governors succeed and others fail. The presence of numerous other actors, both inside and outside of government, who have their own goals and responsibilities also affects the ability of governors to succeed at their jobs. These features of the larger political environment are discussed in Chapter 5.

References and Further Reading

Barrilleaux, Charles. 1999. Statehouse bureaucracy: Institutional consistency in a changing environment. In *American state and local politics,* ed. Ronald E. Weber and Paul Brace, 97–113. London: Chatham House.

Beyle, Thad. 1990. Governors. In *Politics in the American states,* 5th ed., ed. Virginia Gray, H. Jacob, and R. B. Albritton. Boston: Little, Brown.

———. 1992. *Governors and hard times.* Washington, DC: Congressional Quarterly Press.

Beyle, Thad, and Lynn Muchmore. Introduction. In *Being governor: The view from the office,* ed. Thad L. Beyle and Lynn R. Muchmore, 3–11. Durham, NC: Duke Policy Studies Press.

Brudney, Jeffrey L., and F. Ted Hebert. 1987. State agencies and their environments: Examining the influence of important external actors. *Journal of Politics* 49:186–206.

Dalton, Robert. 1983. Governor's views on management. In *Being governor: The view from the office,* ed. Thad L. Beyle and Lynn R. Muchmore, 93–101. Durham, NC: Duke Policy Studies Press.

Dilger, Robert J., George A. Krause, Randolph R. Moffett. 1995. State legislative professionalism and gubernatorial effectiveness, 1978–1991. *Legislative Studies Quarterly* 20(4):553–571.

Dometrius, Nelson C. 1987. Changing gubernatorial power: The measure vs. reality. *Western Political Quarterly* 40:319–333.

Dometrius, Nelson C. 1999. Governors: Their heritage and their future. In *American state and local politics,* ed. Ronald E. Weber and Paul Brace, 38–70. London: Chatham House.

Elling, Richard C. 2004. Administering state programs: Performance and politics. In *Politics in the American states: A comparative analysis,* 8th ed., ed. Virginia Gray and Russell L. Hanson, 261–289. Washington, DC: Congressional Quarterly Press.

Ferguson, Margaret R. 2003. Chief executive success in the legislative arena. *State Politics and Policy Quarterly* 3(2):158–182.

Ferguson, Margaret R., and Jay Barth. 2002. Governors in the legislative arena: The importance of personality in shaping success. *Political Psychology* 23(4):787–808.

Greenstein, Fred I. 1988. *Leadership in the modern presidency.* Cambridge, MA: Harvard University Press.

Gross, Donald. 1991. The policy role of governors. In *Gubernatorial leadership and state policy,* ed. Eric B. Herzik and Brent W. Brown, 1–24. New York: Greenwood.

Hebert, F. Ted, Jeffrey L. Brudney, and Deil S. Wright. 1983. Gubernatorial influence and state bureaucracy. *American Politics Quarterly* 11:243–264.

Herzik, Eric. 1991. Policy agendas and gubernatorial leadership. In *Gubernatorial leadership and state policy,* ed. Eric B. Herzik and Brent W. Brown, 25–38. New York: Greenwood.

Herzik, Eric, and Brent W. Brown. 1989. Introduction: Symposium on governors and public policy. *Policy Studies Journal* 17(4):841–862.

Lipson, Leslie. 1939. *The American governor from figurehead to leader.* Chicago: University of Chicago Press.

Morehouse, Sarah M., and Malcolm E. Jewell. 2003. *State politics, parties, and policy.* 2nd ed. Lanham, MD: Rowman and Littlefield.

National Governors Association Center for Policy Research. 1978. *Governing the American states: A handbook for new governors.* Washington, DC: National Governors Association.

Neustadt, Richard. 1980. *Presidential power: The politics of leadership from FDR to Carter.* New York: Wiley.

Peterson, Kavan. 2003. Governors shy from clemency power. Stateline.org. www.stateline.org.

Ransone, Coleman. B. 1985. *The American governorship.* Westport, CT: Greenwood.

Rosenthal, Alan. 1990. *Governors and legislatures: Contending powers.* Washington, DC: Congressional Quarterly Press.

Schlesinger, Joseph A. 1965. The politics of the executive. In *Politics in the American states,* ed. Henry Jacob and Kenneth N. Vines, 207–238. Boston: Little, Brown.

Sharkansky, Ira. 1968. Agency requests, gubernatorial support, and budget success in state legislatures. *American Political Science Review* 62:1220–1231.

Simonton, Dean Keith. 1987. *Why presidents succeed: A political psychology of leadership.* New Haven, CT: Yale University Press.

Wiggins, Charles W. 1980. Executive vetoes and legislative overrides in the American states. *Journal of Politics* 42(4):1110–1117.

Websites Consulted

Battered Women's Justice Project: www.bwjp.org.

National Governors Association: www.nga.org.

Stateline.org: www.stateline.org.

3

THE ROLE OF THE EXECUTIVE BRANCH IN STATE POLITICS

Cynthia J. Bowling

O ne of the roles fulfilled by governors across the country is that of chief executive, and in that capacity, they are charged by the state constitutions with ensuring that the laws of their states are "faithfully executed." The actual responsibility for carrying out the laws, however, resides with the state bureaucracy, which is the topic of this chapter. The bureaucracy includes all of the state agencies created to write the rules and regulations necessary for executing state laws, implementing programs that enact these laws and policies, and helping create the budgets that make all of these services possible. The numerous state agencies in the governmental bureaucracy are overseen by high-ranking state officials who are chosen in a variety of ways: elected separately from the governors, appointed by the governors and legislatures, and chosen by independent commissions. This chapter will first explain the concept of bureaucracy as a method of organization. Next, it will explore five key themes of state administration: the growth, development, and organization of state administrative agencies; the qualifications, duties, and responsibilities of the primary elected state officials in addition to the governors; the budget process and the actors who participate in it in American states. The chapter concludes with a discussion of the bureaucratic reforms recently implemented by state governments around the country in hopes of improving the work of the executive branch as it pursues its many responsibilities.

BUREAUCRATIC GOALS AND ORGANIZATION

The term *bureaucracy* is often used synonymously with *executive branch*. But by a more general definition, a bureaucracy is a method of organizing people who are pursuing a task (or, more likely, many tasks). The bureaucratic type of organization is found in both public and private institutions; indeed, nearly all large organizations are organized as bureaucracies. Characteristics of a bureaucracy include:

- A division of labor and specialization of function.
- A hierarchical organization, meaning authority flows downward from a single leader at the top while responsibility flows upward to that individual. This organization is shaped much like a pyramid, with a single point at the top and a wide base at the bottom.
- The employment and advancement of persons based on their knowledge and competence, often called a merit system.
- An elaborate set of rules, or standardized operating procedures, governing organizational operations (Elling 2004).

Several of the features listed here do, in fact, describe the state executive branches. But real-life bureaucracies do not necessarily exhibit all of these features, and those in the states are not organized exactly as an ideal bureaucracy would be, largely due to the way in which bureaucratic agencies came into existence. Bureaucracies tend to grow in a piecemeal fashion. Sometimes, existing agencies are given new responsibilities when programs are created. At other times, new agencies or offices are added to meet new needs and implement new laws. The state executive branches are therefore not as tightly organized as the theoretical bureaucracy would be. In some cases, individuals with similar functions are spread across many different divisions. In others, multiple divisions duplicate work or even have contradictory responsibilities. And attention is not always paid to making sure that new laws form a coherent whole with existing laws. Thus, the organization of the state bureaucracy is the product of the piecemeal way in which states make laws.

The shape of bureaucracy theoretically resembles a pyramid. It is broad at the bottom, where many people perform the same tasks. These individuals report to those above them, who have a different set of specialized tasks to perform. Ultimately, some individual sits at the top of the pyramid and bears the responsibility for overseeing the people below. But state bureaucracies do not look quite like this pyramid. In theory, the governor is the individual who sits atop the state bureaucracy. In theory, authority flows down from the governor to others in the executive branch, and responsibility flows up to the governor. However, a public organization has multiple "principals," or persons to whom public administrators must report. So who really has ultimate responsibility for overseeing the bureaucracy? The answer to this question is not as clear-cut as one might expect. The governor, as the chief administrator, obviously influences state agency heads and activities. But state legislatures also have a duty and a desire to oversee what goes on in the bureaucracy. Moreover, some agencies report to independent commissions elected by the public or appointed by the governors. This set of circumstances makes the question of who sits at the top of the pyramid difficult to answer. It also means that making sure the bureaucracy is responsive can be tricky. To whom should it be responsible? While the governor is the official head of the executive branch, the legislature has a legitimate role to play as well. And citizens' groups and agency clientele also demand attention and responsiveness in agency activities.

The existence of multiple principals may result in bureaucracies that do not always function effectively. For this and other reasons, bureaucracies are sometimes controversial. In fact, when people hear the word *bureaucracy,* they often think of something negative. They imagine massive governmental agencies, uncaring administrators, inefficiency or red tape, or waiting in line for hours trying to accomplish a simple and necessary task. Certain public officials may even contribute to this public perception by criticizing the work done by the executive branch. While there are certainly problems in every state government, research shows that, by and large, state bureaucracies are staffed by qualified people who work hard to do their jobs. Indeed, a prominent public administration scholar, Charles Goodsell, wrote a book entitled *The Case for Bureaucracy* in which he documented many findings that rebut common misperceptions of bureaucracies. Describing the responses of citizens who had interacted with the bureaucracy, he stated, "In general, government agencies and government employees in America do their jobs surprisingly well in view of their reputation. . . . Broadly speaking, between two-thirds and three-fourths have reported their encounters with agencies as satisfactory" (Goodsell 2004, 139).

Goals of Bureaucracy

One of the major problems involved in the execution of law is that those in charge often feel pulled toward many different (and maybe even contradictory) goals. The three most important goals of bureaucracy are efficiency, effectiveness, and political/public accountability. But at times, these goals conflict with one another. Efficiency means getting the most out of the dollars spent, and effectiveness is a measure of whether the job that the agency set out to do was achieved. The third goal is peculiar to public entities. Governmental bureaucracies must not only be efficient and effective (or at least strive to be), they must also be accountable to the public and to the elected officials who oversee them. Accountability means making sure that the process of government is legal and constitutional. This goal creates another category of expectations that state bureaucrats must satisfy.

Additionally, public administrators are expected to recognize the values of equity and equality—making sure that everyone is treated impartially and equally. State organizations are bound by the Fourteenth Amendment of the U.S. Constitution to make sure that all citizens are given equal protection and offered the due process of law; accordingly, they must ensure that people are treated equally and fairly and also abide by all rules pertaining to agencies and all procedures outlined for dealing with citizens. Making sure that the bureaucracy lives up to these standards can be costly and time consuming; therefore, maximum efficiency is not necessarily always practical or even possible. The goals of efficiency and effectiveness often conflict with the goals of equity, which presents another major challenge for public bureaucracies.

Not only are the values inherent in state bureaucracies contradictory and therefore unclear, so, too, are the responsibilities. Bureaucracies are expected to act as neutral implementers of state law. They are the arm of state governments with the responsibility to actually put into place the programs and actions required by the lawmakers. Many times, however, state law is both broad and vague, and every law must be implemented along with previously written regulations. All of these features make the implementation of laws a difficult process.

When laws are written in imprecise language, it is up to the bureaucrats to interpret them and craft the rules and regulations to put the laws into force. The job of implementing the law is generally accepted as a legitimate role of the executive branch. Yet when bureaucrats write rules and regulations, they become policymakers, which is a more controversial function. The situation seems to violate the public's sense of who does what in government. Governors and legislators are the officials expected to make policy, and the public can hold these actors responsible for their choices at the next election. However, if bureaucrats—sometimes hired, sometimes politically appointed—must "fill in the blanks" left by vague laws as they write rules and regulations and implement laws passed by elected officials, they are often more involved in policymaking than many people realize. If that is the case, how can the public, in a democratic society where accountability comes from regularly held elections, hope to hold appointed or tenured public administrators accountable for their actions? Herein lies one of the enduring challenges of modern government.

Despite the controversy, bureaucrats do engage in policymaking, and they will continue to do so because they have the requisite skill and expertise. But this does not mean that the public is comfortable with the situation, nor does anyone seem to have any viable alternative if this is, in fact, viewed as a problem. Because of all of these factors, the appropriate role of bureaucracy in a democratic society remains open to debate.

Political actors and people who study state government continue to question how bureaucracy ought to behave in a democratic society. For a long time, political scientists asserted that making law and implementing it were completely separate functions. Lawmaking was obviously political, but carrying out the law was a neutral, technical process. Some argued that this division (sometimes called the politics-administration dichotomy) should exist. Countless other observers, however, contend that such a dichotomy (or strict division) does not exist and most likely cannot possibly exist.

In 1956, political scientist Herbert Kaufman noted that there are really three competing philosophies of administration within a democratic society. The first philosophy asserts that public administration should be viewed within the light of *representativeness*, or accountability to elected officials (associated with legislative control of bureaucratic organizations). But efficiency and effectiveness were lacking in this model. As civil service reforms were passed urging the promotion of public administrators by expertise and merit and the creation of public tenure systems, the idea of *neutral competence* emerged. This second philosophy encouraged administrators to act as neutral, apolitical implementers of public policy. However, administrators were, in fact, engaged in the political process and thus needed direction from a central administrator to work effectively. Thus, the third philosophy, the idea of *executive leadership*, became dominant as the president and governors sought to attain and maintain a position on top of the bureaucratic pyramid. Today, these three philosophies are all present in state administration—representativeness (or responsiveness to legislators or other elected officials), neutral competence in professional administrators and administration, and executive control through gubernatorial offices and organization.

Bureaucratic Personnel

At the national level, the president is the only figure in the bureaucracy who is elected by the public. Everyone else is either hired or chosen through appointment. That is not the case in the state bureaucracies. Instead, many state officials are independently elected and therefore draw their authority from the public. In 2000, there were just over 300 separately elected executive officials covering twelve major departments in all of the states. This figure compares to a nearly identical number of elected officials in 1972. States are obviously not in a hurry to change to a different method of choosing these officials. The number of elected executive officials varies from state to state, though most states elect more than just the governor. Nearly three-fourths elect at least five executive officials. Half of the states elect the state auditor. And in over a fourth of the states, the controller, the secretary of agriculture, and the head of the education department are all elected (Council of State Governments 2003).

These officials are often considered department heads, or officials in charge of large functional policy areas in the state, such as the education department (in charge of kindergarten through twelfth-grade education across the state) or the social services department (in charge of implementing many programs to improve the lives of the state's poorest citizens). In each department are several agencies or programs to accomplish these goals. For instance, the Pennsylvania Department of Labor encompasses several different offices or agencies, including information technology, unemployment compensation, workforce development, safety and labor relations, labor law compliance, and vocational rehabilitation.

Since 1964, the American State Administrators Project has surveyed many agency and department heads across the country. Findings from the most recent survey (Bowling and Wright 2004) indicate that about 3 percent of top offices are elected (mostly the department heads discussed in the preceding paragraphs). The governor appoints about one-fourth of the agency heads with legislative approval and another 17 percent without legislative approval. Independent boards or commissions appoint another 13 percent of state agency heads, and department heads appoint over one-quarter more. Approximately one-fifth of these agency heads are protected by the civil service system and a tenure process and cannot be fired for political reasons.

Note that the governors appoint less than half of the top administrators in the states. Department heads, many of whom are independently elected, appoint over a quarter of agency heads. Such a system is believed to make the state government more accountable to the public, but it also means that the governor is not the sole authority sitting at the top of the pyramid. This situation makes it harder for the governor to oversee the state bureaucracy, and it surely complicates attempts to make substantial changes in how the bureaucracy works.

GROWTH IN STATE BUREAUCRACY

Probably the most striking feature of state bureaucracies today is that they are extremely large and still growing. Since the 1980s, national government leaders have repeatedly announced their intentions to cut back the size of the federal bureaucracy, because of persistently negative public attitudes about burgeoning governments and government spending. Yet in this same period, state bureaucracies have continued to expand. In large part, this growth is linked to a constant increase in the responsibilities undertaken by state governments. On top of that, when the federal government cuts back on the services it provides, it is often up to the states to fill in the gaps.

Thus, the state bureaucracies evolved over time in response to changes in state government activity. As lawmakers created new programs, they often created new units in the bureaucracy to carry them out. The earliest generations of agencies had responsibilities related to broad, well-recognized state needs—in areas such as education, health, highways, agriculture, and finance. As new needs were recognized or particular problems or issues became publicized, agencies proliferated: for example, states developed civil rights commissions, highway safety departments, and drug and alcohol abuse agencies in the 1970s; hazardous waste agencies in the 1980s; and child support enforcement and crime victim compensation agencies in the 1990s. States across the country created such entities in an effort to address emergent issues.

By the middle of the twentieth century, it was not unusual for state bureaucracies to contain 100 to 200 units. In 2000, the fifty states combined employed 3.6 million people on a full-time basis and another 1.3 million on a part-time basis—equivalent to a full-time workforce of about 4 million. Though the general trend since the 1950s has been toward higher levels of state government employment, growth has not occurred at a constant rate. The 1990s, for instance, were marked by slower rates of growth (6.3 percent) than the 1980s (24 percent), despite the nation's population increase of 13.2 percent in the 1990s. Further, growth varied significantly by state during this decade. State employment increased by 25 percent in eight states (most of which experienced higher than average population growth). State employment shrank in eleven states. To further clarify the change, the number of state employees per capita (that is, adjusted for the state population) declined in thirty-eight states in the 1990s (Elling 2004).

Government Spending

One technique for conceptualizing the size of state governments is to examine their total spending. While this method does not tell us anything about individual states, it shows the impact of the states collectively in the national economy. In fiscal year 2003, the states collectively spent $1.1 trillion, including both operating and capital expenditures. That figure represents a 4.5 percent increase over the previous year, with state funds rising by 1.4 percent and federal funds (those transferred from Washington, D.C., to the states) growing by 10.3 percent. The small growth in spending is a reflection of tight fiscal conditions in the states. Between fiscal years 2002 and 2003, seventeen states actually experienced a decrease in spending from state funds. Spending levels cannot be directly compared to earlier years due to changes in the value of the dollar. But statistics show total state spending from all sources (state and federal funds and bonds) was just at $400 billion in 1987. It rose to approximately $700 billion in 1995 and peaked in 2003 at $1.1 trillion. Adjusted for inflation, state spending has grown in real dollars as well (National Association of State Budget Officers, http://www.nasbo.org).

Other measures are needed to account fully and meaningfully for the size of state government. One technique accounts for the amount of resources a state government draws from the private sector. Possible measures quantify government size by comparing state expenditures to the state population or by comparing state spending to some indicator of the size of the state economy. A common method is to assess the size of state government in terms of total state expenditure as a share of total state personal income (Garand and Baudoin 2004). By this measure, state governments have grown dramatically in the modern period. The average size of the states' public sectors (as a share of state personal income) was just over 4 percent in the mid-1940s but had grown to about 14 percent by 2000. State government growth took place in steady increments from 1945 to 1967, though certain decades saw greater variations. For example, in the 1960s and 1970s, during the Great Society programs of the national government, states experienced dramatic surges in expenditures. However, after 1977, the growth in size of the state public sectors stalled (compared to the private sector). Following a high of a bit more than 14 percent, the average size of state governments as a percentage of personal income fell to 12 percent in less than ten years. Declines continued off and on until the mid-1980s, largely as a function of cuts in federal contributions to the states. Average state government size bottomed out in 1985, followed by steady but small increases between 1986 and 2000.

The size of state governments varies across the states even controlling for population. The average state allocates 14 percent of personal income to the public sector, with most states falling between 14 and 18 percent. But the size of government in some states varies from this average. At the top end is Alaska, which has an unusually large public sector (37.3 percent). States at the low end of public sector size include Maryland, Georgia, and New Hampshire.

Observers have offered a host of explanations for the growth in state government over the years. Probably the most widely accepted theory argues that government grows due to economic and social changes that occur with industrialization and urbanization. As societies move away from their traditional agrarian economies, citizens have more discretionary income, which makes them more comfortable with governmental attempts to solve public problems. Some scholars dismiss this argument, pointing instead to citizen demand, political culture, or even the advocacy of public officials who have a vested interest in the growth of government. For whatever reason, state government activities have grown and expanded, as have their expenditures (Garand and Baudoin 2004).

THE BUDGET PROCESS

The decisions on how money is to be allocated are the result of the state budgetary processes. The allocation of state spending, in turn, is a result of political preferences. The ability to set priorities and then to implement public policies through state programs is ultimately determined through the state budget process. Thus, participating in the budget process is a critical job for state officials, which assures that multiple officials will jockey for influence in this regard. According to the National Association of State Budget Officers (2002, pref.), "The budget process is the arena in which a state determines public priorities by allocating financial resources among competing claims . . . the authorities and restrictions on budget players influences each state's ability to achieve policy." Further, the association noted that "it is within the budget process that spending policies for public programs are articulated and debated between the governor, the legislature, and state agencies" (NASBO 2002, 1). The governor can make the state of the state address, and agency heads can generate repeated policy impact statements, but unless money is allocated in sufficient amounts, public policies and programs cannot achieve their full objectives.

The budget process in the states is a perpetual cycle; one budget is hardly completed before preparations for the next year's budget begin. In over half the states, budgets are prepared on an annual cycle. Twenty-three states budget on a biennial cycle (every two years). However, in fourteen of the states that budget biennially, the state legislatures meet annually, giving them a chance to examine the budget and seek revisions in non-budget years. Thus, in a majority of states, even as an agency begins to spend money for one fiscal year, it has already begun calculating how much funding it will need in the next. Additionally, the budget office and individual state agencies must be prepared to provide fiscal statements, spending plans, and even a defense of upcoming expenditures at any given time.

The Budget Office

The budget office is the focal point for the creation of the governor's budget recommendations to the legislature. In this office, all elements of a potential budget come together—economic forecasts, agency requests and defenses of requests, the governor's priorities, and budget analysis. In many ways, this is where the real budget action begins.

The organizational location of the executive budget office differs from state to state. It can be a semi-independent, freestanding agency, located outside of any other department in state government. In this arrangement, the expectation is that the state budget will be less subject to political manipulation, so that it accurately reflects the state's revenue availability and expenditure needs. In most cases, the governor is the direct administrative superior to the budget director. A budget office located outside the governor's office or within another administrative department overseen by the governor lends both credibility and neutrality to the process. Ten states have opted for a semi-autonomous agency outside the governor's office.

In some states, such as Indiana and Pennsylvania, the budget office is a freestanding organization, and in Pennsylvania, the director ranks as a department-level (or cabinet) official. In these states, the budget director or secretary is chosen by the governor and acts as his or her representative in the budget process. But as discussed earlier, establishing the agency as a freestanding entity also places some distance or insulation from the governor's office. In Indiana, the budget agency serves the budget committee, composed of four members of the Indiana General Assembly and the budget director (who is appointed by the governor). The committee is responsible for creating a budget for submission to the governor, who then sends it to the Indiana legislature. In essence, the Indiana budget agency is a liaison between the legislative and executive branches of government, and it provides information to both. It creates more of a total state budget than an "executive" budget.

In New York, the Division of the Budget is described as "an agency within the executive department of New York State government [that] came into existence . . . following constitutional reforms that laid the foundation for a 'strong executive' form of government" (http://www.budget.state.ny.us/division/history/history.html). In this situation, the agency is autonomous in that there is no agency head or administrator hierarchically above the budget director; he or she reports directly to the governor and is not subject to any other administrative forces. The separate organization for the budget office gives it a single mission, in contrast to the situation when the budget office is part of another department focused on multiple tasks. However, the emphasis is on centralization of the process to provide the *governor* with the ability to create an executive budget.

Eleven states locate the budget office within the office of the governor itself, providing an even more direct relationship to the governor and centralization of the budget process within the executive branch. In these states, the governor uses the budget office to create a budget that reflects his or her agenda and priorities. Under this arrangement, the governor and the legislature might not have a consensus on priorities or revenue estimates. If the budget is made outside the governor's office, it is more likely to reflect multiple viewpoints; if it originates in the governor's office, it likely reflects the chief executive's spending goals. Georgia, Montana, and Utah are among the states that centralize the budgeting process within the governor's office.

The rest of the states locate the budget office within another state department. In this arrangement, the budget office assumes only a portion of the mission of that department, and in some cases, the director also reports to the governor through the department secretary. There are several advantages to this form of organization. First, the process of creating the executive budget is fully integrated into the other financial and analytical processes of the state. Second, information from other divisions (such as taxation, revenue, and management analysis) can freely flow horizontally within the organization rather than across several departments and committees. And third, the director can gain some insulation from politics, as information runs through an administrative hierarchy. Typically, the budget office is integrated into the department of finance or the state department of administration, or it may be part of a larger department of management and budget (similar to the Office of Management and Budget [OMB] at the federal level).

The budget director is in charge of integrating agency requests and gubernatorial priorities into a presentable budget to be sent to the legislature. When the budget office is located as a freestanding agency or within the governor's office, the governor directly appoints the budget director. In two states where the budget director heads a semi-autonomous agency—in California and Ohio—the director is appointed by the governor with the advice and consent of the state senate. This arrangement reflects the more neutral role of these agencies as liaisons and tools of both the executive and legislative branches of government.

When the budget office is located within another department, the governor is much less likely to have total control over the appointment of the budget director. In the twenty-nine states with this form of organization, the governor alone appoints budget directors in only seven of the states. In another six states, the governor makes the appointment with the advice and consent of the state senate. However, in all but two of the remaining states, the governor has direct or indirect input into the selection. In ten states, the department head appoints the budget director subject to the governor's approval; in another five states, the department alone has sole responsibility for the appointment. However, unless very chaotic political conditions exist (for instance, if an independently elected commissioner or a department is at political or ideological odds with the governor), it is unlikely that the department head would choose someone the governor did not approve. In one state, however, the selection of the budget head is removed from gubernatorial control entirely. In South Carolina, the Budget and Control Board appoints the budget director.

Regardless of where and how the budget office is organized or when and how the budget director is appointed, the director and his or her office play an integral role in creating a budget that combines administrative and/or gubernatorial (and sometimes legislative) priorities as a starting point for legislative deliberations. The budget director is in charge of a more than year-long process with many different phases. In all but four states (Alabama, Michigan, New York, and Texas), the fiscal year begins on July 1. Alabama's fiscal year starts on October 1, as does Michigan's. New York's fiscal year begins in April, and Texas starts its fiscal year on September 1. In the states with biennial cycles, the budgeting process dominates every other year in the same way that an annual process does. The next sections will describe the steps of the budget process, discussing the administrators involved in each. Table 3.1 details the approximate timetable (recognizing that the states' budget schedules vary), emphasizing the countdown until the beginning of each fiscal year.

Economic Forecasts are Developed

Before any of the work by the governor and the administrative agencies begins, state administrators, fiscal analysts, and economic forecasters are hard at work. Approximately twelve to fifteen months before the start of the next fiscal year, these state officials are diligently trying to forecast that year's revenue growth or deficit. Although sophisticated computer programs extrapolate revenue growth—taking into consideration various economic indicators such as current revenue trends, tax rates, property growth, and interest rates—forecasting state revenues two years into the future can be a tricky business. And if unexpected circumstances occur, such as a major disaster (the 9/11 attacks, for example), unforeseen industrial change, or even unanticipated changes in federal allotments to the states, economic forecasts can be far from the mark. When this happens and agencies have budgeted based on faulty or changing assumptions, states may find themselves quickly out of money. Since most states have some sort of balanced-budget requirement, this situation can cause agencies much hardship. In Alabama, for instance, when state revenues fall short, state agencies are subject to a process called proration, whereby agency budgets are cut by a particular percentage in order to balance the budget with less than anticipated funds. For an agency that is counting on funds to last over the entire budget year, a 10 percent shortfall is devastating.

TABLE 3.1. THE BUDGET PROCESS AND SCHEDULE IN THE STATES

Countdown to the start of the fiscal year	Activities
12 to 15 months	Economic analysis conducted and revenue forecasts prepared for fiscal year (FY)
10 to 12 months	Budget guidelines sent to state agencies for FY
8 to 10 months	Agency requests submitted to governor (or executive budget office)
7 to 10 months	Agency request reviewed by governor and budget office; agencies defend budget requests
6 to 8 months	Governor finalizes executive budget recommendations
6 months	Governor submits executive budget to legislature
2 to 6 months	Agency defends budget requests to legislature; legislative debates and hearings
1 month	Legislature adopts budgets

Thus, these economic forecasts are critical for every agency that receives funding from the state. But forecasting is not an exact science. Usually, there is also some discrepancy in the estimates produced by different governmental organizations. In the national government, both the Congressional Budget Office (CBO) and the OMB make economic forecasts, sometimes with discrepancies of millions of dollars. In addition to the executive branch budget and finance departments that make estimates, some states may also have legislative fiscal offices with purposes similar to the CBO's (to provide independent, nonpartisan information), and these offices supply estimates to legislators. Additionally, independent economic forecasting firms may be used by budget offices and/or groups interested in influencing the budget process.

To help sort through these various estimates, thirty states have some type of council of economic advisers that helps the governor and budget office decide which revenue forecasts to use for the coming budget year. In some states, this is a constitutional or statutory requirement. In others, the governor has created the council by executive order. The makeup of these councils can also vary greatly. Members of some councils are directly appointed by the governor, while other councils are made up of individuals the governor has appointed to different positions. For instance, Alaska's governor's council of economic advisers is composed of the director of the Office of Management and Budget, the commissioner of the Department of Commerce and Economic Development, the commissioners of the Departments of Labor and Revenue (or their designees), and an economist from the state. Alternatively, the Nevada Economic Forum was created by the state legislature. The forum may not contain any employees of state government, including persons employed by institutions of higher education; instead, members are appointed by the senate majority leader, the speaker of the assembly, and the governor.

In all fifty states, either the council and the governor or the governor and his or her budget officer decide on revenue estimates provided by various sources. Each of the following agencies, depending on the particular state and the delegation of authority in that state, may provide the governor, councils, and budget offices with estimates either singly or with the aid of other agencies: the department of revenue, the budget office, the department of taxation, the economic forecast council, the department of finance, the offices of management and budget, and the department of labor. Sometimes, even outside agencies are contracted to provide the estimates.

Budget Guidelines are Sent to Agencies

Once the economic forecasts are decided on, the budget office provides guidelines to all state agencies seeking funding. The budget information sent to the agencies contains technical, legal, and policy guidelines. For instance, the budget office is responsible for providing the uniform documents that the agencies must use to submit their funding requests. The budget office is also typically in charge of implementing new information technology for the budget process, including integrated computing and information systems. Thus, typical guidelines might incorporate instructions for using a new computer system or, in some cases, a new budget process altogether. Part of the information given to the agencies specifies what information needs to be included in their requests. Additionally, the budget office might send out directions on how to calculate particular budget estimates, such as estimates on inflation, debt service for bonds and/or loans, service fees or rental rates, and additional funds needed for personnel lines such as fringe benefit calculations or insurance rates.

Legal and policy guidelines are included as well. These guidelines would be pertinent if, say, a state legislature enacted legislation that required state agencies to detail how they would cut their budgets if a certain percentage budget reduction was implemented (especially appropriate if fiscal hardships are expected). Similarly, a law might allow for a particular rate of growth for a program or change entitlement requirements; for example, state insurance programs might be changed to include a new or enlarged population or different benefits, which might require recalculations of potential expenditures. The governor also will include policy guidelines for the budget office to forward to agencies. The governor might designate (either formally or informally) his or her policy priorities or present each agency with spending targets or ceilings for its requests. Further, the governor might ask that each (or some) agency change amounts within particular lines of the budgets (for example, reduce personnel or administrative costs by a certain percentage). The governor might also introduce expansions to programs he or she favors or seek justification or additional analyses from less preferred areas. Each of these requirements or goals is included in the guidelines sent to agencies or organizations that seek state funds.

Agencies Submit Requests to Budget Office

After receiving the budget guidelines, the agency head prepares a budget request for submission to the budget office and the governor. Budgeting requests typically contain a budget "base" and additional expenditure requests. The budget base, depending on the directions received from the budgeting office, usually contains the expenditure amounts needed to keep the agency's programs running at the current level; alternatively, it might separate out the funds needed for existing services and spending needed for services as they are projected into the next year with increases due to inflation. Further, administrators are usually asked for separate funding requests for capital (building) projects that need to be completed or additions for existing programs.

The agency head's main concern is to secure enough resources so that his or her unit can continue operations at the preferred level. He or she may also hope to expand the resources available to the agency. Agency heads hoping to increase their budgets are labeled budget maximizers. Early budgeting scholars, including William Niskanen (1971), hypothesized that administrators would seek to gain the largest budget possible for their agencies. Additional research, however, concluded that this view was overstated. Niskanen (1991), Aaron Wildavsky (1964 and 1988), and Sydney Duncombe and Richard

Kinney (1987) all concluded that other considerations in making budget requests were relevant. Rather than only caring about increasing the size of their own agencies, administrators are also concerned with maintaining good working relationships with the legislature, the governor, and other administrators. Consequently, they must craft the agency funding requests very carefully, asking for enough resources so that, after the governor and legislature review them, they are left with enough funding to work with. They must take care not to ask for more funds than the legislature or governor are comfortable with. It is a very delicate game to play. Administrators know that the governor and his or her staff, as well as the legislators, will scrutinize the budget requests carefully and will almost definitely pare them down to some extent. Legislators and governors expect administrators to pad their requests so that they are left with the funding they really need after the cuts are made. Thus, the cycle of gamesmanship continues.

According to the 2004 American State Administrators Project, almost 60 percent of the agency heads responded that they had requested an increase in funding during the last budget cycle. However, about 10 percent actually requested decreases in their budgets, and about one-third requested no change. These requests also came after three years of fiscal stress for the states, when many agencies had previously found their budgets decreasing. So state agency heads do not really seem to be budget maximizers after all.

Reports are Analyzed

The budget office analyzes all of the agency requests before consolidating them into a statewide executive budget proposal. In most cases, the analyses are comprehensive and employ specialized techniques. The budget office, the finance/revenue departments, or independent economic commissions will have previously conducted economic analyses to develop guidelines for the agency requests. So at this stage of the process, these economic forecasts are often repeated and/or reconfirmed with new economic data the state has received since the agency guidelines were first created. Also, the budget office staff might analyze national trends or recent business activity to confirm economic trends, for the proposed budget needs to match the realistic financial situation of the state. Further, if additional information about federal funding or intergovernmental budget transfers or grants has been received, it will need to be incorporated into the requests. In some states, revenue from certain funding sources is earmarked for particular state services. For example, in Alabama, education is funded entirely from the Education Trust Fund with designated state revenue sources. Other state agencies must draw their funds from different revenue sources. In these cases, extraordinary care must be used in revenue forecasts because money for appropriated programs cannot be transferred freely if revenue in some areas runs short.

Additionally, the budget office may conduct program evaluations and management reviews (in many states, the budget office might be called the office of management and budget, like the OMB at the federal level). The program evaluations are conducted to determine how efficiently and effectively the programs are operating (Are they spending money wisely and conducting the state's services in the cheapest possible manner? Are they having the desired impact on citizens and community problems?). Sometimes, "doing the right thing" might cost a lot of money, so trade-offs between efficiency and effectiveness exist in state administration. Program evaluations often determine if such trade-offs in a particular program are creating favorable public policy. These evaluations might also determine if the agency's program has enough staff, technology, and funding to accomplish its goals. Evaluators might also identify ways to improve the programs. For budget purposes, an evaluation usually identifies ways that programs might operate more inexpensively. If agencies are requesting more funding, then the evaluation might determine if the funding requested will actually improve the quality of agency services and whether the additional cost is justified for the amount of program improvements outlined.

By contrast, agency requests may be increased during this stage. If demographic changes are detected in the population that needs agency services, then funds to that agency must increase accordingly. This situation is especially likely to occur when the agency operates an entitlement program (one that provides services to any individual or group that meets certain requirements) or when gubernatorial or legislative priorities have been established.

During this stage in the budget process, the budget office staff typically will communicate with agency staff, either formally through budget hearings or informally through meetings and discussions. These meetings can include the governor or his or her representative, agency advocates, legislators, and agency clientele and other advocates. The agency head may be given the opportunity to review and offer advice on the assumptions made by budget office personnel as they evaluated programs and analyzed budget requests. Just as it is important to have specialized, outside sources evaluate programs, it is also important that program staff members be involved because they possess the most knowledge of agency programs and the expertise required to accomplish policy goals. According to the 2004 ASAP survey, 58 percent of the agency heads reported having moderate or high influence on their agency's total budget and about three-fifths reported having moderate or high influence on specific program budgets. So a majority of agency heads feel that their concerns are heard and that they do influence their agency's budgets. The final decisions on the executive proposals, though, lie with the governor (in most states) and/or the budget offices.

Governor Finalizes and Submits Executive Budget

Of the majority of agency heads who feel they have a moderate or high degree of influence on their agency's budgets, almost nine in ten feel that the governor exercises a moderate or high degree of influence on their total budgets, and 82 percent feel that the governor's influence on specific budgets is moderate or high. Over half of the agency heads report experiencing high levels of influence from the governor. Reports show that the majority of agency heads requested increased expenditures, but results from the

2004 ASAP survey indicate that governors proposed increases in administrators' budgets only 35 percent of the time and decreases almost as often (30 percent). Thus, agency heads perceive high influence from governors and not always in ways that favor their agencies with increased funding.

A large part of the executive budget process and analysis by the budget office hinges on producing a balanced budget for submission to the state legislature. Governors often deliver a highly publicized budget address to the legislature (and the public via the media). This address gives governors the opportunity to explain their spending priorities and to attempt to garner support among lawmakers and the public. In all but six states (Idaho, Indiana, Texas, Vermont, Virginia, and West Virginia), the governor is required by either the state constitution (in thirty-four states) or legislative statute (in ten states) to submit a balanced budget for legislative consideration. In Idaho, the governor submits a balanced budget because the legislature *must* pass a balanced budget, making it irresponsible to submit an unbalanced budget that probably would end up being decreased in ways the governor would not approve. In Virginia, the governor must make sure that the actual expenditures do not exceed actual revenue by the end of the appropriation period, so it would again be illogical to propose a budget that was extremely unbalanced (NASBO 2002).

Once the estimates about future revenues are completed, agencies have requested funding, and the governor has placed his or her stamp on the budget, the governor presents the budget to the legislature for consideration. While many actors worked to draft the proposed budget and each left an imprint on it, hoping to assure that certain priorities are well funded, it is the legislature that will adopt the actual spending plan and authorize the funds for it. Nearly all legislatures have essentially unlimited power to do whatever they want with the budget proposal once it is delivered to them.

Legislative Hearings are Conducted

At this point, the governor has created the proposed budget and submitted it to the legislature, but the budget process itself is not complete. In fact, 92 percent of administrators report that the legislature exercises a moderate or high degree of influence on total agency budgets, and 88 percent report that the legislature has at least a moderate level of influence on budgets for specific agency programs. In essence, both the governors and legislatures are intimately involved throughout the budget process. In many ways, the process is a battle determining whose policy objectives will be pursued in the state, so both actors exert a great deal of influence in pursuit of their own goals. In some states and especially in times of fiscal stress, the fight over the state's budget may be quite contentious. The governor's proposals might be adjusted slightly, moderately, or dramatically or even declared dead on arrival.

Legislative budget hearings are one way the legislature exercises influence. In most cases, even after the agency request has undergone review, analysis, and hearings in the executive branch, the legislature holds its own hearings. Such hearings may be less extensive or contentious when legislators are represented within a state's budget committee that helps to create the executive budget. On occasion, agency heads will use the legislative hearings to attempt to circumvent budget cuts (in their preferred areas) that occurred when the budget office and/or the governor reviewed their requests. Agency heads may mobilize legislators favorable to their agency's goals, their agency's clientele, or interest groups to testify on the agency's behalf to add funding to the governor's proposals. At times legislative committees have information that differs from that of the budget office. For instance, they may have their own revenue forecasts, evaluations, or information from interest groups. From varying assumptions, different decisions may result. But finally, legislative committees must send appropriations bills (budget-related bills detailing expenditures for each agency and program) to both houses of the legislature, which must pass the bills just as they would any other piece of legislation.

Legislature Passes Final Appropriations

After the series of budget hearings and legislative debates, the state legislature finally approves a budget for the next fiscal year, concluding a process that began over a year earlier. As the legislature is passing this fiscal year's budget, revenue estimations and planning are already beginning for the next fiscal cycle. But the legislators, like most governors, are also focused on passing a balanced budget. The governor's executive budget submission is simply a starting point for the legislators—they are free to mark up and change the governor's recommendations in committees as they seek to insert their own preferences into the budget. The legislature must pass a balanced budget in forty of the states. This requirement may or may not exist alongside a similar requirement that the governor submit a balanced budget proposal to the legislature.

In California, Hawaii, Missouri, New Hampshire, New York, Pennsylvania, Vermont, and Washington, even though the governor is required to submit a balanced budget, the legislature is under no constitutional or statutory requirement to pass a balanced budget. In several of these states, however, despite the fact that the legislature is not mandated to balance the budget, the governor can only sign a budget in which expenditures meet expected revenue. These states include California, Hawaii, Missouri, and Pennsylvania. In Idaho, Texas, and West Virginia, the legislature assumes the primary responsibility for passing a balanced budget, though the governor need not submit a balanced executive budget. Thus, various constitutional and statutory requirements place responsibilities on the governor and the budget office, the legislature, or both as the "guardian[s] of the purse" in the states.

In the final step of the budget process in most states, the budget bill moves to the governor for his or her signature. As with other legislation, the governor may either sign the bill or, in all states except Maryland, veto it. The State of Maryland treats budget bills differently from other pieces of legislation. When both houses of the Maryland legislature pass the budget bill, it becomes law without any further action by the governor. However, if supplemental appropriations are needed (additional funds for state programs added after the budget bill has passed), they are subject to gubernatorial veto. In forty-three states, the governors also have line-item vetoes. Only Indiana, Maine, Nevada, New Hampshire, North Carolina, Rhode Island, and Vermont do not give their governors some form of item veto. Item vetoes were created so that governors could take out portions of legislation that they deemed detrimental without vetoing what might otherwise be an acceptable bill. Governors use the item veto to remove portions of appropriations bills that they believe are unnecessary or inappropriate public expenditures.

Item vetoes come in various forms. In Arizona, the line-item veto can be used only in bills that contain multiple appropriations. If a single appropriation is placed in a bill that has other purposes as well (such as establishing a law or program), then the entire bill must be vetoed if the governor hopes to quash it. In New Mexico, line-item vetoes apply only to appropriations legislation. In Illinois, the governor can veto appropriation items entirely, reduce the amount of an appropriation, or amend the language of a bill by changing or deleting words (NASBO 2002)

Clearly, the budget process is a long, complicated, and often highly politicized procedure. It represents the culmination of policymaking; without money, programs cannot operate and policy goals will go unfulfilled. The governor and legislators alternately cooperate and contend with one another as they attempt to pass fiscally responsible budgets that reflect all of their political and policy goals. The state agency heads seek to maintain good relationships with their elected officials while keeping their programs operational. This wrangling for position and the signing of the final budget bill represent the height of political drama in what many consider to be a boring, numbers-driven, analytical process.

And it is only the beginning. After the budget is passed, funds must actually be appropriated, revenues invested, and loans obtained in some cases. Audits must be conducted to assure citizens that their tax dollars are used on the programs and items for which the appropriations bills designated them. Three primary individuals in the state oversee the use of state funds: the treasurer, auditor, and comptroller. The next section will discuss each of these officials and their functions within state government.

EXECUTIVES INVOLVED IN STATE FINANCIAL OPERATIONS

As noted, the budget director and his or her office are usually responsible for helping create a state's budget and administration goals. Once the budget is passed, many other state agencies and executive officials are vested with the responsibility to create, implement, and monitor the financial operations of the state government. Among the offices implementing the fiscal operations are the department of revenue, the state treasurer, the state comptroller, and the state auditor. States have all created their own executive organizations, and no two look exactly alike. In some states, these fiscal offices are independent agencies; in others, the revenue department may be a division in a larger finance or administration agency. In most of the states, the treasurer is deemed the chief financial officer; in a few others, such as Texas and Hawaii, the comptroller or director of finance, respectively, performs the treasurer's role. But despite these variations, a general set of financial responsibilities is shouldered by these officials in every state across the country. This section looks at the methods of appointment for the officers who perform these roles, as well as the primary duties of the executives who manage the fiscal processes of state government.

Treasurer (Chief Financial Officer)

In three-fourths of the states, the treasurer, or chief financial officer (CFO), is elected by the citizens in a statewide election. Except in the case of the Vermont treasurer (who serves two years), all of the states elect their treasurers to a four-year term. In Texas, the elected comptroller assumes the treasurer's responsibilities in addition to duties that are typically performed by comptrollers. Another nine states have gubernatorially appointed treasurers or CFOs. In several of these cases, an executive appointed to a different office performs the duties that a treasurer might perform in another state. For instance, in Alaska, a deputy commissioner in the Department of Revenue fulfills the treasurer's role. In Hawaii and Minnesota, the director/commissioner of finance performs the duties associated with the treasurer. Finally, in four other states—Maine, Maryland, New Hampshire, and Tennessee—the treasurer is elected by members of the state legislature to two- or four-year terms.

In most states, the treasurer (or whoever acts as the chief financial officer) has a set of responsibilities associated with being the state's chief banker and investment officer. As the state's banker, the treasurer or CFO focuses on cash management. In many states, this function means assuring that the state has sufficient funds to meet its payroll and guaranteeing that moneys that should flow to particular agencies from the state's general fund or particular trust funds are readily available and transferred appropriately. The treasurer might receive and account for funds that flow into state government through intergovernmental transfers as well as agency fees or deposits. Additionally, the office of treasurer is usually responsible for disbursing any funds drawn on state accounts, such as tax refunds, transfers of funds from one agency to another, or transfers from a state agency to citizens or organizations.

Typically, the treasurer or CFO also operates as the primary investment officer for the state. Citizens normally do not think of states as investors, but to perform state functions efficiently, as well as increase the money available for state services, state funds must be managed wisely. Thus, the treasurer or CFO oversees short-term and long-term investments, manages debt, and borrows money at the lowest cost to state and local governments. Short-term investment of the tax dollars deposited in the state's general fund or special funds such as education or highway trust funds is a necessary part of a state's financial operations. (The general fund is a fund into which most states place the bulk of state revenue and from which most state agencies receive their budgetary allotments.) These funds typically will be expended within a fiscal year, but prudent financial managers cannot allow billions of dollars to sit idle when they might instead be drawing returns that could be used for state services. Consequently, it is often the job of the state treasurer to invest these funds for the short term in an efficient but stable and secure manner.

The treasurer is also typically in charge of longer-term investments. In a majority of states, the treasurer or CFO is in charge of investing state employees' retirement and pension funds. Additionally, over forty states have set up college savings plans, which help citizens fund their children's future education. Citizens put funds into these plans, and the state (the treasurer) invests them so that the interest earned over the next decades will, in effect, allow parents to pay today's tuition rates and receive tomorrow's education for their sons and daughters.

As both banker and investor, the treasurer is often a debt manager as well. The state's CFO is responsible for issuing all bonds for the state, which entails borrowing money when interest rates are favorable and maintaining repayment schedules backed by the state's tax dollars. In many states, the treasurer or CFO is also responsible for counseling, aiding, and overseeing local governments' issuance of bonds and guaranteeing that local governments maintain acceptable levels of debt and proper repayment allowances. In this manner, the treasurer represents the state and local governments to bond rating agencies such as Standard and Poor's or Moody's Investments, which set the cost at which state and local governments can borrow money.

Another way in which state treasurers aid local governments is in creating linked-deposit programs or pooled investments. Larger investments can sometimes yield higher rates of return, so about a third of the state treasurers oversee state and local pooled investment funds in which many local governments place money for short-term investments, earn the higher interest rate accorded larger investments, and receive their share of the interest.

Comptroller (Controller)

In some states, such as New York and Texas, the comptroller is constitutionally elected and performs many of the functions of the chief financial officer or treasurer. If the treasurer is the banker and investment officer, then the comptroller is typically the chief accountant, charged with creating financial systems for managing and recording the state's financial transactions. In this section, the methods for appointing the comptroller, as well as the typical duties of this office, are discussed.

Unlike the treasurers, comptrollers are much less likely to be constitutionally defined elected state officers. Only sixteen states elect their comptrollers. Interestingly, California, Florida, Texas, and New York, the nation's largest states in terms of financial transactions, all elect their comptrollers. In Florida, New York, and Texas, the comptroller plays the role of the chief financial officer; as of January 2003, Florida even dropped the title of comptroller in favor of chief financial officer. In these three states, the comptroller really assumes both the typical comptroller duties that will be discussed and many of the duties of treasurer. And the merger of these offices seems to be efficient, as the banker and investment officer operates within the accounting and financial reporting systems that comptrollers most often oversee.

In the rest of the states, the comptroller is appointed by various officials. In ten of the states, the governor appoints the comptroller, sometimes with the approval of one or both houses of the legislature. In other states, the comptroller is appointed by the agency head or cabinet secretary in charge of the department of finance or management and budget (depending on the state). In some states, among them Alaska and New Hampshire, the governor must approve the appointment of the comptroller.

If the treasurer is the primary banker and investor for the state, the comptroller acts as the chief accountant and/or operations officer. In most states, the comptroller is directly responsible for assuring that state funds are used for the purposes for which they were budgeted and that financial systems allocate and record state transactions appropriately. The comptroller essentially keeps track of all state expenditures and payments. Further, the comptroller in some states has the cash-management responsibilities that other states assign to the treasurer. This job entails disbursing state funds from the general fund to state agencies or local governments and ensuring that the state can meet its financial obligations.

Typically, however, as the state's accountant, the comptroller is in charge of developing and operating the financial accounting systems for the state government. He or she creates a single, centralized system and assists state agencies in using it. In this way, all agencies can utilize the same forms and methods of accounting for public funds. In the last few decades, this job has involved developing computerized systems that can be accessed by employees across all state agencies. These systems might release state funds from the treasury into agency accounts as they are needed, keep track of purchases by state agencies according to the particular item purchased and the account used to pay for it, and generate summarized records of expenditures each month.

As the state's primary accountant, the comptroller is also responsible for providing monthly or quarterly reconciliations of accounts—making sure that the amounts reportedly spent by each agency match the amounts the agency was budgeted. The comptroller must ensure that the state's funds are spent and recorded according to generally accepted accounting principles, a set of professional standards developed by accountants. Also, almost every public organization (local, state, or federal) and most private organizations must provide a comprehensive annual financial report (CAFR). The comptroller is usually responsible for creating this document and providing it to the governor, legislators, and citizens of their state.

Auditor

If the treasurer is the banker and investor and the comptroller is the accountant, then the state auditor is an independent evaluator of state expenditures, accounts, and programs. Most public and private organizations realize that to ensure integrity and accuracy in the handling of financial resources, an independent, or outside, auditor is necessary. Although outright dishonesty is rare among state executives, problems do occur. More common are honest mistakes and human error. The public demands maximum accountability from the government when taxpayer money is concerned, and thus, states have established the office of state auditor to make sure that the treasurer and comptroller are expending moneys correctly and keeping accurate records and that state agencies are using their funds efficiently.

Like the state comptrollers, state auditors are appointed to their offices through a variety of mechanisms. Seventeen states have constitutionally provided elections for the officer in charge of state audits. In another third of the states, the auditor is chosen by the legislature or by a legislative committee. Having the legislature play a primary role in choosing the auditor provides another of the checks and balances that are an integral part of state government. But whether elected by the public or the legislature, the auditor is completely independent of the executive branch and its agencies, in order to remain neutral. Other state auditors are appointed by the governor (in Florida and Indiana), an independent board or commission (in Alaska and South Carolina), or agency heads (for instance, in New Jersey and Oregon).

The state auditor, or director of the division or department of audits, typically plays two important roles in the financial operations of the state. First, he or she acts as an independent accountant or auditor of public funds. To perform this function, the auditor might undertake financial, contract, or investigative audits. A financial audit ensures that public funds have been spent in the manner prescribed by laws and state procedures; in this regard, the auditor will ascertain if moneys were expended on appropriate items for appropriate prices and if the transactions were recorded appropriately. A contract audit determines if a contractor has met its obligations and performed appropriate services or if a bidding process was fair and appropriate to the task; here, the auditor will determine if a company earned a state contract fairly and if it used state funds appropriately. And finally, an investigative audit occurs when an agency employee, an elected official, or a citizen suspects state funds have been spent inappropriately; in such a case, the auditor will gather evidence to confirm or refute that suspicion.

In addition to all the functions directly related to making sure that state funds are expended appropriately, the auditor might also be in charge of performance and/or efficiency evaluations of state programs: in essence, the auditor operates as an independent evaluator of the state's programs. Evaluations of this type ensure that state agencies operate programs that are both effective (following state policies and helping to create the outcomes desired by legislators and agency employees) and efficient (doing the most effective activities that they can with state dollars). The auditor might ask questions such as: Can you do this particular activity more cheaply and still maintain quality? Are there less expensive ways to secure products? Are there other ways to pursue this goal that might lead to better outcomes for agency clients? Above all, the auditor is an independent source for validating and ascertaining efficiency, accuracy, and honesty in state financial and programmatic activities.

KEY STATE EXECUTIVE OFFICERS

Governors make many decision that result in state actions, but so, too, do others within the government. The state legislature, which bears the primary responsibility for making law, is clearly involved in the decision process. And so are a number of actors within the executive branch who, to varying degrees, impact policymaking. These actors may be in step with the governor's preferences—but then again, they may not. Many are elected separately from the governor and may choose to pursue their own priorities, and as the previous discussion illustrated, there are ways in which they can exert influence in the policymaking arena. While the bureaucracies in the states are made up of hundreds of individuals, three top-level officials are most important for understanding the dynamics of policymaking within the executive branch: the lieutenant governor, the secretary of state, and the attorney general. Each of these key officers will be discussed in the following sections. Though some duties of their offices are fairly standard from state to state, there is also a significant degree of variation in how they are chosen, how long they serve, and what responsibilities they fulfill in the state. Despite the fact that all of these actors function within the executive branch of the state, they do not always work toward a common goal. The conflict that sometimes arises among them will also be addressed.

Lieutenant Governor

In many states, the lieutenant governors play some of the same roles as the vice-president of the United States. For instance, most are first in the line of succession should the chief executive not be able to perform his or her duties. Some lieutenant governors preside over the upper chambers of state legislatures, and similar to vice-presidents, they may cast the deciding vote in the legislature should a tie exist. Many lieutenant governors also represent their governments at ribbon cuttings, funerals, and celebratory events. The vice-president may have served in the House or Senate in the nation's capital, and similarly, lieutenant governors often have served in one or both houses of the state legislature as a stepping stone to the executive branch position. And just as the vice-president may hope to rise to the presidency, many lieutenant governors hope to eventually be elected to the highest office in the state.

However, there are also many differences between the vice-president and the lieutenant governors in terms of the responsibilities they assume. Further, the methods of appointment, the powers, and the responsibilities of lieutenant governors differ widely across the states. The most important difference is that many lieutenant governors are elected separately from the governor; they do not run on a single, partisan ticket. Additionally, their power to affect policy and governance in the states varies widely. And a minority of states does not even have a lieutenant governor.

Becoming Lieutenant Governor

Forty-four of the fifty state executive branches include the position of lieutenant governor among their offices. The states that do not have a lieutenant governor are Arizona, Maine, New Hampshire, New Jersey, Oregon, and Wyoming. In forty of the states that do have an office of lieutenant governor, the position was established within the state's constitution, along with the terms of election and the duties of the office. In the other four, the office of lieutenant governor was established by state statute. In Ohio and Rhode Island, state law (as opposed to the constitution) enacted the position of lieutenant governor and its method of popular election. By West Virginia law, the person elected by the senate membership to serve as the president of that body, chosen at the beginning of each two-year legislative term, also serves as the lieutenant governor of the state. Similarly, although Tennessee is not considered by all sources to have an office of lieutenant governor, the speaker of the senate, elected by the senate membership, is also given the statutory title of lieutenant governor. In the other six states, the duties that might fall to a lieutenant governor are divided among other state offices.

In the forty-two states that popularly elect the lieutenant governor by a statewide vote of the citizens, two different practices are followed. In twenty-four states, the governor and the lieutenant governor are elected together. Under this arrangement, the gubernatorial candidate chooses the candidate for lieutenant governor who will run on his or her ticket (nearly always under the same political party). Because the lieutenant governor is chosen by the gubernatorial candidate and seeks election in tandem with him or her, the two often have similar political ideologies and policy goals.

In the nineteen other states that elect the lieutenant governor, he or she runs separately from the candidate for governor. Their campaigns are managed separately, and voters must vote for each officer individually. Voters may choose a governor of one party and a lieutenant governor of the other party. Consequently, the two highest officers of a state may not share the same policy preferences, especially when voters elect a governor from one political party and a lieutenant governor from the opposing political party. In states where the lieutenant governor serves as the president of the senate or plays an active role in the legislative arena, having the governor and lieutenant governor positions filled by members of opposing parties may be particularly problematic for governors seeking to influence legislation and policymaking. For instance, if a lieutenant governor has the power to initiate legislation within the state senate, that official might seek passage of the bills he or she prefers at the expense of the governor's goals. This topic will be explored further in the section detailing powers and responsibilities. As Table 3.2 illustrates, as of July 2003, six states had lieutenant governors who did not share the governor's party attachment.

TABLE 3.2 STATES IN WHICH THE LIEUTENANT GOVERNOR AND THE GOVERNOR DO NOT SHARE PARTY AFFILIATION

State	Lieutenant governor	Governor
Alabama	Lucy Baxley (D)	Bob Riley (R)
Georgia	Mark Taylor (D)	Sonny Perdue (R)
Louisiana	Mitch Landrieu (D)	Mike Foster (R)
Mississippi	Amy Tuck (R)	Ronnie Musgrove (D)
Oklahoma	Mary Fallin (R)	Brad Henry (D)
Rhode Island	Charles Fogarty (D)	Don Carcieri (R)

Source: Data compiled by the author; reflects incumbency prior to the 2003 elections.

D = Democrat   R = Republican

Many of the individuals who become lieutenant governors do so after a lengthy career in politics. They have often served as state representatives and/or state senators, as other executive branch officials such as secretaries of state or attorneys general, or as elected officials within local government, such as a county commissioners or city council members. California lieutenant governor Cruz Bustamante initially developed a taste for politics during a summer internship in Washington with a member of the U.S. Congress. In time, he was elected to the California General Assembly, became speaker of that body, and finally was made the lieutenant governor of one of the largest states of the Union (www.ltg.ca.gov/about/biography.asp). Jennette Bradley, lieutenant governor of Ohio, was elected to that post after serving for eleven years as a member of the Columbus City Council (ltgovernor.ohio.gov/bio.htm). Kerry Healey, Massachusetts's lieutenant governor, also had political experience, having served as the chair of the Massachusetts Republican Party; Healey also has an academic background, with a Ph.D. in political science and years of service as a law and public safety consultant (mass.gov/portal).

Women have been more successful in securing the lieutenant governorship than becoming governor. In fact, only twenty-seven women have been named governors of their states. In July 2004, there were nine female governors, whereas seventeen women served as lieutenant governor, in Alabama, Colorado, Florida, Indiana, Iowa, Massachusetts, Minnesota, Mississippi, Nevada, New Mexico, New York, North Carolina, Ohio, Oklahoma, Pennsylvania, Utah, and Wisconsin.

Members of racial and ethnic minorities are also serving as lieutenant governor, though not in the same numbers as women. In the late 1990s, Joe Rogers and Michael Steele, both African American Republicans, were elected lieutenant governors of Colorado and Maryland, respectively. Currently, there are four minority lieutenant governors: James Aiona of Hawaii, Cruz Bustamante of California, Michael Steele of Maryland, and Jennette Bradley of Ohio. Lieutenant Governor Bradley also has the distinction of being the first African American woman elected lieutenant governor of any state. As the office of lieutenant governor is often a stepping stone for future electoral ambitions, it is likely that minorities and women especially will soon come to governorships, the U.S. House of Representatives, and the U.S Senate in greater numbers.

The office of lieutenant governor also comes with some restrictions on terms of office. In every state with a lieutenant governor except West Virginia (whose lieutenant governor is elected as president of the senate every two years), lieutenant governors serve four-year terms. In over half of these states (twenty-five), lieutenant governors are limited to two consecutive terms in office. In most of these states, if a lieutenant governor leaves office without fulfilling his or her term, the governor is allowed to appoint a replacement until the next regularly scheduled election. This situation may develop if the lieutenant governor resigns from the post or dies while in office or if he or she must vacate the office to assume the duties of the governor. In some states, including Arkansas, a special election may be held to fill the position.

The Powers and Responsibilities of Lieutenant Governors

The powers and duties of lieutenant governors differ from one state to the next. In general, these duties and assignments derive from three main sources: from the state constitution, from state laws, and through assignment by the governor. In some states, the lieutenant governor plays a very active role in policy development as a member of the governor's cabinet and through appointment to various boards and commissions. Also, the lieutenant governor may have constitutionally assigned duties in the legislative process (often presiding over senate proceedings in the states); however, the impact the lieutenant governor may have in the legislature varies. Finally, lieutenant governors are given a variety of administrative duties within the executive branch. Each of these roles—legislative actor, policy adviser, and administrative officer—will be explored in turn.

The Lieutenant Governor as Legislative Actor.   Many state constitutions and statutes grant the lieutenant governor a power similar to that of the vice-president of the United States—the job of senate president. As the senate president, the lieutenant governor acts as the presiding officer of that body. He or she may call the senate to order, declare quorums (the minimum number of legislators that need to be present for a legislative session to occur), direct debates, and moderate points of order. These are the duties that twenty-six of the lieutenant governors perform in the senate, the upper chamber of the state legislature. In Nebraska, the only state with a unicameral legislature, the lieutenant governor is the presiding officer of the legislative body called the senate. In addition, in most of the states where the lieutenant governor is the senate president, he or she may also cast the deciding vote in case of a tie in the chamber. In Georgia, Nebraska, Nevada, Oklahoma, and West Virginia, the lieutenant governor is the senate president but may cast no deciding vote. In one state, Massachusetts, although the lieutenant governor does not preside over the senate, he or she may still cast the tie-breaking final vote.

The lieutenant governor is not, however, generally recognized as the leader of the state senate. Typically, the members of each of the state's senates elect one of their own to become the respective senate speaker or president pro tempore. The speaker or the president pro tem is usually the true leader of the senate—directing debate, appointing members to committees, and assigning bills to committees for debate. But in some cases, the lieutenant governor's powers stretch into this part of the legislative arena. Thus, in seven states, the lieutenant governor appoints senate members to committees—Alabama, Georgia, Mississippi, Rhode Island, Texas, Vermont, and West Virginia. Vermont is a special case, though, as the lieutenant governor is one of a three-person committee, along with the president pro tempore of the senate and another senator elected by the membership, who together make committee appointments. The ability to assign members to committees in the legislature is a powerful tool for lieutenant governors to wield, allowing them to place persons loyal to their agendas onto particular committees. In each of the states mentioned here, the lieutenant governor is elected separately from the governor (they do not run on the same ticket and may not share the same political party), and thus, the lieutenant governor's choice of committee assignments may not be advantageous to the governor's agenda.

Even more important than assigning persons to committees is the power to assign bills to particular committees for debate. Twelve states give the lieutenant governor this power: Alabama, Georgia, Massachusetts, Mississippi, New Mexico, North Dakota, Pennsylvania, South Carolina, South Dakota, Texas, Vermont, and West Virginia. Some committees may look more favorably on a particular bill than others would. For example, a bill dealing with medical benefits for the poor could legitimately be assigned to a health committee, a welfare committee, a labor/workforce committee, or even a ways and means committee, one of which may treat the bill more favorably than the others. The lieutenant governor could essentially push his or her own agenda through the legislature, often to the detriment of or in opposition to the governor. Historically, American fears of a strong executive created this division of power and the establishment of strong lieutenant governorships in order to curtail gubernatorial power. However, in a few states where the governor and lieutenant governor are elected in tandem—Massachusetts, New Mexico, North Dakota, and Pennsylvania—this power may greatly increase the governor and lieutenant governor's ability to promote and propel their shared agenda in the legislative process.

Another role the lieutenant governor plays in the legislative process is as an advocate for particular policy areas and legislation. The fact that the lieutenant governor can assign bills to committees that might further his or her own policy agenda (and stall bills he or she finds unfavorable) has already been mentioned. Although lieutenant governors cannot generally sponsor legislation themselves, they are in a position to influence other legislators to sponsor bills for them and may, in some cases, act

Alabama's Lieutenant Governor

A powerful lieutenant governor may be detrimental to the governor's goals. In the 1998–2002 term of office in Alabama, Don Siegelman (a Democrat) and Steve Windom (a Republican) were elected governor and lieutenant governor, respectively, along with a Democratic majority in the senate. At that time and historically, Alabama's lieutenant governor had played a prominent role in the state senate. Governor Siegelman had been lieutenant governor before being elected governor, so he understood the power of the position. As Lieutenant Governor Windom attempted to promote his own more conservative agenda within the senate by using the tools of committee and bill assignment as well as control of debate, Siegelman and the Democratic senators organized a coup. They attempted to redefine the role of the lieutenant governor by statutorily changing the senate's operating rules at the beginning of a legislative session. Windom made national news by refusing to give up the floor for a vote, even urinating in a jug behind his desk on the senate floor so that he would not have to leave the room. Eventually, however, Windom and the office of lieutenant governor were stripped of much of their power, including the unlimited power to appoint members to committees and bill assignment. Alabama's lieutenant governor is now relegated mainly to presiding over the senate. The officeholder has only limited ability to affect committee and bill assignment.

Former Alabama lieutenant governor Steve Windom (R) was elected in the same year that Lee Siegelman (D) became governor. Windom sparked controversy when his conservative agenda came in conflict with the governor's goals. Alabama's office of lieutenant governor was later stripped of much of its legislative power. (Office of Steve Windom)

as cosponsors of legislation. In other words, due to close working relationships established during senate proceedings, lieutenant governors may have an ability to influence legislative content and legislators' votes that the governor may not possess. In some special cases, lieutenant governors may actually write legislation. For instance, California's Cruz Bustamante's website boasts that he authored a law providing $1 billion of public school textbooks, as well as authoring a bill forcing the attorney general of the state to join the multistate suit against tobacco companies (www.ltg.cs.gov /about/biography.asp).

Finally, the lieutenant governor plays a role traditionally expected of a representative or senator—that of constituent service. Often, a lieutenant governor feels he or she is the person who can help citizens navigate the sometimes confusing processes of the state bureaucracy. On several lieutenant governors' websites, a special form is provided for citizens to state any problems they are having with state agencies and to request the help of the lieutenant governor's office. Indeed, the lieutenant governors often have "constituent service specialists" who serve in this capacity. On the website of New Mexico's lieutenant governor, Diane Denish asserts that part of her mission is to act as an ombudsman and that her office "will strive to provide timely and courteous constituent service to help New Mexicans resolve conflicts with state government" (www.governor.state.nm.us/ltgov/missions.html). The site also provides a link to "constituent services." Through this type of service, a lieutenant governor can establish contact with citizens in a way that the governor generally cannot, for he or she is also in charge of most executive branch agencies.

The Lieutenant Governor as Policy Adviser.   The lieutenant governor also acts as a policy adviser and advocate, and in a sense, this is another way that he or she can influence the legislative process. This advisory role comes to the lieutenant governor primarily from three sources: the state constitution, state statutes, and gubernatorial discretion. In this capacity, the lieutenant governor sits on many boards and commissions that advise both the governor and the legislature. In addition, he or she is often a member of the governor's cabinet or advisory group. In many ways, the lieutenant governor can act as the eyes, ears, and mouth of the governor in numerous policy arenas.

The primary way in which lieutenant governors serve in an advisory capacity is through their membership on the cabinet; over half of all lieutenant governors hold this position. Typically, if the lieutenant governor plays a significant leadership role in the senate, he or she is not included in the cabinet, although exceptions (as in Massachusetts, New Mexico, and North Dakota) do occur. In some states, the constitution or state law provides for the lieutenant governor to sit on particular boards and/or commissions. This creates an institutionalized role for the lieutenant governor in specified policy areas. For instance, by constitutional provision, New Mexico's lieutenant governor sits on the Border Authority, the Community Development Council, and the Board of Finance. Louisiana law provides specifically for the lieutenant governor to oversee the Department of Culture, Recreation, and Tourism, the Louisiana Serve Commission, and the Louisiana Retirement Development Commission. In North Carolina, the lieutenant governor is a member of the Council of State, which oversees the expenditure of tax dollars and conducts business on behalf of the state government.

The extent of the lieutenant governor's constitutional or statutory policy activities can be narrow or broad. Delaware's constitution assigns two specific duties to the position. The first is to act as the presiding officer of the senate, a very common assignment. The second duty is quite unusual. Delaware's lieutenant governor is the chair of the Board of Pardons, which makes recommendations to the governor after pardon hearings. The governor is not bound to the board's recommendation, but the governor cannot grant a pardon in the absence of a recommendation from the board. Constitutions and state laws may place particular policy functions under the control of the lieutenant government or place him or her in an advisory position on boards or commissions that make recommendations to legislatures and governors.

Constitutions and state laws also typically give the legislature and the governor some leeway to assign particular duties or roles to individual lieutenant governors. The legislature or, more often, the governor may appoint the lieutenant governor to a variety of boards and commissions. North Carolina's constitution formally provides only that the lieutenant governor be a member of the Council of State, but it also says that "he shall perform such additional duties as the General Assembly or the governor may assign to him" (Article 3, Section 6). In that capacity, the lieutenant governor in 2005 served on the state board of education, the board of community colleges, and the board of economic development, among others. Additionally, the lieutenant governor has been given the authority to make appointments to other boards and commissions, a function often reserved to the governor.

The extent to which lieutenant governors pursue particular policy goals on these boards and commissions is largely a reflection of the particular individuals holding the office. They can push initiatives in which they are interested or promote highly salient or popular initiatives to increase their own visibility for the next election (or their own bids for the governorship). For example, Lieutenant Governor Denish of New Mexico has adopted two missions for her office—to improve the lives of children by chairing the Children's Cabinet (comprising department secretaries and agency heads who deal with children's issues) and to nurture small business growth. At the other extreme, a lieutenant governor can simply be a name on a ledger, playing only a minimal role on the board if he or she even attends the meetings at all.

When the governor and lieutenant governor are elected in tandem, there is even more possibility for the lieutenant governor to advise the governor on policy. If the two were elected based on a particular agenda, the governor may assign the lieutenant governor to promote particular issues in his or her stead. The lieutenant governor of Wisconsin, Barbara Lawton, reports working with the governor to advance his agenda in economic development and civic engagement. She chairs the Wisconsin Arts Board as well as the Wisconsin Women Economic Development Initiative. In another case, Gayle McKeachnie of Utah is focused, at the governor's request, on issues of the use and management of public lands; she also serves on the Disaster Emergency Advisory Council. Kerry Healey, Massachusetts's lieutenant governor and an expert in law and public safety, has been assigned a broad range of activities by the governor to advance their joint agenda, including serving as the primary contact with local leaders on budgetary issues; chairing commissions for the governor on criminal justice reform, domestic violence, and homelessness; and presiding over the governor's council, which confirms the governor's judicial appointments. Some lieutenant governors are more active in the policy arena than others. Of course, these relationships and roles will change with the election of different individuals to office.

The Lieutenant Governor as Administrative Officer.   The lieutenant governor typically serves as the administrator of various duties in the executive branch, the third of his or her broadly defined roles. Most of the time, this role is limited to activities that arise when the governor is unable to fulfill the obligations of office. In all states with a lieutenant governor, this individual is first in line to assume the governorship should the governor resign from office or die. In the last few decades, most state constitutions and statutes have also provided for the lieutenant governor to temporarily act as governor should the chief executive become temporarily or terminally incapacitated. Further, in most states, the lieutenant governor will actually serve as governor when the chief executive travels out of state. In states without a lieutenant governor, the governor is succeeded by the secretary of state (in Arizona, Oregon, and Wyoming) or the president of the senate (in Maine, New Hampshire, New Jersey, and West Virginia). In Tennessee, the speaker of the senate is also titled lieutenant governor and is first in line to succeed the governor.

In many states, the lieutenant governor also serves as a member of the governor's cabinet. As part of this group of officials who typically head state agencies, the lieutenant governor is present to advise the governor on administrative issues in executive agencies. In some states, the lieutenant governor also oversees particular departments or administrative duties. For instance, the lieutenant governor of Louisiana is the head of the Department of Culture, Recreation, and Tourism. In several states, including North Carolina and Delaware, he or she plays a primary role in state fiscal administration. In North Carolina, the lieutenant governor is a member of the Council of State, which oversees the expenditure of state tax dollars. In Delaware, the lieutenant governor is a member of the State Budget Commission, which reviews executive agency requests for funding that are submitted during each fiscal cycle.

In addition to fiscal administration, lieutenant governors also may direct different agency activities. After the creation of homeland security mandates in the wake of the 9/11 attacks, the lieutenant governor of Nebraska was made director of homeland security, responsible for advising the governor on security policies and implementing state and federal guidelines for improving homeland security. In other states, such as Ohio and Massachusetts, the lieutenant governor is the primary contact for local officials' interactions with state agencies. In Ohio and Indiana, the lieutenant governor serves as the director of the department of commerce. These examples from a sampling of states indicate the great variety of administrative leadership roles lieutenant governors may play.

In states that do not have a secretary of state, other administrative duties fall to the lieutenant governor. These duties include keeping records, recording rules and regulations, publishing state constitutions and statutes, and validating official records (as keeper of the state seal). The most important assignment, however, is the oversight of elections. For example, Utah's lieutenant governor is the chief election officer, facilitating state elections, coordinating with local elections officials, and certifying elections (declaring that elections have been fairly administered and that their results are complete). In the wake of the 2002 Help America Vote Act (HAVA), passed by the U.S. Congress after the problems encountered in the 2000 presidential elections, the duties in this area have increased, as state elections administrators now must meet additional federal mandates and guidelines. This topic will be more fully discussed in the next section, detailing information about the secretaries of state.

In many states, lieutenant governors are key players in the work of the executive and legislative branches of state government. While early lieutenant governors were viewed as weak and unimportant, even by some of the people holding the office, such an assessment is no longer valid in most states. In addition to the many roles these officials play within state government, they also often serve as a link between the public and the state governments. This informational role, in addition to the jobs described previously, serves to raise the visibility of lieutenant governors and may assist those who hope to move up to the highest office in the state, the governorship.

Secretary of State

The executive branches in forty-seven of the American states include the position of secretary of state. Alaska, Hawaii, and Utah are the only exceptions; in these states, the lieutenant governor has been given many of the duties and responsibilities typically associated with the secretary of state's office. In many ways, although most are elected, secretaries of state can be considered the most apolitical of the state executive officials. While no one in an elected position can be completely devoid of partisan leanings and policy preferences, many of the duties of secretaries of state require that the persons holding the job be fair, nonpartisan, and objective. In many ways, the job is clerical in nature: recording licenses for businesses or professionals, archiving state records, and publishing state laws. Other duties require an active engagement in current policies, remarkable implementation skills, and the capability to oversee activities across the state. For example, most secretaries of state are the chief election officials in their states, which requires them to oversee elections in the counties and coordinate statewide elections, as well as monitor and oversee campaign financing. This section explores the methods of appointment of secretaries of state and their terms of office, as well as the vast range of duties and responsibilities that fall under their office.

Method of Appointment

In the forty-seven states that have secretaries of state, the vast majority of these officials are chosen in partisan elections. They do not run on a party ticket with any other state official but are instead individually elected. In fifteen of these states, the secretary is limited to two terms in office. For a number of reasons, one would not expect that a person in this position should necessarily be affiliated with a political party, as many of the duties are clerical or nonpartisan in nature. The idea behind electing a secretary of state directly is to keep that person responsible and responsive to citizen requests. Perhaps no other office in the state touches the lives of so many citizens through its many responsibilities. However, the duties of the secretary of state vary dramatically across the states, and in many states, the secretary serves on several governmental boards and commissions and pushes policy initiatives related to the duties he or she performs. For instance, many secretaries have launched initiatives to increase voter registration and turnout.

Nonetheless, several states do appoint their secretaries of state. In Delaware, Florida, Maryland, New Jersey, New York, Oklahoma, Pennsylvania, Texas, and Virginia, the secretary of state is appointed by the governor. When governors make appointments to these high positions in state government, they exercise some control over the activities of the departments, since the secretary owes some allegiance to the governor. Even when the governor cannot change the duties or responsibilities of a department (most functions of state agencies are determined by state constitution and statutory guidelines), he or she has a greater opportunity to direct state department operations when the official in charge is not elected. In this case, the ultimate responsibility for maintaining quality agency services falls on the governor, who must keep the secretary of state accountable for his or her actions. This approach also gives the perception that the governor and his or her team of officials is in charge of state government activities. In the welcome message of New York's secretary of state, Randy Daniels, he stated that one of Governor Pataki's campaign promises and governmental missions was to "make state government more accessible, efficient, and responsive to the needs of its customers. To conform with this directive, the department of state was reorganized" (www.dos.state.ny.us). In this example, an appointed state official helped to create an organizational structure of state government consolidated within the governor's office.

In Maine, New Hampshire, and Tennessee, the legislatures appoint the secretary of state, via a joint ballot of state senators and representatives. This appointment can also be important for the legislature. Because the secretary is appointed by a diverse group of individuals in the legislature, the supposition is that he or she will fairly administer the office's duties in order to please the legislature and keep the job. In a state such as Tennessee, this appointment is very important because the secretary of state, by law, also serves on a number of state boards and agencies, including the State Funding Board, Tennessee Local Development Authority, Tennessee State School Bond Authority, and the Tennessee Higher Education Commission. Since Tennessee does not have a publicly elected lieutenant governor (the senate pro tem serves as lieutenant governor), some advisory duties fall to the secretary of state. And because the secretary of state is legislatively appointed, the legislature has some control over the office and its functions.

The Powers and Responsibilities of Secretaries of State
Whether elected, appointed by the governor, or appointed by the legislature, secretaries of state all have a host of duties under their jurisdiction. Overseeing many different divisions is a complex job. The California secretary of state boasts a staff of approximately

450 persons (with four field offices) performing services in regard to elections, government and business record keeping, and archiving. The New York department of state is comprised of seventeen different divisions organized into two distinct areas. Even in relatively small states, the responsibilities are vast. The Alabama secretary of state, to cite just one case, has been given over 1,000 different duties by state law. The responsibilities of this office, though they differ across the states, can be grouped into five main categories: elections duties, registration and licensing duties, legislative duties, state publication duties, and recording and archiving duties. Each of these will be discussed in turn, including what the secretaries are perhaps best known for—serving as the keepers of the great seal of their states.

Secretary of State as Chief Election Officer.   In four-fifths of the states, the secretary of state is designated as the chief election officer. This function is arguably the most significant and entails overseeing a host of voter registration, election, and campaign activities. In many cases, the secretary must work with state and local election officials to make sure that registration and election procedures conform to state law as well as federal mandates. In 2002, the National Association of Secretaries of State conducted a survey of secretaries' duties and responsibilities (www.nass.org/sos/duties_survey), and the Council of State Governments conducted a similar study in the same year. Secretaries of state reported performing many of the following duties in the areas of voter registration and education, election activities, and campaign monitoring.

In the area of voter registration and education, many secretaries of state reported that they are charged with conducting voter education programs. Additionally, they typically inform the public about statewide ballot issues and questions. They must also prepare the election-year calendar, including dates for primaries and general elections, and transmit this information to local election offices. Further, within the mandates of the Help America Vote Act (HAVA), states must have a statewide voter registration system. Because of HAVA, secretaries of state must now be in charge of creating voter registration forms and facilitating the statewide voter registration database.

In the area of elections-related activities, secretaries of state may, depending on the particular state, be in charge of testing and approving new voting systems and devices for use in localities across the state. In the same vein, the secretary's office might also supply ballots and other materials (such as registration forms or informational brochures) to local election boards and offices. Further, the office often determines the ballot eligibility of parties; usually, this requires certifying either that the political party received a large enough percentage of the popular vote in the previous election or that it has gathered enough signatures from registered voters to be placed on the state's ballot. Further, the secretary of state receives and verifies the signatures on initiatives and/or referendum petitions (in the states that allow these actions). The secretary also might file certificates and keep current and historical records of election nominations and results, and they might canvass election returns. Finally, the secretary of state's office will usually handle all state vote recounts.

Many secretaries of state are also charged with upholding state campaign finance laws. Among their duties are several recording and regulatory activities. For example, they may: record candidates' expense statements, as well as campaign expenditure statements; keep records of campaign contribution disclosure statements for both individuals and political parties; record lobbyists and political action committee (PAC) contribution disclosures; and collect the personal financial statements that candidates in many states are required to file with the secretary of state's office. Campaigns may also have to file information about loans they have received, and the secretary of state will record these statements as well.

Secretaries of state do not necessarily perform every one of these jobs. Each state is free to assign the jobs to them or to other officials, such as the lieutenant governor. In some of the states, these tasks may be given to a separate election board or commission. As one example, Mississippi's chief elections "officer" is actually a three-person commission comprised of the governor, the secretary of state, and the attorney general. And in Tennessee, the secretary appoints a state coordinator of elections. Despite such variations, however, it is safe to say that elections typically fall under the jurisdiction of the secretary.

As noted earlier, the HAVA was passed by the U.S. Congress in 2002 in response to the voting problems experienced in Florida and other states during the 2000 presidential elections. HAVA created the federal Election Advisory Commission, devised new guidelines and mandates for the states to follow during elections, and authorized the expenditure of millions of dollars in federal funds to help update state and local voting equipment. One of the first HAVA mandates required election officials in each state to develop a plan for implementing federal guidelines and spending federal funds. In most states, this task fell to the office of secretary of state and the state election division. States must comply with many new mandates, including federal accommodations for citizens with disabilities, developing new statewide complaint procedures, creating new identification procedures to reduce fraud in registration and absentee voting, and replacing most of their old voting machines. Undoubtedly, secretaries of state will be directly involved in the changes in responsibilities, processes, and procedures that loom on the horizon.

Secretary of State as Registrar. Most secretaries of state are responsible for maintaining registration lists of the various entities that conduct business within the state and with and for the state government. In many cases, it is the state seal that certifies that a document is a legitimate, official record of a transaction between two parties. Thirty-eight secretaries of state process and/or commission officials to help with this task during transactions that are spread across the state. These are the notaries public who record and certify (often through placing their seal on documents) everything from deeds of sale to banking and loan transactions.

On a broader scale, however, most secretaries of state are vested with the duties of registering entities that conduct business within the state. For instance, a majority of secretaries of state are responsible for registering any corporation that conducts business within their particular state. Lobbyists and PACs, which work to influence legislation within the state, must also register with the secretaries in most states. The secretary of state is also charged with registering trade names or trademarks in a majority of the states. In most states, this office is responsible for implementing and overseeing the Uniform Commercial Code (the guidelines that govern commercial transactions).

The secretaries of states' duties in registration and licensing are also varied. In about half the states with secretaries, charitable organizations must register with the secretary's office. In a few states (ten), securities that are traded within the state must also be recorded with the secretary of state's office. Many responsibilities are assigned due to distinctive state needs as well. Thus, New York's Department of State features the Office of Local Government Services, where citizens can obtain information about programs and policies affecting their communities. It also runs the Division of Cemeteries.

The secretary of state often licenses various professionals to practice their crafts or to do business within the state. The professionals who are licensed by the secretary's office differ on a state-to-state basis according to both necessity and tradition. The professionals who must register with the secretary of state's office in Alabama, Arkansas, and Nevada are sports agents. The Colorado secretary of state is responsible for licensing one set of individuals—bingo-game operators. In North Dakota, the secretary licenses general contractors, and in Maine, auto dealers. The licensing responsibility is most broad in Florida, New Hampshire, Oklahoma, and Texas, where the secretaries license professionals in a wide range of areas, including accountants, beauticians, funeral directors, wrestling commissioners, medical professionals, private investigators, and real estate brokers.

Secretary of State in the Legislative Arena.   Perhaps one of the least recognized responsibilities carried out by the secretary of state involves the legislative process. As already discussed, the secretary is, in most states, responsible for the bulk of election activities, the registration of PACs and lobbyists, and the oversight of campaigns (including campaign finance laws). Thus, he or she plays an active part in ensuring the fair election of legislators. However, his or her duties in the legislative arena extend further still.

Most obviously, the secretary is responsible for handling the bills that are introduced in the state legislature. In most states, he or she records and retains copies of all bills. In twenty states, he or she is responsible for assigning the official act number to bills (for example, House Bill 345 or Senate Bill 256). However, in a few states, the secretary plays a more active role in legislative activities. The National Association for Secretaries of State reports that in Kansas, Minnesota, Missouri, Montana, Nevada, New Mexico, South Dakota, and Wyoming, the secretary is responsible for convening legislative sessions in the state house. In Connecticut, Kansas, and Montana, the secretary convenes the state senates. In a couple of these states, this duty is temporary, lasting only until a speaker is chosen.

In a small number of states, the secretary of state is responsible for enrolling and/or engrossing bills. Engrossing involves checking amendments for style and consistency and incorporating them into the bills passed by each chamber. Next, the bills, along with all passed amendments, are prepared in their final format for presentation to the governor for signature or veto (enrolling).

Secretary of State as Publisher.   Typically, the secretary is responsible for the publication and dissemination of state constitutions. In addition, some secretaries are responsible for publishing session laws as well as a complete listing of statutes. In twenty states, the secretary of state's office publishes the state manual or state directory, a comprehensive listing of state government activities and the officials responsible for each function, along with their contact information.

Further, the secretary of state may play a large role in the administrative rule-making and regulatory processes. In three-fifths of the states, the secretary is responsible for maintaining the official files of the rules and regulations currently in effect by state agencies. In about a third of the states, the secretary publishes the state register of rule-making activity. Similar to the Federal Register, the state registers record all proposed agency rules and the time line for proposed action on the rules. Without this information, members of the public would not be informed of the agency activities and would not be able to comment on regulations that may affect them.

Thus, in many of the states, the secretaries play vital public information roles, keeping businesses and citizens informed of new laws, current regulations, and proposed rules. They also, however, have a number of other archival and custodial responsibilities.

Administrative Rulemaking

Ambiguous legislation routinely gives administrative agencies an opportunity to exercise policymaking authority. At least three factors encourage legislative ambiguity. First, politicians may lack expertise in the technical matters of particular policies. Second, the more specific a piece of legislation is, the more likely it is to offend some member of a politician's constituency. Finally, forging the legislative coalitions necessary to pass legislation is facilitated by the differing interpretations that ambiguity affords. In combination, these factors result in a tendency to pass vague legislation and then let administrators fill in the details.

Administrative agencies use two formal mechanisms—rulemaking and adjudication—to interpret legislative statutes. Rulemaking is a quasi-legislative function that sets standards for future application, while adjudication is a quasi-judicial process that typically applies specific decisions or orders to specific individuals.

Both rulemaking and adjudication are governed by state administrative procedure acts (APAs). At the federal level, the U.S. Administrative Procedures Act, enacted by Congress in 1946, governs administrative decision making by national agencies. At the state level, the Model State Uniform Administrative Procedure Act has served as a model for state APAs, which have been adopted in all fifty states.

(continues)

Administrative Rulemaking *(continued)*

APAs govern agency rulemaking procedures. Although rulemaking traditionally has been subject to fewer procedural restraints than adjudication, there has been a trend toward greater procedural constraints on agency rulemaking, including, for example, the imposition of cost-benefit analysis, legislative and gubernatorial review of proposed rules, and provisions to provide outside parties access to the rulemaking process. These provisions are significant because institutional procedures are seldom neutral in their impact on policy outcomes. Instead, they provide ways for external actors to influence the substantive content of administrative actions.

Although the procedural requirements of the federal APA and the model state APA are similar, state APAs contain very different provisions regarding several important aspects of the rulemaking process. Some states provide numerous opportunities for interested citizens to affect a rule's substance, while others provide only a limited opportunity to do so. In some states, agencies are simply required to present their proposed rules to the state attorney general prior to their enforcement; in others, there are numerous procedural steps and long delays from the time an agency submits a proposed rule to its implementation. The key variation occurs across two dimensions: public participation and rule review.

PUBLIC PARTICIPATION

During the period between the proposal of a rule and its final adoption, the proposed rule is published, which provides an opportunity for concerned citizens or groups to respond. This phase is called the notice and comment period, and its length varies from state to state. Almost all states (forty-seven) provide the opportunity for the public to submit written comments to the agency during the notice and comment period. In addition to the minimum notice and comment provisions common to the federal and state APAs, states sometimes provide additional avenues by which the public may directly influence the administrative rulemaking process. Some states allow for public petitions for hearings either with the agency or with an outside entity reviewing the rule. Some allow the public to petition to delay the rule, or to call for a detailed economic analysis of the rule. In addition, a few states provide adjudicative mechanisms allowing the public to challenge a rule after it has been adopted.

Public participation procedures give citizens a greater feeling of empowerment in the rulemaking process. It is unclear, however, what effect these mechanisms have on the content of agency rules. At the national level, rulemaking studies have suggested that the notice and comment period gives special interests with a stake in the outcome a greater say in the rulemaking process. The broadened avenues of public participation at the state level may serve to exacerbate this influence. Several observers, by contrast, have argued that public participation mechanisms do little to affect the content of administrative rules.

RULE REVIEW

In many states, elected political officials have the power to review and recommend changes in the administrative rules promulgated by state agencies. In some cases, these officials may modify or even strike down rules as part of this process. Loosely categorized under the term *agency rule review*, these powers together give many state officials a potentially powerful tool with which to influence administrative agencies. At the national level, use of the legislative veto has been prohibited since the U.S. Supreme Court held congressional veto of agency rules to be unconstitutional (*INS v. Chadha*, 462 U.S. 919 [1983]). Both legislative and executive review provisions continue to flourish, however, at the state level.

These powers are not without controversy. Administrators often resent their intrusiveness, and agency heads generally feel that they negatively affect agency performance. Many observers have decried them as politicizing the administrative process, and some have suggested that they increase the receptiveness of state government to special interests.

Governors and legislatures frequently engage in struggles over the use of these powers, with the judiciary often being called upon to arbitrate these disputes. The 1990s witnessed several lengthy legal battles over separation of powers issues arising in the administrative rule review provisions. In New York, for instance, the governor was the object of a class-action suit arguing that his use of executive orders to mandate review by the governor's Office on Regulatory Reform was an infringement on legislative powers (*Rudder v. Pataki*, 93 NY2d 273 [1999]). In Michigan, by contrast, legal action was aimed at the legislative branch. The legislature's Joint Committee on Administrative Rules was the object of a lawsuit claiming that its legislative review process, by which it could override rules without the governor's input, was a violation of the governor's constitutional authority (*Blank v. Department of Corrections*, 546 NW2d 130 [1997]). The Michigan case is more typical; state courts have often been called on to consider legislative rule review provisions, and on several occasions, they have struck them down as an infringement on the governor's authority under the state constitution.

Political review of agency rules is a fairly common feature of state government; thirty-eight states have some form of formal rule review power. Formal power indicates the presence of some review mechanism specifying particular rule review authority and procedures. Although legislative rule review powers are generally provided for in statute, state APAs are far less likely to provide for gubernatorial rule review authority.

Governors, however, may derive rule review powers through executive order. Regardless of the source of its legal authority, gubernatorial rule review varies significantly across states in regard to its use. In some states, although the governor technically has the power to exercise executive review of agency rules, that power is never used; others have established routine rule review procedures. In states with formal gubernatorial authority, some are allowed authority to review only proposed rules, while others may review both proposed and existing rules. Some states require gubernatorial approval before proposed rules go into effect, but others do not.

Legislative powers are generally located in a special legislative rules review committee. These powers are even more complex than those of the governor, due, in part, to the variety of committee structures and their relative autonomy in taking action without the approval of the entire body (and, in some cases, the governor as well). Moreover, legislatures vary greatly in the scope of their review authority (such as what rules they may consider) as well as in their power to recommend changes to agency rules, alter them, or rescind them altogether. Therefore, both the procedure and the outcome must be taken into account when assessing legislative rule review power. Powers range greatly: some states allow legislative oversight committees to unilaterally veto all agency rules, but others only allow committees to add their comments to the written record, along with those of other interested actors, during the rulemaking process.

Neal Woods
Department of Political Science
University of South Carolina

Secretary of State as Archivist and Custodian.   The final role of many secretaries of state is that of archivist and keeper of the state's records and general history. In many states, the secretary is the official state archivist. In California, for example, he or she not only oversees the State Archives but also serves as a trustee of the California State History Museum. In Tennessee, the appointed secretary of state serves on many boards and commissions, including the library and archives management board. In Delaware,

Florida, Illinois, Missouri, Tennessee, and Washington, the secretary of state also directs the state's libraries, which house most of the state's historical records.

The secretary of state in almost two-thirds of the states is responsible for archiving all official state records and documents. The responsibilities do not end there, however. In forty-three states, the secretary files and maintains most of the executive records. In many of these states, the governor's signature on some official state documents is not valid unless it is witnessed by the secretary of state. As the keeper of the great seal, the secretary will witness the signature and affix the state seal on the document.

The secretary of state also serves as the record keeper in a number of other areas. In nineteen states, the secretary is responsible for filing bonds for state officers and other employees who need to be bonded. He or she also may serve in a variety of other law enforcement recording functions. For example, in many states, the secretary attests to the governor's signature on extradition papers or legal warrants. In a few states, the secretary actually prepares state extradition warrants (in Louisiana, Maryland, Montana, New Hampshire, and Virginia) or arrest warrants (in Louisiana, Montana, New Hampshire, and Virginia) for use by law enforcement officers.

The secretary of state in a majority of states is also responsible for filing city charters, which is sometimes only part of a greater responsibility as liaison with local governments and citizens. In about a third of the states, the secretary maintains the official records of state lands.

Summary.   The secretaries of state, whether elected (as a majority are) or appointed, are responsible for a vast array of duties. If a particular task is related to elections, recording statutes or bills, licensing professionals, or maintaining archives, it is a good bet that the secretary of state has at least a partial responsibility for the job.

Perhaps, too, in no other governmental role has computing and technology become so invaluable. To process and maintain records, many secretary of state offices are coming to the front line of technology. On many of the secretaries' websites, the term *E-government* appears frequently. Whether referring to computers used for internal record keeping or a computer interface that gives citizens and private companies the ability to access and file required state documents, E-government is a necessity for secretaries of state today. Computers are used in all aspects of record keeping, data processing, and, most recently, touch-screen electronics for voting and elections. Of necessity, secretaries of state are also becoming the keepers of the computer data.

Attorney General

The attorneys general of the states should be considered the chief justice officials. Whether they head only the office of the attorney general or the entire justice department in a state, they serve as the primary legal advisers to state (and local) officials, defense attorneys in litigation against state organizations, and the main prosecutors of state law, both criminal and civil. The sections that follow detail how attorneys general (AGs) come into their offices and describe their official duties and responsibilities.

Method of Appointment

The vast majority of the attorneys general in the states (forty-three) are popularly elected in partisan elections. In all of these cases, the regular term of office is four years. North Dakota, however, had an interesting quandary in the 2004 elections. The attorney general, along with three other statewide elected officers (the secretary of state, commissioner of agriculture, and tax commissioner), was elected to a two-year term in 2004. It will shift back to four years in 2006. North Dakota voters endorsed this change in the June 2000 election with 62 percent supporting it. The rationale behind this temporary change was to shift some of the elections for main state offices to years when the president and governor (and several other state officers) are not running for reelection. This change would decrease the length of the ballot and give voters an expanded opportunity to gather information on fewer candidates. Since there is no term limit for the attorney general in North Dakota, the current AG is eligible to run for office in 2006.

About half of the states that elect their attorneys general, however, do have term limits specified by their state constitutions. Most attorneys general are limited to either two complete terms of office or eight years, though there are various methods of "counting." For instance, in Arizona and Nebraska, after two terms in office, an attorney general can run for office again after four years or one full term. In Montana, individuals are limited to eight out of sixteen years. Thus, they could presumably serve two terms, take another job for eight years, then run again for attorney general.

There is additional variation by state in the way in which attorneys general come into office. In five states—Alaska, Hawaii, New Hampshire, New Jersey, and Wyoming—they are appointed by the governor. Additionally, in Wyoming, the attorney general must be confirmed by the state senate. Two states appoint their AGs in unique ways. In Maine, the attorney general is elected biennially by a joint ballot of state senators and representatives. Although this is a unique situation for attorneys general, there are a couple of secretaries of state and lieutenant governors elected in this manner as well. In Tennessee, the judges of the state supreme court appoint the attorney general to a four-year term, with no constitutional limit on the number of times this official can be reappointed.

Regardless of the method of appointment, the attorneys general perform a core set of tasks, including issuing advisory opinions, acting as legal counsel for state organizations, and enforcing (including litigating) state laws.

Advisory Duties

One of the key roles of the attorney general in each state is to serve as the state's primary legal adviser. Many of the state attorneys general are called on for legal advice and formal opinions on any number of local law enforcement actions, administrative rules, proposed legislation, or executive activities. These opinions serve as official advice on a particular action or activity, but they do not constitute a law, a change in a law, or a court ruling. In fact, if a state agent acts in concert with an attorney general's opinion, the action may still be appealed in court, and the attorney general would then be forced to defend his or her opinion and the state's action.

In general, AGs are prohibited by state constitutions or statutes from rendering legal advice to private citizens, although they often play a role in litigating consumer protection or antitrust actions on behalf of citizens. The next section highlights several of the advisory responsibilities of attorneys general.

State executive officials are vested with the responsibility for enforcing certain federal laws and guidelines and all state statutes and regulations. Sometimes, federal law and state law may seem to be in conflict with one another. At other times, the state rules and regulations may be unclear or offer little information on exactly how a regulation should be interpreted, enforced, or implemented. When in doubt, state executives often call on their attorneys general. In all states except Oklahoma, AGs issue advisory opinions to executive officers on how the laws should be interpreted or implemented. These opinions cover a broad range of topics for a variety of executive officers. For instance, the Delaware secretary of health and social services asked whether the state was obliged to pay for all or part of the malpractice insurance of full-time health-related employees (DE. Op.Atty Gen. 04-IB05). In Nevada, the secretary of state sought a ruling on whether a state or local employee could simultaneously be a member of the Nevada legislature (NV. Op.Atty. Gen. 2004–03). The request for this ruling came after conflicting guidelines were found among the constitution, the advice provided by the Nevada legislative counsel bureau, and prior attorney general opinions. The result of this request was a twenty-six-page opinion. Carole Fischer, the director of the Missouri Department of Revenue, asked the attorney general of her state if a county tax collector could waive interest or penalties on delinquent taxes (MO. Op.Atty Gen. 80–2004). Thus, executives of administrative agencies may ask for official advice on implementation or an interpretation of agency regulations.

Similarly, legislators may seek advisory opinions from the attorney general on how state laws are to be implemented. In a recent case in Arizona, the attorney general was asked by members of the legislature to issue opinions related to the authority of law enforcement officers to interview students in a school and the school board's abilities to create rules governing parental notification (AZ. Op.Atty. Gen. R04–03). In Indiana, in response to the nationwide movement to legalize marriage between persons of the same sex, a member of the state house of representatives asked the attorney general to render an opinion on what the requirements of court clerks were when processing marriage licenses and what may occur if the clerk knowingly disregarded state law (IN Op.Atty. Gen. 2004–4).

The situations under which members of the legislative branch can ask for the attorney general's opinions vary by state. In most states, opinions can be issued to individual legislators or to the legislature as a whole. Some states impose restrictions. In Connecticut and West Virginia, the attorney general may only issue opinions to members of the legislative leadership. In Massachusetts, Minnesota, New York, and Ohio, opinions can only be issued to the legislature as a whole (or, in the case of Ohio, an entire house of the legislature).

The attorney general, as the chief law enforcement officer in the state, may also issue advice and assistance to local prosecutors or district attorneys in about four-fifths of the states. Again, the ability of the attorney general to advise or assist local prosecutors varies. In some states, the attorney general may offer advice or assistance on his or her own initiative. In other states, the attorney general offers advice or assistance at the request of the governor, the legislature, the local prosecutor, and/or when this assistance is ordered by a court or is deemed in the "state's interest."

Many attorneys general also have advisory responsibilities during the lawmaking process. For example, in about three-fifths of the states, the attorney general may issue opinions of the constitutionality (according to the state constitution) of bills or ordinances. Many times, he or she reviews legislation prior to passage and/or prior to the governor's signing of a bill. In addition, whenever state agencies engage in rule-making activities to implement laws, some AGs are involved in the rule-making process. In a majority of states, it is the attorney general's responsibility to review proposed rules for legality under the state constitution or current statutes.

All of these advisory duties are undertaken to help ensure that state governments and all of their agents act in accordance with the national and state constitutions and statutes. Because of the complexity of the law, it is important that the office of attorney general aids governors, legislators, and executive branch agencies in their activities. Doing so through advisory opinions can often save the state from litigation. In addition to advice, however, the attorney general and his or her assistants also perform other duties as chief legal counsel to the state government.

Attorney General as Chief Legal Counsel.   A key activity of the chief attorney for the state government is advising and issuing opinions to the governor, legislators, state agencies, and employees. At times, however, the attorney general must become an even more active counsel for state government. One of the ways in which he or she acts as the state's chief legal counsel is in the area of intergovernmental law. In all fifty states, it is the office of the attorney general that defends the state government in the U.S. district courts or the Supreme Court when state law is challenged on the grounds that it violates the U.S. Constitution or federal statutes. Many times, this challenge is based on a perceived violation of the Fourteenth Amendment, which effectively prohibits the *state* government from violating its citizens' rights to due process or equal protection under the law. The office of attorney general or its delegate has been a state's prime respondent in many cases; one recent example is the case of *Lawrence v. Texas* (2003), in which the state of Texas was forced to defend its same-sex sodomy laws against charges that they violated the equal protection clause in the U.S. Constitution.

Another way in which the attorney general acts as chief counsel for a state in the intergovernmental arena is in disputes with other states. For instance, AGs can conduct litigation on behalf of the state in federal courts as well as in other states' courts. They also may prosecute actions against other states (or defend their own state from other states' litigation) in the U.S. Supreme Court. A recent example is the boundary dispute between two states that culminated in the U.S. Supreme Court case of *Virginia v. Maryland* (2004).

Federal regulatory agencies (such as the Environmental Protection Agency, the Interstate Commerce Commission, and the Occupational Safety and Health Administration) and agencies that protect individual's rights (including the U.S. Department of Justice) often have numerous rules and regulations that state agencies must follow. When a breach of these rules is perceived, the state attorney general becomes the chief representative for the state's citizens, administrative agencies, or the state as a whole in the federal regulatory agency hearings. It is the AG's job to defend the actions of the state and prove that its actions fall within the federal guidelines.

The attorney general also serves as chief counsel to state administrative agencies. In all states except Florida, the AG conducts litigation on behalf of state agencies against citizens or organizations. Alternatively, in some states, the AG may conduct litigation *against* an agency on behalf of the state. Also, the attorney general in some states represents the public before an administrative agency during informational hearings or rule-making procedures. Thus, a special arrangement in Tennessee allows the consumer advocate division of the office of attorney general to represent the public during hearings establishing public utility rates. In every state except Kentucky, the AG prepares legal documents for state administrative agencies.

In most of the circumstances presented in this section, the attorney general acted as chief legal counsel, preparing legal documents and defending the state or its agencies when citizens, other states, or federal agencies perceived wrongdoing. The next section discusses the attorney general's role as the main enforcer of state laws.

Attorney General as Enforcer of State Laws.   The executive branch of state government is in charge of making sure that the laws of the state are faithfully executed. In most cases in which the law is broken, the attorney general and his or her assistant attorneys general must become involved in litigation to punish offenders and/or enforce state law.

One arena in which the attorney general may act is in the realm of local prosecution. According to Dillon's Rule, local governments are the "creations" of state government. Thus, it seems appropriate that one of the responsibilities of the AG lies in his or her authority in many areas of local prosecution. Although the states can prescribe guidelines for their activities in local prosecution, almost all attorneys general have some authority in this area. For example, in all states except Arkansas, Connecticut, North Carolina, and West Virginia, the office of the AG has at least some authority to initiate prosecutions at the local level. In the majority of cases, the attorney general may intervene in local cases already under prosecution. He or she may also assist the local prosecutor; sometimes, the AG is asked to participate by the local attorneys, governor, legislature, or others, but at other times, the AG acts on his or her own initiative. In about half of the states, the attorney general can even supersede the local prosecutor. As an example, the state attorney general became involved in a local case in 2005 in Alabama. Attorney General Troy King asked that the death penalty be considered in the case of an individual convicted in local proceedings of murdering an Opelika, Alabama, police officer.

Further, attorneys general in all fifty states may initiate civil proceedings on behalf of the citizens of the state. In a majority of states, the attorney general's office initiates and prosecutes criminal activities directly. These cases may occur in many areas. The AG can commence legal proceedings against governmental employees for illegal actions against state agencies or against persons under contract with state organizations for failing to live up to the terms of the contract.

One area that most attorneys general have been concerned with in recent years is consumer protection and advocacy. In forty-two states, the AG's office now has separate divisions to handle these situations. In all but four states (Georgia, Montana, Tennessee, and Wisconsin), the attorney general receives consumer complaints and may elect to prosecute companies for acts such as breaching safety regulations or engaging in unfair business practices like bait and switch advertising (advertising one product but delivering another of lesser quality).

Additionally, the office of attorney general plays a primary role in regulating and prosecuting antitrust laws in most states. When a business is seen as breaking antitrust regulations through the creation of monopolies or unfair business practices, to cite one example, the AG may commence civil or criminal proceedings against that business. A good recent illustration was the attorney general's promises to prosecute price-gougers (persons who raise prices dramatically to take advantage of a lack of competition or sudden demands for products caused by natural disasters or other emergencies) following the 2005 hurricane disasters in Alabama, Mississippi, and Louisiana. Attorneys general may commence lawsuits on behalf of consumers in their states, the state government itself, or local governmental entities such as cities, counties, or special districts.

Since the mid-1990s, an additional enforcement role has developed that has national implications. The attorneys general of many of the states are now banding together through their professional association and initiating multistate lawsuits. Thus, many attorneys general cooperated to jointly prosecute tobacco companies on behalf of their citizens and state governments. When the failure of tobacco companies to reveal important health information was made public and when the states realized the massive costs to both individuals' health and the government in terms of health insurance and disability, the AGs in most states joined together to seek compensation for these costs. This action resulted in a multicompany (the tobacco companies as an industry) settlement, with millions of dollars awarded to each state and new regulations required for tobacco products and advertising. The National Association of Attorneys General also provides a network within which AGs are working together to prevent Medicaid fraud and discuss right-to-die issues, antitrust regulations, and consumer protection. Recently, Alyon (a company sponsoring adult websites), Microsoft, and State Farm Insurance have all been on the receiving end of litigation brought by multiple attorneys general working in concert.

Summary.   As this section has discussed, most attorneys general are elected, although a few are appointed by the governor. Their primary responsibilities involve giving opinions and advice to the governor, legislature, and administrative agencies; acting as the state's chief legal counsel; defending the state or its agencies against allegations of wrongdoing or breaches of federal regulations; helping to draft rules and legislation; and prosecuting violators of state law.

Recently, the activism of the attorneys general in protecting citizens against consumer fraud or illegal business practices has increased. Moreover, AGs are more likely than ever to work in concert with other states' attorneys to prosecute offenders. Not only is the attorney general the chief enforcer of state law, it seems he or she is also the chief protector of the well-being of the citizenry.

REFORMING THE EXECUTIVE BRANCH

Given the confusion and contradiction in the many jobs and goals of state bureaucracy, it is perhaps not surprising that reforming the executive branch has been a recurrent theme in state politics. As noted in the first section of this chapter, the state bureaucracies have increased in both size and scope over the last century. In many ways, the changes in state policymaking and the growth of state bureaucracies were reactionary in nature. That is, as needs arose and were placed on the agenda by state citizens, elected officials, or changes in intergovernmental interactions, states responded by adding functions and agencies in a piecemeal or almost haphazard fashion; in the process, state government growth exploded in every direction. In short, state government has at times been "uncoordinated, unconsolidated, and uncontrolled" (Bowling 2003:1127).

In the early twentieth century, the changes that led to increased executive power and centralization originated from the 1912 Taft Commission's recommendations at the federal level and spread through several successive waves of reform at the state level (Garnett 1980).

New York produced plans to reorganize in 1915. Although the actual reorganizations did not occur at that time, the effort produced an impetus for later changes in New York and other states. In 1917, Illinois became the first state to enact major reorganizations, and twenty-five other states followed over the next two decades (Bowman and Kearney 1986). In 1926, New York did pursue a sweeping reorganization, consolidating over 150 agencies into no more than 25 statutorily defined departments.

A wave of state reform also followed the national government's efforts following the report of the 1937 Brownlow Commission, as well as the "little Hoovers" that were spawned in the states from the Hoover Commissions at the federal level immediately after World War II. The purpose of all of these efforts at both the state and federal levels was to improve the organization and efficiency of government after rapid increases in the size and scope of their operations. These movements echoed the tenets of scientific management, an approach toward organization asserting that if the correct structure or organization is created for bureaucracies, then efficiency, effectiveness, and accountability will follow. One of the earliest observers of state reorganizations, A. E. Buck (1938), noted that the first approaches to state government reforms included a concentration of authority under the governor and appointed department heads, an integration of functions into fewer departments, the reduction of independent boards, the creation and coordination of staff services, and the creation of a governor's cabinet. The focus was on reorganization, consolidation, and centralization.

These trends continued and escalated from the 1960s to the 1980s into what Ann Bowman and Richard Kearney (1986) described as the "resurgence of the states." Even greater reforms became evident as constitutional changes occurred. Almost forty states experienced broad constitutional changes or ratified new constitutions altogether. The governors and legislatures gained institutional powers, and most specific administrative provisions (including the delineation of department functions) were erased from state constitutions. The governors, especially, gained more ability to organize or reorganize executive agencies and to appoint agency heads. Further, the personnel and professional resources of the governors' offices increased, so that the chief executives gained the ability to coordinate and control the executive branch. This was also the period of the "superdepartment," when many states consolidated agencies into twelve to twenty functional departments headed by governor-appointed executives (Bowman and Kearney 1986; Bowling and Wright 1998).

In the 1970s and 1980s, faltering national and state economies, devolution (or return) of policy implementation and programs to the state governments from the national government, and decreased federal funding led to a need for states to "do more, do it better, and do it cheaper" (Bowling 2003, 1131). Since the inception of the United States, citizens have distrusted the administration of government. As the size and scope of government grew and even as state citizens both demanded more and relied more on state services, they also worried more that government was inefficient and too costly. Citizens suspect that the bureaucracy wastes state resources. Such resources come from the public, of course, typically through taxation. Citizens often complain about high taxes and call for tax reductions. They do not, however, wish for services to be cut.

So in the 1990s and into the twenty-first century, states have had to work smarter or, to use the language of the late 1990s, "reinvent" themselves. The ideals of bureaucracy, as noted earlier in this section, emphasize the importance of hierarchy. Thus, one approach to reforming state bureaucracies is to make them more like the ideal bureaucracy—more tightly organized and hierarchical. Public administration scholars prior to the early 1970s emphasized this approach. Later reformers argued that the ideals of bureaucracy were actually part of the problem. They argued that such organizations were too inflexible and too difficult to change.

There were other problems as well. In a traditional bureaucracy, authority resides at the top level, and the lower-level workers, who have the greatest responsibility for actually delivering the government services, have little influence on how things will be done. Further, the multiple layers of the organization make communication up through the ranks too time consuming and difficult, which leads to even greater difficulty in responding to feedback from outside the bureaucracy.

Two prominent reform approaches directed at these shortcomings have found support across the states. Total Quality Management (TQM) is one of these trends. TQM argues that poor executive branch performance arises from badly designed management practices. Further, government agencies should view those they serve as customers purchasing a service. So, as in private business, TQM encourages governmental agencies to emphasize the needs of the customers—those who interact with the agency. Other ideals of TQM are:

- Emphasizing group or team problem solving
- Eliminating some of the layers of employees
- Giving lower-level employees more authority
- Emphasizing results to measure and encourage quality and improvement.

The ideas put forward by TQM advocates found wide support in the states. By the middle of the 1990s, thirty-two states had undertaken at least some reforms recommended by TQM (Saffell and Basehart 2005).

Reinventing government is another reform strategy. In 1992, David Osborne and Ted Gaebler released their best-selling book *Reinventing Government: How the Entrepreneurial Spirit Is Transforming the Public Sector*. This book contains many examples of the complex administrative issues that confront state government and the ways in which many state executives are successfully coping with these issues. President Bill Clinton and Vice-President Al Gore adopted many of the tenets of the strategy for use at the national level, and states from Florida to Oregon began reinventing some administrative services and state programs (Brudney, Hebert, and Wright 1999).

At the same time, the National Commission on State and Local Public Service (in the vein of the reform commissions mentioned earlier), chaired by former Mississippi governor William Winter, set out to develop recommendations to improve state and local governance. Many of the Winter Commission's recommendations also overlapped with the tenets of reinvention. The reinventing government strategy shares the customer focus of TQM but is less optimistic that government officials will be able to achieve the reform goals. It advocates having government make decisions about what ought to be done and what services should be provided. However, it argues that government does not have to actually provide those services; instead, outside actors, such as private or nonprofit organizations, should provide many of these services because they can do so at a lower cost. The idea of contracting out, or privatizing, governmental services also opens the door for competition among multiple organizations that hope to be hired to provide the services, which should lower costs further. This idea removes the monopoly that government has always had on the delivery of certain services. Nearly all states have adopted some of the ideals embodied in the reinventing government approach.

Using the 1994 and 1998 American State Administrators Project surveys, Jeffrey Brudney, F. Ted Hebert, and Deil S. Wright (1999) and Brendan Burke and Deil Wright (2002) studied the extent to which state agency executives reported implementing components of the reinventing government strategy in the states. Burke and Wright reported that by 1998, the reinvention-related initiatives listed in Table 3.3 had been either partially or fully implemented by state agencies.

The recommendations that were most likely to be adopted involved measuring state programs or improving planning or services. The recommendations least likely to be adopted were the initiatives that would have increased administrative discretion (Bowling 2003). This outcome probably relates to the continued friction between allowing administrative officers "too much power" in a democratic society, and continued distrust of government among the citizenry. The desire to improve efficiency is not necessarily as dominant as the desire to control bureaucratic actions.

TABLE 3.3   **PERCENT OF STATE AGENCY HEADS REPORTING PARTIAL OR COMPLETE IMPLEMENTATION OF REINVENTION RECOMMENDATIONS IN THEIR AGENCY**

Reinvention recommendation	Percent partially or fully implementing
Strategic planning	87%
Training programs to improve customer service	83%
Quality improvement programs to empower employees	79%
Benchmarking	73%
Creation of customer service measurement systems	64%
Decentralization of decisionmaking	60%
Increased procurement discretion	45%
Reduction of agency hierarchy	44%
Simplification of human resource rules	34%
Greater discretion to "carry over" funds	23%

Source: Adapted from Table 4, Brendan F. Burke and Deil S. Wright. 2002. Reassessing and reconciling reinvention in the American states: Exploring state administrative performance. *State and Local Government Review* 34, 1:7–19. With permission of Carl Vinson Institute of Government, University of Georgia (www.vinsoninstitute.org).

One of the most difficult and controversial features of the reinventing government approach is the component that calls for contracting out for governmental services. Some of these services can easily be performed by nongovernmental actors—garbage collection, roadwork, building maintenance, and so on. Contracting for other sorts of services, however, is much more problematic. Some governmental services are quite different from services provided by the private sector, among them adoption and foster care for children, mental health treatment, and prisoner incarceration. Some states have experimented with contracting out various services, including the running of prisons. However, such privatization has not been as successful as its proponents had predicted. Costs have declined in some cases, but the cost savings have at times been the result of a decline in quantity or quality of services rather than greater efficiency, as advocates had argued.

The 2004 American State Administrators Project also asked agency heads about reinvention initiatives, as well as privatization and contracting out. Almost two-thirds of the agency heads who responded reported that their state had engaged in reinventing government reforms. Of the administrators in states experiencing reinvention, 69 percent of the administrators stated that their agency had been impacted by the reforms. When these administrators considered the effects of reinvention reforms on state government, over three-quarters responded that the effects of reforms on their particular agency were at least fair, and 45 percent found the reforms good or excellent.

The ASAP also asked agency heads about privatization and the use of contracts. Fully 65 percent of the respondents reported contracting out some of their agency's services. The agency heads were then asked to report how contracting out has impacted their agency's service to the public. Table 3.4 highlights their responses.

Thus, at least from the perspective of state agency heads—those most often in charge of implementing privatization and granting contracts—the movement toward privatization is creating more positive benefits than negative effects. Indeed, very few administrators reported decreases in the quality of services, in the ability to respond to pub-

TABLE 3.4   AGENCY HEADS' REPORTS ON EFFECTS OF CONTRACTING OUT (PERCENTAGE RESPONDING)

Effect on agency service	Increased	Neither increased nor decreased	Decreased	Total
Quality of service	56%	38%	6%	100%
Cost of service	35%	28%	37%	100%
Ability to respond to public needs	58%	31%	11%	100%
Agency accountability for service delivery	41%	46%	13%	100%

Source: Data compiled by the author.

lic needs, or in accountability to the public. In almost two-thirds of the cases, costs either stayed the same or decreased. The use of contracting out is continuing to increase, and administrators report that when decisions are made to contract for services, the decision making generally is not controversial or contentious. And universally, administrators reported that public satisfaction with contracted services was moderate to very high (only 3 percent of agency heads rated public satisfaction as low or very low). As more agencies try to do more, do it better, and do it with fewer funds—and with the extremely high perceptions of public satisfaction—contracting out is a trend that is here to stay. In fact, it may be one of only a handful of reforms and reinventions that actually survives the next round of reform that will inevitably come.

QUALITY OF STATE GOVERNMENT

As this chapter has detailed, a great many actors are charged with the myriad responsibilities inherent in executing state law. Should the citizenry feel their laws are in good hands? How can one determine how well the states are conducting the business of their people? In many ways, this is actually quite hard to answer. States are much more likely now to benchmark performance (that is, to try to measure current performance levels, comparing them with past performance or other agencies/programs), evaluate programs on multiple criteria, and utilize performance-based budgeting (tying expenditures and costs to program performance within the budget document). And yet, there is no one best way to evaluate programs. Criteria change often, and different states and agencies use varying measurements, making comparisons extremely difficult. Moreover, evaluations can be shaped to reflect the most beneficial components of the agency's programs. Any individual is biased about the quality of his or her own work, and the funding for external evaluations is minimal. From the evidence presented here, it is clear that citizens are paradoxically suspicious of government but not likely to disapprove of the services states provide or their experiences with agency interactions (Goodsell 2004).

The Government Performance Project, a joint project between academics and *Governing Magazine* (www.governingmagazine.com), evaluated the performance of all fifty states on a plethora of criteria in 1999, 2001, and 2005. The latest evaluations look at how well the states are administering their money, people, infrastructure, and information. The grades ranged from As for Utah and Virginia to Cs for Alabama and California. This broad range reflects the diversity of the states as well as the fact that they have experienced diminishing resources through fiscal stress and have responded in differing ways. Some states are cutting back on program analysis and oversight capabilities, reducing capital maintenance, and letting staff positions go unfilled. Other states are actually improving their capacity to oversee programs by maintaining positive financial practices and improving human resources systems, as well as increasing and utilizing the information technology that both increases administrative efficiency and brings government information closer to the citizenry (Barrett and Greene 2005). In times of fiscal crisis, the national government often pulls back, leaving states to fill in the gaps. Ironically, it is at such times that citizens of the states are in the greatest need. States do not have the luxury of turning their backs on those in need, and they continually struggle to change, grow, and adapt in order to improve their ability to respond. While these efforts are not always successful, state capacity to serve its citizens has increased, and signs point to continued improvement in the coming years.

REFERENCES AND FURTHER READING

Barrett, Katherine, and Richard Greene. 2005. Grading the states: The year of living dangerously. *Governing Magazine.* http://governing.com/gpp/2005/intro.htm.

Bowling, Cynthia J. 2003. State government administration, impacts of reform movements. In *The encyclopedia of public administration and public policy,* ed. John Gargan, 1127–1131. New York: Marcel Dekker.

Bowling, Cynthia J., and Deil S. Wright. 1998. Change and continuity in state administration: Administrative leadership across four decades. *Public Administration Review* 58(5):429–445.

———. 2004. American State Administrators Project. Unpublished data. Auburn University, Auburn, AL.

Bowman, Ann O'M., and Richard C. Kearney. 1986. *The resurgence of the states.* Englewood Cliffs, NJ: Prentice-Hall.

Brudney, Jeffrey, and Deil S. Wright. 2002. Revisiting administrative reform in the American states: The status of reinventing government during the 1990s. *Public Administration Review* 62(3):353–361.

Brudney, Jeffrey, F. Ted Hebert, and Deil S. Wright. 1999. Reinventing government in the American states: Measuring and explaining administrative reform. *Public Administration Review* 59(1):19–30.

Buck, A. E. 1938. *The reorganization of state governments in the United States.* Morningside Heights, NY: Columbia University Press.

Burke, Brendan, and Deil S. Wright. 2002. Reassessing and reconciling reinvention in the American states: Exploring state administrative performance. *State and Local Government Review* 34(1):7–19.

Council of State Governments. 2003. *The book of the states.* Lexington, KY: Council of State Governments.

Duncombe, Sydney, and Richard Kinney. 1987. Agency budget success: How it is defined by budget officials in five Western states. *Public Budgeting and Finance* 7(1):24–37.

Elling, Richard C. 2004. Administering state programs: Performance and politics. In *Politics in the American states: A comparative analysis,* 8th ed., ed. Virginia Gray and Russell L. Hanson, 261–289. Washington, DC: Congressional Quarterly Press.

Garand, James C., and Kyle Baudoin. 2004. Fiscal policy in the American states. In *Politics in the American states: A comparative analysis,* 8th ed., ed. Virginia Gray and Russell L. Hanson. Washington, DC: Congressional Quarterly Press.

Garnett, James L. 1980. *Reorganizing state government: The executive branch.* Boulder, CO: Westview.

Goodsell, Charles. 2004. *The case for bureaucracy,* 4th ed. Washington, DC: Congressional Quarterly Press.

Kaufman, Herbert. 1956. Emerging conflicts in the doctrines of political science. *American Political Science Review* 50(4):1057–1073.

National Association of State Budget Officers (NASBO). 2002. *Budget processes in the states.* Lexington, KY: NASBO.

Niskanen, William A., Jr. 1971. *Bureaucracy and representative government.* Chicago: Aldine.

———. 1991. A reflection on bureaucracy and representative government. In *The budget-maximizing bureaucrat: Appraisals and evidence,* ed. Andre Blais and Stephane Dion, 3–21. Pittsburgh, PA: University of Pittsburgh Press.

Osborne, David, and Ted Gaebler. 1992. *Reinventing government: How the entrepreneurial spirit is transforming the public sector.* New York: Penguin.

Saffell, David C., and Harry Basehart. 2005. *State and local government: Politics and public policies,* 8th ed. New York: McGraw-Hill.

Thomas, Clive S., and Ronald J. Hrebenar. 2004. Interest groups in the states. In *Politics in the American states: A comparative analysis,* 8th ed., ed. Virginia Gray and Russell L. Hanson, 100–128. Washington DC: Congressional Quarterly Press.

Wildavsky, Aaron. 1964. *The politics of the budgetary process.* Boston: Little, Brown.

———. 1988. *The new politics of the budgetary process.* Glenview, IL: Scott, Foresman.

Wright, Deil S., and Cynthia J. Bowling. 1997. An administrative revolution in the American states: A half-century perspective. *Madison Review* 2(3):7–13.

Websites Consulted

www.ltg.cs.gov/about/biography.asp
www.governor.state.nm.us/ltgov/missions.html
www.dos.state.ny.us
www.nass.org/sos/duties_survey
www.ltg.ca.gov/about/biography.asp
www.budget.state.ny.us/division/history/history.html
www.ltgovernor.ohio.gov/bio.htm
www.mass.gov/portal

U.S. Supreme Court Cases

Blank v. Department of Corrections, 564 NW2d 130 (1997)
INS v. Chadha, 462 US 919 (1983)
Lawrence v. Texas, 538 US 904 (2003)
Rudder v. Pataki, 93 NY2d 273 (1999)
Virginia v. Maryland, 540 US 56, 157 (2004)

Opinions of State Attorneys General

AZ. Op.Atty.Gen. R04-003 (March 26, 2004)
DE. Op.Atty.Gen. 04-IB05 (February 10, 2004)
IN. Op.Atty.Gen. 2004-4 (April 29, 2004)
MO. Op.Atty.Gen. 80-2004 (April 8, 2004)
NV. Op.Atty.Gen. 2004-03 (March 1, 2004)

4

THE PEOPLE WHO SERVE

SEEKING, WINNING, AND HOLDING THE OFFICE

Margaret R. Ferguson

A remarkable variety of men and women have held the office of governor in the United States over the years. Some grew famous, heading to the White House after leaving their state capitals. Others grew infamous, even serving jail time in a few instances. Except for the handful who succeeded to the office, all of the governors had at least one thing in common—they had to pursue and win the chief executive position. This chapter looks at the process of getting to and holding the governorships in the states. The first section examines the rules pertaining to who can seek the office. There are relatively few formal and legal requirements for being governor but many informal rules, which are probably more critical in determining who actually seeks and ultimately wins the office. The second section describes the processes involved in filling the office. As the governorship has become more valued and sought after, the election process has become more costly and time consuming. Modern gubernatorial campaigns are high-tech endeavors, planned and carried out by professionals, and candidates typically have to raise and spend a great deal of money to secure the office. This reality affects not only how gubernatorial hopefuls approach the race but also the sorts of people who can even contemplate such a run. Modern campaigns for governor, like other campaigns for high-level office, are increasingly candidate centered. And though political parties remain important, they no longer influence campaigns to the extent they once did. The third section discusses who the governors are. It presents a portrait of those who hold the office today, including their demographic characteristics and the professional experiences they bring with them to the job. Though they are a somewhat more diverse group than their predecessors, governors remain disproportionately white and male even in the twenty-first century. The fourth section describes the job of governor itself and what those who hold this office do on a daily basis. The chapter concludes with a discussion of what comes next for the nation's governors. For some governors leaving office, the transition from public official to private citizen is a difficult one. This is most often true when a governor is forced to exit the office before he had hoped. Some will return to private life. Many others will seek, and a few will win, higher office—making the transition to ambassador, senator, or president.

SEEKING THE OFFICE

Those who seek and win the governorship are, in many ways, an elite group. They are often better educated than the average citizens of their states, and they typically have proven themselves by winning and serving in other elective offices. Neither of these credentials is required of governors, in a legal sense, but realistically, candidates with a legitimate chance of gaining the coveted office usually have distinguished themselves in some way.

According to the U.S. Constitution, there are only three requirements for seeking the presidency: potential candidates must be natural-born citizens, have resided in the United States for at least fourteen years, and be at least thirty-five years old. An enduring tenet of the American belief system is that virtually anyone can grow up to become president, but clearly, the realistic criteria for seeking the presidency are far more restrictive. In truth, only a handful of people at any given time can reasonably hope to mount a serious campaign for the office, and the same might be said of the highest elected position in state government. The next sections will address the two sets of requirements—legal and informal—that come into play in seeking the governorship in states across the country.

Legal Requirements

In most states, the legal requirements for seeking the governorship are quite minimal and fall into four categories: minimum age, citizenship (state and/or country), state residency, and voter qualification. Two states, Kansas and Massachusetts, do not set a minimum age, but in the rest, the age requirement ranges from a low of eighteen years to a high of thirty years. By far the most common minimum age is thirty, the standard in thirty-four states.

All states but three specify that the governor must be a U.S. citizen. Thirty-three states merely require current citizenship; others stipulate a minimum number of years of citizenship, ranging from a low of five years (in five states) to a high of twenty years (in Mississippi). Other states require seven, ten, or fifteen years of U.S. citizenship. Unlike the U.S. president, a governor does not have to be a natural-born citizen. Twelve states go further and require state citizenship in addition to U.S. citizenship. The state citizenship requirement can be as short as thirty days (in Rhode Island) to as long as seven years (in Alabama, Alaska, and Tennessee).

Though only a dozen states have set state citizenship rules, all but three have established state residency requirements. In seven states, the governor must simply be a resident of the state, but in most others, a minimum length of state residency is required, ranging from just thirty days (again in Rhode Island) to ten years (in Missouri). The residency requirement in the other states is between one and seven years.

Thus, most states establish the governor's connection to the state via residency rather than citizenship rules. In fact, all but one of the states that does not have a state citizenship requirement does have a residency requirement. Only Kansas fails to establish any citizenship or residency requirements (indeed, it sets no legal requirements at all for those seeking the governorship). State residency requirements are intended to assure that those who seek the governorship have some bonds with the state. Much as the U.S. Constitution requires members of Congress to be residents of the states they represent, these rules tie the governor to the state. Without such rules, a person could conceivably simply move into the state and immediately seek the governorship. (The ability to win, of course, is another question altogether.) Having lived in a state also makes a governor more likely to understand and respond to the needs of the citizens. While one does not have to have lived in the state from birth, some length of residency enhances the prospects of this understanding.

The last category of requirements for seeking the governorship is being a qualified voter. Twenty-nine states specify that the governor must be a qualified voter. Only four states set a minimum length of time for this qualification.

Clearly, then, the legal requirements for seeking the governor's office are rather modest. In fact, most adults who have been in a state for more than a few years probably would meet them easily. Of course, that does not mean they all would have a legitimate chance of gaining the office. In every state, there are informal requirements for the governorship that are much more taxing than the legal/constitutional ones just described—and more significant in determining who will succeed in pursuit of the office.

Informal Requirements

Making a run at the governor's office is an enormous undertaking. The vast majority of people who possess the legal credentials for being governor would never realistically be able to attain the office, nor would they have any interest in doing so. Nevertheless, there are a good number of people who do have their eyes set on the office, and they tend to have a few things in common beyond meeting the legal requirements.

In the modern era, seeking the governorship requires a sizable amount of money. Though the funding needed to wage a credible race varies considerably from state to state, the cost of campaigning has gone up across the board. Consequently, although gubernatorial candidates need not be wealthy themselves, they must be connected with others who have money or who at least have access to it. Further, given the other expectations surrounding the office, the candidates nearly always hail from at least a middle-class background. And again, monetary factors come into play, because acquiring the education and experience normally expected of these candidates requires money. Thus, only a small subset of those with gubernatorial aspirations can really make a serious run for the office.

Next, with few exceptions, candidates for governor have already held an elected office. As a result, they have experience at building electoral support, in addition to on-the-job experience. And winning the governorship is easier for those who have won a statewide election in the past. Among other things, they can count on a certain amount of name recognition created over the years by the news coverage, press releases, and so on that come with holding a statewide elective office. Prior experience in office also makes a candidate better prepared for the job of governor. Having been in the state legislature, for example, makes a potential governor more knowledgeable about the workings of state government. Voters tend to expect governors to bring a significant amount of experience to the office, not launch their careers there.

That relatively rare group of individuals who do win the governorship as their first elective office have typically developed name recognition and job experience in some other arena (as a businessperson or an actor, for example). While there is some evidence that the number of governors coming to office without prior experience has been on the increase, it is still an uncommon trajectory. Also, those who manage this feat are usually remarkable in some way—such as superstar Arnold Schwarzenegger in California or George W. Bush of Texas (son of a former president). Such individuals often make up for their lack of experience in seeking office by launching expensive media campaigns.

Other informal requirements include having connections to the political party establishment. Though the power and effectiveness of the party structure differs in each state, seeking the governorship without the blessing of key party leaders is an exceedingly difficult proposition. In many states, the party elite exercises a great deal of control over the nominations process. In these states, winning the governorship without the endorsement of the state party is nearly impossible.

Finally, voters tend to expect a certain personal profile of their governors. They formerly had a strong preference for men, but this bias is no longer as entrenched as it once was. However, other personal features remain important. Governors are nearly always married, very often have children, and typically express some religious affiliation (usually with one of the mainline religions). They are also disproportionately white. While minorities such as African Americans and Hispanics have had a degree of success in winning governorships, the reality is that seeking the office is a much more daunting challenge for minorities in most states in the Union.

Becoming governor is not an easy task. Beyond meeting the modest legal requirements, candidates are normally expected to possess substantial informal credentials. This combination of formal and informal requirements assures that almost all of those who finally win the office derive from a rather elite group.

GUBERNATORIAL ELECTIONS

A large majority of states (thirty-four) hold their gubernatorial elections at the same time as congressional midterm elections, which are held in non–presidential election years (Table 4.1). Nine states elect their governors in presidential election years. In the two states where governors serve two-year terms, the elections are held on even-numbered years, so every other gubernatorial election coincides with a presidential election. Five states (Kentucky, Mississippi, Virginia, Louisiana, and New Jersey) choose their governors in odd-numbered years, when no national elections are being held. Holding state elections in non–presidential election years is believed to focus the elections on state issues and to avoid "polluting" them with sweeping national political trends. In other ways as well, gubernatorial campaigns and elections are becoming divorced from national elections.

In the early part of the twentieth century, it was common for a party to gain or lose a governor's office in step with national party gains and losses. Voters tended to vote straight party tickets—giving all of their votes to their chosen party. This pattern has occurred less frequently since the 1960s. Instead, it is now common for voters to split their tickets, voting for a Democratic governor, a Republican president, and a Democratic U.S. senator, for example. Noted state politics scholars Malcolm Jewell and Sarah Morehouse (2001) assert that voters are acting more independently in gubernatorial races (rather than following strict partisanship) and that this is the result of campaign-specific factors such as the candidates who are running, the nature of the campaigns they wage, and the issues they bring to the debate. Gubernatorial elections are about far more than partisanship and ideology—though these factors remain important, too.

TABLE 4.1   GOVERNORS' ELECTIONS BY STATE AND YEAR

Elections held in midterm years (non–presidential election years)				
Alabama	Florida	Maine	New Mexico	South Carolina
Alaska	Georgia	Maryland	New York	South Dakota
Arizona	Hawaii	Massachusetts	Ohio	Tennessee
Arkansas	Idaho	Michigan	Oklahoma	Texas
California	Illinois	Minnesota	Oregon	Wisconsin
Colorado	Iowa	Nebraska	Pennsylvania	Wyoming
Connecticut	Kansas	Nevada	Rhode Island	
Elections held in odd-numbered years (neither congressional nor presidential election years)				
Kentucky	Louisiana	Mississippi	New Jersey	Virginia
Elections held in presidential election years				
Delaware	Missouri	North Carolina	Utah	West Virginia
Indiana	Montana	North Dakota	Washington	
Elections held every even-numbered year				
	New Hampshire		Vermont	

Source: Council of State Governments (2003).

Electing the governor is a two-stage process. First, candidates must be selected to run for the office, and then, the general election that actually chooses the governor must take place. In most of the states, the general election enables voters to choose between the standard-bearers of the two major parties. In a few states, candidates from third parties occasionally win, and other states have elected independent candidates, that is, those who run without a party affiliation.

The Nomination Process

The nomination is the first phase in choosing who will ultimately serve as governor. In earlier times, party elites handpicked the candidates for public offices, including the governorship. More recently, the general trend across the states is to give the parties' voters, rather than their leaders, the greatest influence over nominations for the general election.

In the states today, parties choose their candidates through primary elections. Primaries involve voters going to the polls to select among potential nominees. Democratic voters cast primary ballots for Democratic hopefuls; Republicans choose among Republican candidates. Though states have different rules as to who is allowed to participate in a primary election, the general idea is that the voters who consider themselves Democrats or Republicans ought to be empowered to determine who will carry their party's banner in the general election. The widespread use of primaries is a relatively recent development. In the late nineteenth century, nominations for statewide races were made by state party conventions made up of delegates selected earlier at county conventions. This practice put the choice of nominees squarely in the hands of a relatively small political elite.

The use of primaries has been hailed as a democratic reform because it takes the power out of the hands of the few party leaders who formerly chose the nominees and places it in the many hands of the people the party is supposed to represent. Wisconsin was the first state to employ the direct primary, beginning in 1903. By 1917, a majority of states had adopted the practice. The spread of the direct primary weakened political parties, since it distributed power across the voters rather than allowing party leaders to hold on to it. This outcome was actually just what members of the Progressive movement who advocated for primaries sought. They wanted to open up the nominating process by breaking the party leaders' hold on selecting candidates and, it was hoped, do away with the practice of having party leaders tell elected officials what to do once they obtained their offices.

Some states leave the decision making almost completely in the hands of the primary voters, while others have created mechanisms (either by law or by tradition) that enable party leaders to express their preferences to the voters going to the polls in the primaries. Some argue that party leaders (such as delegates to state party conventions) are better able to judge the qualities of potential nominees than are the party's voters and are therefore better able to choose good candidates (that is, those with a decent shot at winning the general election). Others argue that the party's voters are best able to discern which candidates will serve their needs most effectively.

Recruiting Candidates

Potential candidates need to be identified and placed on the ballots. In the vast majority of cases today, candidates for governor are self-recruited: individuals with ambition for the office step forward to seek their party's nomination. In this relatively simple process, potential candidates often must obtain a certain number of signatures on a petition or pay a modest filing fee to have their names placed on the ballot. In other states, the party convention has a hand in placing names on the ballot. All of these procedures are meant to assure that only the names of serious candidates appear on the ballot.

There is normally no shortage of candidates for office where there are two active political parties in a state. However, the likely success of a party at the ballot box affects how many people are willing to come forward to seek its nomination. In the South as recently as the early 1980s, the Democratic Party had an unquestioned advantage in gubernatorial elections (and most other state elections as well). This one-party system meant that multiple candidates sought the Democratic nominations, but viable Republican candidates were hard to come by. In those few states where the Republican Party held a distinct advantage, potential Democratic candidates were in short supply.

At present, both parties are competitive enough to attract candidates for the nomination for the governorship in all states. Though one party has a distinct numerical advantage over the other in some states, the parties are more competitive in nearly all the states than ever before, which makes the process of recruiting candidates easier; parties need not beat the bushes to entice candidates to come forward. However, when a party has a reasonable chance at winning the election, more candidates may seek the nomination, meaning the party must choose among multiple contenders. This situation makes the process of selecting a nominee more costly and perhaps more difficult.

The events that occur during the nomination process can have consequences for a candidate's prospects in the general election. For that reason (among others), it is important to examine the nomination process more closely.

Preprimary Endorsements

Some observers worry that the use of direct primaries to select party nominees has weakened political parties. While the direct primary is more democratic, critics contend that it has robbed the state parties of their principle role. In response to these concerns, some states have tried to give both the people and the party leaders a voice in the process. In these states, the nominations systems allow party leaders to provide formal input on their preferred nominees while still involving the party voters in the final decision making. The party leaders' input is given in the form of endorsements for specific candidates.

There are three types of endorsements (Table 4.2). Some states have created *formal preprimary endorsements*, which are made by a party convention. These endorsements are made by both parties in Connecticut, Rhode Island, New York, North Dakota, Colorado, Utah, and New Mexico. In several of these states, the party leadership had chosen the nominees in the past. When the state legislatures moved to create direct primaries, the parties maneuvered to have endorsements provided for by law. States vary as to the actual significance of the party endorsement process. In some states, winning a certain percentage of the votes at the party convention is the only means for a candidate to get on the primary ballot. In other states, the endorsee is automatically placed on the ballot, while other candidates must qualify by petition. In still other states, the endorsee is nominated unless challenged by a candidate who gets a specified percentage of the convention vote.

The second form of endorsement is *endorsement based on party rules.* In states where this type of endorsement is used, the party convention does name an endorsee, but there are no tangible benefits for that individual (such as being placed automatically on the ballot). This method gives the party leadership the opportunity to give its recommendation to the voters, though the effects of the endorsement are not as significant as in the formal preprimary endorsement states. This type of endorsement is used in Massachusetts and Minnesota for both parties and by Republicans in Delaware and Democrats in California.

The final category of endorsement is the *informal endorsement* made by party leaders, usually behind closed doors. This kind of endorsement may be made only sporadically. Informal endorsements, while giving voice to the desires of the party elite, do not carry the weight of the legal endorsements described previously. Informal endorsements are used in Illinois, Pennsylvania, Ohio, Michigan, and Louisiana.

Endorsements are typically made by state party conventions. These conventions meet several months before the primary election and are made up of delegates from across the state. Some delegates are chosen by local party organizations; others are chosen at local caucuses, which are attended by voters who possess sufficient political interest to participate at this early stage. If there is competition for the election of delegates, those who hope to serve in that capacity may be asked to identify the candidates they support for endorsement in major statewide races. Delegates are normally party activists and loyalists who have worked in party campaigns in the past. Some also have held a state or local position in the party, such as county Democratic chair, or held elective office, such as a seat in the state legislature.

What effect do these delegates have on the process? One line of thought holds that, as party activists, convention delegates should be well qualified to judge the strengths and weaknesses of potential nominees and that they can, therefore, best choose good candidates for the general election. A contrary line of thought suggests that convention delegates are likely to hold strong opinions about policy issues and have ideological leanings that may not necessarily reflect the views of the state's party members as a whole. If the latter perspective is accurate, the nominees that the conventions endorse will not necessarily win the overwhelming support of the primary voters.

Overall, state party conventions resemble national presidential nominating conventions in that they provide an opportunity for the party to showcase its ideas and rising stars and for delegates to politick and socialize with fellow partisans. Unlike the presidential conventions, however, the state conventions sometimes offer a bit of suspense, for it is not always obvious which candidates will be endorsed.

Given the fact that some states do give their party elite input into the nominations process, one might wonder how much influence the elites actually have. The answer depends on the endorsement rules. As noted earlier, in some states, having the endorsement of the convention means the endorsee will run unopposed in the primary, thus being guaranteed the party's nomination. In other states, the endorsee does have competition but is advantaged by the endorsement and therefore well placed to win the nomination. Research by state politics scholars Jewell and Morehouse found that in states that permit the strongest form of endorsement (formal preprimary endorsement), less than half of the endorsees were challenged in the primary. The figure remained essentially constant from 1960 to 1998. For the second category of endorsements, based on party rules (rather than law), endorsees were more likely to face opposition in the primary. This happened in three-fourths of the races. However, in these contested primaries, the endorsee won over 80 percent of the time between 1960 and 1980. The success of endorsees dropped in the later period: they won only half of the time between 1982 and 1998.

It appears that the success of endorsements in determining the eventual nominee depends on several factors. Most important, some state parties seem much more committed to the endorsement principle than others and place a greater emphasis on making sure the endorsee faces no opposition in the primary. Other considerations are also significant. For an endorsee to do well in the primary, he or she needs to be a strong candidate. When the convention is divided (or for some other reason it has a hard time choosing a candidate to endorse), the endorsee does not fare as well in the primary election. Finally, endorsements are most helpful to the endorsees when they carry with them tangible benefits. In some states, the endorsement of the party convention is accompanied by benefits such as the backing of party activists in the campaign and funding from the party organizations and from individuals. In other states, the party provides the endorsee with campaign funding and advisers to generate polling, media outreach, and other professional services. In only a handful of states does state law prohibit the party organizations from contributing funds to candidates in contested primary elections (Jewell and Morehouse 2001).

The principle behind the use of direct primaries is to empower the party's voters to choose its nominee. A primary election that has a single name on the ballot obviously does not give the voters a true choice in the matter. Between 1968 and 1998, 69 percent of primaries were contested (had more than one candidate). Given the strength of incumbents, it is not surprising that primaries are much more likely to be contested when no incumbent is running in that party's primary. States with party endorsements also

TABLE 4.2   TYPES OF PREPRIMARY ENDORSEMENTS BY STATE

Legal party endorsement by convention	Endorsement based on party rules	Occasional informal endorsements by party leaders
Colorado	California (Democrats)	Illinois
Connecticut	Delaware (Republicans)	Louisiana
New Mexico	Massachusetts	Michigan
New York	Minnesota	Ohio
North Dakota		Pennsylvania
Rhode Island		
Utah		

Source: Data compiled by the author with information from Jewell and Morehouse (2001).

have fewer contested primaries: only half of the primaries were contested in the ten states with endorsements, compared to three-fourths of the primaries in the other states. A party is also more likely to have a contested primary when it has a better chance at winning the general election. Such a positive situation for the party's nominee makes seeking the nomination appealing to more candidates.

Party primaries serve multiple purposes. In one sense, they are a means for the political party to choose its standard-bearer. Given that goal, the party is probably better off to limit the number of candidates on the primary ballot so that the primary is not actively contested and the state's partisans are not divided or upset by a raucous party fight. However, when the primary is viewed as a democratic enterprise, having a single candidate on the primary ballot essentially defeats the very purpose of holding direct primaries. These two strands of thought illustrate the controversy that continues to exist about how party nominees should be chosen.

Types of Primaries

The rules for participation in choosing party nominees for the governorship have been changed to include essentially all voters who identify with a party. Not surprisingly, though, only a small percentage of those who are eligible to participate actually do so. To assess how successful the move to primary elections has been, one needs to examine how many party members actually take part in the nominations process.

Voter participation in the nominations process varies significantly over time and across the states. Turnout is determined by multiple factors, some structural (related to legal arrangements and party rules) and some more transient (such as the personalities of the candidates or the likelihood of a party winning in the general election). Though

TABLE 4.3   STATE REQUIREMENTS FOR VOTING IN PRIMARY ELECTIONS

Completely closed				
Arizona	Connecticut	Delaware	Florida	Kentucky
Maryland	Nevada	New Mexico	New York	Oklahoma
	Pennsylvania		South Dakota	
Closed but some voters may shift on election day				
Alaska	California	Colorado	Iowa	Kansas
Maine	Massachusetts	Nebraska	New Hampshire	New Jersey
North Carolina	Ohio	Oregon	Rhode Island	West Virginia
Wyoming				
Open but voter must select primary publicly				
Alabama	Arkansas	Georgia	Illinois	Indiana
Mississippi	Missouri	Tennessee	Texas	Virginia
Completely open				
Hawaii	Idaho	Michigan	Minnesota	North Dakota
South Carolina	Utah	Vermont	Washington	Wisconsin
Nonpartisan				
	Louisiana			

Source: Data compiled by the author with information from Jewell and Morehouse (2001).

the decision to go to the polls is a personal one, turnout across the states and the parties is somewhat predictable.

As Table 4.3 illustrates, state laws differ regarding who may vote in primary elections. Primaries can be classified as open or closed, but variation exists within these broad categories as well. For example, in ten states, voters are not required to register their party preference in advance, but they must express a choice or request a ballot of only one party when they go to the polls. In ten other open-primary states, voters are not required to make their party preference public at all—neither in advance nor at the polling place. They can choose to vote in either primary and then keep the primary in which they participated private. In these states, voters can easily move from one party primary to another from year to year.

Three states have used a variation on this type of primary, known as a blanket primary. In a blanket primary, voters can participate in the primaries of both parties (though not for the same office): thus, a voter can participate in the Democratic primary for governor, in the Republican primary for U.S. senator, in the Democratic primary for U.S. House member, and so forth. (A recent U.S. Supreme Court decision has invalidated this type of primary.) Finally, one state, Louisiana, uses another type of open primary, known as a nonpartisan primary. In this one- or two-stage voting process, all candidates for the governorship (of all parties) appear on the same ballot. In the first stage of voting, if one candidate receives a majority of the vote, he or she wins the election (and no general election is held). If no candidate wins a majority at this stage, then a runoff election is held between the top two vote-getters. The candidate receiving a majority of the vote in the runoff takes the office.

Closed primaries also take multiple forms. The more rigid form of the closed primary (used in twelve states) requires that voters be registered with a party in advance of a primary election. To vote in the other party's primary, voters must change their party affiliation in advance of the election. Sixteen states give a bit more flexibility, allowing voters to change their party affiliation as late as election day. The rules in some closed-primary states are so flexible that, in practice, the system functions essentially like an open primary. Open primaries and the more flexible versions of closed primaries make participating in primary elections easier, which tends to encourage turnout in these states, all things being equal.

Turnout in primary elections is somewhat lower in states where the party exerts a lot of control over the nominations. Further, in states that are dominated by one party (where either the Democrats or the Republicans nearly always win the governorship), turnout is higher in the dominant party's primary election. For example, until fairly recently, most southern states were overwhelmingly dominated by the Democratic Party (in state-level races at least). In these states, the Democratic primary was almost always the election in which the governor was actually chosen. Since the Republican candidate had essentially no chance of winning in the general election, the person the Democrats nominated would almost surely be the next governor. This situation encouraged turnout in the Democratic primary while discouraging turnout in the Republican primary.

Turnout in primaries is lower than turnout in the general election. Research shows that between 1968 and 1998 in states where the parties were closely matched, roughly half as many people voted in the primaries as voted for the parties' candidate in the November election. In states where one party usually won the contests for statewide offices, turnout in that party's primary as a percentage of those voting for the party's candidate in the general election was substantially higher than for the party that usually lost.

It is clear that regular voters are somewhat different from people who rarely or never vote. Voters are better educated, wealthier, have higher-status occupations, and have a greater interest in politics. The more of these features a voter possesses, the more frequently he or she votes. Not surprisingly, then, primary voters are likely to rank even higher in these qualities than persons who vote only in general elections (Jewell and Morehouse 2001). Primary voters have stronger party attachments than do general election voters.

As one would expect, voters who call themselves Democrats and who vote in a primary generally vote in the Democratic primary. However, the laws in some states make this relationship more or less likely to hold true. In open-primary states (or in flexible closed-primary states), it is possible for a Republican to vote in the Democratic primary or vice versa. It is also possible for independents to participate in one of the two major party's primaries, despite their lack of attachment to the party. This fact raises the possibility that voters may choose to participate in a primary for strategic reasons. In the South during the 1970s, for example, a Republican, knowing his or her party's candidate had no chance of winning, might choose to vote in the Democratic primary so as to have some influence on the choice for governor. Or as the Republican Party began to build momentum but did not really have a contested primary, a Republican might vote in the Democratic primary in hopes of choosing the weakest Democratic nominee thereby helping the Republican candidate in the general election. This practice is called raiding, and it does not seem to happen very often. Yet it can be done under the law in some states. Some voters do bounce back and forth between primaries over time, apparently because of the appeal of certain candidates or certain issues rather than a desire to raid the other party.

Who Wins?

When it comes to the general election, the partisanship of voters is the best predictor of how they will cast their ballots. But in primary elections, voters must choose among candidates who share a party affiliation, so partisanship does not explain their choice. Predicting primary elections is therefore different in some respects from predicting the general election outcome. Because the primaries are not predicted by partisanship, certain factors that are important in the general election are much more important in the primary, such as the candidate, the issues they address, and the quality of the campaigns they wage. Given the central importance of television and radio advertising for the campaign, a candidate's ability to raise money to pay for advertisements is even more important in the primaries than it is in the general election, where most voters depend on partisan attachments to decide how to vote. The short answer to the question of who wins, therefore, is that the person who spends the most money gets the most votes—at least in the overwhelming majority of cases. In another sense, though, this answer raises the question of who raises the most money and why.

When sitting governors decide to seek reelection, they nearly always easily win the nomination of their party. It is rare for the incumbent to have any serious competition for the nomination, and it is exceedingly rare for the sitting governor who seeks renomination to fail to get it. In the 157 state elections that took place from 1988 to 1998, the governor sought reelection in 91 of them. Only 43 of these governors had substantial competition in the primary. In these 43 contested races, 30 of the sitting governors prevailed with more than 60 percent of the vote. Only 2 of the incumbent governors seeking reelection lost their primary bids in this ten-year period (Jewell and

Morehouse 2001). This pattern of incumbent successes in the primaries continued into 2002.

Incumbents almost always get their party's nomination because of a variety of benefits commonly referred to as the incumbency advantage. These benefits are wide ranging. For one thing, incumbents have the kind of name recognition that no one else in the state can typically match. In the course of doing their job, governors get free advertising as the media cover them at work. Incumbents, by definition, have also run for the office before and thus have experience in planning and winning a statewide race. They also may have a campaign apparatus that is still partially in place from the prior race.

In addition, incumbents know how to raise money because they have done so in the past, and they most likely can look to their former contributors to become contributors again. Would-be challengers are often scared off by this campaign wealth and decide not to seek the nomination. And in most instances, challengers who do come forward to fight for the nomination are no match for the incumbent. Viable candidates—those who might really have a shot at the governorship—will likely wait for an open seat, after the incumbent has retired.

Incumbents also benefit from their credentials. Voters tend to look for candidates with experience, and incumbents have experience in the office. They also have a record that they can point to. Of course, this record can be a detriment as well as a benefit, as a governor will be held accountable by the voters for the state's conditions. When an incumbent has managed the job poorly or has taken controversial steps (such as raising taxes), the record becomes a liability rather than a benefit. As the statistics for the races between 1988 and 1998 show, however, the benefits of incumbency normally far outweigh the costs, especially in the nominations phase.

Since incumbents are hard to beat, the first question a prospective candidate for governor should ask is whether the incumbent is likely to run. In the states that limit their governors to two terms, it is fairly easy to predict when a seat will come open. In states where gubernatorial terms are not limited, prospective candidates must wait for cues from the incumbent as to when he or she will decide to step down. Individuals hoping to run for the office when their own party holds the governorship must face the reality that it is very hard to defeat an incumbent in the primary. Gubernatorial hopefuls of the other party must also understand that incumbents seeking reelection win about three-quarters of the time. There may be a good reason to run anyway (to work on building a name, perhaps, or to get more experience in running a statewide race), but the chances of prevailing are small. This topic will be addressed in the discussion of the general election later in this chapter.

The candidate who spends more money in the campaign typically wins, and incumbents almost always have more money to spend than their challengers. Because of these two facts, it is hard to determine how much of the incumbent's success is attributable to campaign spending as opposed to incumbency itself. Understanding the separate effects of spending requires looking at primary elections in which no incumbent is running.

Although the biggest spender normally wins the nomination, spending the most money does not guarantee a win. When a candidate has a lot of money to spend but not much experience or name recognition, an opponent who has these credentials may win despite spending less money. Nevertheless, those who fall far behind in raising and spending money are not likely to win. The importance of money will be discussed more fully.

The General Election

The previous sections discussed the first phase of the electoral process, the nomination. This section will cover the second phase, the general election, beginning with a discussion of the general election campaign. The modern campaign is highly competitive and expensive and the subject of a great deal of media and public attention. But some expert observers question the significance of the campaign itself for deciding who actually wins. These observers point to other factors that determine the outcome of elections.

Some things are clear. When candidates are perceived as being strong, they attract weaker opponents and therefore have an easier time winning. The same tends to be true when they have a large war chest. Further, we know that the strongest candidates are usually incumbents. They are widely perceived as tough to beat, which affects who will decide to run against them. However, we also know that incumbents occasionally lose. Given this possibility, some challengers do decide to make a run for the office, and consequently, the outcome of an election is never fully predictable.

The winning candidate is usually the one who manages to tap into the issues that are important to the voters. This candidate is able to focus the issues in such a way that the people are convinced that his or her position is closest to their own. The campaign is directed in large part toward achieving these outcomes.

The Campaign

As noted in the earlier section on nominations, the candidate who spends the most money usually wins the election. Though outspending the opponent is not a guarantee, it normally results in success. Money is particularly important in the modern period because television advertising plays such a major role in the campaign—and voters get most of their information from television. They get much less information from reading newspapers (since they spend much less time doing this). Further, especially in large states, a potential voter is far more likely to see a candidate on television than in person at a rally. Rallies tend to reach the party faithful, whereas television has a far wider reach. Television advertising is therefore much more likely to entice voters to cross party lines and to reach those who do not have a firm party attachment.

A good television campaign (sometimes called an air war) is necessary—it is incredibly difficult to win without one. But a candidate must also run a good ground war. According to state politics experts Jewell and Morehouse, the ground war includes appearing at meetings and rallies across the state, holding press conferences, and conducting interviews with the local media. These activities, which are more easily accomplished in smaller states for logistical reasons, are vital because they help to form connections between the candidate and the local party organizations, which may then lend their assistance throughout the campaign and help to get voters to the polls.

Depending on the availability of resources and the preferences of the candidate, modern campaign organizations may include many hired professionals carrying out a range of responsibilities. In the past, the political parties usually ran the campaigns, but today, the candidates themselves are in charge. They raise most of their own money, and they make the decisions about whom to hire and what activities and strategies to pursue.

For candidates, a key priority in building a campaign team is hiring the best consultants available. Candidates for major offices such as the governorship will want consultants with prior experience managing a statewide race. They will also look for those with a strong winning record. And as one would expect, quality consultants will also be the most expensive to hire. Because consultants perform different jobs, a well-financed campaign may hire several different consultants to perform the various essential jobs.

Above all, some individual must be placed in charge of running the campaign—from planning strategy to managing the work of volunteers and other campaign staffers. In addition to a campaign manager, a skilled and experienced press secretary must be hired to prepare press releases and interact with reporters. This individual will also work to make sure the campaign receives adequate news coverage and that the coverage is as positive as possible. Next, the campaign should have a person in charge of advertising, particularly for radio and television, where most voters get their information. The advertising specialist must coordinate with the candidate and the campaign manager to plan the themes that will be featured in the ads. The ad specialist is usually also in charge of creating the ads (perhaps with the help of other professionals) and arranging when and where to air them. If possible, the campaign will also hire a professional pollster. Polls are useful not only as indicators of who intends to vote for the candidate but also to help identify the strengths and weaknesses of the campaign's message among different elements of the electorate. Some campaigns try to get by with polls conducted in a more ad hoc manner by regular staff members (not professional pollsters), usually because resources are limited. But there is a danger in doing this, in that a poorly prepared poll will likely generate inaccurate information that might actually do more harm than good. The fund-raiser is another important campaign figure. This person is often an active party member in the state rather than a hired outside consultant. Having extensive experience in raising funds for the party in the state is likely a prerequisite to doing a good job raising contributions for the campaign.

Incumbent officeholders have many advantages as they put together their campaign teams. Unlike challengers, they already have professional staffs in place. In addition, they can draw on individuals from the gubernatorial staff to do campaign work. These staff members have often been with the candidate over time, so they and the candidate know one another well. They also typically have extensive political experience in the state and long-standing relationships with other political actors. To work on the campaign, staff members must take a leave of absence from the governor's office and formally become part of the campaign staff, ensuring that state employees do not engage in purely political activities while still drawing their state salaries.

The gubernatorial campaign described here might be considered an ideal that can be created when a candidate has as much money as he or she needs and wants to develop a professional campaign apparatus. But not every candidate understands or appreciates the importance of a solid campaign organization, and others are unable to raise sufficient funds to support such a staff. The personality of the candidate may also play a role. For example, some candidates try to control too many of the details of the campaign themselves, which is usually a big mistake. Modern gubernatorial campaigns have simply become too complicated to be managed by the candidate while he or she also does the work of running for office (and perhaps serving in office as well if he or she is an incumbent).

Despite the fact that campaigns are usually very candidate centered today, the political parties continue to be vital players, too. They may help to establish or pay for phone banks, voter registration drives, and get-out-the-vote (GOTV) activities. In recent years, some parties have gone further, actually producing and running independent advertisements in support of their candidates or in opposition to their opponents. While such ads can be most useful to the candidates, they themselves have little or no influence over the content of these ads. As such, it is possible that the ads may end up having unintended negative consequences.

Interest groups also sometimes play a role in campaigns. They often submit questionnaires to the candidates meant to establish and then advertise whether the candidate shares the group's ideals. Interest groups sometimes hold candidate forums to encourage the candidates to pay attention to the concerns of the interests they represent. They may also advertise a candidate's past voting behavior (especially if he or she was a legislator or a member of Congress), either approvingly or disapprovingly. Interest groups at times endorse a candidate and encourage their members to support the endorsee. If they have enough money to do so, interest groups may run television ads supporting or opposing candidates. Some also run "issue-advocacy" ads that do not explicitly advise viewers to vote for or against a particular candidate but that nevertheless support or criticize the viewpoint or past behavior of a candidate. This distinction is important, since campaign finance regulations are more restrictive on ads that explicitly advocate voting for a particular candidate. Much like ads run independently by the political parties, independent ads run by interest groups may be either helpful or hurtful to a candidate. The preferred candidate may benefit from favorable advertising achieved without cost to the campaign but may suffer from negative fallout among other voters who do not share the group's positions.

Interest groups that are closely allied with the candidate's party are the most likely to be helpful to the gubernatorial hopeful. Republican candidates, for example, can often benefit from the efforts of business groups, gun rights groups, antitax groups, and

Christian conservative groups. Democratic candidates can often count on labor unions, teacher groups, African American and Hispanic groups, feminist and prochoice advocates, and environmental organizations (Jewell and Morehouse 2001). Clearly, modern gubernatorial campaigns involve the activities of a great many people, both inside and outside the formal campaign apparatus.

Campaign Strategies

Once the campaign apparatus is in place (or at least key elements of it), the campaign team must devise a strategic plan. Candidates and their teams must make hundreds of choices over the course of the campaign in response to changing events. They may have to adapt their original plan when the political landscape changes. Each of these strategic decisions ultimately rests with the candidate him- or herself, drawing on the advice of campaign experts. Given limited financial resources, choices have to be made about the types and timing of advertising. Given limited time and energy, candidates have to choose how to allocate their time as well as that of their campaign staffs.

Timing is a particularly important consideration because research shows that voters pay relatively little attention until the later stages of the campaign—specifically, the last month. Despite this fact, there are sometimes reasons why a candidate must hit the airwaves early, such as to build name recognition, to satisfy the desires of key supporters, or to match ads being run by the opponent.

In addition to the timing and placement of ads, candidates must decide on their content. Different types of messages are appropriate at different points in the campaign. Early ads generally are targeted at building name recognition and introducing the candidate to the electorate (especially if he or she is a challenger). These ads may emphasize family background, education, and experience. The next ads typically focus on key issues the candidate feels will speak effectively to potential voters. Final ads return to central themes and are targeted at getting core and swing voters to the polls.

Along the way, candidates have to decide whether to focus on presenting a positive image of themselves or to produce negative ads about their opponents. Negative ads may offer valid content that the voters have a right to know. However, they can also take the form of personal attacks and allegations that may or may not have merit. This choice is a tricky one. If the opponent has gone negative (begun airing negative ads), the pressure builds to match those negative ads. Failing to do so may give the appearance that the ads are accurate or that the candidate being attacked is weak and ineffectual. Research indicates that voters pay attention to and remember negative ads, so they are often quite effective. However, other research finds that voters become disillusioned by the tendency of campaigns to go negative; in fact, they may actually end up turned off by the whole process.

In addition to buying advertisements, campaigns attempt to attract free publicity in the form of media attention. The larger the state, the more candidates must depend on the media to get the word out, as there is no other viable means of reaching distant voters. Candidates take steps to try to attract media attention. They sometimes develop gimmicks, such as working in various jobs to illustrate the state of the economy and the needs of the voters or taking a bus trip and stopping at towns across the state to talk to voters along the way. Candidates (particularly challengers) also hold press conferences in significant settings, such as steel mills that are closing down or decrepit public school buildings, to draw attention to particular issues.

Many states also hold so-called debates for the gubernatorial candidates, which usually turn out to be more like joint press conferences, with very little true debate between the candidates. Such joint public appearances are more appealing to the challenger than to the incumbent or the obvious front-runner. A joint appearance has the effect of elevating the challenger—putting him or her on the same level with the sitting governor. This effect is sought after by the challenger and preferably avoided by the incumbent. Ideally, these debates attract a significant number of viewers, giving them the opportunity to hear the candidates speak at length (compared to the typical news sound bite) about issues and their positions. Such events also help the viewers to make determinations about the personalities and political skills of the candidates. Voters (and the media) will consider whether the candidates seem intelligent, prepared, and able to think quickly on their feet.

Incumbents (or front-runners) and challengers often adopt different sorts of campaign strategies. For incumbents, financial resources are usually plentiful, so larger campaign staffs and more frequent advertising spots can be acquired. Yet incumbents cannot completely control the content of the campaign. They will normally be judged by their records in office, which can be good or bad for their reelection prospects. Poor economic conditions negatively impact incumbents at the polls. If a governor raised taxes in the previous term, he or she will also have some serious explaining to do on the campaign trail.

Challengers do not have a record they have to defend, though their performance in other former offices might be scrutinized. Challengers will work to paint a negative picture of the incumbent while presenting themselves as the natural alternative. Occasionally, candidates will identify new issues that have not been part of the public debate and encourage voters to identify them with those issues. Some candidates, for instance, have settled on establishing a state lottery as an innovative (and seemingly cost-free) way to address state budgetary problems. Such issues do not always attract the attention of voters in the way the candidate intended. But if they do, this approach can be an effective means of distinguishing the challenger from an incumbent who is already a known quantity for the voters.

The final challenge of the campaign is to make sure that supporters turn out to vote. At the same time, however, candidates will hope to discourage those likely to vote for the opponent from going to the polls. Because negative campaigning has been found to decrease turnout, candidates may target negative ads in parts of the state where the opponent is strongest. They and their parties will likely organize cars and drivers to help people get to the polls if needed, and they will make calls on election day to be sure that supporters follow through and actually vote.

Campaign Spending

Gubernatorial campaigns are expensive, what with hiring consultants, airing ads, and raising money, and the costs continue to rise. Elections in 1998 cost more than they did four years earlier. Candidates in governor's races in the thirty-six states holding elections in 1998 spent a combined $469 million, compared to $418 million in 1994, a 13 percent increase (Jewell and Morehouse 2001). But the increases, when adjusted for inflation, are not as great as they first seem. For example, 1994 spending was only 6.5 percent more than the amount spent in 1990; whereas the 1990 figure was 7.2 percent higher than the figure four years earlier. The greatest shift in spending took place between the 1982 and 1985 races, when the increase in real dollars represented a 32 percent jump. The 1980s marked the beginning of the modern gubernatorial race, which involved polling, television, direct mail, and television ads—all of which caused the cost of campaigns to skyrocket.

While it is true that campaigns are more expensive, on average, than they used to be, it is also true that spending continues to vary quite a lot across elections and across states. As might be expected, races in larger states tend to be more costly than those in smaller states. Candidates in California and Texas, the two largest states by population, were the first- and second-biggest spenders, respectively, in gubernatorial races in the 1990s. Campaigns for governor in California between 1982 and 1994 cost an average of $51 million, yet even this high figure is eclipsed by the $125 million campaign in 1998. Texas's gubernatorial races averaged $44 million from 1982 to 1994. But New York's 2002 governor's race topped both of these, at a cost of nearly $147 million (Beyle 2004).

Clearly, the population of a state is positively related to spending on the campaign; it is simply more expensive to run a race in a large state. But this is not the only predictor of spending levels. Some smaller states where the two parties are increasingly competitive have also experienced some very expensive races.

Recent gubernatorial elections continue to show that winners most often outspend losers. In 2002, the average expenditure among those who won the governorship was $9.8 million. Losers spent, on average, about $100,000 less on their campaigns. Data from recent years also tend to show that Democratic gubernatorial hopefuls spent more, on average, than did their Republican counterparts, although this was not true during every election cycle. In 2002, for instance, Democratic gubernatorial candidates outspent Republicans by a little over $2 million on average. The average spent by Democrats was higher than that spent by Republicans in 1999, 2000, and 2001. But in 1994, Republican gubernatorial candidates outspent Democrats by over $400,000 on average.

As noted earlier, campaign spending is partly driven by the size of the state. In order to reach larger populations, candidates must buy more media advertising. So total dollars spent does not really tell us much about the impact of spending on the election outcome. Another way to conceptualize campaign spending, then, is to examine the amount spent for each vote cast. In 1998, the amount spent per general election voter in the gubernatorial race was highest in Nevada (at $22.97). In three large states with very high total spending, the cost per vote was much lower. In Texas, New York, and Florida the cost per vote cast for governor ranged from $3 to $8. Obviously, it costs more to reach voters who are spread out geographically.

Even these figures on the spending per vote do not tell us a lot about what the campaign dollars actually "buy" for the candidate. Incumbent governors do not need to spend as much money to win as do candidates in open-seat races. Races involving incumbent governors cost $6 per voter, while open-seat races cost about $10 per voter. There is, of course, a bit of irony here. Incumbent governors do not need to spend as much to win their races, but they are better able than other candidates to raise money for their campaigns.

Campaign Finance

Money is important at all stages of the electoral process. Money is necessary to get the nomination, and it is even more critical in garnering enough votes in the general election to win the governorship. Consequently, candidates must spend a lot of time and other resources attempting to attract contributions to pay for their campaigns. This necessity raises a variety of concerns about the healthy functioning of the democratic system in the United States.

Since the Watergate scandal of the 1970s, many questions have surrounded the propriety of big campaign contributions. People worry that groups or individuals give money to candidates in order to buy their support. In general, they often have a gut feeling that money corrupts politics. In response to these concerns, nearly all states have chosen to place at least some restrictions on campaign spending and other unseemly activities. At a minimum, all states prohibit bribery and vote buying. They also require some form of disclosure and reporting of campaign receipts and expenditures. A number of states have gone further to create new finance systems in which some or all of the campaign is funded by public dollars in exchange for the acceptance of spending limits.

Disclosure and Contribution Limits

The most basic set of laws designed to control the flow of money in the electoral system focuses on disclosure and contribution limits. These laws are also the most widely adopted types of campaign finance rules.

Disclosure rules require candidates to report the sources of their campaign funds and show how these funds were spent. Increased use of the Internet has made this process much easier. Today, all state elections agencies are online, and nearly all states provide some type of online filing capability for candidates. Easy access to these data also makes it much easier for observers to keep an eye on where candidates are getting their money and what they are doing with it. Public attention of this sort is just what disclosure laws are meant to elicit. The idea is that candidates and contributors will police their own behavior if they know they are being closely observed. The easier it is for the public, the press, and other interested groups to access this information, the more effective disclosure will be in encouraging candidates to be careful about where they get their money and how they spend it.

Most states have also established contribution limits. These limits target those who wish to give money to candidates and their campaigns—individuals, corporations, political action committees, unions, and so forth. According to state elections scholars John Bibby and Thomas Holbrook (2004, 65), "Thirty-five states have imposed some limits on individual contributions. . . . Forty-three have prohibited or placed limits on corporate contributions; thirty-eight have restrictions on direct labor union contributions; thirty-six limit PAC contributions; and forty-four prohibit or limit contributions from state-regulated industries." By contrast, four states (Colorado, New Mexico, Texas, and Utah) place no restrictions on either individual or PAC contributions. Some states have established time periods during which contributions are prohibited, such as during the state legislative session, in an attempt to separate the giving of money from the most important work of state government.

Effectiveness of Campaign Finance Rules

Most candidates and contributors will voluntarily abide by state campaign finance laws. However, no attempts at controlling the flow of money into campaigns will ever be perfect. Certain individuals will always find ways around the laws, and states will most likely continue to adapt to these new strategies. The key to how successful the restrictions are is how effectively they are enforced. Twenty-six states have established independent commissions to oversee the conduct of campaigns. Unfortunately, these commissions have been underfunded in nearly all states, and as a result, enforcement has not been as effective as it could be. To prevent those who wish to break the law from doing so, there must be a perception that breaking the law is risky. Aggressive enforcement conveys this sense of risk to would-be violators. Some state legislatures in 2001 and 2002 took steps to give more adequate enforcement tools to the responsible agencies. Such changes clearly require that a majority of legislators view the control of campaign funds as a significant concern facing their state. But since legislators seek contributions themselves, they may be of two minds on the question of finance reform.

Public Funding

Given the huge importance of money in campaigns, attempts to restrict or control the flow of funds into public campaigns have not been fully successful. As a result, some states have taken more dramatic steps to change the way gubernatorial elections are financed. They have created public funding mechanisms for their gubernatorial elections.

The idea of public funding is to control the sources of the money that campaigns receive. Contributions for political campaigns often come from interest groups and others who presumably hope to gain something by supporting a candidate. Interest groups, in particular, are controversial in that many voters seem to believe that PACs can buy support from public officials by contributing to their campaigns. Whether such arrangements happen or not (they are surely quite rare), the appearance of such impropriety is destructive to the democratic process. Public funding removes or at least diminishes the influence of groups with vested interests on state campaigns.

Another argument in favor of public funding is that it levels the playing field, making political office available to a broader range of people. Because extremely wealthy individuals who seek public office may spend as much of their own money as they choose, candidates who may be more qualified but lack a large personal fortune are at a major disadvantage. Public funding makes a run for office more accessible to those with less wealth.

Another concern often expressed by election observers is that campaigns are just too expensive. They assert that candidates are engaging in a sort of arms race—wherein each candidate opts to spend more in order to keep up with the opposition. These observers view high spending on campaigns itself as a problem.

Public funding for campaigns is one way to remove (or at least lessen) all of these concerns. Fifteen states make public funding directly available to gubernatorial candidates and to candidates for other statewide offices. According to court decisions, states cannot require candidates to accept public funding. They also cannot limit the amount of money candidates are allowed to spend, though they can limit the size of contributions. What the states can do is to require those candidates who accept public dollars for their campaigns to also abide by spending limits. It is not clear how much this approach will really change things.

Given the ability of some candidates to raise major amounts of money, coupled with the huge benefits of spending aggressively on campaigns, those who want to regulate the flow of campaign funds face a real challenge. When it comes to public funding, it is clear that a candidate who is having difficulty raising sufficient money to mount a campaign will readily accept the public dollars and the spending caps that accompany them. But candidates who are able to raise enough money on their own will likely choose to decline the public funds and their accompanying spending caps unless there is some enticement for them to do otherwise. One way to address this dilemma is to make the amount of public funding high enough to be tempting to candidates in both of these situations. But if the caps are set too high, then the concern about exorbitant spending on campaigns is left unanswered. Some states attempt to respond to this concern by providing extra support to candidates who, having accepted the public funds, find that their opponents (who declined public funding) have outspent them.

Typically, to be eligible for public funding, a candidate must demonstrate that he or she can mount a legitimate campaign. States usually measure this by requiring that the candidate raise a certain amount of money on his or her own from fairly small contributors.

Given that participation in public funding is discretionary, it is, of course, possible that candidates will simply choose not to participate. One study (Malbin and Gais 1998) examined elections in eleven states between 1993 and 1996 and found that four of six incumbents and eleven of sixteen challengers accepted the funding and spending limits. Democrats accepted the money more often than Republicans. Further, candidates were more likely to participate in public funding when the caps were perceived to be high enough to mount a good campaign. When the caps were set too low, candidates were more likely to opt out. Among these races, no correlation was found between accepting funding and winning. So critics of public funding overall who fear that those who accept the limits will be disadvantaged do not seem to be correct. As laws have continued to change, some states have experienced increases in the number of candidates choosing to accept public funds.

Most states use a taxpayer checkoff to pay for their public funding systems. In some states, the checkoff results in a reduction of taxpayer refunds; in others, the checkoff is not paid for by the individual taxpayer. Particularly in states where the taxpayer actually makes the contribution, participation in the checkoff program is rather low. In recent years, participation has been only about 10 percent, meaning the legislatures have had to supplement these funds to cover the costs of the program. And if state legislators do not support such a system, they may not choose to add the additional resources. However, the systems adopted in four states in the 2000 elections were adopted by voter initiative, which indicates that voter preferences may prevail in certain states even when the elected officials are not inclined to support the funding systems. This trend continued into the 2001 and 2002 elections.

Public funding systems in the states are relatively new, with several states only adopting them in the late 1990s. So it is a bit premature to comment on what effect public funding has had on the many concerns the systems were meant to address. Early experience does, however, seem to show that campaign spending has gone down in the states that have public financing.

VOTING IN THE GENERAL ELECTION

After all of the money is spent, all the ads are run, and all the rallies are held, the election arrives. Voting is one of the essential rights of U.S. citizenship, yet for much of the history of the country, state and national laws allowed only relatively limited participation in the voting process. Many people fought long and even bloody battles to guarantee the rights of all citizens to participate in choosing their public officials. However, despite the essentially universal right to vote that is now in place in the states, relatively few people actually turn out for elections, whether for the U.S. president or for state officials such as the governor. The level of turnout is higher in some states and regions than others and in certain types of elections. This section will first examine who tends to vote and why and then consider how those people who show up at the polls decide whom to vote for.

Turnout

The U.S. Constitution gives the states a great deal of control over elections. As a result, states traditionally have had many different rules regarding the time and place of elections and who can participate. Historically, some states erected discriminatory laws and practices designed to make it difficult or impossible for African Americans to vote. Such rules often infringed on the voting rights of poor whites as well. All of these practices were outlawed by various federal laws and U.S. Supreme Court decisions culminating in the 1960s.

Though they can no longer discriminate by race, states still establish rules about registering to vote, and these rules vary to a significant degree. By federal law, states cannot demand that a citizen reside in the state for more than thirty days in order to vote in state elections. Some states retain the thirty-day residency requirement, meaning new voters must register at least thirty days in advance of an election in which they hope to vote. Other states allow registration on election day itself. Generally speaking, it is easier today to register to vote than it has ever been. States have instituted mail-in registration, online registration, and other changes due to the federal Motor Voter Act. This law requires states to allow people to register to vote at motor vehicles bureaus, welfare offices, and other governmental offices they might visit for other reasons.

Overall, states have taken steps to make the ballot box easily accessible to all potential voters. Given these legal changes and other factors, states saw some increase in turnout in the 1990s (compared to the 1980s). Between 1997 and 2002, the average turnout for governors' races across all fifty states was 43.5 percent. This average, however, masks significant variation from one state to the next. North Dakota, Minnesota, and Montana, for instance, averaged a turnout of 60 percent or more over this period. Nine other states had turnouts of 50 percent or more. Meanwhile, nineteen states recorded turnouts of less than 40 percent across their gubernatorial elections, and Kentucky had the lowest average turnout by far, at only 19.4 percent.

In large part, turnout is driven by characteristics of individual voters. Older people are more likely to vote than younger people on average. Moreover, those with higher incomes and higher education levels also are more likely to cast their votes. So a significant portion of the variation in turnout can be attributed to socioeconomic differences among the states. However, other state-level factors are involved as well.

To some degree, differences in state turnout simply represent the historical differences of the states themselves, though that is not a full explanation. First, some regional differences are significant. Southern and border states, for example, consistently have the lowest voter turnout rates, and indeed, there is a long tradition of very limited participation by regular citizens in these areas, because governance was believed to be the job of a small, aristocratic elite in earlier times. The highest turnout is seen in small, sparsely populated states. Next, the level of competition between the parties affects how many people choose to vote. When the parties are fairly evenly matched, potential voters become more interested in elections and are more likely to vote. Another factor is the stringency of state registration laws.

Though states have generally moved toward making registration easier, variations persist and continue to affect turnout. The easier it is to register, the more likely people are to do so. And where more people are on the voter registration rolls, more voters show up on election day. Research shows that registration laws play a significant role in determining how many people vote. The turnout for states with the most flexible registration laws (where registration is permitted ten days or less before the election) averages 54.3 percent. In those states with the strictest registration rules, the average turnout is nearly 11 percent lower (43.5 percent). Average turnout across all the states is 53.9 percent. The timing of gubernatorial elections is also important. Turnout tends to be highest in presidential election years. Therefore, those states that elect their governors in presidential election years have higher voting percentages for the governor's race as well. Eight of the nine states that elect their governor in presidential years had a turnout of 49 percent or more (compared to the fifty-state average of 43.5 percent).

How Voters Decide

Previous sections discussed the question of who decides to go to the polls and cast a vote. But what accounts for the choices these voters make once they step into the voting booth? The best predictor of how a person will vote is party affiliation. The vast majority of people who have a party attachment cast their ballots for their party's candidate for governor. One study examined data from thirty-five of the thirty-six states holding gubernatorial elections in 1986, 1990, and 1994. In these elections, 79 percent of the voters who voted for a major party's candidate and who identified with a party voted for the party's candidate for governor; this was true for both Democratic and Republican voters. Partisanship is an especially strong predictor of the vote when the parties are more polarized. When the two parties stand for quite different policies on major issues, voters seem even more inclined to stand by their party when voting for governor.

Partisanship and Ideology

In evaluating the outcomes of state elections, it is important to consider the many forces that swirl around these contests. Scholars point to both state- and national-level effects on voter choice. Some researchers believe that voting for governor is a sort of referendum on the presidency, which suggests that voters respond to national forces when they decide how to vote for governor. According to this theory, when voters approve of the president's performance, governors who share the president's party benefit. Others say that state elections should be viewed as separate from national elections and that they are most influenced by state-level, rather than national-level, influences. According to this school of thought, voters consider the performance of the incumbent governor (when he or she is seeking reelection) and especially how well the economy seems to be doing. If the voters feel better off financially than before the governor took office, they will vote to reelect that individual. This type of voting is called retrospective voting, since it involves looking back over the governor's term and making a decision based on prior performance.

Researchers do not agree about which is most important for state elections—national factors or state factors. But the bulk of evidence seems to point to state-level influences. The high degree of incumbent success provides some evidence that state-level factors are supreme. As noted earlier, incumbents are quite successful when they seek reelection. In the 1940s and 1950s, about two-thirds of governors who ran were reelected. That percentage climbed steadily, and in the 1990s, 82 percent of incumbent governors won.

In addition to the voter's partisanship, his or her ideology is also central. Ideology is especially important for predicting the vote when the candidates are far apart ideologically—when a liberal Democrat is facing a conservative Republican, for example. In such cases, ideological differences are most apparent to voters, and they feel motivated to vote for the candidate whose ideology is closest to their own (this is normally the candidate for their own party, too, when they have a party attachment).

Short-Term Factors

As noted, most people who have a party attachment vote for their party's candidate. Further, most people stick to their party attachment over time. But if these two ideas were to always hold, the majority party would always win. The truth is, however, that while the majority party typically does quite well, it does not always prevail. Short-term factors sometimes intervene to determine the outcome of an election.

One of the major short-term factors is incumbency. Another related short-term factor is the issues, which often affect the incumbents' success directly, since it is the current officeholder who has a record that can be scrutinized by the press, the opponent, and the public. But sometimes, the issues raised in the campaign help to determine the outcome of the election quite apart from incumbency effects. Certain issues are particularly significant. For example, a major issue that often affects campaigns and elections is taxation. Not all governors who raise taxes lose, but they often suffer at the ballot box. Similarly, a poor state economy is bad for an incumbent (of whatever party). The reverse also seems to hold. When voters view the state's economy as strong, they reward the governor with their votes. Unfortunately for governors, some research finds they are more likely to suffer from blame than they are to benefit from positive assessments. These issue-based decisions are further examples of retrospective voting. Particularly controversial policy positions or scandals also may contribute to a vote against an incumbent. Thus, when abortion becomes a key issue in a campaign, voters often base their choices on how close the candidates' beliefs are to their own position on the subject.

In sum, partisanship is the best predictor of election outcomes. About 80 percent of partisans stick with their party's nominee. However, the parties are typically well matched in the states today, with the candidates for both major parties usually having a fighting chance—especially when no incumbent is running. Jewell and Morehouse (2001, 200) summarized it this way: "In states where neither party dominates, the outcome of elections depends heavily on the quality of candidates nominated by each party, the record of the incumbent (if one is running), the extent of factionalism in each party, and the ability of each party and its candidate to build a coalition among party loyalists and other voters." Researchers and political observers are sometimes surprised by the outcome of elections, but these general trends are highly predictive of what is likely to happen in the future.

WHO ARE THE GOVERNORS?

American governors were once considered "goodtime Charlies." They often had doubtful credentials, and some were corrupt or inept. Things are quite different today. Though the standard picture of the American governor is still a white, male lawyer, many other types of people have joined the gubernatorial ranks. It is important to understand the background of governors because the experiences and beliefs that people bring to the office affect how well they perform the job, in addition to affecting how others view them, what policy issues they pursue, and which parts of the job they choose to put the most effort into. The changing personal features of governors also help shape the public's view of the office. For all of these reasons, it is vital to understand who holds the office, not just what the office entails.

Demographics

Hundreds of different people have occupied the governor's offices over the years. Some states have lots of turnover in the office from term to term, while others elect the same person over and over. Between 1951 and 1981, for example, the average number of governors per state was 7.3. The state with the most new governors was South Dakota (10). Utah had the fewest, electing only 4 men over those thirty years (Beyle 2004).

It is not surprising that the majority of governors today, as in the past, are white men. However, the face of the governorship is changing. Women, Asian and Latino men, and one African American have joined the ranks.

Gender

The American governorship was long the exclusive domain of white men. In fact, by 1965, only two women had held governorships: Nellie T. Ross of Wyoming and Miriam A. "Ma" Ferguson of Texas. Each of these women followed her husband into the office, and they were both elected on the same day, November 9, 1924. Governor Ross was sworn in first, so she is considered the first female governor. Several women sought but did not achieve the office between the end of Ma Ferguson's term and 1967, the year Alabama elected a female governor. Lurleen Wallace sought the governorship at the behest of her husband, George Wallace, who was barred by state law from seeking a second consecutive term.

Though early women governors were often surrogates for their husbands, they did pursue some policies of their own. However, it was not until 1975 that a woman was elected to the governorship in her own right. Ella Grasso of Connecticut, the first woman governor who did not follow her husband into office, had a groundbreaking career in many ways. She was the first woman to be elected floor leader in the Connecticut house of representatives. She served two terms in the U.S. Congress before running for the governorship. She then served one term as governor and was elected to a second term. She resigned early in her second term, however, due to illness and died a year later.

Since Governor Grasso's election, a fairly steady stream of women have served as governors across the country (Table 4.4). As of May 2005, twenty-seven women have occupied the office in twenty-one states, and Texas, Arizona, Connecticut, and Kansas have each had more than one female governor. Ann Richards was Texas's second female governor (1991–1995), and unlike Ma Ferguson, she was definitely a political actor in her own right. Governor Richards was a fierce campaigner who worked hard to overcome tough competitors in both the primary and general elections. Though she was not reelected to a second term, she has remained a highly visible figure in the national Democratic Party. Three women have served as governor of Arizona. Two, Rose Mofford and Jane Dee Hull, succeeded to the position from the secretary of state's office. Hull sought and won a term of her own, serving from 1997 through 2003. Janet Napolitano became the third female governor for the state of Arizona when she was elected in 2002. Connecticut has had two women serve in the office, the first being Governor Grasso. The second, Governor Jodi Rell, succeeded to the post from her position as lieutenant governor in July 2004 after Governor John Rowland resigned. Kansas has also elected two women, Joan Finney (1991–1995) and Kathleen Sebelius (2003–present).

In addition to the four states that have had more than one woman in the governorship, Alabama, Delaware, Hawaii, Kentucky, Louisiana, Massachusetts, Michigan, Montana, Nebraska, New Hampshire, New Jersey, Ohio, Oregon, Utah, Vermont, and Washington have each had one female governor. Two of these women succeeded to the office (Jane Swift of Massachusetts and Olene Walker of Utah); the rest were elected. Nancy Hollister served as governor of Ohio for only nine days between the resignation of Governor George Voinovich and the swearing in of Governor-Elect Bob Taft.

Nine women held governorships in July 2004, the largest number of female governors to hold office at a single point in time; these women accounted for nearly 20 percent of the nation's governors. The previous record was six female governors, in 2003. Women have now held the governorship in every region of the country and in nearly half of the states. Obviously, the notion that chief executives have to be male is slowly receding from the public belief structure.

There is reason to expect that women will increasingly seek and win the office in the years to come. First are the changing public attitudes. Voters are more comfortable than ever before with voting for women for high public offices, and as a result, women are able to raise money for their campaigns just as well as men. Another reason for the change is that more and more women are serving in the positions that are traditionally the proving grounds for the governorship. As more women work their way up the political ladder, more of them will be in line to make a strong run for the governorship. And the more women who serve, the easier it will be for future women to seek and obtain the office. It seems most likely that the more traditional states (especially those in the South) will be the last to have a substantial number of women governors. However, the Deep South state of Louisiana elected its first female governor in 2004, so even in the Bible Belt, the prospects for women are good.

TABLE 4.4   FEMALE GOVERNORS

Name	State	Term in office
Lurleen Wallace (D)	Alabama	1967–1968
Jane Dee Hull (R)	Arizona	1997–2003
Rose Mofford (D)	Arizona	1988–1991
Janet Napolitano (D)	Arizona	2003–present
Ella Grasso (D)	Connecticut	1975–1980
M. Jodi Rell (R)	Connecticut	2004–present
Ruth Minner (D)	Delaware	2001–present
Linda Lingle (R)	Hawaii	2003–present
Joan Finney (D)	Kansas	1991–1995
Kathleen Sebelius (D)	Kansas	2003–present
Martha Layne Collins (D)	Kentucky	1984–1987
Kathleen Blanco (D)	Louisiana	2004–present
Jane Swift (R)	Massachusetts	2001–2003
Jennifer Granholm (D)	Michigan	2003–present
Judy Martz (R)	Montana	2001–present
Kay Orr (R)	Nebraska	1987–1991
Jeanne Shaheen (D)	New Hampshire	1997–2003
Christine Todd Whitman (R)	New Jersey	1994–2001
Nancy Hollister (R)	Ohio	12/31/98–1/11/99
Barbara Roberts (D)	Oregon	1991–1995
Miriam A. "Ma" Ferguson (D)	Texas	1925–1927; 1933–1935
Ann Richards (D)	Texas	1991–1995
Olene Walker (R)	Utah	2003–present
Madeleine Kunin (D)	Vermont	1985–1991
Christine Gregoire (D)	Washington	2005–present
Dixy Lee Ray (D)	Washington	1977–1981
Nellie Tayloe Ross (D)	Wyoming	1925–1927

Source: www.gendergap.com/government/governor.htm.

Christine Todd Whitman

In 1993, the citizens of New Jersey elected their first woman governor in Christine Todd Whitman. She served as the state's fiftieth governor until 2001, when she was appointed as President George W. Bush's Environmental Protection Agency (EPA) administrator. Governor Whitman's distinguished political career includes being the first woman and first governor to respond to a presidential State of the Union address, in 1995. She was a tough campaigner during the 1994 midterm elections, when eighteen of the twenty-two candidates for whom she campaigned won. The leaders of the Republican Party called her a superstar, and she was seriously considered as a possible running mate for 1996 presidential candidate Bob Dole. Whitman's favorability grew from her moderate Republicanism and her economically conservative and socially progressive ideology, which she learned growing up in a politically active family.

Christine Todd Whitman, the first elected female governor of New Jersey, was later administrator of the U.S. Environmental Protection Agency (2001–2003). (Office of Governor Christine Whitman)

Parents Eleanor Schley Todd and Webster Todd introduced young Christie to politics. Both were state Republican Party leaders, and Eleanor was even considered a possible gubernatorial candidate herself. Christie was twelve when, in 1956, she attended her first Republican National Convention, where she and a young Steve Forbes presented President Dwight Eisenhower with a homemade golf tee holder as he left the stage for the evening. She has not missed a convention since. In 1964 and 1968, Christine Todd worked for Nelson Rockefeller's presidential campaign, and today, she still calls herself a Rockefeller Republican. The term generally refers to a Republican who is fiscally conservative but socially liberal—thus, a moderate Republican.

Balance, partnerships, and listening are themes that characterize Whitman's public life. She officially began her political career as a staff member in the U.S. Office of Equal Opportunity, where she designed a "listening tour" in 1969 to learn why more young people were not drawn to the Republican Party. Ever since, she has found herself in public life listening and acting on what she

has learned. Whether it was as a Somerset County freeholder, a post to which she was elected for two terms, as a cabinet member for former New Jersey governor Tom Kean, or as governor in her own right, Christine Todd Whitman worked to build relationships with the citizens of New Jersey, whom she referred to as her New Jersey family.

Governor Whitman was an effective communicator, often using specific examples and stories from her wealth of experience to relate to her New Jersey family. In her first inaugural, she promised to "trust and listen to the people . . . for as long as I am governor." And she expressed the hope that the citizens, as "one family," would work together in partnership with government to "make New Jersey first." Her goal was to make the state "a better place to live, work

(continues)

Christine Todd Whitman *(continued)*

and raise a family." As she emphasized listening and partnerships, she referred to specific individuals in her speeches, indicating the personal tone with which she infused her oratory. Whether it was Monica Jones and the "Women in Trades program" discussed in her 1997 state of the state address or newborn John Kueny and the "four E's" of her 2000 state of the state address, Governor Whitman relied on personal experiences and thereby demonstrated her connection with her audience.

The personal tone with which Whitman infused her public addresses may have been a direct response to the criticism she received during her first campaign for governor and her early term in office. The most common criticisms of candidate Whitman were that she lacked toughness as well as any basic understanding of the concerns of average New Jerseyans. New Jersey newspapers dubbed her "candidate lite" and ran stories with such derisive titles as "Christie's Clueless." Her political opponents used her family wealth against her to paint her as "out of touch" and even "dishonest" in her tax-cutting and economic reform measures. As a candidate and first-term governor, she was commonly described as "aloof," "distant," "measured," and "tentative," so it is no wonder that she worked so hard to forge connections with the audiences in her later speeches to emphasize her collaborative style.

Governor Whitman would be remembered in New Jersey for her environmental legacy. She began planting the seeds of her environmentalism in her 1997 state of the state address, which paved the way for her EPA appointment in 2001. In the address, she discussed efforts to keep New Jersey "clean and green" and her proposal to preserve thousands of acres of open space across the state. She also made it clear she wanted to encourage "environmentally friendly businesses [to] expand or locate in New Jersey," further demonstrating her attention to balance, which would eventually be her challenge as EPA administrator.

As governor, Whitman's emphasis on partnerships and balance never overshadowed the fact that she was, indeed, the leader of the state. In fact, the New Jersey governorship is the most powerful in the country, since the position is the only statewide elected office. All other state officials in New Jersey are appointed by the governor. This fact may have created a special challenge for Whitman when she became President Bush's EPA administrator. Not used to clearing decisions before announcing them, Whitman was now in the position of having to credit the Bush administration for policy proposals. In fact, she often linked her leadership style at the EPA to one of Bush's campaign promises: "Government should be citizen-centered, results-oriented, and whenever possible, market-based. Government should be guided not by process but by performance." While the themes resonate with Whitman's gubernatorial rhetoric—partnerships, bal-

Race and Ethnicity

The governorship, like nearly all facets of American government, continues to be dominated by whites. Though state legislatures, the U.S. House, and, to a much lesser degree, the U.S. Senate have increasingly been populated by people of diverse racial and ethnic backgrounds, the governorship has remained more elusive for minority group members. Women have made significant inroads over the years, but people of racial and ethnic minorities have been less successful. In 1982, the California Democratic Party chose Los Angeles mayor Thomas Bradley as its nominee for governor. Mayor Bradley,

ance, and results—now these themes were credited to the president.

As EPA administrator, Whitman made her share of mistakes, including one early one that set the tone for the rocky nature of her tenure. In March 2001, she attended a meeting of G-8 ministers on climate change, during which she articulated the president's commitment to reducing greenhouse gas emissions, including carbon dioxide, and the commitment the administration made in 1992 at the Kyoto Convention. Her words would come back to haunt her. Less than two weeks later, the Bush administration in effect stated just the opposite, and a White House spokesperson said "it was a mistake" to include carbon dioxide in the list of pollutants she had mentioned. The reversal found Whitman's credibility in serious jeopardy. In the wake of the incident, she was described as "embarrassed," "undercut," "wounded," and "whipsawed," with one report suggesting she might even resign. Whitman did not resign, but over her short tenure, she would find herself in other uncomfortable situations concerning everything from EPA policy on safe arsenic levels to drilling in Alaska.

To manage her image at the EPA, Whitman attempted to justify her decisions by relying on the credibility of science. In fact, her legacy at the EPA will be that reliance on science. She used science, scientific studies, and solid research analyses to reinforce her decisions. Following Whitman's resignation from the EPA in 2003, an article in the publication *Science* claimed that she strengthened the role of research in decision making at the EPA. Her appointment of a science adviser to the EPA was also praised. And she did have some notable policy successes, including cutting diesel emissions and ordering General Electric to pay for the removal of polychlorinated biphenyls (PCBs) from the Hudson River (these chemical compounds are used in manufacturing to lubricate or cool electrical equipment). In the past, manufacturing plants deposited the used chemicals into the nearby water supply; recent research showed that PCBs are harmful to humans who eat fish contaminated with the chemicals in large enough quantities.

Moderation or balance was the hallmark of Whitman's public life. As governor, she regularly spoke of partnerships and collaboration, but as EPA chief, her attempts to balance business and economic interests with environmental policy were not so readily received. However, Carl Pope, Sierra Club's executive director, commented that she "did the best she could" under the circumstances. In May 2003, Christine Todd Whitman resigned her post as the first governor appointed to the position of administrator of the Environmental Protection Agency. In her resignation letter, she cited the agency's "enviable record of success" and reiterated her unwavering loyalty to the Bush administration. A woman of many firsts was able to return home to her beloved New Jersey, where she will undoubtedly continue to be active in public life.

Kristina Horn Sheeler
Associate Professor of Communication Studies
Indiana University at Indianapolis

the first African American candidate for governor in the modern period, came within a single percentage point of being elected governor of the most populous state in the Union. Yet polling data show that racial prejudices continued to hamper African American candidates. Enough people to make up several percentage points of the California electorate admitted to pollsters that they would not support Bradley because of his race. The true percentage of those harboring such concerns is probably actually even higher, since people often are reluctant to admit their prejudices to pollsters.

Douglas Wilder, the first African American to actually win the governorship, was elected in Virginia in 1989. Governor Wilder served for a single four-year term (Virginia remains the only state to prevent its governor from serving successive terms). His election such a short time after Bradley's defeat in California is noteworthy, especially since the first (and, to date, the only) African American governor was elected in a traditional southern state. His career, in fact, included many firsts. Wilder was first elected to the exclusive state senate in 1969, and he was elected the state's first black lieutenant governor in 1985. Wilder was the first black to win a statewide election in Virginia; the first black to win a statewide executive office in the South since Reconstruction; and as lieutenant governor, he was the highest-ranking black elected official anywhere in the United States (Yancey 1988, 8).

Wilder's career is a remarkable success story. He managed to break into important state-level offices despite his second-class status growing up. Yancey (1988, 16) described the odds he faced: "Wilder felt the full sting of Southern racism growing up in the forties and fifties. He went to dilapidated, segregated schools, was denied admission to Virginia law schools, and had no chance of joining a prestigious law firm. He had none of the advantages blacks growing up in the sixties and seventies started to have."

Though Wilder got much of his support in all of his political races from African American voters, he also drew a substantial number of votes from whites. In fact, Bradley's race in California and Wilder's in Virginia illustrate that black candidates for statewide office must draw a significant number of white voters to win. So Wilder's relatively high percentage of the white vote was part of the reason for his success. He was viewed as a moderate who de-emphasized race and was therefore able to appeal to middle-class whites. Wilder nevertheless raised more than half of the money for his campaign for lieutenant governor from black contributors: middle-class blacks were especially important supporters for Wilder, illustrating the continued dramatic importance of black voters.

Prevented from seeking a second consecutive term under Virginia law, Wilder made a run for the Democratic nomination for president in 1991 but dropped out in 1992, having insufficient money to continue. He left the governorship at the end of his term in 1994.

The preceding quote from Yancey seems to imply that as generational changes occur—as a new generation of African Americans grows up in this country after the fall of Jim Crow laws and the end of segregation—the door should open to more blacks seeking statewide office. Yet this does not seem to be happening. Wilder remains the sole African American to win the governorship even as late as 2005.

There have, nevertheless, been other important African American leaders in state politics. Two African Americans were elected lieutenant governor in 1974—Mervyn Dymally of California and George Brown of Colorado. In 1998, Colorado elected Joe Rogers, the second African American to hold its office of lieutenant governor. His selection as one of the highest-ranking black elected officials was even more significant because he was a Republican. Nevertheless, none of these lieutenant governors has gone on to seek and win the governorship. Democrats in the state of New York chose

Carl McCall, the state comptroller, as their candidate for governor in 2002. He received 33 percent of the vote but was defeated by the Republican incumbent, George Pataki.

Other minority groups have also struggled to assert themselves in state politics. Five Hispanic men have been elected to the governorship, but this has occurred in only three states. These Hispanic governors are Jerry Apodaca (New Mexico), Raul Castro (Arizona), Toney Anaya (New Mexico), Bob Martinez (Florida), and Bill Richardson (New Mexico). However, even in states with significant Hispanic populations, wins for Hispanic governors have been few and far between. When Bill Richardson was elected in New Mexico in 1992, he was the first Hispanic to win a governorship since the mid-1980s. The candidate he defeated was also Hispanic, guaranteeing that no matter the outcome, New Mexico would have a Hispanic governor when the campaign was over.

New Mexico has clearly been the most fertile ground for Hispanics seeking the governorship, which is perhaps not surprising given the fact that nearly half of the state's population (42 percent in 2003, according to the U.S. Census Bureau) is Hispanic. The other two states to elect Hispanic governors in the modern period, Arizona and Florida, also have sizable Hispanic populations. In each of these states, the percentage of Hispanics exceeds that in the national population (25 percent in Arizona and 17 percent in Florida, compared to 12.5 percent in the nation as a whole). Other western states with substantial Hispanic populations, such as Texas (32 percent), California (32 percent), and Nevada (20 percent), are likely locations for future Hispanic governors. In 2002, Tony Sanchez made a respectable run against Texas governor Rick Perry, though he could not ultimately unseat an incumbent Republican (the final tally was 58 percent for Perry, 40 percent for Sanchez). California lieutenant governor Cruz Bustamante unsuccessfully sought to replace Governor Gray Davis in the 2003 recall election that ultimately elected Arnold Schwarzenegger. Much as in the experience described regarding women and blacks, the advent of viable Hispanic candidates is a precursor to actually electing Hispanic governors. So an increasing number of Hispanic state legislators, members of Congress, and lieutenant governors will likely give rise to Hispanic governors in the future.

Hispanic Americans come from many different countries with different political leanings. Cuban Americans, especially in Florida, tend to vote Republican whereas Mexican Americans, many of whom are located in California, Texas, Arizona, and New Mexico, tend to be Democrats. These partisan tendencies are borne out by the party affiliations of Hispanic candidates in these states. Martinez of Florida was unusual in being that state's first governor of Hispanic descent. He was also only the second Republican to win the office in Florida since Reconstruction. The other Hispanic governors, in states dominated by Mexican Americans, have all been Democrats. Though the party divisions among Hispanic voters may make winning national office difficult for Hispanic candidates, they should not be so problematic in state and local races. Hispanic candidates in Florida are more likely to come from the Republican Party, while candidates in states dominated by Mexican Americans (such as the western states of Arizona, New Mexico, Texas, and California) will likely produce Hispanic candidates who are Democrats. In any case, Hispanic candidates will be most likely to succeed in states with substantial Hispanic populations. To date, they have had almost no success outside of these states.

There have also been a handful of governors of Asian or Pacific Islander heritage, with all but one of them serving in the state of Hawaii. When Gary Locke of Washington was inaugurated in 1997, he was the first Asian American to be elected governor in one of the contiguous forty-eight states.

These few examples aside, racial minority group members have experienced somewhat less success in statewide elected offices than have women. However, more minority candidates seem to be jockeying for position these days, obtaining the offices with the necessary prestige to someday seek the governorship. It seems likely that it is simply a matter of time before successful African American and Hispanic candidates will emerge to capture the governor's offices, given the percentage these groups make up in the electorate of many states.

Another question arises: to what extent might a "black and brown" coalition offer a minority candidate a chance in a state where no one minority group has a sufficient number of voters to shape the outcome? In Texas as of 2000, African Americans and Hispanics together made up 42 percent of the population. If a candidate could appeal to both racial/ethnic groups and get these voters to the polls, this could be a powerful voting bloc. However, such a coalition, while promising, would be difficult to achieve. For various reasons, questions remain as to how likely blacks and Hispanics are to join together behind common candidates.

Education

Today's governors are, by and large, highly educated. Though this was not always true through history, most modern governors have pursued a good deal of formal schooling before arriving at the state's highest office. Even in the early part of the twentieth century, over half of the governors had attended college. In the 1940s, nearly 90 percent had at least some college education (though they did not all attend long enough to earn a degree). Between 1951 and 1981, the average governor had earned a college degree and then pursued some postgraduate education. This trend continued into the 1990s and beyond. Now, it is nearly unheard of for a person without a college education to seek and win the office of governor. Further, most governors have gone beyond a bachelor's degree to earn advanced degrees, especially in the study of law. In 2004, nineteen sitting governors had law degrees. Seventeen governors held bachelor's degrees as their highest level of education, four held master's degrees, one held a Ph.D., one an MD, and one was a doctor of veterinary medicine.

Clearly, then, governors have become a well educated group. The American public has been becoming more highly educated over recent decades, but governors have outpaced the general public in average level of education. Of course, having more education does not guarantee success in the office, but it should make those who enter the office better prepared to undertake its many responsibilities. In the past, there were some regional differences in governors' levels of education. In the 1970s, governors in the South had achieved the highest education levels, for example. But today, governors across all regions and in both major parties are likely to have postgraduate education, which is one of several indications of the high quality of the individuals currently holding the office.

Governors' Backgrounds

When candidates seek elected office, they bring with them many collected experiences. Their personal backgrounds, their life experiences, and their work histories all contribute first to the decision to seek the office and then to the success they have once elected. Some people begin planning to run for governor at a young age. Others may not expect to seek the office but find at some point that events have come together to make it seem like a good idea. One way of thinking about who runs for governor and why is to assess how many opportunities a person has to seek the office. As was noted earlier, some states experience a lot of turnover in the governor's office. In a state such as Virginia, which even now allows its governor to serve only a single term, there is a race for an open seat every four years. In states that allow an individual to serve two consecutive four-year terms, turnover may happen every four years or perhaps less frequently. This information is important because those who hope to be elected governor must make a decision on when to run, whether to go up against an incumbent of their own party in the primary (an unlikely and most likely unpopular option), or whether to wait until no incumbent is in the race. Also, given an open seat, other candidates of the same party are likely to come forward as well, which would require further negotiation and perhaps fighting a battle for the nomination.

Most people who desire the governorship seek it while occupying some other office: state legislators, lieutenant governors, and members of the U.S. Congress all may be potential candidates for governor. For various reasons, other candidates will choose the governor's race as their first foray into politics. In many cases, these are individuals who have already made a name for themselves in other arenas—perhaps as celebrities or wealthy businesspeople. For these individuals, the governorship may be either a long-time goal or a novel idea arrived at after pursuing a markedly different career.

Occupations

Many people who seek the governorship and other elected offices first seek law degrees. The skills required for being a good lawyer are similar to those needed for public leadership: verbal ability, skill at debate, and prowess at developing personal relations, among others. Law careers also offer flexibility of scheduling, giving potential candidates the time necessary to seek and even serve in electoral office. Few jobs are better suited to a person with political aspirations. Lawyers are also generally well paid and have access to the financial resources required to wage increasingly expensive gubernatorial election campaigns. Almost half of all governors who served between 1951 and

1981 were lawyers. Another 8 percent of governors during this period called themselves lawyers/businessmen. The number of lawyers among the governors remained at just under 50 percent in 2004 (twenty-two).

Businesspeople made up the next largest group of people seeking and holding the office, accounting for 20 percent of all governors between 1951 and 1981. These two groups—lawyers and businesspeople—have comprised a majority of governors over the years in every state, and they were also the major groups in both parties and in all regions of the country. Yet there were differences in terms of party affiliations. Businesspeople were more common in the Republican Party while Democratic governors were more likely to be lawyers.

Other professions are also commonly represented in the governorships, including educators, news reporters, bankers, dentists, engineers, farmers, ranchers, and even at least a couple of actors. Governors are therefore typically well trained and have considerable professional accomplishments before seeking the office.

Much as governors outpace the general population in level of education, they are also more likely to be members of professions. In the period during which nearly half of the governors were lawyers, less than 1 percent of the adult males in the country were lawyers. Even in 2005, less than half of American adult males can be classed as white-collar workers. Thus, governors are an elite group in terms of their education and their professional experience and are not reflective of the general population in this regard. However, it makes sense that those who have the position, ambition, and prestige to seek and win the governorship and serve in the office should be somewhat different from the rest of population. Governors comprise a small group, and having taken the office, they tackle a job requiring patience, negotiation skills, organizational ability, and empathy so that they can understand and respond to the needs of others. Those who rise to such levels in government are typically drawn from the ranks of the successful in other occupational arenas.

Former Offices Held

Individuals who seek the U.S. presidency have often amassed both legislative and executive experience. Eighteen former governors, for example, have gone on to become president. There are many proving grounds where presidential hopefuls can develop the knowledge and skills to prepare them (at least in part) for the presidency. But the situation for governors is different. There is no clear proving ground to prepare for being governor. No other single job or office provides experience in the varied responsibilities that governors have.

As noted, most people who run for governor have already run for and won some other office. Often, these are lower offices in the executive branch, such as lieutenant governor or attorney general. Other people make a run for the governorship from the state legislature. Given the immense demands placed on governors, prior experience in professional occupations in addition to elective office is nearly essential to success in the governor's office.

When asked what background they believed would best prepare a candidate for their position, governors themselves offered a variety of answers. This variance no doubt arose from the variability of the job itself. As illustrated in Chapter 2, governors serve many different roles. Nevertheless, nearly every governor who was asked expressed the belief that experience in the state legislature was critical. Through legislative experience, a prospective governor acquires knowledge about the problems facing the state, an understanding of the lawmaking process, and perhaps ready-made political allies among former colleagues. Almost everyone, therefore, agrees that prior legislative experience is important if not essential to success as a governor.

Gaining executive experience to prepare for the administrative aspects of the governorship is more problematic. Even though there are many lower-level executive offices, none is similar enough to the governorship to really prepare an individual for the chief administrative component of the job. One possible place to gather administrative experience is in a local executive position, such as mayor. For various reasons, however, few local elective officials move straight from there to the governorship. As mayors are typically known in only subsections of the state, they tend to have a difficult time in winning the governorship. Those mayors who do seek the governorship often come from the state's largest cities. This tendency may raise internal political problems, as people outside the mayor's home city may be suspicious of his or her allegiances. Perhaps voters suspect a former mayor would not serve all parts of the state equally. History shows that mayors seeking the governorship face a tough challenge. However, that is not to say that local experience is absent among governors. Many governors (16 percent between 1981 and 2002) began their political careers in local offices.

Due to the central importance of the chief legislator role, the state legislature is increasingly a proving ground for governors. Historically, many governors have been state legislators before assuming the top office. The percentage was 18 percent in the period between 1900 and 1949. The percentage increased to 23.8 between 1950 and 1980. Just looking at the 1970s, nearly 30 percent of governors came from the state legislature. Though the percentage dropped slightly between 1981 and 2000, it increased again in the early twenty-first century. In 2004, just under 50 percent of governors (twenty-three out of fifty) had formerly served in one or both chambers of the state legislature.

At one time, law enforcement posts were common proving grounds for the governorship. Thus, nearly 20 percent of governors in the early twentieth century had held law enforcement positions, serving, for instance, as county and city attorneys, district attorneys, U.S. attorneys, Central Intelligence Agency (CIA) and Federal Bureau of Investigation (FBI) personnel, judges, and state attorneys general. But the percentage of governors coming from this background has decreased in recent years. Again, if one thinks of former offices held as on-the-job training for the governorship, most law enforcement positions do not necessarily provide much helpful experience for would-be governors. Of course, some law enforcement positions are exceptions in this regard, in that high-level judges and attorneys general most likely acquire a substantial amount of vital administrative and leadership experience.

Most states have several statewide elected executive offices, and many individuals who seek these lower-level executive posts ultimately hope to move up to the governorship. The lieutenant governorship is a particularly common stepping stone. The percentage of governors coming from another state executive office remained at around 20 percent from the early 1900s into the 1980s. This percentage climbed to 27 percent in the period between 1981 and 2002. Well over half of these executive officers were lieutenant governors.

As Chapter 3 illustrated, the roles and responsibilities of the lieutenant governors vary substantially from state to state. In a handful of states, the lieutenant governor actually has more influence in the legislature than does the governor. Across the states, the lieutenant governorship offers the name recognition (if not always the experience) needed to launch a run for the governorship. It is not surprising that this is a common path to the highest office. However, being lieutenant governor does not guarantee promotion to the governorship. Between 1981 and 2001, more than two-thirds—69 percent—of the lieutenant governors who ran for governor lost. Other candidates seeking the governorship from state executive office experienced similar rates of defeat.

Occasionally, prospective gubernatorial candidates come from positions in Washington, D.C. As the governorship in the states has been granted more power and more responsibility, the position has become attractive to a wider array of hopefuls. In recent years, some members of the U.S. Congress have been included in these ranks. This situation is particularly striking given that members of Congress have very high reelection rates; in fact, an incumbent member who seeks reelection is all but guaranteed a victory. Consequently, seeking the governorship is a much riskier endeavor than seeking reelection to Congress. Further, while members of Congress can seek office for as many terms as they choose, the terms of governors are typically quite limited. That a member of Congress is willing to give up the relative safety of Congress to seek the governorship illustrates how coveted the office has become. The percentage of governors coming from seats in the U.S. Congress hovered around 10 percent for most of the twentieth century, but that number was on the rise as the twenty-first century approached. Between 1981 and 2003, 16 percent of governors were former members of Congress. Most of the Congress members who won the governorship came from the U.S. House, but a handful of U.S. senators sought and won the governorship as well. In some states, members of Congress do not have to give up their seats in Washington to seek the governorship, and as a result, these states have had a comparatively large number of "congressional governors." But congressional governors have been chosen in over half the states across the country.

There are, of course, many other paths to the governorship. Unelected administrative posts and local elective offices provide a handful of governors. Federal administrative posts such as U.S. secretary of state and secretary of commerce have produced a few as well. High-level political party officers also sometimes seek the governorship. Governor Haley Barbour of Mississippi, former chair of the Republican National Committee, is the most recent example.

Still other governors have held no prior public office. Governor Arnold Schwarzenegger may be the most unusual example, though another actor, Ronald Reagan, sought and won the California governorship many years before. The number of governors in this category seems to be growing: between 1981 and 2002, 14 percent of governors had held no prior elective office.

The Body and the Terminator

Most governors start out in other elective positions and gradually seek higher offices as they move toward the top executive position. But a few governors have followed decidedly different paths—making their names outside of politics and then translating that public familiarity into public office. Ronald Reagan of California, for example, was a movie actor and president of the Screen Actor's Guild before being elected to the governorship. Jesse Ventura of Minnesota and Arnold Schwarzenegger of California are noteworthy for the unusual paths they pursued to the governor's mansion. Most governors do not have their own action figures.

THE BODY

Reform Party governor Jesse Ventura (born James George Janos) brought an unusual résumé to his race for the Minnesota governorship in 1998. Ventura, a Vietnam veteran, had been a professional wrestler, an actor, a navy Seal, and a radio shock jock. His term as mayor of Brooklyn Park, Minnesota, was his only political experience, and clearly, this stint as mayor was not the source of his popularity. Instead, his flamboyant personality, personified in his wrestling name of Jesse "the Body" Ventura, explains a lot about his appeal.

Minnesota, unlike most states, allows voters to register on election day. Because of this rule, a lot of people who had never voted before, especially young men, were able to arrive at the polls, register to vote, and cast their votes in support of the outsider candidate who would stun nearly everyone by becoming Minnesota's governor. Ventura defeated two very well-known

Jesse Ventura, former Navy Seal, professional wrestler, and actor, became governor of Minnesota in 1999 as a member of the Reform Party. (Office of Governor Jesse Ventura)

political figures, Democrat Hubert "Skip" Humphrey III and Republican Norm Coleman.

Ventura had a love-hate relationship with lawmakers, the media, and the public alike. His term as governor was marked by various scandals and plenty of controversy. He made derisive statements about religion,

(continues)

The Body and the Terminator *(continued)*

among other topics, during an interview with *Playboy* magazine. He got into a shouting match with college students on the steps of the state capitol. His decision to make extra money by moonlighting in multiple jobs while serving as governor raised questions about conflicts of interest. His additional jobs included a guest appearance as a referee in the World Wrestling Entertainment's (WWE's) Summerslam, a book deal, acting in an episode of his favorite soap opera, and serving as a television sports commentator for the now defunct XFL.

Despite his unorthodox governorship, he did manage to accomplish some of his goals in office (enacting property tax reform, advocating light rail, securing health care endowments, and promoting trade). Critics asserted he could have been much more successful had he adopted a less controversial stance with legislators, but confrontation seemed to be the hallmark of his leadership and his life. Ventura eventually broke with the national Reform Party and later declined to seek a second term of office.

Ventura built his campaign around being a "regular guy" and speaking about the needs of groups he asserted were ignored by the two major parties, especially young people. This message got through to potential young voters, who were instrumental in getting him into office. He recognized this fact in his inaugural address: "We must not fail, because if we do, we could lose this generation. And we must not let that happen. It's those young people, it's those disenchanted voters we've reached out to and brought back to the system. We have to keep striving to do that." It is clear that Ventura was a different kind of governor who changed politics in Minnesota (at least temporarily). What is less clear is what lasting effect his governorship will have. After leaving the office, he hosted a short-lived talk show on cable channel MSNBC called *Jesse Ventura's America*. In 2004, he taught a study group at Harvard University's Kennedy School of Government. He continues to be involved in wrestling and the

WWE and has maintained a presence on the political scene as well. Supporters occasionally raise the possibility that he will run for president one day. While being interviewed by Ventura at a WWE Wrestlemania event, Donald Trump asserted his willingness to support him should he ever return to politics. Ventura declared, "We need to put a wrestler in the White House in 2008."

THE TERMINATOR

In the summer of 2003, opponents of California governor Gray Davis mounted a petition drive, ultimately gathering more than enough signatures to trigger a recall election. Eighteen states allow for such elections, which force the elected official to face the voters before the end of his or her term. But instead of facing an opponent, the incumbent faces a question of retention. Voters decide to keep the governor (vote against the recall) or remove him or her from office (vote for the recall). In California, the recall ballot also contained a separate section allowing voters to choose a replacement from among 130 candidates should Davis be removed from office. Thus, if more than 50 percent of voters supported the recall, Governor Davis would be removed and another candidate would be elected governor. Most of the 130 candidates were not meaningful contenders. Two, however, eventually emerged as viable opponents: a Democrat, Lieutenant Governor Cruz Bustamante, and a Republican, bodybuilder turned movie superstar Arnold Schwarzenegger. Schwarzenegger, like Ventura, had made his name far outside the political arena. After being named Mr. Olympia seven times, Schwarzenegger starred in many blockbuster movies, notably the *Terminator* films and other action movies such as *Total Recall* and *Collateral Damage*. (Interestingly, both Ventura and Schwarzenegger appeared in the science fiction film *Predator*.) Though he initially seemed an unlikely candidate for governor, he was ultimately elected, defeating Bustamante after the effort to recall Davis was successful. Schwarzenegger capitalized on his celebrity during the campaign. He announced his intention to run on the *Tonight Show* with Jay Leno and made multiple appearances on other national television talk shows. He quoted lines from his movies and did not shy away from his image as a movie star. As the election neared and polls showed Schwarzenegger was gaining on Bustamante, the news media pressed Schwarzenegger for details of what he intended to do as governor. He mostly ignored their questions, choosing less confrontational (and less challenging) venues to discuss what he wanted to talk about. Schwarzenegger peppered his campaign speeches with reminders of his movie appearances, uttering lines such as "hasta la vista" and promising to "pump up" Sacramento.

In the end, Gray Davis was recalled, as 55.4 percent of voters favored his removal. On the next question on the recall ballot, Schwarzenegger was chosen to replace Davis, gaining 48.6 percent of the vote while his next closest competitor, Bustamante, garnered only 31.5 percent. This was obviously a substantial margin, especially since there was another Republican in the race (Tom McClintock, who gained 13.5 percent of the vote). California political insiders, particularly Democrats in the state legislature, did not receive the governor very warmly. First, they were angered by having their own governor removed before the end of his term. Second, they doubted that the new governor would have the skill necessary to successfully perform the job.

Surprisingly, early on the governor and state legislators on both sides of the aisle managed to overcome their differences and accomplish a variety of economic reforms to combat the state's economic woes. Schwarzenegger was popular with the public—both Democrats and Republicans. In May 2004, his popularity stood at 65 percent, the highest for any California governor in forty-five years. His support among Democrats was 41 percent.

However, conflicts between Governor Schwarzenegger and the legislature arose sporadically during the first year of his term. In July 2004, they deadlocked and

Former champion bodybuilder and movie superstar Arnold Schwarzenegger became governor of California in 2003 after Governor Gray Davis was recalled and removed from office by voters. (Office of Governor Arnold Schwarzenegger)

failed to pass the budget on time. The governor mocked legislators, asserting they were like kindergartners who needed a "time-out." And he had this to say about his legislative colleagues to a group of supporters: "They cannot have the guts to come out there in front of you and say 'I don't want to represent you. I want to represent those special interests: the unions, the trade lawyers' . . . I call them girlie men. They should get back to the table, and they should finish the budget." The phrase *girlie men* is a reference to a well-known *Saturday Night Live* skit. References to his former life as an actor/celebrity have continued to mark his term. When he spoke to a congressional committee in Washington, he employed another of his well-known movie lines, "I'll be back."

Perhaps not surprising given the controversial nature of his governorship, *(continues)*

The Body and the Terminator *(continued)*

Schwarzenegger's honeymoon with the public did not last. His job approval ratings plunged from 69 percent to 40 percent in one year. Frustrated by attempts to work with the Democrats in state government, in 2005 he decided to bypass the legislature and go directly to the people. He called a special election for the consideration of his proposed referenda. Key proposals included spending controls for state government, merit pay for public school teachers, privatizing public pensions, and a proposal to give a panel of retired judges the responsibility for drawing state legislative district lines (removing the power from the legislature).

Schwarzenegger's decision to hold a special election rather than simply wait for the 2006 election was costly and therefore controversial. Observers asserted he called the special election to garner national media attention; he is widely believed to have his eye on an eventual run for the White House. He launched a massive $50 million television campaign in support of his proposals. Teachers' unions quickly organized in opposition to the governor's plan, and other groups followed suit, launching their own massive media campaigns in hopes of defeating the governor's initiatives.

In the end, opponents of the governor prevailed. Voters defeated all four of Schwarzenegger's proposed reforms, despite the governor's aggressive campaigning in support of them. Political observers saw this defeat as bad news for Schwarzenegger's hopes for reelection. In addition, it casts doubt on his possible national political aspirations. However, the governor may have an opportunity to overcome this defeat. It seems the key for Schwarzenegger will be to figure out how to function within the state political system rather than attempting to be the perpetual outsider. The governor who has asserted repeatedly that he is not a "politician" (as if that is a nasty word) will probably have to learn to work with the other politicians in state government if he hopes to actually get anything done to address the challenges facing the state. He will need to stop trying to be the "governator" and become simply the governor.

Clearly, there is no single path that a gubernatorial hopeful must follow in order to seek the governorship; they arrive there by many different career routes. In most instances, governors have served in other elective offices. Such a background offers experience that ought to bolster a candidate's abilities, including the ability to convince the voters of his or her qualifications for the job. Membership in the state or national legislature also helps to foster critical lawmaking skills. High-level offices including lieutenant governor, attorney general, and U.S. senator or House member also offer name recognition and access to financial and political resources that make a run for the governorship more likely to succeed.

BEING GOVERNOR

According to at least one former chief executive, the governorship is the "greatest job in the world." But it takes quite a lot of work to get there, and holding the office surely requires far more. Demands are enormous, family and personal time are scarce, and tenure is often quite limited. Nevertheless, the possibility of leaving a stamp on the state leads many qualified people to seek the office. Once they get there, governors probably face greater challenges than they ever dreamed. This section examines what it is like to actually hold the office. It examines the benefits and burdens of serving as governor. It concludes with a discussion of where governors go after leaving the state's highest office, revealing that their futures are as varied as are their backgrounds.

Workload

Given the many responsibilities and many different roles governors have, their workload is extremely heavy. One of the biggest challenges they face is figuring out how to budget their time. They have to make choices, because they cannot possibly do all that they might wish to. Budgeting time is difficult, however. To some extent, the workload of the governor is predetermined. Some ongoing jobs and time commitments simply cannot be avoided. Then, too, crises inevitably occur that demand the governor's attention for some period of time. When this happens, he or she will have no choice but to put other commitments aside and address the crisis at hand. Other parts of the job are more discretionary. While each of the many roles (chief of state, chief legislator, and so on) must be fulfilled by every governor, the degree of attention paid to each role and the time set aside for it is affected by the preferences of the individual governor. Some governors truly enjoy the legislative process and therefore dedicate relatively more of their time to the chief legislator role. Some enjoy the pomp and circumstance of the office and the symbolic role of the governor, and they like using the office's prestige to honor and recognize state citizens. Due to the preferences of each of the governors and the circumstances surrounding their offices, the workload naturally varies. What is certain is that they all work long hours each day, and to at least some extent, all governors end up sacrificing personal and family time while holding the office.

The National Governors Association surveys the states' chief executives about how they spend their time and what their average workday is like. One key finding is that the governors' schedules vary depending upon the time of the year. For example, in the early months of the year, when most state legislatures are in session, governors spend significantly more time and resources on legislative matters than they do when the legislature adjourns or when legislative business slows. Other times of the year are devoted to preparing the budget for submission to the legislature. The workload and time allocation also vary by the year in the governor's term. In the first year in office, governors (and their staffs) devote a lot of time to making appointments to executive offices, boards, and commissions. Election years, both legislative and gubernatorial, also bring a set of responsibilities to which the governors must devote time and energy (NGA 1978).

Governors receive a seemingly unlimited number of requests to speak to community groups, participate in parades and celebrations, and preside at the grand openings of new business enterprises. In addition to these many public appearances, they must also manage the state bureaucracy. They are expected to meet regularly with agency heads and staffers, with the press and the public, and with their own staff members. On top of that, governors must take care to maintain a positive relationship with the legislature and, hopefully, to have a bit of time left over for some sort of personal life. Given these extraordinary demands, careful scheduling of the governor's time is critical. Scheduling choices are potentially critical in part because those who spend time with the governor typically exercise more power in the administration.

According to the NGA, governors devote nearly 30 percent of their time, on average, to managing state government, most of it spent in meetings with agency heads, staff members, and board or commission members. The next largest time commitment involves working with the legislature (16 percent), followed by meeting the general public (14 percent) and ceremonial functions (14 percent). It is not uncommon for governors to work nights and weekends, putting in well over forty hours of work per week. In fact, former governors warn their new colleagues against overcommitting themselves and thereby losing out on the chance to spend time with family or set aside time for private contemplation. Former governors also advise their new colleagues to establish a schedule that allows for adequate rest. Exhausted people do not respond well to pressure, they caution.

The NGA survey shows that governors spend the majority of their time doing the essential work of state government, that is, acting as chief executives and chief legislators. Their ceremonial public roles, though perhaps important for the image of the position, fall behind their executive and legislative roles. Intergovernmental concerns receive significant but limited time and attention from the governors. Expressly political activities take a back seat to all of these commitments, though official gubernatorial activities can and do serve political purposes.

Within these broad categories of responsibility, governors hold press conferences (often weekly or more frequently), grant interviews with individual reporters, receive visitors to their offices, and make hundreds of phone calls and scores of public appearances—all on top of the managerial and legislative work they must do. Of course, modern governors do not have to tackle all of this responsibility on their own, since much of the work of the office is performed by staffers. Nevertheless, a very significant amount must be handled by the governor personally.

The Governor's Office

The early governor's office consisted, quite simply, of the governor and perhaps a single personal assistant. However, much like the chief executive of the nation, the governor in every state across the country is now surrounded by a collection of professional staffers who provide a variety of services. An augmented support staff is critical to enable the governor to accomplish the many tasks for which he or she has responsibility. Furthermore, there are many duties associated with the office that need not be handled directly the governor. The staff (when it functions well) takes on all the work that it can manage so that the governor is free to perform the duties that must be handled by the chief executive personally. High-level staffers may even act as stand-ins for the governor, making appearances or giving speeches on his or her behalf when the governor is unable to do so.

Inevitably, changing demands have led to changes within the governor's office. It has become more structured, specialized, formalized, and hierarchical. Gubernatorial staffs today provide both political and administrative assistance. In addition to helping carry out the many tasks entailed in the workings of the governor's office, staffers also provide guidance on political matters, identifying and researching key policy issues and mapping strategies for achieving the governor's goals.

The size of gubernatorial staffs has certainly grown in step with the increasing complexity of the governorship. In 1956, the average size of gubernatorial staffs (including clerical and professional personnel) was eleven, with a range in size from three to forty-three people. The average size rose to thirty-one in the early 1980s, and in 2003, the average number of employees in the governor's offices across the states was fifty-nine. In nearly every state, the size of the governor's office grew in that twenty-year period. On average, the governor's offices have grown by almost twenty-four people over this time span.

Of course, the size of the governor's office staff is closely related to the size of the state. Governors in larger states tend to have even greater responsibilities than their counterparts in smaller states, and their staffs have grown accordingly to assist the governors with this added complexity. In 2003, Florida, New Jersey, New York, and Texas had the largest gubernatorial staffs. Meanwhile, more sparsely populated states had much smaller staffs: in Nebraska, the governor's staff numbers thirteen, and the governors in Iowa, North Dakota, Vermont, and Wyoming all have fewer than twenty staff members. However, it does seem that there is a certain minimum size necessary to carry out the work of the governor's office regardless of the size of the state.

A typical governor's office might include one or more of the following employees: a press secretary, an executive secretary/chief of staff, a legal adviser, a speechwriter, a budget director, and a commissioner of administration. It will likely also include staffers assigned by the political party. The particular mix of staffers and the duties they fulfill is largely determined by the governor's individual preferences. Put another way, the makeup of the staff reflects, at least in part, the governor's orientation to the job.

Some staffers do the work of actually running the office. For instance, one or two people will be responsible for performing the delicate balancing act required to set the governor's schedule. In consultation with the chief executive, they will try to make sure his or her time is used wisely. Staffers must also manage the enormous volume of phone calls, mail, and electronic mail that arrives every day. Much of this correspondence does not require the governor's direct involvement, though some of it does. Part of the job of the staff is to know the difference—to determine which part needs to be passed on to the governor and which part can be handled without taking up his or her time.

Nearly every governor's office has a chief of staff or designates some other staffer to fill this position. The chief of staff oversees the office and its personnel. He or she assures that everything that needs to be done is being handled. The chief of staff should also conserve the governor's time and coordinate the many activities of the office. He or she may act as a gatekeeper, determining who has access to the governor and who does not. Some observers worry that a strong chief of staff may control the flow of information too tightly and therefore restrict the issues and arguments that reach the governor's ears. A governor in this situation may become isolated from the political realities of the state. Further, chiefs of staff with their own agendas may filter the information reaching the governor in such a way as to bias his or her decision making. Yet governors obviously cannot serve as their own chiefs of staff. The administrative detail involved in managing the office and running it on a daily basis would distract the chief executive from the more weighty elements of the job that only he or she can handle.

Other staffers help the governor in communicating with the state. Public relations specialists write press releases to inform the public about the governor's work. Staffers help the flow of communication travel the other direction as well. A major part of their job involves keeping the governor posted on political developments in the state, the nation, and perhaps the world. Other vital tasks involve providing the governor with the expertise and research support to shape the agenda on the many major policy issues facing the state. Still other staffers will assist in shepherding the governor's legislative agenda through the legislature. Intergovernmental relations liaisons provide a link between the governor's office and the other levels of government. Since the work done at each level of government in the United States affects every other level, this liaison role is often critical in advancing the governor's goals.

In addition to those working directly in the management of the governor's office, other support staff have become increasingly valuable. Budgeting and planning agencies, once part of the larger bureaucracy, are being moved closer to the governor's office today. In 1960, thirty-seven states had planning departments, but only three of those were situated in the governor's office. By the mid-1970s, all states had planning departments. In more than half of the states (twenty-nine), they were directly under gubernatorial control (Bowling 2003). Such support agencies provide the chief executive and his or her advisers with the data and expertise they require for successfully planning the governor's agenda.

Staffers tend to be rather young—many are in their thirties—but despite their youth, they are generally well qualified and ambitious. Nearly all have university degrees. Many have advanced degrees in law (especially), political science, or history. Some hope to move into political office themselves in the future. Often, those who helped to run the election campaign become the foundation of the governor's staff. Some observers have raised concerns about this, since the skills and judgment associated with successfully running a campaign and those necessary to successfully administer the governor's office are not always congruent.

One should not underestimate the enormous management challenge associated with running a governor's office, particularly in the larger states. The size of the operation, budgets, and personnel roster of large states such as New York and California dwarf those of most private businesses in this country and even the governments of some small countries in the world.

Not everyone agrees that the growth in the gubernatorial staff is a positive development. Some observers who express concern over the increasing size fear that office staff may perform some of the work that the public expects the governor to perform. And unlike the governor, who is elected, hired staff members cannot be held accountable to the public. In some cases, such concerns have resulted in attempts to cut back on the size of the staff. Often, in order to accomplish this, staff from other offices are "loaned" to the governor. In this way, they can provide assistance in the governor's office without being listed among the staff members. Such arrangements also serve the beneficial purpose of increasing gubernatorial ability and scope.

Pay and Perquisites

Financial compensation for governors has remained fairly constant over the years (when adjusted for inflation), though salary levels have always varied significantly across the states. As one would expect, the largest, most populous states tend to offer the highest salaries, while smaller states compensate their governors at lower levels. Cross-state variations reflect, in part, differences in the cost of living in the states. However, such salary variation also speaks to the relative emphasis a state places on the work of government and the office of governor in particular. Setting the salaries of public officials is always a controversial process. Often, members of the public resent it if their public officials earn a great deal more than the average citizen of the state. Yet the pay of public officials ought to be commensurate with the pay of individuals at the highest levels in other arenas, such as business and industry. Moreover, failing to establish reasonable pay and other benefits for the office can have negative consequences for the states themselves. Benefits need to be at least somewhat appealing so that highly capable people will be attracted to the office. While the salary package associated with the office is surely not the only reason people seek the governorship, a minimal level of compensation must be provided so that the job is not filled only by the very wealthy or by unqualified individuals willing to work for little pay. Salaries should also be high enough so that incumbents are not tempted to turn to illegal or unethical means to supplement their income.

In the early 1940s, the average gubernatorial salary across the forty-eight states was just over $8,000. At $25,000 per year, New York offered the most generous compensation, whereas South Dakota's governor earned the smallest salary, just $3,000 per year. In 1951, two states set the governor's salary at $25,000 (the highest level), while Maryland's governor earned the least, at only $4,500. The average salary in 1974 was $37,121, with the governor of New York earning the most at $85,000.

Despite the dramatic change in the prestige and power of the governorship over the years, average salaries, when adjusted for inflation, have remained fairly stable. The average salary in 2003 was over $100,000. New York's governor continued to be the highest earner, at $179,000. Converting earlier salaries to 2003 dollars shows that salaries have not changed much in real dollars.

In addition to salary, today's governors normally benefit from various other forms of compensation. Every state provides its governor with a state automobile, and all but eleven states make a state airplane available for the governor's use. Twenty-four states provide the governor with a helicopter, and twenty provide all three modes of transportation. Most governors also receive a travel allowance to offset the costs of travel associated with the duties of office. In addition to these benefits, all but five states provide an official residence for the governor and his or her family. These homes are often stately mansions that serve both as a private residence and as a public space for state events.

Salary and other compensation for elected public officials are often controversial topics. On occasion, a loud public outcry accompanies pay raises for public officials. However, as the previous section made clear, those who seek the governorship today are an elite group and would no doubt be top earners in whatever field they chose. Moreover, they would certainly earn a great deal more in the private sector than they do as governors. So while the earnings of governors have increased over the years, current salaries seem appropriate and commensurate to the responsibilities of the office.

Leaving Office

Eleven states allow their governors to seek an unlimited number of terms. The remaining states place some restriction on service, either setting an absolute limit or stipulating the number of consecutive years in which an incumbent can hold the office. Due simply to these regulations, an incumbent will generally not serve in the governor's office for more than eight years in most states. Consequently, though there are certainly exceptions, governors by and large serve a relatively brief time in the office and then move on to other pursuits.

On occasion, incumbents leave office by other means. Some may not be interested in pursuing as many terms as they are allowed to seek. Rarely, governors may lose their bids for their party's nomination. Somewhat more often, an incumbent may seek reelection but fail to win. Between 1970 and 2002, there were 466 separate gubernatorial elections and 275 incumbent governors seeking reelection. Some 78 percent of these incumbents were successful in their reelection bids. But sixty-seven of them did lose: fifteen of these lost in their own party primary, and fifty-two lost in the general election (Beyle 2004). Finally, governors occasionally leave office before their term is up, for a range of reasons. They may choose to accept a federal executive appointment or to take some other elected office (as when Governor Bill Clinton resigned the governorship to become president). They may resign for reasons of illness or because they are accused of wrongdoing or involved in a personal scandal. Very rarely, governors leave in the midst of their terms against their will through recall or impeachment.

In August 2004, Governor James McGreevy (Democrat of New Jersey) announced his intention to resign before the end of his term. He made his resignation effective on November 15 so that rather than holding a special election, the president of the state senate (another Democrat) would become governor as state law specified. McGreevy's administration had been hounded by claims of wrongdoing in office. However, it was apparently his personal problems that finally caused him to leave. He admitted publicly that, though married to a woman, he was gay and had participated in an extramarital affair with a man (for whom he apparently arranged a state job). McGreevy asserted that his personal scandal would hamper the work of state government and that he therefore felt he should leave the office early. Situations in which governors decide to leave office prematurely do occasionally occur, but they are quite rare.

Impeachment

Most of the time, when governors leave the office, it is because they are defeated at the polls; are no longer eligible to run; or have chosen not to run for professional, political, or personal reasons. There are a few instances, however, when governors leave office due to other factors.

All of the states except Oregon have established provisions allowing for the impeachment of the governor for wrongdoing. The word *impeach* means "to bring charges against." Impeaching a public official is similar to charging an individual with a crime. After impeachment, hearings are held and votes are taken. If the public official is convicted of the charges specified in the impeachment, he or she is removed from office.

Similar to the process established in the U.S. Constitution, each of the states divides the powers of impeachment, on the one hand, and trial and conviction, on the other, between two separate bodies. Again much like the rules specified by the Constitution for impeachment of federal officials, the lower house of the state legislature holds the power of impeachment in all but two states. Alaska designates the senate as the body with the power to impeach, as does Nebraska—since the senate is Nebraska's only legislative chamber. As the entity charged with impeaching officials, the lower body performs an investigation into the issues that have been raised, much like a grand jury investigation. If its members (or, more likely, a committee responsible for the impeachment investigation) feel the concerns are serious enough, they will draft articles of impeachment to be presented to the entire chamber for a vote. Nineteen states specify that a simple majority vote is required to impeach the governor, while eight states call for a two-thirds majority. Twenty-three states have provisions for impeachment but do not specify a certain number of votes. The articles of impeachment become the basis of the trial to be held in the other chamber.

The majority of states designate the upper chamber of the legislature as the body with the power to conduct impeachment trials. Alaska, which gives the senate the power to impeach, gives the house the power to conduct the trial and vote to convict. Three states include state judges in the process of trying the governor on impeachment charges. Missouri calls for a commission of seven imminent jurists to be formed by the senate to try the governor. In Nebraska, the provision for trial and conviction stipulates that a court of impeachment be composed of the chief justice and all district judges in the state. New York's law specifies that a court for a trial of impeachment will be made up of the president of the senate, members of the senate (or the major part of them), and judges of the court of appeals (or a major part of them).

Again like the federal model, most states require a higher percentage of votes to convict and remove the governor from office than to impeach him or her. Forty-five states specify that a two-thirds majority is necessary to convict and remove the governor from office. Those three states that create a court of impeachment also require a supermajority of the members voting to convict in order to remove the governor.

All states relieve the governor of his or her duties on impeachment and designate an acting governor. In most states (forty-two), the acting governor is the lieutenant governor. Two other states (Arizona and Wyoming) designate the secretary of state as acting governor, while five others name the president of the senate to the post. If the governor is not convicted of the impeachment charges, he or she returns to duty. If, however, the governor is convicted, then he or she is removed from office and replaced. Again, most states designate the lieutenant governor to fill the position on the governor's conviction. In some of the states that do not have an elected lieutenant governor, another official (such as the president of the senate) carries the additional title of lieutenant governor and succeeds to the governorship if it is vacant. In three states, the secretary of state is first in line to succeed to the governorship.

The use of the impeachment process is rare. Impeachment is designed to be an extraordinary tactic employed only under rather extreme circumstances. Given the fairly short length of gubernatorial terms, legislatures typically decide to defer to the voters, allowing them to remove the governor in the next election rather than put the state through the painful process of impeachment. Impeachment and the trial that follows are debilitating to the work of the state government and disturbing to the sense of well-being in the state. Most of the time, therefore, impeachment is avoided if at all possible. In certain cases when the legislature is considering impeaching the governor, he or she will choose to resign rather than face impeachment. Most recently, for example, Governor John Rowland of Connecticut resigned the office in the summer of 2004 in the face of an impeachment movement following a federal corruption investigation. Only seven governors in U.S. history have been impeached, convicted, and removed from office. Nebraska and North Carolina both impeached and convicted their governors in 1871. However, in the case of Nebraska's governor David Butler, the impeachment hearings were later expunged from the record, and Butler was renominated for governor in 1888. Four governors were impeached just a few years apart in the early 1920s, one in New York, one in Texas, and two in Oklahoma. Each of these cases involved misuse of public funds or misuse of the power of the office. The most recent impeachment and conviction of a governor took place when Arizona removed Governor Evan Mecham in 1988.

Recall

Governors in nineteen states can be involuntary removed from office before their terms are up by the actions of the public. This mechanism is known as a recall. Over the years, many governors have been the subject of more or less serious recall efforts. In every state that allows a recall, advocates must gather a specified number of signatures in order to put the recall question to a vote. Then, a specified vote is required to remove the governor from office. States vary significantly in how many signatures are required to request a recall election. The fewer the signatures required, the easier it is to pursue a recall election.

The governors facing recall efforts are typically caught up in some partisan turmoil and lack the full support of their party. Three different recall attempts were launched against Governor Barbara Roberts of Oregon in the early 1990s, though none gathered enough signatures to actually trigger a recall election. There have been many other attempts, but only two governors have actually been recalled in the history of the country. The first was Governor Lynn Frazier of North Dakota, recalled in 1921. The other came in 2003 when California governor Gray Davis was recalled after a very high-profile recall election. Davis was ultimately replaced by movie superstar and former world-class bodybuilder Arnold Schwarzenegger.

In most states, the number of petitions required to request a recall election is quite high and therefore hard to achieve. The recall is somewhat easier in California. It is therefore possible that at least in California, recalls may become more common in the future. However, the public generally prefers to remove unwanted incumbents from office through more typical means—defeat in the next regularly scheduled election. After all, the next gubernatorial election (in all the states) can never be more than four years off.

Death

Unfortunately, governors sometimes die in office. In fact, this has occurred fifty-one times since 1900. Most recently, Governor Frank O'Bannon of Indiana died while serving in 2003, and two years earlier, Governor Mel Carnahan was killed in a plane crash while campaigning for a U.S. Senate seat. All states have established a succession process, whereby another officer (typically the lieutenant governor, the president of the senate, or the secretary of state) takes over the office on the governor's death.

What happens when the governor is ill or incapacitated is less straightforward. But when Governor O'Bannon fell ill unexpectedly and lived for a few days before succumbing, the procedure to be followed in Indiana was clear. Indiana law spells out succession procedures not only in the case of the death of the governor but also in the case of gubernatorial incapacity. Under Indiana law, the state's supreme court is charged with determining whether the power of the governorship should be transferred to the lieutenant governor during a governor's incapacity. In 2003, on the request of the leaders of both chambers of the legislature, the supreme court named Lieutenant Governor Joe Kernan to serve as acting governor, and on O'Bannon's death, Kernan became governor. In states without clear procedures to be followed during periods of gubernatorial incapacity, the lieutenant governor will likely serve as acting governor in practice, though the propriety of that is not entirely clear.

Indiana law also specifies that the governor shall name a new lieutenant governor should the office become vacant, but many other states do not have procedures specified to fill a vacancy in that office. This situation has led some states to reconsider the question of succession in recent years. Worries about terrorist attacks have caused some legislatures to specify a longer list of offices to succeed to the governorship in case several top public officials should be lost at one time. States are likely to clarify these procedures in coming years.

Life after the Governorship

In some states, an individual can seek the governorship many times. For that reason, it occasionally seems that a particular governor has set up permanent residence in the governor's mansion. However, with the exception of those few who die while holding the office, every governor eventually faces the question of where to go from there. In states with limited terms, the question comes up sooner rather than later. When Virginia's governor is elected, for example, he or she is an automatic lame duck and will, by law, be out of office in just four years.

For some politicians, the governorship is their greatest political ambition. Others see the office as a rung on the ladder toward a higher position (or positions). A governor's ultimate career aspirations certainly impact the life he or she pursues on leaving the governor's office. Age at leaving office is another important factor, as is the availability of a window of opportunity to pursue some higher office.

Governors may also aspire to a federal executive appointment, a seat in the U.S. Senate, or even the highest elective office in the country—the presidency. All of these are, of course, coveted positions, and many different variables have to line up for governors to succeed in realizing their hopes of moving to the higher office. One key variable is the likelihood of winning the office. As noted earlier, members of Congress who seek reelection nearly always win. So governors aspiring to the Senate have a much better shot at a win when there is an open seat. Governors are well placed to pursue a Senate seat, since they have already waged at least one successful statewide campaign.

Positions in the executive branch do not necessarily come open at regular intervals. Though a block of positions is handed out at the beginning of a new presidential administration, other jobs change hands sporadically throughout a president's term. Such offices are "campaigned for" using more behind-the-scenes techniques. Four former governors served in high-level positions in President George W. Bush's administration: as secretary of health and human services (Tommy Thompson of Wisconsin, Mike Leavitt of Utah), as administrator of the Environmental Protection Agency (Christine Todd Whitman of New Jersey, Mike Leavitt of Utah again), and as director of the Office of Homeland Security (Tom Ridge of Pennsylvania, who was serving as governor at the time of the September 11, 2001, attacks). Ridge was the first director of the newly created homeland security agency. Two governors of New Hampshire have served as chief of staff in the White House: Sherman Adams (1949–1953) for President Eisenhower and John Sununu for President George H. W. Bush (1983–1988) (Beyle 2004). Other governors have moved into leadership positions in the private sector or in higher education.

Terry Sanford of North Carolina, Lamar Alexander of Tennessee, and Tom Kean of New Jersey all became university presidents after leaving the governorship.

Though the path is only available to a limited number of governors, some will seek the White House. Indeed, four of the past five presidents of the United States were governors first: Jimmy Carter (of Georgia), Ronald Reagan (of California), Bill Clinton (of Arkansas), and George W. Bush (of Texas). Other recent governors, such as Michael Dukakis (of Massachusetts), have earned their party's nomination to the presidency but lost in the general election. In all, governors were candidates for either the presidency or the vice-presidency in forty-seven of the nation's fifty-four presidential elections. The current high profile of the governorship in the states encourages many ambitious politicians who aspire to the presidency to seek the governor's office along the way. Recent history indicates the governorship is a very viable springboard to the White House.

The majority of governors simply return to private life on leaving the office. It could be that the governorship was their ultimate goal or that time and circumstances made seeking higher office impractical. For older governors, the governorship may have been the crowning achievement of a long career and the time after the governorship is to be dedicated to retirement. However, governors today tend to be younger than their predecessors were. These youthful governors may look around and realize that, though they are only in their mid-forties, they have already achieved their highest political goals. Many former governors return to their earlier jobs—often, lucrative legal careers. The name recognition and experience associated with their political careers make former governors very attractive to potential clients. As a result, these individuals may end up representing clients before the legislature, state agencies, or state courts. It is hard to imagine a lawyer better placed to provide such services than a former governor.

It is perhaps not surprising that governors spend a lot more time and energy thinking about entering the office than they do about leaving it. A number of them, especially those who leave the office earlier than they intended, may find the transition to private life disorienting and difficult. While most states have taken steps to provide assistance during the transition to incoming governors, none have given much thought to the outgoing officeholder. Governors find themselves in a strikingly different life on leaving the office. They suddenly lose the many perks of the office, such as staff and drivers. The National Governors Association has taken steps to encourage these men and women to plan for the worst-case scenario of being ousted from office so that the transition will be as painless as possible. But with their time and resources being limited, especially during a campaign, governors probably do not really heed this advice. Further, it is not only the governors leaving office unexpectedly who may find the transition to private life difficult. Those who have chosen to leave or who are not allowed to seek reelection are not surprised by the end of their term, but they may still find the change disconcerting. As Vermont governor Madeline Kunin (1994, 19) said, "There are two climaxes in political life: rising to power and falling from it." The rising to power is certainly more pleasant, as it is accompanied by the adoration and attention of throngs of supporters. Falling from power—or simply giving it up—is a much more solitary endeavor.

REFERENCES AND FURTHER READING

Beyle, Thad. 2004. The governors. In *Politics in the American states: A comparative analysis*, 8th ed., ed. Virginia Gray and Russell Hanson, 194–231. Washington, DC: Congressional Quarterly Press.

Beyle, Thad, and Lynn R. Muchmore. 1983. *Being governor: The view from the office*. Durham, NC: Duke University Press.

Bibby, John F., and Thomas M. Holbrook. 2004. Parties and elections. In *Politics in the American states: A comparative analysis*, 8th ed., ed. Virginia Gray and Russell L. Hanson, 62–99. Washington, DC: Congressional Quarterly Press.

Bowling, Cynthia J. 2003. State government administration, impacts of reform movements. In *The encyclopedia of public administration and public policy*, ed. Jack Rabin, 443–448. New York: Marcel Dekker.

Council of State Governments. 2003. *The book of the states*. Lexington, KY: Council of State Governments.

Jewell, Malcolm, and Sarah M. Morehouse. 2001. *Political parties and elections in American states*, 4th ed. Washington, DC: Congressional Quarterly Press.

Kunin, Madeline. 1994. *Living a political life*. New York: Knopf.

Malbin, Michael J., and Thomas L. Gais. 1998. *The day after reform: Sobering campaign finance lessons from the states*. Albany, NY: Rockefeller Institute Press.

National Governors Association Center for Policy Research. 1978. *Governing the American states: A handbook for new governors*. Washington DC: National Governors Association.

Partin, Randall W. 1995. Economic conditions and gubernatorial elections. *American Politics Quarterly* 23(1):81–95.

Ransone, Coleman. 1956. *The office of governor in the United States*. Tuscaloosa: University of Alabama Press.

Sabato, Larry. 1983. *Goodbye to good-time Charlie: The American governorship transformed*, 2nd ed. Washington, DC: Congressional Quarterly Press.

Yancey, Dwayne. 1988. *When hell froze over*. Roanoke, VA: Taylor.

Website Consulted

http://www.gendergap.com/government/governor.htm

5

THE POLITICS OF THE EXECUTIVE BRANCH

Jennifer J. Hora and Margaret R. Ferguson

Modern governors are key leaders in the states and nation. States have granted to their executives greater formal powers, and the people seeking the office are more qualified, prepared, and ambitious than ever before. As a result of these changes, governors have the opportunity to achieve lofty goals, if they choose to pursue them. However, they are not "all-powerful actors," nor should they be. In a democratic system, no single actor should be able to predominate. Despite the many changes empowering modern governors, they cannot always achieve their goals, and they almost never can achieve such goals on their own. Instead, many other actors both inside and outside government also influence the policy decisions and daily work of the state.

All state governments, like the federal government, have a system of separated powers. They each have three branches (legislative, executive, and judicial), and all but Nebraska further divide the legislative branch into two chambers. In all of the states, the governor shares the work of administering the laws with scores of other executive branch officials and even with state legislators. All of these actors depend on the courts to interpret the laws and occasionally to act as mediator. The separation of powers demands that governors work with their legislatures and executive agency officials in order to make and implement the laws. As a result, the nature of the legislature and the executive branch impacts the work of the governor. On top of this, the states are relatively open systems, which means that many actors outside of government also exert influence on what state governments do. Governors must interact with these individuals as well.

Governors do not dictate state policy. But they often can prevail. Achieving success requires strategy, dedication, and a clear focus. Successful governors maneuver their ways through the complicated state political systems by mobilizing their formal and informal powers and tapping into positive relationships with the public and other governmental actors.

The state political context forces governors to take account of a host of factors beyond their own political and policy goals. They must consider the goals and likely behavior of key legislators and interest groups. They must attend to prominent bureaucrats, since some actors within their own executive branches may hope to impede their goals. And always, the state and federal court systems are present, holding the duty of assuring that state law is in step with the state and, ultimately, the national constitution.

The fact that governors do not hold all of the power does not mean that they are always locked in battle with others. In reality, there are times when governors, the public, most legislators, and interest groups all unite behind common goals. In such instances, governors—acting in concert with the legislators, interest group leaders, bureaucrats, and potentially countless others—can quickly and easily move their goals toward speedy adoption. However, unanimity of purpose is not always present; in fact, it is more likely the exception than the rule. Under normal circumstances, some or all of these actors have preferences that conflict (in small or large part) with those of the governors. When conflict occurs, the governors are faced with a variety of challenges. They may attempt to forge some kind of agreement or compromise that will enable them and other key state actors to work together. However, compromise may not be possible, or for some reason, it may not be what the governor chooses. The personality of the governor may mean he or she dislikes compromise; while the personality of another may cause him or her to shy away from major conflict and seek a negotiated agreement. Sometimes, a governor who is willing to put up a fight may determine it cannot be won or is not advisable—it may not be worth the cost in time, favors, goodwill, or other political resources. In these cases, the governor may simply withdraw to wait for better circumstances. At other times, the governor may decide the moment is right to do battle with the opposition.

When governors decide to pursue goals that clearly conflict with the aims of other important state actors (such as legislative leaders), they will likely face fierce opposition that must be overcome. A smart governor chooses these battles wisely, since undertaking a fight of this type uses up lots of resources. Losing such a battle is even more costly to the governor in terms of political capital—such as, support among the public and respect within the legislature. A governor who knows the battle cannot be won will usually withdraw, but on occasion, he or she may decide to undertake the fight anyway, viewing it as the first round in a longer contest that can eventually be won. Or a governor may believe so strongly in a policy goal that he or she is willing to lose in order to make a point or draw attention to a pressing issue.

The reality of having to work with other actors, necessitated by the separation of powers, complicates the governors' job. But this is not the only complicating factor. Other factors broaden the arena in which they must function. The United States is also a federal system with multiple levels of government, a fact that impacts on the governors' ability to lead as well. Consequently, they must sometimes work with the national government to achieve their goals. They may go to Washington to lobby directly or set up Washington offices to monitor the national government on a regular basis. They may also work closely with the state congressional delegation in hopes of getting positive outcomes in Washington.

Furthermore, functioning as they do within a federal system, governors often must interact with leaders of other states. They may work with other governors to win approval in Washington for a certain program, or they may simply join with other states to adopt solutions to problems that affect multiple states. Governors of a region facing high levels of pollution, for example, may find it useful to work together. But states sometimes find themselves in disagreement with their neighbors as well, and when this occurs, governors may have to work with leaders of nearby states to devise practical solutions. Such disagreements are occasionally rather heated and may even land the states in federal court if a solution cannot be reached.

Given the U.S. system of government, some people argue that state governments are unnecessarily complicated. They believe that having so many statewide elected offices is inefficient and that it also makes the governor's job harder than it has to be. At the national level, the president has a team of executive officials who are chosen by and owe allegiance to the president. The governor does not have this luxury. Instead, he or she faces a much more complicated political environment full of likely supporters and potential opponents. This chapter will examine some of the other prominent actors in the states and the nation and how they affect the governor's ability to lead. These actors include the legislatures, interest groups, the bureaucracy, the media, the courts, the national government, and other states.

GOVERNORS AND THE LEGISLATURE

The state legislature is the governor's most important partner in state governing. The structure and makeup of the legislature therefore has a major impact on the governor because these two branches of state government must constantly interact. Any change in one of the branches ultimately can alter how the two of them work together. When the nature and composition of the legislature changes, the executive branch must change as well or otherwise respond in order to maintain its status in the political arena.

Legislators themselves have specific ideas about shaping policy in addition to political goals they set out when running for office. While the governor serves a statewide constituency, legislators serve narrower interests. They try to please the constituents who voted them into office and contributed to their campaigns, whereas the governor must maintain a much broader policy focus. The legislators' own sets of policy goals may or may not converge with the goals of the governor. If they do not, the result can be conflict between the governor and the legislature, which means the governor does not always achieve what he or she set out to accomplish.

The fact that the legislature writes the laws under the system of separated powers can create a contentious relationship between the executive and legislative branches when they are not working toward the same objective. If governors want to achieve the goals they set out, they must learn to cooperate with and cajole their state legislators. Most governors have more formal powers today than in the past, but the bargaining position of the governor still differs from state to state because the constitutional powers of both the executive and legislative branches differ, and that can play a major role in how these two government actors work together.

In particular, three aspects of the legislative branch significantly impact legislative-executive relations: the professionalization of the legislature, divided government, and term limits. Professionalism of the legislature refers most simply to whether membership is a full or part-time position and whether legislators have access to the other resources necessary to be effective lawmakers. Divided government results when the governor's party does not hold a majority in one or both chambers of the state legislature. Legislative term limits, adopted by some states, restrict the number of terms legislators may serve. Since the 1970s, all of these legislative characteristics have changed and, in turn, have altered how the two most visible branches of state government interact. Each of these concepts is discussed in general in the next sections, followed by a discussion of how professionalization, divided government, and term limits impact the relationship between the executive and legislative branches of state governments.

Legislative Professionalism

The professionalism of a legislature is a key feature affecting how the institution will interact with the executive branch of the state. A professional legislature is one in which the members devote the majority of their time to their jobs as legislators and do not pursue other careers simultaneously; they also receive good monetary compensation for serving as legislators. In contrast, a nonprofessional, or citizen, legislature is made up of members who typically receive low compensation and only work a few weeks or months of the year as legislators. Citizen legislators do not view being a legislator as their primary employment; they expect to perform the necessary work in the state capital in a short period of time and return home to their other jobs.

Scholars of state politics generally measure professionalism by examining three features: time in session, monetary compensation, and staffing. Judging by these measures, states as a whole are moving toward having more professional legislatures.

The first element of professionalization is time spent in session. The legislatures in some states, such as Massachusetts, Michigan, New Jersey, and New York, meet annually and throughout the entire year on a regular basis. Conversely, those in states such as Montana and North Dakota meet only once every two years and typically for only a few months. Still other states' legislatures meet every year but have sessions that last less than two months; Utah and Wyoming fall into that category.

Salaries paid to state legislators are the second element of legislative professionalism. New Hampshire has by far the lowest compensation, paying only $200 for the entire two-year term an elected representative serves. More typical on the low end of the compensation scale are Arkansas, Indiana, Mississippi, Rhode Island, South Carolina, and Texas, which all pay between $10,000 and $15,000 per session and also provide a modest per diem (to cover the cost of attending legislative sessions) for the days the legislature is in session. On the opposite end of the scale are the states with well-compensated legislators. Illinois, Michigan, and Pennsylvania, for example, all pay upward of $50,000 and offer a generous per diem as well. The most highly compensated state legislators are in California, where they received $99,000 per year as of 2003, along with a $121 per diem allowance for daily expenses.

Availability of support staff is the final element of legislative professionalism. On average, citizen legislators have only one staff person each to aid them in their duties, whereas professional legislators have about nine people. Members of the legislature rely on staff for various types of assistance, from organization to research and from providing constituent service to overseeing the bureaucracy. Clearly, representatives with the support of nine staff members can be more productive in terms of policy output than their colleagues in less professionalized states. This greater level of productivity is also more expected of professional legislators, who work for the state on a full-time basis.

Using these three measures—time spent on the job, compensation, and staffing—the National Conference of State Legislatures classifies legislatures into three categories: full-time, part-time (citizen), and hybrid. Eleven states have full-time legislatures, in which legislators spend a majority of their available work hours as legislators; they are highly compensated and have relatively large staffs. Seventeen states have part-time legislatures; their legislators spend approximately half of their available work time as legislators, receive total compensation of approximately $15,000 per session , and have only one staff person each. The third category, the hybrid legislature, falls between these first two categories. Legislators in the seventeen states with hybrid legislatures spend more time on the job than citizen legislators, are compensated at a higher level, and have approximately three staff persons to assist them.

In addition to days on the job, salary, and number of staff assisting them, the more professionalized legislatures differ from less professionalized ones in other ways as well. They have more organizational tools, such as larger and better-organized committee structures, and more formalized procedures, such as internal rules to keep the legislature on task. All of these features affect how state legislators interact with their governors and how the governors must approach the legislators.

Though states have generally moved toward greater professionalization, not everyone agrees that this is a positive development. One fear is that professional legislators are no longer like the people they represent. Instead of being regular citizens taking time off from their jobs and going to the state capital to represent their neighbors for a month or two, these individuals work for state government full time. They often live in the capital on a nearly permanent basis and commute to the home district only on weekends. The fear is that these professional legislators are too distanced from the citizens they are supposed to represent. Some feel that being a career politician rather than a citizen legislator changes how one thinks and acts. Critics argue that this distance results in a legislature that is out of touch with the needs of the communities it represents.

Given the recent trend toward greater professionalism, the citizen legislatures of today may one day become professional bodies. However, it may also be that the amateur nature of the legislature in some states actually reflects the desires of the population and that the citizens may oppose developments directed at changing the status quo. It is unlikely, for example, that states such as New Hampshire and North Dakota will ever achieve the level of professionalization that California and New York have, nor does it seem necessary for such a change to occur. Further, some states with professionalized legislatures have recently made changes that may result in the legislatures becoming *less* professional. California, the state with the most professionalized legislature of all, has instituted term limits for its members and leaders, a move that is likely to decrease the professionalism of the legislature in the long term. However, given the enormous size and complexity of the state of California, the legislature will likely work to adapt to the new limitations to continue to complete the necessary work of lawmaking in the state.

Impact of Professionalism on Legislative-Executive Relations

The level of professionalization of a state legislature impacts how legislators interact with the executive branch of government. Traditionally, the governor is the primary agenda setter in the state: the governor speaks with one voice, commands media attention, and is the clear face of the state. He or she is also responsible for the state of the state address and holds a statewide constituency. Legislators typically cannot come close to such a level of prominence. Thus, the governor has an advantage in relations with the legislature, since he or she can typically establish the central issues to be considered by the lawmakers. However, as a legislature becomes increasingly professionalized, it can compete with the governor for agenda-setting responsibility.

Agenda Setting.   Legislators in a more professional legislature have greater resources than those in a less professional legislature, enabling them to set the state's agenda for the year. In particular, legislative leaders in chambers that meet year-round can challenge the governor's primacy in setting the agenda and commanding media attention if they choose to do so. This challenge to the governor's agenda-setting authority is especially likely to take place if the legislative leader does not share the governor's party affiliation and if the media see this person as the opposition leader.

Citizen legislators working in the capitol for fewer than sixty days a year obviously offer less of a challenge to the governor. They do not have the capacity to demand sustained media attention—they are only officially working at the capitol for a fraction of the year. Additionally, governors participate in politics at the national level, as members of the National Governors Association, and often act as go-betweens for the state and national levels of government. A legislator maintaining another full-time job and residence outside the state capital cannot compete for political power. This disparity in time devoted to the job tends to work to the benefit of the governor in legislative-executive relations.

Professionalized state legislatures controlling the length of their sessions, as compared to legislatures bound by constitutional restrictions on the number of days they can meet, have the opportunity to more fully deliberate and debate on legislation. Further, the more professional legislatures can keep pace with governors' initiatives and counteract them quickly (when necessary), rather than either having to wait for a legislative session that could be months away to take action or, in some states, having to wait for the governor to call an emergency session.

In states with more professionalized legislatures, members have higher rates of re-election. Since they serve more terms and for more days during each term and also have more resources at hand, these legislators certainly have a greater ability to achieve their policy goals, even when they are not in line with those of the governor. When a legislature contains many long-time members with extensive experience, the governor must take greater care to work with these members and consider their goals and preferences.

The discussion so far seems to depict power as a sort of seesaw arrangement: if the governor has more power, the legislature must have less. This may be an accurate characterization in some cases. However, there are clear indications that the legislature gaining power, does not necessarily mean the governor has less power; in fact, this can be a win-win situation, in which improved institutional characteristics within the legislature can actually mean governors are more effective, too. Research has shown that governors and professional legislatures can work together to achieve their collective goals. Consequently, it would seem that more effective and efficient professional legislatures can actually lead to more productive governors and not have a negative impact on how these two institutions coordinate with each other. In addition, there is some evidence that as one branch of government gets stronger, the other branch will as well; more equally matched competition between the two branches forces both the legislature and the executive to be more savvy political actors. The balance of power is not, therefore, necessarily shifted from the governor to the legislative branch as the legislature becomes more professional. If this is true, then executive-legislative relations should, on the whole, become more harmonious as legislatures become more professionalized.

Executive Branch Oversight.   In addition to lawmaking and representation, legislatures are also responsible for overseeing the bureaucracy. It is in this area of responsibility that differences between more and less professional legislatures are most obvious, and these differences have real consequences for governors. Clearly, a state legislator who works another job full time and spends only a short number of days working at the capitol cannot closely monitor numerous state agencies. Oversight—which includes duties such as policy and program evaluation, review of administrative rules, and review and control of federal funds—is difficult to perform when the legislative body is in session for less than sixty days per year. Further, given a limited number of days in session, amateur legislators will likely choose to spend their time on issues relevant to the needs of their constituents rather than on the more abstract job of executive oversight. The task of evaluating and reviewing executive agencies is not as publicly visible as passing new legislation, and despite requiring a great deal of work, it can often result in little or no change in how policies are actually carried out. When choosing how to allocate their time, part-time legislators simply cannot spend as much time and energy on agency evaluation as their more professional counterparts can. Then, too, many of these evaluation and review activities are enhanced by competent staff members. Citizen legislators who have only one or two staff members each do not have the luxury of assigning them significant review activities.

Governors, by contrast, are keenly interested in oversight of the bureaucracy. The tendency of the legislature to review the bureaucracy is important to the governor because as head of the executive branch, it is important to him or her that government agencies operate as smoothly as possible. The legislature has the ability to oversee agencies' activities and correct minor problems before they become major ones and before the media and the public become involved. And smoothly operating agencies make the executive branch appear strong.

Legislators occasionally employ the executive oversight process to promote their own agendas. Should their agendas conflict with the governor's preferences, the governor may find this an unwelcome contribution. Given this possibility, amateur legislatures are potentially less dangerous to the governor's control of the bureaucracy, which may well suit the chief executive.

Divided Government

Prior to the 1970s it was common for states to have unified party government: one party controlled both houses of the state legislature as well as the governorship. This situation has changed significantly in the intervening years, and today, many governors must learn how to operate in a political environment where the opposing party holds at least one of the state's legislative chambers—that is, where a divided government exists.

The term *divided government* encompasses a variety of political arrangements. Both chambers of the legislature may be unified in opposition to the governor, or the legislature itself may be divided, with one party holding a majority of the seats in one chamber and another party controlling the other. All of these situations create challenges for the governor.

A majority of state legislatures operate under the control of either the Democrats or the Republicans, but in a significant number of states since the mid-1970s, the chambers have been controlled by different parties. At least one-fifth of the states have had split partisan control of the state legislature at some point in that period. In some years, as much as one-third of all state legislatures experienced split control. Further, it occasionally happens that a legislative chamber itself is split evenly between parties, so that neither party holds a majority in the chamber. In fact, since 1990, there have been seventeen such instances across sixteen different chambers. Beyond this, at least half the states regularly operate with one chamber of the legislature controlled by the party opposite the governor's party. Obviously, then, the states as a whole are not typically functioning under unified government.

Since 1984, more than half of the states have had divided government. The percent of states with divided government exceeded 60 percent twice, in 1988 and 1996. As these statistics show, divided party control is more of a normal phenomenon in state government rather than an anomaly.

For legislatures and governors in this situation to operate and to create public policy, they must cooperate. Of course, working cooperatively is always necessary, albeit never easy, but it seems that divided government may make this even harder.

Impact of Divided Government on Legislative-Executive Relations

Divided government has a significant effect on legislative-executive relations, and it is often blamed for the strife that occurs between the legislative and executive branches of state government. While unified government, in which the governor and both chambers of the legislature are of the same party, does not guarantee harmonious relations between the two, divided government does present unique challenges. An increase in divided government may weaken the governor's powers; it may mean he or she faces disorder and disunity in the state capitol. Research shows that legislators who are members of the opposing political party are less likely to support the governor's policy initiatives. Put another way, if the opposition party holds the majority in one or both chambers, a governor may have a very difficult time getting his or her goals accomplished.

Coordination and coherence drop when the legislative and executive branches of government are run by opposing parties. Even under the best of circumstances, in which the two branches are trying to cooperate and keep each other informed, it is difficult for them to coordinate and settle on one coherent course of policy change. Under less than ideal circumstances, open hostility can occur. When both chambers of the legislature are united under the party banner opposite to the governor's party, they can, in fact, stand up to the governor, and palpable conflict may result.

Divided government can lead to a blame game, as has been seen at the national level. When opposing parties control different branches, they can each blame the other for a lack of government action, and citizens find it hard to parse out who is really at fault. Efficiency has never been a strong feature in governments in the United States, since they are designed to encourage deliberation and careful consideration, not speed. Divided government is sometimes indicted for pushing deliberation and consideration to an extreme level. Indeed, many researchers blame gridlock, or the failure to pass new legislation, solely on divided government. Not all researchers agree, but divided government does make an easy target for the public and the media.

Though there is disagreement on whether divided government is the disaster that some suggest, it is widely acknowledged that divided government does make passage of certain types of policy more difficult to achieve. Policy that is more conflictual in nature is made even more challenging by divided government. Certain policy areas, such as health care, agriculture, and the environment, are minimally affected by divided government, but policies in other more contentious areas are doomed by stalemate under divided government. In fact, policy creation often grinds to a halt in challenging areas such as crime, education, and welfare when divided government prevails. Bill passage in these areas especially slows when the legislature itself is divided. Given the blame game and the difficulty in devising policy in conflictual areas, both the legislature and the executive branch can avoid responsibility for creating a problem and accountability for fixing it when neither party is in control of both branches. This situation is a significant failure in a democratic system, since the public must be able to hold its governmental actors accountable for their actions. Nonetheless, public opinion shows that citizens actually like their governments *more* when they operate under divided control. Some evidence at the national level even suggests that voters like divided government enough to purposely create it at the ballot box. It is possible that voters at the state level behave this way as well and split their tickets on purpose. So while citizens often become frustrated with divided government and are dissatisfied that things appear to not get done, they also, in some unpredicted way, find this situation appealing. Perhaps some elements of the public see divided government as an additional check in the separation-of-powers system. Be that as it may, it is undisputed that divided government leads to greater discord in legislative-executive relations

Term Limits

The implementation of term limits has altered the nature of legislative-executive relations. When a state imposes term limits, it restricts elected officials to serving a certain number of years and/or terms in office. Some states have created consecutive limits, meaning an elected official can serve no more than twelve years without sitting out a term. Other states have created lifetime limits, meaning that once an official has reached the maximum years of service allowed, he or she cannot serve in that office again.

Starting in the early 1990s, instituting term limits for state legislators became the subject of a major public policy debate. Citizens felt their voices were not being heard by representatives who served long terms and appeared not to be intimidated by the threat of defeat at the next election. The impression that state legislators were very difficult, if not impossible, to unseat started a grassroots movement to change the rules of the game so that legislators could not be reelected indefinitely.

As of 2005, fifteen states have instituted term limits for their legislators. However, in three of those states, the year of impact has not yet been reached, so only twelve states have actually started to see the consequences of this move. Six other states had term limits at one time that were later repealed either by the legislature (in two states) or by the state supreme court (in four states). State term limits are not all the same.

Only six of the fifteen states have enacted lifetime limits for those serving in the state assembly. In the other nine states with term limits, the limit is on consecutive terms served, meaning that legislators can run again after a set period of time out of office, typically two years. Legislators may also move from one chamber to another and thereby remain in the legislature.

In 1996, Maine and California became the first states to put legislative term limits into effect, followed by Colorado, Arkansas, and Michigan in 1998. Between 2000 and 2004, term limits took effect in seven other states. Three other states—Nebraska, Louisiana, and Nevada—have passed term-limit legislation that will go into effect between 2006 and 2010.

The limits placed on legislative service range from a low of six years on members of the house in California, Arkansas, and Michigan to a high of twelve years in both the house and the senate in Oklahoma, Louisiana, and Nevada. All other bodies have limits of eight years.

Advocates for term limits expected them to change the face of the state legislatures. However, evidence shows that the legislatures operating under term limits look very similar to those without term limits. Contrary to the predictions of the advocates, the characteristics of legislators do not substantially change when term limits are applied. Those elected under term limits are similar to legislators in other states in terms of gender, age, minority status, religious affiliation, family income level, and ideology. While advocates pushed for term limits as a way to involve new segments of the population, this has yet to materialize in the states with term-limited legislators.

Indeed, several of the predicted impacts of imposing term limits have not materialized. Predictions such as significant increases in the number of women and minority representatives or substantial changes in the characteristics of people serving in the legislature have not been realized. But one prediction—that power would shift away from the legislature relative to other political actors—is, in fact, occurring. Since states began creating them, term limits have significantly altered the balance of power between the legislative and executive branches of government.

Impact of Term Limits on Legislative-Executive Relations

While term limits have not yet substantially changed the nature of state legislatures themselves, they have altered the relationship between the legislative and executive branches of government. Contrary to the hopes of term-limits proponents, the roles of governors and other executive branch officials have been strengthened in states where the terms of legislators are limited, and the relative power of the legislative branch has declined.

The term-limit movement was led by citizen groups hoping to give more power to the people, but all evidence indicates that power has simply shifted between the branches of government, not back to the citizens. Obviously, this was an unintended consequence: citizens thought they were giving themselves more power, but instead, it is the governor who has benefited.

Perhaps the most substantial shift of power is evident in the loss of leadership in the legislature due to expired terms. Traditionally, leadership positions—speaker of the house, senate president, majority and minority party leaders, and committee chairs— have been held by representatives with long terms of service. Legislative leaders are the lawmakers who shepherd policies through the legislative process. In 2004, in the twelve states operating under term limits, thirty-two legislators holding leadership positions were forced to leave office because their term limits had been reached. All states lost at least one leader, and several states lost three or more. Additionally, 122 committee chairs were not able to run for reelection in these twelve states. Some states, such as Oklahoma and Arkansas, saw losses of as many as sixteen chairs or cochairs, which has left a leadership vacuum in these states.

Speakers in state legislatures without term limits have an average of twenty-four years of experience, compared to only six years in states with term limits. Inevitably, there is a change in dynamics when legislators in high leadership positions lack experience in coordinating decision making within and across the branches of government. By contrast, all governors are full-time officials, and they typically have a great deal of experience in government. This experience, coupled with a strong legislative liaison office, increases the governor's power in policymaking compared to the power exercised by legislative leaders. The governor's office is now the entity with more information and experience, and legislatures are increasingly dependent on the executive branch for expertise as they face difficult lawmaking challenges.

Legislatures have realized they need to develop ways to cope with the changes brought by term limits. New leaders and chairs, particularly those with little legislative experience, must spend time learning the legislative process. To respond to this need, several states have instituted training programs for new leaders in order to pass down the institutional memory; they are also selecting new leaders before the old leaders actually step down. It is possible that as legislatures create more coping mechanisms, they will regain some of the power in policy leadership that they have lost with term limits, but, initially at least, this change has meant a gain in power for governors.

Another impact of term limits is that they discourage cooperation between branches of government. Prior to term limits, legislators were aware they would be working with the governor for years to come and would have plenty of time to leave their marks. Legislators hoping to serve their constituents for many years did not want to develop a reputation for being antagonistic toward another branch of government. Being term limited, by contrast, lessens the incentive to be collegial with the executive branch; since members are out of office after a set number of years no matter what their working relationships are in state government. Additionally, term limits might actually create an incentive to behave antagonistically toward the executive branch because such antagonism increases a member's profile and name recognition—and name recognition (however it comes about) might be extremely useful for an elected official who will be out of a job in the near future. Having a high-profile reputation might help a member run for another, perhaps higher government office. But of course, this state of affairs has a negative effect on legislative-executive relations.

Some evidence indicates that as well as discouraging cooperation between branches, term limits dampen cooperation within the legislative branch itself. Again, the individuals serving do not look across the aisle and see potential colleagues for years to come. Instead, they see competitors in their drive to become known as individuals who get things done in the short time in which they serve. There is also evidence of more conflict between leaders in legislatures with term limits than in legislatures without them. The same ideas apply. Knowing you may well work with another individual, whether of the same party or not, for years to come creates a norm of behaving agreeably even if you disagree with his or her policy recommendations. Knowing the relationship is only a short-term working arrangement changes that dynamic. Such discord in the legislature may, on the one hand, work to the disadvantage of the governor, who has to build relationships with multiple actors rather than being able to focus on cultivating relations with key leaders. On the other hand, this discord within the legislature may simply mean the governor can take the lead, since legislative leaders cannot.

Changing Executive Power.   Term-limited legislators have much less time to fulfill their duties as policymakers. Traditionally, governors have excelled at the role of agenda setter, gathering support for new policies while leaving the duties of actual policymaking mainly to the legislatures. Policymaking requires knowledge of the processes as well as the specifics of individual policies. But legislators operating under term limits have much less time to acquire the necessary skills. The governor's office, supported by ample staffing and knowledgeable agencies, is then put in the preferred position of power in the policymaking arena. The governor's role in the policy process increases.

This situation may especially pertain when the legislative leaders are in a lame-duck position (unable to be reelected) and the governor has a longer, if not indefinite, time in office. The dynamics of their roles in policymaking are altered. Often, substantial policy change takes years to pass and implement; it is possible that the governor is the only actor who will serve long enough to oversee the many different phases of policy creation.

Actors in the political process perceive this change in relative power. A survey of lobbyists who work to influence policy outcomes revealed that they now think that governors, agency heads, interest groups, and even legislative staff members have become more influential over policy development than legislators. This opinion represents a substantial shift—after all, passing legislation to implement new policies or change old ones is traditionally the primary role of legislators. If these other actors now play a larger part in that process, the legislature's role in state politics has been redefined.

The legislators themselves perceive a change in relative power as well. A survey of legislative leaders across all fifty states found that, compared to their peers in states without term limits, the leaders in term-limited states indicated significantly higher gains in influence by the governor, bureaucracy, courts, and committee staff. Furthermore, the legislative leaders in states with term limits also indicated that committee leaders and senior members have lost influence compared to those in states without term limits.

A survey of all legislators picked up on this change in perception of power as well, with the governors and members of the bureaucracy being seen as gaining power over legislative outcomes relative to legislators after term limits took effect. Both leaders and rank-and-file legislators perceive that they now play a smaller role in policy development than they did before term limits were implemented. Furthermore, these legislators believe that the executive branch experienced a net gain in power because of this change. The advocates of term limits were not, of course, pushing for more power in another branch of government; they were hoping for more citizen input. With the exception of more input from interest groups, this has certainly not been the outcome. From that perspective, the term-limit movement has not been a success. Nevertheless, it has had the effect of improving the governor's position in legislative-executive relations. Governors are more powerful in lawmaking as a result of legislative term limits.

This shift in relative power is especially clear in the state budget process. When the governor and the legislature disagree about the budget, the legislature has less leverage when negotiating with the governor in states with term limits. Budget policy impacts nearly all other state policies, and given the global importance of the budget, decreased budgetary power means legislatures in term-limited states have less power in general. It seems that the legislature's loss is the governor's gain in this arena, too.

Many changes are taking place today in all fifty state governments. Professionalization, divided government, and term limits each alter the structure of state legislatures. It is difficult to say whether there has been a substantial shift overall in the balance of power between the legislature and the executive branch. Some changes, such as professionalization and divided government, seem to detract from the governor's power, whereas legislative term limits seem to add to it. Multiple trends have influenced and will continue to influence the manner in which the two branches interact.

The Nature of Executive-Legislative Relations.   Legislative professionalism, divided government, and legislative term limits have combined to substantially change the nature of executive-legislative relations and will continue to do so in the years ahead. In particular, term limits have only very recently started to impact on these dynamics. All of these developments need to be watched in the future to see how they will continue to alter executive-legislative relations.

Professionalization of the legislature may initially give legislators more policy control, as they can play a more active and ongoing role in state policy. However, the ultimate impact may be smoother and more productive state-level government all around. Professionalization can lead to a better working relationship between the governor and the legislature, and it may actually give the governor better partners to work with in pursuit of sound policy production.

Divided government is more of an unknown feature in terms of how it contributes to the dynamic between the legislative and the executive branches. When the legislature is united in its opposition to the governor, with both chambers being of the opposite party, perhaps divided government strengthens the legislature's relative power. At least to the public casually observing politics, it looks as if the legislators are more powerful because they can present a unified front and hold up the governor's policy proposals. When the two chambers themselves are controlled by different parties, it is more difficult to predict how the balance of power between the two branches will be affected.

Term limits are the only clear change that reduces the power of the legislature and adds to the governor's overall power. While most legislatures grappling with the implementation of term limits are developing coping skills, such as leadership training and other ways of passing down institutional knowledge, term limits do make it more difficult for legislators to play a dominant role in policy development. They simply do not serve long enough to walk a policy through agenda setting, bill adoption, implementation, and evaluation. Other actors—such as interest groups, agency heads, and, perhaps most important, the governor—play a more active role in all steps of policy development because they have greater longevity. Clearly, this lessens the legislature's overall political power and diminishes its relative position in dealing with the governor.

The relationship between the governor and the legislature has a large impact on the overall operations of government in the state. A governor must constantly be aware of all the activities in the state capitol and consider how he or she will react when a new bill is announced. Will the governor sign the bill and create new state law? Or will he or she veto the bill and hunker down for a battle between the branches? Because the interaction between these two branches sets the pace for all the work of state government, the relationship between the legislature and the governor is the most important element of the political environment for determining gubernatorial success.

GOVERNORS AND INTEREST GROUPS

While governors and legislators are arguably the most important players in terms of what state government does, governors must interact with many actors beyond the members of the legislature. Some of these actors, though working closely with public officials, are not public officials themselves. Interest groups are chief among the extragovernmental actors that influence the role of the governors in the states.

An interest group is "an association of individuals or organizations or a public or private institution that, on the basis of one or more shared concerns, attempts to influence public policy in its favor" (Thomas and Hrebenar 2004:102). Interest groups represent individuals, businesses, and other entities that have a stake in governmental decision making. Many of these groups promote the goals of interests from outside government. However, governmental actors may also act as interest groups as they attempt to influence the actions of state government.

Most members of the public seem to have negative attitudes about interest groups. They are perceived as serving narrow, specialized concerns and are often thought to be destructive to the public good. To be sure, interest groups have, at times, participated in inappropriate or illegal activities, and such experiences are probably why the public is so skeptical. Yet at the same time, Americans join these groups by the tens of millions. It is undeniable that many different interests find a voice through these organizations and that the presence of these many and varied groups has significant consequences, both positive and negative, for the governor's place in the political system in the states.

Though these groups are sometimes viewed in a negative light, they are also a necessary outlet for those outside of government hoping to have their voices heard. James Madison, one of the founding fathers of the United States, wrote about the potential dangers of groups (he used the term *factions*) for the success of the young American government. However, he also noted that such groups are inevitable in a free society and must therefore be controlled or put to good use rather than destroyed. Since the government guarantees the rights of people outside of government to express their opinions and pursue their own goals, interest groups inevitably form. Madison also argued that because the country is so vast and the interests would be so varied, no one group could gain too much power or do too much damage. This argument has not always worked so well at the state level. An individual state is obviously a much smaller entity than United States: the land area is smaller, the people are less diverse, and the economy likely depends on fewer industries. Due to these circumstances, certain interest groups have sometimes been formidable actors in state governments. Observers often mention that the Anaconda Steel Company essentially dominated politics in Montana into the 1960s, just as the gaming industry continues to exert a great deal of influence in the politics of Nevada today. However, the power that a single interest is able to exercise often depends on what other groups exist. When, for example, a state has one key industry, such as coal mining, the needs of that industry and its supporters will likely be taken very seriously by the state government. Their needs may, in fact, be better tended to than the needs of other groups or even the collective needs of the rest of the state. Such lopsided politics can occur when only a small number of groups organize to pursue their interests. When more groups organize and work for their goals, the outcomes are less one-sided and more likely to benefit multiple groups. Though some states continue to be dominated by a single interest, the states as a whole generally have more diverse interest group systems today than ever before. This change is worth examining briefly because the number of groups and the power they exercise certainly impacts the governor's ability to get things done in the state.

A state interest group system is defined as the "array of groups and organizations, both formal and informal, and the lobbyists who represent them working to affect public policy within a state" (Thomas and Hrebenar 2004, 103). The effect that interest groups have on the work of the governor and the rest of the executive branch depends on the state interest group system. Groups may impact the governor in at least two primary ways. First, the policy influence of groups can be either helpful or destructive for the governor's goals. Interest groups may exert power independent of and potentially in opposition to the governor, which may limit the governor's ability to achieve his or her policy goals. Conversely, groups may find common ground with the governor and join him or her in pursuit of similar goals. Second, groups may benefit or hurt the governor in a more strictly political sense in that they often participate actively in the gubernatorial campaign and election.

From the governor's perspective, interest groups and their goals may come into play in multiple ways. Groups may donate money to the governor's campaign (or to that of the opponent) by forming political action committees (PACs). They may seek the governor's public support of a particular group goal. They may lobby the legislature or the governor's office on legislation of interest to both the group and the governor. They may also lobby those in the executive branch who are responsible for writing the rules and regulations that put state laws into effect. Groups can be extremely effective at this point, since activities of this type are often less open to public scrutiny. Further, such rule making is critical to the effect that laws will actually have in a state. Again, groups may be on the same side as the governor or in opposition to the governor's stated or unstated preferred position. Given this basic fact, an interest group may either contribute to a governor's success (by acting as a partner) or serve as a roadblock to the governor's goals at various junctures along the way.

Interest Group Systems

In the twenty-first century, many groups representing myriad different interests operate in the states, but this has not always been the case. Before 1900, there were few organized groups, and only a very narrow range of interests was represented. By the 1930s, five broad categories of interests could be identified: business, labor unions and professional groups, education, agriculture, and local government. However, since state governments did not really do too much during that period, sometimes entire legislative sessions would pass without witnessing any activity by these groups.

After the 1960s, the picture was very different. State interest group systems gradually became more pluralistic. That is, there was a notable increase in the number of groups lobbying and also in the variety or range of these groups. New sorts of interests organized themselves to advocate on behalf of various social issues (the needs of the poor or the handicapped, for example), underrepresented groups (such as women and racial minorities), and concerns about the quality of government (on taxation or term limits, for instance). Some groups are active across all of the states; others are particular to one or a few states.

In addition to being more numerous and varied, interest groups are now more active than ever before. They lobby more intensively than was the case in the 1960s or 1970s. They have more regular contact with public officials and use more sophisticated techniques.

Some groups remain on the scene for a long time. Others have short life spans. David Lowery and Virginia Gray (1995) have found that in many cases, a group stops lobbying government because the group itself ceases to exist. This situation is most likely to involve membership organizations (rather than business or industry groups). Nonetheless, the number and variety of groups forming in the states has continued to expand into the twenty-first century. The presence of these many and diverse groups illustrates the importance of state government. The number of groups in the states first skyrocketed at the same time that state governments took on increasingly important roles in the federal system—in the 1960s and 1970s. Though change has certainly occurred since then, states continue to be key actors in American government, and interest groups continue to work to influence them.

Most of these groups are not primarily political organizations. They often form due to some common economic or social interest (such as businesses forming a trade association or parents of children with special needs joining together to seek help for their kids). Such organizations serve the needs of their members in many ways, providing resources and information, creating outlets for social interaction and support, and so forth. However, pursuing the interests of a group's members often necessitates political activity at some point. Having made this jump into the public arena, groups perform many vital services for the states. They give voice to needs that may not have been heard before. They educate public officials and open a line of communication between citizens and their government. They also sometimes work to help certain officials gain office (or to prevent others from doing so).

This last role, their work in campaigns and elections, is one of the more controversial features of interest groups' activities. Understandably, groups view certain public officials as supportive of their goals and see others as unsupportive. And they sometimes work to assist their "friends" obtain and retain office. Presumably, public officials who benefit from such help will remember this in the future, which causes some people to worry that this connection might corrupt the political process.

What Do Interest Groups Do?

Groups work to influence the decisions of state government. They direct their attention to all branches of government, though people often think most of their work is in the legislature. In fact, groups hope to influence lawmaking by governors and legislators, rule making by the executive branch, and even decisions made by state courts.

Groups use multiple tactics to achieve their goals. Though these activities vary greatly, they are all essentially directed at influencing government. The tactics can be classified into two broad categories: direct strategies and indirect strategies. Direct strategies refer to those activities aimed directly at government officials to influence their decision making. Such strategies include lobbying legislators and the governor, testifying at legislative hearings, and drafting sample legislation. They require access to decision makers, which not all groups have. Indirect strategies are not directly aimed at public officials. Instead, these activities have to do with gaining access to or influencing the environment in which governmental decisions are made. Indirect activities include working on election campaigns and donating money to them, as well as developing and funding public relations campaigns.

When groups have connections to public officials, they are most likely to pursue the direct approach and simply contact these individuals and ask for their support. The most common type of direct contact is called lobbying. Through this process, members of interest groups or their representatives (sometimes hired lobbyists) attempt to influence public officials or build positive relationships that may be useful in some future situation. In the course of this interaction, lobbyists often give public officials information designed to both educate the official and sway his or her opinion. A minority (about 25 percent) of lobbyists at the state level are "contract lobbyists," typically hired because of their knowledge of the political system and their connections to public officials. The most common type of lobbyist is the "in-house lobbyist," meaning employees of organizations, corporations, or other groups. These lobbyists tend to have a great deal of technical knowledge about their areas of interest. A final type might be referred to as "citizen or volunteer lobbyists." They commonly represent small nonprofit or community organizations that lack the resources to employ full-time employees or hired lobbyists.

While groups lobby all parts of state government, they direct the majority of their lobbying efforts to legislators, who are generally fairly accessible to them. Lobbyists target legislative leaders and legislators serving on committees of relevance to their policy interests, since these members exert the greatest influence on pertinent legislation. Different groups, of course, have different goals. Further, the goals of a particular group will change over time. Groups may advocate for new legislation, attempt to halt legislation that has been introduced, or simply work to maintain good relations with government officials in preparation for future support. Achieving the passage of new legislation is a major challenge, requiring the marshaling of considerable resources to carry legislation through the many steps of the state legislative process. Halting unwanted legislation is typically easier, as a group needs simply to defeat it at a single point in the process; thus, they can focus on specific activities, such as getting the support of a friendly committee chair (Thomas and Hrebenar 2004). Although rules and the stringency with which they are enforced differ markedly from state to state, groups lobbying state legislatures are required to register in all states today. In this way, the states hope to monitor those who are attempting to influence state legislators.

Though lobbying legislators is the most common lobbying activity, groups commonly combine this approach with other lobbying activities, such as lobbying the executive branch or even lobbying the governor directly. Lawmakers (in concert with the governor) make the law, of course, but they grant authority to the executive branch to draft the rules and regulations that carry out the laws. Sometimes, executive branch agencies exert a significant amount of influence over how laws are actually carried out, especially when it comes to complicated technical matters.

Consequently, lobbyists often monitor executive branch activities and testify before agency hearings. The minutiae of legislative implementation are commonly vital to groups whose members will be impacted by new laws. Not all states require those lobbying the executive branch to register their activities, so less is known about how common their activities are. It seems likely that fewer groups lobby executive agencies than lobby the legislature, but for groups interested in laws of a highly technical nature, executive rule making may be even more important than the adoption of the law by the legislature.

A small subset of interest groups might be able to contact the governor directly and request a meeting or ask for his or her support for group goals. All governors have extremely busy schedules, and their time is precious and their attention scarce. If a group has access to the governor, this can be a very effective means of getting the governor's support. However, this technique is not available to the vast number of groups.

Interest groups most directly affect the work of the governor in their positions as allies or opponents in the policymaking process. If groups share the governor's goals, they can be valuable resources, working jointly toward their policy aspirations. When groups are in disagreement with the governor, they may serve as opponents in the process. Depending how well organized they are and how open their access to key legislative leaders is, such groups may be formidable opponents.

Indirect tactics employed by interest groups exert a different influence on the governor's work in the state. Many groups form political action committees through which they can contribute money to state election campaigns. All states establish legal guidelines for such contributions (see Chapter 4), but collectively, PAC moneys make up a significant portion of the funds received by gubernatorial candidates. Groups give campaign funds to candidates who share their policy goals in hopes that after the election, they will have a friend in the governor's mansion. Incumbents typically benefit from higher levels of PAC contributions because they typically win reelection and the interest groups the PACs represent hope to maintain access to the likely winner. However, under extraordinary circumstances, groups may mobilize in support of a challenger and contribute to his or her campaign. They might also fund and produce ad campaigns in support of or in opposition to particular candidates.

Beyond the election cycle, groups sometimes launch public relations campaigns to mobilize public support or opposition to legislation being considered by the state legislature. To the extent such groups' preferences coincide with the governor's, their public relations campaigns may either benefit or harm the goals of the governor. For example, if a legislature facing financial constraints is considering legislation to cut funding in public education, parents' or teachers' groups may launch a television campaign to make others in the state aware of the cuts being considered. This sort of public relations campaign is most likely to be used by groups lacking access to internal decision makers. But if the campaign is successful, it will mobilize others in the state to contact their public officials and, it is hoped, sway their opinions on the issue.

What Impact Do Interest Groups Have?

Political scientists coined the term *iron triangles* to describe relations among government and interest groups. The idea was that the actors involved in decision making in any policy area fell into three categories—the points of a triangle. One point represented important members of the legislature—most likely, key members of committees responsible for the policy. The second point represented actors in the executive branch who were responsible for writing the rules and regulations to carry out the laws. The third point represented actors outside of government that were concerned about the topic—interest groups. At first glance, it might seem that the actors representing the three points of the triangle were in conflict with one another. Those writing the laws may have had different goals than those in the public who would be affected by them or those who actually had to put the laws into force. However, what often happened was that the various groups represented in the triangle settled into comfortable arrangements. They knew one another and knew each other's needs and goals. As a result, they often worked together, coming to collective decisions on critical issues that arose in their policy domain.

More recently, researchers have characterized the collections of important actors within particular policy arenas more broadly. These entities, often called issue networks or subgovernments, bring other actors, such as experts from outside of government into the fold. However, the general point remains. A limited, predictable set of actors is likely to be interested in governmental decision making in any given policy arena.

Strikingly, one of the most powerful figures in the states—the governor—does not really occupy a point on the triangle or a place within the network. In theory, since the governor heads the executive branch, one could assume that the point assigned to the bureaucracy is the governor's entrance to the triangle, but this may not really work in practice. As noted elsewhere in this volume, while the governor sits at the top of the executive branch organizationally, he or she cannot always direct the decision making of the bureaucracy. Indeed, many bureaucrats are chosen separately from the governor and do not necessarily feel an allegiance to the chief executive's goals. Governors may therefore have to struggle against all of the members of these networks when they hope to make significant changes in the status quo. At that point, another set of actors—those in the bureaucracy—may get involved and impact the ability of the governor to lead.

GOVERNORS AND THE BUREAUCRACY

Since the governor carries the title of chief executive, it would be natural to assume that he or she controls the executive branch. And to some extent, this is true, for the governor is ultimately responsible for ensuring that the laws of the state are faithfully executed. Governors have also gained greater formal powers to assist them in playing this role. They appoint many executive branch officials (though not all of them), and they exert a significant amount of control over the budget requests for executive agencies. However, governors are not the only actors attempting to influence the state bureaucracies. Since legislatures write the laws that the executive branch is charged with implementing, legislators often hope to influence how those laws are executed. Further, since legislators delegate a significant amount of discretion to executive branch officials, they retain the right to oversee how that discretion is exercised. In addition to these two actors, executive officials themselves sometimes seek to make their own choices. These officials typically possess knowledge and expertise that leads them to form preferences regarding how the laws implemented by their agencies should be managed. Even when such administrators are appointed by the governor, they may not always agree with the governor's policy positions. Agency heads with significant experience and a broad set of political supporters outside the governor's mansion may actually be able to pursue their policy interests to the exclusion of the governor's goals.

This scenario is another example of the overlapping authority created by the separation-of-powers system in the states. Should governors desire to exert significant influence over the work of the executive branch, they may face opposition from legislators and from high-level bureaucrats themselves. The struggle to control state bureaucracy is one of the ongoing sagas of state politics, but it is important to understand that this is not simply a power struggle between the governor and other actors. Multiple actors have legitimate reasons for trying to influence what the bureaucracy does. The competing claims are at least in part a result of different philosophies about who should control the bureaucracy, and these different philosophies have been around for a long time.

Herbert Kaufman (1956), a prominent scholar of public administration, labeled these competing theories "representativeness," "neutral competence," and "executive leadership." Representativeness, or control of the bureaucracy through popularly elected legislative officials, was preeminent early in the country's history. The primacy of the representativeness doctrine was replaced by the idea of neutral competence during the Progressive reform movement. Neutral competence advocated for expertise and objective standards in the administration of government. An emphasis on executive leadership emerged early in the twentieth century, in reaction to the fragmentation created by adherence to the first two values. This doctrine advocated greater gubernatorial control over the bureaucracy. As noted earlier, the argument has definitely not been settled. Each institution has its own goals. Administrative agencies struggle for autonomy, governors push for their own political aims as they exert policy leadership, and legislators try to direct state agencies down paths consistent with their goals (either as individual legislators or as the legislative institution). In addition to having a legitimate claim on control of the bureaucracy, all three sets of actors (the governors, the legislators, and the bureaucrats) are today more professional and have more resources to influence the bureaucracy if they want to. So all three could exert control over the bureaucracy, which leads to the obvious question of who really does exert that control. Does the governor dominate in this domain, or do the other actors and their motivations limit the governor here? One answer to this question is, it depends. The situation has changed substantially over time. In the mid-1960s, a survey of state administrative agency heads found that governors and legislators were each influential in certain ways but that legislators seemed to have an edge. A majority of administrators reported that the legislature had more control over their agencies, yet many of these same individuals viewed the governor as more supportive of the agencies' goals. More recently, the general trend has seemed to favor the governors. In the decades following the first surveys, more and more agency heads have reported that the governor exerted the greatest level of control over their agencies. At the same time, legislative influence seems to have declined.

Aside from general control of the bureaucratic decision making, one might also wonder who controls decisions about the money allocated to the various agencies. In the 1960s and early 1970s, agency heads said that legislatures were more likely than governors to reduce their budgets. But in the 1980s and 1990s, governors seemed to engage in this budget cutting more than they had before. Further, more and more agency heads said that both the governor and the legislature engaged in budget oversight activities. This finding emphasizes again that the governor does not have free rein even in the executive realm. But if governors are not the only prominent actors in the executive branch, they are nonetheless critically important ones. Part of their success in recent decades seems to have arisen from the greater formal powers that have been vested in the governorship. As Chapter 2 explained, today's governors have a great many tools available to them, which have been vital for those hoping to exert influence in the bureaucracy. At the same time, legislatures have definitely not given up on the goal of influencing the executive branch. Their influence continues to be felt on occasion, especially in the budgetary arena. However, if there is a battle between the governor and the legislature for executive control, the governor has the preferred position. Being a single actor gives the chief executive an edge. Legislatures rarely act in pursuit of a unified goal, for they are made up of hundreds of members. The tools the governor possesses also give him or her an advantage. Finally, legislators are likely to place less emphasis on exerting influence in this arena. As legislatures have become more professionalized, legislators must worry about lawmaking, campaigning, and constituency work, all of which typically take precedence over the job of overseeing the bureaucracy (Bowling, Ferguson, and Wright 2002; Wright 1967).

GOVERNORS AND THE MEDIA

The high profile of the governorship in the states both grows from and benefits from modern mass media. The media, especially television, have contributed to the stature of the governor by the coverage they have given to the office. Media outlets pay more attention to the governor than to any other state governmental actor, which is reflected in their coverage. Knowing this, governors are attuned to shaping the coverage they receive in the media. In addition, they employ their access to the media in fulfilling the many roles of their office. Finally, the media may focus attention on public problems and thereby force governors to add those problems to their own agendas. While the relationship between governors and the media may occasionally be difficult, both sides generally benefit from working closely together.

As noted, state and national news media outlets dedicate more attention to the governors than to any other state figures. The fact that the governor is a single individual (as opposed to a legislature that may be made up of hundreds of members) makes the chief executive easier to cover. The singular nature of the office also seems to capture the attention of the public. And the governorship is perhaps easier to comprehend than the tens of committees doing the work of state legislature.

This high media profile has both positive and negative consequences for the governor. The American media collectively function as a watchdog, monitoring the decisions and behaviors of governmental actors. As a result, they may uncover or report on misconduct by the governor or members of his or her administration. Additionally, the media may assess the performance of the governor's administration. They may compare the governor's actions to the promises spelled out in the campaign. They may also compare the current governor to his or her predecessor, either favorably or unfavorably. While this is clearly part of the role of a free press, the governor's office would certainly prefer to receive only positive coverage and, if possible, to control the information the media report.

Consequently, all governors and their staffs dedicate a lot of time and energy to trying to influence the content of reporting about the administration. Governors often hold press conferences and issue press releases and private interviews, in an attempt to shape the way in which the media cover them. They hope to influence both the character and the content of the coverage they receive.

Second, given the media's preoccupation with the governorship, the states' chief executives have unique access to media coverage, which can be used in pursuit of their goals. Unlike any other state official, governors can nearly always get coverage if they want it. Clearly, all governors have to pay attention to their relationship with the media, and the smart ones will work hard to make sure that the relationship is a positive one.

Good media coverage can draw the attention of the public to a governor's key goals. The flow of ideas between the public and the governor is carried by the media, and if people are impressed enough by the governor's arguments, they may be motivated to contact their legislators on his or her behalf. Access to the media can therefore be a powerful tool in enabling a governor to mobilize support. Indeed, there is no other mechanism by which a governor's ideas can be spread so widely to so many audiences.

Yet the relationship with the media is not wholly under the control of the governor. In addition to the press interactions the governor can plan for, other media coverage will result from events that arise during his or her term in office. Reporters may bring forth allegations that the governor must respond to. And when reports on the state's economy are published in the media, the governor is expected to comment. In other words, a governor is not completely free to define the topics the media will address.

When a crisis occurs, for example, the chief executive must react publicly to fulfill the managerial role and to assuage the fears of the public. The media will be the means by which the public is made aware of the governor's actions, and how well he or she does will surely be reflected in the reporting that follows. When a governor falters in leadership, the media will carry that information to the public. When a governor appears strong and in charge, the public will view that through the media as well.

The media may also play a more direct role in public policymaking. Given their ability to draw the attention of the public to the stories they present, the media may actually bring policy questions to the forefront by granting them broad coverage. If the public responds to media stories about a given policy with sufficient attention, the governor may be forced to make that policy a priority and add it to the agenda he or she will pursue in the state legislature. For example, workplace safety might be placed in the public spotlight by media coverage of a fire or explosion at a facility that had not been appropriately inspected. If questions persist and are serious enough to cause criticism and concern among the public or interest groups, the governor may have no choice but to address the issue. Otherwise, he or she will appear out of step with or unconcerned about the needs of the public.

Most governors are reasonably comfortable in their relationship with the media, since it was through running media-based campaigns that they managed to get elected to office. Still, some governors are better at interacting with the media than others; some like this part of the job much more than their colleagues do. As a result of their own attitudes (and perhaps those of their close advisers), some governors hold numerous press conferences and give frequent interviews, making themselves regularly available to the media. Others are suspicious of the media or perhaps just protective of their limited time and therefore stay more remote from the media. Such an approach, though perhaps understandable, would not seem to be the best choice for a public official who will clearly depend on the media in subsequent endeavors (both pursuing future policy goals and seeking future office).

Modern governors are in the media spotlight, which is both a benefit of the office and a potential liability. Those who are good at communicating with the public via the media (and who avoid major scandals) will, on balance, benefit from this high profile. Others may struggle with this role and therefore fail to capitalize on the potential benefits it offers.

GOVERNORS AND THE COURTS

Though the separation of powers defines the responsibilities of the executive, legislative, and judicial branches as distinct from one another, it also sets up a system in which each branch has some control over and some opportunity to influence the other branches. Governors and legislatures most obviously work closely together in making law; the governors and their representatives lobby the legislators directly to identify their goals and if necessary work toward a compromise when those goals do not align with the administration's. But relations between the governor and the courts are different. These two branches do not have constant contact with one another, and governors would typically not attempt to directly influence court decisions by lobbying judges. Nevertheless, governors both influence and are influenced by the decisions of the courts. In many states, they have a hand in choosing the judges who will sit on the state bench. This appointment power surely offers at least the possibility that the governors' reach may extend beyond the legislative and executive arenas into the judicial arena. For their part, the courts regulate the relationships among state governmental actors, sometimes passing judgment on gubernatorial actions and refereeing disputes between governors and legislatures.

In a number of states, judges are chosen by popular election. But many other states give this authority to other actors, notably the governor, the legislature, and judicial selection panels. These states reformed their mechanisms of choosing judges so that judges would not be so explicitly involved in electoral politics. In theory, having governors, legislators, and merit selection committees choose judges means that judicial qualifications and fitness for office will be given greater emphasis than political considerations. However, it would be naive to assert that governors and legislatures make such decisions without political motivations. On the contrary, governors are keenly aware that their choices for judgeships—particularly for higher courts with appellate jurisdiction—will have long-standing consequences. Consequently, they (and their administrations) devote considerable care to this process. Judges often remain on the bench long after governors have left office, so in states where governors get to choose judges, they exercise some influence over judicial decision making. At the same time, judges, once placed on the bench, are not beholden to the public officials who put them there, and though governors choose judges they believe share their political philosophy, the judges often surprise them. Having appointed a judge to a state court, governors retain no further formal influence over their decisions.

Occasionally, governors interact with the state courts in ways other than through the judicial appointment process. Courts may, for example, be called on to settle disputes between the executive and legislative branches. Though such disputes rarely end up in court, they do arise on a frequent basis. Relationships between governors and legislatures are not always harmonious. In fact, the system of separated powers that is employed by all states sets up these two branches to be in conflict with one another. As the responsibilities of states have grown, relations among governors and legislatures have become even more complicated as everyone jockeys for position in a changing political context. On top of this are the traditional differences that have always marked legislative-gubernatorial relations. Individuals in high political office typically have strong personalities and perhaps large egos, traits that may lead to personality conflicts and perhaps jealousy over the relative political strength of one actor or another. Further, while governors serve the entire state, legislators serve much smaller segments, where the needs of local people, businesses, and industries may be at odds with the overall needs of the state (at least as they are perceived by the governor). When these long-standing sources of conflict are exacerbated but the existence of divided government, as occurs in many states, it is not surprising that governors and legislatures often do not get along. Closely tied to the fact of divided party control is the idea of party competition. When one party has a large majority, a minority party that hopes to have any impact at all on state policy must go along with that majority, at least to some degree. Where the parties are closely matched, however, governors and legislators of different parties may actually be discouraged from agreeing, in the interest of setting one party apart from the other in preparation for the next election. The consequences of such disagreements between the legislative and executive branches are broad-ranging and potentially very significant. In most cases, the disagreements are managed without too much disruption to the state lawmaking process, but in other instances, it falls to the courts to serve as referee.

Courts may be called on to define the powers of the other branches of state government. The dynamic state environment and the shifting responsibilities of states (versus the national government) can give rise to disputes over the limits of legislative and executive authority. When governors and legislators cannot solve such disagreements, they often turn to the courts for resolution. In at least a third of the states, for instance, courts have issued rulings on the subject of legislative involvement in the appropriation of federal funds. The spending of these funds has traditionally been controlled by governors, but some legislatures have asserted a right to influence this process. Other questions have arisen as to the constitutionality of the legislative veto (a veto sometimes used by legislators) and the appropriate use of the veto by governors. Since the 1970s, governors have increasingly and creatively made use of the item and amendatory vetoes—one of the side effects of enhanced gubernatorial involvement in the legislative arena, whereby governors attempt to get the most out of the tools at their disposal. When legislatures feel the governors have gone too far, they may attempt to employ political mechanisms to send signals to the chief executive. When that approach fails, the dispute may end up in court. The state courts are then in the position of weighing the relative powers of the other two branches, a very delicate job indeed. Critics of such judicial oversight worry that the courts are poorly positioned to gather accurate political information about the other two branches when they are in conflict. More important, judicial handling of political disagreements tends to result in absolute decision making rather than nuance and compromise. Such decisions may permanently shift the balance of power from one branch to another in a way that may harm the system overall. For whatever reason, legislatures are more commonly on the losing end in such disputes: across the states, when the judiciary has weighed in on disagreements between the legislative and executive branches, it has tended to favor greater executive authority at the expense of legislative power. An extreme example arose in Wisconsin in 1988. Wisconsin allows its governor a "partial veto," which gives the chief executive the ability to create new words from an assortment of letters left from vetoed sections of budget bills. Legislators took Governor Tommy Thompson to court, protesting against 37 of his 290 item vetoes and arguing that he used the partial veto to change legislative intent (a clear violation of the separation-of-powers doctrine). Governor Thompson did use the veto aggressively. He changed the length of time a juvenile could be held in a secure detention facility from forty-eight hours (the language in the bill adopted by the legislature) to ten days (the governor's preferred language). Wisconsin's high court did not support the legislators' claims. Instead, it indicated (by a four-to-three vote) that the governor's power extended to individual letters, spaces, and punctuation marks in an appropriations bill. The court majority ruled that the governor could use the veto however he chose as long as the end result was a "complete, workable bill" that the legislature could have passed in the first place. Other state courts have not granted the governor as much discretion as in the Wisconsin case, but they nevertheless have interpreted the law to the benefit of gubernatorial power.

The responsibility of the courts sets them apart from the other branches of government. Whereas governors and legislatures are engaged in the political process of drafting legislation and building coalitions to gain or block passage of that legislation, courts come into play after such decisions have been made. Judges must wait for questions to be brought to them, and then they must pass judgment based on the case at hand. Court decisions often have broad-ranging political consequences—for example, when a court orders the legislature to restructure its education funding system—and the other branches of government must respond to such decisions and their consequences. And finally, though the courts are more insulated from the influence of the governor than is the legislature, governors do have some opportunity to affect the decisions of courts (by choosing the judges) and the consequences of those decisions (by influencing legislative decision making in response to court rulings).

GOVERNORS AND WASHINGTON

The discussion thus far has examined how actors within state government and in the larger state political context affect the work of the governor. But the governor's environment is more complex still. Since the United States is a federal system, state governments always function within an environment of multiple power centers: while state governments (and governors) exercise a significant level of autonomy, they are also undeniably affected by the actions of the national government and even by the choices of surrounding states. This fact means that governors must devote attention to relationships beyond state borders. It also means that as the heads of state governments, governors must grapple with the problems created for the states by their neighbors and the national government, as well as work to maximize the benefits that might result from actions emanating from Washington.

As David Walker (2000, 21) explained:

What federalism means specifically in terms of the territorial division of powers and of the appropriate mode of relationships between the two constitutionally recognized levels of government (national and state) has been the subject of con tention, even violent conflict, during the past two hundred years. In part, this is because the Framers for good and practical reasons left many questions relating to federalism unanswered or unclear . . . and in part the contention stems from their overriding desire to create a "flexible instrument concerned with the functions and the practice of government."

The relationship between Washington, D.C., and the states has always been a dynamic one. In early arrangements, the states tended to have the most power. Later periods saw a huge growth in the size and activities of the national government. While states have remained important all along, their areas of authority have fluctuated. Scholars of federalism have identified multiple phases of federalism in U.S. history. During each phase, the relationship between the states and the national government has shifted somewhat. In the latest phase, the rhetoric of national government, if not always the actual decisions, has emphasized the "devolving" of powers to the states. The idea of devolution is that the national government should hand over more power and responsibilities to the states, since they are closer to the people and therefore better able to actually serve the public interests. This devolution sometimes means more power for the states and, as a result, for the governors. In that sense, devolution has emboldened governors. However, devolution at times has meant that states have greater responsibility but lack the resources needed to do their work. Given this reality, governors attempt to influence decision making in Washington to protect against potential negative outcomes and to encourage outcomes more beneficial to themselves and their states.

Broadly speaking, governors have two priorities when lobbying Washington. They must respond to actions of the national government, and they must attempt to influence those actions in ways that will benefit their states.

States often have the job of administering programs developed by the national government. As a result, a significant burden may fall on the states, especially if the national government does not provide sufficient funds to put its programs into effect. Another major component of the relationship between the national and state governments in the modern period is the flow of money going to the states (and localities). Though recent cutbacks in federal spending have changed the situation dramatically, the national government has been a major source of income for the states.

The dependence of the states on the national government for funds (which has varied significantly over time) is reason enough for governors to devote considerable time and energy to developing relationships in Washington. Congress generally decides how the money will be distributed to the states and localities and for what purposes it will be used. Congressional revisions of distribution formulas, changes in eligibility requirements for grants, and reductions in congressional appropriations can all have extremely significant consequences for the states. Governors must at least be well aware of such changes, and preferably, they will manage to influence the changes to help their states and preserve the support they depend on. During periods of federal government retrenchment, rather than working to build affirmative national government support, governors must work to cushion the impact of federal cutbacks and unfunded mandates or to just hold on to what they have. They know that shifts in responsibility from the national government to the states will ultimately place greater challenges on their own desks.

Governors must advocate for positive changes and also attempt to protect their states against negative ones. To pursue these goals, they have undertaken both individual and joint political lobbying activities. Individual governors employ intergovernmental coordinators, set up offices in Washington, and occasionally participate in lobbying activities themselves. Governors are represented collectively by various national, partisan, and regional associations. The two types of lobbying serve somewhat different purposes. Individualized lobbying is directed at state-specific needs, while collective action is typically geared toward generalized benefits for multiple states.

Individualized Lobbying

Nearly all governors have developed individualized links with Washington, employing various techniques to create these linkages. The most obvious connection between a state and the national government is the state's delegation to Congress. Congress is also where many of the decisions that the governors are concerned about take place. Since members of Congress each represent a district (in the House of Representatives) or a state (in the Senate), one might assume that they are the natural voice of the states in Washington. However, over the last decades, governors have increasingly questioned whether they can depend on their representatives in Washington to fully speak for the needs of the state back home. The stakes have been growing as well, especially because of the states' mounting dependence on Washington for funds. There are good reasons for this skepticism. Members of Congress, in their quests to represent the state (or district), address the desires of their constituencies and the groups and interests that combined to elect them to office. They rarely have reason to be particularly concerned with the policy and operational concerns of the state government. In short, they represent the state, not the state government. For this reason, governors eventually came to believe that a more direct lobbying process, emanating from state government, was needed.

In the 1960s and 1970s, they began to set themselves up as the chief lobbyists for their states. Most governors have hired an intergovernmental relations (IG) coordinator (a federal-state relations manager) for their offices to assist them in carrying out this role. The duties of these officials historically have differed from state to state. Some provide an early-warning function, advising governors of pending rules, regulations, or congressional actions that might impact state government. Other IG coordinators work to maximize federal moneys coming to the states by offering technical assistance to grant writers. These officials are also critical in that they are a central coordination point for the many intergovernmental activities being undertaken by the governor and his or her cabinet agencies. Such coordination helps to eliminate duplicated effort and to make sure that all important fronts are covered. Finally, IG coordinators serve to bring a gubernatorial perspective to negotiations taking place between federal agencies and various parts of the state executive branch. This function is an important one, since even members of the state executive branch do not always speak for the governor.

In addition to the IG coordinator within the governor's office, many (though not all) governors have established state offices in Washington. The thinking is that the interests of the state government can be represented most effectively through a Washington outpost of state personnel who maintain a presence with federal agencies and with congressional staffs. Officers located in Washington are more aware of the nuances of actions taken by the administration and Congress, and they are better placed to assess the state-federal implications of the positions advanced by the governor. Having officers located in Washington also makes it possible for representatives from multiple states to coordinate with one another and work out compromises acceptable to a variety of states and their interests. Most of the Washington offices are actually located in the same building, the Hall of the States, which enhances the possibilities for joint action.

New York was the first state to set up an office in Washington, in 1941. By 1976, about half the states had Washington offices, and by the mid-1980s, there were thirty. The number peaked at thirty-six in the late 1990s, but declined to thirty-one as of 1998. All but two of these offices are established by the governor's office and under the direct control of the governor; the other two regularly represent the interests of the governor. These offices are clearly outposts of gubernatorial interests. Further evidence of this fact is that some state legislatures have established their own offices in Washington. The small decline in the number of governors' offices in Washington in recent years emphasizes that not all governors feel that maintaining such an office is worth the considerable resources required—particularly during difficult economic times. The majority, however, remain convinced of the necessity of such a constant presence in the nation's capital.

Some governors have avoided creating offices in Washington for reasons unrelated to the scarcity of resources. State politics scholar Jennifer Jensen (2000) found that in some states, governors actually feel political pressure *not* to establish such offices. For example, in states where the public tends to be distrustful of Washington (particularly western states), governors view clearer connections to Washington as a political liability rather than a benefit. Other patterns can also be discerned. Governors from states with more professionalized legislatures are more likely than others to establish Washington offices, as are younger and more ambitious governors. While the governors' personal choices are partially responsible for establishing state offices in D.C., other forces outside the governors' control are also vital in determining how the states' chief executives go about establishing relations with the national government.

Governors as Lobbyists

In addition to having representatives carrying the states' concerns to Washington, governors themselves sometimes take on this role. They communicate with members of Congress, with officials of the federal executive branch, and even occasionally with the president directly. First, governors must work with the Congress, which of course holds the power to make laws. The governor as chief lobbyist relates to Congress on two levels—on issues specific to the home state that require some interaction between a governor and the state's own congressional delegation and on issues that have general importance to the states or state governments.

Governors also sometimes work through the federal executive branch. Here, they employ different strategies, depending on the question at hand. If a topic is important enough for the governor's personal attention, he or she will communicate directly with the appropriate cabinet secretary or someone at the White House, including the president. Less important issues are usually handled by a member of the governor's cabinet, who contacts a federal regional office or works through a lower-level division of the national executive branch (Beyle and Muchmore 1983).

The predominant concern of governors is necessarily their own states. Their relationships with their state delegations in Congress (or leaders key to state interests) are therefore more critical than their ability to exert influence on Congress in general. However, despite the apparent natural connection between a state's governor and its members of Congress, these relationships are not always successful. Some governors find their delegations open to state government needs; others find the relationship much more challenging. It seems that the success of these relationships depends greatly on personal friendship and interaction. It is worth noting here that members of Congress, particularly senators, may be wary of their governor because they may view him or her as a potential rival at some point in the future. Governors often do have aspirations for higher office, and it is possible that this ambition may complicate what is already an uneasy coalition (Beyle and Muchmore 1983).

Collective Lobbying Efforts

The National Governors Association is the largest and perhaps best known of the governors' organizations. Once largely a social organization, the NGA is increasingly concerned with lobbying the national government on behalf of the governors. It is one of the major public interest associations working in Washington, with lobbying, research, and state service staff dedicated to speaking for the collective interests of the nation's governors. It maintained this broad-based role through the 1980s. However, as the partisan composition of the nation's governors shifted to a Republican majority, the NGA struggled to adapt to the changing goals of its member governors. The NGA staff, accustomed to the preferences of its majority Democrat members, most often tried to work with federal agencies in order to increase federal programs and funding for the states. The ideological shift that occurred after the elections of 1994 meant that a majority of governors now preferred less government, and ultimately, they became somewhat suspicious of the NGA's orientation. Some Republican governors chose to work directly with the new Republican leadership in the U.S. Congress on their policy concerns, rather than working through the NGA. As a consequence, the NGA and its Democratic governor members were shut out of the process.

Other collective organizations also represent the nation's Republican and Democratic governors and speak for the governors of particular regions. The Republican Governors Association (RGA) was founded in 1963 to serve as the official public policy and political organization of the nation's Republican governors. This organization devotes it energies to representing the political ideas of the state Republican parties to lawmakers in Washington, as well as to raising and distributing money to assist Republican governors in their reelection bids. Similarly, the Democratic Governors Association (DGA) was founded in 1983, explicitly to assist Democratic gubernatorial candidates. In addition to this electoral role, the DGA works through the governors' policy forum series to develop positions on federal and state issues that affect the states.

Western and southern governors have also formed their own associations, bringing together chief executives of both parties who share similar political and economic challenges in their states. The Western Governors' Association (WGA) focuses on issues of regional concern, working to develop solutions to common problems and developing information that is made available to business and educational leaders. The WGA facilitates the forming of coalitions of governors to advocate for shared western interests before Congress and the executive branch. Each year, the chair of the WGA develops a strategic agenda. The 2004–2005 agenda included protecting threatened and endangered species, preparing for drought, ensuring water quality, and restoring and maintaining healthy forests and rangelands in the West.

Similarly, the Southern Governors' Association (SGA) offers the chief executives of the states in the South an arena for the exchange of ideas and for representing the common interests of their states. The SGA supports the work of the governors by providing a bipartisan forum to help shape and carry out national policy and to solve state and regional problems. It tracks national laws and regulations that will have an impact on the southern states and advocates for the states' interests before Congress and the executive branch.

Effectiveness of Lobbying Efforts

In the 1970s, governors reported that their interactions with Congress as an institution were not particularly effective. Reflecting on these activities, they stated that Congress was largely indifferent to their requests. Though governors continued to testify before Congress, most felt that neither their testifying nor the petitions and resolutions they passed were particularly helpful. More recently, however, governors have occasionally played significant roles in national policymaking. Some examples of this success involved lobbying about particular issues of concern; others were more general in nature. Governors acting jointly took steps to employ the constitutional amendment process and force the national government to be more cognizant of the needs of state governments. After a series of meetings hosted by Virginia governor George Allen in 1994 and 1995, the thirty Republican governors adopted an agreement (the Williamsburg Resolve) proposing a constitutional amendment that would "allow three-fourths of the states to initiate constitutional amendments, and to repeal federal legislation or regulations that burden state or local governments, subject to congressional authority to override the state-sponsored measures by a two-thirds vote of both houses." In addition, Governors Mike Leavitt (of Utah) and Ben Nelson (of Nebraska) organized the Conference of the States; the intent was to issue recommendations in the form of a "states' petition," which was to be ratified by state legislatures and presented to Congress. This group also called for three constitutional amendments: a "states' initiative," a "mandates amendment," and a "national reconsideration amendment." The states' initiative called for constitutional revision allowing a supermajority of states to propose constitutional amendments. The mandates amendment was meant to prohibit Congress from imposing conditions on the receipt of grants unless the conditions were tied directly to the purposes for which the funds were appropriated. And finally, the national reconsideration amendment would allow a majority of state legislatures to force the Congress to reenact any law that was rejected by a supermajority of state legislatures (Dinan 1997).

Amending the national constitution is an extremely difficult process, and it almost always requires that the national government, not the states, propose the change. For this reason, in part, the governors advanced their requests. And for the same reason, none of their proposals actually came to pass. Nevertheless, these instances of collective action on the part of governors emphasize their joint concerns and the power they can wield if they work together.

The governors have been more successful in securing the passage of legislation directed at forcing Congress to pay attention to state governments. The Unfunded Mandates Reform Act (UMRA) called for the Advisory Commission on Intergovernmental Relations (ACIR) to conduct a cost-benefit analysis of all existing mandates and to recommend the repeal of mandates that were particular burdens for state and local governments. In addition, the Congressional Budget Office was instructed to compute the cost to state and local governments of all newly proposed legislation (with a few spelled-out exceptions). Bills containing intergovernmental mandates could no longer be considered on the floor unless accompanied by a cost estimation report. If such a bill appeared on the floor without the required cost estimation, opponents could then raise a point of order, which would prevent further consideration of the measure unless a majority of the chamber voted to reject the point of order. While this law clearly has not done away with burdensome mandates on state governments, it has caused Congress to reconsider the costs of some legislation and make changes to proposed laws. At other times, Congress considered the cost concerns of state governments but did not change the proposed legislation. Further, UMRA is not self-executing. It requires a member of Congress to take the initiative and raise a point of order. It cannot force members to protect state interests over other interests they may have. However, it has been somewhat successful in at least two ways. It helps to make sure that Congress at least considers the effects of its legislation on state governments, either in committee or on the chamber floors. And it influences congressional decision making by creating a presumption against mandates and making those who hope to install them responsible for justifying their creation (Dinan 1997).

Governors continue to lobby individually and collectively with Congress to press for their positions. This lobbying reached new heights in 1994 when the Republican Party took the majority of both houses of Congress and the governorships. The entire class of Republican governors met regularly with Republican members of Congress to discuss state concerns about proposed legislation. Also, smaller bipartisan groups of governors with common policy interests drafted bills and lobbied Congress and the president. Individual governors with particular policy expertise joined with congressional committees in drafting legislation.

Though not all attempts at gubernatorial influence have proven effective, there are several noteworthy examples of success. The Family Support Act of 1988 grew from the recommendations of a six-governor task force led by Governors Bill Clinton of Arkansas and Michael Castle of Delaware. The group worked closely with the House Ways and Means Committee and the Senate Finance Committee as they considered the legislation. Similar activities surrounded congressional consideration of the 1996 welfare reform bill entitled the Personal Responsibility and Work Opportunity Reconciliation Act (PRWORA). Governors John Engler (of Michigan), Tommy Thompson (of Wisconsin), and Tom Carper (of Delaware), all innovators in welfare policy, worked with the Ways and Means Committee staff throughout 1995 to draft a welfare reform bill. Engler spent a great deal of time in Washington testifying before committees and lobbying individual members. As the legislation moved forward in the process, the governors formed a six-member bipartisan task force consisting of Republicans Leavitt, Thompson, and Engler and Democrats Lawton Chiles (of Florida), Bob Miller (of Nevada), and Roy Romer (of Colorado). The task force was charged with the goal of working out legislation that could break the deadlock between the Democratic president (former governor Bill Clinton) and the Republican Congress. From there, governors resorted to individual negotiation to achieve passage of the revised legislation. Engler and Iowa governor Terry Branstad finally worked with the conference committee to help the House and Senate reach final agreement and pass the bill.

Governors (individually and collectively) were also important advocates for passage of the Transportation Equity Act for the Twenty-first Century (TEA-21). This legislation, the most expensive and extensive public-works legislation ever passed by Congress, was passed in part because of the work of the governors and the NGA. In April 1997, the NGA launched an initiative called Transportation Revenues Used Solely for Transportation (TRUST), a coalition of more than 700 public and private organizations dedicated to increasing and protecting Highway Trust Fund money. The NGA's strategy called for governors to testify before Congress and visit directly with their states' members of Congress. Republican governors also worked with the leadership in both chambers to assure that this legislation would be a congressional priority (Marbach and Leckrone 2002).

The preceding examples aside, even when governors dedicate themselves to a particular cause, they do not always achieve their goals. Extensive gubernatorial lobbying was ultimately unsuccessful, for instance, in the case of Medicaid reform, and without doubt, gubernatorial lobbying of Washington is time consuming and costly for governors. Yet the examples of gubernatorial intergovernmental success do show that governors can influence congressional decision making. The fact that the Republicans held a majority in Congress and the governorships at the time surely helped this relationship along, but partisanship is not the full explanation for why congressional leaders came to pay attention to the nation's governors. In fact, evidence from the 1990s shows that state officials were most effective when they formed bipartisan groups and lobbied in a bipartisan manner. Further, when governors demonstrate particular expertise in policy areas, Congress is more likely to listen to what they have to say (Dinan 1997).

The influence of governors is felt in other ways as well. Sometimes, federal officials actually reach out to them for their input (rather than the other way around). Thus, President Clinton worked closely with the nation's governors as he prepared his health care reform proposal. Though not all governors were pleased with the plan, President Clinton did make sure that the legislation included a substantial role for the states and their governors. Republican leaders in Congress also actively sought the ideas of Republican governors.

Governors are definitely more successful in Washington today than they were in the past. While earlier governors had often felt frustrated in their interactions with Congress, their counterparts in the 1990s were clearly considered key players in the national decision-making process. What is not clear is how long such a relationship will persist. As the Republican leaders in Congress become more comfortable in their positions, they may seek less input from those outside Washington.

GOVERNORS AND OTHER STATES

Relations with Washington, D.C., are the most important intergovernmental connections for the states, since the national government frequently makes decisions that affect the governors and their states and sometimes provides funding to pay for state needs. For these reasons, governors necessarily spend a great deal of time and resources managing this relationship. However, the fact that the United States is a federal system also means that states and their governors occasionally interact with the governors and other leaders of surrounding states. The regional governors associations discussed earlier are evidence of the shared problems and needs of states within particular regions. Western governors have particular challenges in common, such as retaining access to sufficient stores of clean water. Southern governors share challenges related to economic development and high levels of poverty and poor educational outcomes. Given these shared needs, it is not surprising that governors would join together to discuss the problems and attempt to construct solutions, while also working together to lobby Congress and the executive branch in Washington. In addition to this collective regional activity directed at the solution of common problems, governors often interact with neighboring chief executives for other reasons. For instance, states occasionally have border disputes with their neighbors that can only be resolved via negotiation between the states' governors. Similarly, environmental challenges may arise if one state feels it is left to deal with the pollution created by a neighboring state and dumped into the air or water. A governor faced with pollution created by an adjacent state might lobby that state's governor to pursue regulations or laws to rectify the problem. If such negotiations fail and a solution cannot be found, states may end up suing one another in federal court. Such incidents are relatively rare and quite costly; governors would much prefer more amicable solutions to disagreements with nearby states.

Governors work individually and collectively to influence the national government. They work through offices in Washington and in their home states. They make connections themselves or work through proxies such as staff members or federal-state liaisons. Whatever mechanism they ultimately employ, the job of cultivating and maintaining relationships with the national government continues to be a critical aspect of being governor.

Despite their prominent place within their states and the role they play in the country as a whole in the twenty-first century, governors must nonetheless share the political environment with many other significant actors. State legislatures are equal partners in lawmaking, and they cannot be compelled by the governors to follow their preferred paths. Modern governors have many tools they can employ in this environment, but legislators have the resources and the motivations to make their own contributions as well. Interest groups and the media are additional players at the state level. These actors may contribute to gubernatorial success, but they may equally stand in the way of governors' goals. This reality means that chief executives must direct considerable attention to building relationships with these and other state-level actors if they hope to achieve their aims at home. State courts, the third branch of the state government, can also play a significant role in state politics. They stand as a potential referee, helping to define the powers of the governors and the legislatures. Their decisions typically work to the benefit of governors, but this is not always the case. Finally, given the multitiered nature of government in the United States, governors must devote time and energy outside their states as well. They often lobby Washington in hopes of influencing national decision making. In the past, they seemed to find this a difficult and rather thankless task, but modern governors have played significant parts in key national government reforms. Similarly, by choice or necessity, they often interact with the governors and other leaders of neighboring states either to settle disputes or to forge potential solutions to common problems. Regional governors' associations facilitate these relationships, but individualized contact between states takes place as well. In the complicated arena of U.S. politics, governors must share the stage with many other actors, but they very often take the leading role.

REFERENCES AND FURTHER READING

Bell, Dawson. 1999. Reducing rancor in Michigan. *State Legislatures* 25(10):22–24.

Berry, William D., Michael B. Berkman, and Stuart Schneiderman. 2000. Legislative professionalism and incumbent reelection: The development of institutional boundaries. *American Political Science Review* 94(4):859–874.

Beyle, Thad. 2004. The governors. In *Politics in the American states: A comparative analysis*, 8th ed., ed. Virginia Gray and Russell L. Hanson, 194–231. Washington, DC: Congressional Quarterly Press.

Beyle, Thad, and Lynn R. Muchmore. 1983. Governors and intergovernmental relations: Middlemen in the federal system. In *Being governor: The view from the office*, ed. Thad L. Beyle and Lynn R. Muchmore, 192–205. Durham, NC: Duke Press Policy Studies.

Bowling, Cynthia J., and Margaret R. Ferguson. 2001. Divided government, interest representation, and policy differences: Competing explanations of gridlock in the fifty states. *Journal of Politics* 63(1): 182–206.

Bowling, Cynthia J., Margaret R. Ferguson, and Deil S. Wright. 2002. Governors, legislatures and the bureaucracy. Manuscript prepared for the 2nd Annual State Politics and Policy Conference, Milwaukee, WI, May 23–25.

Bowman, Ann O'M., and Richard C. Kearney. 2005. *State and local government*. Boston: Houghton Mifflin.

Carey, John M., Gary Moncrief, Richard Niemi, and Lynda Powell. 2003. Term limits in the state legislatures: Results from a new survey of the 50 states. Manuscript prepared for the American Political Science Association Annual Meeting, Philadelphia, PA, August 28–31.

Carey, John M., Richard G. Niemi, and Lynda Powell. 1998. The effects of term limits on state legislatures. *Legislative Studies Quarterly* 23(2):271–300.

Clarke, Wes. 1998. Divided government and budget conflict in the U.S. states. *Legislative Studies Quarterly* 23(1):5–22.

Conlan, Timothy J., James D. Riggle, and Donna E. Schwartz. 1995. Deregulating federalism? The politics of mandate reform in the 104th congress. *Publius* 25(3):23–40.

Dilger, Robert Jay, George A. Krause, and Randolph R. Moffett. 1995. State legislative professionalism and gubernatorial effectiveness, 1978–1991. *Legislative Studies Quarterly* 20(4):553–571.

Dinan, John. 1997. State government influence in the national policy process: Lessons from the 104th Congress. *Publius* 27(2):129–143.

Dometrius, Nelson C. 1999. Governors: Their heritage and their future. In *American state and local politics*, ed. Ronald E. Weber and Paul Brace, 38–70. London: Chatham House.

Drage Bowser, Jennifer, Rich Jones, Karl T. Kurtz, Nancy Rhyme, and Brian Weberg. 2003. The impact of term limits on legislative leadership. In *The test of time: Coping with legislative term limits*, ed. Rick Farmer, John David Rausch, and John C. Green, 119–132. Lexington, MA: Lexington.

Fiorina, Morris P. 1992. An era of divided government. *Political Science Quarterly* 107(3):387–410.

———. 1994. Divided government in the American states: A by-product of legislative professionalism? *American Political Science Review* 88(2):304–316.

———. 1997. Professionalism, realignment, and representation. *American Political Science Review* 91(1):156–162.

———. 1999. Further evidence of the partisan consequences of legislative professionalism. *American Journal of Political Science* 43(3):974–977.

Francis, Wayne L., and Lawrence W. Kenny. 1997. Equilibrium projections of the consequences of term limits upon expected tenure, institutional turnover, and membership experience. *Journal of Politics* 59(1):240–252.

Jensen, Jennifer M. 2000. Establishing a state lobbying office in Washington: Factors that matter. Paper presented at the annual meeting of the American Political Science Association, Washington, DC, August 21–23.

Kaufman, Herbert. 1956. Emerging conflicts in the doctrines of political science. *American Political Science Review* 50(4):1057–1073.

Lowery, David, and Virginia Gray. 1995. The population ecology of Gucci Gulch, or the natural regulation of interest group numbers in the American states. *American Journal of Political Science* 39(1):1–29.

Marbach, Joseph R., and J. Wesley Leckrone. 2002. Intergovernmental lobbying for the passage of TEA-2. *Publius* 3(1)2:45–69.

Moncrief, Gary. 1999. Recruitment and retention in U.S. legislatures. *Legislative Studies Quarterly* 24(2):173–208.

Moncrief, Gary, and Joel A. Thompson. 2001. On the outside looking in: Lobbyists' perspectives on the effects of state legislative term limits. *State Politics and Policy Quarterly* 1(4):394–411.

Moncrief, Gary, Joel A. Thompson, and William Cassie. 1996. Revisiting the state of U.S. state legislative research. *Legislative Studies Quarterly* 21(3):301–335.

Moncrief, Gary, Joel A. Thompson, and Karl Kurtz. 1996. The old statehouse, it ain't what it used to be. *Legislative Studies Quarterly* 21(1):57–72.

Mooney, Christopher Z. 1995. Citizens, structures, and sister states: Influences on state legislative professionalism. *Legislative Studies Quarterly* 20(1):47–67.

National Conference of State Legislatures. Legislative term limits: An overview. www.ncsl.org/programs/legman/ABOUT/termlimit.htm.

———. Legislator compensation 2003. www.ncsl.org/programs/legman/03table-legcomp.htm.

———. Tied state legislative chambers: 1966–present. www.ncsl.org/Programs/Legman/about/tiedcmblist.htm. January 29, 2003.

———. Divided government in the states. www.ncsl.org/programs/legman/elect/divgov.htm. March 17, 2003.

———. Size of state legislative staff: 1979, 1988, 1996, and 2003. www.ncsl.org/programs/legman/about/staffcount2003.htm. May 6, 2004.

———. Historic partisan control. www.ncsl.org/programs/legman/elect/hstptyct.htm. November 3, 2004.

———. NCSL Backgrounder: Full-time and part-time legislatures. http://www.ncsl.org/programs/press/2004/backgrounder_fullandpart.htm. October 2005.

Peery, George, and Thomas H. Little. 2003. Views from the bridge: Legislative leaders' perceptions of institutional power in the stormy wake of term limits. In *The test of time: Coping with legislative term limits*, ed. Rick Farmer, John David Rausch, and John C. Green, 105–118. Lexington, MA: Lexington.

Rosenthal, Alan. 1996. State legislative development: Observations from three perspectives. *Legislative Studies Quarterly* 21(2):169–198.

Squire, Peverill. 1997. Another look at legislative professionalization and divided government in the states. *Legislative Studies Quarterly* 22(3):417–432.

———. 1998. Membership turnover and the efficient processing of legislation. *Legislative Studies Quarterly* 23(1):23–32.

Thomas, Clive S., and Ronald J. Hrebenar. 2004. Interest groups in the states. In *Politics in the American states: A comparative analysis*, 8th ed., ed. Virginia Gray and Russell L. Hanson, 100–128. Washington, DC: Congressional Quarterly Press.

Walker, David B. 2000. *The rebirth of federalism*. New York: Chatham House, Seven Bridges.

Wright, Deil. 1967. Executive leadership in state administration: Interplay of gubernatorial, legislative and administrative power. *Midwest Journal of Political Science* 11(1):1–26.

———. 1982. *Understanding intergovernmental relations*, 2nd ed. Monterey, CA: Brooks/Cole.

6

THE EXECUTIVE BRANCH

STATE BY STATE

ALABAMA

•••••••••••••

ALABAMA ELECTED EXECUTIVE BRANCH OFFICIALS

Governor   Lieutenant Governor
Attorney General   Auditor
Commissioner of Agriculture and Industries
Secretary of State   Superintendent of Education
Treasurer
http://www.governor.state.al.us/

•••••••••••••

If one person has shaped the modern Alabama governor's office more than any other, it would be George C. Wallace. Through his four terms in office, starting in 1962 and including his first wife's abbreviated term in office before she died, Wallace had a major impact on the politics and government in Alabama for over thirty years. By combining a populist appeal to the "average" Alabamian with a traditional message for those who sought to continue the segregationist past, Wallace came back from his first gubernatorial defeat to win the office. He acknowledged his winning association with segregationists at his first inaugural address by proclaiming, "Segregation now, segregation tomorrow, and segregation forever!" Barred at the time from succeeding himself, he had his first wife, Lurleen, run for the office; Alabamians knew that if they elected Lurleen, they would put George back in power. Wallace used his position in the Alabama governor's mansion to rail against the civil rights movement of the 1960s, and he eventually carried his message to the national level by making three runs for the White House. However, his message attracted the attention of those who despised him as well: while campaigning for the Democratic nomination in 1972, he was shot and left paralyzed. Later, when he ran for his fourth term as governor, Alabamians found a repentant Wallace, who gave up his claims for segregation in favor

Governor George Wallace confronts deputy attorney general Nicholas Katzenbach on the steps of the University of Alabama in an attempt to block integration, June 11, 1963. (Library of Congress)

of reconciliation with blacks in his state. In his last campaign for the governorship, he received an unprecedented level of support from black voters.

The state of Alabama is known for the men who have dominated the political landscape, particularly as governor. This situation was most likely due to the fractured nature of Alabama politics, most notably the conflict between north Alabama and the middle part of the state, known as the Black Belt. The conflict between the two regions can be traced back to the granting of statehood in 1819. From the controversy over the location of the state capital and the composition of the state legislature, through

the divisions created by the Civil War (the mostly white farmers of the north were reluctant to join the Confederate movement supported by slave-owning planters), to the marches and police beatings at Selma's Edmund Pettus Bridge and in Birmingham during the 1960s civil rights movement, Alabama has seen its share of conflict.

This conflict played out within its politics as well, even though the Democratic Party was the majority party in the state until the 1980s. Conflicts within the party split along a progressive-conservative line, and the election of governors was the most apparent evidence of this split. Jim "Big Jim" Folsom was the most notable progressive governor. While he served in the 1940s and 1950s, he invited a visiting black member of Congress to the governor's mansion at the beginning of the civil rights movement. He believed the Alabama legislature's declaration against the *Brown v. Board of Education* decision to be nothing more than "hogwash." Running for his first term as governor as a progressive, Folsom campaigned with a hillbilly band, The Strawberry Pickers, and a "suds bucket" to illustrate his promise to clean up state government. Once in office, he advocated programs such as pensions for the aged, the paving of farm-to-market roads, and greater funding for education. Like other Alabama governors, he used his own powers of persuasion to advance the needs of the state (as he perceived them). This approach has not always worked, however. Most recently, Republican governor Bob Riley sought to revise the state's tax structure, calling for a more progressive and "Christian" approach, but Alabamians defeated his proposal by a wide margin. Even if the governor is charged with leading the state, the state may decide not to follow its chief executive—indicative of a weak governor system such as Alabama's. The Alabama governorship has a formal structure that offers little power; the power that governors can wield is personal, and it does not always carry the day.

This structure is reflected within Alabama's constitution, which states that the executive branch of government "shall consist of a governor, lieutenant governor, attorney general, state auditor, secretary of state, state treasurer, superintendent of education, commissioner of agriculture and industries, and a sheriff for each county." To serve as either governor or lieutenant governor, candidates must be at least thirty years old, citizens of the United States for at least ten years, and residents of Alabama for a minimum of seven years prior to the election. For the other executive offices, individuals must be twenty-five years old, citizens of the United States for seven years, and residents in the state for five years prior to the election. All executive officers serve four-year terms, and the governor is allowed to be reelected but can only serve two terms in a row. In addition, all statewide elected officers must, by constitutional requirement, reside in the state capitol. This requirement does not apply to the lieutenant governor, and it is suspended in cases of "epidemics."

The constitutional powers of the governor include ensuring that "the laws be faithfully executed" and "giving information of the state of the government, and recommending for its consideration such measures as he may deem expedient." The governor also has the power to recommend a budget to the legislature and to request reports from other officers and departments within state government. The Alabama governor can call the legislature into special session and can limit the legislature's discussion to matters he or she considers necessary. The governor also oversees more than twenty departments. Heads of these departments meeting collectively constitute a cabinet.

Another constitutional power that the governor possesses is the package veto, along with the line-item veto power for appropriations bills. The legislature can override a governor's veto with only a simple majority of each chamber, however. In addition, the governor can propose amendments to a bill, and if the legislature approves the amendments and removes the objectionable aspects of the measure, the bill can then become law. Bills without a governor's signature become law after six days, unless they are passed during the closing days of the legislative session. If a bill is not approved by the governor within ten days after the end of the legislative session, it dies under a pocket veto.

The governor can also grant reprieves, paroles, and pardons and commute sentences of individuals convicted of criminal acts, with the exception of cases involving the impeachment of officers. First, however, a board composed of the attorney general, secretary of state, and state auditor reviews clemency requests and forwards a recommendation to the governor. If the board fails to report to the governor on a request within sixty days, the governor may grant the request. At the end of the legislative session, the governor must report his or her action on all requests, along with the recommendations by the board. The governor is also the commander-in-chief of the state militia and volunteer forces.

Among the governor's informal powers is the ability to designate the speaker of the state's house of representatives and the president pro tempore of the state senate. During recent times, the influence of the governor has weakened, while the legislature has asserted its own power.

If, at any time, the governor appears unfit for office or of "unsound mind," the state supreme court, acting on the official request of two officers in the line of succession (but not the lieutenant governor), can remove the governor from office. In the event that another executive officer (attorney general, state auditor, state treasurer, superintendent of education, or commissioner of agriculture and industries) is deemed to be of "unsound mind," the state supreme court can remove that individual, based on a recommendation by the governor. The governor is then eligible to appoint a replacement, who serves until the next scheduled election.

The lieutenant governor's constitutional power is to serve as president of the state senate; he or she can only vote in that chamber in the event of a tie. If the governor dies, is removed, or resigns from office, the lieutenant governor is next in line of succession, followed by the president pro tempore of the state senate, the speaker of the house of representatives, the attorney general, the state auditor, the secretary of state, and the state treasurer. If the governor is out of the state for more than twenty days, the lieutenant governor serves as acting governor until the governor returns.

The duties of the secretary of state include keeping the great seal of the state and signing all commissions and grants of the state, as well as maintaining all the official acts of the state. The commissioner of agriculture and industries is responsible for exercising regulatory control over products, business entities, and the movement and application of goods and services.

J. Michael Bitzer

References

Alabama State Constitution, Secs. 112–138.

Stewart, John C. 1975. *The governors of Alabama.* Gretna, LA: Pelican.

Thomas, James D., and William H. Stewart. 1988. *Alabama government and politics.* Lincoln: University of Nebraska Press.

Additional Resources and Recommended Readings

Carter, Dan. 2002. *The politics of rage: George Wallace, the origins of new conservatism, and the transformation of American politics.* New York: Simon and Schuster.

Lesher, Stephan. 1994. *George Wallace: American populist.* New York: Addison-Wesley.

ALASKA

• • • • • • • • • • • •

ALASKA ELECTED EXECUTIVE BRANCH OFFICIALS

Governor
Lieutenant Governor
http://www.state.ak.us/

• • • • • • • • • • • •

In 1867, the United States completed a deal with Russia to purchase the Alaskan Territory—all 365 million acres of it. It was not until nearly 100 years later, however, that the people of Alaska were able to choose their first elected governor. Since then, the state executives who serve the people of Alaska have been faced with a number of challenges, which include trying to spur economic growth, balancing governmental and tribal relations with Native inhabitants, and dealing with the special relationship the state has with the U.S. federal government, the owner of approximately 61 percent (220 million acres) of the state's land.

On December 2, 2002, Republican Frank Murkowski was sworn in as governor of Alaska. Although Murkowski is the tenth governor to serve in Alaska since it received statehood in 1959, he is only the eighth person to hold the state's highest office. Democrat William A. Egan, who served as Alaska's first governor from 1959 to 1966, was defeated in his run for reelection by then-Republican Walter J. Hickel. However, after Hickel stepped down from his position as Alaska's chief executive to serve as secretary of interior under President Richard Nixon, Egan was elected once more to serve as governor from 1970 to 1974. Hickel also resurfaced in the realm of gubernatorial politics, this time as a member of the Alaskan Independence party. After twenty years and three political defeats, he again took up residence in the governor's mansion. On his election in 1990, Hickel became one of only six third-party candidates to win a gubernatorial election to that point in U.S. history.

Alaska's governor is primarily responsible for the "faithful execution of the laws." In other words, he or she is in charge of implementing and administering public policy enacted by the state legislature. At the same time, the governor serves as the commander-in-chief of the state military and is responsible for numerous other activities in the political operations of the state. For example, he or she is in charge of appointing the heads of many state agencies, as well as justices to the district, superior, and supreme courts. The governor also delivers a state of the state address at the start of each legislative session, which details statewide concerns and offers recommendations for addressing these issues. In addition, the governor has the power to call special sessions of the legislature, in which the houses convene to discuss matters specifically outlined in a gubernatorial proclamation. Finally, the governor has been granted the power of executive order to reorganize the executive branch (unless overturned by the legislature).

One of the most important duties performed by Alaska's governor is the submission of a yearly fiscal budget to the state legislature. Although the legislature is not bound to the governor's proposed budget, it serves as a starting point or a foundation on which the legislature can build. This approach enables the governor to set the tone of budgetary deliberations and helps ensure that the governor's budgetary desires are considered from the outset of legislative decisions.

The governor is assisted by the lieutenant governor, who performs all duties prescribed by law for the office as well as those assigned by the governor. If the governor is temporarily unable to fulfill the duties of the office, the lieutenant governor fills in as acting governor as needed. If the governor dies while in office, is disqualified from office, or otherwise resigns

the position for any other reason, the lieutenant governor succeeds to the office. In the history of Alaskan statehood, there has only been one instance in which the lieutenant governor succeeded to the position of chief executive. When Governor Hickel resigned his position to become the U.S. secretary of interior in 1969, he was replaced by Lieutenant Governor Keith Miller. Miller was, however, defeated in his bid to be elected governor in 1970, and up to this point in Alaska's history, no lieutenant governor has ever made a successful run to become governor in a general election.

The lieutenant governor is responsible for overseeing both the division of elections and the review and filing of administrative regulations. He or she is also the keeper of the seal of the state and responsible for publishing and distributing the state constitution.

The rest of the executive branch is made up of a number of departments in charge of a wide variety of statewide functions. They include, among others, the Department of Revenue, the Department of Health and Social Services, the Department of Fish and Game, and the Department of Public Safety. There are currently fifteen such departments in Alaska, which has a constitutional limit of twenty. Within each of these principal departments is a network of governmental offices, agencies, and departments in charge of the daily operations of state government. According to the state constitution, each principal department is under the governor's supervision, with department heads being selected by executive appointment and legislative confirmation and serving "at the pleasure of the governor, except as otherwise provided in this article with respect to the secretary of state."

The individual who receives the most votes in the general gubernatorial election is selected to serve as governor for the state. The only requirements for running for the office are that the individual must be at least thirty years old, a qualified voter, a U.S. citizen for no less than seven years, and a resident of Alaska for at least seven years immediately prior to filing for office. This last qualification seems to be uniquely appropriate to consider in Alaska, given that only one of its governors, William Egan, was a native Alaskan. Alaska's governor serves for a term of four years and is limited to two full terms. However, an individual who has served as governor for two full terms can run again after another full, four-year term has passed. While serving as the state's chief executive, the governor cannot hold any other "office or position of profit," either federally or statewide.

The lieutenant governor must meet the same qualifications of age, voter status, citizenship, and residency as the governor. Candidates for the office of lieutenant governor run jointly with the gubernatorial candidates in the general election. They are elected as a team, so that the person running as lieutenant governor on the winning governor's ticket is selected to serve in office.

Although being governor in the state of Alaska carries with it a number of the same duties that other state executives have, the unique geography and history of the country's "last frontier" produce various political responsibilities not held by governors in many other parts of the

United States. In the year 2000, the U.S. Census Bureau reported that Native peoples made up nearly 16 percent of Alaska's population, which places a substantial responsibility on the governor of Alaska, for he or she must deal with state and tribal relations, state and federal relations, and federal and tribal relations. This triangle of interaction between three governing structures places a significant burden on the Alaska state executive to maintain good relationships with many different governmental actors.

Another important job of the executive in Alaska involves economic development. Although economic growth and vitality are the goals of almost any state executive, the context in which the governors of Alaska find themselves creates a unique set of problems. Because Alaska is a far northern state that must rely almost entirely on a few natural resources to maintain and support its economy, the governors are faced with unique difficulties in attempting to spur economic growth. In 2003, Governor Murkowski developed a program based on the slogan "Alaska's Jobs for Alaska's People." The purpose of the program was to encourage Alaskan businesses and corporations working in the state to hire Alaskan citizens. The governor argued that the program was needed because employers hired too few Alaskan workers and too many from out of state. In 2001 alone, over $1 billion in wages went to people from out of state—wages that were being spent in other states, which significantly harmed Alaska's economy. Murkowski's initiative was designed, among other things, to encourage employers with a set of incentives to maintain a workforce that was at least 90 percent Alaskan. This move would not only provide quality jobs for the people of Alaska but also help to ensure that the money paid out for work there would also be spent in Alaska. This example illustrates how the state executives of Alaska must confront the difficult economic challenges posed by the fiscal realities of the nation's forty-ninth state.

Joseph J. Foy

References

Alaska State Constitution of 1956, Art. 3.
Alaska State Department of Public Assistance, DPAweb. November 2003. Governor launches Alaska hire, sets 90% goal. http://dpaweb.hss.state.ak .us/node/view/232.
Institute for Social and Economic Research, University of Alaska Anchorage. Alaska Humanities Forum. October 2001. Trends in Alaska's people and economy. http://www.iser.uaa .alaska.edu/Publications/Alaska2020.pdf.
McBeath, Gerald A., and Thomas A. Morehouse. 1994. *Alaska politics and government.* Lincoln: University of Nebraska Press.
U.S. Census Bureau. 2000. *State and county QuickFacts: Alaska.* http:// quickfacts.census.gov/qfd/states /02000.html.

Additional Resources and Recommended Readings

Hammond, Jay S. 1996. *Tales of Alaska's bush rat governor: The extraordinary autobiography of Jay Hammond, wilderness guide and reluctant politician.* Fairbanks, AK: Epicenter.
———. 2002. *Chips from the chopping block: More tales from Alaska's bush rat governor.* Fairbanks, AK: Epicenter.
Haycox, Stephen W. 2002. *Frigid embrace: Politics, economics and environment in Alaska.* Corvallis: Oregon State University Press.
Hickel, Walter J. 2002. *Crisis in the commons: The Alaska solution.* Oakland, CA: Institute for Contemporary Studies.
Miller, Keith H. 1997. *Prudhoe Bay governor: Alaska's Keith Miller.* Anchorage: Todd Communications.
Strohmeyer, John. 1997. *Extreme conditions: Big oil and the transformation of Alaska.* Marina del Ray, CA: Cascade.

ARIZONA

● ● ● ● ● ● ● ● ● ● ● ● ●

ARIZONA ELECTED EXECUTIVE BRANCH OFFICIALS

Governor   Attorney General
Corporation Commissioners
Secretary of State   State Mine Inspector
Superintendent of Public Instruction
Treasurer
http://az.gov/

● ● ● ● ● ● ● ● ● ● ● ●

When it was granted statehood in 1912, Arizona became the last of the contiguous states to be admitted into the Union. However, even prior to its admission, the history of Arizona was such that it would rival even the most interesting developments in any other part of the country.

Although the territory was known initially for its lawlessness and propensity for attracting prospectors who were only interested in finding a quick fortune in the mineral-rich land, those who saw opportunities in farming and ranching were simultaneously developing Arizona for the long term. The mix of various types of individuals who were attracted to the territory is reflected in those who were selected to serve in the office of the executive. Some of the territorial governors, such as John Goodwin (1863–1866) and John C. Fremont (1878–1882), were primarily interested in finding ways of opening Arizona's vast mining potential, while others, including Richard C. McCormick (1866–1869) and Alexander O. Brodie (1902–1905), made efforts to develop Arizona's agricultural potential. Still others represented another side of the territorial politics of Arizona, such as Conrad M. Zulick (1885–1889), who was serving time in a Mexican prison when he was appointed to the office of territorial governor by President Grover Cleveland, and Frederick Tritle (1882–1885), whose administration bore witness to the famous shoot-out at the OK Corral.

After the bid for Arizona's statehood was accepted, the people chose George W. P. Hunt to serve as their first governor. Hunt would go on to be elected to the executive office of the state seven times. He served as governor from 1912 to 1919, 1923 to 1929, and 1931 to 1933.

Hunt and the executives who would follow him had the challenging task of developing all of the potential resources that would make Arizona what it is today. Economically, the state is said to be driven by the "five Cs": copper, cattle, cotton, citrus, and climate, referring to the mining, agricultural, and tourism sectors of the Arizona economy. Likewise, perhaps in accordance with the state's frontier and pioneer legacies, the politics of Arizona were designed primarily around the goal of limiting the power and

George W. P. Hunt, first governor of Arizona, served for seven terms between 1912 and 1933. (Library of Congress)

influence of government. Arizona has a vibrant history of democratization throughout its politics, including the initiative, referendum, and judicial recall, and it was not until the administration of Jack Williams in 1970 that the state allowed its executives to serve for four-year terms. Prior to 1978, Arizona's governors were limited to two-year terms. These attempts at weakening government through the diffusion of power into the hands of everyday citizens have sometimes made it difficult for the Arizona state executive to exercise leadership. However, through the application of various personal and institutional resources available to them, a number of the governors have left a profound mark on the nation's forty-eighth state.

Proposition 100, passed in 1992, amended the selection process for the governor. It was through this initiative process that Arizona's state constitution was changed from requiring an absolute majority for the election of the governor to a system requiring a simple plurality (getting more votes than any other candidate). Prior to this amendment, if the highest vote getter in a general election did not receive at least 50 percent of the votes cast, then a runoff election was held between the top two candidates for the office. Now, in electing the governor in Arizona, only one round of elections is held. In the unlikely event of a tie, the election is decided by a joint ballot of the two houses of the state legislature at the start of its next general session. To qualify to serve as governor of Arizona, a person must be at least twenty-five years of age, a citizen of the United States for a minimum of ten years prior to the election, and a citizen of the state for at least five years.

There is no lieutenant governor to serve in the event of the governor's death, removal, or inability to fulfill the duties of office. If the governor, for whatever reason, is no longer able to serve, then the duties fall first to the secretary of state and then to the other members of the executive. This situation became an important feature in shaping the history of the Arizona executive. In 1977, Secretary of State Wesley Bolin replaced Governor Raul Castro, who left the Arizona governor's office to become the U.S. ambassador to Argentina. However, Bolin's tenure as governor was cut short by a fatal heart attack on March 4, 1978, leaving the executive office to be filled by the thirty-nine-year-old attorney general, Bruce Babbitt. Babbitt later went on to serve as secretary of the interior under President Bill Clinton.

Turning to the powers and duties assigned to the executive, the Arizona governor is charged with the faithful execution of all state laws and acts as the head of the executive office. He or she also serves as commander-in-chief of the state's military forces and, except in cases of treason or impeachment, has the power to grant pardons, reprieves, and commutations to those convicted of crimes. If there is a vacancy in any of the executive offices other than the governorship, the governor has the ability to fill that office through appointment. The governor may also call special sessions of the state legislature when necessary and is charged with delivering a state of the state address at the beginning of each legislative session. In these ways, the Arizona executive seems typical when compared to the governors of other states. However, as previously noted, certain features make the Arizona governorship stand out. The state constitution purposefully built institutional limitations into the executive office so as to temper gubernatorial strength. For example, the governor may serve any number of four-year terms but cannot serve more than two consecutively. Additionally, although the governor has both a package and a line-item veto, those powers are subject to legislative override; furthermore, the governor cannot veto items approved by citizens via a referendum. Finally, the governor is limited in the ability to surround him- or herself with like-minded individuals in the executive, in that all five state executives—governor, attorney general, treasurer, secretary of state, and superintendent of public instruction—are elected separately, not as a part of a team. Combined, these characteristics ensure the relative institutional weakness of the Arizona governor's office, as the governor is limited in his or her ability to push legislation or set forth a unified executive program and vision for the state.

The attorney general is the chief legal counsel for the state. He or she also acts as a watchdog for victims' rights, consumer affairs, civil rights, and the welfare of children and the elderly. The secretary of state is the chief elections officer, registers all lobbyists and charitable organizations, commissions all notaries public, files secured financial transactions under the Uniform Commercial Code, and is the official custodian of the great seal of Arizona. The state treasurer provides banking, cash management, investment, and accounting services for the state, as well as serving as the chief financial officer.

An additional check on the governor of Arizona is the power of the people to recall the chief executive. In the late 1980s, the people collected enough signatures on a petition to recall Governor Evan Mecham, but the recall election never actually occurred because Mecham was already facing impeachment charges for embezzlement and obstruction of justice. Mecham was impeached in February 1988 and was removed from office after being found guilty of high crimes and misdemeanors later that year. Secretary of State Rose Mofford, who became Arizona's first female governor, replaced Mecham following his conviction.

Despite the limitations that exist in terms of gubernatorial power and leadership, Arizona has a history of innovative and resourceful executives who have shaped the development of the state. One such example was Governor Ernest McFarland, who used his legal expertise in the field of irrigation law to help resolve seemingly endless disputes over one of Arizona's most scarce and vital resources—water. However, the most influential of all of Arizona's executives remains Governor Hunt, whose dedication to populism helped to create the state constitution, establishing one of the most democratized states in the nation. Hunt's "maverick" political spirit lives on today, as Arizona continues to defy national trends in its executive office. Three women have served as governor, and following the election of 1998, women filled all five of Arizona's executive offices—something largely unseen throughout the rest of the country. It is a fitting legacy for the pioneering traditions of the Grand Canyon State.

Joseph J. Foy

References

Arizona State Constitution of 1911, Art. 5.
Ballot propositions of the state of Arizona. General election of November 3, 1992. Prepared by the secretary of state of Arizona. Reprinted online at http://www.azsos.gov/ election/1992/Info/PubPamphlet/PubPam92.pdf.
Goff, John F. 1983. *Arizona biographical dictionary.* Cave Creek, AZ: Black Mountain.
Scott, Jeffrey. 2004. Arizona government and general history. http://jeff.scott.tripod.com/azhistory.html.

Udall, Morris K. 1984. Arizona: Where we came from, where we're going. *Congressman's Report* 22(1) (April 1984). http://dizzy.library.arizona.edu/branches /spc/udall/congrept/98th/8404.html.

Wagoner, Jay J. 1970. *Arizona territory, 1863–1912: A political history.* Tucson: University of Arizona Press.

Additional Resources and Recommended Readings

American Law Sources Online. Arizona. http://www.lawsource.com.

Arizona Legislative Information System (ALIS). http://www.azleg.state.az.us.

Arizona Newspapers. United States Newspaper List (USNPL). http://www .usnpl.com/aznews.html. A collection of media resources for the state of Arizona.

McClory, Toni. 2001. *Understanding the Arizona constitution.* Tucson: University of Arizona Press.

Sheridan, Thomas E. 1995. *Arizona: A history.* Tucson: University of Arizona Press.

ARKANSAS

• • • • • • • • • • • •

ARKANSAS ELECTED EXECUTIVE BRANCH OFFICIALS

Governor	Lieutenant Governor
Attorney General	Auditor
Land Commissioner	Secretary of State

Treasurer

http://www.arkansas.gov

• • • • • • • • • • • •

In serving as the states' chief executives, many governors are sometimes caught in the middle within the American federal system. Due to the division of power between the national, state, and local governments (referred to as federalism), questions about "who reigns supreme" are often at the heart of the conflict between the national government and the fifty state governments. This conflict was particularly evident in the 1950s and 1960s, when the modern civil rights movement began using the power of the national government to overcome segregation and discrimination within the states, most notably in the South. Arkansas's governor Orval Faubus found himself caught between the wishes of his state's residents and the dictates of the national government.

Following the landmark decision by the U.S. Supreme Court in *Brown v. Board of Education 1954,* Governor Faubus sought to wield his executive power to resist the dictates of the national government. He used the commander-in-chief power given to him by the state constitution to resist the integration of Central High School in Little Rock sending the Arkansas National Guard to prevent nine black students from entering the school. Faubus reported that he took these steps because he believed that white supremacists were planning to go to the Central High School and that "blood would run in the streets" if the integration was allowed

Arkansas governor Orval Faubus was an outspoken opponent of school integration. (Library of Congress)

to proceed. After a series of confrontations, President Dwight D. Eisenhower sent in the 101st Airborne Division to escort the black students into the high school and serve as a source of protection against angry whites both outside and inside the facility.

The following year, after one of the black students graduated from Central High School, Governor Faubus requested that the legislature give him the power to close public schools if integration was continued. The general assembly granted him that power, and Faubus shut down the public school system in Little Rock. The action of granting the governor the power to close public schools was later ruled unconstitutional, and eventually, the public schools were integrated.

The executive officers of the state of Arkansas include a governor, lieutenant governor, secretary of state, treasurer, auditor, attorney general, and commissioner of state lands. While Arkansas is typical in dividing its executive power between several constitutional officers, the state constitution does vest "supreme executive power" in the governor. All officers are elected for four-year terms and can run for reelection once.

The governor must be a U.S. citizen, at least thirty years old, and a state resident for a minimum of seven years. The state constitution also holds that no member of the U.S. Congress can hold the office of governor while serving in Congress. The chief executive, as noted earlier, serves as commander-in-chief of the military forces of the state, and he or she can give "information by message concerning the condition and government of the State" to the legislature, which is commonly referred to as the state of the state address. The governor is also the keeper of the seal of the state.

The governor has some legislative authority. Once a bill is passed by both chambers of the general assembly, the governor may sign the bill into law or veto the legislation. The general assembly may, however, override the veto with only a simple majority of those members elected to both the house and the senate. If the governor chooses not to sign or veto the bill within five days after it is presented, the bill becomes law. If the legislature has adjourned, the governor has up to twenty days after the adjournment to veto the bill. The governor also has the power of line-item veto over appropriations by the legislature.

Another constitutional power that the governor possesses is the power to grant "reprieves, commutations of sentences and pardons after conviction." The governor, on exercising this pardoning power, must report to the general assembly his or her reasons for doing so. The governor also has the power to both call

a special session, in which he or she specifies the business that the legislature must consider, and adjourn the legislature if there is a disagreement between the two chambers.

The legislature can impeach the governor with a simple majority vote in the house of representatives, while the state senate conducts the trial. Conviction by the state senate requires a two-thirds vote, with the chief justice sitting as the presiding officer of the trial. The governor may request that the legislature, by a two-thirds majority vote, remove the following constitutional officers: auditor, treasurer, secretary of the state, attorney general, judges of the supreme and circuit courts, chancellors, and prosecuting attorneys.

The governor has the power to appoint over 500 individuals to various boards and commissions. However, the terms of most boards are staggered to prevent the governor from stacking them with allies. These staggered terms have frustrated many chief executives hoping to exercise influence over state government operations. As the former governor David Pryor once remarked when asked what would best increase his influence over state government, "What this state needs most is a few good funerals" (Blair 1988, 147).

Among the most useful resources that the governor possesses are the free passes to the Oaklawn Park Race Track that he or she can give out. Each pass costs only $1, but possessing a free pass signifies that the holder is close to the chief executive; therefore, these passes are highly sought after.

In addition to serving as presiding officer of the state senate, the lieutenant governor also serves as acting governor whenever the governor is out of the state. While the position of lieutenant governor was created in 1915, the first person to serve in the post did not actually take office until 1926. A vote on a constitutional amendment to establish the lieutenant governor's office was held in 1915, and voters favored the amendment, but the speaker of the house declared that the amendment did not pass because it did not receive a majority of the highest total vote. Ten years later, however, the speaker's decision was overturned when it was ruled that only a majority of those voting was needed in order for a ballot issue to be approved. So in 1926, the 1915 vote was declared to be valid and the position of lieutenant governor was formally recognized.

The constitutional duty of the secretary of state is to keep "full and accurate records of all the official acts and proceedings of the governor." Additional duties include overseeing the elections process within the state, as well as overseeing the capitol and its grounds. The other constitutional offices are assigned duties by the legislature; if there is a vacancy in one of these offices, the governor has the power to appoint an individual for the remainder of the term in office.

The attorney general serves as the state's chief law enforcement officer, while the auditor serves as the general accountant for the state by paying the state bills and the salaries of a number of its officers. The treasurer, by contrast, receives all moneys due to the state and provides reports to the governor and other state officers regarding state-held funds.

The power of the state land commissioner is to oversee the recovery of taxes on delinquent property. In addition, he or she is responsible for historical preservation, natural resources and mineral leasing, and handling donated lands to the state.

J. Michael Bitzer

References
Arkansas Constitution, Art. 6.
Blair, Diane D. 1988. *Arkansas politics and government: Do the people rule?* Lincoln: University of Nebraska Press.

Additional Resources and Recommended Readings
Beals, Melba Pattillo. 1994. *Warriors don't cry: A searing memoir of the battle to integrate Little Rock's Central High.* New York: Pocket.
Urwin, Cathy K. 1991. *Agenda for reform: Winthrop Rockefeller as governor of Arkansas, 1967–1971.* Little Rock: University of Arkansas Press.

CALIFORNIA
• • • • • • • • • • • •

• • • • • • • • • • • •

When gold was discovered at Sutter's Mill in 1848, people from all over the world began to flock to California in search of their fortunes. Over a century and a half later, California remains the destination of all types of people looking for prosperity within the state's enormous economy. In terms of demographics, California is the most diverse state in the nation, and it remains the most populous state as well. According to the 2003 population figures, it is home to over 35.5 million people, or approximately 12 percent of the entire population of the United States. Additionally, according to economic data released in 2004, California has the largest state economy in the nation. In fact, if California were its own country, it would be home to the eighth-largest economy in the world, and if Los Angeles were a state, it would have the fourth-largest economy in the United States. Much like the state's people, the businesses contributing to the vast wealth of California are also incredibly diverse, ranging from agriculture to computers, entertainment to aerospace, and mining to manufacturing. All of these factors combine to make the job of governor in the state of California one of the most challenging in the world. It is no wonder, then, that some of the most important and influential leaders in American history have served in the executive office of the Golden State.

The executive branch in California is headed by a number of statewide officials—the governor, lieutenant governor, secretary of state, attorney general, state treasurer, state controller, superintendent of public instruction, insurance commissioner, and members of the Board of Equalization. Each of these officials is separately elected to serve the state. The "supreme power of the executive office," however, is placed in the hands of the governor, whose job it is to assure that the laws of the state are faithfully executed. To accomplish this daunting task, the governor is assigned a number of institutional powers and resources. One source of power is the yearly address that he or she gives to the state legislature, in which the governor can define the political agenda for the state as well as present legislative priorities for the coming year.

The governor is also responsible for submitting the state's yearly budget to the legislature. Additionally, in order to remain on top of all of the complex demands in a state as large and economically demanding as California, the governor can draw information and updates from state administrative agencies and their employees at any time. The governor is also endowed with the constitutional authority to reorganize any aspect of the executive branch, except those aforementioned elected offices. Finally, the chief executive of California is also the commander-in-chief of the state's military, which he or she "may call forth to execute the law."

The governor of California is limited to serving no more than two four-year terms. To qualify for office, a gubernatorial candidate must have been a citizen of the state and of the United States for at least five years leading up to the election. Although the lieutenant governor is chosen in the same election, the governor and lieutenant governor are not elected jointly as members of the same team. Consequently, the governor and the lieutenant governor are often members of different parties, as is the case currently with Republican governor Arnold Schwarzenegger and Democratic lieutenant governor Cruz Bustamante. This division between the top two executive officials makes a unified vision for the state difficult to establish, and beyond that, state law allows for the lieutenant governor to approve or disapprove legislation passed while the governor is out of the state. The lieutenant governor is also first in the line of succession

should anything happen to the sitting governor. In addition to this power, the lieutenant governor serves as president of the state senate but is only allowed to cast a tie-breaking ballot.

In working with the legislative branch, the governor of California has two types of vetoes. The first is a package veto that can be used to reject any legislation passed by the state legislature. The governor also has item veto power over appropriations, which means that he or she can selectively veto parts of an appropriations bill without rejecting the rest of the act. As a result, the governor has substantial control over state spending, as well as over the types of programs and government actions that are either maintained or allowed to die out because of funding issues. Both the package and item vetoes are, however, subject to legislative override. Such an override requires at least a two-thirds vote in both houses. In this way, each of these two branches of the state government has a check on the other's activities.

As a part of the role of chief executive, the governor of California is also given the power to make appointments to fill vacancies that might occur in any of the other executive offices. However, his or her ability to fill these vacancies is subject to approval and confirmation by the state senate and assembly. Finally, the governor is required to report to the legislature any time he or she chooses to exercise the office's constitutional power to grant reprieves, pardons, or commutations of sentences for individuals convicted of crimes. These checks and balances, built into the state constitution, reflect historical concerns about concentrating power in a single branch of government and the desire to limit the unilateral capabilities of the state executive.

The state of California also provides for a direct, democratic check on the governor in the form of a recall vote, by which the citizens of the state can petition to have an early election to remove the sitting governor while simultaneously electing a replacement. The recall rules in California require only that the signatures of 12 percent of the eligible population be gathered within 160 days after the process has begun. The impetus for a recall can be anything; it is usually brought on by a lack of popular support for the governor or his or her activities among the electorate. In 2003, Arnold Schwarzenegger became the thirty-eighth governor of California following the recall of Governor Gray Davis. Due to surges in unemployment, state budgetary problems, and a continuing governmental inability to address a number of statewide needs, Davis's popularity sagged from a high of over 60 percent to a record low approval rating of a mere 24 percent. Schwarzenegger's subsequent election was monumental, as he became only the second person in U.S. history to take over after the recall of a sitting governor. The first time that had occurred in the United States was over eighty years earlier: in 1921, North Dakota governor Lynn Frazier was successfully recalled and was replaced by Ragnvald A. Nestos.

Perhaps the most famous of the Golden State governors was Ronald Reagan. Reagan defied political odds when he became governor of California even though he had not previously held any public office. Although an active Democrat for a number of years, he began to embrace a number of conservative philosophies that earned him the backing of the Republican Party in his bid for the state's chief executive office. Reagan's ideological program left its mark on the state, as he not only helped to return fiscal conservatism to state spending levels in an effort to balance the budget but also reformed the state's welfare system. After serving as governor of California from 1967 to 1975, Ronald Reagan went on to become the president of the United States. In doing so, "the Great Communicator" became the first California governor to occupy the Oval Office.

The lieutenant governor has many responsibilities in California, among them serving as president of the state senate as well as serving as a regent of the University of California and as a trustee of the California State University system. The lieutenant governor often carries out other duties, such as leading a variety of programs related to health, infrastructure, trade, and education. The secretary of state is the chief elections officer and the overseer of campaign finance laws. He or she oversees the chartering of corporations, the commissioning of notaries public, and the state archive. The attorney general is the chief law officer. As such, it is his or her duty to "see that the laws of the state are uniformly and adequately enforced." The attorney general coordinates statewide narcotics enforcement efforts; participates in criminal investigations; and provides forensic science services, identification and information services, and telecommunication support. In addition, the AG is responsible for protecting consumers from fraud. The treasurer is the state's lead asset manager, banker, and financier. He or she manages and invests public moneys on behalf of state and local government. The primary functions of the state controller are to provide sound fiscal control over both receipts and disbursements of public funds; to report periodically on the financial operations and condition of both state and local government; to make certain that money due the state is collected through fair, equitable, and effective tax administration; and to provide fiscal guidance to local governments.

The challenges facing the California executive include but are not limited to the traditional concerns of fostering economic growth, providing governmental services, and balancing the state budget. However, the governor's office is also faced with difficult issues related to the high level of immigration, which impacts the state in a variety of ways in terms of jobs, resources, the environment, and public education, to name just a few. Recent demographic studies estimate that immigration into California accounts for approximately one-third of all immigration into the United States. At the turn of the millennium, California also had to deal with problems within the energy sector of its enormous infrastructure, as rolling blackouts caused power shortages that affected everything from residential to corporate activities. Another obstacle confronting the chief executive is how to balance efforts to attract and main-

Ronald and Nancy Reagan at the victory celebration for California governor at the Biltmore Hotel in Los Angeles. (Ronald Reagan Library)

tain businesses in the state with the environmental and employment concerns that result from such a large, robust economy. These are but a fraction of the difficult issues that come with the job of governor of the state of California.

Joseph J. Foy

References

California State Constitution of 1879.
Saffell, David C., and Harry Basehart. 2005. *State and local government: Politics and public policies*, 8th ed. New York: McGraw-Hill.
Simmons, Charlene W. 2004. To faithfully execute the law: California's executive branch agencies, 1959–2003. Sacramento: California Research Bureau. http://www.library.ca.gov/crb/04/02/04–002.pdf.

U.S. Bureau of the Census. 2004. *California QuickFacts.* http://www.census.gov.

U.S. Department of Labor. Bureau of Labor and Statistics. 2004. California economy at a glance. http://www.bls.gov.

Additional Resources and Recommended Readings

Gerston, Larry N., and Terry Christensen. 2002. *California government and politics: A practical approach.* Belmont, CA: Wadsworth.

Grodin, Joseph R., Calvin R. Massey, and Richard B. Cunningham. 1993. *The California State Constitution.* Westport, CT: Greenwood.

Janiskee, Brian P., and Ken Masugi. 2002. *Democracy in California: Politics and government in the Golden State.* Lanham, MD: Rowman and Littlefield.

Newslink. 2004. California Newspapers. http://newslink.org/canews.html.

State of California. 2005. Official homepage of the governor of the state of California. http://www.governor.ca.gov/state/govsite/gov_homepage.jsp.

COLORADO

• • • • • • • • • • • •

COLORADO ELECTED EXECUTIVE BRANCH OFFICIALS

Governor	Lieutenant Governor
Attorney General	Secretary of State

Treasurer

http://www.colorado.gov

• • • • • • • • • • • •

Starting in 1858 and reaching its peak in 1859, the Colorado gold rush drew settlers from all over the nation. These individuals began seeking their fortunes in gold in the area around Denver, which today serves as Colorado's state capital. Like most mining booms, Colorado's rush involved a huge influx of people followed by their rapid departure when the resources began to run dry. However, even after the so-called Fifty-niners vacated the area, Colorado found its permanent place within the frontier West. With the help of the territorial governor, John Long Routt, who had prepared the area for admission into the Union, Colorado became the nation's thirty-eighth state on August 1, 1876. In recognition of his efforts, the people of Colorado elected Routt to serve as their first governor (from 1876 to 1879) and again as their seventh governor (from 1891 to 1893). Since Colorado's establish-

ment as a state, the executives who have served the people have confronted a number of economic transitions, as the state's economic base has shifted from mining to agriculture and from agriculture to manufacturing. The governors have played vital roles in attempting to resolve continuing disputes over land and resources. Over the years, these executives have assisted Colorado in becoming a true economic hub in the Rocky Mountain West, and they have helped to draw businesses and people back to the state in search of their fortunes.

Colorado's executive branch is constitutionally limited to twenty departments. It is headed by five statewide officials—the governor, lieutenant governor, secretary of state, state treasurer, and attorney general. All five of these public officials are limited to serving two consecutive, four-year terms. Such limitations went into effect in 1991 following a constitutional amendment, with the rationale for limiting the terms of those officials in the executive branch being expressly written into the state's constitution. According to Article 4, Section 1, term limits are applied to these executive offices "in order to broaden opportunities for public service and to guard against excessive concentrations of power." David Ottke, the executive director of the Colorado Term Limit Coalition, noted that term limits also ensure "that we have a competitive election every eight years" (Hughes and Pankratz 2002, E-03). The voters of the state, for a number of reasons, have embraced the application of term limits on their elected, statewide officials. In fact, it was through public referenda in 1991, 1994, 1996, and 1998 that term limits were applied by the people on their elected officials.

The head of the executive branch is the governor, who is responsible of overseeing the execution of state law. The governor is assisted in this task by the lieutenant governor. These officials, who are chosen together as a team in a statewide election, must be at least thirty years of age, U.S. citizens, and citizens of the state of Colorado for at least two years prior to election. If for any reason the governor is unable to fulfill his or her duties as chief executive of the state, the lieutenant governor assumes that role. However, the lieutenant governor can also function as a vital partner to the governor in the executive office. How active the lieutenant governor is largely depends on his or her working relationship with the governor. Jane Norton, currently serving as the state's forty-sixth lieutenant governor

under Bill Owens, is an example of an actively involved lieutenant.

Norton serves as the chair for the eleven-member Colorado Commission on Indian Affairs. Historically, Colorado was inhabited by a number of Plains tribes, including the Apache, Cheyenne, Ute, Arapaho, Comanche, and Kiowa. The Navajo also settled in southern parts of the state. Today, the Ute continue to constitute a large part of the demographic landscape in Colorado, and the lieutenant governor acts as a medium between their interests and those of the state. She has also been active in implementing health insurance reform throughout the state. In addition, Norton serves as a delegate on the Aerospace States Association, which is vital to maintaining over 100,000 jobs in the aerospace industry in the state. Although some of these responsibilities are statutorily defined, the good working relationship between Norton and Governor Owens enables her to be more proactive in setting the agenda for her office.

Along with the governor and lieutenant governor, three other statewide officials round out the executive office. Similar requirements of office are placed on these three officials, although in order to serve as secretary of state, treasurer, or attorney general, a candidate need only be twenty-five years of age. To qualify for the position of attorney general, a candidate must have the additional credential of being a licensed attorney in good standing within the state. The secretary of state oversees the collecting, screening, and communication of information, in addition to managing state elections and working to enhance commerce. The state treasurer provides banking, investment, and accounting services for all funds and assets deposited in the treasury. The attorney general has primary authority for enforcement of consumer protection and antitrust laws, prosecution of criminal appeals and some complex white-collar crimes, the statewide grand jury, training and certification of peace officers, and certain natural resource and environmental matters. In addition, the AG is the chief legal counsel and adviser to the executive branch of the state.

If there is a vacancy within any of the other executive offices, the governor is granted the power to fill the position via appointment. Such an appointment requires the approval of the senate. In addition to these elected offices, the governor's cabinet consists of the heads of a number of departments ranging from agriculture to education and technology to trade.

As chief executive, the governor serves as commander-in-chief of the state militia, among his or her other duties. As commander-in-chief, the governor may call on the armed forces of the state to assist in the faithful execution of public law, unless they are otherwise called into the service of the federal government. This power was used on a number of occasions by Governors Albert Wills McIntire (1895–1897) and James Hamilton Peabody (1903–1905), who called on the National Guard to calm violence that erupted during mining strikes at the turn of the twentieth century. In addition to calling on the National Guard for assistance in executing the law, the governor can ask officers in the executive branch to report to him or her any information relating to their positions. The governor uses these reports to stay abreast of the needs and activities of the state and applies this information to the yearly state of the state address at the commencement of each new legislative assembly. The governor is also required to report to the assembly about all state incomes and expenditures, and he or she must also—under oath—make a semiannual reporting of all state accounts. This requirement helps to maintain transparency and complete public accountability for all state spending and financial allocation for goods and services. Finally, the governor has the power to grant reprieves or pardons to or commute the sentences of those individuals convicted of any crime except treason or in cases of impeachment. In an effort to prevent an abuse of this power, however, the governor is required to give a full report of his or her actions in this regard to the legislative assembly.

In dealing with the legislature, the governor has the power both to convene special sessions and to adjourn regular sessions of the legislative assembly. If the legislature passes an act that does not meet the approval of the governor, he or she may veto that legislation by returning it to the originating house with objections noted. The legislature can override this veto with a two-thirds vote in both legislative chambers. In addition to this package form of veto, the governor also has a special item veto that may be applied to specific elements of an appropriations bill. Consequently, the governor may reject parts of the spending bill while leaving the rest intact. If the item veto is used by the governor, then the parts of the bill that were rejected return to the assembly, where legislators will reconsider the elements individually and may override the veto in the manner previously described.

One of the most important jobs of the executive of a state such as Colorado is maintaining a vibrant and efficient public utilities program. Although the Colorado Public Utilities Commission itself is the result of legislative actions, it was Governor Benjamin Harrison Eaton who, in 1885, made the initial attempts at regulating public utilities through the appointment of the state's first railway commissioner. Since that time, regulation has been an essential element of the governor's job description, especially given the lopsided distribution of the state's population in conjunction with limited water resources. Additionally, as previously noted, the role of the executive in the state of Colorado often involves attempting to balance the needs of a population undergoing economic transitions and reforms. Following the initial gold rush, the state had to be remade economically if it was to develop and thrive. The initial transition was to agricultural production, which required executive action to expand irrigation throughout the state. Following the agricultural period, Colorado began to move into manufacturing, relying heavily on gubernatorial efforts to attract military bases and production facilities to the state.

Today, Colorado remains a central area for military development and research, as Colorado Springs is home to both the North American Aerospace Defense Command (NORAD) and the U.S. Air Force Academy. Although Colorado's relationship to the U.S. military and to weapons research and manufacturing has benefited the economy in some ways, it has also created strains requiring executive initiative to help resolve spillover issues that come from such partnerships. For example, Governor Owens, who was reelected by the largest majority in Colorado history in 2002, was forced to deal with ecological and transitional employment ramifications following a round of layoffs at Rocky Flats, a major nuclear weapons plant based in northern Colorado. These are but a few of the significant challenges facing the executive department of Colorado as it seeks to continually diversify its economic base, attract new business, and increase the quality of life of those who live in the Centennial State.

Joseph J. Foy

References

Colorado State Constitution of 1876, Art. 4.

Hughes, Jim, and Howard Pankratz. 2002. Term limits for DAs, other referendums outcomes are mixed on ballot questions. *Denver Post*, November 6.

Schmidt, David D. 1989. *Citizens as legislators: The ballot initiative revolution.* Philadelphia: Temple University Press.

State of Colorado. Department of Regulatory Agencies, Colorado Public Utilities Commission. 2004. A brief history of the Public Utilities Commission. http://www.dora.state.co.us/puc/about/AboutHistory.htm.

———. Governor's Office. 2004. Governor Bill Owens's official website. http://www.colorado.gov/governor/.

———. Lieutenant Governor's Office. 2004. Lieutenant Governor Jane E. Norton's official website. http://www.colorado.gov/ltgovernor/ index.html.

Additional Resources and Recommended Readings

DenverPost.com. http://www.denverpost
.com.

Lamm, Richard D., and Duane A. Smith.
1984. *Pioneers and politicians: 10
Colorado governors in profile.* Boulder:
Pruett.

Rocky Mountain News. http://www
.rockymountainnews.com.

State of Colorado. Colorado Department of
Personnel and Administration. 2004.
Colorado State Archives. http://www
.colorado.gov/dpa/doit/archives/
resource.html.

CONNECTICUT

● ● ● ● ● ● ● ● ● ● ● ●

CONNECTICUT ELECTED EXECUTIVE BRANCH OFFICIALS

Governor	Lieutenant Governor
Attorney General	Secretary of State
Treasurer	Comptroller

http://www.ct.gov/

● ● ● ● ● ● ● ● ● ● ● ●

Connecticut appears to have two distinct identities. On the one hand, it is the wealthiest state (when measured in per capita income) and the home of quaint, pristine New England villages, where the town meeting still enjoys a high degree of civic participation and pride. On the other hand, Connecticut is home to some of New England's most bereft cities, former manufacturing havens that have lost jobs and revenue to cities in the Sun Belt or abroad. The cities of Connecticut deal with crime, social need, and revenue scarcity with some of the trappings of old-fashioned, "machine"-style politics. Connecticut ironically serves as a model of democratic practice while also displaying some of troubling aspects of politics and government. State leadership, especially as exercised by Governor Jodi Rell, has led the way in reforming the ethics laws of the state to forge a brighter future, more consistent with the best of democratic governance.

Connecticut has several nicknames, including the Nutmeg State and the Land of Steady Habits, but its official nickname is the Constitution State. Connecticut historians claim that the state's initial constitution, drafted in 1639, was the first to establish a modern democratic government. Connecticut colonists specified distinct legislative and executive branches and officers, rights of citizens, and forms of government in the document called the Fundamental Orders. The first governor of the Connecticut colony, John Haynes, was a popular choice. He was elected in 1639 to his first one-year term. Under the Fundamental Orders, the sitting governor could not run for reelection, but Haynes was appointed as the deputy governor at the end of his year as governor. After reestablishing his eligibility to serve, he ran for and won a second term in 1641—and in every odd-numbered year after that until his death in 1653. Even though the state had a strict term limit for its governor, Haynes found a way around it and was able to serve as the chief executive eight separate times!

Unlike some of the other New England states with constitutional roots in colonial times, Connecticut modernized its constitution consistently into the late twentieth century. One of the primary focuses of the state constitutions shaped during the period of the Articles of Confederation (predominantly in the 1780s) was the limitation of executive power; this limitation is clear in Connecticut's two neighbors to the north, Vermont and New Hampshire. Both of these states still limit the governor's term to two years (though a governor can be reelected indefinitely if he or she has voter support). Since 1950, Connecticut governors have served four-year terms of office, and they can be elected to as many terms as the candidates and voters choose. And in that period, three governors have served into three terms—Democrats John Dempsey and William O'Neill and Republican John Rowland. None of these men completed all three terms, however.

In addition to the governor, Connecticut voters elect five officials to serve on the executive leadership team. The lieutenant governor is the presiding officer in the state senate, stands in when the governor is incapacitated, and takes over if the governor dies or resigns from office. The lieutenant governor also serves as the chairperson over specialized coordinating committees, such as the state's mental health cabinet. The secretary of state maintains important state government records, such as business registrations, campaign finance reports, and elec-

Connecticut governor M. Jodi Rell (Office of Governor M. Jodi Rell)

tions documentation. One of the most important duties of the Connecticut secretary of state (like his or her equivalents in other states) is the implementation of the Help America Vote Act of 2002, whereby a state government must ensure the accuracy and consistency of voting equipment and information for all voters.

The Connecticut governor receives financial advice and support from an elected treasurer and comptroller. The treasurer is responsible for the sound maintenance of collected income, sales, and other taxes; relations with banks that issue debt on behalf of the state; and responsible investment and payout of pension funds for government employees. The comptroller pays the government's bills (for example, for the purchase of goods to be used by government agencies), reports on the state's budget, and handles government employee payrolls and fringe-benefit administration. These duties of the treasurer and comptroller may seem mundane, but they are crucial to the state's economic operation in three ways. First, the state could lose millions of dollars each year if its investments were handled poorly. Second, the government's employees and contractors appreciate smooth functioning of payment processes. And possibly most important of all, the $13.5 billion state budget could be subject to corrupt actions such as embezzlement and misuse of funds if the treasurer and comptroller were not diligent in their roles as fiscal watchdogs.

The attorney general of Connecticut is the legal representative of all governmental agencies and also serves as a protector of the constitutional rights of the state's citizens. The attorney general's office may defend state agencies and services when they are sued, but it also oversees state operations in a proactive manner to ensure that state employees are not breaking the law while carrying out the state's duties. For example, the attorney general scrutinizes service contracts to make sure that they are not awarded in a biased or discriminatory manner. In the area of citizen protection, the Connecticut attorney general polices businesses and individuals who try to commit fraud on unsuspecting consumers. Two major focuses in this area include telemarketing and E-mail scams.

The attorney general's website offers tips to citizens to protect against these types of fraud and provides a hotline for reporting problematic sales operations. Around the country, state attorneys general are vigilant in their efforts to protect citizens and the public interest, and this elected post is seen as a stepping stone to higher office. Connecticut is no exception; Joseph Lieberman, the state's junior U.S. senator who ran as the vice-presidential candidate on the Democratic national ticket in 2000, is a former Connecticut attorney general.

The Connecticut governor has a great deal of support from other actors in leading the state and its policies. But the governor's greatest ongoing responsibility is crafting the state budget, whereby service priorities are enhanced or reduced—given more money or less for the coming year. The state budget process could be likened to a chess game between the executive and legislative branches of government. In this game, the governor has the first two moves. First, each January, the governor announces his or her priorities in the state of the state message. Much like the president's State of the Union address, this is a widely publicized speech made directly to the legislature, but since the cameras are rolling, the entire state population is part of the audience. Next, the governor has the opportunity to fill in the details of the broad outline presented in the state of the state message. He or she has a specific bureaucratic agency charged with the job of forecasting tax revenues and agency expenses, the Office of Policy and Management (OPM). With the governor's close guidance, OPM prepares the $13.5 billion revenue and spending plan for adoption by both houses of the state legislature. If it chooses, the legislature can disregard the governor's proposed budget, but it will do so at its own peril because of the governor's veto power. The veto is the governor's tool to cancel any legislative action. When a bill comes to the governor's desk from the legislature, he or she can choose to not sign it or even to cross out portions of it. As an example, if the legislature passes a bill to create new state universities in the eastern and western halves of the state but the governor only supports the western university, he or she can use the line-item veto and cross out the disfavored budget item. Connecticut's governor has one of the strongest line-item vetoes in the country, with a three-fifths majority of legislators required to overturn the governor's decision to omit a legislative priority.

In most ways, the Connecticut governor has benefited from the modernization of executive powers within the state, including unlimited terms of office and strong budgetary and veto powers. But reform is an ongoing battle. The most recent governor of Connecticut, John Rowland, resigned in disgrace after being caught in a corruption scandal in 2004. Governor Rowland purportedly received "in-kind" bribes, whereby the state awarded construction contracts to certain contractors in exchange for having those contractors perform work on additions to his personal residence. When Lieutenant Governor Jodi Rell ascended to the governor's office, she quickly embarked on ethics and contracting reforms to reduce the likelihood of corrupt practices in the state's administration. Among the contracting reforms were: the standardization of contracting laws, education of government employees on fairness in purchasing practices, the enhancement of public access to contracting decisions, and harsher penalties for contracting abuses. When "old-style" politics and corruption rears its ugly head in Connecticut, it can be balanced with reform-oriented policy, under the leadership of a strong and progressive governor's office.

Brendan Burke

References

Connecticut Attorney General's Office. Consumer issues. 2005. http://www.cslib.org/attygenl/mainlinks/tabindex3.htm .

Constitution of the State of Connecticut. 2005. http://www.sots.state.ct.us/RegisterManual/SectionI/ctconstit.htm.

Lockard, Duane. 1959. *New England state politics.* Princeton: Princeton University Press.

McKee, Clyde, and Stefanie Chambers. 2003. Connecticut's challenged political systems. *New England Journal of Political Science* 1:183–190.

Rell, Jodi. 2004. A blueprint for restoring integrity in state government. http://www.ct.gov/governorrell/cwp/view.asp?A=1793&Q=277410.

Additional Resources and Recommended Readings

Feinberg, Barbara Silberdick. 2001. *Joseph Lieberman: Keeping the faith.* Brookfield, CT: Millbrook.

Weicker, Lowell P., Jr. 1995. *Maverick: A life in politics.* Boston: Little, Brown.

DELAWARE

• • • • • • • • • • • • •

Governor	Lieutenant Governor
Attorney General	Treasurer
Auditor of Accounts	Insurance Commissioner

http://www.delaware.gov/

• • • • • • • • • • • • •

Delaware, the second-smallest state in the Union, has a diversity to its geography that is at odds with its size. The southern portion of the state, secluded on the eastern reaches of the Chesapeake Bay, is a beautiful region of isolated marshes and long, sandy beaches. To the north is the city of Wilmington, a bustling banking and financial center and home to a thriving petrochemical industry. Millions pass through Delaware each year on their way from Washington, D.C., and Baltimore to New York City via Interstate 95. For its size, Delaware has a surprisingly large impact on the nation's economy. The First State provides a model for average legislative and executive powers, featuring a balance between citizen and governmental influence appropriate to the distinct nature of this 96-mile-long state.

Like Rhode Island, Delaware is a state that would seem more like a community than most others, if not for the distinctive nature between the state's northern and southern reaches. The state capital of Dover has a population of only 32,000 people, so the legislature and governor operate in a community that feels like a small town. The state house of representatives, with forty-two members, and the state senate, with twenty-one members, have the short legislative session and small staff of a "citizen" legislature; yet the average pay in these two bodies is at the higher end of the scale ($33,400 per session), likely in keeping with the higher cost of living in the center of the eastern seaboard.

Executive powers in Delaware might be seen as a combination of weakness and strength. The governor must share power with five other separately elected officials. The lieutenant governor is elected separately from the governor, though at the same time. The state constitution specifies the duties of the lieutenant governor as president of the state senate and as chair of the Board of Pardons. The formal duties involve properly facilitating senate meetings and breaking tie votes when the body is deadlocked. From there, the lieutenant governor's duties are relatively dependent on the energies of the officeholder and the support he or she gets from the governor. For example, as lieutenant governor, John Carney played prominent roles in establishing health care and education policies by leading committees on these issues. In some states, the lieutenant governor is seen as a symbolic and unimportant job—the "governor-in-waiting" if some misfortune befalls the top officeholder. But in Delaware, lieutenant governors have a good record of rising to the position of governor once the incumbent resigns or is forced out of office by term limits.

The other elected positions in the Delaware cabinet include the attorney general, responsible for legal functions of state government; the auditor of accounts, an independent evaluator of the state's financial records and transactions; the insurance commissioner, who establishes regulations under which private insurance companies must operate within Delaware's borders; and the state treasurer, who is responsible for the collection of taxes and the proper investment of the state's large cash balances and resources. In some states, these functions serve the governor directly, as he or she appoints the officeholders. There are advantages in such a system, as it will be the governor's job to ensure that the officeholder carries out the job properly. However, there is also an argument for democratic control, as exists in Delaware. Citizens may or may not know the name of the auditor of accounts (let alone understand the job), but this individual may take his or her mandate from the citizenry seriously. The current attorney general of Delaware is active in confronting tobacco companies, examining securities fraud, and enforcing consumer protection laws. The auditor of accounts has expanded his mission to include the investigation of fraud complaints against the state's civil servants. Furthermore, the independence of the

state auditor insulates the governor. Since the separately elected auditor undertakes investigations of financial wrongdoing or mismanagement, Delaware's governors do not have to scrutinize their own employees when they are under investigation, and they are protected from allegations that their appointees are not subject to the same scrutiny as other state officials.

The governor of Delaware has other limitations to his or her powers, based on the participation of other political actors. The state constitution strongly limits the governor's power to appoint agency and department heads and judges (who are not elected in Delaware). The benign-sounding language of the constitution states that the governor may appoint his or her favored candidates for office without senate confirmation unless "the salary, fees, and emoluments of office shall exceed five hundred dollars annually." In other words, the governor may choose volunteers to work with his or her office without the state senate's involvement; all other appointments require legislative confirmation. Thus, the legislature has a hand in the appointment of a number of the state's administrative officials, as well as in the establishment of the $2.4 billion state budget.

The governor's judicial powers are rather limited compared to those of chief executives in other states. The Board of Pardons makes recommendations to the governor on the commutation of criminal penalties; the governor cannot issue a pardon without a recommendation having been made, though he or she can ignore or go against the recommendation.

The governor's other formal powers are consistent with those of most other U.S. governors, giving strength to the office. The Delaware governor is allowed to serve up to two consecutive, four-year terms; the last three elected governors, Pierre DuPont, Michael Castle, and Thomas Carper, all chose to do so. Thirty-nine of the fifty states allow their governors to serve for eight years. Three states are more restrictive than Delaware in limiting the governor's terms, while in the remaining eight states, the only limitation is the number of times that the public is willing to reelect the incumbent. Is eight years a sufficient time for a Delaware governor to make his or her mark on the state? It would appear so, as Governor Carper has moved on to the U.S. Senate, Governor Castle now serves in the U.S. House of Representatives (which is a statewide position in the small state of Delaware), and Governor DuPont was sufficiently prominent to make a run at the 1988 Republican presidential nomination.

Like the president, the governor cannot write legislation; he or she can propose bills but will need a sponsor in the legislature to introduce legislative initiatives. Yet national and state executives have historically held the power to veto any legislative action of which they disapprove. The strongest possible veto power is the line-item veto. With this tool, a governor can reject only the portions of a bill that are disfavored and maintain the portions that he or she likes. Say, for example, that the governor is presented with a budget bill to fund road construction across the state. If he or she does not want to fund the five roads proposed in the southern portion of the state but *does* support the five northern roads in the measure, the governor can simply cross the southern roads out of the budget bill. If he or she has some support in the legislature to prevent a bill's override, or rejection by a supermajority of votes, the governor with a line-item veto has special strength in crafting the legislation that crosses his or her desk. Delaware's governor holds this most influential form of the veto; in fact, this is the only area in which the Delaware chief executive could be characterized as having above-average powers.

With all of this in mind, is the governor of Delaware an administrative weakling? Given the skills and abilities the governors themselves bring to the office, as well as Delaware's stature as a state that is much more powerful than its size would suggest, the answer to this question is, probably not. The current governor, Ruth Ann Minner, held positions in the Delaware House of Representatives from 1974 to 1982 and in the state senate from 1982 to 1992. She also served as lieutenant governor from 1993 to 2001 and has been governor since then. Governor Minner's leadership has been clear in several of the state's services, bridging her legislative and executive careers. She led the expansion of state conservation lands and initiated administrative reorganizations to streamline the state bureaucracy while serving in the senate and as lieutenant governor. In a move on the forefront of controlling sprawl (unplanned commercial and residential land use growth), she pushed for the formation of the "Livable Delaware" initiative, and she continues to support it as governor. Under this program, the state provides incentives to encourage planned growth and to protect open spaces and natural resources. Delaware has a population of less than 800,000, but it moved up from the forty-seventh most populous state to the forty-fifth since the 1980s. Under Governor Minner, it is one of only a few states that are taking the lead on the issue of managing land use, which is usually left to municipal governments.

Finally, the potential of the Delaware governor has been made clear in Governor Minner's response to potential terrorist threats. She has initiated several policies under her executive order authority (that is, the ability of the governor to unilaterally establish policies affecting the governmental workforce and its duties), and these policies have been followed with legislative action. Among the cooperative actions between Governor Minner and the legislature are: (1) a bill to ensure that state employees who are called up to active duty as members of the National Guard will forfeit no pay during their military service, (2) emergency health powers legislation to enhance the acquisition of public health information related to potential terrorist attacks and to clarify the chain of command in the event of a chemical or biological terrorist incident, and (3) increased penalties for making false threats of chemically or biologically related terrorist incidents.

Delaware is an average state when it comes to its executive's powers. But just as the great potential of its diverse financial and industrial economy outstrips its place as one of the smallest states, the governor of Delaware can rise above these average powers and resources as the need arises.

Brendan Burke

References

Minner, Governor Ruth Ann. 1999. Livable Delaware agenda. Dover, DE: Office of State Planning Coordination. http://www.state.de.us/planning/livedel/details.htm.

State of Delaware. Delaware Constitution, Art. 3. http://www.delcode.state.de.us/constitution/index.htm.

———. State Auditor. 2004. Message from R. Thomas Wagner Jr. http://www.state.de.us/auditor/default.shtml.

———. State Treasurer. 2004. Welcome to our website! M. Jane Brady, attorney general. http://www.state.de.us/attgen/index.htm

Additional Resources and Recommended Readings

Boyer, William W. 2000. *Governing Delaware: Policy problems in the first state.* Newark: University of Delaware Press.

Bushman, Claudia L., Harold B. Hancock, and Elizabeth Moyne Homsey, eds. 1988. *Proceedings of the House of Assembly of Delaware State, 1781–1792, and of the Constitutional Convention of 1792.* Newark: University of Delaware Press.

Harmon, Robert B. 1990. *Government and politics in Delaware: A selected guide to information resources.* Monticello, IL: Vance Bibliographies.

Martin, Roger A. 1984. *A history of Delaware through its governors, 1776–1984.* Wilmington, DE: McClafferty.

Phelan, James L. 1973. *The company state: Ralph Nader's study group report on Dupont in Delaware.* New York: Grossman.

FLORIDA
• • • • • • • • • • • •

FLORIDA ELECTED EXECUTIVE BRANCH OFFICIALS
Governor   Lieutenant Governor
Attorney General   Chief Financial Officer
Commissioner of Agriculture
http://www.fl.gov/

• • • • • • • • • • • •

Like most governors, Florida's chief executive is responsible for overseeing a vast governmental structure and a multitude of activities within the Sunshine State. Florida is the nation's fourth-largest state, with a diverse citizenry, geography, and economy. However, most Florida governors consistently have to deal with one phenomenon that many other governors may never encounter—hurricanes. During 2004, for instance, Florida experienced Hurricane Charley, a category-four storm that left a swath of destruction across the state's midsection. Governor Jeb Bush, the state's forty-third chief executive, served as the point man for dealing with the natural disaster and coordinating state efforts to rebuild and repair. When natural disasters such as hurricanes occur, governors must manage activities and provide services to their states' citizens. Like all chief executives, Florida's governors must incorporate these responsibilities into their broader range of jobs. However, Florida's chief executive must share power and authority with other popularly elected officials within state government, a situation found in many other states.

The executive branch in Florida is divided into several offices. An executive branch with this division of powers is commonly referred to as a "plural" executive. As in most states, the chief executive officer in Florida is the governor, who is vested with "supreme executive power." However, the governor must share this executive power with a cabinet composed of an attorney general, chief financial officer, and commissioner of agriculture. In addition, there is a lieutenant governor, who succeeds the governor if he or she leaves the office for any reason. Other officers include the secretary of state and commissioner of education, who are appointed by the governor. Prior to constitutional changes in 2003, the position of chief financial officer was fulfilled by a treasurer and a comptroller; now, those two positions are merged into one office.

With this cabinet structure, Florida divides executive power and authority among multiple officials. Usually taking place every other Tuesday, cabinet meetings are held in the state capitol building. Staffers for each of the four cabinet members brief their respective officials prior to the meeting. The cabinet may meet in the form of a board, a commission, or a department: for example, it might sit as the state Board of Executive Clemency, with the governor and other cabinet members determining whether to commute a prisoner's sentence or grant pardons. Other departments, commissions, or boards that the cabinet may convene as include the state's Board of Administration, Division of Bond Finance, Department of Veterans' Affairs, Department of Highway Safety and Motor Vehicles, Department of Law Enforcement, Department of Revenue, Administration Commission (which also serves as the Florida Land and Water Adjudicatory Commission), Electrical Power Plant and Transmission Line Siting Board, Board of Trustees of the Internal Improvement Trust Fund, and Financial Services Commission.

At every cabinet meeting, the staff of each agency submits an agenda and information to the governor and other cabinet members. Each cabinet member also has a staffer who reviews the proposed agenda and material and in turn prepares material for the cabinet official. Citizens may participate at any point in the process, and they generally do so at the cabinet meetings. Following discussion, a voice vote is taken by the cabinet to act on a given agenda item.

The governor is formally responsible for ensuring that the laws "be faithfully executed," and he or she is also responsible for the "planning and budgeting for the state." In addition, the governor serves as commander-in-chief of all military forces of the state and can call out the militia in order to "preserve the public peace, execute the laws of the state, suppress insurrection, or repel invasion." The governor is limited to two four-year terms, but unlike some other states, Florida has no constitutional require-

Florida governor Jeb Bush (Office of Governor Jeb Bush)

ments regarding age or residency for the chief executive. All other statewide elected officials can serve an unlimited number of terms.

Like all other governors, Florida's chief executive has the formal constitutional power of the veto. He or she may decide to reject a bill that was approved by the legislature, but the legislature may override the governor's veto by casting a two-thirds vote in each chamber.

The governor also has the power to propose a budget for the state. In preparing that budget, the chief executive uses the Office of Planning and Budget, which collects the requests from all state agencies and compiles the budget. Unlike the situation in other states, however, the governor's budget in Florida is only a set of recommendations and is not introduced as a bill for consideration by the legislature. The legislature may take or reject the governor's recommendations in drafting a bill of appropriations, otherwise known as the budget bill.

Another constitutional power that the governor possesses is the power to fill, by appointment, a vacancy in any state or county appointed office for the remainder of the term of office. If there is a vacancy in a position that is elected by the voters, the governor can appoint someone for the remainder of the term of office if it is less than twenty-eight months. If the term of the vacant elected office is longer than twenty-eight months, then the appointee will stand for election at the next general election.

In running for governor, candidates are able to handpick their lieutenant governors. Although very little formal or constitutional power is associated with the office, the lieutenant governor can be assigned duties and responsibilities by the governor. The state's first female elected to that office, Lieutenant Governor Toni Jennings, served as Governor Bush's liaison during Hurricane Charley and gave many press interviews to keep the public aware of the governmental assistance being provided to those affected by the natural disaster.

Beyond picking their running mates, Florida's governors can use informal powers to benefit their office. Most notably is the power that comes with the chief legislator role. Each year, the governor, by constitutional provision, is required to deliver a message to the legislature "concerning the condition of the state." During what is commonly called the state of the state address, the governor can direct the atten-

tion of the public and the media to propose legislation and announce other plans and initiatives. This informal power—known as the power of the bully pulpit—allows the chief executive to gain the public's attention and focus the legislature's consideration on his or her programs.

Just as the governor shares some legislative power, both by constitutional and informal means, the legislature shares some executive power. Most notably, this derives from the power of impeachment, the ability to remove the chief executive from office. In addition, Florida's governor may be removed from office by his or her own cabinet. On receiving the petition of three cabinet members, the state supreme court may declare the governor incapacitated for office and remove him or her. The governor may be restored to office by the "written suggestion" of the governor, the legislature, or three cabinet members.

Besides electing a governor, all of Florida's voters elect an attorney general. The attorney general is responsible for a variety of legal activities, most notably serving as the official representative of the state whenever the state is taken to court. In addition, the attorney general is responsible for enforcing the state consumer protection and antitrust laws, as well as representing the state whenever there is an appeal in a criminal case. The attorney general serves as legal adviser to the governor and the cabinet and can issue legal opinions at the request of public officials regarding state laws and constitutional issues.

The next statewide elected official is the commissioner of agriculture, who is given a four-year term and is not term limited. The position originally was designated as the commissioner of immigration, with responsibility for overseeing agriculture activities as well as attracting settlers to the states. In the 1885 state constitution, the position was changed to agriculture commissioner. Currently, the commissioner of agriculture has a variety of duties, including regulating the animal industry, overseeing food safety, and licensing activities.

The final popularly elected statewide official is the chief financial officer, who administers the Department of Financial Services. This officer is responsible for numerous government activities, including consumer protection, overseeing the state

fire marshal, regulating the funeral and cemetery industry, and administering the state's workers' compensation program.

J. Michael Bitzer

References
Florida Constitution of 1968, Art. 4.
Huckshorn, Robert J. 1998. *Government and politics of Florida.* Gainesville: University Press of Florida.

Additional Resources and Recommended Readings
Colburn, David R., and Richard K. Scher. 1980. *Florida's gubernatorial politics in the twentieth century.* Tallahassee: University Press of Florida.

GEORGIA

• • • • • • • • • • • •

GEORGIA ELECTED EXECUTIVE BRANCH OFFICIALS

Governor	Lieutenant Governor
Attorney General	Public Service Commissioners
Commissioner of Agriculture	Commissioner of Labor
Insurance and Safety Fire Commissioner	
Secretary of State	State School Superintendent

http://www.ga.gov

• • • • • • • • • • • •

Georgia's chief executive office has often been filled with characters. Akin to the Long family, which built a dynasty in another southern state, Louisiana, Georgia's father-and-son team of Eugene and Herman Talmadge rose to power and occupied the highest office in the state. One of the most notable events involving the Talmadges was the "three-governors" incident. After being elected to an unprecedented fourth term as governor, Eugene Talmadge, sick on the campaign trail from a liver condition, died prior to his inauguration in 1947. The state was then

left with a political vacuum, and several men tried to fill it, most notably Eugene's son, Herman. However, two other men—the retiring governor, Ellis Arnall, and the first lieutenant governor of the state, M. E. Thompson (of the anti-Talmadge faction)—claimed the chief executive's office. Prior to 1946, the state of Georgia did not have a lieutenant governor.

The constitution of 1945 did not make succession clear. Three different interpretations arose as to what would happen to the state's chief executive office if the individual who won the November election died prior to being sworn in. The first interpretation was that the incumbent governor would continue to serve until a new governor was selected (an interpretation preferred by Arnall, the sitting governor), while the second interpretation held that the lieutenant governor–elect, on being sworn into office, would automatically assume the governorship, as provided in the constitution (an interpretation supported by Lieutenant Governor Thompson). However, the Talmadge forces relied on a third interpretation, in which the general assembly was given power to select the chief executive; since the legislature was dominated by Talmadge supporters, this was their favored interpretation. During the election campaign and Eugene's obvious illness, his supporters encouraged Herman to run as a write-in candidate. Under their interpretation, the general assembly would pick either the second or third candidate in the general election to assume the governor's office. The Talmadge machine then wanted Herman to be either the second or third candidate in order to qualify for the legislative runoff selection process.

With the beginning of 1947, Arnall and Thompson received an opinion from the state's attorney general supporting their interpretations of the succession process. On January 11, Arnall announced he would resign the office once the new lieutenant governor was sworn in. However, a few days later, the general assembly met in session, with mobs of 2,000 to 3,000 people watching the proceedings. Most individuals in both the legislature and the mob were Talmadge supporters, and, as Herman recalled, "some of them [were] armed, some of them drunk"

(http://www.georgiaencyclopedia.org). Supporters of Thompson were also there, and they claimed to have put "knockout drops" in the drinks given to Talmadge supporters.

Chaos continued until the legislature officially counted the votes from the general election; it was then discovered that Herman had actually come in fourth, behind two other write-in candidates. The vote was immediately challenged, and an envelope with votes from Herman Talmadge's home county was quickly "discovered." With these votes, Herman took the lead. However, it was later revealed that all of the newly discovered votes were written in the same handwriting, that the voters had cast their ballots in alphabetical order, and that some of the voters resided in the local cemetery. With the state's National Guard supporting Talmadge and the State Guard supporting Arnall, Georgia was close to experiencing an open revolt and perhaps a coup. Despite Talmadge being declared governor by the legislature, he and Arnall continued the standoff. When Arnall left the capitol, Talmadge ordered the locks changed on the governor's office. The next day, Arnall returned to his office only to find himself "waiting for the governor just like any other citizen" (http://www.georgiaencyclopedia.org). Arnall occupied an information booth in the capitol until a pro-Talmadge legislator dropped a firecracker in the booth. Arnall then moved to his nearby law office and continued to claim the chief executive's position until Lieutenant Governor Thompson was ready to take over.

Once Arnall resigned and Thompson claimed the authority to be acting governor, other state officers became involved. The secretary of state, as the official keeper of the seal of Georgia, refused to let the seal out of his reach, even going so far as to sleep with it. The seal was needed to make documents legal in the state. The state treasurer refused to honor any spending requests by Talmadge. State government was quickly devolving into chaos, and both Talmadge and Thompson appealed to the state's supreme court to resolve the issue.

Later claiming that political enemies on the high court were out to sabotage his father, Talmadge lost his appeal when the supreme court declared Thompson acting governor. The court also declared that a special election was to be held in 1948 to determine who would complete the remainder of the term. It was then that Herman Talmadge declared that he would go before the "court of last resort" in the state—the people. In the special election of 1948, Talmadge easily defeated Thompson to complete his father's term, and he defeated Thompson again in the 1952 election for governor. (This story is recounted at the secretary of state's website: http://www.sos.state.ga .us/capitolguide/appendixc.htm.)

Other Georgia governors have not experienced the chaos that surrounded the 1946 election, but many have been colorful in their own right. Lester Maddox won the governorship based on his opposition to civil rights and the desegregation of his former restaurant. He defeated Ellis Arnall (of the three-governors incident) after a campaign in which he wielded the pick handles that he kept at his restaurant's front door to prevent blacks from entering. After his one term in office, Maddox

Georgia governor Eugene Talmadge announces he will seek another term. His death in 1947 prior to inauguration to his fourth term gave rise to the "three-governors" incident. (Library of Congress)

went on to serve as lieutenant governor, the only former governor to do so. Another famous Georgia governor would become president in 1976. Jimmy Carter sought to counter the racist image that plagued the Peach State.

The governor in Georgia is like many others in the South, an executive officer who must share power with other elected officials. He or she must share executive power with a lieutenant governor, secretary of state, attorney general, commissioner of insurance, superintendent of schools, commissioner of labor, and commissioner of agriculture, along with separately elected public service commissioners. This diffusion of executive power among several offices dilutes the power of the chief executive to effectively administer and oversee the executive branch of government in Georgia.

To be elected governor, one must be at least thirty years old, a U.S. citizen for fifteen or more years, and a Georgia resident for a minimum of six years prior to the election; these requirements apply to the lieutenant governor as well. Governors and lieutenant governors are limited to serving two consecutive four-year terms in office. The other constitutional officers must be twenty-five or older, U.S. citizens for ten years, and Georgia residents for four years prior to the election. In addition, the attorney general must be an active member of the Georgia State Bar for seven years prior to the election. There are no constitutional limits to the number of terms statewide officers other than the governor and lieutenant governor may serve.

The governor is responsible for "faithfully" executing the laws, and he or she "shall be the conservator of peace throughout the state." In that regard, the chief executive is the commander-in-chief of the various military forces in the state. Georgia governors may give state of the state addresses to the legislature and may call for elections to fill vacancies in the state senate and house of representatives. If a vacancy occurs in one of the statewide constitutional offices, the governor may appoint, subject to senate confirmation, an individual to serve in that capacity until the next general election.

The governor has the power to exercise a veto over legislation passed by the general assembly. If the governor vetoes a bill, the assembly can override that veto with a two-thirds majority vote in each chamber. If the governor fails to sign a bill within six days of its passage by the general assembly, the bill automatically becomes law. If the legislature adjourns for more than forty days prior to the regular six-day expiration, the governor may have until the end of the forty days to act on the measure; if the governor chooses not to sign the bill after forty days, the bill becomes law.

The constitution states that the governor must submit a budget within the first five days of a legislative session. To prepare the budget, he or she may use the Office of Planning and Budget, which typically prepares the entire document for the governor's submission. Once the legislature passes an appropriations bill, the governor may exercise a line-item veto, which the legislature can override with a two-thirds vote in each chamber.

The constitution grants authority to the lieutenant governor to serve as president of the state senate and to exercise other duties assigned by the governor. As in other states, the attorney general provides legal counsel and represents the state in court. The secretary of state is responsible for overseeing the corporations, elections, professional licenses, and archives, as well as managing the state capitol. The superintendent of schools oversees 180 school systems across the state, while the commissioner of labor oversees unemployment compensation and other employment-related activities, in addition to inspecting carnival rides and amusement parks. The commissioner of agriculture is responsible for promoting agricultural activities and the interests of the state's farmers, while the insurance commissioner is responsible for overseeing regulated industries and providing consumer protection.

J. Michael Bitzer

References

Fleischmann, Arnold, and Carol Pierannunzi. 1997. *Politics in Georgia.* Athens: University of Georgia Press.

Georgia State Constitution of 1983, Art. 3 and Art. 4.

Additional Resources and Recommended Readings

Cook, James F. 1995. *Governors of Georgia, 1754–1995.* Augusta, GA: Mercer University Press.

Henderson, Harold P., and Gary L. Roberts, eds. 1988. *Georgia governors in an age of change: From Ellis Arnall to George Busbee.* Athens: University of Georgia Press.

HAWAII

• • • • • • • • • • • •

HAWAII ELECTED EXECUTIVE BRANCH OFFICIALS
Governor   Lieutenant Governor
http://www.state.hi.us

• • • • • • • • • • • •

With President Dwight D. Eisenhower's signing of the Admission Act on March 18, 1959, Hawaii became the last U.S. territory to be admitted into the Union. The granting of statehood to Hawaii was brought about with the help of John A. Burns who, following William Frances Quinn, became the state's second elected governor in 1962. Burns served in that role for three consecutive terms, and in his twelve years in office, he established a precedent of leadership that has left its mark on Hawaiian executive politics to the present day. For starters, Burns helped to establish the Democratic Party's dominance of Hawaiian state politics that lasted four decades. Burns also laid the foundation for Hawaiian social and economic policy that continues to this day. Not only did he appeal to the wide swath of ethnic groups that made up Hawaii's population, he also worked closely with the powerful union groups in state government and private enterprises to establish fair labor and employment practices. His efforts to solve racial problems and promote civil rights led one Honolulu reporter to describe him as "likely the most important political figure of the latter half of the 20th century here in the islands" (Burlingame 2000). Governor Burns laid the foundations of government and politics in the Aloha State, and he defined a lasting role and function of the Hawaiian executive office.

The governor of Hawaii is limited to serving no more than two four-year terms. The same is true for the lieutenant governor, who is elected along with the governor as a member of the same ticket. Both the governor and lieutenant governor are required to be at least thirty years of age and residents of the state for at least five years prior to their election.

Elected governor of Hawaii in November 2002, Linda Lingle is the state's first female governor and the first Republican to be elected to the post in more than 40 years. (Office of Governor Linda Lingle)

These positions are full-time jobs, and the executive officeholders are constitutionally barred from holding any other office while serving as governor or lieutenant governor.

The governor is charged with upholding all laws passed by the state legislature, as well as enforcing decisions made by the courts. In fulfilling these responsibilities, he or she is granted a number of executive powers. Relative to most other states, the governor of Hawaii has a high degree of institutional power and authority, which stems primarily from the extremely centralized organization of Hawaiian government. Very little authority has been granted to the county governments that comprise the local municipalities of the state. Other than

the city of Honolulu, which occupies a unique position in the state, Hawaii has only two levels of local government—state and county. Concomitantly, Hawaii does not have any independent school districts; instead, the state government directly controls schools. This unusual arrangement allows much more freedom for state action in the everyday lives of the citizens of Hawaii, and it increases the power and authority of the governor and the executive departments that head the state.

Among the powers of office held by the governor are those granted to him or her as commander-in-chief of the state's armed forces. These powers enable the governor to call into service the state militia to enforce the laws and maintain peace throughout the state. Additionally, at the start of each legislative session—and at those times the chief executive may deem appropriate—the governor must deliver a state of the state address in which he or she identifies the primary needs facing the state and offers recommendations on how to address them. The governor also has the power to draft the budget of the state and submit it for legislative review and approval. Consequently, the chief executive has significant powers in setting priorities for state spending and for programs and functions that the state will provide for its citizens. Finally, the constitution offers the governor the power to grant pardons, reprieves, and commutations of sentences for those individuals convicted of any crime and, with the approval of the legislature, to pardon individuals *before* they are convicted (even in cases of impeachment). This power is much broader than the clemency powers granted to governors in most states.

The executive branch of Hawaii is limited to no more than twenty departments, though the governor may, if necessary, establish temporary agencies or departments beyond these twenty to be charged with limited functions. Headed by the governor, these departments can be created or dissolved according to gubernatorial will. The governor appoints all department heads, with the senate playing an advisory role and offering either its consent or its rejection on all gubernatorial appointments. The governor also has the power to remove each of these officials after their appointment, except for the attorney general. Removal of this chief legal officer requires an act of the state senate. Similar to the ability to appoint executive officers, the governor has the power to appoint all of the justices that serve within the state's judicial system. This power, along with the extensive pardoning powers granted to the chief executive, makes the governor a highly influential member of the state's legal system.

Another important characteristic of the Hawaiian executive office is the relationship between the lieutenant governor and the rest of the executive branch. Not only is the lieutenant governor the first in line for succession should anything happen to the governor, he or she also serves as acting governor if the chief executive is out of the state. In addition, the lieutenant governor serves concurrently as the secretary of state, making the position a full-time responsibility and one in which the officeholder has a great deal of influence on a number of state activities. Elected in

1994, Mazie Hirono, the first Asian immigrant in the United States elected to serve as lieutenant governor, was incredibly active in defining statewide educational policy. She served as the president of a number of teaching and policy commissions and also helped to start the first universal prekindergarten program, known as Pre-Plus. Although Hirono was defeated in her bid for governor in 2002, her tenure demonstrates how influential the lieutenant governor can be as a member of the executive department. Similarly, another lieutenant governor, Benjamin Cayetano, left a mark on the state's educational system through the development of Hawaii's A+ Program, a large-scale afterschool program to help children from homes with working parents. Cayetano's work in this area is another example of how active the lieutenant governor can be in shaping Hawaiian politics and policy.

Following his time as lieutenant governor, Cayetano also served as governor of the state of Hawaii, from 1994 to 2002. On his election, he became the nation's first Filipino governor. His tenure in office demonstrated the pressures placed on the Hawaiian executive office, as he was forced to deal with severe budget shortfalls and declining tax revenues. These issues added up to significant problems for Cayetano, who also had to try to maintain a balanced budget, as required by state law. Such countervailing forces place a significant strain on the ability of the state to provide needed resources and programs for the people. Succeeding Cayetano to office was Governor Linda Lingle, who broke through two barriers with her election: she was a member of the Republican Party, breaking forty years of Democratic dominance in the state executive office, and also the first woman to lead Hawaii since it was admitted into statehood. Lingle was able to win office largely because of the economic challenges facing the state.

Joseph J. Foy

References

Boylan, Dan, and T. Michael Holmes. 2000. *John A. Burns: The man and his times.* Honolulu: University of Hawaii Press.

Burlingame, Burl. 2000. Burns mystique lives after 25 years. *Honolulu Star Bulletin,* March 31, 2000. http://

starbulletin.com/2000/03/31/features /story2.html.

Burris, Jerry. 2002. Democrats' "revolution" spanned 40 years. *HonoluluAdvertiser.com,* November 10, 2002. http://the.honoluluadvertiser .com/article/2002/Nov/10/op/ op05ajerry.html.

Hawaiian State Constitution of 1978, Art. 5.

Additional Resources and Recommended Readings

Fuchs, Lawrence H. 1983. *Hawaii pono: A social history.* San Diego: Harvest, Harcourt Brace Jovanovich.

Honolulu Advertiser. http://www. honoluluadvertiser.com/.

Honolulu Star-Bulletin. http://www .starbulletin.com/.

IDAHO

● ● ● ● ● ● ● ● ● ● ● ●

IDAHO ELECTED EXECUTIVE BRANCH OFFICIALS

Governor   Lieutenant Governor
Attorney General   Controller
Secretary of State
Superintendent of Public Instruction
Treasurer
http://www.accessidaho.org/

● ● ● ● ● ● ● ● ● ● ● ●

Idaho is one of the country's most rural states, and as such, it faces a number of problems imposed by geographic isolation. For example, rural areas throughout Idaho have significant needs for support in infrastructure, telecommunications, health care, education, governance, transportation, employment training, business services, and even library systems. It often falls to the governor to address these issues, which forces the state executive of Idaho to find creative solutions. In 1997, to combat these rural problems, Republican governor Phillip Batt signed Executive Order 97-02, authorizing the continuation of the Idaho Rural Development Council, which was established in 1991 by Governor Cecil Andrus as a part of a national plan for rural economic development. Dirk Kempthorne, who was elected to serve as governor in 1999, reauthorized this executive order in an attempt to overcome the adverse effects of rural isolation. Issues of ruralism are, however, just a few of the many problems that are faced by the governor of Idaho, and in attempting to understand how these problems are dealt with, it is important to understand the nature and composition of the executive branch.

The seven officials that constitute the executive branch in the state of Idaho are the governor, lieutenant governor, secretary of state, state controller, state treasurer, attorney general, and superintendent of public instruction, all of whom are publicly elected. Unlike in some other states, the governor and lieutenant governor in Idaho are separately elected.

Each of these executive officers holds the position for a term of four years, and there are no term limits for these officials. Unelected members of the executive branch of the state of Idaho serve within one of twenty departments as defined by law. As of 1975, the executive branch became constitutionally limited to only twenty departments, although temporary agencies may be established for specific purposes as long as they do not exist for more than two years.

To qualify for election to the office of governor, lieutenant governor, or attorney general, a person must be at least thirty years of age. For the other four officers, the qualifying age is only twenty-five. The attorney general has an additional requirement for eligibility, which is that he or she must be "admitted to practice in the Supreme Court of the state or territory of Idaho, and be in good standing at the time of . . . election." Finally, all persons running for an executive office in Idaho must be U.S. citizens who have resided within the state for at least two years prior to the election.

In case there is a tie in the vote for executive officials, the decision is turned over to the state legislature, where both houses put together a joint ballot to elect the individual who will take office. Such a decision does not require a special ses-sion of the legislature, as the state constitution dictates such a balloting will take place after the legislative branch convenes for its regular session.

The powers of the governor of Idaho, as codified in the state constitution, are many and varied. The chief job of the executive is the faithful execution of the laws. The governor also serves as the commander-in-chief of the state's militia, except in times when these forces are called into the service of the federal government. In 1899, Governor Frank Steunenberg exercised this power, calling in state and federal troops to help suppress a riot in the Coeur d'Alene mining district. The governor also has the power, with senatorial approval, to appoint through nomination all executive officers that are not elected to their positions.

The pardoning power possessed by Idaho's governor is quite different from that of the chief executives in most other states. Idaho has a Board of Pardons that has the power to grant reprieves and remissions of fines and forfeitures, to grant conditional or unconditional pardons, and to commute sentences after individuals have been convicted. The Board of Pardons functions primarily within the jurisdiction of the legislature. It is the legislative branch, not the governor, that establishes the meetings of the board, the application process to be heard by the board, and the regulations for the board's proceedings. The only power that the governor has in issuing reprieves or remissions is in the interim period when the board of pardons is not in session. During these times, the governor, except in cases of impeachment or treason, is granted a temporary power of reprieve until the next session of the Board of Pardons, which determines the ultimate fate of the convicted person.

In working with the legislature, the governor has the responsibility, at the start of each legislative session, to give a report on and offer recommendations for dealing with issues facing the state. The governor may also give such addresses from time to time as is deemed necessary for problems needing more immediate attention from the legislature. The governor can also demand written reports from executive officers and managers of state institutions. Whenever necessary, he or she may require these reports to be written under oath. The governor can then use the reports given by the state officials to compile his or her assessment of the state in order to better recommend to the legislature an informed view of what lies ahead and how it should be handled. The governor may also, in special circumstances, call an additional session of the legislature to deal with a specific and well-defined issue that requires legislative attention. In these cases, the legislators may only deal with the issues that are expressly the purpose for their convening.

In the state of Idaho, all laws passed by the legislature are subject to executive approval or veto. If a governor does not approve a bill, it goes back to the originating house with recommendations on how it should be amended. The legislature then must reconsider the bill and either amend it in an effort to gain the governor's approval or attempt to override the veto and make the bill into law over the governor's objections. To override an executive veto, there must be support from at least two-thirds of the members of both legislative houses.

In addition to this veto power, the governor also possesses a form of line-item veto for appropriations bills. This veto enables the governor to reject a portion of any bill that appropriates funds and send just that part of the bill back to the legislature with recommendations. The legislature then follows the same process used with a regular veto to either amend the measure or override the governor's line-item veto.

An additional responsibility and power of the governor is shared with a number of other officials of the executive branch—service on the state's Board of Examiners. The Idaho Board of Examiners is made up of the governor, secretary of state, and attorney general. Its purpose is to examine all claims against the state—save for those involving salaries or compensation of state officials—before the state legislature is allowed to act on the claims. If and only if the board approves a claim, action can be passed by the legislature in regard to that claim.

The official duties of the lieutenant governor are to preside over the state senate when it is in session, to fill in for the governor when he or she is out of the state, and to perform such duties as the governor may deem necessary for the good of the state. The secretary of state is responsible for overseeing the election process, facilitating business activity, and providing timely and accurate information to the citizenry. The controller is the chief fiscal officer of the state, paying the state's bills and employees, maintaining all accounting and financial records, and performing preaudit procedures. The state treasurer operates as the central chief fiscal officer and banker of moneys collected by Idaho. The treasurer's office acts as the state's bank, receiving and disbursing all funds and investing idle state moneys and funds for local government and state agencies. The attorney general provides legal representation to the state.

The chain of succession in Idaho follows that of many other states. If the governor is unable to fulfill the duties of office, the powers and duties of the supreme executive fall to the lieutenant governor, who also serves as the president of the senate. If neither the governor nor the lieutenant is able to perform in the designated capacity, the responsibilities are then "devolved to the president pro tempore of the Senate." There are a number of instances listed within the state's constitution that would warrant transferring power from the governor to the lieutenant governor or president pro tem, including the governor's failure to qualify for office; death; resignation; absence from the state; impeachment; conviction of treason, felony, or other infamous crime; or disqualification for any cause. In cases in which any other state or district office is vacated, the governor is granted the power to appoint an able, qualified individual to serve in that office. Normally, this would require the consent of the senate, but when the senate is not in session, the governor may appoint someone to fill the role until the senate reconvenes. Once the senate convenes, the governor can nominate the individual for the office, and the senate has the ability to consent to or reject the nomination. Gubernatorial appointees who fill vacant offices serve in that capacity until the next successor is selected in the usual manner provided for by state law.

Ever since Boise was established as the state capital in 1865, officials there have had a difficult time servicing areas throughout the state due to the sparse population and large land area. To try to connect all areas of the state, Governor Kempthorne called for the creation of the Office of Science and Technology in January 2004. Such an office would, according to Kempthorne, help to boost the state's economy, provide statewide informational resources, and supplement intrastate commerce. The creation of such an office, the appointment of officials to head it, and the directing of nearly $100,000 to help start the new agency all demonstrate a number of ways in which the governor can use the constitutionally prescribed authority to address pressing state issues in Idaho.

Joseph J. Foy

References

Frank, Diane. 2004. Idaho governor calls for tech office. *Federal Computer Week*, January 13. http://www.fcw.com/geb/articles/2004/0112/web-idaho-01-13-04.asp.

Idaho State Constitution of 1890, Art. 4.

Office of the Governor. Executive Department, State of Idaho, Boise. Executive Order No. 2003–01. Continuation of the Idaho rural partnership, repealing and replacing executive order 2001–01. http://www2.state.id.us/gov/mediacenter/execorders/eo03/eo_2003_01.htm.

U.S. Census Bureau. 2000. *State and county QuickFacts: Idaho.* http://quickfacts.census.gov/qfd/states/02000.html.

Additional Resources and Recommended Readings

Access Idaho. Idaho's official website. http://www.accessidaho.org.

Andrus, Cecil, and Joel Connelly. 1998. *Cecil Andrus: Politics western style.* Seattle: Sasquatch.

Batt, Phil. 1999. *The Compleat Phil Batt: A kaleidoscope.* Meridian, ID: Eva Gay Yost.

Gunzburger, Ron. 2004. Politics1: Online guide to Idaho politics. http://www.politics1.com/id.htm.

The Idaho Statesman. http://www.idahostatesman.com.

Smylie, Robert. 1988. *Governor Smylie remembers.* Moscow: University of Idaho Press.

ILLINOIS

• • • • • • • • • • • •

ILLINOIS ELECTED EXECUTIVE BRANCH OFFICIALS

Governor	Lieutenant Governor
Attorney General	Controller
Secretary of State	Treasurer

http://www.state.il.us/

• • • • • • • • • • • •

The Illinois governor has historically presented a study in contrasts. The governorship was regularly regarded, by outside observers, as among the nation's strongest chief executive posts, but the position was long deemed politically subordinate to Chicago's mayor, regardless of which party filled the governor's chair. The state was considered a leader in administrative reform, having adopted a general merit system in the first decade of the twentieth century, but the Illinois governor symbolized "job-oriented politics" in which the elected chief executive oversaw one of the nation's most extensive state patronage operations.

These situations no longer exist. The 1976 death of Chicago mayor Richard J. Daley removed from the scene the man who was reputedly the last of the big city political bosses and certainly the state's most powerful Democratic politician. None of his successors filled the void, and none was able either to elect and influence a Democratic governor or to thwart the objectives of a Republican governor. In 1990, the U.S. Supreme Court held that the government could not hire, promote, or fire persons for political reasons, effectively ending the widespread patronage system developed by Governor James Thompson (1977–1991), in which virtually every state job under his direction was filled on the basis of partisan loyalty.

History shows the state has had twenty-one Republican governors and nineteen Democratic chief executives, but Republicans tended to dominate for long periods. They won all but two elections from 1856 to 1932. There was a reasonable rotation between parties from 1928 through 1976, as neither party could elect two different individuals successively over this period. That situation changed in 1976 with the election of the Republican Thompson to the first of his four terms. He was followed by Republican governors Jim Edgar (1991–1999) and

George Ryan (1999–2003). This Republican string of twenty-six consecutive years in the governor's office ended only when Governor Ryan, beset by scandals, did not seek reelection and Democrat Rod Blagojevich (2003–) won the office.

The Illinois governor had relatively little authority under the state's first two constitutions (1818 and 1848), but the position was considerably improved by the constitution of 1870, which would serve as the state's fundamental law for just over a century. On the basis of the provisions of that Reconstruction-era charter, outside observers ranked the Illinois chief executive among the nation's most powerful governors throughout the first two-thirds of the twentieth century. Voters adopted a constitutional amendment in 1884 to grant the governor an item veto over appropriations bills, although governors rarely used this power. The legislature in 1917 reduced more than 100 agencies into nine code departments whose directors were appointed by the governor, subject to senate confirmation. As a result of these alterations, one survey in 1938 rated the Illinois governor the third most powerful chief executive after those of New York and Virginia; another in 1965 found the Illinois governor was tied for second with the chief executive of New Jersey, following the New York governor. The authors of the present constitution, adopted in 1971, retained much of the previous charter's approach and language in the state's executive article. They made only a few significant changes in the structure of the executive branch but materially upgraded the governor's veto power and management authority.

The present-day basic law provides that all elected executive officials must be U.S. citizens, at least twenty-five years old, and residents of the state for at least three years preceding their election. Each officer holds a four-year term, with no limits on reelection. In addition, voters since 1978 have chosen all offices in non-presidential election years. This document also requires that candidates for governor and lieutenant governor run on a joint ballot, eliminating the possibility of these officeholders representing different political parties.

Under the 1971 constitution, the Illinois governor exercises "the supreme executive power" and is responsible for "the faithful execution of the laws." In addition, the state's Civil Administrative Code grants the governor general administrative responsibility over various semi-independent agencies, boards, and commissions. He or she appoints all officers not otherwise provided for (subject to the advice and consent of the senate), may remove any official he or she appoints "for incompetence, neglect of duty, or malfeasance in office," and may refuse to reappoint without cause merit system executives at the close of their four-year terms. The governor fills vacancies in the independently elected offices of attorney general, secretary of state, comptroller, and treasurer.

The governor serves as commander-in-chief of the state militia and may use these forces "to enforce the laws, suppress insurrection or repel invasion." He or she also may grant reprieves, commutations, and pardons. Illinois governors rarely used the latter authority in the past, but Governor Ryan issued 4 pardons and commuted 167 death sentences to life without parole two days before leaving office in 2003. A longtime opponent of capital punishment, Ryan had suspended executions three years earlier.

The constitution also directs governors to participate in the legislative process in three ways: they must report to the general assembly at the beginning of each term "on the Condition of the State and recommend such measures as deemed desirable," including a proposed budget for the operation of state government; they may convene the legislature or the senate alone in special session and limit the agenda by "stating the purpose of the session"; and they must consider every bill passed by the general assembly. Already the holder of a formidable veto, the Illinois governor received substantially enhanced authority to review legislation from the framers of the 1971 constitution. The governor's control over a bill's fate is among the most comprehensive in the fifty states.

Under the expanded provisions, the governor has sixty calendar days to consider legislation, rather than the ten days (excluding Sundays) afforded by the previous constitution. As in the prior charter, the governor may sign a bill into law, allow a bill to become law without his or her signature by taking no action within the prescribed time frame, veto the entire bill, or exercise a line-item veto over appropriations bills. Most important, the 1971 constitution granted the governor two additional veto options—a reduction veto, by which the chief executive may decrease any appropriation, and an amendatory veto, by which the governor may return any bill, together with spe-

cific recommendations for change, to the legislature.

This constitution reduced the required override vote of a full veto from two-thirds of the members of both legislative chambers to three-fifths of the lawmakers in both houses and provided that a simple majority in each house may override a reduction veto or an amendatory veto. These changes did not, however, reduce the potency of the governor's veto. The first three governors elected under this charter each used the various vetoes extensively and successfully. The legislature overrode fewer than 6 percent of all vetoes during this period.

The authors of the 1971 constitution also granted the governor extensive authority to reassign functions or reorganize agencies that are directly responsible to the governor's office by executive order, subject to rejection by a majority of either house of the general assembly. Governors have used this management tool sparingly, although in 1995, Governor Edgar combined several related agencies into a single department of natural resources. The combination of these formal powers—particularly the unlimited tenure potential, the extensive management authority, and the far-reaching veto power—continued to rank the Illinois chief executive among the nation's top five governors in terms of formal power at the close of the twentieth century, according to external evaluations. Researchers who study state politics have long classified the formal powers of governors based on four categories: tenure potential (length of term and chances for reelection), the veto, budget power, and appointment power. More recent formulations of this power index include two additional components: the number of separately elected public officials in addition to the governor and party control of the state legislature.

The present charter designates the lieutenant governor, attorney general, and secretary of state, in that order and then as provided by law, to serve as acting governor in the event of a governor's disability and to become governor if the chief executive dies, resigns, is convicted on impeachment, or fails to qualify for the office. The governor may personally determine if he or she is "seriously impeded in the exercise of his [or her] powers" and relinquish official duties until "prepared to resume office." Conversely, the charter provides that the general assembly determines by law when a governor is unable to serve and when that disability is removed, subject to review by the state supreme court. The governor and all executive and judicial officers may be removed by impeachment by a majority of the house of representatives and conviction by two-thirds of the senate. The 1971 constitution, however, does not specify any grounds for impeachment but provides only that the house "may determine the existence of cause for impeachment."

This charter modified the remainder of the Illinois executive branch to some degree, although it retained the multiple elected offices of lieutenant governor, attorney general, secretary of state, comptroller (replacing the auditor), and treasurer. The document eliminated an elected superintendent of public instruction and specified few duties for the other offices. Curiously, while retaining the position of lieutenant governor, the framers of this constitution eliminated the lieutenant governor's responsibility of presiding over the state senate and provided that this person has only those duties delegated by the governor or prescribed by law. At least one holder of the position in the 1990s considered it so ineffectual that he announced his intention to resign in order to host a radio talk show in Chicago. Lieutenant Governor Robert Kustra, however, changed his mind when he saw the possibility of succeeding to the governor's office due to Governor Edgar's heart problems. Governor Edgar regained his health and did not vacate his office; the lieutenant governor also completed his term when the "show biz" opportunity was withdrawn.

Today, the duties of the lieutenant governor include serving as chair of the Illinois River Coordinating Council and chair of the Illinois delegation of the binational Great Lakes Commission. As the chief legal officer of the state, the attorney general has the constitutional duty to act as legal adviser to and legal representative of state agencies. The secretary of state's office manages information for state citizens, provides services such as programs for seniors and children, and manages a tissue- and organ-donating initiative. The comptroller maintains the state's central fiscal accounts, orders payments into the treasury, and issues warrants against any funds held by the treasurer. The treasurer is the state's banker. He or she is responsible for the safekeeping and investment of taxpayers' moneys. The attorney general manages a do-not-call list and other measures to protect consumers. The treasurer has four primary duties, including accounting for all of the state's funds; overseeing and disbursing county, city, town, and school tax distributions; paying the state's bills; and paying the state's employees. The secretary of state oversees state elections.

Constitutionally, the Illinois governor occupies a preeminent position among peers in other states. The occupant of the office has an opportunity to not only lead the state but also become a national political and governmental figure. In most cases, under the 1971 constitution, Illinois governors have not achieved these distinctions. The jury is still out as to whether the extensive formal powers necessarily will lead to success in office in the future.

James McDowell

References

Beyle, Thad. 2004. The governors. In *Politics in the American states: A comparative analysis,* 8th ed., ed. Virginia Gray and Russell L. Hanson, 194–231. Washington, DC: Congressional Quarterly Press.

Fenton, John H. 1966. *Midwest politics.* New York: Holt, Rinehart and Winston.

Garvey, Neil F. 1958. *The government and administration of Illinois.* New York: Crowell.

Gove, Samuel K., and James D. Nowlan. 1996. *Illinois politics and government: The expanding metropolitan frontier.* Lincoln: University of Nebraska Press.

Illinois Constitution of 1870.

Illinois Constitution of 1971.

Additional Resources and Recommended Readings

Howard, Robert P. 1988. *Mostly good and competent men: Illinois governors, 1818–1988.* Springfield: Illinois State Historical Society.

Ranney, Victoria. 1970. *Con-Con: Issues for the Illinois Constitutional Convention.* Urbana: University of Illinois Press.

INDIANA
• • • • • • • • • • • •

INDIANA ELECTED EXECUTIVE BRANCH OFFICIALS
Governor   Lieutenant Governor
Attorney General   Auditor
Secretary of State
Superintendent of Public Instruction
Treasurer
http://www.state.in.us/

• • • • • • • • • • • •

Indiana's governor is the nominal head of an executive branch that contains several separately elected statewide officials. Believing in the Jacksonian principle that public officials should be chosen by voters, the framers of Indiana's constitution of 1851 provided for the election to four-year terms of a governor and lieutenant governor and for the election to two-year terms of a secretary of state, auditor, treasurer, and superintendent of public instruction. The state legislature later provided for election to two-year terms of an attorney general, a state supreme court clerk, and a state appellate court clerk.

Indiana is widely regarded by external observers as a strong Republican state, principally because of its support of twenty-one of twenty-five of that party's presidential candidates in the twentieth century. Because of this nearly constant support for Republican presidents, one might expect nearly all state officials to be Republicans, too, but this is not necessarily the case. Although Indiana chooses governors in presidential election years, presidential coattails have not always proved long enough for state Republican candidates. During this period, voters selected thirteen Republican and twelve Democratic governors and tended to favor one party for several consecutive elections. Republicans won four times straight, from 1916 to 1928, and Democrats won three successive elections, from 1932 to 1940. In more recent times, this trend has been even more pronounced, with Republicans winning five times in a row (1968 to 1984) and Democrats winning the next four times (1988 to 2000). Republican Mitch Daniels, a former corporate executive and national budget director, ended the Democrats' sixteen-year hold on the governor's office by winning in 2004. Daniels became Indiana's twenty-first Republican governor; he was preceded by twenty-three Democrats (most of whom served in the nineteenth century), one Jeffersonian Republican, three Whigs, and one nonpartisan chief executive.

Indiana's constitution requires that candidates for governor and lieutenant governor be U.S. citizens for at least five years, residents of the state for the five years "next preceding . . . election," and at least thirty years old. The qualifications remain the same, but constitutional and statutory changes adopted since the 1970s altered both the manner

of selection and the tenure of Indiana's executive officials. The constitution prescribes no citizenship, age, or residence requirements for the lesser elected executive officials.

The lower statewide offices were the first to benefit from constitutional modifications. Voters in 1970 approved an amendment that extended the terms of the secretary of state, auditor, and treasurer to four years and allowed these officials to serve two consecutive terms. In 1972, voters adopted an amendment that requires the general assembly to determine the selection and tenure of the superintendent of public instruction. The legislature initially (in 1973) made the position appointive by the governor but decided in 1974 to make the position elective for unlimited four-year terms.

The Indiana Constitution initially provided that the governor was not "eligible more than four years in any period of eight years," which meant that the state's chief executive could not seek immediate reelection. From 1851 through 1972, in fact, only Democrat Henry F. Schricker sought and won election twice as governor (from 1941 to 1945 and from 1949 to 1953). In 1972, Indiana voters ratified an amendment that permits governors to serve two consecutive four-year terms. Through the election of 2000, all governors elected under this provision also won a second term.

The state constitution at first also required the separate election of the governor and lieutenant governor. On occasion, although not often, voters selected the state's top two officials from different political parties. This outcome did not always produce negative consequences, but voters in 1974 adopted an amendment that requires candidates for governor and lieutenant governor to run on a joint ballot in the general election.

Until 1976, Indiana's political parties selected all candidates for statewide office, including nominees for U.S. senator, in state conventions consisting of delegates often handpicked by county chairs. Governor Otis Bowen (1973–1981), one of the state's most popular chief executives who was assured of renomination by any procedure in 1976, supported enactment of a direct primary law by the 1975 general assembly against the wishes of his state party organization. As originally enacted, the statute required parties to select candidates for U.S. senator, governor, and lieutenant governor in the May primary election. In the 1980s, declining interest in the state political conclaves caused the legislature to return selection of the lieutenant governor to the convention system. This change has not reinvigorated the party conventions because successful gubernatorial nominees traditionally select their running mates following the primary election and delegates simply ratify their choices.

The general assembly has the constitutional authority to remove all statewide officials from office for "crime, incapacity, or negligence" by either impeachment or joint resolution, but lawmakers have yet to employ either method.

Indiana is one of few states that have a detailed constitutional provision concerning gubernatorial disability and succession. Originally, the constitution provided only that the powers and duties of the governor's office "devolved" on the lieutenant governor whenever the gover-

nor was removed from office, died, resigned, or was otherwise unable to serve. Voters in 1978 ratified a provision similar to the Twenty-fifth Amendment to the U.S. Constitution. Under its terms, a governor may step aside temporarily by declaring in writing to the house speaker and senate president pro tempore an inability "to discharge the powers and duties" of the office, but he or she can resume the position with a written declaration that no inability continues. If these legislative officials feel that a governor is unfit to serve, they may jointly file a written declaration to that effect with the state supreme court. The state high court is required to decide within forty-eight hours if a gubernatorial inability exists. In either case, the lieutenant governor serves as acting governor until the inability is removed.

Dormant for almost a quarter century, procedures that nobody wanted to employ were in place in September 2003 when a massive stroke felled Governor Frank O'Bannon. Lieutenant Governor Joseph Kernan served first as acting governor, then succeeded to the office when O'Bannon died. The amendment also permitted him to fill the vacant office of lieutenant governor by nominating a candidate to be confirmed by a joint session of the general assembly. Prior to these events, the Indiana legislature had, in its 2001 and 2003 sessions, passed a proposed amendment to establish a constitutional line of succession in the event the offices of both governor and lieutenant governor are simultaneously vacant. Under this provision, an official serves as acting governor until a joint legislative session elects a governor. The amendment provides that the house speaker is first in line to act as governor, followed in order by the senate president pro tempore, treasurer, auditor, secretary of state, and superintendent of public instruction. The attorney general is not included because the position is statutory, not a constitutional office.

The Indiana governor is limited to two terms, has only indirect control over the state budget, and possesses an officially weak veto power. Due to this combination of factors, outside observers traditionally considered the Indiana governor among the nation's weakest state executives. However, the occupant of this office is the chief executive of the state by constitutional provision, various statutes, and a landmark state supreme court decision. In 1941, a Republican-dominated legislature attempted to strip many appointive powers from the newly elected Democratic governor Schricker. The state supreme court held that the governor has general responsibility for the management of state government, including the power to appoint and remove state administrative personnel, exclusive of the duties of other elected officials (*Tucker v. State,* 218 Ind. 614 [1941]). The governor's authority includes an extensive ability to appoint other state officials, influence the state budget and spending practices, and take part in the policymaking process.

The governor is granted considerable power by both the state constitution and statutes to fill vacancies in other executive or judicial offices and to name the directors and some secondary officials of the several hundred administrative agencies within the executive branch. None of these appointments requires legislative confirmation, and all officials serve at the governor's pleasure. By a 1970 constitutional amendment, the governor's appointment power extends to the selection of state supreme and appellate court judges and by statute to trial courts in selected counties. Under the state's version of merit selection and retention of judges, the plan is officially nonpartisan, but Republican governors picked only Republican judges and Democratic governors only Democratic judges through 2004.

The governor's influence over the state budget is indirect but nevertheless significant. The governor appoints the director and assistant directors of the state budget agency that prepares the state budget for submission to the legislature and administers the state spending plan following its adoption. As these officials serve at the governor's pleasure, they usually concur with the chief executive's views on revenue and spending approaches. Likewise, agency heads appointed by the governor tend not to make "unacceptable" (to the governor) spending requests.

Important as these powers are, they are less visible to the public than the governor's legislative powers. The Indiana Constitution directs the governor to participate in the lawmaking process in three ways—delivering a message at the beginning of a legislative session, signing or vetoing bills at the close of a session, and calling special sessions of the general assembly.

The governor delivers an annual state of the state message to a joint meeting of the legislature at the opening of each legislative session. This presentation has become largely perfunctory and symbolic in recent years—the governor's address is tailored for a television audience and usually takes place after the deadline for introducing bills has passed. However, the governor's speech helps establish both a legislative agenda and public expectations of what the general assembly might accomplish in the session.

The governor must act on all bills passed by the legislature. A constitutional amendment ratified in 1972 gives the governor seven days to take action on bills, with three options: he or she can sign the bill into law, let the bill become law without a signature on the eighth day, or veto the bill and return it with his or her objections to the chamber of origin. Voters in 1990 further amended the veto procedure by restricting legislative consideration of a veto to the next regular session following passage of a bill. The Indiana governor does not have an item veto over appropriations bills, and the legislature may override a veto by a simple majority in each chamber (fifty-one votes in the house, twenty-six in the senate). For these reasons, the Indiana veto is technically one of the weakest in the nation, although it is apparently not so ineffective in practice. Lawmakers overrode fewer than 10 percent of governors' vetoes from 1967 to 2002.

Governors may also call the general assembly into special session at any time. Usually, special sessions were needed in the past when lawmakers could not complete work on the state budget under the previous sixty-day, biennial session approach. The move to annual legislative sessions beginning in 1971 was expected to reduce, if not end, the need for frequent special sessions, but governors neverthe-less found it necessary to call eight special sessions between 1977 and 2004. The majority of these sessions resulted from failures to enact budgets.

In addition to these major powers, the governor may also grant reprieves, issue pardons, and commute sentences; serve as commander-in-chief of the state's "military and naval forces" (although an appointed adjutant general actually directs the state National Guard); issue executive orders to establish certain policies; and serve as a member of many state boards and commissions.

The adoption of constitutional amendments enhancing the office's tenure potential and modifying the veto power, coupled with the adoption of annual legislative sessions, substantially improved the role of the state's chief executive in the policymaking process. Researchers who study state politics classify the formal powers of governors based on four categories: tenure potential (length of term and chances for reelection), the veto, budget power, and appointment power. More recent formulations of this power index include two additional components: the number of separately elected public officials in addition to the governor and party control of the state legislature. By this assessment, the contemporary Indiana governor is among the nation's top twenty chief executives (Beyle 2004).

James McDowell

References

Barnhart, John D., and Donald F. Carmony. 1951. *Indiana's century old constitution.* Indianapolis: State Constitution Centennial Commission.

Beyle, Thad. 2004. The governors. In
*Politics in the American states: A
comparative analysis*, 8th ed., ed.
Virginia Gray and Russell L. Hanson,
194–231. Washington, DC:
Congressional Quarterly Press.
Indiana Chamber of Commerce. *Here is
your Indiana government, 2003–2004.*
Indianapolis: Indiana Chamber of
Commerce.
Indiana Constitution of 1851.
Watt, William J. 1981. *Bowen: The years as
governor.* Indianapolis: Bierce
Associates.

**Additional Resources and
Recommended Readings**
Madison, James H. 1986. *The Indiana way:
A state history.* Bloomington: Indiana
University Press.
McDowell, James L. 2001. Indiana's
venerable constitution: 150 years old
and counting. *Traces of Indiana and
Midwestern History* 13(4):24–31.

IOWA

• • • • • • • • • • • •

IOWA ELECTED EXECUTIVE BRANCH OFFICIALS

Governor	Lieutenant Governor
Attorney General	Auditor
Secretary of Agriculture	Secretary of State

Treasurer
http://www.iowa.gov/state/main/index.html

• • • • • • • • • • • •

Iowa provides a classic example of the evolution of a state's governor from figurehead to leader, a development that took place only in relatively recent times. For some 120 years after the state's entry into the Union in 1847, the Iowa governor was generally viewed as having "hardly any power," even "less power than the lowliest legislator." Considered by lawmakers as "the most helpless individual in state government," the Iowa chief executive occupied primarily "a ceremonial office" with any influence "due solely to persuasion" (Hahn 1971, 163). This overwhelmingly negative assessment of the Iowa governor was well founded in constitutional language and political practice, stemming from the long dominance by the Republican Party in the state.

As initially scripted by a Democratic-dominated convention in 1846 and revised by supporters of the new Republican Party in 1857, Iowa's constitutions severely restricted the governor's office in regard to leadership opportunities. Governors served only a two-year term and were traditionally limited to two terms, making it difficult for them to achieve their agendas. The chief executive had only a package veto but seldom used this power, being hesitant to alienate the legislature, considered the more powerful branch of state government. The governor's limited appointment power was further curtailed by a number of independent boards and commissions, whose members served longer terms, and his or her executive authority was abridged by the separate election of several other statewide officials, who generally enjoyed long tenure limited only by death or resignation. The governor was also politically handicapped by the legislature's control of patronage and jurisdiction over positions in the state administration, as well as the extent to which lawmakers exercised their oversight authority over executive agencies. Due to the combination of a low tenure potential, modest appointment opportunities, and a relatively weak veto power, outside assessments commonly placed the Iowa governor in the lower half of state chief executives in terms of formal authority.

The more serious disadvantage, however, derived from the curious political arrangement that made governors virtually dependent on the usually Republican-controlled Iowa legislature for their nominations. Because Iowa lawmakers traditionally were influential party people in their districts, this legislative faction became the dominant factor within the state's prevailing political party. Until the latter part of the twentieth century, Republican lawmakers in essence determined Republican candidates for governor and lieutenant governor, most of whom, not surprisingly, had extensive legislative backgrounds. Further, lawmakers also tended to rotate nominees between northern and southern areas of the state on a regular basis.

This unusual political and governmental pattern is the product of a state that was and remains relatively more politically, economically, and socially homogeneous than most. Iowa voters chose Democrats as their first two governors (from 1846 to 1854) and selected a Whig for their third (from 1854 to 1858). An influx of residents from northern states who supported the fledgling Republican Party,

however, not only led to the adoption of a new constitution in 1857 but produced a total turnabout in political direction. Republicans served as twenty-one of the state's twenty-two governors over the next seventy-four years (between 1858 and 1932), a period interrupted only by the election of a Democrat (from 1890 to 1894) during the Populist period. Democrats would not occupy the governor's office again until the Depression era (between 1932 and 1938). But with the passing of the most serious economic problems, Republicans regained the support of Iowa voters and dominated gubernatorial politics for the remainder of the twentieth century. Over the state's history, thirty Republicans and nine Democrats have served as governors.

Democrats interrupted Republican successes in 1956, despite President Dwight Eisenhower's landslide reelection, choosing Herschel Loveless, who benefited from rural concerns over farm price supports and property taxes and urban opposition to an increased sales tax. Loveless exercised a rare veto in 1957, rejecting the legislature's sales tax increase, an action that helped him win a second term in 1958. Following the single term of Republican Norman Erbe (1960–1962), Democrats swept into power in 1962 with the election of Harold Hughes, who campaigned successfully on the issue of selling liquor by the drink. Hughes won reelection in 1964 and 1966 and moved on to a U.S. Senate seat in 1968.

When Hughes departed the Iowa statehouse, Republicans reclaimed the governor's office and held it for the next thirty years, although only two persons were elected—Governors Robert Ray for fourteen years (1968–1982) and Terry Branstad for sixteen years (1982–1998). Democrat Tom Vilsack, a former state senator, won in 1998 in what observers considered upset victories in both the primary and general elections, and he won a second term in 2002. In the latter part of the twentieth century, however, substantial revisions of Iowa's constitution, beginning with the addition of an item veto for appropriations bills in 1968 and extension of the governor's term to four years in 1974, materially strengthened the chief executive's position. State politics scholars classify the formal powers of governors based on four categories: tenure potential (length of term and chances for reelection), the veto, budget power, and appointment power. More recently the index has been updated to include two additional components: the number of separately elected public officials in addition to the governor and party control of the state legislature. According to this measure, combined with a perceived improvement in the Iowa governor's personal attributes, the state's chief executive ranking rose to among the top quarter of the nation's governors at the beginning of the twentieth century.

The Iowa governor is vested with "the supreme executive power" of the state and is elected jointly with his or her party's candidate for lieutenant governor in nonpresidential years. Aspirants for these positions must be U.S. citizens, residents of the state for a minimum of two years prior to election, and at least thirty years of age. The governor sees to it that the laws are faithfully executed; commands "the Militia, the army, and navy" of the state; transacts all executive business; grants reprieves, commutations, and pardons for all offenses except treason and impeachment; fills vacancies if no other method is provided; and keeps the great seal of the state of Iowa for official use.

The governor has the traditional powers for working with the legislature, including the constitutional duty of communicating to legislators on the condition of the state and recommending measures deemed expedient at the opening of every regular session. The chief executive may also summon legislators "on extraordinary occasions" and "state the purpose for which they shall have been convened" and adjourn the legislature should the two chambers disagree on a time of adjournment. The governor is charged with calling a special election to fill a legislative vacancy.

Iowa's governor must either sign or veto all bills within three days of receipt, excluding Sundays. The governor returns a vetoed bill, together with objections to the chamber where the bill originated, for reconsideration. A two-thirds vote of each house is necessary to override a veto. The governor must also sign or veto any bills presented during the last three days of a legislative session, depositing these measures with the office of the secretary of state within thirty days of adjournment. The governor may veto any items of an appropriations bill, with the remainder of the bill becoming law. All vetoed appropriations items are subject to two-thirds override votes in each legislative chamber.

Iowa's lieutenant governor has those duties provided by law and assigned by the governor. In the case of the death, impeachment, resignation, removal from office, or other disability of the governor, the lieutenant governor assumes the powers and duties of the chief executive until the governor is acquitted of impeachment charges or the disability is removed. The Iowa Constitution does not specifically define the term *disability* or clarify procedures for determining it, and it provides an order of succession only in the event of a gubernatorial vacancy when the lieutenant governor is "incapable" of performing the governor's duties. In that event, the senate president or the house speaker performs these duties. If neither legislative leader is able to serve, the Iowa legislature meets in joint convention to elect a governor and lieutenant governor.

The state's political climate is no longer "conservative, cautious, and 'standpat'" (Rogow 1961, 869). Nor is the state "unembarrassedly out of step" at the onset of the twenty-first century (Barone and Cohen 2001, 590). Among the most Republican of states as late as the 1960s, Iowa has become more politically competitive in recent years, ranking near the midpoint of the nation's two-party states, and it has delivered its electoral votes to Democratic candidates. Iowa remains the nation's leading corn producer, but service industries and manufacturing have been far more important segments of the state economy since the 1970s. The contemporary Iowa governor reflects the state's altered political and economic complexion.

James McDowell

References

Barone, Michael, and Richard E. Cohen. 2001. *The almanac of American politics 2002*. Washington, DC: National Journal.

Beyle, Thad. 2004. The governors. In *Politics in the American states: A comparative analysis*, 8th ed., ed. Virginia Gray and Russell L. Hanson, 194–231. Washington, DC: Congressional Quarterly Press.

Hahn, Harlan. 1971. *Urban-rural conflict: The politics of change*. Beverly Hills, CA: Sage.

Iowa Constitution of 1857.

Rogow, Arnold A. 1961. The loyalty oath issue in Iowa. *American Political Science Review* 55:869. Quoted in Hahn, 18.

Schambaugh, Benjamin F. 1934. *The constitutions of Iowa*. Iowa City, IA: Athens Press.

Additional Resources and Recommended Readings

Schwieder, Dorothy. 1996. *Iowa: The middle land*. Ames: Iowa State University Press.

KANSAS

• • • • • • • • • • • •

KANSAS ELECTED EXECUTIVE BRANCH OFFICIALS
Governor   Lieutenant Governor
Secretary of State   Attorney General

http://www.accesskansas.org/

• • • • • • • • • • • •

Most people envision Kansas as a vast wheat field, an image befitting a state legitimately labeled "the nation's breadbasket." But this tranquil image belies the state's torturous and contentious origin. Established as a territory in 1854 by the Kansas-Nebraska Act, the region soon became "Bleeding Kansas" and served as the principal battleground between proslavery and antislavery forces before the onset of the Civil War. Proslavery forces largely from Missouri gained control of the territory and drafted a constitution permitting slavery, but Congress refused to admit Kansas as a slave state. When slavery opponents (or Free Staters)—settlers with roots in New England and the Great Lakes states—became a majority, they drafted a constitution banning slavery. But Congress again refused Kansas admission, this time because southern Democrats did not want another Republican-leaning state in the Union. Only after several southern states seceded was Congress able to admit Kansas in 1861, on the eve of the outbreak of hostilities between the North and South.

Kansas's political genealogy largely established the partisan preferences that other Great Plains states would follow. In its first century of statehood (from 1861 to 1961), Kansas voters elected as governor twenty-seven Republicans and only six Democrats, while choosing two Populists in the 1890s. Kansas exhibited traditional Republican conservatism for most of this period but for a brief dalliance with Populist and Progressive reform efforts around the turn of the twentieth century. Republican dominance was so great that no Democratic governor was reelected until George Docking won two consecutive two-year terms in 1956 and 1958. To put it another way, Republicans held the chief executive office for 86 of the Sunflower State's first 100 years.

George Docking's governorship did not usher in a Democratic revival, but competition for the office became more evenly matched. From 1961 to 2003, Republicans elected five chief executives and Democrats three, and Republicans held the office just twenty-two years to the Democrats' twenty over this time frame. One of the Democrats elected was Docking's son Robert, who was the first Kansas governor elected more than twice, winning four consecutive two-year terms (from 1967 to 1975). After the advent of the four-year term in 1974, Republicans controlled the governorship for sixteen

Kansas governor Kathleen Sebelius (Office of Governor Kathleen Sebelius)

years, a tenure Democrats will match given the election of Kathleen Sebelius as the forty-fourth Kansas governor in 2002. Governor Sebelius is the second woman (both Democrats) to hold the state's top office, the first being Joan Finney (1991–1995). At least some of the recent Democratic success can be traced to infighting between Christian conservatives and traditional Republicans for control of their state party.

Constitutional changes changing the governor's tenure potential from unlimited two-year terms to two consecutive four-year terms, enhancing the veto power, and granting authority to reorganize state agencies by executive order substantially increased the Kansas governor's formal powers. Researchers classify the

formal powers of governors based on four indicators: tenure potential (length of term and chances for reelection), the veto, budget power, and appointment power. Recent updates of the power index include two additional components: the number of separately elected public officials in addition to the governor and party control of the state legislature. By this measure, Kansas's governor was relegated to the lower third of the nation's chief executives four decades ago but ranks "moderately strong" at the beginning of the twenty-first century. It must be noted, however, that the constitution of 1861, though substantially amended, treats the governor's office somewhat sparingly.

Kansas voters elect four executive branch officials—the governor, lieutenant governor, secretary of state, and attorney general—whose qualifications for office "are provided by law." The Kansas legislature has not established any formal qualifications for governor. Voters elect all state executive officials to four-year terms in even-numbered, nonpresidential election years and choose the governor and lieutenant governor on a joint ballot. No person may be elected to more than two consecutive terms as governor or lieutenant governor, but there are no term limits for the secretary of state or attorney general.

The governor and "all other officers under this constitution" may be removed by impeachment for and conviction of treason, bribery, and other high crimes and misdemeanors. The process requires a majority vote in the lower house to impeach and a two-thirds vote in the upper chamber to convict. The lieutenant governor becomes governor if that office is vacated for any reason. If the governor becomes disabled, as determined by state law, the lieutenant governor assumes the powers and duties of the governor until the disability is removed. The secretary of state and the attorney general are the next two officers in line to serve as governor.

The governor exercises the state's "supreme executive power" and is responsible for enforcing the laws of the state. His or her legislative obligations include communicating in writing to the lawmakers information on the condition of the state, although the governor customarily recommends "measures as he [or she] deems expedient" in a state of the state message. Governors may call legislators into special session on their own initiative or in response to a petition signed by at least two-thirds of the members of each chamber, and he or she may dismiss the legislature should the two houses disagree on the time of adjournment. The constitution also requires a governor to collect reports from each executive department and all state institutions and transmit these to the legislature.

The Kansas chief executive serves as commander-in-chief of the state militia and may call out these forces to execute laws, suppress insurrection, and repel invasion. The governor is assigned a "pardoning power" and is the keeper and official user of the great seal of Kansas for state-sanctioned documents. Under the state's version of the Missouri Plan for merit selection of judges, the governor appoints members of the state supreme court. All of these powers, however, are relatively minor in comparison to the governor's formal authority to reorganize the executive branch, influence state finances through the budgetary role, and employ a strong veto, including an item veto over appropriations bills.

The governor may transfer, abolish, consolidate, or coordinate all or part of any state agency or its functions if "necessary for efficient administration" by issuing executive reorganization orders. In exercising this authority, the chief executive must include in an order the proposed disposition of records, property, and personnel and the transfer of unexpended appropriations of each affected agency, submitting the order to both legislative chambers on the same day. A reorganization takes effect on July 1 after the governor's submission, unless either house of the legislature disapproves it by majority vote within sixty calendar days.

Kansas's chief executive officially has full responsibility over the state's budget, subject to the legislative appropriations process, but much of the actual work on the state's spending plan is the responsibility of the state division of the budget. This unit determines the manner in which state agencies and institutions propose and justify their requests for biennial expenditures. The budget office reviews these proposals and compares them with the projections of a "revenue estimating committee" to form the basis for the governor's formal budget recommendations to the legislature. Essentially, as one budget directory expressed it, "we ask the governor what kind of balance he wants at the end of the year" (Loomis 1994, 43). This division then furnishes staff support to the legislature to formulate the budget and administers the budget after its adoption.

The existence of a "legislative veto" by either chamber over a governor's proposed executive reorganization and the role played by the state budget division in the financial planning process serve to tone down the chief executive's actual authority in these areas. However, the veto power is undeniably strong. The Kansas governor has ten calendar days after a bill is presented in which to sign or veto the measure. In the case of appropriations bills, the governor must also act within the same time frame but may veto individual items. In either instance, the bill is returned to the house of origin, which has thirty calendar days to reconsider the measure and attempt to override the veto by a two-thirds majority. If the override attempt is successful, the second house must also successfully negate the governor's veto within thirty calendar days. The legislature by law must reconvene "at a time sufficiently beyond adjournment" to reconsider any bills vetoed too late in a session for override endeavors.

Kansas voters in recent years have tended to switch between major party candidates for governor. Whether this decision results primarily from dissension within the Republican ranks, an increase in media-oriented and candidate-centered campaigns, or a growing independence among the electorate remains open to debate. What is not in dispute is that regardless of party label, Kansas governors remain routinely conservative and customarily deal with a Republican-controlled state legislature. Further, Kansas governors, state legislators, and lobbyists traditionally work out an agenda acceptable to all parties. One longtime observer of Kansas politics noted that "agreement on the nature of the agenda does not, however, imply consensus on the solutions," but this process tends to minimize conflict (Loomis 1994, 52). Taken together, these factors may mitigate against a Kansas governor making more vigorous use of the authority granted the position.

James McDowell

References

Barone, Michael, and Richard E. Cohen. 2001. *The almanac of American politics 2002*. Washington, DC: National Journal.

Beyle, Thad. 2004. The governors. In *Politics in the American states: A comparative analysis*, 8th ed., ed. Virginia Gray and Russell L. Hanson, 194–231. Washington, DC: Congressional Quarterly Press.

Council of State Governments. 2004. *Book of the states 2004*. Lexington, KY: Council of State Governments.

Kansas Constitution of 1861.

Kansas Legislative Research Department. 2002. *Legislative procedure in Kansas*. Topeka: Kansas Legislative Research Department.

Key, V.O., Jr. 1956. *American state politics: An introduction*. New York: Knopf.

Loomis, Burdett A. 1994. *Time, politics, and policies*. Lawrence: University Press of Kansas.

KENTUCKY

• • • • • • • • • • • •

Governor	Lieutenant Governor
Secretary of State	Attorney General
Treasurer	Auditor of Public Accounts

Commissioner of Agriculture
http://kentucky.gov/

• • • • • • • • • • • •

While some would not associate the Bluegrass State with the "banana republics" of South America, the history of Kentucky has been witness to a coup d'état. In the 1899 gubernatorial election, the Democratic candidate for governor, William Goebel, used a mixture of agrarian populism and an urban alliance in his bid for the chief executive spot. Goebel was a controversial figure prior to running for governor, having killed a political enemy in a duel. His campaign to become the Democratic candidate was marred by controversy; Goebel won the nomination on the twenty-sixth ballot.

This combination of controversy led to a tightly contested election that fall, with the Republican candidate, William Taylor, winning the general election by 2,300 votes, as decided by the State Board of Elections. Incensed with the result, Goebel declared the election was a fraud, and the Democratic-controlled legislature met to investigate the election. Sensing that the legislature would attempt to overturn the election results, Republicans filled the state capitol while Goebel headed toward the building with his Democratic allies.

On January 30, 1900, as Goebel reached the capitol, an unknown assassin shot him. This act prompted the legislature to declare him the governor, only to learn four days later that he had died. Following Goebel's death, the Democratic lieutenant governor assumed the office. The Republicans challenged the election decision, but the state courts upheld the legislature's ruling, and the Republican Taylor left the state.

While modern-day gubernatorial politics in Kentucky have not been as fatal as the 1899 election, the executive branch, both in terms of campaigning for office and governing, still reflects the deep divisions within the Bluegrass State. Political observers note that Kentucky is divided regionally into sections that often compete with one another: from the Appalachian east through the central bluegrass section to the western part of the state, which is more "southern" than the rest. In addition, the urban areas of Louisville and Lexington add another element to the diversity and competition within the state. This geographic division has led to politics based on factions, much like that seen in many southern states.

As is the case with a majority of the state executive branches, Kentucky has multiple elected statewide executive officers: the governor; lieutenant governor; attorney general; secretary of state; auditor of public accounts; treasurer; and a commissioner of agriculture, labor, and statistics. This division of executive power originally weakened the chief executive, but in recent times, the office of governor has been strengthened by both personal and official powers. As the Kentucky Constitution asserts, the "supreme executive power of the Commonwealth shall be vested in a Chief Magistrate, who shall be styled the 'governor of the Commonwealth of Kentucky.'"

Governors of Kentucky have key official powers that enhance their capacity to influence government operations; among these is the power to veto legislation, as well as to issue line-item vetoes of appropriation bills, which can be overridden by a majority of legislators. The governor also has the power to appoint individuals to twelve cabinet-level agencies, as well as to some of the 330 boards and commissions within the executive branch. The governor can appoint some midlevel managers within the bureaucracy as well. Another institutional power that the governor possesses is the power to call special sessions of the legislature. These special sessions are strictly limited to the topics the governor specifies. If the legislative chambers cannot agree on a time of adjournment, it is the governor's prerogative to adjourn the legislature. Like other governors, the Kentucky chief executive serves as the "Commander-in-Chief of the army and navy," but he or she cannot (by constitutional restriction) personally command the militia in the field, unless directed by the legislature to do so. The Kentucky governor has the power to commute sentences and grant reprieves and pardons, except in the case of impeachments. The governor must file a "statement of reasons" for his or her decision in granting the pardons and reprieves.

Among the most powerful of the governor's resources is the power to create the budget. In Kentucky, the governor controls the process and personnel that create the budget, and he or she is seen as an influential player in the budget negotiations with the general assembly. While the legislature can change the governor's proposed budget, the governor often has the last word by using the threat of a line-item veto against any items found to be objectionable.

In addition, the governor possesses informal powers, such as the power to bargain and persuade, the power of patronage and pork-barrel politics, and the power to use his or her position in the state's highest office to gain popular support. Governors can capitalize on the prestige of the office to achieve their goals. They also spend a great deal of time in their ceremonial role, representing the state government when visiting dignitaries come to the state or giving speeches at new senior citizen centers.

The second-ranking officer of the state is the lieutenant governor. Unlike the governor, the lieutenant governor has seen the power of the office decrease over time. The lieutenant governor, elected jointly with the governor, performs duties as set by the governor and the legislature. Unlike in other states, he or she cannot exercise constitutional authority whenever the governor leaves the state. In a referendum to approve constitutional amendments in 1992, the lieutenant governor's office was stripped of its powers of confirming gubernatorial appointments as well as presiding over the state senate.

The voters, who cast a single vote applicable to both offices, jointly elect the governor and lieutenant governor. In the event of a tie between two different candidates for each office, the legislature is empowered to determine who will be the governor and lieutenant governor. Both executive officers must be at least thirty years old and have been Kentucky residents and citizens for at least six years prior to the election. The governor can run for reelection for another term but is only allowed to serve for a total of eight years. For the other constitutional officers, the age requirement remains at thirty, but the residency requirement is only two years prior to the election.

If the governor is either physically or mentally incapacitated, the state attorney general may petition the state supreme court to have the governor declared unfit. The decision by the court must be unanimous, and the lieutenant governor assumes the office until the state supreme court finds the governor fit to resume office.

As for the other constitutional officers, their powers have also been eroded over recent time. For example, in the 1990s, the general assembly restricted the powers of the state treasurer and the superintendent of public education (a position that was eliminated in 1992). The legislature also controls the activities of the secretary of agriculture through the appropriations process.

J. Michael Bitzer

References
Kentucky Constitution of 1891, Secs. 69–96.

Miller, Penny M. 1994. *Kentucky politics and government: Do we stand united?* Lincoln: University of Nebraska Press.

Additional Resources and Recommended Readings
Harrison, Lowell H. 1985. *Kentucky governors, 1792–1985.* Lexington: University Press of Kentucky.

LOUISIANA

•••••••••••••

•••••••••••••

Many states have seen their fair share of colorful chief executives, but probably no other state can match the long line of governors Louisiana has generated. Starting with the Long dynasty of the 1930s through the modern governors, Louisiana's chief executives have captured the bayou style of politics and often reflected the flamboyance of Cajun politics, which can be summarized by the infamous line of Huey P. "the Kingfish" Long: "I am *sui generis* [one of a kind], just leave it at that" (http://www.sec.state.la.us/60.htm). Many of Louisiana's governors continued in the tradition of the Kingfish; it was Huey Long, however, who left an indelible print on the executive branch of Louisiana.

Huey Long, governor from 1928 to 1932, dominated Louisiana politics both during his lifetime and after his death in 1935. Elected on a platform of expanding governmental services and the promise to make "every man a king," Long created a viable two-party system in Louisiana: those who pledged their allegiance to Long and the "anti-Longs." Once in the governor's mansion, Long consolidated his grip on power and government by rewarding his supporters and punishing his opponents. Only two years into his term as governor, he was elected to the U.S. Senate, but he remained governor due to a falling out between himself and the lieutenant governor, Paul Cyr. Following Long's senatorial election, Cyr declared the governor's office vacant and proclaimed himself governor by taking the oath of office. In a unique turnabout, Long declared the office of lieutenant governor vacant and successfully argued that the president pro tempore of the state senate (a Long ally) should become lieutenant governor. Long succeeded in ousting Cyr and replacing him with his ally, and the Kingfish also got his slate of candidates, particularly an ally running for governor, elected. Long then gave up the office but continued to exercise near-complete control over Louisiana politics from his Senate seat in Washington, D.C. The Long legacy continued with the election of Huey's brother, Earl, to the governorship in 1948 and in 1956 after succeeding to the office in 1939.

In the modern day, the Long legacy has faded, but Louisiana has continued to see a cast of unique characters fill its governor's office. Most notable was the governorship of Edwin Edwards, who served four terms in office. First elected in 1972 and reelected four years later, Edwards put together a winning coalition of Cajun and black voters. However, in his third term in office, he was indicted on federal charges of mail fraud, obstruction of justice, and public bribery. He came in second in the general "open" election of 1987 to Buddy Roemer, at which point Edwards was thought to be politically dead. However, after Roemer switched parties and became a Republican and then ran for reelection, Edwards ran yet again for governor. His run was intended not so much to spite Roemer but instead to prevent a former leader of the Ku Klux Klan's, David Duke, from winning the governorship, which he did manage to do. Allegations of wrongdoing continued to plague Edwards, and he was ultimately convicted in federal court and sentenced to ten years in prison. Following the two terms of Republican Mike Foster, Louisiana voters elected their first woman as governor in 2003—Kathleen Babineaux Blanco, a former lieutenant governor. Governor Blanco endured an early test of her leadership when portions of her state were devastated by the 2005 hurricane Katrina. She endured some criticism, but time will tell how her leadership will ultimately be viewed.

The 1974 state constitution of Louisiana creates a plural executive branch, with nine officers specified: the governor, lieutenant governor, secretary of state, attorney general, treasurer, commissioner of agriculture, commissioner of insurance, superintendent of education, and commissioner of elections. In order to hold any statewide elective office, a candidate must

Huey Long rose from poverty to national prominence by ruthlessly building a powerful political organization in Louisiana and shrewdly appealing to the populist sentiments of the state's poor. (Library of Congress)

be at least twenty-five years old, an "elector" of the state, and a U.S. citizen and state resident for a period of five years prior to the election. The office of attorney general has the additional requirement of being "admitted to the practice of law" for at least five years prior to the election. No statewide officer can concurrently hold another public office. All statewide elected offices have a term of four years, with only the governor being restricted to two consecutive terms.

The governor, as "chief executive officer of the state," is responsible for seeing that the laws "are faithfully executed," as mandated by the Louisiana Constitution. Other constitutional responsibilities include giving a state of the state address to the legislature to "make reports and recommendations and give information . . . including its [the state's] complete financial condition." The governor is also responsible for submitting two budgets, one focusing on operating expenses and the other focusing on capital, or major, expenditures of the state. Once the legislature has passed an appropriations bill, the constitution gives the Louisiana governor the power to exercise a line-item veto, which can be overridden by the legislature with a two-thirds vote. The governor is also responsible for ensuring that the appropriations for the state "shall not exceed anticipated revenues," thereby requiring a balanced budget.

The governor has the constitutional power to appoint, subject to confirmation by the state senate, the department heads of various state agencies and members of commissions and boards that are not popularly elected. The various state agencies include: Civil Service, Education, Environmental Quality, Health and Hospitals, Labor, Public Safety and Corrections, Natural Resources, Revenue, Social Services, Transportation and Development, and Wildlife and Fisheries. In addition, the governor has the power to remove any department head who was appointed.

The legislature can remove the governor through the impeachment process. The house of representatives impeaches the governor, while the state senate holds a trial and, on a two-thirds vote, convicts and removes the chief executive from office.

The lieutenant governor of Louisiana has little constitutional power. The governor may delegate duties and power to the lieutenant governor, who may also serve as acting governor when the chief executive is out of the state. Otherwise, the role and duties of the lieutenant governor are limited. Currently, this individual oversees the Department of Culture, Recreation, and Tourism, as well as the Louisiana Serve Commission and the Louisiana Retirement Development Commission. As a policymaking board, the Louisiana Serve Commission focuses on national service efforts in the state and functions as a clearinghouse for national service programs operating in the state. The Retirement Development Commission works to attract retirees to the state.

If a vacancy occurs in the governorship, the lieutenant governor succeeds to the office, with the secretary of state, attorney general, and treasurer next in the line of succession. Following these elected officials is the presiding officer of the senate and then the leader of the house of representatives. Should a vacancy in the office of lieutenant governor occur, the governor nominates an individual, who is confirmed for the office by a majority vote of each house of the legislature.

Louisiana's secretary of state has a wide variety of duties and responsibilities. In addition to being the keeper of the great seal of the state, he or she oversees the publication of all enacted laws and the archives of official state documents. The secretary is also responsible for serving as the chief election officer, which entails preparing ballots, publicizing all election returns, and administering elections laws. Prior to 2004, a commissioner of elections was responsible for issues concerning voter registration and for overseeing the custody of voting machines. However, these duties have been folded into the secretary of state's responsibilities, and the commissioner is now appointed by the secretary of state.

The treasurer of Louisiana is responsible for the "custody, investment, and disbursement of public funds" for the state and is constitutionally responsible for reporting on the state's financial condition to the governor and the legislature. The commissioner of agriculture is constitutionally responsible for the "promotion, protection, and advancement of agriculture" in the state, while the commissioner of insurance oversees and regulates the insurance industry within Louisiana.

All elected statewide officials except the governor are constitutionally required to appoint a "first assistant," who is subject to senate confirmation. If the elected official must vacate the office, then the first assistant succeeds to the office. If the unexpired term of office is more than one year, a special election is held to fill the position for the remaining term of office.

In addition, first assistants assume the office while the elected official is temporarily absent from the state, similar to the lieutenant governor's responsibility in serving as acting governor while the governor is out of the state.

J. Michael Bitzer

References
Kurtz, Michael L., and Morgan D. Peoples. 1992. *Earl K. Long: The saga of Uncle Earl and Louisiana politics.* Baton Rouge: Louisiana State University Press.
Louisiana State Constitution, Art. 4.
Williams, T. Harry. 1981. *Huey Long.* New York: Knopf.

Additional Resources and Recommended Readings
Brinkley, Alan. 1982. *Voices of protest: Huey Long, Father Coughlin and the Great Depression.* New York: Vintage.
Haskins, James S. 1995. *The first black governor: Pinkney Benton Stewart Pinchback.* Trenton, NJ: Africa World.
Reeves, Mariam G. 1998. *The governors of Louisiana.* Gretna, LA: Pelican.

MAINE

• • • • • • • • • • • •

MAINE ELECTED EXECUTIVE BRANCH OFFICIALS
Governor
http://www.state.me.us/

• • • • • • • • • • • •

Maine is a unique state in the Union due to its relative geographic isolation, its natural wonders, and its independent and eclectic population. It is the only state with just one bordering neighbor in the Union (New Hampshire), and it actually shares a far longer border with Canada. It also has a 3,500-mile-long coastline, despite being ranked as the twelfth-smallest state in terms of landmass. One of its most famous current residents is suspense author Stephen King.

Maine is an outlier in several political aspects, as well, serving as a leader in election campaign finance, term limits for elected officials, and "green" environmental stances. And relative to their peers in most other states, Maine's governors have a greater potential to work in a manner dominated by issues rather than partisan stances.

The state of Maine, formed in 1820 when Massachusetts divided its territory, embraced the Republican Party from its early years. The party of Abraham Lincoln had an almost uninterrupted run of dominance in national and state elections until 1954, when Democrat Edmund Muskie pulled off an upset in the gubernatorial race. Muskie's election marked the abrupt beginning of a period of party competition within Maine. Ever since, though an incumbent governor might win reelection to a second term, Maine's voters have not elected a new face from the incumbent party to be their governor. As further evidence of the less partisan orientation in the Maine executive, the state has elected Independent governors on three occasions in this competitive era (James Longley in 1974 and Angus King in 1994 and 1998).

Political Scientist Daniel Elazar has contended that the political paths of the American states are determined by cultural roots. Maine (indeed, all of northern New England) is characterized as "moralistic," community-based, concerned about the public interest, and led by attention to issues. These factors may explain why the state has supported nonpartisan leadership in recent times. The last governor, Angus King, earned high marks for activist policies, including his environmental stances and his support for education funding. Under his administration, the state purchased laptop computers for all middle-school students. At the same time, he pursued efforts acceptable to conservatives, such as tough-on-crime

initiatives and the limitation of human service funding. Governor King parlayed his experience as a broadcaster on public television into a charismatic and conciliatory governorship, pursuing other nonpartisan issues such as economic development, land use policies to control sprawl, and opposition to Native American gaming facilities. Even though Maine moved from an Independent to a Democratic governor following King's retirement in 2002, the transition has proven seamless. Governor John Baldacci now pursues many of the same policies related to the balancing of economic development needs and the maintenance of Maine's quality of life.

Maine's governor is among the best-situated New England governors with regard to formal powers, which may also explain the ability of recent chief executives to lead based on the issues. Since Maine was formed thirty years after the founding of the nation, the state's constitution reflects some modern components not found in the documents of the thirteen original ratifying states. The Maine document may reflect some of the lessons learned in the country's early history, including the benefit of a greater sharing of power between an executive and the legislature.

Like the American president, the Maine governor is allowed two four-year terms in office. Since 1960, the tendency has been for the state's governors to serve two terms. During that time, only Governor Longley, the first Independent governor, failed to win reelection to a second term. Each Maine governor in recent decades had at least sufficient time, if not the skills, to make a mark on the policies of the state. It is interesting to note that the governors, while popular enough to win reelection, do not ensure the fortunes of their political parties; as mentioned earlier, Maine consistently has chosen to move from the Democratic Party to the Republican Party and back again, with the insertion of Independents on occasion, once an incumbent's eight years have passed.

The governor is the only elected executive in Maine. The rest of the cabinet members, including the lieutenant governor, serve at the appointment of the governor. Indeed, the national officials that represent Maine in Congress tend to be statewide officials as well; the small state has two U.S. senators, of course, but only two members in the U.S. House of Representatives, one for the northern and inland portions of the state and one for the coastal and more urban south. A cabinet without separately elected officials enables the Maine governor to be a true executive, with little visible infighting for the policy agenda. The governor also does not need to satisfy the legislature while making other appointments to the cabinet. For the most part, he or she can choose leaders for state agencies without legislative endorsement.

If there is a limitation to the Maine governor's powers, it is most evident in the ability to craft the budget, which currently stands at $5.3 billion. The governor is able to draft the initial budget, including his or her own priorities for taxation and spending, but legislators have unlimited power to revise the budgetary appropriations bills, inserting their own spending priorities and deleting the governor's if they so choose. In addition,

the Maine governor has only a weak veto power, whereby he or she must reject entire unfavorable bills rather than just the specific aspects of bills that are unacceptable. In forty-three of the states, if the governor finds that the legislature has attached some kind of disagreeable spending to a state budget appropriation bill, he or she can excise the specific spending item and sign the remaining portions of the bill into law. However, in Maine and six other states, the governor is limited to two choices: veto the entire bill, including many specifics that he or she favors, or let the indiscretion stand if it is deemed sufficiently insignificant. The state of Maine, with its distressed economy, has suffered through fairly consistent budget woes involving revenue deficits in recent decades, made more severe in times of national economic stress. The lack of a line-item veto only worsens the difficulties faced by governors in presenting the legally required budget that balances revenues and expenditures.

The state has modernized its budgetary capacities to enhance both executive and legislative capacity in recent years. In 1996, the legislature passed a bill mandating "performance budgeting." Under this reform, state agencies must base their programmatic effort on a strategic plan that includes an overall agency mission and results-oriented goals and objectives. They must report the impacts of service changes related to funding revisions through performance measures. If an agency requests additional funding, it must project the impact of the new funding on agency results. This reform is an advantage for both the legislature and the governor because it enhances the dialogue around funding requests, giving both sides in the budget process better information about the impacts of state spending. Governor Baldacci has enhanced state budgeting by asking Maine's citizens for input on their priorities via the state's website, with the intent of using this information to create a better match between citizen demands and government programming.

Among the governor's other formal powers and duties is the pardoning of criminals; among his or her informal duties is service as the chief diplomatic representative for state government, hosting important visitors and dignitaries. Governors are increasingly involved in economic development initiatives that cross national borders. The Maine governor is expected to promote the state's products abroad and to recruit businesses and industries to relocate to Maine. He or she can lead the way on giving potential industries tax breaks and other incentives such as infrastructure construction to encourage relocation to Maine in a competitive environment. Economic development has been a hard sell in Maine in recent times, though the Pine Tree State has lately become a more popular destination because it offers natural assets and an alternative to the fast pace of its neighbors to the south and west.

The Maine governor oversees seventeen executive branch agencies with 14,300 state employees. The state's direct capacity to serve citizens has grown most prominently under the current circumstances of fiscal stress through "E-government" initiatives. The citizens of Maine may benefit from a growing range of online capabilities to transact with the government, including applying for driver's, hunting, and fishing licenses; registering automobiles; paying traffic tickets; and gaining information about public services such as state park availability. Though Maine is a small state physically, weather and other factors can make mobility difficult. Much of its geographic area is remote, with few roads and limited population. E-government has enhanced the ties between the citizens and their state government. The governor, through the relatively strong powers of the office and through the state's issue-oriented politics, is at the forefront of modernizing Maine's governmental capabilities.

Brendan Burke

References

Baldacci, Governor John Elias. The budget balancing education tool. http://www.maine.gov/governor/baldacci/issues/budget/.

Cody, Howard. 2003. Maine: Recent politics in a "place apart." *New England Journal of Political Science* 1(1):201–212.

Constitution of the State of Maine, Art. 5. http://janus.state.me.us/legis/const/.

Lockard, Duane. 1959. *New England state politics.* Princeton: Princeton University Press.

Maine State Planning Office. State of Maine performance budgeting web page. http://www.state.me.us/spo/sp/stratplan/.

Palmer, Kenneth T., G. Thomas Taylor, and Marcus A. LiBrizzi. 1992. *Maine politics and government.* Lincoln: University of Nebraska Press.

Additional Resources and Recommended Readings

Lippman, Theo, Jr., and Donald C. Hansen. 1971. *Muskie.* New York: Norton.

Pierce, Neal. 1976. *The New England states: People, politics, and power in the six New England states.* New York: Norton.

MARYLAND

• • • • • • • • • • • •

• • • • • • • • • • • •

Historian George Callcott (1985) has written that Maryland likes to call itself "America in miniature." This small state certainly draws some of its nature from Washington, D.C., the seat of the national government, as many federal workers commute to their jobs from suburban Maryland. The Free State also draws its identity from both the industrial North and the agrarian South; during the Civil War, Maryland joined the Union but saw violent protests by Confederate sympathizers in response to the movement of Union troops to the front lines through Baltimore. Maryland is home to high-technology industries as well as pastoral farmland and attractive tourist destinations on the Atlantic shore and Chesapeake Bay. Do these competing state identities make the governor of Maryland average in powers and responsibilities among the chief executives of the fifty states? They probably do not—the Maryland governor enjoys greater than average formal powers and has tended to be at the forefront of governmental reforms at least during the second half of the twentieth century and beyond.

Maryland's early roots tended toward a conservative restriction on executive powers, as can be seen in the state constitutions of the eighteenth and early nineteenth centuries. The Free State adopted its first constitution in October 1776, three months after the last British proprietary governor sailed back to England. This document kept powers of appointment to the legislature in the hands of landowners and in turn allowed the legislature to choose the governor. The governor's main powers during early statehood related to the appointment of magistrates and other local government officials. The constitution was rewritten in 1851, 1864, and 1867. Since then, the document has been amended over 100 times. Steadily over the years, the governor's statutory powers have been increased—and most would argue that during the twentieth and twenty-first centuries, savvy Maryland governors have made the most of their abilities. There was a period during the 1960s and 1970s when the office was tainted by scandal, but otherwise, Maryland chief executives have led in the economic advancement of the state.

The Maryland governor serves a four-year term, with the same ability as the U.S. president to serve two such terms if the voters approve. There is another parallel between the U.S. and Maryland executives regarding tenure in office: the two-term limit was set after a long-standing executive left office. As president,

Franklin Delano Roosevelt was elected to four terms, and in Maryland, Governor Albert C. Ritchie won his office four times, between 1920 and 1935. Ritchie was popular and successful at modernizing state government and the bureaucracy, but the state decided to encourage new blood in the governorship at least every eight years. Maryland's governors typically do serve out their two terms in office, demonstrating a reasonable level of popularity with the state's voters. Since the 1950 election, Maryland governors have served for eight years with just two exceptions: Spiro Agnew resigned after two years to become Richard Nixon's vice-president in 1968, and Blair Lee only served two years after rising from the lieutenant governor's office following the scandal-induced resignation of Marvin Mandel in 1977. Other governors, such as Millard Tawes in the 1960s and William Donald Shaefer in the 1980s, presided over booming growth and managed politics and the state bureaucracy effectively.

The Maryland governors of the twentieth century almost invariably worked to modernize the state's government structure. Part of the modernization involved the reduction of statewide elected offices. In some states, the voters choose from a "long ballot" of state officials, deciding on their choices for governor, lieutenant governor, secretary of state, secretary of insurance, secretary of education, and other leaders of specialized services. This variety of elected officials can create problems for the governor, just as it can create disagreement over the executive agenda. For example, if a governor is elected on a pledge to increase the availability of charter schools in the state while a secretary of education is elected with a promise to abolish charter schools, a coherent policy will be difficult to pass. Maryland has moved toward prevailing wisdom in executive leadership by limiting its elected executive officials to four: the governor (who runs for election with the lieutenant governor as part of a team, just like the president and vice-president), the attorney general, and the comptroller. Under Maryland's system, the governor is able to set policy by choosing nineteen other department heads, spanning agency functions such as agriculture, business and economic development, juvenile services, and transportation, to name a few. But at the same time, two other elected officials provide checks and balances to the governor's power. The attorney general, who represents the state's interests in all legal matters, can bring suit against the governor if necessary from an independent stance. And the comptroller audits state spending across the government—including spending by the governor. It would be difficult for either of these officials to confront the governor if he or she had the ability to fire them. But only the voting public has that power.

The state budget is the key to growth and development of public services, involving both the people who deliver services (including teachers, state troopers, environmental regulators, and the like) and physical assets (such as schools, universities, highways, ports, and parks). If the public, the elected officials, and the governor are willing to pay more in taxes, then public services should increase. But rarely do citizens support higher taxes. The budget process is a tug-of-war between political actors and services to provide the best mix of services at the lowest cost. Over time, Maryland has especially focused on the development of its public assets such as its highway and public transportation networks, as well as promoting its tourism industry—witness new publicly supported baseball and football stadiums for the Baltimore Orioles and Ravens. At the same time, the state maintains a relatively low tax burden in comparison to the other states. Part of the explanation for this balance is the strength of the governor's budgetary powers.

The Maryland governor has more control over the state budget than all but one other governor (the Free State's executive holds a tie for these powers with the governor of West Virginia). Most states have a budget process that is similar to the national government's. Governors, like the president, develop and send their budgets to the legislatures, which are under no obligation to adopt the executives' proposals. In Maryland, there is a limitation on the legislature: it cannot pass a budget that is larger than the one proposed by the governor. This constraint is an important one. Individual members of the state's general assembly usually have pet projects within their home districts, and sometimes, they are costly. If all legislators add their own districts' priorities to the budget, spending can become excessive. The Maryland governor is able to constrain this growth, if he or she chooses. The governor has a strong veto power, whereby individual line items that fund programs and projects the governor finds unappealing can be struck out.

In the end, it is clear that the Maryland governor has strong constitutional grants of power, and most of the recent governors have used these powers skillfully to enhance the quality of life within the state. The governor has even been effective in establishing policy beyond the state's borders when Maryland shares interests with its neighbors. One of the state's most treasured assets is the Chesapeake Bay. Marylanders as well as out-of-state visitors enjoy the bay for fishing, boating, nature watching, and swimming. But the natural beauties of the bay are threatened by industry and development in Maryland as well as in "upstream" states, the homes of rivers that feed into the bay. Two of the most recent governors of Maryland, Schaefer and Parris Glendening, led efforts to reduce pollution from Maryland's businesses and industries that reached the bay. In addition, Governor Glendening worked with his counterparts in Virginia, West Virginia, Pennsylvania, and New York to be more conscientious about water pollution issues that harmed the Chesapeake. Governor Glendening's skills at negotiating and fostering cooperation with other states earned him a role as the chairman of the National Governors Association in 2000 and 2001.

Brendan Burke

References

Bowman, Ann O'M., and Richard C. Kearney. 2002. *State and local government*, 5th ed. Boston: Houghton Mifflin.

Callcott, George H. 1985. *Maryland and America: 1940 to 1980*. Baltimore: Johns Hopkins University Press.

Constitution of Maryland. http://www.mdarchives.state.md.us/ msa/mdmanual/43const/html/const.html.

Department of Natural Resources, State of
Maryland. 2003. Chesapeake 2000—the
Renewed Bay Agreement.
http://dnrweb.dnr.state.md.us/bay/res_pr
otect/c2k/index.asp.

Fenton, John H. 1957. *Politics in the
border states.* New Orleans: Hauser.

Gray, Virginia, and Russell L. Hanson, eds.
2004. *Politics in the American states: A
comparative analysis,* 8th ed.
Washington, DC: Congressional
Quarterly Press.

**Additional Resources and
Recommended Readings**

Horton, Tom. 2003. *Turning the tide:
Saving the Chesapeake Bay.*
Washington, DC: Island.

Rascovar, Barry, and Mike Lane. 1998. *The
great game of Maryland politics.*
Baltimore: Baltimore Sun.

Smith, C. Fraser. 1999. *William Donald
Schaefer: A political biography.*
Baltimore: Johns Hopkins University
Press.

MASSACHUSETTS

● ● ● ● ● ● ● ● ● ● ● ● ●

MASSACHUSETTS ELECTED EXECUTIVE BRANCH OFFICIALS

Governor	Lieutenant Governor
Attorney General	Auditor

Secretary of the Commonwealth
Treasurer
http://www.mass.gov/massgov2/index.html

● ● ● ● ● ● ● ● ● ● ● ● ●

The Massachusetts governor has slightly below average powers in comparison to the other American governors. But given the persistent strength of the state's legislature and the ongoing party difference between the legislative and executive branches in the state, the Massachusetts governor rises above expectations when realizing even limited achievements. The state has produced several prominent national leaders by way of the governor's office, so it must provide some good training for higher politics. Prominent Massachusetts governors include two signers of the Declaration of Independence, John Hancock and Samuel Adams, and one man who later rose to be president—Calvin Coolidge. More recent officeholders included John Volpe, who became secretary of transportation and ambassador to Italy; Michael Dukakis, who gained the Democratic nomination for the presidential election in 1988; and Paul Cellucci, who was a recent ambassador to Canada.

Massachusetts is a state central to many of the proudest chapters in American history, including the establishment of governorships with limited powers. The Bay Colony's first governor was John Milton, elected in 1629 while still in Britain before coming to America. Milton set the tone for visionary leadership through a speech that promoted the new colony as a "City on a Hill," with a political system and community above all others, in the service of God. Massachusetts is proud of having the oldest written constitution in the world that is still in effect. While this is largely due to the absence of any constitutional convention to rewrite and streamline a document first developed in 1780, this oldest constitution does allow its reader to see the classical language and content from colonial times, giving a sense of the importance of throwing off the monarchy and developing shared government with the citizenry of the state.

The Massachusetts Constitution has been amended approximately 120 times, and many of the revisions have enhanced the powers of the governor. For example, at the outset, the governor was subject to annual elections, but through amendment, the term of office grew to two and then four years; current rules allow a governor to be elected to two terms for a total of eight years. In early times, the governor served much as a citizen-politician, with a short time of service in Boston. The job was uncomplicated and largely ceremonial, but it grew in complexity as the state's economy and government structure gained in size and stature. Legislators also served for one year at first, but the length of their terms eventually increased to two years. This situation may seem to give an upper hand to the governor, until one considers that legislators can serve an unlimited number of terms.

The Massachusetts governor is not the only state official elected on a statewide basis. He or she is supported by a lieutenant governor of choice, who serves as a kind of teammate in running the executive office. But since the drafting of the 1780 constitution, the governor must also serve alongside several other elected officials. These include: the secretary of the commonwealth, who handles clerical duties involved in record keeping, elections, and archives; the treasurer and receiver general, who is responsible for collecting state income and sales taxes and administering the popular state lottery; the attorney general, who serves as chief litigator for the state, responsible, among other things, for protecting the public interest through enforcement of state laws; and the state auditor, who renders independent audits of the state's financial transactions and operating programs.

The treasurer, attorney general, and auditor all have important roles in offsetting potential abuses of power by the Massachusetts governor. Since they are elected by the citizenry rather than appointed by the governor, they will not shy away from properly reviewing legal and financial matters that affect the governor. The secretary of the commonwealth seems to have less of a justification for separate election, except possibly for his or her role in maintaining fair elections. But all of these constitutional officers draw support from the constituency that elects them, and as a result, they develop programs responsive to the needs of the public in order to promote their own reelection. For example, the attorney general is actively engaged in maintaining consumer protection via lawsuits against shady businesses.

The Massachusetts Constitution defines one other group of elected officials who reduce the governor's authority—but only at the margins. Since the outset, the citizens of the Bay State have elected an eight-member executive council. This group provides advice to the governor on smaller matters. It advises the governor on pardons, though he or she does not need to heed the council's advice. In addition, the council assists with the choice of judges, notaries, and justices of the peace. New Hampshire also has such an executive council but claims with apparent accuracy that its council has a hand in much more important gubernatorial decisions, including fiscal matters.

In addition to the separately elected officials, Massachusetts governors are limited in their authority to appoint state executive department heads. The state's bureaucracy has grown over time because of the early development of the state and because Massachusetts has tended to take an activist approach to the duties and responsibilities of government. Many state services were established during the Progressive era, around 1900, through the formation of independent service authorities and commissions. The initial intent of establishing an independent body was to limit the ability of corrupt politicians to abuse important services, especially for financial gain. The danger of this corruption has declined, but the governor still cannot lead these independent bodies in keeping with his or her agenda. Massachusetts retains dozens of these independent bodies, which oversee horse and dog racing, water resources, toll roads, public universities, and myriad smaller functions. The Massachusetts governor is allowed to reorganize the state government's structure at the outset of his or her term in office. Thus, he or she could streamline the number of independent commissions and agencies, but only if the legislature approves the governor's redesign plans. Furthermore, the legislature

is given an "up-or-down" vote on the reorganization; it cannot select the parts of the reorganization that it likes and amend out any unfavorable aspects. With this rule in place, the governor must be careful when proposing reorganizations so that no important legislative coalition is offended; should that happen, the reorganization plan could fail in the up-or-down vote.

Power is an important commodity in the establishment of the Massachusetts budget. The state allocates approximately $25 billion to a range of public safety and corrections programs, welfare and public health benefits, transportation projects, education services from kindergarten through the university level, economic development initiatives, and recreational and environmental programs. In recent decades, Massachusetts governors have been confronted with a difficult budget situation made worse by the fact that many have represented the Republican Party, while the legislature has consistently been in the hands of the Democratic Party. The voters appear to favor a government divided between the parties, as Democrats have served as governor in only twenty-two of the past fifty-five years. But no Republican governor has served more than six years at a time. This situation contrasts dramatically with that in the state senate, where leaders such as William Bulger served as majority leader from 1970 to 1995. In the general assembly, Thomas Finneran has served as the speaker only since 1996, but he does so with an iron hand. In most polls, Massachusetts citizens recognize Speaker Finneran as the most powerful person in state government, to the chagrin of former Republican governors Paul Cellucci and Jane Swift and the current office-holder, Mitt Romney.

The rules of the budget are written in a manner that favors the strong Democratic Party leadership. The Massachusetts state process is similar to the national process, whereby the president proposes the budget but the legislature can change the details as much as it wants, adding its own funding priorities and deleting the president's at will. But the Massachusetts governor has one power that can block Democratic spending priorities, and that is the line-item veto. Once the legislators have rewritten and revised the governor's budget, they must send their budget back to the governor for a final signature before the financial plan goes into effect. The governor can strike programs that he or she feels are excessive from the budget bill before signing it. The Massachusetts governor can also use this power of striking offending particulars in other legislative bills, as nothing becomes law without the governor's participation.

While both the constitutional rules regulating the executive and the historical political situation in Massachusetts favor the Democratic legislature over the often Republican governor, the Republican Party and its governors have their moments. Governor Romney is not afraid to use the veto when the legislature oversteps its limits, and he has proposed major reorganizations and reforms to the operating procedures for state services. In the past, the Republicans benefited extensively from the chief executive's power to appoint the lieutenant governor to serve out the governor's term in the event that he or she resigns. For example, Governor

Mitt Romney was elected governor of Massachusetts in November 2002, the first Mormon ever elected to the Bay State's highest office. (Office of Governor Mitt Romney)

William Weld appointed Lieutenant Governor Cellucci to serve out his term when he resigned to lobby for the job of ambassador to Mexico. This move gave Cellucci the advantage of running as an incumbent in the 1998 election; people tend to vote for the person in office over a challenger when they do not know much about the candidates. When this strategy worked for Governor Cellucci's reelection, he turned around and used the same strategy himself, appointing Lieutenant Governor Jane Swift as his replacement in 2001 when he became ambassador to Canada. Governor Swift ended her career with her resignation in 2002, endorsing Mitt Romney as her successor. The comparatively weak Republican governors of

Massachusetts can prevail when they are sufficiently clever in the face of the Democratic legislature.

Brendan Burke

References
Constitution of the Commonwealth of Massachusetts. http://www.mass .gov/legis/const.htm.

Jonas, Michael. 2002. Beacon ill. *Commonwealth* 7(5):38–43.

Massachusetts General Assembly. 2004. Speaker of the House Thomas M. Finneran. http://www.mass.gov/ legis/member/tmf1.htm/.

Massachusetts Office of the Governor. 2002. Mitt Romney. http://www .mass.gov/portal/index.jsp?pageID=gov2 homepage&L=1&L0=Home&sid=Agov2.

Office of the Massachusetts Attorney General. 2004. *The attorney general's commitment to consumer protection.* http://www.ago.state.ma.us/sp.cfm? pageid=967.

Perry, George S., ed. 1978. *Our Massachusetts state government: A collection of essays.* Boston: Massachusetts Teachers Association.

Additional Resources and Recommended Readings
Beatty, Jack. 1992. *The rascal king: The life and times of James Michael Curley, 1874–1958.* Reading, MA: Addison-Wesley.

Bulger, William. 1996. *While the music lasts: My life in politics.* Boston: Houghton Mifflin.

Kilgore, Kathleen. 1987. *Volpe: The life of an immigrant's son.* Dublin, NH: Yankee.

MICHIGAN

● ● ● ● ● ● ● ● ● ● ● ● ●

MICHIGAN ELECTED EXECUTIVE BRANCH OFFICIALS

Governor	Lieutenant Governor
Attorney General	Secretary of State

http://www.michigan.gov/

● ● ● ● ● ● ● ● ● ● ● ● ●

Michigan is a state divided, both geographically and politically. Consisting of two peninsulas separated and nearly surrounded by three of the five Great Lakes (and touched by a fourth), Michigan has been a predominantly moralistic state in which a growing individualistic strain reflects the increased involvement of interest groups and regional conflict in state policymaking.

The state's four constitutions testify to these frictions. Michigan's earlier basic laws each represented the moralistic views of the state's New England forebears but also exhibited the widespread nineteenth-century belief in Jacksonian democracy. During the wave of state constitutional reform and revision that swept the United States in the 1960s and 1970s, Michigan produced the nation's first "new" state fundamental law in 1963. The document significantly improved the governor's authority and position, but organized interests were able to thwart the larger goals of the reformers and retain various advantageous provisions from the previous (1908) document.

Election results from the past half century suggest that Michigan is politically competitive, as three Democrats and three Republicans occupied the governor's office from 1949 to 2003. However, over this period, Republicans served as the state's chief executive for thirty-two years, reinforcing Michigan's status as a bastion of Republican strength in state politics. Governor Jennifer Granholm, elected in 2002, is the first woman and only the eighteenth Democrat among the forty-seven individuals who have served as Michigan's chief executive. Twenty-seven Republicans and two Whigs complete the roster. The state's first three constitutions permitted unlimited two-year terms, and Democrats controlled the state's early years, choosing eight of the first ten governors through 1854. Thereafter, Republicans prevailed, electing the next eight governors through 1882 and twelve of fourteen over the remainder of the nineteenth century. Republicans extended their dominance of the governor's office through the twentieth century, winning fifteen of twenty-two gubernatorial elections and holding the office for sixty-eight years.

In the first third of the twentieth century, Democrats elected a governor only in 1912, when the split between progressives and traditionalists in the national Republican Party divided the state's Republicans as well. Although Democrats showed signs of resurgence during the Franklin Roosevelt presidency, they elected governors only in 1932, 1936, and 1940, losing the office in the midterm elections. By 1946, as one observer noted, the state reverted to "its dominantly Republican bias because of inept, corrupt, and conservative Democratic state politicians" (Fenton 1966, 11). One exception to this generalization, however, was the election of liberal Frank Murphy in 1936. During his single term, Murphy helped establish Michigan's Democratic Party as a prolabor party and aided in making Detroit–Wayne County an important component in state and national party politics.

Governor Murphy's efforts did not produce immediate success for Michigan Democrats, but they did provide the groundwork for a liberal-labor, issue-oriented coalition that reintroduced two-party politics to the Wolverine State. His work also ushered in the "modern era" of the Michigan governorship that began with the election of Democrat G. Mennen Williams, a "liberal icon of Michigan politics," to the first of six two-year terms in 1948 (Browne and VerBerg 1995, 78–100). Over the next half century, both Republicans and Democrats occupied the position for extended periods. The state's 1963 constitution extended the governor's term to four years, and the first beneficiary of this change was Republican governor George Romney. An automobile executive, Romney spearheaded the drive for a constitutional convention and won the governor's office the following year. Romney (1963–1969) won a pair of two-year terms and a four-year term in 1966.

Governor Romney resigned at the midpoint of his third term to join President Richard Nixon's cabinet and was succeeded by William Milliken (1969–1983), who then won three terms on his own. Governor Milliken's nearly fourteen years in office make him Michigan's longest-serving chief executive. Democrat James Blanchard held the office from 1983 to 1991 but lost a close race to Republican John Engler (1991–2003), whose three terms at the close of the century gave Republicans control of the state's top position in thirty-two of the previous forty years. These periods of lengthy gubernatorial service apparently irritated some Michiganders, who secured passage of a constitutional initiative in 1992 to set a limit of two terms for all elected executive branch offices. The exceptionally lengthy tenure of other state officials likely helped spur the term-limits initiative. Two Democrats held the office of secretary of state for forty years (James Hare, 1955–1971, and Richard Austin, 1971–1995), and one Democrat served as attorney general for thirty-six years (Frank Kelley, 1963–1999). This provision did not apply to Governor Engler, the incumbent at the time of its adoption, and was first applicable to Governor Granholm, elected in 2002.

Candidates for Michigan governor and lieutenant governor must be at least thirty years of age and registered voters in the state for a minimum of four years preceding their election. A gubernatorial candidate is chosen in a direct primary election and is elected on a joint ballot with the party's candidate for lieutenant governor. The governor's running mate, however, is chosen in a state party convention along with candidates for secretary of state and attorney general, the only other elected executive branch officials. Voters elect all four offices to four-year terms in nonpresidential years.

As chief executive, the Michigan governor exercises more than the traditional authority of taking care that the laws be faithfully executed and transacting all necessary business. The 1963 constitution substantially improved the governor's administrative control and budgetary role. The charter consolidated more than 100 independent agencies into "not more than 20 principal departments . . . grouped as far as practicable according to major purposes." The governor may reorganize these departments or reassign functions by executive orders, subject to legislative disapproval by a majority vote in both houses. The chief executive also is constitutionally empowered to initiate court proceedings to force compliance with or restrain violations of any constitutional or legislative mandate by officials of all state agencies and local governments, except the state legislature. The governor appoints the heads of all principal departments, other than those departments headed by other elected officials, subject to senate confirmation. These department heads, however, serve at the governor's pleasure.

The chief executive appoints members of boards and commissions, subject to senate confirmation, and may remove these officials only as prescribed by the constitution or statute. Despite the constitutional consolidation of numerous agencies into executive departments and an extensive civil service system, a study in the late 1980s estimated that the Michigan governor continued to appoint some 2,700 individuals to more than 270 advisory boards and professional standards agencies (Browne and VerBerg 1995). In addition to this rather extensive appointment power, the governor has the authority to remove or suspend any elective or appointive state officer, except legislative or judicial, for gross neglect of duty or for corrupt conduct in office. The governor also fills vacancies in the offices of secretary of state and attorney general.

The Michigan governor's legislative role is enhanced by additional budgetary powers established in the 1963 constitution. In addition to the standard practice of communicating to the legislature at the beginning of each session "information as to the affairs of the state" along with measures considered "necessary or desirable," the governor also must submit a detailed, balanced budget, setting forth all proposed expenditures and estimated revenues. Further, the governor submits at the same time a series of proposed appropriations bills that outline the proposed expenditures and any necessary legislation to provide for necessary revenues to meet the proposed budget. The governor is also mandated to reduce authorized appropriations when actual revenues fail to match estimated revenues for a prescribed fiscal period, although he or she may act only with the approval of the appropriating legislative committees.

The governor has both a package veto for all legislation and an item veto for appropriations bills, each subject to override by a two-thirds vote of both legislative chambers. In one of the more specific bill consideration procedures found in any state constitution, the Michigan document provides that the governor must act on a bill within fourteen days "measured in hours and minutes from the time of presentation." Finally, the governor may "convene the legislature on extraordinary occasions," but the need for special sessions is rare because the professionalized Michigan legislature is in session virtually year-round.

Michigan's chief executive discharges the typical military and judicial powers. The governor is commander-in-chief of the state's armed forces and may call them out to assist in executing the laws and to "suppress insurrection and repel invasion." In the judicial domain, the governor may grant reprieves, commutations, and pardons, except for impeachments, but they are subject to statutory regulations and procedures.

The governor may be removed from office either by impeachment or a recall election, but no Michigan chief executive has faced either procedure. In the event of the governor's death, resignation, or removal from office, the lieutenant governor (followed by the secretary of state, attorney general, and other persons designated by law, in that order) serves the remainder of the governor's term. On the joint application of the senate president pro tempore and the house speaker, the state supreme court may determine the "inability" of a governor to serve. Only the state high court may determine "if and when the inability ceases."

State politics scholars characterize the formal powers of governors based on four elements: tenure potential (length of term and chances for reelection), the veto, budget power, and appointment power. More recently this power index has been adapted to include two additional components: the number of separately elected public officials in addition to the governor and party control of the state legislature. The enhanced authority granted the Michigan governor in the 1963 constitution did not translate into a substantial improvement in the state's gubernatorial power rankings using this traditional framework. Michigan's chief executive placed in the middle of the pack under the prior charter but advanced only slightly to a "moderately strong" rating at the beginning of the twenty-first century. The imposition of term limits apparently negated the additional governing authority granted Michigan's governor in the view of external observers. Certainly, no future governor will have the time to "become one of the major policy innovators in the United States," as did Governor Engler (Barone and Cohen 2001, 771). However, current and future governors will have the opportunity to employ controls over administrative organization and state revenues and expenditures if they desire to use them. Outside assessments to the contrary, the Michigan governor has the potential to be among the nation's most significant state chief executives.

James McDowell

References
Barone, Michael, and Richard E. Cohen. 2001. *The almanac of American politics 2002.* Washington, DC: National Journal.

Beyle, Thad. 2004. The governors. In *Politics in the American states: A comparative analysis*, 8th ed., ed. Virginia Gray and Russell L. Hanson, 194–231. Washington, DC: Congressional Quarterly Press.

Browne, William P., and Kenneth VerBurg. 1995. *Michigan politics and government: Facing change in a complex state.* Lincoln: University of Nebraska Press.

Fenton, John H. 1966. *Midwest politics.* New York: Holt, Rinehart and Winston.

Michigan Constitution of 1963.

Additional Resources and Recommended Readings
Sikkenga, Raymond. 1987. *Doers and dreamers: The governors of Michigan.* Spring Lake, MI: River Road.

Weeks, George. 1991. *Stewards of the state: The governors of Michigan*, 2nd ed. rev. Ann Arbor: Historical Society of Michigan.

MINNESOTA

• • • • • • • • • • • •

MINNESOTA ELECTED EXECUTIVE BRANCH OFFICIALS

Governor   Lieutenant Governor
Attorney General   Auditor
Secretary of State
http://www.state.mn.us

• • • • • • • • • • • •

Minnesota is part of the northern tier of politically progressive and moralistic states that demonstrate a high level of civic involvement, as indicated by its nation-leading voter turnout of 77 percent in 2004. Historically the home of a long list of liberal and forward-looking political figures, the state is well known for the enduring public service of, among others, Harold Stassen, Hubert Humphrey, Eugene McCarthy, and Walter Mondale and the more recent brief but tempestuous tenure of Jesse Ventura. But Minnesota and its political practitioners have also experienced a long and turbulent history that predates the state's entry into the Union.

At the 1857 constitutional convention, the fifty-nine Republican and fifty-five Democratic delegates refused to convene in the same room. This bitter rivalry resulted in the two parties meeting separately and each devising its own document. Eventually, a conference committee of five delegates from each party negotiated compromise language that, after acrimonious debate, each side independently accepted. But neither party's delegates would sign a document inscribed by delegates from the other party, necessitating two copies of the final statement. The two documents, however, were not identical and actually contained over 300 grammatical, punctuation, and spelling differences. Although evaluations suggest there were no substantive differences in the two versions, Republicans signed a thirty-nine-page charter and Democrats approved a thirty-seven-page constitution. The Republican document apparently attained official status in 1860 when three amendments were appended to that version by Republican governor Alexander Ramsey.

Following Minnesota's admission as the thirty-second state, voters elected a Democrat as its first governor but then embarked on a long relationship with the Republican Party that began with "massive support for the Union in the Civil War" and continued with the backing of protestant Scandinavian immigrants who affiliated with "the anti-slavery, anti-liquor, and anti-Catholic Yankees in the Republican party" (Fenton 1966, 76). Governor Ramsey, who as a Whig had been appointed the first territorial governor in 1847, won election in 1860 as the first of twelve consecutive Republicans to serve as chief executive through 1898. Through 1930, in fact, Republicans elected seventeen of the state's first twenty-one gover-

nors and so dominated state legislative, congressional, and presidential voting that Minnesota was virtually a one-party state for its first seven decades.

Republicans elected five governors and Democrats three from 1898 to 1930, but the turn-of-the-century era of protest produced a one-term Democrat (1898–1900), a two-term Republican (1900–1904), and Democrat John Albert Johnson, a "reform" governor whose widespread populist and progressive support threatened to end the Republican dynasty. Dealing with a Republican legislature, Governor Johnson secured bipartisan backing for a number of third-party platform planks and gained a national reputation and backing as a presidential candidate. However, he died after abdominal surgery in 1909, causing Minnesotans to weep in the streets at the loss of the "people's governor" (Mitau 1970).

Johnson's death during his third term ended Minnesota's first sustained Democratic leadership, but the progressive approach continued under a Republican return to power, including enactment of a statewide direct primary law that called for selection of state legislators on a nonpartisan basis.

Republicans elected four of the next five governors, but all was not harmonious within party ranks. When Governor Winfield Hammond, the lone Democrat, died of a stroke in 1915 after eight months in office, Republican lieutenant governor Joseph Burnquist succeeded to the office.

Winning two additional terms in 1916 and 1918, Governor Burnquist held office during the period when the radical Nonpartisan League (NPL) became a driving force in North Dakota politics and spread eastward into Minnesota, making inroads into the Republican Party. Using a public safety commission officially designed to ensure patriotism to attack members of the "socialist-oriented" and antiwar NPL as "traitors," Governor Burnquist succeeded in stifling the NPL but also drove Scandinavian progressives from the Republican Party. Prosperity kept the state in Republican control throughout the 1920s, but the 1929 economic collapse brought the Farmer-Labor Party to the forefront of the Minnesota political scene.

Supported by Scandinavians and Germans who had left the Democratic Party, the Farmer-Labor Party had modest success in the 1920s and elected the charismatic Floyd Olson as governor in 1930. A self-described "radical—not a liberal," Governor Olson actually functioned more as a New Deal Democrat and spent considerable time toning down the "frankly socialist" organization he headed (Fenton 1966). Olson was elected three times, but his death in 1936—like that of Democratic governor John Johnson in 1909—terminated an effective alternative party in Minnesota politics. Republicans regained the governor's office in 1938 and elected four chief executives over the next sixteen years.

During this period, political necessities brought about the 1944 fusion of the state's two anti-Republican options into the Democratic-Farmer-Labor Party (DFL) under the leadership of Hubert Humphrey. Success did not come immediately, but after a decade, the DFL ushered in a new, competitive political era in Minnesota politics. Over the next half century, beginning with the election of DFL governor Orville Freeman in 1954 and ending with the election of Republican Tim Pawlenty in 2002, the two major parties each elected five governors, with DFL chief executives serving twenty-six years and Republicans elected for twenty-two years. Suggesting that Minnesotans had not completely lost their taste for quirky politics, the other four years of this period were served by Governor Jesse Ventura of the Reform Party, who won a three-way race in 1998 with 37 percent of the vote. Governor Ventura, a former professional wrestler and movie actor, changed his affiliation to Independent and did not seek a second term. His confrontations with the Minnesota legislature also led to an unsuccessful attempt to amend the state constitution in order to establish a unicameral legislature.

Minnesota's governor, regardless of party or personal qualities, still operates under provisions of the state's original 1858 constitution. Both the governor and the lieutenant governor must be at least twenty-five years of age, residents of the state for a minimum of one year, and U.S. citizens. They serve unlimited four-year terms and, since a 1998 amendment, are elected on a joint ballot.

The governor takes care that the laws are faithfully executed; serves as commander-in-chief of the state's military forces and may call them out to execute the laws, suppress insurrection, and repel invasion; serves with the attorney general and chief justice on a board of pardons that may grant reprieves and pardons in all cases but impeachment; and appoints "notaries public and other officers provided by law" with the advice and consent of the senate. The chief executive also fills vacancies in the other elected executive offices of secretary of state, auditor, and attorney general, as well as "the other state and district offices hereafter created by law."

In dealing with the legislature, the governor is expected to communicate to each session of the legislature "information touching the state and country." He or she has extensive veto power, including an item veto over appropriations bills and, effectively, a pocket veto: any bill passed during the final three days of a legislative session does not become law if the governor does not sign it and deposit the bill with the secretary of state within fourteen days after adjournment. In other instances, the governor must act on a bill within three days, excluding Sundays, after it is presented; if he or she fails to act, the measure becomes law without the governor's signature. The legislature may override vetoes by a two-thirds vote of the membership of each chamber.

The governor, secretary of state, attorney general, and all judges may be impeached for "corrupt conduct in office or for crimes and misdemeanors." Impeachment requires a majority vote in the house, and conviction on charges requires a two-thirds vote of "senators present." Convicted parties are removed from office and may be subject to indictment and trial under state law. The governor, lieutenant governor, secretary of state, attorney general, legislators, and all judges are subject to recall by voters for "serious malfeasance or nonfeasance" during their terms or for "conviction during the term of office of a serious crime." A recall petition must be signed by not less than 25 percent of the number of voters casting ballots for the office at the most recent general election. An official recalled from office may not be appointed to fill the vacancy.

Researchers who study state politics describe the formal powers of governors based on four indicators: tenure potential (length of term and chances for reelection), the veto, budget power, and appointment power. More recently scholars have updated the index to include two additional components: the number of separately elected public officials in addition to the governor and party control of the state legislature. The formal powers of Minnesota's governor have traditionally been rated as "moderate," though the ranking increased to "moderately strong" after an increase in the term from two years to four years in 1962. In Minnesota, where the populist tradition remains strong, the governors have presided over a state that, despite its sometimes tempestuous politics, has continually practiced "good government" with traditionally strong commitments to education and social services.

James McDowell

References
Barone, Michael, and Richard E. Cohen. 2001. *The almanac of American politics 2002.* Washington, DC: National Journal.

Elazar, Daniel J., Virginia Gray, and Wyman Spano. 1999. *Minnesota politics and government.* Lincoln: University of Nebraska Press.

Fenton, John H. 1966. *Midwest politics.* New York: Holt, Rinehart and Winston.

Minnesota Constitution of 1858.

Minnesota's Constitution(s). 2005. Saint Paul: Minnesota Historical Society. http://www.mnhs.org.

Mitau, G. Theodore. 1970. *Politics in Minnesota,* 2nd ed. rev. Minneapolis: University of Minnesota Press.

Additional Resources and Recommended Readings

Davy, Frank A., and Theodore M. Knappen. 2005. *Life of John Albert Johnson: Three times governor of Minnesota.* Whitefish, MT: Kessinger.

Frank, Stephen I., and Steven C. Wagner. 1999. *We shocked the world! A case study of Jesse Ventura's election as governor of Minnesota.* New York: Harcourt Brace College.

MISSISSIPPI

• • • • • • • • • • • •

MISSISSIPPI ELECTED EXECUTIVE BRANCH OFFICIALS

Governor

Lieutenant Governor

Attorney General

Auditor

Commissioner of Agriculture

Commissioner of Insurance

Secretary of State

Treasurer

http://www.state.ms.us

• • • • • • • • • • • •

The state of Mississippi is often seen as a land of contrasts—a land of magnolia trees that epitomize the grace of the South but also a land of racial tension, epitomized by the fight over civil rights in the 1960s. Others see it as a state mired in poverty and dependent on agriculture as its main commercial product. However, in recent times, the state has experienced considerable industrialization, among other things, becoming home to the space technologies laboratory of the National Aeronautics and Space Administration (NASA). The state has also witnessed growth in urban areas, such as Jackson and Gulfport. Mississippi is often characterized as a state where public services, especially education, receive little attention; however, in the 1980s, it led many states in reforming its educational system. The contrasting images and realities of Mississippi make it an interesting study.

The political structure of Mississippi's state government reflects that sense of contrast, particularly in its executive branch. While charged by the constitu-

tion with being the chief executive and responsible for ensuring that the laws "are faithfully executed," the governor of Mississippi is considered among the weakest in the nation in terms of formal power. He or she must share executive power with thirteen other officers (individual officials as well as members of two commissions), all of whom are elected by the voters. This division of power is reflective of Mississippi's history of Jacksonian democracy, in which it was thought best to divide power so that it could not be abused by any one governmental official. Another principle of Jacksonian democracy held that officials should have short terms in office and be unable to succeed themselves. In Mississippi, however, only governors could not succeed themselves in office, until a constitutional amendment was passed in 1986 eliminating this prohibition.

Because of this division of executive power, most political analysts describe Mississippi's government as being a legislature-dominated system. However, governors sometimes can use informal powers to achieve their goals, as was exemplified by the fight over the adoption of a state lottery to pay for education reforms in 1990. The governor at the time, Ray Mabus, used a simple argument—the legislature should allow the people to decide whether to adopt a lottery or not. After the state senate defeated the lottery proposal, Mabus used the legislative defeat as an effective public relations tool. He went around the state claiming the state senate had told the people "to shut up, your right to vote does not matter" (Krane and Shaffer 1992, 150) on this issue. Citizens began to flood the state capitol with angry calls, and their demands soon convinced the legislature to allow a referendum on the issue (which the public, perhaps ironically, ultimately defeated). Clearly, the governor had wielded an effective informal power in his use of publicity in this regard.

The formal constitutional power of Mississippi's executive branch is "vested in a governor," who holds office for four years and can serve a maximum of two terms. The constitutional requirements for serving as chief executive consist of being at least thirty years of age, a U.S. citizen for twenty years or more, and a state resident for a minimum of five years prior to the day of the election.

Like many other governors, the Mississippi chief executive has the constitutional power to "give the legislature information on the state of the government, and recommend for consideration such measures" as he or she believes are important to enact. The governor also has the power to call a special session of the state legislature, together with the au-thority to determine the legislature's business during that session. Mississippi's governor has one of the strongest powers of veto in the nation, since it takes two-thirds of the entire membership of both legislative chambers to override the veto, not just two-thirds of those present and voting. In addition, the governor is the commander-in-chief of the state's army, navy, and militia, except when they are called into service by the national government.

The governor of Mississippi, like other governors, has the power to grant reprieves and pardons; however, anyone seeking a pardon from the governor must first publish a request in a county newspaper for thirty days and indicate the reasons why he or she should be pardoned. Only after the thirty days have passed may the governor grant the pardon.

Even though the governor must share power with other elected officials, the Mississippi chief executive can make over 500 appointments to the 135 commissions and boards that oversee state agencies. Thus, the governor does have some power to influence and shape the direction of state government, albeit indirectly. In addition, the governor can make appointments to judicial positions whenever they become vacant. Along with the power of appointment, the governor can suspend the state treasurer and county treasurers and tax collectors, and he or she can make a temporary appointment while an investigation is conducted. In addition, the governor may remove members of the state supreme court or lower courts. The governor must present an address to the entire legislature as to the reasons for removing justices. However, those whom the governor has targeted for removal may appeal to the entire legislature, which then can vote on whether to uphold the governor's decision to remove the justices.

Among the other officers of the executive branch is the lieutenant governor. Mississippi's lieutenant governor succeeds the governor if the chief executive must resign or leave office. Like the governor, the lieutenant governor is limited to two consecutive terms; however, unlike the governor, he or she may sit out one term and then run for reelection for another set of two terms. The lieutenant governor serves as president of the state senate, and whenever there is a tie within the senate, he or she may cast the deciding vote. According to the state constitution, whenever the state senate meets as "the committee of the whole" (a parliamentary technique that generally allows more flexible debating), the lieutenant governor is allowed to "debate all questions." When the governor is absent from the state, the lieutenant governor assumes the office on a temporary basis; this power can often lead to mischief, particularly when the governor and lieutenant governor are from opposing political parties. The governor and lieutenant governor are chosen separately in Mississippi (some other states choose them by joint election).

Another executive branch officer is the secretary of state, who is popularly elected to four-year terms of office. Candidates for secretary of state may run for consecutive offices and are constitutionally required only to be at least twenty-five years old and a resident of the state for five years preceding the election. One of the main responsibilities of the secretary of state is to be the "keeper of the capitol"; more im-

portant, the secretary is responsible for keeping a "correct register of all official acts and proceedings of the governor." In addition, a state treasurer and an auditor of public accounts are separately elected to four-year terms, with no constitutional limit on their tenure in office; however, they must also be at least twenty-five years old and state residents for five years prior to their election. The state treasurer is responsible for ensuring the "condition of the treasury." The state constitution authorizes the governor to pay a "surprise" visit to the treasurer and request verification of the state's accounts.

Other executive branch officers include the attorney general, the commissioner of agriculture, and the commissioner of insurance. The attorney general is the state's chief legal officer and is responsible for bringing lawsuits and defending the state in court. In addition to overseeing activities regarding drugs, gaming, and environmental issues, the Mississippi attorney general supervises a division of consumer protection, which investigates unfair or illegal business practices. The agriculture commissioner oversees the Department of Agriculture and Commerce, which promotes and regulates agricultural production in the state. The commissioner of insurance is charged with overseeing the implementation of all laws pertaining to insurance companies, associations, agents, and adjusters. In addition, the insurance commissioner is also the state fire marshal, responsible for investigating all fires that occur in the state. The attorney general, agriculture commissioner, and insurance commissioner are all elected to unlimited four-year terms in office.

Along with the agriculture and industry commissioners, Mississippi voters elect three members each to the Public Service Commission and the Highways Commission, with responsibility to oversee these executive agencies. Commissioners for the Public Service and Highways Commissions are elected from the same multicounty districts, and both commissions serve as policymaking bodies. The Highways Commission oversees the distribution of funds for constructing roads and streets, while the Public Service Commission regulates all for-hire transportation (taxis and the like), as well as communication, electric, gas, water, and sewer services in the state.

The governor and other civil officers of the state can be removed from office by impeachment and conviction by the legislature. Two-thirds of the members present in the state house must vote to impeach the official, and two-thirds of the members present in the state senate must vote for conviction and removal, with the chief justice of the state supreme court presiding over the trial.

J. Michael Bitzer

References

Krane, Dale, and Stephen D. Shaffer. 1992. *Mississippi government and politics: Modernizers versus traditionalists.* Lincoln: University of Nebraska Press.
State of Mississippi Constitution of 1890, Art. 5.

Additional Resources and Recommended Readings

Parker, Joseph. 1993. *Politics in Mississippi.* Salem, WI: Sheffield.

MISSOURI

• • • • • • • • • • • •

MISSOURI ELECTED EXECUTIVE BRANCH OFFICIALS

Governor	Lieutenant Governor
Attorney General	Auditor
Secretary of State	Treasurer

http://www.state.mo.us

• • • • • • • • • • • •

With the signing of the Louisiana Purchase in 1803, Missouri began its progress toward statehood—a process that would almost be derailed by the debate concerning slavery. However, thanks to the Missouri Compromise in 1820, Missouri was granted statehood as a "slave" state, Maine entered the Union as a "free" one, and the balance between the two categories of states was preserved in the U.S. Congress.

The struggles of Missouri's early days, beginning with the expedition of Meriwether Lewis and William Clark and their resulting attempts to establish solid governance and prosperity in the region, mirror the current challenges of Missouri state government. As part of the Louisiana Purchase, Missouri represented a new area of the country with unclear boundaries and a somewhat confused sense of self. It was wedged between the

Great Lakes region and the South, between the European-dominated East and the Native American–dominated central and western parts of the United States. Settlers in the frontier states struggled to find their identity and relate to the Native Americans in the region.

Most Americans know of Missouri as the Show Me State. While there is much debate regarding the actual origin of the nickname, it has become representative of the resolute, conservative, and clever nature of Missouri's citizens. And as evidenced from a closer look at the state's executive branch, this term might also be an appropriate characterization for their government as well.

Over the course of its history, Missouri has had a total of only four constitutions, beginning with the first in 1821 and followed by subsequent ones in 1865, 1875, and 1945. The Missouri Constitution begins with a bill of rights, powerfully affirming citizens as architects of government and government as promoters of the general welfare.

The Missouri Constitution, in addition to the Reorganization Act of 1974, called for a number of executive departments, each with a very specific focus. The constitution mentions a total of sixteen departments: the Office of Administration and the Departments of Agriculture, Conservation, Corrections, Economic Development, Elementary and Secondary Education, Health and Senior Services, Higher Education, Insurance, Labor and Industrial Relations, Mental Health, Natural Resources, Public Safety, Revenue, Social Services, and Transportation.

Missouri has a somewhat complicated organization within its executive branch.

Under each of the sixteen departments are a number of subunits, which vary quite significantly from one another. "Divisions" are the largest section, and they unite smaller groups below them, such as "units," "commissions," "bureaus," and "sections." Examples include the Air Conservation Commission (under the Department of Natural Resources), the Agriculture Business Development Division (under the Department of Agriculture), and the Office of Consumer Affairs (in the Department of Mental Health).

The appointment powers of the governor are extensive. He or she is responsible for appointing the heads of all departments in state government, and with the approval of the senate, the governor also appoints all members of state boards and commissions as well as all members of the boards for colleges and universities. After a judicial nominating commission submits candidates, the governor also appoints supreme court and appellate justices. A public vote is required, however, for retention. This method of appointment for justices was initiated in Missouri in 1940 and subsequently adopted in multiple other states. It is even referred to as the Missouri Plan.

In addition to the governor and lieutenant governor, four statewide offices are elected within the executive branch of Missouri state government. The lieutenant governor and governor must both be at least thirty years of age, citizens of the United States for fifteen years, and residents of Missouri for ten years in order to be qualified candidates. The constitution also stipulates that the state auditor must meet the same qualifications, but there are somewhat looser requirements for the remaining offices of treasurer, secretary of state, and attorney general. The only qualification required for both the secretary of state and the attorney general is that they be residents of Missouri for one year prior to the election. The state treasurer, however, in addition to the one-year residency requirement, must also have been a citizen of the United States for fifteen years. All of these elected positions within the executive branch are on the ballot during a presidential election. Each official serves a term of four years. Two-term limits are in place for the governor and the state treasurer only.

With respect to the actual powers of the governor, the Missouri Constitution is quite broad and general, stating the following: "The governor shall take care that the laws are distributed and faithfully executed, and shall be a conservator of the peace throughout the state." Additional formal and informal powers have been enumerated via statute and custom, including the power of appointment to fill vacancies in the general assembly, the power to pardon, and the responsibility of serving on numerous boards and commissions. As "conservator of the peace," the governor is in charge of the state militia and can call on it if the need arises.

One of the other major responsibilities of the governor is submission of the budget to the assembly thirty days after it convenes. Compared to the situation in other states, the power of the governor with respect to the budget is relatively strong. He or she has the power not only of the line-item veto (the power to reject individual lines of the legislative budget) but also of the appropriation item veto.

This power, which can be employed on legislation other than budget bills, allows the governor to reject individual items (sentences, paragraphs, or words) related to appropriations. In Missouri, the governor can veto words that establish the purpose of the moneys vetoed, though the governor cannot use this veto to change the purpose of appropriations. The governor can also reduce the budget without legislative approval; however, he or she cannot reorganize departments without the approval of the assembly. And the governor is required by the constitution to both sign and submit a balanced budget to the legislative branch.

As in many states, the lieutenant governor is ex officio president of the senate. Additionally, the lieutenant governor is a member of many state boards and commissions, including the Board of Public Buildings, the Board of Fund Commissioners, and the Missouri Finance Development Board, among others. The office of the lieutenant governor is characterized by service to citizens—especially Missouri's most vulnerable ones. For example, in the realm of education policy, the lieutenant governor plays an important advisory role to the Department of Elementary and Secondary Education. By statute, he or she also serves a unique role as the state's official advocate for the elderly and therefore devotes a great deal of time to working with Missouri's Department of Health and Senior Services. In recent years, the office has been lauded for its development of two service organizations—Missouri Volunteer and the Missouri Community Service Commission. And finally, the lieutenant governor works on issues of affordable housing, economic development, veterans' affairs, and tourism.

Recent evaluations of Missouri's state government and, in particular, the executive branch have touted their adoption of high objectives and goals and their subsequent effective communication of those objectives to the lowest levels of state organizations. The budget office, in particular, has focused on improving performance measures and incorporating them into the budgetary process as a basis for its decisions and allocations. Fiscally, Missouri faces many of the same struggles as other states—rising Medicaid costs; shifts in revenue leading to budgetary shortfalls; and the maintenance of a qualified, appropriately sized state workforce.

In summary, the Show Me State's executive branch can be characterized as a complex system of agencies and departments headed by a governor with strong enumerated powers. All of these organizations and individuals work together to deal with the most pressing issues of the day in a manner illustrated by the state motto: *Salus populi suprema lex esto*, translated as "Let the welfare of the people be the supreme law."

Christine Kelleher

References

Davis, Ron. 2004. *Official manual: State of Missouri 2003–2004.* Published by the secretary of state as authorized by: *Revised Statutes of Missouri*, 2000, Section 11.020. Election qualifications for statewide offices. http://www.sos.mo.gov/elections/elect_qualification.asp.

Government Performance Project—Missouri. http://results.gpponline.org.

Missouri State Constitution. http://www.moga.mo.gov/const/moconstn.htm.

National Association of State Budget Officers. 2002. Budget processes in the states. http://www.nasbo.org/Publications/PDFs/budpro2002.pdf.

Additional Resources and Recommended Readings

Foley, William. 2004. *Wilderness journey: The life of William Clark.* Columbia: University of Missouri Press.

MONTANA

• • • • • • • • • • • •

MONTANA ELECTED EXECUTIVE BRANCH OFFICIALS

Governor

Lieutenant Governor

Attorney General

Auditor

Secretary of State

Superintendent of Public Instruction

http://www.state.mt.us

• • • • • • • • • • • •

The history of the executive office of the state of Montana reflects the frontier of which it is a part. The history of the West calls to mind a great mix of pioneers attempting to settle a vast and open land. Even the most cursory look into Montana's gubernatorial past reveals that history as it came to life. Montana has had three governors who were born outside the United States. Governors Frank H. Cooney and Stan Stephens were born in Alberta, Canada, and Governor John Hugo Aronson was born in Sweden. Interestingly enough, Montana has also elected two governors born in the same small town in Missouri: the state's first governor, Joseph K. Toole, and Governor William Elmer Holt were both born in Savannah, Missouri. It was not until 1937 that Montana elected a governor who was a true native son, as Roy E. Ayers became the first Montana governor born inside state lines. Judy Martz was the state's first female governor. Elected on November 7, 2000, she moved from serving as lieutenant governor under Marc Racicot to leading her own administration. She retired at the end of her term in 2004. Brian Schweitzer then became the state's first Democratic governor since 1988.

The challenges facing the Montana state executive's office are those that one might expect from one of the most rural states in the country. Montana averages 6.2 people per square mile, compared to the U.S. average of nearly 80. Economic sustainability, health care, and education are but a few of the major issues arising from the geographic isolation of the state. One of the most significant debates is the competition between the timber and logging industry and environmental groups. Each of these groups hopes to control what is done with one of the largest natural resources in Montana, its trees. It is therefore up to the governor to try to balance the pristine natural wonders of the nation's "last best place" with attempts to nurture industrial development and economic sustainability. The governor must lead the state in its attempts to overcome these and many other obstacles.

The highest executive offices of Montana are the offices of governor, lieutenant governor, secretary of state, attorney general, superintendent of public instruction, and state auditor. These state officers are elected to serve four-year terms, and all have specific duties entrusted to them as expressly stated in Article 6, Section 4 of the state constitution, as well as other duties of office as established by state law.

The governor and lieutenant governor are elected jointly as members of the same ticket in both the primary and general elections, while the other executive officers are elected separately. To qualify for these offices, a person must be at least twenty-five years of age, a U.S. citizen, and a resident of the state of Montana for at least two years prior to being elected. Additionally, a person seeking the office of attorney general must be in good standing—and eligible to practice law—within the state of Montana, as well as having actively practiced for at least five years prior to election. Likewise, the superintendent of public instruction must hold "at least a bachelor's degree from any unit of the Montana university system or from an institution recognized as equivalent by the board of public education for teacher certification purposes."

If the governor is unable to fulfill his or her duties in office, the lieutenant governor serves as acting governor. When the lieutenant governor's office becomes permanently vacant, either because the lieutenant governor was called on to serve as governor or because of death, resignation, or inability to fulfill the duties according to law, then the governor appoints a qualified person to serve out the lieutenant governor's term. If both the governor and lieutenant governor are unable to serve, state law provides for legal succession until the next general election; at that time, a new governor and lieutenant governor will be elected to serve out the remainder of their predecessors' terms. Likewise, if any of the other four elected executive offices (secretary of state, attorney general, superintendent of public instruction, and auditor) is vacant for any reason, the governor is given the power to appoint a qualified individual to serve until the next general election; the individual elected to office at that point will serve out the remainder of the term for which his or her predecessor was elected.

The issue of succession has played an important role in Montana's executive history. After his election to the governor's office in 1933, John Erickson resigned to take up an appointment to the U.S. Senate. His vacant seat was filled by Lieutenant Governor Frank Cooney, who succumbed to heart failure in 1935. Cooney was replaced by William Elmer Holt, who was then president pro tempore of the Montana senate. Holt served as governor until 1937. In 1962, Montana lost another governor during his time in office when Donald G. Nutter died in a plane crash. He was replaced by Lieutenant Governor Tim Babcock.

Montana's executive branch is constitutionally limited to twenty principal departments, the heads of which are appointed by the governor. All executive offices and agencies (with special exceptions for temporary commissions) are arranged within these twenty departments in an attempt to keep the executive branch operating in an orderly manner. It should be noted that the governor, lieutenant governor, secretary of state, attorney general, superintendent of public instruction, and auditor are not bound to assignment within these twenty departments and therefore are not included within the constitutional limitation when considering the size of the executive branch.

The governor of Montana has significant authority to determine the state's budget. At the beginning of each legislative session—and at any other time deemed necessary or appropriate—the governor delivers a budgetary message in which he or she offers information and recommendations on those issues that need to be addressed. In addition, the governor prepares the budget that will be submitted to the legislature prior to a fiscal period. This means that the governor not only determines the budgetary agenda but also has a great deal of discretion over setting the levels of spending for programs in the state.

The governor's veto power in Montana is not as simple as in a number of other states across the country. Instead, there are various elements to this power that make for a unique system of interaction between the governor and the legislature. Each bill passed by the legislature is subsequently sent to the governor for approval. However, certain legislative actions are not subject to gubernatorial veto. Among them are "bills ratifying proposed amendments to the United States constitution, resolutions, and initiative and referendum measures." If the governor signs the bill or takes no action on the legislation within ten days of receiving it, the measure becomes law. If the governor decides to veto the bill, it is resubmitted for the consideration of the legislature, along with the reasons why it was not acceptable. If the governor returns the bill with recommendations for amendment, the legislature can choose whether or not to amend and resubmit it to the governor. The governor cannot, however, return the bill for amendment more than once, and therefore, the only way for the legislature to pass a bill that has received a second gubernatorial veto is with an override vote in both state houses. For an override to be successful, it must receive a two-thirds vote in both of the state houses. If the governor vetoes a bill that has been approved by two-thirds of those legislators present when the legislature is not in session, the bill (along with the governor's reasons for the veto) is submitted to the secretary of state. The secretary of state then polls the remaining members of the legislature by mail, sending each a copy of the governor's veto message. If two-thirds or more of the members of each house vote to override the veto, the bill becomes law. The legislature can also reconvene at any time to reconsider a bill that has been vetoed. Additionally, the governor of Montana is given a special line-item veto for appropriations, which means that he or she can veto parts of an appropriations bill without rejecting it as a whole. Such a veto gives the governor even more control over the budget and spending. However, a line-item veto is subject to the same override process that was described previously.

In addition to the appointment, budgetary, and veto powers, the governor has a number of other duties assigned by law. He or she is the commander-in-chief of the state's militia and is given the power to pardon, reprieve, or commute sentences assigned to individuals found guilty of an assortment of crimes. Also, the governor is in charge of overseeing the different departments within the executive branch, as well as a variety of other state institutions. As such, the governor has the power to demand executive and state officers and managers to submit in writing (under oath if necessary) information pertaining to their work and duties. The governor may also form an investigative committee to look into the activities, conditions, and functions of any executive office or state institution.

The powers of the Montana governor help not only to balance legislative demands and those of various state agencies but also to foster the well-being of citizens across a state roughly the size of Germany. In 1996, Governor Racicot, perhaps the most popular governor in Montana's history, spoke about the difficulties of bringing scientific advancement and innovation to rural states such as Montana, as well as the necessity of such research for modernizing and streamlining economic, environmental, and social forces throughout the state. These same issues faced Democratic Governor Ted Schwinden, whose "Build Montana" economic plan led to the creation and support of the Science and Technology Alliance in 1985. The goal of this alliance was to find new uses for Montana's vast raw materials. Innovation and leadership are, therefore, two critical aspects of the gubernatorial history of Montana.

The role of lieutenant governor in Montana is largely undefined in terms of constitutional responsibilities. It is primarily left up to the governor to decide what part the lieutenant governor will play in his or her administration. However, the constitution explicitly forbids the lieutenant governor from exercising any executive power expressly delegated to the governor.

In the 2004 elections, Democratic gubernatorial candidate Brian Schweitzer used the lieutenant governor's office to increase his electoral advantage. Realizing the need to sway Republican swing voters, Schweitzer looked beyond his party to find a lieutenant to serve with him in the executive. In a bold move that helped carry him on to electoral victory, Schweitzer asked Republican senator John Bohlinger to be his running mate. Since that time, Bohlinger has continued to build bridges between the two major parties, attending legislative caucuses and meeting with legislators to push for their support on a number of executive initiatives.

The attorney general of Montana assumes the role of the state's chief legal and law enforcement officer. He or she also serves as the director of the state's Department of Justice, which places the attorney general in charge of the state's law enforcement branches and county attorneys. The attorney general also retains a permanent seat on both the State Board of Examiners and the State Land Board. One of the more unusual elements of legal authority retained by the attorney general is the power to offer legally binding opinions to the legislature and other state departments and agencies. All of these functions combine to make the attorney general a critical player in the faithful execution of public law across the state.

Although the office of secretary of state was originally established over a century

ago, in 1889, the current secretary, Brad Johnson, is only the nineteenth person to hold that post. Given the lack of turnover in the secretary of state's office, the tenure of the secretary was limited in 1992 to two four-year terms in any sixteen-year period. This limitation was put in place due to the influence the secretary has over a number of the state's electoral, administrative, and other public and private sector rules and regulations. These functions are distributed across six administrative divisions under the secretary's oversight: elections and legislative services, business services, management services, administrative rules, records management, and information services.

Montana has a rugged frontier history whose effects are being felt even today. Through creative ways of balancing industry and environment, technology and natural resources, and business and agriculture, the state executive office has helped to maintain Montana's reputation as "the last best place" and set the foundation for further growth in a rural landscape.

Joseph J. Foy

References

Montana State Constitution of 1972, Art. 6.

Morrison, John. 1997. *Mavericks: The lives and battles of Montana's political legends.* Moscow: University of Idaho Press.

Racicot, Marc. 1996. Remarks to the Future of Science in Rural America Third Annual EPSCoR Conference, Bigfork, MT, May 30. http://www .discoveringmontana.com/racicot/spch/ epscor96.htm.

U.S. Census Bureau. 2000. *State and county QuickFacts: Montana.* http:// quickfacts.census.gov/qfd/states/ 02000.html.

Additional Resources and Recommended Readings

Lee Enterprises. Montana Forum. A collection of news and articles from five of Montana's top selling news agencies. http://www.montanaforum.com/.

Malone, Michael P., Richard B. Roeder, and William L. Lang. 1991. *Montana: A history of two centuries.* Rev ed. Seattle: University of Washington Press.

Merrill, Andrea, and Judy Jacobson. 1997. *Montana almanac.* Helena, MT: Falcon.

Montana State Historical Society. http://www.his.state.mt.us/.

Weaver, Kenneth L. 2002. *Governing Montana at the grass roots: Local government, structure, process, and politics.* Bozeman: Montana State University, Local Government Center.

NEBRASKA

• • • • • • • • • • • •

Nebraska Elected Executive Branch Officials

Governor	Lieutenant Governor
Attorney General	Auditor of Public Accounts
Secretary of State	Treasurer

http://www.nebraska.gov

• • • • • • • • • • • •

Born in political controversy, Nebraska is historically identified as the home of some of the nation's most progressive political figures. Nebraska is recognized for operating with the only nonpartisan, unicameral state legislature in the country, and it is also known as the nation's most Republican state, based on its presidential voting in the last half of the twentieth century. Although it is a leading agricultural state in which nearly 95 percent of the land is given over to farms—a greater portion than in any other state—Nebraska has an economy that is dominated by service industries, particularly insurance and finance. More than two-thirds of the state's people reside in the metropolitan areas of Omaha and Lincoln, the capital.

Nebraska was formed from territory opened for settlement by the disputed Kansas-Nebraska Act of 1854. Initially crafted by Illinois senator Stephen Douglas to support a St. Louis–Great Salt Lake route as part of a proposed transcontinental railroad, the final bill allowed settlers to determine whether to permit slavery in the new territory. This provision renewed the expansion of the slavery dispute and may have accelerated the onset of the Civil War. Following the war's end, the Union Pacific Railroad began building a line west from Omaha, and in 1867, Nebraska became a state. Nebraska's statehood, however, came over the veto of President Andrew Johnson, who feared that the certain addition of two Republican U.S. senators would ensure his conviction on impeachment charges.

Caught up in the Populist cause toward the end of the nineteenth century, Nebraska became the platform for William Jennings Bryan, the "silver-tongued orator of the Platte," who won the Democratic presidential nomination three times but espoused policies too extreme for most of the nation. Swept by the Progressive movement of the early twentieth century, Nebraska produced George Norris, one of the nation's most independent political figures. As a member of Congress, Norris led the fight against the autocratic rule of House Speaker Joseph Cannon, and as a U.S. senator, he helped pass the Twentieth Amendment (the "lame-duck" amendment) to the U.S. Constitution, authored legislation that created the Tennessee Valley Authority (TVA), and from Washington persuaded Nebraskans to adopt a nonpartisan and unicameral state legislature.

Despite these flirtations with more radical policies and politicians, Nebraska has traditionally been a conservative Republican bastion, as suggested by a review of occupants of the governor's office. Among the thirty-nine individuals who have served as the state's chief executive, twenty-five were Republicans, twelve were Democrats, and two were elected by a Populist-Democratic alliance, or fusion ticket (from 1895 to 1901). Republicans elected twelve of the first fifteen governors from 1867 to 1909, but Democrats made some inroads between 1909 and 1941, electing six of the next ten governors. One observer, however, attributed this "deviation from Republicanism" more to "recurrent agrarian distress" than any other factor (Key 1956, 243). While agricultural problems continued, Nebraskans' dissatisfaction with New Deal policies returned the state to its Republican roots for the next two decades, with voters choosing five Republicans and one Democrat as governors from 1941 to 1961.

Beginning with the 1960s, however, the Cornhusker State became more politically competitive. Voters elected four Democrats and four Republicans as governors between 1961 and 2003, and Democrats served for twenty-six years compared to sixteen years for Republicans during this period. Republican Mike Johanns, a onetime Democratic county official and Republican mayor of Lincoln, became the first Republican governor in four decades to win reelection with his victory in 2002. Governor Johanns, however, resigned in the midst of his second term to accept a cabinet position as secretary of agriculture. Lieutenant Governor Dave Heineman, whom Johanns initially appointed to the position in 2001, succeeded Johanns as governor.

Nebraska's second constitution, adopted in 1875, assigns traditional powers to the chief executive that are very similar to those in other states, with two exceptions that will be noted. The extent of the governor's budgetary and veto powers, however, places this position slightly above average in terms of formal authority among the nation's governors. Despite being a "fairly strong" governor, Nebraska's chief executive has typically played a caretaker role, seldom using the position to shape public debates, influence the legislature, or lead the party. One governor who did take an active policy role, Republican Norbert Tiemann (1967–1971), was denied a second term by voters after he persuaded the legislature to enact both an income tax and a general sales tax to produce a more balanced revenue system. Nebraska voters also historically have preferred governors, regardless of party, with "bland public personas." One mid-1980s assessment concluded, in fact, that "charisma is not critical to success in Nebraska politics" (Welch 1984, 40).

Nebraska governors originally could serve an unlimited number of two-year terms, but a 1966 constitutional amendment imposed a limit of two consecutive four-year terms. One of six elected executive officers, the governor runs on a joint ballot with the lieutenant governor in even-numbered, non–presidential election years. Both candidates must be at least thirty years of age, U.S. citizens, and Nebraska residents for the five years preceding their election. Voters also elect a secretary of state, auditor, treasurer, and attorney general simultaneously with the governor and lieutenant governor. Voters in 1938 rejected, by a nearly three-to-one margin, a proposed amendment to allow the governor to appoint the secretary of state, attorney general, and treasurer, with legislative consent. The state has made no further attempt to shorten the long ballot.

The governor is vested with the "supreme executive power" and is mandated to take care the state's affairs are "efficiently and economically administered." To this end, the constitution provides that the chief executive "may" give information to the legislature on the condition of the state at the beginning of each session, at the close of his or her term of office, or on request of the legislature, as well as submit topics for legislative consideration deemed "expedient." The governor may also call special sessions and limit the lawmakers' agenda to business "for which they were called together."

More significantly, the state's fundamental law requires the governor to submit to the legislature "a complete itemized budget of the financial requirements" of all state agencies, departments, and institutions and to prepare a budget bill for introduction by the speaker of the legislature. The legislature may not appropriate funds in excess of the governor's recommendations, except by a three-fifths majority, and excessive amounts are subject to veto by the chief executive. The Nebraska governor's veto power is among the nation's strongest. The governor may veto any bill and veto or reduce any "item of appropriations," subject to a three-fifths override vote. The governor, however, must act within five days, excluding Sundays, after a bill is presented.

The governor appoints the heads of all statutory executive departments with the consent of the legislature but has sole authority to remove these officials. Except for judges, the governor fills all vacancies in elected state offices on his or her own authority and fills vacancies in nonelective state offices, with legislative consent. Together with the attorney general and secretary of state, the governor serves as a board to grant reprieves, pardons, and commutations for offenses other than treason and impeachment. As commander-in-chief of the state militia, the governor may call out the state's armed forces to execute laws, suppress insurrection, and repel invasion.

The Nebraska governor may be removed from office by impeachment and conviction "for any misdemeanor in office." David Butler, the state's first governor (1867–1871), remains the only Nebraska chief executive impeached and convicted, and his politically motivated removal led framers of the state's second constitution in 1875 to create a unique impeachment system. Rather than placing the procedure entirely within the legislative branch, the constitution provides for impeachment by a joint legislative session and a trial before the state supreme court, with a two-thirds vote of the justices necessary for conviction. With the adoption of unicameralism, the system was modified to provide for impeachment by a majority of the one-house legislature. One authority considers this system "on a par with criminal prosecutions in a regular court of law" that gives "substantial protection to the accused" (Sittig 1984, 101). Perhaps due to this change, the Nebraska legislature has not considered impeaching any official since the 1890s.

Should a governor be impeached or be otherwise removed from office or if he or she should die or resign, the lieutenant governor and then the speaker of the legislature are constitutionally in line to serve the remainder of the governor's term. Should the governor be absent from the state or suffer an "inability," the powers and duties of the chief executive devolve on the lieutenant governor and, if necessary, the speaker of the legislature "until the absence or inability ceases."

One other political dispute resulted in a significant alteration in the lieutenant governor's already modest powers. When the lieutenant governor cast a tie-breaking vote on a controversial bill in 1981, opponents—including the governor—argued that a bill could become law, as the state constitution prescribed, only if approved by "a majority of all members elected." The state high court agreed, ruling that the lieutenant governor could not cast a tie-breaking vote on legislative matters except on the question of final passage of a bill.

One student of Nebraska politics concluded in the mid-1980s that "unexciting leaders" proved satisfactory in a state that practiced politics with a high degree of civility and was largely devoid of political scandals (Welch 1984, 40, 55–56). Events since the mid-1980s have produced little to alter that judgment. During that time frame, governors have continued to allow the legislature to advocate and advance its own agenda. However, as the formally nonpartisan legislature shows definite signs of more openly partisan politics, Nebraska's governors may necessarily be forced to abandon their traditional passive approach and take a more active public policy role.

James McDowell

References

Barone, Michael, and Richard E. Cohen. 2003. *The almanac of American politics 2004.* Washington, DC: National Journal.

Key, V. O., Jr. 1956. *American state politics: An introduction.* New York: Knopf.

Miewald, Robert D. 1984. *Nebraska government and politics.* Lincoln: University of Nebraska Press.

Nebraska Constitution of 1875.

Sittig, Robert. 1984. The Judiciary. In *Nebraska government and politics,* ed. Robert D. Miewald. Lincoln: University of Nebraska Press.

Welch, Susan. 1984. The governor and other elected executives. In *Nebraska government and politics,* ed. Robert D. Miewald. Lincoln: University of Nebraska Press.

Additional Resources and Recommended Readings

Olson, James C., and Ronald C. Naugle. 1997. *History of Nebraska.* Lincoln: University of Nebraska Press.

NEVADA

• • • • • • • • • • • •

NEVADA ELECTED EXECUTIVE BRANCH OFFICIALS

Governor	Lieutenant Governor
Attorney General	Controller
Secretary of State	Treasurer

http://www.nv.gov/

• • • • • • • • • • • •

At the turn of the nineteenth century, Nevada was considered a stronghold of the Silver Party, which advocated the free coinage of silver as well as the issuing of large amounts of paper currency. Members of the Silver Party were committed to these inflationary measures as a means of easing the financial burdens of the nation's debt-ridden farmers, as well as bailing out the depressed mining industry. Composed largely of factions that had split from the major parties, the Silver Party swept through the state, capturing the governor's office and a number of other state offices between 1895 and 1911.

Governors John E. Jones and Reinhold Sadler were both members of this populist political group. Additionally, after the Democratic Party had co-opted a number of the group's issues on a national level, a Silver-Democratic coalition was led by Governor John Sparks from 1903 to 1908 and Governor Denver S. Dickerson from 1908 to 1911. Although the third-party experiment in Nevada lasted for slightly less than two decades, such success by a populist organization offers insight into the political and social context of serving as chief executive in the country's Battle Born State.

The state of Nevada entered into a period of political realignment in terms of ideology and partisanship at the turn of the twenty-first century. Large increases in the number of people entering the state, the ever-increasing influence of the Nevada Gaming Commission on politics, and the vast population concentrated in the southern half of the state are all contributing factors to this shift, and the state executive office must confront these new needs as well as the old problems as it seeks to serve the people of Nevada.

To become governor of the state of Nevada, one must be at least twenty-five years of age, a qualified elector, and a resident of the state for a minimum of two years preceding the election. It is also worth noting that an individual who holds a federal office is ineligible to run for governor while occupying that national seat. The governor of Nevada is term limited, so a person cannot be elected to serve in this post more than twice. Each term lasts for four years.

As in most other states, the governor has the primary responsibility to ensure the faithful execution of the laws of the state. Except in cases of impeachment, the governor is also given the power to pardon, to offer reprieves or commutations of sentences, and to provide remission for fines or forfeitures. Although state law often dictates when such measures are appropriate and how such actions should be carried out, the governor is given discretion in terms of when and how these powers are used. The governor is also the commander-in-chief of the state's military forces, when they are not called into the service of the federal government, and has the power to make both civil and military officials submit reports in writing about any duties, responsibilities, or activities relating to their office or position.

The governor is responsible for a number of duties in regard to the state legislature. The chief executive is required to deliver an opening address before the start of each legislative session, communicating what he or she feels to be the important issues facing the state and offering recommendations as to how they should be confronted. The governor may also call a special session of the legislature if there is a matter that must be dealt with and the state houses are not in session. When the legislature is specially convened, however, it may only deal with the issue or issues for which it was originally called into special session. It may not attempt to look into any other legislative activity. Further, when there is disagreement between the two houses about when to adjourn a session, the governor may call for adjournment.

The remaining officials at the top of the executive branch for the state of Nevada are the lieutenant governor, secretary of state, treasurer, controller, and attorney general. The lieutenant governor, who must have the same qualifications for office as the governor, is not elected with the governor on a ticket. Lieutenant Governor Lonnie Hammargren, a Republican who served under the Democratic governor Bob Miller, told the state legislature, in 1997, that it should seek to rectify that situation in the future. Hammargren explained that the governor and his or her lieutenant should run as members of the same ticket because "cooperation, not confrontation, is the key to good government" (Vogel and Whaley 1997).

Even though the governor and lieutenant governor are not elected as members of the same team and might have strong political differences, the lieutenant governor is still expected to fill in for the governor should he or she becomes unable to fulfill the duties of the office. The lieutenant governor also serves as the president of the senate, with the ability to cast a vote. The secretary of state, treasurer, attorney general, and controller are not bound to the same eligibility requirements as the governor and lieutenant governor. Instead, any elector is eligible for these state offices. However, like the governor and lieutenant governor, they are limited to serving only two four-year terms.

The governor, attorney general, and secretary of state together comprise the Board of State Prisons Commissioners, as well as the Board of Examiners. As commissioners of the Board of State Prisons, these three members of the executive branch have the power to supervise all matters that relate to the state prison, within the boundaries of written law. Of even greater interest is the role they play as the Board of Examiners, which evaluates all claims against the state except for salaries and compensation of state officials that are elucidated by law. In 1998, for example, Governor Bob Miller, Attorney General Frankie Sue Del Papa, and Secretary of State Dean Heller awarded nearly half a million dollars to plaintiffs in nine law suits brought against the state for abuses of civil rights and discrimination and for accidents in which the state was deemed to be at fault.

Perhaps the most exceptional aspect of serving as governor of Nevada relates to the economic context in which the state is grounded. Nevada's connection with legalized gambling makes it thoroughly unique among the states; and one of the governor's duties is to appoint and oversee members of the Nevada Gaming Commission. The NGC and especially its chair wield considerable power in regulating and overseeing the state's largest industry. Traditionally, the chair of the commission has been an individual from northern Nevada, an unwritten compromise intended to help balance the considerable political power held by the population centers in the southern portion of the state. However, in 2001, Governor Kenny Guinn went against the trend and appointed a Las Vegas attorney to head the commission.

The power that the Las Vegas area holds over politics in the state is not just due to the economic influences of the gaming industry. Approximately two-thirds of the state's total population is concentrated in Clark County, where Las Vegas is located. Consequently, the governor faces a difficult dynamic in seeking to distribute resources across the state to everyone who might need them while simultaneously keeping the large southern population happy and thereby maintaining a solid base of power. Additionally, recent growth in the state's population has raised new challenges. The governor must try to adapt to the influx of new citizens whose demands may not fit well with old government policies. For example, between 1990 and 2000, the population of Nevada grew by 66.3 percent, as opposed to the national average of 13.1 percent. This tide of new residents pouring into the state has shifted the balance of power among the parties. As analyst Lou Cannon has observed, "Democrats outnumbered Republicans by nearly 40,000 in 1992; today, Republicans hold a much smaller 4,000-vote edge."

The political history of the Nevada governor's office is filled with the excitement of populism. Shifts in political ideology and partisanship from the Republican days after Lincoln's presidency to the Silver Party days at the turn of the nineteenth century led to Democratic dominance in the state for a number of years; subsequent changes brought a reemergence of Republicanism at the turn of the twenty-first century. The ways in which the state executive has dealt with these changes is a reflection of social trends as well as leadership and innovation coming from the governor's office. How that office will deal with the new challenges emerging today will help to define the state for years to come.

Joseph J. Foy

References
Bicha, Karel Denis. 1976. *Western populism: Studies in an ambivalent conservatism.* Lawrence, KS: Coronado.

Cannon, Lou. 1998. Demographic changes leave Nevada senator in jeopardy. *Washington Post,* September 25. http://www.washingtonpost.com/wpsrv/politics/campaigns/keyraces98/stories/nv092598.htm.

King, R. T. 1994. *Hang tough! Grant Sawyer: An activist in the governor's mansion.* Reno: University of Nevada Oral History Program.

McMath, Richard. 1993. *American populism: A social history.* New York: Hill and Wang.

Morrison, Jane Ann. 2001. Nevada Gaming Commission: Guinn picks panel chief. *Las Vegas Review-Journal,* October 2. http://www.reviewjournal.com/lvrj_home/2001/Oct–02-Tue–2001/business/17126167.html.

Myles, Myrtle Tate. 1974. *Nevada's governors from territorial days to the present.* Reno: Nevada Publishers.

Vogel, Ed, and Sean Whaley. 1997. Lawmakers open 1997 session. *Las Vegas Review-Journal,* January 21. http://www.reviewjournal.com/lvrj_home/1997/Jan-21-Tue-1997/news/4716172.html.

Whaley, Sean. 1998. Board settles claims against state. *Las Vegas Review-Journal,* April 16. http://www.reviewjournal.com/lvrj_home/ 1998/Apr-16-Thu-1998/news/7323581.html.

Additional Resources and Recommended Readings

Davies, Richard O. 1998. *The maverick spirit: Building the new Nevada.* Reno: University of Nevada Press.

Douglass, William A., and Robert A. Nylen. 2004. *Letters from the Nevada frontier: Correspondence of Tasker L. Oddie, 1898–1902,* ed. William A. Douglass and Robert A. Nylen. Reno: University of Nevada Press.

Las Vegas Review-Journal Online. http://www.reviewjournal.com/.

Ralston, Jon. 2004. *The anointed one: An inside look at Nevada politics.* Las Vegas: Huntington Press.

Raymond, C. Elizabeth. 1992. *George Wingfield: Owner and operator of Nevada.* Reno: University of Nevada Press.

NEW HAMPSHIRE

• • • • • • • • • • • •

NEW HAMPSHIRE ELECTED EXECUTIVE BRANCH OFFICIALS

Governor   Lieutenant Governor

http://www.state.nh.us

• • • • • • • • • • • •

The motto of New Hampshire, "Live Free or Die," generally suggests a state government that has little power and that limits its intervention in the lives of its citizens. The state is mountainous and scenic, and it may project a remoteness appropriate to its independent citizens. But New Hampshire also has a time line spanning all of American history. It was first settled in 1623; it provided most of the troops who performed the actual fighting at Bunker Hill during the Revolutionary War; and as the ninth state to enter the Union, it cast the deciding endorsement of the U.S. Constitution.

Most of the attention given to the New Hampshire state government is related to its unique "citizen" legislature. The Granite State's house of representatives has 400 members, the second-largest legislative body in the United States (only the U.S. House of Representatives is larger, with 435 members). New Hampshire is just 180 miles long, averaging 50 miles in width; its population is slightly over 1.2 million people. Each of the 400 members of the house represents about 30,000 individuals. Thus, each representative serves a small number of people and an even smaller geographic area within the state. A further component of the citizen link in the statehouse is the pay given to the legislators: they earn $200 per legislative term (plus mileage expenses). Clearly, politics in New Hampshire is an avocation, not a profession, as is reflected in the legislature's membership. College students, homemakers, and retired people serve alongside attorneys and businesspeople. State policy has a distinct closeness to citizen concerns, rather than to the moneyed interests that prevail in some neighboring states with professional legislatures.

Is the governorship of New Hampshire also a low-paying avocation? Is power as dispersed in the governor's mansion as it is in the statehouse? The answer to these questions is mixed. The governor's salary in 2001 was $93,263—far better than the typical legislator's but only about half as much as the pay of the New York governor ($179,000). New Hampshire governors since 1955 have served four or six years, with the exception of Hugh Gallen, who died in office in 1982, and his interim successor, who served briefly until the inauguration of a newly elected governor. Some of the more recent governors have continued their political careers by moving on to higher offices, among them Judd Gregg, a member of the U.S. Congress, and John Sununu, who peaked as White House chief of staff. Gregg and the last governor of the state, Jeanne Sha-

Jeanne Shaheen, elected in 1997, became the first female governor of New Hampshire. (Office of Governor Jeanne Shaheen)

heen, may have higher political aspirations in years to come.

In some ways, the governor of New Hampshire is more powerful than his or her peers. The governor is the only official elected to statewide service; he or she runs for office with the lieutenant governor and then shares in the appointment of the state's attorney general, secretary of state, and other specialized department and agency heads. In other states, the lieutenant governor and many other members of the cabinet (insurance commissioner, secretary of education, state auditor, and so on) are elected separately from the governor, giving these other officials a mandate independent from the governor. This situation can lead to sticky relations. For example, if a governor is elected on a pledge of reducing taxes but an education secretary is elected on a platform of enhancing school funding through higher taxes, conflict will probably follow.

The dynamic of shared power in New Hampshire is unique among the fifty states. While there are no competing elected agency heads, the state's citizens do elect five individuals to the Executive Council. This body supports the governor on policy decisions such as those involved in developing the budget. Each council member is elected from a geographic area of the state, for the same two-year terms as the governor. The governor has the power to convene the Executive Council, so he or she sets the agenda regarding when the business of state government will occur. But the Executive Council has the power to veto any action of the governor. If the governor and the Executive Council do not agree on an issue, that issue will not move forward for consideration by the state legislature. In an additional restriction on gubernatorial power—but an expansion of democratic dialogue and debate in New Hampshire—all meetings of the Executive Council are open to the public. Other state governors can shield their policies from public scrutiny until they move into the legislature.

Does the Executive Council act at odds with or in support of the governor? The tendency appears to be the latter. Presently, all members of the council are Republicans, sharing the party affiliation of Governor Craig Benson. For the most part, because of the open status of meetings, relations between the governor and the council are amicable. At times, the council serves as an expert advisory body in support of the governor, such as on the state's long-term planning of roads and other infrastructure. Interestingly, while no governor has served for more than six years in recent times, members of the Executive Council may serve much longer and thus work with many governors. In 2001, Councilor Bernard Streeter retired after thirty years of continuous service.

Organizations similar to the Executive Council existed in the other New England states at the nation's founding, but these have been reduced, altered, or eliminated over time. Meanwhile, New Hampshire maintains its ties to the original idea of limited government and executive power in additional ways. Only New Hampshire and Vermont still hold gubernatorial elections every two years. Consequently, the governor has about one year to set policy after his or her election before having to start a reelection campaign. But the idea of a two-year term is in keeping with the notion of serving in the state capitol for a short period before returning to the private sector work of a good citizen. This tendency prevailed from colonial times until about 1950. Since then, the tenure of the governors in nearly all states has expanded. Yet it is still relatively short, at either four or six years.

The American governor has long held an important check on the legislature's actions through the veto power. This mechanism allows the governor to strike language from legislation of which he or she disapproves. The strongest veto power is the line-item veto, whereby a governor can pull a specific sentence or broader wording from a bill. If the governor does not want to fund abortion clinics in a human services budget bill, for instance, he or she can delete this specific funding line. It should come as no surprise that, in keeping with the limited power granted originally in the New Hampshire Constitution, the Granite State's governor has a weaker veto power, without the ability to strike line items. If the New Hampshire governor does not like the specific funding line, he or she has to veto the entire bill, potentially endangering the funding of programs that he or she favors. Only six other states have as weak a veto power, three of which are in the northeast (Vermont, Rhode Island, and Maine). The standard elsewhere is to grant the governor the line-item veto.

As mentioned previously, the New Hampshire governor has a power-sharing arrangement with various actors in government in most other ways. The Executive Council collaborates in the development of a $1.3 billion budget, and it advises the governor on agency leadership appointments for a workforce of 11,700 employees. The state's responsibilities include public health and safety, secondary and higher education, cultural affairs, environmental protection, and economic development.

In most states, there is a tension between many of the public interests over which the governor presides. For example, growth related to economic development efforts may have detrimental effects on the natural environment. New Hampshire is ripe for this kind of conflict, as population growth in the southern part of the state has been rapid since the mid-1990s. Contributing to the increase in sprawl that is occurring around the country's major cities, many New Hampshire residents work in the Boston area, one hour to the south. New residential subdivisions reduce the natural space in New Hampshire's forests and hills. The state's response to balancing growth and environmental needs is to place responsibility for these competing concerns in the same agency, the Department of Resources and Economic Development (which also handles tourism support). Another difficult aspect of adding a large number of new residents is a burgeoning need for other services, such as those provided by schools and public health facilities. Despite the downturn in state government budgets nationwide, New Hampshire's citizen-focused executive office and legislature have maintained an effective relationship for policy setting in the new century.

The governor has symbolic duties as well, some cheerful and others more disheartening. An unfortunate early challenge for Governor Benson arose when the state's symbol—a rocky outcropping in Franconia Notch State Park that formed the face of "The Old Man of the Mountain"——collapsed. (See the image, before the collapse, at http://www .nhstateparks.org/ParksPages/OldMan/ OldMan.html.) Many throughout New England were saddened by the loss of this impressive natural wonder, and others quickly demanded its restoration. The governor ordered a period of open public input and formed the Revitalization Task Force, observing that the most fascinating aspect of the "Old Man" was its creation by natural forces over time. The governor presides over ceremonies and has held historical duties in the past, such as the declaration of Fast Days. From early Puritan times, the governor occasionally declared a day of prayer and fasting, especially related to plantings and harvest. Up until 1991, the governor still could declare this state holiday, which has since been converted into Civil Rights Day.

The links between New Hampshire's early traditions and current governance are many, such as the citizen legislature, the Executive Council as a check on the governor's power, and short-lived terms for the governor. These institutions have operated successfully since the early 1600s, and they will likely survive for many more with only minor revision.

Brendan Burke

References
Anderson, Leon W. 1980. *Three hundred years: New Hampshire's unique governor-council government, 1680–1980.* Kirkland, WA: Phoenix.

Clement, John. 1987. *New Hampshire facts.* Dallas: Clements Research.

Constitution of the State of New Hampshire, Art. 41–59. http://www.nh .gov/constitution/governor.html.

Gilbreth, Donna. 1997. Rise and fall of Fast Day. Concord: New Hampshire State Library. http://www.nh.gov/nhinfo /fast.html.

Additional Resources and Recommended Readings
Lockard, Duane. 1959. *New England state politics.* Princeton: Princeton University Press.

Pierce, Neal. 1976. *The New England states: People, politics, and power in the six New England states.* New York: Norton.

Rosal, Lorenca Consuelo. 1988. *God save the people: New Hampshire history.* Orford, NH: Equity.

NEW JERSEY

● ● ● ● ● ● ● ● ● ● ● ●

NEW JERSEY ELECTED EXECUTIVE BRANCH OFFICIALS
Governor
http://www.state.nj.us/

● ● ● ● ● ● ● ● ● ● ● ●

The combination of strong executive powers aligned with a professional legislature, as well as a relatively strong, white-collar-oriented economy, have made New Jersey a noted site for policy activism and achievement in recent decades. The state's governors have gained prominence as a result. Interestingly, New Jersey's Republican governors are more active policy leaders than even the Democratic governors in other regions across the country. These Republican governors have led on topics such as environmental protection, the maintenance of effective welfare benefits, and statewide planning for economic development and growth.

New Jersey's first and very concise (2,000-word) constitution of 1776 created a relatively weak executive. Power was placed in the hands of the legislature, even the power to decide on and appoint the governor for a one-year term. While other states held the same limited powers for their governors in the times of the Articles of Confederation, New Jersey was different in that it did not update its constitution to include the separation of powers following the framing of the U.S. Constitution. In fact, it waited until 1844 to hold a constitutional convention, during which the length of the first document was tripled; the new document included a bill of rights and incorporated the philosophy of separating legislative, executive, and judicial powers. But the state's legislature still held firmly to most of its powers, limiting the governor to one three-year term of office and maintaining its ability to appoint most of the agency leaders at the pinnacle of the state government.

During the 1800s and early 1900s, the state endured a power struggle between large and influential businesses, especially railroads, and a modest wave of modernizing reform. New Jersey was home to many waves of immigrants, who came to work in the factories and in the extraction of natural resources. The state also grew as many workers chose a suburban life within New Jersey's borders, working by day in New York City or Philadelphia and returning by night to Jersey City, Camden, and smaller suburbs. Political machines controlled the cities and state government, but when Woodrow Wilson left the presidency of Princeton University in 1910, he became a Progressive governor for two years before mounting his successful run at the U.S. presidency. His only major accomplishment during his time as governor was to create more fair and open elections, but he planted the seeds for change,

Woodrow Wilson served only two years as governor of New Jersey before being elected the twenty-eighth president. (Library of Congress)

as the government organization would be modernized and made more responsive to citizens' needs during the next few decades.

The modernizing reforms were included in the state constitution of 1947, which endures today with minor amendments. Because of this constitution, the New Jersey governor is recognized as having among the most favorable circumstances for governance among the fifty American states. In conjunction with a strong legislature that seats well-paid members with plenty of staff resources, the New Jersey state government is positioned to enact well-crafted policies through professional deliberation.

The 1947 constitution expanded the tenure of the New Jersey governor. Some legislators realized that governors might serve as good leaders of the major political parties, but rarely could a governor who served only three years in the capital create a leadership coalition. Thus, the legislature supported expanding the time that the governor could serve in office. The term of office was ultimately extended to four years, and the governor could be reelected an unlimited number of times. He or she was only prevented from serving more than two terms in a row. In essence, a governor could serve for eight years, sit out for four, and reenter the executive office for eight more years. Since 1947, however, most governors have served eight years.

The New Jersey governor has the most centralized leadership alignment found within the American states. In most states, citizens elect several different statewide officers, including attorneys general, treasurers, state auditors, and possibly independently elected lieutenant governors. In New Jersey, only the governor is elected on a statewide basis. The state does not even have a lieutenant governor. When the citizens of New Jersey think about the statewide electoral accountability of their government, they can only think of the incumbent governor. Statewide successes can be credited to the governor, and when things go wrong, voters need only focus on that one office to create desired change.

New Jersey's state government was like that of most other northeastern states prior to 1947, in that the long time line of its history and the needs of an urban and industrial society led to growth in bureaucratic services over time. By 1947,

the state's departments, agencies, commissions, and independent authorities were numerous, and they varied in their reporting to and from the governor. The 1947 constitution limited the possible number of state departments to twenty, so that fewer functions would report directly to the governor. Today, the list of state officials includes the attorney general; the secretary of state; the state treasurer; and the commissioners of agriculture, banking and insurance, commerce, community affairs, corrections, education, environmental protection, health and senior services, human services, labor, military and veterans affairs, personnel, and transportation. The governor even holds the ability to appoint judges. In most of these appointments, he or she must obtain the endorsement of the state senate, but this is a short list requiring outside approval. Within the twenty-department limit, the governor can reallocate and reorganize the 53,400 state employees in whatever manner he or she sees as most responsive to the needs of New Jersey's citizens.

The governor has relatively common powers in terms of building the $26.3 billion state budget. He or she prepares estimates of available revenue and compiles the requests for staff and funding within the state's agencies. The governor can add his or her own priorities to a recommended budget, which is transferred to the legislature at approximately the same time that the governor makes the state of the state speech to New Jersey's citizens. The legislature can revise the governor's budget as it sees fit, but ultimately, the budget returns to the governor, as his or her signature is required before the revenue and spending plans go into effect. The budgetary powers of the New Jersey governor are very similar to those of the U.S. president. They are stronger than in some states, where the governor must write the budget with a committee of other officials. The New Jersey governor can set the agenda for subsequent budget discussions on his or her own.

The governor has had one more important constitutional power since 1947: the veto. There are three forms of veto in New Jersey, including the absolute veto of entire bills, which is found in all other states; the line-item veto, found in most states; and the less common conditional veto. The line-item veto involves the reduction of appropriations bills. If the governor disagrees with budgetary specifics in legislation that arrives on his or her desk, the veto pen can be used to remove the offending funding. The rest of the bill remains intact. As long as the legislature cannot muster two-thirds of its membership to override the governor's changes, they will stand once the bill becomes permanent law. The conditional veto allows the governor to revise the language of legislative bills. With this power, he or she can add wording or change specific language; if the changes are acceptable to the legislators, they can pass the governor's bill into law with a majority vote. If the governor's language changes are unacceptable and the legislature does not pass the revised bill, then the entire bill is killed and the legislature's policy-writing process must start over again.

New Jersey governors muster these powers on a variety of important issues.

During Governor Christine Todd Whitman's tenure in office, environmental issues were significant, as air and water pollution became dominant issues for the Garden State's citizens. Between 1992 and 2000, Governor Whitman championed incentives to reduce air pollution and increase conservation among major polluters, funded protections of the state's watersheds and the cleaning of beaches, and developed one of the first statewide initiatives to protect open space and concentrate new development in already built regions of the state. This agenda was passed with the support of the legislature. Whitman's success as governor earned her the attention of President George W. Bush, who chose her to lead the U.S. Environmental Protection Agency in 2000.

The governorship has been a rather chaotic place since Whitman's departure. Upon Whitman's resignation, the governorship was filled by three state senate presidents who served as acting governors as prescribed by state law since New Jersey does not have a lieutenant governor. State law further prescribes that the senate president will continue to serve his/her office while serving as acting governor. James McGreevey was elected and took office in January 2002 and served until resigning in November 2004 after admitting to having an affair with a male state employee. Though McGreevey announced his intention to resign in October of 2004, he delayed stepping down until November so that a special election would not be held and the Democratic state senate president Richard J. Codey would serve as acting governor until the next regularly scheduled election. Codey declined to seek election and former US Senator Jon Corzine was elected governor in the November 2005 election. Corzine took over the governorship in January 2006.

It is not always easy for the New Jersey governor to lead according to plan, especially when funding is tight. As the state grew in population, citizens increased their demands for first-rate services. The state adopted a statewide sales tax in the 1960s but resisted an income tax until it was absolutely necessary to fund the bureaucracy. Two governors, Brendan Byrne and James Florio, both won the governorship by declaring that they would not raise taxes. Governor Byrne managed to create a 2 percent income tax in 1974 and even won reelection, but when Governor Florio saw the need to raise the income tax rates to as much as 7 percent, he was not as lucky. He lost his reelection bid in 1993.

Despite a somewhat slow start, New Jersey has increased its gubernatorial (and legislative) capacity since 1947, which has enabled it to become one of the better-run and most policy-active states. The citizens of New Jersey demand as much.

Brendan Burke

References

Beyle, Thad. 2004. The governors. In *Politics in the American states: A comparative analysis*, 8th ed., ed. Virginia Gray and Russell L. Hanson, 194–231. Washington, DC: Congressional Quarterly Press.

Gray, Virginia, and Russell L. Hanson, eds. 2004. *Politics in the American state: a comparative analysiss*, 8th ed. Washington, DC: Congressional Quarterly Press

New Jersey State Constitution 1947. http://www.njleg.state.nj.us/ lawsconstitution/constitution.asp.

Office of the Governor, State of New Jersey. 2004. James E. McGreevey. http://www.nj.gov/governor/.

Office of Management and Budget, State of New Jersey. 2004. Fiscal 2005 budget in brief. http://www.state.nj.us/treasury /omb/publications/05bib/pdf/bib.pdf.

Salmore, Barbara G., and Stephen A. Salmore. 1993. *New Jersey politics and government: Suburban politics comes of age*. Lincoln: University of Nebraska Press.

Additional Resources and Recommended Readings

Aron, Michael. 1994. *The governor's race: A TV reporter's chronicle of the Florio/ Whitman campaign*. New Brunswick, NJ: Rutgers University Press.

Pennachio, Matthew. 1996. *A charter revised at Rutgers: The New Jersey Constitutional Convention of 1947*. New Brunswick, NJ: Rutgers University.

Worton, Stanley N. 1997. *The reshaping of New Jersey: A history of its government and politics*. Trenton: New Jersey Historical Commission.

NEW MEXICO
• • • • • • • • • • •

NEW MEXICO ELECTED EXECUTIVE BRANCH OFFICIALS
Governor   Lieutenant Governor
Attorney General   Auditor
Commissioner of Public Lands
Secretary of State   Treasurer
http://www.state.nm.us

• • • • • • • • • • • •

New Mexico is a state rich in racial and ethnic diversity, and its demographic composition in turn has a significant effect on the governor's office. For example, with a population that is 42.1 percent Hispanic, New Mexico is proportionally the most Hispanic state in the Union according to the 2000 Census. In New Mexico, Hispanics are a diverse group, 428,261 people chose to label themselves "Other Hispanic," compared with 330,049 who responded "Mexican," 4,488 "Puerto Rican," and 2,588 "Cuban."

Such diversity has been reflected in the governor's mansion, as New Mexico has had five Hispanic governors, including current governor Bill Richardson, who was born in Mexico and raised in a bilingual household. Richardson took office in 2003 and was elected by the largest margin any candidate had received since 1964. In 2004, five of New Mexico's seven elected executive officials were of Hispanic decent. Among them is Secretary of State Rebecca Vigil-Giron, who at the time of this writing is the highest-ranking Hispanic female in the United States.

In addition to the large Hispanic population, New Mexico has a higher number of Native Americans than most other states. In the year 2000, 9.5 percent of its population was identified as Native American. One of the executive agencies appointed and overseen by the governor is the New Mexico Indian Affairs Department (NMIAD). Its primary responsibility "is to further strengthen the government-to-government relationship between the State and Tribal Governments as well as improving the well-being of Native American Indian people." The NMIAD attempts to fulfill its responsibilities to the Native peoples of New Mexico by "recognizing and respecting the sovereign status of Tribal Governments, enhancing and improving communication and outreach, assisting in developing policies that may result in positive resolution to issues impacting Native American Indian people, utilizing intergovernmental and intra-agency coordination and collaboration, and institutionalizing an implementation process that provides a framework for how the State and Tribal Governments will exercise agreed upon policy and principles" (NMIAD 2004). These activities laid the foundation for the work done and the policies pursued by this state executive agency.

New Mexico governor Bill Richardson (Office of Governor Bill Richardson)

The diversity in terms of who serves as governor and in the types of executive agencies present in New Mexico demonstrates the effect of demographics on the governor's office and provides insight into the context in which New Mexico's executive serves. However, these population effects are not the only factors surrounding the governor's office. A number of economic, political, and social forces come together to create challenges that the chief executive must face on a day-to-day basis.

The elected officials that make up the executive branch of the New Mexico state government are the governor, lieutenant governor, secretary of state, state auditor, state treasurer, attorney general, and commissioner of public lands. Further, the governor oversees a number of other offices and departments designed to carry out the duties of the state executive. For example, Article 5, Section 14 of the state constitution establishes the state Transportation Commission, whose six officials oversee the state's highways and transportation networks. The governor, with the advice and consent of the state senate, appoints the members of this commission to serve for staggered, six-year terms. The Transportation Commission is but one example of a department established to assist the governor in his or her attempts to faithfully execute the laws of New Mexico. The same is true for the aforementioned New Mexico Indian Affairs Department. These and other state agencies provide additional resources of support for the governor and help form the rest of the executive branch of the state's government.

The governor and lieutenant governor are elected jointly as members of the same ticket. Once elected, the lieutenant governor serves as president of the senate, and when the senate's vote is evenly divided, the lieutenant governor casts the tie-breaking vote. Also, if for any reason the governor is no longer able to serve, the lieutenant governor assumes the gubernatorial role. If both the governor and lieutenant governor are unable to serve, succession then falls to the secretary of state, followed by the president pro tempore of the senate.

The eligibility requirements for the governorship of New Mexico follow largely the same formula as in other states across the country. To serve as governor, a person must be thirty years old, a U.S. citizen, and a citizen of New Mexico for at least five years prior to the election.

To qualify for the office of attorney general, a person must also be an attorney in good standing, licensed by the New Mexico Supreme Court. A similar requirement is placed on persons seeking the office of superintendent of public instruction, as they must be trained and experienced educators.

The term limitations for the governor in the state of New Mexico are slightly different than those in many other states in that, after serving two full terms in office, the governor may again run for the post after one full term has intervened. However, the difficulty for most state executives in New Mexico is not in seeking a third term but achieving a second one. Although the first governor, William C. McDonald, took office in 1912, it was not until 1995 that Republican Gary E. Johnson became the first governor of New Mexico to serve two full, four-year terms.

A key responsibility of the governor, as in all states, is to oversee the faithful execution of the laws. To make this happen, the state constitution entrusts the executive with a number of powers, including the ability to appoint executive officials whose selection is not otherwise provided for by law or election. These officials and all public institutions are required to give the governor a full accounting report annually, and they may be called on by the governor for reports thirty days prior to a legislative session. The governor of New Mexico also acts as commander-in-chief of the state militia, which places him or her in the position of calling on the military forces (as long as they are not in the service of the federal government) if they are needed to help keep the peace or execute the laws. The governor also has the power to pardon individuals convicted of crimes, except in cases of treason or impeachment.

When she took office on January 1, 2003, Diane Denish became New Mexico's first female lieutenant governor. In this capacity, she is responsible for a number of executive and legislative functions across the state. Not only does the lieutenant governor serve as chief executive whenever the governor is out of the state or otherwise unable to perform the duties of office, he or she is also the president of the state senate. In an administrative capacity, the lieutenant governor serves on a number of state boards and agencies. Currently, Lieutenant Governor Denish is a member of the State Border Authority, the Community Development Council, the Workforce Development Board, and the Board of Finance, and she chairs the Children's Cabinet (a board composed of various directors of state agencies that work with children).

The attorney general of the state of New Mexico serves in a dual capacity as the chief legal officer of the state and chief counsel in all cases in which the state is an involved or interested party. In her capacity as attorney general, Patricia Madrid has spearheaded a number of reforms and initiatives to expand the capacity and abilities of the state's law enforcement agencies. Madrid was New Mexico's first female to be elected to the district court bench in 1978, and two decades later, she became the first female attorney general. She was subsequently reelected to a second term in 2002.

As the third officer in the line of executive succession, the secretary of state of New Mexico performs the role of chief executive whenever the governor and lieutenant governor are out of state or unable to perform their duties in office. The secretary also performs an important legislative function for the state, calling the house of representatives to order—and serving as the interim speaker of the house at the beginning of each new legislative session until a permanent speaker is elected from that body. Administratively, the secretary is responsible for overseeing state elections, regulating central aspects of commerce in the state, and providing service to various state boards. An additional role of some import performed by the secretary of state is to oversee the public printing of all proposed amendments in both English and Spanish prior to a public vote; this is but one of the many informational duties carried out by the secretary of state in his or her capacity as a public servant serving the diverse public needs of the people of New Mexico.

The auditor is responsible for the collection, management, and oversight of tax revenues generated and allocated by the state. Along with the auditor, the state treasurer's office provides a number of important financial services for the state and the citizenry. First, it acts as the state's central bank, maintaining account records of taxpayer moneys collected by the state. Second, the treasurer's office invests state revenues to increase the financial resources available to the state. The treasurer performs this investment role for both state and local governments, accounting for billions of dollars. Finally, the treasurer sits on a number of state boards and is actively involved with advising and reporting to a number of administrative agencies across New Mexico.

Although the governors of New Mexico have a number of constitutionally and legally ascribed powers, the political and economic realities they confront continually force them to be flexible and innovative to keep the state running. For example, the federal government employs approximately one-fourth of the state's working population, which creates an interesting dynamic between the state and federal governments because of the vast amount of land and resources under federal control; the governor must be flexible in order to meet the challenges this situation poses. Likewise, much of the state's wealth is derived from the mining of its vast mineral resources. However, that sector of the economy has declined over the last few decades, requiring the creation of innovative policies, often spearheaded by the state executive, to diversify the state's economy and sustain the levels of prosperity many in the state expected. One attempt that Governor Richardson made to maintain steady growth in the economy was to launch a campaign in 2004 to bring more manufacturing jobs to the southern parts of the state. The governor's ongoing "Make it in New Mexico" campaign is a $100,000 effort to advertise to companies contemplating a move overseas, in hopes of inducing them to keep their businesses in the United States and locate them in New Mexico. Although the final results of this campaign remain to be seen, it stands as an example of the innovative efforts the governor must put forth in attempting to benefit the state as a whole.

Joseph J. Foy

References

de la Garza, Rodolfo. 1996. *Ethnic ironies and the 1992 elections.* New York: Westview.

Hanrahan, Rorie. 2004. State launches $100,000 "Make it in New Mexico" campaign. Official Press Release, New Mexico Economic Development Department, April 8, 2004. http://www.edd.state.nm.us/PRESS/news.php?_fn=view&_rn=20001380.

Maurillo, Virgil E. 1990. *New Mexico government and politics.* Lanham, MD: University Press of America.

New Mexico Department of Transportation. 2004. Transportation Commission. http://nmshtd.state.nm.us/main.asp?secid=11393.

New Mexico Indian Affairs Department. 2004. Mission statement. http://www.state.nm.us/oia.

Smith, Tim R. 1996. The New Mexico economy: Where do we go from here? Federal Reserve Bank of Kansas City. New Mexico Economic Forums. http://www.kc.frb.org/spch&bio/fornm96.htm.

Additional Resources and Recommended Readings

Albuquerque Journal Online. http://www.abqjournal.com/.

Albuquerque Tribune Online. http://www.abqtrib.com/.

Gunzburger, Ron. 2004. Politics1: Online guide to New Mexico politics. http://www.politics1.com/nm.htm.

Santa Fe New Mexican Online. http://www.sfnewmexican.com/.

University of New Mexico. Online Archive for New Mexico (OANM). http://elibrary.unm.edu/oanm/.

NEW YORK

• • • • • • • • • • • •

NEW YORK ELECTED EXECUTIVE BRANCH OFFICIALS

Governor   Lieutenant Governor
Attorney General   Controller

http://www.state.ny.us

• • • • • • • • • • • •

New York governors have had a number of major political successes in the nation's history. Four have become presidents (Martin Van Buren, Grover Cleveland, Theodore Roosevelt, and Franklin Delano Roosevelt), two others rose as high as the vice-presidency (George Clinton and Nelson Rockefeller), and five more peaked as party nominees for the presidency in three different elections (DeWitt Clinton, Samuel Tilden, Charles Evans Hughes, Al Smith, and Thomas Dewey). Power defines the New York governor, as he or she holds the highest level of institutional powers among American governors. However, the New

York governor is virtually assured of a competitive relationship with at least one other potent subnational politician, the mayor of New York City. Oddly, the New York governorship and the New York City mayoralty are distinct political tracks; one has to go back to the pastoral times of the early nineteenth century to find a person who held both posts during his political career (the energetic DeWitt Clinton again).

The governor of New York is one of eight American governors allowed to run for the job in perpetuity. There is no limit to the number of four-year gubernatorial terms that one may consecutively pursue in New York. Mario Cuomo served for twelve years, and Nelson Rockefeller served for fourteen, only resigning as governor to become vice-president. When one is allowed to sit for many years as the governor, one builds up a base of personal support by participating in the hiring of numerous political appointees in patronage positions. The long-serving governor also develops a familiarity with all policy areas and political actors, making it less taxing to develop strategies over time. In fact, the greatest danger to the most successful long-standing New York governors seems to be the call of higher office. Governor Cuomo, for instance, had an ongoing if reluctant interest in the presidency through the 1988 and 1992 elections, before being voted out of office in favor of George Pataki in 1994.

The governor of New York competes for attention with only two other statewide elected state officials (not counting the lieutenant governor, who is elected jointly with the governor)—the comptroller and the attorney general. It is possible that the governor could conflict with these political actors on budgetary matters and legal issues. But since the statewide election is dominated by the governor, the victor can generally claim a broad mandate for his or her policy stances. In some states, the lieutenant governor is elected independent of the governor and may serve as a rival for power and attention, but in New York, the lieutenant governor is more like the U.S. vice-president, serving in support of the chief executive, especially in legislative matters.

In some ways, the execution of statewide policy and administration is watered down for the New York governor.

Despite a reorganization in 1925, the structure of the state's government retains many remnants of the Progressive era of the early twentieth century. One of the structural reforms of that era was the formation of specialized independent commissions and service authorities, which would be isolated from the influence of corrupt mayors and governors. But the ethical and well-intentioned governor can be equally constrained. One of the most powerful politicians in the state's history, Robert Moses, was actually the administrator of eleven different specialized authorities devoted to the construction of infrastructure, especially in New York City and the surrounding environs. He served as chair of many of these authorities from the 1930s until the 1960s, through the terms of several mayors and governors who tried to fire him for insubordination. Independent bureaucratic forces such as those under Moses reveal one of the few chinks in the armor of New York's gubernatorial strength.

Currently, the other significant authority in potential opposition to the New York governor resides in the administration of higher education (especially the State University of New York). With a budget of $3 billion and seventy-four university, college, and community college campuses throughout the state, this system provides countless jobs—the economic base for communities both large and small—and impacts the capacity of a large percentage of the state's citizens. Governor Pataki has downsized a number of agencies and functions of New York state government since the mid-1990s, but he has had little success with reducing the scope of the decentralized higher education system. Even a governor as powerful as New York's faces limitations.

New York's governor has budgetary powers similar to most other chief executives in the American states. The governor presents a spending proposal to the state legislature, which has the power to increase the plan if there is a supermajority inclined to do so. But the sheer size of the state's budget sets New York apart from almost all of the other states. New York's state government raises and spends fully $100 billion per year, with duties carried out by 187,000 civil servants and many other employees in companies and nonprofit agencies that contract to do the state's work. This huge budgetary force is only compounded when one factors in the largest city in the United States and its separate governmental organization.

The governor of New York benefits from the strongest type of legislative veto. If the legislature presents policies or funding ideas within a bill that the governor does not support, he or she can cancel the specific offending items and retain the remaining portions of the bill that the governor finds acceptable.

The New York governor presides over a confusing array of divisions, commissions, offices, and authorities within twenty cabinet-level departments. The simplest measure of the bureaucracy, the listing of civil service units on the state's webpage, counts 101 separate entities without any categorization or outline, from the State University of New York to the Battery Park City Authority and the Office of Cyber Security and Critical Infrastructure Coordination.

New York City and the state have mustered their resources on behalf of an ac-

New York governor George Pataki (Office of Governor George Pataki)

tivist vision of government since at least the beginning of the Progressive era, at the turn of the twentieth century. Less attention has been devoted to the streamlining and reorganization of the state bureaucratic structure, despite common and even repeated efforts to do so in the other American states. Syracuse University's Maxwell School of Citizenship and Public Affairs has given all state governments letter grades on the performance of their management systems; New York's overall grade was a C– in 1999, forty-sixth out of the fifty states, though the grade was improved to a C+ by 2001. (The reports of the Government Performance Project, available at http://www.maxwell.syr.edu/ gpp, offer a full description and comparison to other states.) One of Governor Pataki's active efforts to streamline state government is focused on public education, which is among the most convoluted and costly of all service areas. The Commission on Education Reform has proposed simplifying the aid formulas used by the state to award funding to local school districts and revising the formulas in favor of the neediest communities. At the same time, the commission, with Governor Pataki's endorsement, has proposed new accountability standards, whereby students, schools, and teachers all will be tested and rewarded or sanctioned based on performance of their different roles and responsibilities in the educational system. Lastly, the commission has recommended that the school bureaucracy be brought under Governor Pataki's authority, producing one less independent authority within the state's overall bureaucracy.

The New York governor enjoys a range of formal and informal powers. As chief executive of the state with the most important city in the country, the governor is highly visible to the entire nation. On occasion, he or she will play a vital role in managing New York City through times of crisis, such as following the city's bankruptcy in 1975 and in the wake of the September 11, 2001, terrorist attacks that destroyed the World Trade Center (WTC) in lower Manhattan.

The governor can call on the power of executive orders, revising laws, budgets, and policies that affect the government's civil service structure and effort. This power is significant because it allows the chief executive to bypass the legislature's financial and policymaking authority in some important ways. While Mayors Rudy Giuliani and Michael Bloomberg have been most responsible for the direct recovery of the city in the wake of 9/11, Governor Pataki has used his executive order power to help restore the city's fortunes. Policy changes within the eighty-two executive orders passed since 9/11 include: the easing of contracting regulations for road construction, forensic testing, and training for firefighters; a number of provisions relating to court cases and compensation related to life insurance; banking regulations, including closings and access to funds for WTC victims; establishment of a scholarship fund for the children of WTC victims; establishment of a state director of public security; and multiple extensions of property tax payment deadlines.

The governorship of New York is a substantial job, among the most complex and responsible in the nation. The state's finances and workforce rank it among the largest business entities in the world. It should be no surprise that during good times and bad, a number of New York governors have gone on to become candidates and even worthy incumbents in the highest positions in American politics.

Brendan Burke

References

Caro, Robert A. 1974. *The power broker: Robert Moses and the fall of New York.* New York: Knopf.

Liebschutz, Sarah F., Robert Bailey, Jeffrey M. Stonecash, Jane Shapiro Zacek, and Joseph F. Zimmerman. 1998. *New York politics and government: Competition and compassion.* Lincoln: University of Nebraska Press.

New York State Commission on Education Reform. 2004. Ensuring children a sound basis for education—final report. http://www.state.ny.us/pdfs/finalreportweb.pdf.

New York State Constitution, Art. 4. http://assembly.state.ny.us/leg/?co=6.

Pataki, Gov. George E. World Trade Center Emergency Executive Orders. http://www.state.ny.us/sept11/wtc_exeorders.html. Accessed June 2004.

Additional Resources and Recommended Readings

Benjamin, Gerald, and Norman T. Hurd. 1984. *Rockefeller in retrospect: The governor's New York legacy.* Albany: Rockefeller Institute of Government.
———. 1985. *Making experience count: Managing modern New York in the Carey era.* Albany: Rockefeller Institute of Government.
Cuomo, Mario M. 1994. *The New York idea: An experiment in democracy.* New York: Crown.
Giuliani, Rudolph. 2002. *Leadership.* New York: Hyperion.
Ward, Robert. 2002. *New York State government: What it does, how it works.* Albany: Rockefeller Institute of Government.
Zimmerman, Joseph. 1981. *The government and politics of New York State.* New York: New York University Press.

NORTH CAROLINA

● ● ● ● ● ● ● ● ● ● ● ●

NORTH CAROLINA ELECTED EXECUTIVE BRANCH OFFICIALS
Governor
Lieutenant Governor
Attorney General
Auditor
Commissioner of Agriculture
Commissioner of Insurance
Commissioner of Labor
Secretary of State
Superintendent of Public Instruction
Treasurer
http://www.ncgov.com/

● ● ● ● ● ● ● ● ● ● ● ●

As one of the original thirteen colonies, North Carolina, the Tar Heel State, designed its constitution of 1776 to reflect the times, and the times clearly opposed a strong, central chief executive. The governor of the newly independent state was selected by the popularly elected legislature for a one-year term and could only serve for three terms in six years. The power of the chief executive was severely limited, so much so that in order to exercise executive authority, the governor often had to obtain the concurrence of the seven-member Council of State, which was also chosen by the state legislature. All state officers had to be of the "Protestant" faith in order to hold their offices. Only after the constitution of 1835 did the governor's

power expand somewhat, most notably in the fact that the term of office was lengthened to two years instead of one. With the constitution of 1868, the governor was popularly elected to a four-year term of office. Yet the executive branch would be characterized by its weakened nature for the next 100 years, during which the governor had to share power with numerous other officials.

The most recent state constitution, written in 1972, stipulates that the "executive power of the State shall be vested in the governor." Unlike other states, North Carolina does not vest *supreme* executive power in the governor because several other officers are also specified in the executive branch: a lieutenant governor, secretary of state, auditor, treasurer, superintendent of public instruction, attorney general, commissioner of agriculture, commissioner of labor, and commissioner of insurance. These officers, along with the governor, make up the Council of State. The Council shares with the governor the authority to convene a special session of the state legislature and must approve all state land transfers and many state financial transactions.

All of these executive officers dilute the governor's ability to oversee affairs of North Carolina's state government. However, the governor can appoint, with the advice and consent of a majority of the state senate, department secretaries to his or her cabinet. The departments include administration, cultural resources, revenue, health and human services, commerce, environment and natural resources, corrections, transportation, juvenile justice and delinquency prevention, and crime control and public safety.

In addition, the governor may appoint individuals to over fifty different licensing boards that oversee a range of occupations within the state, such as the North Carolina Board of Athletic Trainer Examiners, the North Carolina Board of Occupational Therapy, and the North Carolina State Board of Examiners for Electrical Contractors. However, the governor does have to share the appointment power with other government officials and bodies, including the lieutenant governor, both houses of the general assembly, and some Council of State members.

The governor is elected to a four-year term and can run for two consecutive terms of office. One governor in North Carolina history has served for four terms: Jim Hunt assumed the chief executive's office in 1977 and served until 1985 and was elected again to serve two more terms from 1993 until 2001. The lieutenant governor is also restricted to two consecutive, four-year terms. Both the governor and the lieutenant governor must be at least thirty years old, U.S. citizens for five years, and state residents for two years prior to the election.

On the death, resignation, or removal of the governor, the lieutenant governor assumes the office. Whenever the governor is out of the state, the lieutenant governor serves as acting governor until the chief executive's return. If the governor is unable to perform the duties of the office due to physical incapacity, he or she may write to the attorney general declaring the incapacity; the lieutenant governor then assumes the office on an acting basis. If the governor is unable to perform the duties due to mental incapacity, the general assembly may, by a two-thirds vote in each house, remove the governor. If the legislature is not in session, a majority of the Council of State may convene the legislature in a special session to hold such a vote.

Among the duties of the chief executive is to provide "information of the affairs of the State" in what is commonly referred to as the state of the state address, in which the governor provides proposals for the legislature to consider. The governor has the power to submit a budget to the legislature and is responsible for ensuring that "the laws be faithfully executed." He or she also serves as commander-in-chief of the state's military forces. Further, the governor may grant "reprieves, commutations, and pardons," but unlike the chief executives of some other states, the North Carolina governor is not required to submit these decisions and the reasons for them to the legislature.

The governor has the power to recall the legislature back into special session, with the advice of the Council of State. He or she has other legislative powers as well, including the power to issue vetoes of legislation. The chief executive of the Tar Heel State has the notable distinction of being the last governor in the United States to be granted the power of the veto: only in 1996 did the voters approve a constitutional amendment giving the governor the ability to reject a law passed by the general assembly. The legislature may override the governor's veto with a three-fifths majority vote in both houses.

Along with the power to succeed the governor, the lieutenant governor also serves as president of the state senate. Like the vice-president of the United States, the lieutenant governor has the power to break ties in the senate. He or she can also be assigned other duties by the governor.

North Carolina's attorney general oversees the state's Department of Justice and acts as the legal representative for state agencies. The attorney general is also responsible for overseeing the State Bureau of Investigation, as well as investigating issues of consumer fraud.

The North Carolina state auditor is responsible for evaluating the financial accountability and program performance of state agencies, while the state treasurer serves as the chief banker and investment officer of the state. In this capacity, the treasurer administers the public employee retirement system and is responsible for other financial matters for the state.

Like his or her peers in other states, North Carolina's secretary of state oversees various business activities and is in charge of preserving and maintaining state records and documents. However, unlike secretaries in some other states, the North Carolina secretary of state is not the keeper of the seal of the state; that responsibility rests with the governor.

The other popularly elected officers of the state oversee specific areas of government. They include the commissioner of agriculture, who ensures product and measurement standards as well as food and drug safety, and the superintendent of public instruction, who is in charge of overseeing the state's kindergarten through high school education programs. In 2004, these two officers were at the center of an electoral controversy. Due to the failure of electronic voting machines in one county, the winner of both offices remained a mystery for months following the November election. The courts were left to sort out how these offices would be filled, whether by special election or other means. There are two other elected officials in the executive branch: the commissioner of labor, who oversees the health and safety of the state's workers, and the commissioner of insurance, who regulates the various insurance companies and agents within the state.

If any official of the Council of State dies or resigns from office, the governor has the power to appoint another individual to serve until a successor is elected. Most recently, the state's commissioner of agriculture, the daughter and granddaughter of former North Carolina governors, was convicted of illegal campaign fundraising and perjury. After her resignation from office, the governor appointed an acting agriculture commissioner.

The state constitution stipulates that "removal of the governor from office for any cause shall be by impeachment," with the state house of representatives serving to impeach the chief executive and the state senate serving as the jury for the charges. When the governor or lieutenant governor is impeached, the chief justice of the state's supreme court presides over the trial. Conviction by the state senate requires a two-thirds majority vote, with a majority of the body serving as a quorum in which to hold the trial.

J. Michael Bitzer

References

Constitution of 1971, Art. 2 and Art. 3.

Fleer, Jack D. 1994. *North Carolina government and politics.* Lincoln: University of Nebraska Press.

Luebke, Paul. 1998. *Tar Heel Politics 2000.* Chapel Hill: University of North Carolina Press.

Additional Resources and Recommended Readings

Covington, Howard E., and Marion A. Ellis. 1999. *Terry Sanford: Politics, progress and outrageous ambitions.* Durham, NC: Duke University Press.

Crabtree, Beth G. 1968. *North Carolina governors, 1585–1968: Brief sketches.* Raleigh, NC: Division of Archives and History, Department of Cultural Resources.

Drescher, John. 2000. *Triumph of good will: How Terry Sanford beat a champion of segregation and reshaped the South.* Oxford: University of Mississippi Press.

McKinney, Gordon. 2004. *Zeb Vance: North Carolina's Civil War governor and Gilded Age political leader.* Chapel Hill: University of North Carolina Press.

NORTH DAKOTA

• • • • • • • • • • • •

NORTH DAKOTA ELECTED EXECUTIVE BRANCH OFFICIALS

Governor	Lieutenant Governor
Agriculture Commissioner	Attorney General
Auditor	Insurance Commissioner

Public Service Commissioners
Secretary of State
Superintendent of Public Instruction

Tax Commissioner	Treasurer

http://www.nd.gov

• • • • • • • • • • • •

North Dakota is historically considered a Republican state, and its list of governors bears out that description. Twenty-four of its thirty-one governors were elected as Republicans, only seven as Democrats. However, many of these Republican chief executives, particularly those chosen in the first half of the twentieth century, had little in common with Republicans in other parts of the country. These Republicans were affiliated with and strongly supported by the Nonpartisan League (NPL), a farmers' political organization founded in North Dakota in 1915 that united progressives, radicals, and reformers to gain control of state government and create state-owned institutions for the benefit of farmers. In the view of one observer, the NPL also "aroused the most bitter and uncompromising opposition both from within and from outside the boundaries of the state" (Key 1956, 250).

This group's efforts effectively produced a three-party system in North Dakota that impacted the direction of state policy by determining which candidates occupied the governor's office. Most of the time, the decision was rendered by primary battles between the two Republican factions. On some occasions, however, the defeated Republican faction supported the Democratic candidate in the general election. The NPL's political impact was short-lived in other parts of the upper Midwest, but it remained significant in North Dakota and influenced the state's politics into the 1970s. When the group switched its support to the Democratic Party in 1956, the NPL helped elect governors of that party over the next two decades.

In the period when the NPL's political involvement was strongest, North Dakota was the scene of some of the nation's most turbulent gubernatorial politics. After gaining control of the state Republican Party in the 1916 primary, the insurgent NPL routinely engaged in bitter and uncompromising political confrontations with the more conservative "regular" Republican bloc, while the Democrats played a relatively minor role. These battles produced the recall of one governor in 1921, resulted in four individuals serving as chief executive in little more than seven months between 1934 and 1935, and elected a Democrat to three terms as governor (from 1939 to 1945), although

Republicans dominated other state offices and national balloting.

The NPL's initial achievements were the election of Lynn J. Frazier as governor in 1916 and his reelection in 1918 and 1920. During Governor Frazier's tenure, the NPL pushed through several revolutionary proposals, including the establishment of state-operated enterprises—a grain mill and elevator and the Bank of North Dakota, both supervised by the Industrial Commission consisting of the governor, attorney general, and agriculture commissioner. The NPL program also included the introduction of a graduated income tax and an inheritance tax in 1919 and a constitutional amendment adopted in 1920 for the recall of public officials.

Opponents of Governor Frazier and the NPL, chafing from the postwar economic distress and citing scandals in his administration, immediately used this procedure to force a recall election that removed the governor and members of the Industrial Commission from office. Governor Frazier was the first and only American governor removed by this method until the California recall of Gray Davis in 2003. North Dakota voters proved quickly forgiving, however, electing the deposed chief executive to the U.S. Senate as a Republican in 1922. Frazier served three terms until losing in a renomination attempt in 1940.

Quiet during the 1920s, the NPL experienced a resurgence during the Great Depression years, electing the controversial and flamboyant populist William Langer as governor in 1932. Langer, however, was removed from office two years later, convicted of campaign law violations for allegedly coercing contributions from recipients of federal aid. Lieutenant Governor Ole Olson completed the term, but Democrat Thomas Moodie defeated Langer's wife in the 1934 gubernatorial election. An investigation proved that Moodie had voted in a Minnesota election in 1932, and the state supreme court removed him from office after only five weeks for failing to meet residency requirements. Walter Welford, the newly elected Republican lieutenant governor, then became North Dakota's fourth governor in seven months. But the saga was not complete.

After three additional trials, Langer succeeded in overturning his conviction in 1935 and sought to resume his political career. Governor Welford narrowly won the 1936 Republican primary, but Langer then ran as an independent and won a tight three-way contest with 36 percent of the vote over Welford and Democrat John Moses. Langer failed to unseat a Republican incumbent in the 1938 U.S. Senate primary but did defeat U.S. Senator Frazier in 1940. He won the first of his four terms that year and served until his death in 1959. Meanwhile, conservative Republicans continued North Dakota's three-way politics, deserting the NPL faction's gubernatorial candidates in the next three elections and helping to elect Moses, the more business-oriented Democrat.

Twenty-one of the state's first twenty-five governors were Republicans, of whatever political shading, but the state has become more competitive in recent years. Three of the six governors since 1960 have been Democrats, including William L. Guy (1961–1973), whose twelve years in office make his the longest gubernato-

rial tenure in state history. Aided by the switch of the NPL to the Democratic side after 1956, Guy won a pair of two-year terms (1961–1965) and two four-year terms (1965–1973) after voters amended the state constitution to double the governor's term. North Dakota voters also showed their independence from national trends during this period, electing Democrats Arthur Link (1973–1981) and George Sinner (1985–1992) in the face of Republican presidential landslides. The state's electorate also chose Republicans Allen Olson (1981–1985), Edward Schafer (1992–2000), and John Hoeven (2000–).

State politics researchers have developed an index of the formal powers of governors based on four elements: tenure potential (length of term and chances for reelection), the veto, budget power, and appointment power. Scholars have recently added two additional components: the number of separately elected public officials in addition to the governor and party control of the state legislature. Using this framework, North Dakota's move to more traditional two-party politics and modifications in the state constitution resulted in a marked improvement in the governor's power rankings, from dead last in the 1960s to the moderate-to-strong category at the close of the twentieth century. The North Dakota chief executive possibly would rank among the most powerful but for the fact the position is one of thirteen elected statewide executive offices. The additional officials are the lieutenant governor, agriculture commissioner, attorney general, auditor, insurance commissioner, three public service commissioners, secretary of state, superintendent of public instruction, tax commissioner, and treasurer. The governor and lieutenant governor must be at least thirty years old, residents of the state for five years, and "qualified electors." They are elected on a joint ballot and may serve unlimited four-year terms. The lieutenant governor fills any vacancy in the governor's office, and the secretary of state acts as governor if the lieutenant governor's office is vacant or that official is unable to serve.

All other state officials must be at least twenty-five years of age and may serve unlimited four-year terms, except for the public service commissioners; they serve six-year terms, with one of the three positions on the ballot every two years. In the 2004 elections, candidates for agriculture commissioner, attorney general, secretary of state, and tax commissioner received only two-year terms in order to move these offices to off-year elections beginning in 2006.

The governor and other state and judicial officers may be recalled or removed by impeachment by a majority of elected house members and conviction by two-thirds of elected senators. Grounds for impeachment include "habitual drunkenness, crimes, corrupt conduct, or malfeasance or misdemeanor in office."

In addition to the general authority to see that "the state's business is well administered and that its laws are faithfully executed," the North Dakota governor is required to present information on the condition of the state; he or she recommends legislation to every regular and special session of the legislature and may call the assembly into special session. The governor must consider all bills passed by the legislature, either signing them into law, vetoing them, or exercising an item veto over appropriations bills. Two-thirds of the members of both legislative chambers may override a veto. The governor has three legislative days to act if the assembly is in session or fifteen weekdays if the assembly has adjourned. Otherwise, these bills become law.

North Dakota's chief executive also serves as commander-in-chief of the state's military forces and may mobilize them to execute law and maintain order. He or she may grant reprieves, commutations, and pardons and fill vacancies in any offices, subject to senate confirmation, for which "no other method is provided by this constitution or law." The governor also prescribes additional duties for the lieutenant governor, whose only constitutional authority is presiding over the state senate and casting tie-breaking votes.

Unique to the North Dakota governor is his or her service, along with the attorney general and agriculture commissioner, on the state's Industrial Commission, which regulates the state's oil industry, oversees the state-owned North Dakota Mill and Elevator, and supervises the Bank of North Dakota. All state funds are deposited in this bank, which has been the nation's only state-operated financial institution since 1919.

The relative tranquility of North Dakota's political climate in the present day, a marked contrast to its tumultuous political past, disguises the fact that the state is undergoing significant changes. The traditional view of the state as a predominantly rural and agricultural state is no longer totally apt. The decline in its farm-based economy may not be offset by sufficient increases in the state's service

Lynn Frazier, the first North Dakota governor elected from the Nonpartisan League. (Library of Congress)

industries, however. About half of the state's population now resides in its few metropolitan areas, but that population is declining. North Dakota experienced the smallest percentage gain (0.5 percent) of any state in the 2000 Census, and the Census Bureau has estimated the state has since lost 1.3 percent of those residents.

James McDowell

References

Key, V. O., Jr. 1956. *American state politics: An introduction.* New York: Knopf.

North Dakota Constitution of 1889.

Remele, Larry. 1988. *North Dakota history: Overview and summary.* Bismarck: State Historical Society of North Dakota. http://www.state.nd.us /hist/ndhist.htm.

Additional Resources and Recommended Readings

Robinson, Elwyn B. 1995. *History of North Dakota.* Fargo: Institute for Regional Studies, North Dakota State University.

OHIO

• • • • • • • • • • • •

OHIO ELECTED EXECUTIVE BRANCH OFFICIALS

Governor	Lieutenant Governor
Attorney General	Auditor
Secretary of State	Treasurer

http://ohio.gov/

• • • • • • • • • • • •

Ohio, the Buckeye State, is a place of great political importance to the United States, serving as the birthplace of seven U.S. presidents—Ulysses S. Grant, Rutherford B. Hayes, James A. Garfield, Benjamin Harrison, William McKinley, William H. Taft, and Warren G. Harding. Only the state of Virginia can boast a larger group (eight).

Before achieving statehood in 1803, Ohio was part of the Northwest Territory, which included much of the area west of Pennsylvania. In 1787, Congress passed the Northwest Ordinance, the first step toward organized government in the region. Ohio became the first state west of the Allegany Mountains to join the Union (and the seventeenth state overall), and its first constitution was adopted in 1812. Because this document gave too much power to the legislative branch and overlooked pressing issues regarding management of the state debt and the state banking system, a new constitution was adopted in 1851. Subsequent conventions in 1873 and 1912 did not result in new documents, but instead, numerous amendments dealing with Progressive reforms to government, home rule provisions, and term limits were passed. The constitution of Ohio, like that of many states, begins with a bill of rights.

The executive branch in Ohio consists of six elected individuals: the governor, the lieutenant governor, the attorney general, the auditor of the state, the secretary of state, and the treasurer. All of these offices are term limited to two consecutive four-year stints. Additionally comprising this branch of government is the State Board of Education; the adjutant general; the governor's cabinet; and other boards, departments, and commissions responsible for implementing state laws.

As in most states, agencies play a critical role in the legislative process in Ohio. The agencies are staffed by experts on specific policy domains, who are often called on to provide information or testimony in legislative meetings or committees. Additionally, most agencies appoint a legislative liaison to monitor what is going in the state legislature. There are over 100 agencies in the state of Ohio, ranging from small agencies dedicated to very specific programs and policies to large ones with billion-dollar budgets. The Department of Health and Human Services and Department of Education routinely dwarf the others with the size

and scope of their budgets; for example, in 2000, they had operating budgets of $9.6 billion and $6.8 billion, respectively. Other agencies with large budgets include the Board of Regents, Administrative Services, Transportation, and Corrections, which together accounted for approximately two-thirds of the state's full budget in 2000.

Unlike the situation in other states, the specific departments within the executive branch of Ohio were not created in the constitution but rather by law; they are described in the Ohio Code. Currently, there are twenty-one departments: Administrative Services, Aging, Agriculture, Alcohol and Drug Addiction Services, Budget and Management, Commerce, Criminal Justice Services, Development, Environmental Protection Agency, Health, Insurance, Job and Family Services, Mental Health, Mental Retardation and Developmental Disabilities, Natural Resources, Public Safety, Rehabilitation and Correction, Taxation, Transportation, Workers' Compensation, and Youth Services.

The executive branch of the state of Ohio also contains a number of boards and commissions, including the Board of Regents, the Board of Tax Appeals, the Civil Rights Commission, the State Lottery Commission, and the Retirement Study Council. These boards and commissions report directly to the governor.

The governor is elected to a four-year term in nonpresidential years. The primary responsibilities of the office include proposing the budget, appointing directors for state departments, and signing bills passed by the state legislature. The lieutenant governor also is elected to a four-year term. He or she is a member of the governor's cabinet and presides over meetings in the chief executive's absence. The lieutenant governor may also be appointed to a cabinet office in the executive branch if the governor chooses to do so.

The attorney general of Ohio is the state's head lawyer, providing legal advice to all of the other branches of state government. In addition to issuing formal legal opinions and managing a staff of lawyers, the attorney general is responsible for protecting the interests of citizens. The primary responsibility of the secretary of state is monitoring and executing elections, in addition to keeping records of laws and resolutions passed by the general assembly. He or she also appoints all members of the election boards in all of Ohio's counties.

The treasurer is, in essence, the state's money manager. The treasurer's office is responsible for controlling and monitoring the state budget as well as state investments. The treasurer maintains fiscal records and creates detailed reports of revenues, expenditures, and debt in the state. The state's auditor audits all public offices in Ohio. Additionally, he or she distributes state moneys to towns, villages, schools, universities, and other recipients of government funds.

The adjutant general is the only statewide official other than certain members of the Board of Education to be gubernatorially appointed. The adjutant general serves as the military "chief of staff," advising the governor, who, according to the constitution, is "commander-in-chief of the military and naval forces of the state, except when they shall be called into the service of the United States." Under the adjutant general are over 300 employees, as well as 15,000 soldiers who can be called on in times of need or disaster.

The State Board of Education consists of eleven members elected from individual districts across the state as well as eight members appointed by the governor (in conjunction with the advice and approval of the senate). The State Board of Education selects and appoints the superintendent of public instruction. Members of the board are elected or appointed to four-year terms as well; however, there is no limit as to the number of terms they can serve.

Both the governor and general assembly are very involved in the budget process in Ohio. The process begins with the governor working closely with the Office of Budget and Management to create initial suggestions and recommendations, which are ultimately published in the executive budget. Once the budget is completed, the governor is required to present it to the general assembly within four weeks of its convening (an exception is made when a new governor takes office). From there, the legislature takes over, turning the governor's budget into legislation and debating it in committee and on the floor until acceptance. The governor has the power of item veto, according to the constitution. Also required by the constitution is a balanced budget.

Recent evaluations of the state government of Ohio have lauded the management of programs devoted to repairing schools in all of the state's 613 districts. Additionally, the state worked to downsize the Transportation Department. Ohio has historically not been known for effective long-term planning with respect to its expenditures and revenues, and therefore, these advances are even more notable.

The importance of Ohio to electoral politics in the United States became even more evident in the 2004 presidential election. The secretary of state was thrust into the spotlight while dealing with provisional ballots and election irregularities, including voting machine failures and long lines. The race was too close to call on election night but was certified shortly after despite continued protests. This experience is one of many possible illustrations of the importance of the decisions and activities of state executive branches to politics at every level in the federal system.

Ohio's state seal contains a picture of a rising sun with thirteen rays, symbolic of the thirteen colonies. It also has a bundle of wheat with seventeen arrows, indicating Ohio's position as the seventeenth state to join the Union. This imagery is important in depicting Ohio's place in the larger United States—a bridge linking the original colonies to the rest of the nation.

Christine Kelleher

References

The Government Performance Project— Ohio. http://results.gpponline.org.
A guidebook for Ohio legislators. 2005. Published by the Ohio Legislative Service Commission. http://www.lsc.state.oh.us/guidebook/.
Ohio Constitution. http://www.legislature .state.oh.us/constitution.cfm.
The state government book. 2004. http:// www.obm.ohio.gov/mppr/stategovbook .pdf.

Additional Resources and Recommended Readings

Clayton, Andrew. 2004. Ohio: The history of a people. In *Ohio and the world, 1753–2053: Essays toward a new history of Ohio*, ed. Geoffrey Parker, Richard Sisson, and William Russell Coil. Columbus: Ohio State University Press.
Ohio governor's website. http:// governor.ohio.gov/.

OKLAHOMA

● ● ● ● ● ● ● ● ● ● ● ●

OKLAHOMA ELECTED EXECUTIVE BRANCH OFFICIALS

Governor	Lieutenant Governor
Attorney General	Auditor and Inspector
Commissioner of Charities and Corrections	
Commissioner of Insurance	Commissioner of Labor
Corporation Commissioners (3)	
Superintendent of Public Instruction	Treasurer

http://www.ok.gov/

● ● ● ● ● ● ● ● ● ● ● ●

Some scholars consider Oklahoma a state of competing images. Indeed, even the state's name is a combination of two Choctaw Indian words, meaning "red man." Another example of this competing images theme is apparent when trying to decipher what region of the country the state actually belongs to. The U.S. Census classifies the Sooner State as "southern"; the territory sent delegates to the Confederate Congress, and it is considered by some southern scholars to be a "border" state of the region. Others consider the state to be more midwestern, with its cowboys, Native Americans, and oil-drilling images. The state's history reflects this conflict, as it was originally composed of two separate territories, the Indian Territory and the Oklahoma Territory, prior to being granted statehood in 1906.

However, in writing its original constitution, Oklahoma followed the pattern of neighboring states when it came to the executive branch: it created multiple offices and divided executive power among various elected officials. This division of executive authority was more akin to the structure put in place by its southern brethren. In terms of formal executive power, the governor of Oklahoma is relatively weak, having to deal with multiple other officials who oversee administrative offices that the governor cannot touch.

Although it was originally made up of seventeen elected officials, the executive branch in Oklahoma today consists of twelve popularly elected officers: the governor, lieutenant governor, state auditor and inspector, attorney general, state treasurer, superintendent of public instruction, commissioner of labor, commissioner of charities and corrections, commissioner of insurance, and three corporation commissioners. The governor, with the consent of the state senate, appoints the secretary of state. With the exception of the commissioners of insurance, charities and corrections, and labor, all executive officers must be at least thirty-one years old and have been "qualified electors" of the state for a minimum of ten years. The minimum age for com-

missioners of insurance, charities and corrections, and labor is twenty-five. The terms of office are four years, with only the governor being limited to serving two successive terms. In the event of a tied election for one of the offices, the two houses of the legislature, by joint ballot, elect the individual who will fill the office. All candidates for each office run independently of the others, so that, for example, a Republican governor may be elected along with a Democratic lieutenant governor.

Among the governor's formal constitutional powers is the power to call a special session of the legislature and have it consider only matters that the governor designates. A governor's veto can only be overridden by a two-thirds majority vote in each chamber. The governor also has the pocket veto power, which means that any bill he or she does not sign within fifteen days following the legislature's adjournment dies. Further, the governor has the power of a line-item veto for appropriations bills. In addition, if the legislature enacts a bill with the "emergency clause" attached and the governor vetoes the bill, a three-fourths vote is required by both legislative chambers to override that veto. This combination of veto powers is usually a strong weapon of choice for the chief executive in exerting influence on the legislature. Another formal power permits the governor to fill offices if vacancies arise (in some instances, with the consent of the state senate); the governor's appointee must stand for election when the voters next go to the polls.

Along with the lieutenant governor, state auditor, superintendent of public instruction, and president of the Board of

Agriculture, the governor serves on the Commission of the Land Office, which is responsible for overseeing public and school lands in the state. Finally, the Oklahoma governor can appoint individuals to agency leadership positions. With the appointment power, he or she can influence the direction and activities of administrative agencies within state government. However, the governor must share power with other executive officers, elected separately from the chief executive and accountable only to the voters. The governor must also share power with 31 constitutionally created executive branch agencies, boards, and commissions, along with 230 separate bodies that oversee activities ranging from higher education to the Santa Claus Commission (an agency that purchases Christmas toys for children in state orphanages).

The governor does have some direct authority over agencies in state government through the cabinet system. Following a reorganization plan in 1989, the governor can now appoint, with senate confirmation, cabinet secretaries to oversee such areas as natural resources, commerce, education, and veterans' affairs.

Informally, the governor serves as the chief legislator, the ceremonial head of the government, and the leader of the political party. Most notably, the informal power of the governor is the power to persuade, negotiate, and bargain with other executive officers, the legislature, and governing boards and commissions. This power can be extremely useful; for example, when Governor Raymond Gary (1955–1959) sought to "persuade" reluctant legislators to vote for his programs, he would often call them into his office.

Governor Gary would then break out a map of the state and indicate where a road was being planned for the particular legislator's district. Then he would say, in so many words, "I guess we'll just have to cancel that." At that point, of course, many legislators' minds were quickly changed.

In addition, the governor is responsible for interacting with a large number of Native American tribes within the state. Second only to California in the number of residents who are Native Americans, the state is home to the headquarters of thirty-nine tribes. This presence of Native Americans requires the governor to deal with federal, state, and tribal relations.

Other statewide elected officers in Oklahoma oversee distinct areas of administration within state government. In addition to the power of succession if the governor should have to leave the office, the lieutenant governor serves as president of the state senate, casting a vote only in the event of a tie in the chamber.

For the position of state auditor and inspector, candidates must have three years of experience as an "expert accountant" in order to fulfill the office's duties to "examine the state and all county treasurers' books."

The Corporation Commission is a relatively powerful group within the executive branch in Oklahoma. The three members are elected for six-year terms and regulate business activities in the state that are deemed essential for public welfare, most notably railroads, utilities, oil and gas drilling, and motor carrier transportation. The commission's orders carry the weight of law, and its actions can only be reviewed by the state supreme court. Touching a large segment of the Oklahoma economy, the commission is completely autonomous from the governor.

The final constitutional authority within the executive branch is the Board of Regents, which oversees Oklahoma State University and "all Agriculture and Mechanical Schools and Colleges." The governor has the power to appoint eight of the nine members, with confirmation by the state senate, to eight-year terms of office.

J. Michael Bitzer

References

Markwood, Chris. 2000. *Oklahoma government and politics.* Dubuque, IA: Kendall/Hunt.

Morgan, David R., Robert E. England, and George G. Humphreys. 1991. *Oklahoma politics and policies: Governing the Sooner State.* Lincoln: University of Nebraska Press.

Oklahoma State Constitution of 1907, Art. 6.

Scales, James R., and Danney Goble. 1982. *Oklahoma politics: A history.* Norman: University of Oklahoma Press.

Additional Resources and Recommended Readings

Burke, Bob. 2000. *Good guys wear white hats: The life of George Nigh.* Oklahoma City: Oklahoma Heritage Association.

OREGON

• • • • • • • • • • • •

OREGON ELECTED EXECUTIVE BRANCH OFFICIALS

Governor   Attorney General
Commissioner of Labor and Industries
Secretary of State
Superintendent of Public Instruction
Treasurer
http://www.oregon.gov

• • • • • • • • • • • •

The modern history of the state of Oregon can be described as a tale of conflict and compromise between proponents of environmental protection, on one hand, and industrial development, on the other. For example, in the late 1960s, a movement known as the New Urbanism began to take hold throughout Oregon. The term *New Urbanism* was synonymous with *environmentally friendly expansion* in a state that was seeing massive influxes in population and industry. According to William Toll of the Oregon Historical Society, the movement to protect the environment through controlling urban growth was largely initiated by Republican governor Tom McCall, and it would later become a defining hallmark of Neil Goldschmidt's terms as Portland's mayor and Oregon's governor. Environmental issues continued to dominate Oregon politics well into the 1990s, as the state's population and commerce base were being pushed toward expansion alongside a concomitant desire to protect undeveloped lands. The conflict between these two competing policy goals plagued Oregon governor John Kitzhaber, who was forced to deal with the fallout from environmental effects of a long history of industrialization along the Willamette River. Thus, it is fair to say, at least in terms of the last half century, that the politics of the executive are often linked to the politics of the environment in the state of Oregon.

Beginning in 1987 and continuing through 2004, there has been a period of prolonged Democratic control in the Oregon governor's office. During this nearly twenty-year span, Oregon elected its first female governor, Barbara Roberts, who served as chief executive from 1991 until 1995. These decades have also been characterized by the passage of a number of policies and programs that one might expect from a Democratic-dominated government. However, even in the Republican period from 1939 to 1967, the activities of a number of the governors generally served to advance traditional liberal policy issues. For example, Governor Mark O. Hatfield (1959–1967) followed a traditionally conservative path by cutting taxes, but he also helped to establish policies one might not expect from a Republican governor, including a state-supported birth control program and a ban on capital punishment. And while serving as a U.S. senator, Hatfield voted against increasing military appropriations and the Vietnam War. None of these latter actions would be commonly associated with a member of the national Republican Party. They did, however, define the nature of Republican politics in many parts of the Pacific Northwest. Therefore, in order to fully understand the context of gubernatorial leadership in Oregon, one must also understand the political environment in which these governors operate.

The governor of Oregon is limited to serving two four-year terms within a twelve-year period. To qualify for office, all gubernatorial candidates must be at least thirty years of age and residents of the state for five years prior to their election. Further, they must not occupy any other state or national office. Like most state executives, the Oregon governor has a primary responsibility to oversee the faithful execution of the laws. Accordingly, a number of powers are vested in the executive office that make the governor a powerful actor in the state. For example, he or she has two types of veto power that provide increased leverage over legislative activities. First, the governor is granted the power of a blanket form of veto over bills that have passed the legislative assemblies. This package veto enables the governor to send a bill back to the legislature with recommendations if it does not meet executive approval. The reconsidered bill needs approval from two-thirds of the members of both houses if the governor's veto is to be overridden. In addition to this all-or-nothing type of veto, the governor is also given "single-item" veto power over appropriations and emergency bills. This power enables the governor to eliminate specific elements of a bill without preventing other, necessary parts from being passed into law. The legislature can also override line-item vetoes but in doing so, it must follow the same process as for overriding a full veto. Therefore, the governor not only oversees the execution of the law but also plays a vital role in the lawmaking process.

In addition to these primary executive responsibilities, the governor is granted a number of other powers that affect the politics of the state of Oregon. For example, he or she is the chief commander of the state's military forces, which can be employed in cases that involve insurrection or invasion; these forces may also be called on in extreme situations in which they might be needed for the execution of the laws of the state. The governor is also required to deliver a message to the legislature about the conditions and needs of the state, which can, in turn, help set the agenda for legislative activity. As a result, the governor has a great amount of power to set priorities and statewide expectations for action in terms of legislation and appropriation. The governor may also, in extraordinary circumstances that require immediate action, call an emergency session of the legislature. In terms of day-to-day operations of the state government, the governor is charged with overseeing the transactions and duties of state officials and their departments. He or she is also granted pardoning power, except in cases of treason. Finally, the governor can appoint officials to offices that have been vacated when the legislature—which is normally responsible for filling office vacancies—is not in session. In all of these ways, the governor is an important player in the field of Oregonian politics.

Five other statewide officials are elected to complete the executive branch. These officials are the secretary of state, treasurer, attorney general, commissioner of labor and industries, and superintendent of public instruction. Along with Arizona and Wyoming, Oregon does not have a lieutenant governor, which often brings up questions as to who is next in line should the governor be unable to serve. In the event of an emergency or other circumstance that causes a vacancy in the governor's office, the secretary of state assumes the role of governor. Following the secretary of state in the line of succession, in order, are the state treasurer, the president of the senate, and the speaker of the house of representatives.

Oregon's governors have at times played significant roles in defining national standards for environmental policy. Republican governor Tom McCall (1967–1975), for instance, pushed the historic Bottle Bill through his state's legislature. This bill resulted in the first mandatory bottle-deposit law in the United States, which was designed to reduce the amount of waste across the state of Oregon. However, even though a number of McCall's proposals were targeted at protecting the ecosystem, he did support both the timber and nuclear industries in various ways, at times siding with the economy over the environment. Following in the footsteps of his predecessor, Democratic governor Robert Straub (1975–1979) also attempted to balance environmental protection with economic development in the state. As governor, Straub helped to promote industry and environmentalism by courting certain low-pollution businesses and drawing them to Oregon through a system of financial incentives. Straub's goal was to expand the state's infrastructure while maintaining a higher level of environmental standards than almost any other state in the nation. These are but two examples of how Oregon's supreme executives have set the tone for both inter- and intrastate policy in terms of balancing the often-competing goals of environmentalism and industrialization.

An additional note of import in understanding the burdens imposed on the executive office in the state of Oregon is that it remains one of only five states that do not impose a sales tax as a means of generating revenue for state coffers. This factor, especially in combination with the limits placed on property taxes in the state during the mid-1990s, can hobble the chief executive in his or her efforts to push certain programs and proposals because it limits the tax base that generates the revenue needed to pay for state projects. When a state cannot generate high amounts of revenue, the governor's ability to seek new, innovative programs or to fully fund existing ones often suffers. Therefore, understanding the economic context of a state can help shed some light on the difficult choices frequently faced by state executives.

On February 10, 2003, Governor Ted Kulongoski addressed the affiliated tribes of the Northwest. As a part of his speech, he reminded the audience of the efforts made by the Oregon state government (and its executive) to garner federal aid to assist the depleted salmon populations in the state. This brief reference to Kulongoski's speech should remind students of Oregon politics of the importance placed on environmental policies in the state, as well as the role the governor must play in furthering these policies while simultaneously maintaining a strong economy and industrial base. It also helps demonstrate the vital contribution the governor makes as an advocate for and mediator between competing state and tribal demands. Such efforts helped define the politics of the executive office as far back as the 1930s in Oregon, and the continued emphasis on such actions has influenced the Democrat-dominated executive since the mid-1980s.

Joseph J. Foy

References

Dietrich, William. 1995. *Northwest Passage: The great Columbia River.* New York: Simon and Schuster.

Kulongoski, Theodore R. 2003. Winter Conference keynote speech to the affiliated tribes of Northwest Indians. Portland, Oregon, February 10. http://governor.oregon.gov/Gov/speech_021003.shtml.

Oregon Historical Society. 2004. Gubernatorial history in Oregon. http://www.ohs.org/education/focus_on_ oregon_history/Gubernatorial-History-Home.cfm.

Oregon Secretary of State. State Archives. 2004. Governors. http://arcweb.sos.state.or.us/banners/governors.htm.

Oregon State Constitution of 1857, Art. 5.

Sahadi, Jeanne. 2004. Tax-friendly places 2004. *CNNMoney.* http://money.cnn.com/2004/04/05/pf/taxes/taxfriendly_2004/.

Toll, William. 2004. Oregon Historical Society website. *The Oregon History Project. Portland neighborhoods 1960s–present: The new urbanism.* http://www.ohs.org/education/oregonhistory/narratives/subtopic.cfm?subtopic_ID=222.

Additional Resources and Recommended Readings

Dodds, Gordon B. 1986. *The American Northwest: A history of Oregon and Washington.* Arlington Heights, IL: Forum.

Harden, Blaine. 1996. *A river lost: The life and death of the Columbia.* New York: Norton.

Oregon State governor's office official website. http://governor.oregon.gov/.

The Oregonian Online. http://www.oregonlive.com/oregonian/.

Walth, Brent. 1994. *Fire at Eden's gate: Tom McCall and the Oregon story.* Portland: Oregon Historical Society Press.

PENNSYLVANIA

• • • • • • • • • • • •

PENNSYLVANIA ELECTED EXECUTIVE BRANCH OFFICIALS

Governor   Lieutenant Governor
Attorney General   Auditor
Treasurer
http://www.state.pa.us/

• • • • • • • • • • • •

In 2002, President George W. Bush nominated the sitting governor of Pennsylvania, Tom Ridge, as his director of the Department of Homeland Security. The most crucial job of defending the domestic front against terrorism thus went to a capable governor. Why did President Bush choose a governor? A governor is a good choice for such an important position because governors know how to balance accomplishments against the sharing of powers with a strong legislature and court system and because being governor of a large state with diverse interests and a large staff of civil servants bears some similarities to handling the coordination and management of the many crucial duties of our most important domestic agency for opposing terrorism.

The Pennsylvania governorship should be a good proving ground for individuals interested in higher national political roles, as the state affords its chief executive greater than average institutional powers and one of the most active state economies in the nation. Despite this confluence of forces, however, the Pennsylvania governor rarely rises to high national prominence. The exceptions have been Gifford Pinchot, the founder of the U.S. Forest Service and a noted conservationist; Richard Thornburgh, the U.S. attorney general under President George H. W. Bush; and Governor Ridge.

Pennsylvania's constitution reflects the fact that it was written later than other New England constitutions, granting its governor stronger institutional powers and a more effective administrative ability. William Penn wrote the First Frame of Government in 1681 as a broad explication of the role of government, but the merchant class would change the governing document relatively frequently during colonial times. After the national Constitution was framed, an enduring Pennsylvania constitution was written in 1790; it established relatively strong central powers, especially in the area of appointing a working cabinet to support the governor. The national and Pennsylvania documents benefited from lessons learned under the Articles of Confederation, which established a limited central government and executive. There was some reduction in the overall appointment power of the Pennsylvania governor when the constitution was revised in 1838; this was in keeping with the creation of the long ballot and greater electoral accountability in the Jacksonian era. Meanwhile, the state of Pennsylvania was well on its way to major business investments in canals and railroads, under the leadership of strong governors. Manufacturing was important early in the 1800s, and prominent industries arose in steelmaking, coal mining, and, for a time, oil drilling.

With such a rich economy, the population of Pennsylvania swelled as immigrants arrived from European shores. The growing state required a larger bureaucracy, so the number of agencies under the Pennsylvania governor grew. Needs as varied as regulation of the insurance industry and workplace conditions, care for the poor and infirm, and corrections and public safety meant that the state had 139 different agencies in 1922. The organization was streamlined with the help of the governor and members of a supporting commission who retooled the state's administrative code. The state revised its constitution most recently in 1968, through a constitutional convention. The most significant acts of the convention related to its support of the national civil rights legislation of the early 1960s, but the governorship was affected in a positive way as well, as the chief executive was allowed to run for reelection to an extra term.

Pennsylvania is similar to most states with regard to the length of time that its governor can serve—eight years, if he or she serves one four-year term and is then reelected to a second. Some states' governors are allowed an indefinite number of four-year terms, others may serve an unlimited number of two-year terms (though these governors rarely exceed an eight-year tenure in office), and the Vir-

Tom Ridge, former governor of Pennsylvania, was the first secretary of the U.S. Department of Homeland Security. (Office of Governor Tom Ridge)

ginia governor is limited to one four-year term. As we see in the case of the U.S. president, eight years seems to be a sufficient amount of time to have a significant impact on public policy.

There are some other similarities between the powers of the Pennsylvania governor and the U.S. president, notably in their ability to reorganize the government's agencies and to appoint officials in the state bureaucracy. Like the president, the Pennsylvania governor needs the approval of the senate. When the governor chooses departmental leaders or "secretaries," he or she needs the approval of two-thirds of the senate. This rule limits the governor's choices for leadership of the bureaucracy, but in the spirit of checks and balances, it ensures that the governor selects reasonable candidates on behalf of the needs of Pennsylvania's citizens. The senate is largely concerned that the governor's candidates be qualified for the specialized jobs of the bureaucracy (that is, a public safety specialist should run the Pennsylvania State Police, a human services expert should be in charge of the Public Welfare Department, and so on). The Pennsylvania governor is also supported by several citizen commissions, on issues such as women and minority affairs, rural development, and environmental awareness in state operations.

The governor runs with the lieutenant governor as a partner, or team, much like the U.S. president and vice–president. But unlike the situation in the national government, the voters of Pennsylvania also elect several other members of the executive team that leads the state. Other separately elected officials include the state's attorney general, the state treasurer, the state auditor, and judges of the unified judicial system—a relatively limited list of individuals with their own electoral accountability outside of the governor's overall mandate from the people of the state. In theory, the other elected officials in Pennsylvania pose an appropriate offset to the authority of the governor. The attorney general presents legal advice and represents the state in the court system and thus should be a neutral party in case the executive office is involved in any wrongdoing. The treasurer protects the public purse and should not be beholden to the governor to foreclose the possibility of misusing public funds. Likewise, the state auditor, as the watchdog over government finances and operations, could not perform his or her police-like function over the governor without independently elected authority.

Probably the most influential role that the Pennsylvania governor plays involves the fiscal resources of the state and its $22 billion budget. The governor prepares a budget with input from legislative leaders as well as the various agencies of the state government and presents the recommended budget to the legislature; after that, the legislature can change dollar figures and funding priorities as it chooses. In essence, the budgetary power of the Pennsylvania governor is similar to that of the U.S. president. The governor makes a state of the state speech in January, just as the president makes the State of the Union speech. Both present the policies and budget of the executive for the coming year, but it is up to the legislature to honor the executives' priorities. For this reason, the norm of discussing the budget with legislative leaders has arisen in Pennsylvania. In the Keystone State, the legislature and executive do spend some time reaching for a consensus on priorities before the budget is actually written.

Eventually, the legislature finishes its deliberations and presents a budget bill for the governor to sign. Here, the last of the formal powers of the governor—the veto—may come into play. If the legislature includes priorities that are unacceptable to the governor, he or she can either veto the bill in its entirety or, in the most powerful alignment, strike an offending item with a line-item veto. The governor of Pennsylvania has this particularly effective veto and thus in a way has the final say on budgetary and other legislative priorities.

Pennsylvania's governor is the designated leader when dignitaries visit the state, and he or she also has the power to overturn criminal convictions through the pardoning process. Lastly, the governor has the ability to write executive orders, which determine the policies and procedures used within the state's bureaucracy. In this way, the governor can enact programs that the legislature might not support or advance programs more quickly, without having to wait for the legislature to act. Those who defend the use of executive orders point out that the governor is the official in charge of the government's civil service workforce and bureaucratic agencies. The executive order has been used by Pennsylvania governors to pass major gubernatorial initiatives in many instances. Two prominent examples are Governor Robert Casey's ban on certain abortion procedures in state public health clinics and Governor Ridge's movement to allow experimental, independent charter schools to operate alongside schools in the traditional public school system.

With a set of institutional powers that mimic the national executive's in several ways and with the state's large, diverse economy and professionally inclined legislature, Pennsylvania should be a strong proving ground for an individual interested in national office and leadership. But regardless of his or her political aspirations, the person who serves as Pennsylvania's governor occupies a most important office at the helm of the sixth-largest economy among the American states.

Brendan Burke

References

Beyle, Thad. 2004. The governors. In *Politics in the American states: A comparative analysis*, 8th ed., ed. Virginia Gray and Russell L. Hanson, 194–231. Washington, DC: Congressional Quarterly Press.

Constitution of Pennsylvania, Art. 5.

Governor's Office of the Budget, Commonwealth of Pennsylvania. 1999. *The budget process in Pennsylvania.* http://www.oit.state.pa.us/budget/lib /budget/budgetprocess/index.htm.

Pennsylvania Historical and Museum Commission. 2003. Pennsylvania history: People, places, events, things. http://www.phmc.state.pa.us/bah /pahist/overview.asp?secid=31.

U.S. White House. 2004. Biography of Secretary Tom Ridge. http://www .whitehouse.gov/homeland/ridgebio .html.

Additional Resources and Recommended Readings

Casey, Robert P. 1996. *Fighting for life.* Dallas: Word.

Cooke, Edward Francis, and G. Edward Janosek. 1979. *Guide to Pennsylvania politics.* Westport, CT: Greenwood.

Swetnam, George. 1990. *The governors of Pennsylvania, 1790–1990.* Greensburgh, PA: McDonald-Sward.

Wolf, George D. 1981. *William Warren Scranton: Pennsylvania statesman.* University Park: Pennsylvania State University Press.

RHODE ISLAND

• • • • • • • • • • • • •

RHODE ISLAND ELECTED EXECUTIVE BRANCH OFFICIALS
Governor   Lieutenant Governor
Attorney General   Secretary of State
Treasurer
http://www.ri.gov/index.php

• • • • • • • • • • • • •

One of the distinct characteristics of Rhode Island's executive office is its relative lack of institutional (formal) power in comparison to the state legislature. As in other New England states, the Rhode Island governor's power has its roots in colonial times. Once the state moved from the Articles of Confederation, it retained a weak state executive. After all, Rhode Island was the last of the thirteen colonies to ratify the Constitution because it did not want to concede power to a kinglike executive.

This is not to say that Rhode Island governors consistently lack power and influence—or even coercion—within their state's system of politics and administration, for they do not. In addition, they are consistently in the public spotlight. Rhode Island, a state with just over 1 million residents living in an area of only 1,045 square miles, can at times feel more like a community than a state. As a result, citizens are better able to reflect on the personal successes and failures of their governors than residents of other American states.

Edward DiPrete, governor from 1985 to 1991, was indicted for bribery and extortion involving state contractors and landlords. His successor, Bruce Sundlun, is credited for resolving the banking crisis that resulted from the 1991 declaration of insolvency of the Rhode Island Share and Depository Indemnity Corporation (RISDIC). In 2003, newly elected Governor Donald Carcieri worked to calm the nerves of Rhode Islanders by reforming state building inspections; these reforms came in the wake of a fire at a nightclub called The Station that killed 100 patrons.

Rhode Island history includes one of the most famous power grabs in the history of state government. The state's governors are allowed some degree of power to reorganize the state government system at the opening of their terms, as long as the state senate supports the proposed changes. When Democratic governor T. F. Green took office in 1935, the Republican Party had long dominated the state legislature. In what has been called the New Year's Day 1935 "bloodless revolution," Green staged a dramatic takeover of power on the very night of his inauguration. But Republicans retained a 22-to-20 majority at the beginning of Green's term, and they were, not surprisingly, unwilling to support the governor's power grab. With these numbers, the governor had little hope of passing his modernization of the state organization.

However, two of the Republican senators were from districts with contested elections. The Democratic lieutenant governor refused to swear in these two senators, leading to a 20-to-20 deadlock in the chamber. After a quick recount of the ballots, Governor Green declared the two Democratic candidates winners, and with a brief Democratic majority in the general assembly, he was able to replace the entire state supreme court and pass his bill to reorganize the structure of the bureaucracy and the budgetary authority of the governor. The Republicans regained power in the 1936 election, but the new governor, William Vanderbilt, continued the modernization with further mild revisions to the state civil service system (Stanton 2003).

The 1935 reforms notwithstanding, the institutional powers of the Rhode Island governor remain among the weakest among the American states. This characterization is based on measures of power comparing the governors across the states. This measure takes account of the governor's powers in four categories: tenure potential (length of term and chances for reelection), the veto, budget power, and appointment power. Additionally, the power index includes two political components: the number of separately elected public officials in addition to the governor and party control of the state legislature. In 1994, Rhode Island finally moved to a four-year term for its governors, leaving neighboring Vermont and New Hampshire as the only states that hold gubernatorial elections every two years. Despite this change, the powers of Rhode Island's governor are weak compared to most other chief executives across the country.

Two-year terms limit the time that a sitting governor can actually govern. With such a short tenure between elections, he or she must learn the new job quickly, make a mark on the state's politics and policy, and then begin to prepare for a reelection campaign, all within one year. This time frame restricts what the governor can accomplish. It is possible that this is less of a disadvantage in small states, for in a small geographic area, the campaign is easier to pursue: the governor of Rhode Island can literally be driven from one corner of the state to the opposite corner in less than two hours. But under the old system, a governor had little room for error. A mistake at the outset of the first term might still be remembered by voters when the new election came around. Between 1950 and 1994, only two governors served a single two-year term. However, during that same period, only one governor served as long as the two four-year terms enjoyed by Governor Lincoln Almond starting in 1994.

The Rhode Island governor has moderate power and ability to choose the officials at the peak of the government's organization. The arrangement is similar to that of the national executive, where the president appoints the cabinet, with the approval of the Senate. However, unlike the president, the Rhode Island governor must serve with four other separately elected officials at the top of state government: the lieutenant governor, the attorney general, the secretary of state, and the general treasurer. Currently, all four of the separately elected officials are Democrats, whereas Governor Carcieri is a Republican. A situation like this can be difficult for the governor if the other elected officials differ from the chief executive in policy stances. Such divisions may reduce the strength of the message emanating from the governor's office. Currently in Rhode Island, while the other officials have a much smaller bully pulpit (less access to the media) than the governor, the attorney general has established some visibility through lawsuits related to the 2003 nightclub fire and the issue of gay marriage inspired by judicial acts in neighboring Massachusetts. So the governor often has to share the spotlight with other statewide elected officials.

The Rhode Island governor also oversees the state bureaucracy, with its budget of $2.9 billion and its workforce of 15,800 employees. The largest categories of the state government are human services (including public health, mental health, and social services) and education, with substantial programming also in the areas of transportation, public safety, natural resources, and general government or administrative functions.

The structure of the bureaucracy is largely the same as it was following Governor Green's 1935 reorganization, though in some instances, new agencies and components have emerged to handle new needs. For example, the Public Welfare Department was an innovation in 1935, but it is now broken into units to deal with human services; mental health; corrections; and children, youth, and families. One important function that was added after 1935 involved the formation of the Economic Development Corporation, to recruit new industries to Rhode Island as well as to focus on retaining existing industries and employers.

The Rhode Island governor is responsible for writing the budget that allocates funds across the state's public services,

but the legislature can revise the initial proposal as much as it wants. The governor sets the agenda through the budget message and the state of the state message, a speech he or she delivers at the beginning of each legislative session. While legislators can ignore priorities and positions taken by the governor, they do so at their own peril. If the governor's initial message has resonated with the citizenry, it will be difficult for the general assembly to brush aside the popular funding programs that the governor supports.

However, the legislature can and frequently does include the priorities of individual members and their constituencies (supporters), above and beyond the wishes of the governor. The governor's option for removing spending he or she views as wasteful is the veto power. Barring a supermajority vote in the legislature, the governor can delete the general assembly's legislative actions. The veto makes the governor the gatekeeper.

In one way, though, the Rhode Island governor's veto power is weaker than that in most other states. In many states, governors can eliminate parts of a bill while signing the rest of it into law. But in the national government and a handful of states, including Rhode Island, the executive has only a general veto power: he or she must sign or veto the entire bill. Most states' governors, by contrast, have an item veto power. The item veto allows the governor to delete lines within a spending bill or another bill that he or she opposes. This veto is one of the typical governor's greatest powers. The item veto provides a quality control on the final version of bills that are passed, helping the governors make sure that laws reflect their preferences. This is not the case in Rhode Island. Instead, the governor must make strategic calculations, deciding if it is worthwhile to lose some small amount of specific funding from bills that may also include larger gubernatorial priorities.

The governor's limited veto power and the steady Democratic Party domination within the Rhode Island legislature (while the governors are often Republicans) make for a less potent governor within the Ocean State as compared to other states. But on occasion, the Rhode Island governor can work through the limitations to set the agenda and lead the effort for favored changes.

Brendan Burke

References

Constitution of the State of Rhode Island and Providence Plantations, Art. 9. http://www2.sec.state.ri.us/special_projects/0304_Owners_Manual/pdf/riconst.pdf.

Lockard, Duane. 1959. *New England state politics.* Princeton: Princeton University Press.

Moakley, Maureen, and Elmer Cornwell. 2001. *Rhode Island politics and government.* Lincoln: University of Nebraska Press.

Office of the Secretary of State, State of Rhode Island and Providence Plantations. *The Rhode Island government owner's manual, 2003–2004.* http://www2.sec.state.ri.us/special_projects/0304_Owners_Manual/.

Stanton, Mike. 2003. *The prince of providence: The true story of Buddy Cianci, America's most notorious mayor, some wiseguys, and the Feds.* New York: Random House.

Additional Resources and Recommended Readings

Levine, Erwin L. 1963. *Theodore Francis Greene, the Rhode Island years.* Providence: Brown University Press.

Tantillo, Charles. 1968. *Strengthening the Rhode Island legislature.* New Brunswick, NJ: Rutgers University Press.

West, Darrell, Thomas Anton, and Jack Combs. 1994. *Public opinion in Rhode Island, 1984–1993.* Providence: Brown University Press.

SOUTH CAROLINA

• • • • • • • • • • • •

SOUTH CAROLINA ELECTED EXECUTIVE BRANCH OFFICIALS

Governor	Lieutenant Governor
Adjutant General	Attorney General
Commissioner of Agriculture	
Comptroller General	Secretary of State
Superintendent of Education	Treasurer

http://www.myscgov.com/

• • • • • • • • • • • •

Like its sister state to the north, the Palmetto State had an early aversion to executive authority. In its first constitution of 1776, South Carolina gave the general assembly power to choose a "president and commander-in-chief" either from its own body or from "the people at large." However, while the "president" shared legislative power with the general assembly, executive power was generally restricted, due to the fears over concentrated executive power. This concern regarding executive power is still evident in South Carolina's modern executive branch, although some consolidation of executive authority has occurred in recent years.

Nine constitutional officers make up the executive branch of South Carolina. While "supreme executive authority" is placed in a "Chief Magistrate" (otherwise known as the governor), eight other executives wield significant authority over various areas within state government. Elected separately from the governor, the other constitutional officers are the lieutenant governor, secretary of state, treasurer, attorney general, comptroller general, superintendent of education, commissioner of agriculture, and adjutant general.

The qualifications for governor and lieutenant governor include being at least thirty years old, a U.S. citizen, and a citizen and resident of the state for a minimum of five years prior to the day of the election. The term for both offices is four years, with one reelection permitted. If an election produces a tie, then the legislature elects the governor from those candidates who tied for the office.

The governor's constitutional powers include serving as commander-in-chief of the state's militia, ensuring that the "laws be faithfully executed," giving the legislature "information on the condition of the State" (in the state of the state address), and "recommending for its consideration such measures as he deems appropriate." The governor has a qualified power to issue clemency, in that he or she can only grant reprieves or commute sentences of death to life imprisonment. All other pardons and clemencies can be regulated by the legislature.

The governor has the constitutional authority to convene a special session of the legislature, but there is no requirement that the legislature only consider the governor's proposals for the session. The chief executive has the power to veto legislation, with the legislature needing a two-thirds majority vote in both chambers to override the veto. The governor also has the power to use the line-item veto on sections of appropriations or budget bills. If the governor chooses not to sign a bill, it becomes law within five days after being presented to the chief executive. If the legislature should adjourn, however, the governor has until the end of the first two days of the next legislative session to veto bills; failing that, they become law.

The governor, along with other constitutional officers and judges, may be impeached by the state house of representatives. A two-thirds majority vote is required to impeach. The state senate then serves as the trial body for the impeachment, and a two-thirds vote is also required to remove an official from office. In the case of a governor being impeached, the chief justice of the state supreme court presides over the trial.

The governor may request that the legislature remove any other constitutional officer based on "willful neglect of duty, or other reason or cause, which shall not be sufficient ground of impeachment." Following notification and after the accused officer has had an opportunity to present a defense, a two-thirds vote by each chamber of the legislature is needed to remove the officer.

The lieutenant governor serves as president of the state senate and has the ability to break a tie vote in the chamber. In the event of the impeachment, death, or resignation of the governor, the lieutenant governor assumes the office. If the governor temporarily leaves the state, the lieutenant governor has "full authority to act in an emergency."

If the governor is unable to discharge the duties of the office, he or she may write a letter to the president pro tempore of the state senate and speaker of the state house of representatives, asking that the lieutenant governor assume the office as acting governor. If the attorney general, secretary of state, comptroller general, and state treasurer determine by a majority that the governor is incapacitated and submit their opinion to the legislature, the general assembly may remove the governor, and the lieutenant governor can then serve as acting governor.

The secretary of state is responsible for registering corporations and businesses within the state. He or she also is responsible for dealing with the incorporation (or recognition) of cities and special purpose districts, or governments, as well as keeping records on the annexation of lands by cities.

South Carolina's treasurer is responsible for investing, managing, and safekeeping the state's funds. The treasurer is also responsible for receiving and disbursing funds, as well as developing policies related to the state's use of bonds. Whenever payroll checks or payments are made by the state, the comptroller general oversees these activities. Further, the comptroller general is responsible for inspecting state agencies and their accounting practices and supervising the collection of property taxes and various programs.

Along with the treasurer and comptroller general, the governor and chairs of the House Ways and Means and Senate Finance Committees compose the State Budget and Control Board. This government agency is responsible for aiding the governor in creating an executive state budget for submission to the legislature, along with overseeing such programs as the retirement pension system and procurement policies for state agencies.

The commissioner of agriculture is responsible for regulating and overseeing agricultural aspects of the state, including directing the various state farmers' markets. The adjutant general is responsible for overseeing the state's militia.

There has been some movement toward consolidating state government agencies and making the governor more of a chief executive. Following the "lost trust" scandal, which claimed many political lives within the state legislature, a comprehensive reorganization and restructuring of state government was enacted in 1993, giving the governor the power of appointing cabinet officials. Currently, the governor appoints secretaries to oversee the following areas: alcohol and other drug abuse services; commerce; corrections; health and human services; insurance; juvenile justice; labor, licensing, and regulation; motor vehicles; parks, recreation, and tourism; probation, parole, and pardon services; public safety; revenue and taxation; social services; and the State Law Enforcement Division.

Most recently, between 2004 and 2005, the governor submitted a proposal to change how five of the constitutional offices are chosen. The governor asserts that the lieutenant governor should run for election as part of the governor's ticket; while the adjutant general, the secretary of state, the superintendent of education, and the commissioner of agriculture should become appointive rather than elected positions. The legislature, viewing such a proposed restructuring as a move to increase gubernatorial power was not very enthusiastic about the governor's proposals. They did give consideration to shifting some officers to the governor's cabinet (notably secretary of education and secretary of state). All of these changes must be made by constitutional amendment; a process that requires a vote by both chambers of the state legislature and then a public referendum on the questions. Such a referendum may take place in the coming years but significant questions regarding the balance of power in South Carolina government clearly remain.

J. Michael Bitzer

References

Constitution of South Carolina, Art. 4 and Art. 15.

Graham, Cole Blease, Jr., and William V. Moore. 1994. *South Carolina politics and government.* Lincoln: University of Nebraska Press.

Additional Resources and Recommended Readings

Bass, Jack, and Marilyn Thompson. 2003. *Ol' Strom: An unauthorized biography of Strom Thurmond.* Athens, GA: Longstreet.

Robertson, David. 1993. *Sly and able: A political biography of James F. Byrnes.* Winter Park, FL: World Publications Promotions.

South Carolina Office of the Governor. 2005. Contract for change. Government restructuring. http://www.scgovernor .com/uploads/upload/NR-c030205- ContractRestrucDOC.pdf

SOUTH DAKOTA

• • • • • • • • • • • •

SOUTH DAKOTA ELECTED EXECUTIVE BRANCH OFFICIALS

Governor   Lieutenant Governor
Attorney General   Auditor
Commissioner of School and Public Lands
Secretary of State   Treasurer
http://www.state.sd.us/

• • • • • • • • • • • •

South Dakota is often identified by outsiders as the home of liberal Democratic U.S. senator and 1972 presidential candidate George McGovern. Although the state has actually not cast its electoral votes for a Democrat since 1964, the two parties were fairly closely matched in five of seven presidential elections from the 1970s to the 1990s. In terms of state politics, however, a long-standing indicator of interparty competition indicates there is no more routinely Republican state than South Dakota. Considered the third most Republican state in the mid-twentieth century, it ranked as the second most Republican state at the beginning of the twenty-first century (Ranney 1965; Bibby and Holbrook 2004).

Populist but not radical, progressive but not extreme, South Dakotans did not embrace the inflammatory politics practiced in neighboring states—by the Nonpartisan League in North Dakota or the Farmer-Labor Party in Minnesota. Mindful of agrarian and social issues, they elected Populist Andrew Lee as governor in 1896 and 1898 and supported William Jennings Bryan in 1896 and Theodore Roosevelt's third-party effort in 1912. On the cusp of the reform movement, South Dakota was the first state to adopt the initiative and referendum as constitutional provisions, in 1898.

Republicans, however, have dominated the state's politics and its governor's office throughout South Dakota's history. Of the thirty persons who have served as governor, there are twenty-four Republicans, one Populist, and five Democrats. In fact, Democrats elected only three governors from 1889 to 1971, for just one decade of total service in the state's first eighty-two years.

When Democrat Richard F. Kneip won three gubernatorial elections in the 1970s, his success initiated a brief flirtation with two-party politics. Democrats won a majority of statewide offices as Kneip won two-year terms in 1970 and 1972 and a four-year term in 1974 after voters amended the state constitution to extend the governor's tenure. Kneip, however, did not complete this term, resigning to become ambassador to Singapore, and Republicans returned to power with the election of Governor William Janklow in 1978.

Widely regarded as the state's most dominant and controversial political figure since the mid-1970s, Janklow was in and out of public office from 1975 to 2003. Attorney general from 1975 to 1979, he won two terms as governor (1979–1987), lost a U.S. Senate primary in 1986, practiced law over the next eight years, and then defeated an incumbent Republican governor in the 1994 primary and won two more terms (1995–2003). In this latter period of service, Janklow proved popular with voters for cutting state payroll taxes, reducing property taxes by 30 percent, and abolishing the state inheritance tax. But in one of the few states that has no personal or corporate state income tax, these policies left a serious revenue shortfall for his successor. Janklow won South Dakota's at-large U.S. House seat in 2002 but saw his congressional career cut short when he was convicted in 2003 of vehicular manslaughter. Janklow was sentenced to 100 days of imprisonment, which he served in a county jail. His vacant congressional seat was filled in a special election by Democrat Stephanie Herseth, who had narrowly lost the 2002 election.

The South Dakota governor has always possessed the conventional authority associated with this office. But it was not until the state's voters enacted a sweeping variety of constitutional changes in 1972 that the governor's power rankings improved from the lower third to the upper third among the nation's chief executives. These rankings are derived from studies classifying the formal powers of governors based on four categories: tenure potential (length of term and chances for reelection), the veto, budget power, and appointment power. Some of these changes to the powers of the governor merely clarified constitutional language, but others substantially enhanced the governor's jurisdiction.

Under the revised document, voters jointly elect the governor and lieutenant governor to four-year terms in non–presidential election years. Candidates for both offices must be U.S. citizens, at least twenty-one years old, and residents of the state for two years prior to their elections. Since 1974, no person may be elected to either office for more than two consecutive terms. Voters also choose five other statewide officers (attorney general, secretary of state, auditor, treasurer, and commissioner of school and public lands) to four-year terms in presidential election years. As of 1992, persons holding these offices are limited to two consecutive terms.

The governor and all state and judicial officers may be removed from office by impeachment by a majority of the house of representatives for "drunkenness, crimes, corrupt conduct, or malfeasance or misdemeanor in office," followed with conviction by a two-thirds vote of members elected to the senate. In the event of a vacancy in the governor's office, the lieutenant governor succeeds to the position and has the powers of the chief executive. Should a governor be unable to serve due to "continuous absence from the state or other temporary disability," the lieutenant governor acts as governor until the disability is removed. The governor fills a "permanent vacancy" in the office of lieutenant governor by nominating a candidate who must be confirmed by a majority of both legislative chambers. The South Dakota Supreme Court has exclusive jurisdiction to determine if a disability exists in the governor's office or a permanent vacancy exists in the lieutenant governor's office.

The governor's traditional powers include serving as commander-in-chief of the state's armed forces; filling vacancies in any office for which no constitutional or statutory provision is made; and granting pardons, commutations, and reprieves, except for convictions of impeachment. The chief executive also delegates powers and assigns duties to the lieutenant governor, whose only constitutional responsibilities are presiding over the senate and casting tie-breaking votes.

The governor's legislative powers include giving the legislature information concerning the affairs of the state and recommending measures at the beginning of each session and at other times thought necessary. He or she may call either or both houses of the legislature into special session and limit the agenda by "stating the purposes" of the session. The governor has both a package veto and an item veto over appropriations bills and must take action on all measures presented to him or her; without a signature, they become law. When the legislature is in session, the governor has five weekdays after receiving a bill to sign or veto the measure and fifteen days to take action following a recess of more than five days or final adjournment. The legislature may override a veto with a two-thirds vote of members elected to each chamber.

The governor also has authority to return a bill "with errors in style or form," together with specific recommendations for change. If the legislature approves these changes by a majority vote in each house and the governor certifies that the revised bill conforms to his or her recommendations, the bill becomes law. If the governor refuses to certify a bill, it is returned to lawmakers as a vetoed measure.

The constitutional change that most improved the South Dakota governor's power position was a reorganization of the executive branch that took effect in 1974.

But for the elected constitutional officers, all agencies, boards, and commissions are allocated among no more than twenty-five principal executive departments "to provide an orderly arrangement in the administrative organization of state government." The governor appoints each department head, subject to senate confirmation, for a term coincident with his or her own, but the chief executive may remove them sooner. He or she may change the organization and functions of any department "for efficient administration" by executive order. Such orders become effective within ninety days unless they are rejected by a majority of members elected to each legislative chamber.

The improved governing authority of the South Dakota governor, who is almost always supported by substantial partisan majorities in both legislative chambers, has made the governorship more influential than ever before in state history. However, the state's small and relatively stable population (ranking forty-sixth in size in the nation) plus a low tax base and modest

tax effort combine to neutralize the chief executive's position. The success of future governors will depend on the office-holder's ability to supplement these upgraded constitutional and statutory powers with personal and political skills.

James McDowell

References
Barone, Michael, and Richard E. Cohen. 2003. *The almanac of American politics 2004.* Washington, DC: National Journal.
Bibby, John F., and Thomas M. Holbrook. 2004. Parties and elections. In *Politics in the American states: A comparative analysis,* 8th ed., ed. Virginia Gray and Russell L. Hanson, 62–99. Washington, DC: Congressional Quarterly Press.
Ranney, Austin. 1965. Parties in state politics. In *Politics in the American states: A comparative analysis,* ed. Herbert Jacob and Kenneth N. Vines, 61–99. Boston: Little, Brown.
South Dakota Constitution of 1889.

Additional Resources and Recommended Readings
Schell, Herbert S. 2004. *History of South Dakota,* 4th ed. rev. Pierre: South Dakota State Historical Society.

TENNESSEE
• • • • • • • • • • • •

TENNESSEE ELECTED EXECUTIVE BRANCH OFFICIALS
Governor
http://www.state.tn.us/

• • • • • • • • • • • •

In England, the War of the Roses was a bloody campaign, launched between two rival families for the crown of English government. Each family adopted a rose to symbolize its fight for the English throne. The United States experienced its own version of the War of the Roses, but

the American battle was a spirited contest for the chief executive office of Tennessee. Actually, the 1886 election for governor was a familial rivalry that was more humorous and spirited than bloody. Two brothers, Robert L. Taylor (a Democrat) and Alfred A. Taylor (a Republican), both campaigned for the Tennessee governorship in 1886. Bob's supporters wore white roses on their lapels, while Al's supporters wore red roses on theirs. Compared to the English version, the Tennessee war proved to be a more harmonious affair. Following the brothers' nominations by their respective parties, both appeared together on joint campaign stops, with Bob remarking that "the red rose and the white rose bloom together and shed their odors upon the same atmosphere, and gently struggling for supremacy, glorify the twilight hours" (Taylor 1982, 354). The two candidates would end up debating each other fifty times in the span of three months. Bob, the white-rose candidate, eventually went on to win the election, while his red-rose brother would later win the governorship in his own right in 1920.

Unlike most other states, Tennessee has an executive branch that is solely composed of a governor, who exercises "supreme executive power" under the constitution of 1870. Only four states have a governor who is the only statewide elected officer. To hold the office of governor, an individual must be at least thirty years old, a citizen of the United States, and a citizen of the state for a period of seven years prior to the election. In addition, the constitution prevents any sitting member of a national or state office from holding the governor's chair simultaneously. Governors are limited to two consecutive terms in office, but they can wait four years and then run again for the office. As Tennessee does not have a separately elected lieutenant governor, the president of the state senate has the statutory title of lieutenant governor and suc-

ceeds to the executive office on the death, resignation, or incapacity of the governor.

Among the governor's formal constitutional powers is that of commander-in-chief of the state's army and navy (even though Tennessee is a landlocked state), but the governor cannot call the militia into service without a formal declaration by the general assembly. The governor can grant reprieves and pardons, except in the case of impeachment.

The governor of Tennessee also oversees a vast system of government agencies, commonly known as the bureaucracy. Three forms of agencies run the day-to-day activities of the state government: staff, line, and semiindependent departments. Staff departments are generally specialized entities that aid in the operation of other state agencies. These departments oversee such matters as personnel, revenue, and finance and administration. Line departments are responsible for delivering services to the general public; examples include the departments of education, commerce, corrections, environment and conservation, and transportation, among many others. The semiindependent departments can be purely advisory, service-oriented, or regulatory in nature, such as the Alcoholic Beverage Commission or the Tennessee Bureau of Investigation.

As with all other chief executives, the governor of Tennessee has the power to veto legislation. In Tennessee, if the governor vetoes a piece of legislation, the legislature may override that veto with a simple majority vote in each chamber. Tennessee is one of only six states in the nation that require only a simple majority vote by the legislature to override a governor's veto. If the governor fails to sign an enacted bill into law after ten days, the bill automatically becomes law. If the ten-day period extends after the legislature goes out of session, the governor must still veto the bill to prevent it from becoming a law. In many other states, if the governor simply does not sign the bill, it dies (this is commonly referred to as a pocket veto). However, Tennessee's governor must veto the bill.

Like many other governors, Tennessee's chief executive has the power of a line-item veto, by which he or she may strike provisions from appropriations bills and sign the remainder into law. If the legislature overrides the line-item veto by a majority vote, then the spending becomes law.

Another important constitutional power that the chief executive possesses is the power to call the legislature back into special session as well as determine the purpose of the session. In addition, the governor has the constitutional power to deliver "information on the state of the government, and recommend for their consideration such measures as he shall judge expedient." This task is often accomplished through the state of the state address, which most governors deliver at the beginning of a legislative session.

While the Tennessee governor has some constitutional powers over the legislature, the general assembly of Tennessee has certain key powers over the executive branch, most notably through the power of impeachment. Under the Tennessee constitution, the state house of representatives has the power to impeach the governor and to present its case to the state senate, while the state senate tries the individual for conviction, with the chief justice of the state supreme court presiding over the trial. Tennessee's impeachment process is very similar to the national government's impeachment.

For many chief executives, the relationship with their legislature is critical to gaining approval for gubernatorial programs. From the 1930s to the 1960s, Tennessee's governorship was considered the stronger of the two political branches; the governors often named the leaders of both legislative chambers, as well as the individuals who would be legislatively appointed to the office of secretary of state, treasurer, and comptroller. This practice, however, declined in the 1970s when Tennessee's general assembly asserted power over its own internal affairs.

Although Tennessee's governor is the sole statewide elected executive officer, there are other executive officers who have duties in state government. The constitution specifies that the secretary of state, the treasurer, and comptroller of the state are appointed by the general assembly, with the state supreme court appointing the state's attorney general and reporter.

The role of the secretary of state is to keep all the acts and resolutions that have been adopted by the legislature and signed into law by the governor. In addition, he or she is responsible for keeping other records as assigned by the legislature, including articles of incorporation by businesses.

The treasurer is responsible for overseeing the various financial operations, including the payments and collection of revenues, of the state government. The treasurer also oversees the retirement fund and other programs. The comptroller, elected by the general assembly for two-year terms, serves as the official auditor of state and local financial records.

The attorney general is the state's chief legal officer and has the authority to represent the state in legal proceedings. In addition, the attorney general can issue opinions and legal advice to state agencies and officials. Finally, the attorney general serves as the "reporter" of opinions by the state supreme court and the court of appeals.

Tennessee is notable in that one of its governors went on to become both president and governor of another nation and state, respectively. Sam Houston served as the Volunteer State's chief executive from 1827 to 1829, prior to departing for the soon-to-be Republic of Texas and then state of Texas.

J. Michael Bitzer

References

State of Tennessee Constitution of 1870, Art. 3.

Taylor, Robert L., Jr. 1982. Tennessee's War of the Roses as symbol and myth. *Tennessee Historical Quarterly* 41:337–359.

Vile, John R., and Mary Byrnes. 1998. *Tennessee government and politics: Democracy in the Volunteer State.* Nashville: Vanderbilt University Press.

Additional Resources and Recommended Readings

Greene, Lee Seifert, David H. Grubbs, and Victor C. Hobday. 1982. *Government in Tennessee.* Knoxville: University of Tennessee Press.

Olshfski, Dorothy F., and T. McN. Simpson. 1985. *The Volunteer State: Readings in Tennessee politics.* Nashville: Tennessee Political Science Association.

Phillips, Margaret I. 1978. *The governors of Tennessee.* Gretna, LA: Pelican.

TEXAS

● ● ● ● ● ● ● ● ● ● ● ●

TEXAS ELECTED EXECUTIVE BRANCH OFFICIALS

Governor   Lieutenant Governor
Attorney General
Commissioner of the General Land Office
Comptroller of Public Accounts
Secretary of Agriculture
http://www.texas.gov/

● ● ● ● ● ● ● ● ● ● ● ●

Sam Houston, two-time president of the Republic of Texas and the seventh governor of the state, remains one of the most colorful characters in all of American history. His life's odyssey was deeply entwined with the political beginnings of one of the nation's largest and most influential states. A former congressman and governor of the state of Tennessee, Houston took an active role in defining Texas during the thirty-year period in which it was a Mexican colony, an independent republic, a part of the Confederacy, and an American state. Elected as governor of Texas two years before the start of the Civil War, Houston ran on a primarily antisecessionist platform. However, despite his election, Texas did secede from the Union in 1861, and Houston was removed from office. Through it all, he remained loyal to the people of Texas, as he turned down President Abraham Lincoln's offers to send federal troops to keep Houston in power and Texas a part the Union because he feared the bloodshed and violence that would result. Despite his notorious drinking binges, Houston remained a powerful figure in the history of Texas politics. So great was his love of the state, it is said that of the last three words Sam Houston spoke before passing away, two of them were "Texas." The third was "Margaret," the name of his third wife, who was by his side as he passed.

Over fifty years later, Texas's amazing gubernatorial legacy continued with the election of the nation's second female governor, Miriam Amanda Ferguson, who was elected once in 1924 and nearly a decade later in 1932. Ferguson, whose husband, James, was impeached while serving as governor from 1915 to 1917, was embroiled in a number of political controversies, ranging from bribery for a number of state projects to improper use of her pardoning power. One of her most memorable actions as governor, however, was when she took a stand against the Ku Klux Klan and attempted to ban the wearing of hoods and masks in public, which would have effectively shut down a number of the group's public operations. But the state supreme court overturned this act. Ferguson's second term as governor, from 1933 to 1934, was less controversial, although her liberal use of her gubernatorial pardoning power continued. This time, however, not too many people objected to her pardoning hundreds of criminals because the release of prisoners from state facilities decreased the finan-

Infamous Texas governor Miriam "Ma" Ferguson (Library of Congress)

cial drain on the state—an important issue during the Great Depression. Despite the controversies and corruption of her years as governor, Ferguson's impact on history remains crucial to the role of women in politics and a part of executive politics throughout the state of Texas.

The executive branch of the Texas government is composed of a governor who is constitutionally designated as the "Chief Executive Officer of the State," a lieutenant governor, an agriculture secretary, a secretary of state, a comptroller of public accounts, a commissioner of the general land office, and an attorney general. All of these officials, with the exception of the secretary of state, are elected by the state's citizens to four-year terms. The governor and lieutenant governor are not elected as members of the same ticket but instead run for office separately. This situation can create an interesting dynamic between the two officials should their visions for the state be at odds. In fact, because six of the seven executive officials are separately elected and therefore accountable only to their voting constituencies, the state of Texas has what is often referred to as a plural executive. This dispersion of power, built into the state constitution as a means of curbing the accumulation of power in the executive branch, is often cited as evidence of a relatively weak gubernatorial office, for the executive officials are not directly accountable to the governor for their offices.

To qualify to be governor or lieutenant governor, a person must be at least thirty years of age and a citizen residing in the state of Texas for at least five years prior to the election. Once elected, neither the governor nor the lieutenant governor may hold any other civil, military, or corporate office, nor may they be employed as a member of any other profession. This stipulation is intended to keep private interests out of the executive office so that the needs of the state as a whole are looked after in an appropriate manner.

The veto powers of the governor of Texas mirror the "all-or-nothing" types of blanket vetoes held by a number of other governors throughout the United States. On receiving legislation from the legislature, the governor may sign, reject, or simply ignore the bill. With a two-thirds majority in both houses, the governor's veto can be overridden. If ten days pass and the governor has neither signed nor vetoed the bill, the bill becomes a law as if he or she had signed it. Among the other powers granted to the governor are command of the state's armed forces when they are not in the service of the federal government, the ability to convene special sessions of the legislature, the power of pardon except in cases of treason and impeachment, and the ability to fill vacant public offices by appointment. The governor is also expressly charged with the responsibility of representing the state of Texas in dealings with other states and the federal government.

An additional responsibility assigned to the governor of Texas, apart from the typical state of the state addresses given by most governors across the nation, is a requirement to report to the legislature after each session to offer a full accounting and estimate of how much money will be required for any new pieces of legislation passed during the session. This requirement allows the governor a more active role in making sure the legislators are aware of the fiscal resources necessary for the faithful execution of the laws they have just codified.

The office of lieutenant governor in the state of Texas spans both executive and legislative functions. In fact, the lieutenant governor is considered to be a member of both branches. Elected separately from the governor in a statewide race, the lieutenant governor has the traditional role of fulfilling the duties of the chief executive if he or she is unable to do so; further, the lieutenant governor serves as the head of the state senate. This position gives the lieutenant governor a significant amount of leverage over the creation and adoption of legislation by the state legislature. He or she performs traditional roles as the head of the senate, such as answering all questions of procedure and casting votes in the case of ties, and beyond that, the lieutenant governor is responsible for determining which bills are heard and for establishing standing and select committees (and appointing committee leadership). The lieutenant governor also serves on a number of important boards, including the Legislative Budget Board, the Legislative Redistricting Board, the Legislative Council, the Legislative Education Board, and the Legislative Audit Committee. This vast amount of traditional executive and special legislative responsibilities makes the lieutenant governor of Texas one of the most powerful lieutenants in the United States. Some would argue the lieutenant governor is actually more powerful than the governor.

The attorney general's power is also considerable within Texas government. As chief counsel for all state agencies, the attorney general and his or her staff defend state agencies whenever they are sued in court. In recent years, several Texas attorneys general have had experience serving as state supreme court justices.

Among the other executive officers in Texas, the commissioner of the General Land Office, otherwise known as the land commissioner, has evolved into a powerful position. Elected by the people since 1869, the land commissioner is responsible for overseeing the state's public properties, including the land that contains gas, oil, and mineral deposits. Because of the abundance of natural resources in the state and his or her power to grant leases to develop these resources, the land commissioner has become an important player in the executive branch.

Among the other critical executive officers in Texas is the comptroller of public accounts, who is the state's tax collector and, following the abolishment of the state treasurer's office in 1996, a powerful figure. The comptroller estimates the revenue that the state will collect in the coming year, and the legislature may not appropriate more than that amount unless it does so by a four-fifths vote. The agriculture commissioner, an elective office created by the legislature and not by the state's constitution, regulates and promotes agricultural interests in the state.

Other actors also exert significant authority in Texas. Established in 1891, the Railroad Commission of Texas (RRC) is one of the oldest existing regulatory commissions in the United States. Although established as an institution to regulate the railroad industry just prior to the turn of the twentieth century, the RRC has since had its mission expanded to incorporate a number of other statewide industries, including departments in charge of the oil and gas industries and utilities, rail and pipeline safety throughout the state, surface mining of coal and uranium, and safety in the petroleum and gas industries. The RRC also handles state-sponsored research on new fuels as possible alternatives to current sources for meeting energy demands in the state. Such a wide range of oversight and administration activities relating to some of the most critical sectors of the Texas economy makes the RRC an incredibly powerful agency and its members very powerful actors in Texas politics. To try and contain the potential abuses of the commission's authority, three commissioners serve as members of the executive branch and are selected via statewide election to serve six-year terms, with one commissioner being elected every two years to head the commission. If anything happens to one of these commissioners while serving in his or her RRC capacity, the governor appoints a replacement until the next general election.

In general, the executive office of the state of Texas is on a par with—and in many ways is purposefully designed to be weaker than—those in most other states in terms of powers and responsibilities. What is it, then, about the state of Texas that makes the governor such an important national leader? For one thing, the political economy of Texas is expansive and diverse, with the leading industries being petroleum and natural gas, agriculture, steel, banking, insurance, and tourism. Texas has such a massive resource base in these areas that the U.S. economy is heavily dependent on the fiscal and economic decisions made by the Texas government. For example, 60 percent of the nation's petrochemical production capacity is located within the borders of Texas, as is 25 percent of the nation's overall oil-refining capacity. With such a depth of resources, it is easy to see how actions taken by the governor in areas of the state economy often have national ramifications.

Another factor that places Texas at the forefront of a number of national issues is its proximity and historical ties to Mexico. The racial and ethnic composition of Texas is diverse, with large concentrations of Mexican Americans throughout the state. In 2004, at the close of a border governors' conference, Governor James Richard "Rick" Perry of Texas called on Mexico to open its energy markets in order to allow for greater U.S. investment. Perry also highlighted the importance of working together with Mexico to strengthen the borders and reduce the flow of immigration into the United States, which potentially threatens domestic security. In representing both economic and security interests in speaking to Mexico on behalf of Texas and the United States, Perry illustrated another important and unique role that the governor of Texas plays in state and national politics.

The colorful histories of Sam Houston and Miriam "Ma" Ferguson are but two chapters in the political history of Texas and the executives who have overseen the numerous duties that come with being at the helm of this incredible state. From its early foundations up to the election of Governor George W. Bush to the presidency of the United States, Texas has been a leader nationally in terms of politics, economics, policies, and programs. Of course, national leadership might be expected of such an enormous state in terms of square mileage, population, and resources. Geographically, Texas is the second-largest state in the country behind Alaska, with a land size of approximately 268,601 square miles, and it is second only to California in terms of population, with about 21 million people. Texas also remains at the forefront of natural resource production and mining, as the gas and oil industries continue to be central to both Texas and American politics. But size does not mean everything, and it has taken a number of strong executive figures in Texas's history to push the Lone Star State into the national spotlight.

Joseph J. Foy

References

Colyandro, John. 2000. Texas growing cleanly. *Austin Review Online.* http://www.austinreview.com/articles/2 000_07/texasgrowth.htm.

Huddleston, John D., and Miriam Amanda Wallace Ferguson. *The handbook of Texas online.* Texas State Historical Association. http://www.tsha.utexas .edu/ handbook/online/articles/view /FF/ffe6.html.

Massey, Barry. 2004. Border governors conference: Texas governor calls on Mexico to further open energy markets. *Santa Fe New Mexican Online.* http:// www.santafenewmexican.com/news /2865.html.

Railroad Commission of Texas official website. http://www.rrc.state.tx.us/.

Texas State Constitution of 1876, Art. 4.

University of Texas at Austin, Liberal Arts Instructional Technology Services. 2004. Texas politics—The executive branch. http://texaspolitics.laits. utexas.edu/ html/exec/.

U.S. Census Bureau. 2004. *State and county QuickFacts: Texas.* http:// quickfacts.census.gov/qfd/states/ 48000.html.

Williams, John H. 1994. *Sam Houston: The life and times of the liberator of Texas, an authentic American hero.* New York: Touchstone.

Additional Resources and Recommended Readings

Acuña, Rodolfo. 1981. *Occupied America: A history of Chicanos,* 2nd ed. New York: Harper and Row.

Barta, Carolyn. 1996. *Bill Clements: Texan to his toenails.* Austin: Eakin.

Halter, Gary M. 2001. *Government and politics of Texas,* 3rd ed. New York: McGraw-Hill.

Hendrickson, Kenneth, Jr. 1995. *The chief executive in Texas: A study in gubernatorial leadership.* Austin: University of Texas Press.

Ivins, Molly, and Lou Dubose. 2000. *Shrub: The short but happy political life of George W. Bush.* New York: Random House.

McEnteer, James. 2004. *Deep in the heart: The Texas tendency in American politics.* New York: Praeger.

State of Texas, Office of the Executive, governor's official website. http://www.governor.state.tx.us/.

University of Texas at Austin, University Libraries Online. Texas government and information. http://www.lib.utexas .edu/government/texas.html.

UTAH

• • • • • • • • • • • •

UTAH ELECTED EXECUTIVE BRANCH OFFICIALS

Governor	Lieutenant Governor
Attorney General	Auditor

Treasurer
http://www.utah.gov/

• • • • • • • • • • • •

The history of the executive office in Utah is, in many ways, intimately connected to the tenuous relationship between the federal government and the large Mormon population that settled the Utah Territory. For the first six years, Brigham Young served as territorial governor (1851–1857), before President James Buchanan appointed Alfred Cumming to the position in 1858 in an attempt to end the practice of polygamy in the state. Fearing armed opposition, federal troops escorted Cumming to the capitol. After a yearlong military presence, the situation was put to rest when Young agreed to relinquish the governorship. True cooperation between the Utah Territory and federal representatives was long in coming, however. Following the end of the initial conflicts, Young established the so-called Shadow Government of the Deseret, which would conduct its business after the official business of the territorial government was concluded. Young appointed himself to serve as the governor of this organization. Throughout its history as a territory and state, Utah has confronted a number of attempts by the federal government to regulate its political activities, largely because the regulations and laws of the national government have come into conflict with the religious and political dictates of the Mormon community. It was often the governor's responsibility to serve this religious community, as well as attempt to act as a mediator in state and federal interactions. The socioreligious context is crucial to an understanding of the role of the executive in the state of Utah.

Five officials—the governor, lieutenant governor, state auditor, state treasurer, and attorney general—comprise the executive branch in Utah. Each of these executive officers serves four-year terms. Utah remains one of fourteen states that do not impose term limits on their executives. At the head of the executive branch are the governor and lieutenant governor, who are elected as a team. They appear on the ballot together, and a vote for the governor is considered a vote

for the lieutenant governor as well. A simple majority elects these officials, with ties (although unlikely to occur) being decided by both houses of the state legislature. To qualify for the office of governor or lieutenant governor, a person must be thirty years or older at the time of election. All other officials must be at least twenty-five, and the attorney general must be admitted to practice before the state supreme court and in good standing with the American Bar Association. All executive officers must be qualified electors, having lived in the state of Utah for at least five years preceding their election.

The powers and responsibilities vested in the governor of the state of Utah follow a traditional executive model. The governor is the chief executive and responsible for the faithful execution of the laws of the state; he or she is also the commander-in-chief of the state's military forces (except when they are in the command of the federal government). The governor is charged with transacting all executive business with all governmental officials, be they civil or military, and he or she is required to deliver a general address reporting on the needs and conditions of the state during each general legislative session. Further, the governor may call and adjourn special sessions of the legislature in extraordinary circumstances, and he or she has the power to appoint state and district officials (with the advice and consent of the legislature) when their election or appointment is not otherwise provided for or when their offices are prematurely vacated. The governor may, at any time, appoint legal counsel to serve in a gubernatorial advisory position.

The governor of Utah is given two different types of veto power, depending on what type of bill or legislative act is under consideration. For legislation that does not directly involve appropriations, the governor is given a package veto to either completely accept or reject the legislation. If the governor accepts a bill, he or she signs it into law. If the governor does not act on a bill by either signing it into law or vetoing it within ten days, the bill becomes a law as if it had been signed.

If the governor chooses to veto a bill, it is returned to the legislature along with his or her recommendations for amendment. The legislators then reconsider the bill in its entirety, factoring the recommendations into their deliberations, and either amend it and send it back to the governor for approval or attempt to override the veto. For the legislature to override an executive veto, a two-thirds vote is required in both houses. If such an override occurs, the bill becomes law.

The second type of veto power given to the governor is a line-item veto for all legislative acts involving appropriations. In these cases, the governor may remove any item of appropriation from a bill before signing it into law. Those items that the governor applies this selective form of veto to do not become law unless they are subjected successfully to a legislative override, as described in the preceding paragraph. Giving the governor this type of power is an attempt to prevent legislators from attaching spending riders to legislative acts that the chief executive

would otherwise approve. It enables the governor to play a more active role in balancing the budget and containing legislative spending.

In terms of pardoning powers, the governor again has two types of authority granted by the state constitution. First, he or she appoints members to the Board of Pardons and Paroles, with the advice and consent of the senate. The board may, by majority vote, grant reprieves, pardons, and paroles; commute punishments; or secure remissions of fines and forfeitures, except in cases of treason or impeachment. Additionally, the governor can take direct action in offering pardons and reprieves for any case except impeachment or treason when the board is not in session. These gubernatorial actions last until the board reconvenes and can consider the case. It is possible for the governor to suspend the execution of a sentence in a case of treason until the legislature is in session and can consider the case. However, it is the legislators who will have final review of the conviction and sentencing, and the governor is bound to execute their decision once it is final. If the legislature does not act on a suspension of sentence in the case of treason during its session, then the governor is also bound to execute the sentence.

The other members of the state executive—the state auditor, treasurer, and attorney general—perform duties similar to those carried out by their peers in most other states. The lieutenant governor of Utah serves a dual role as successor to the governor and as de facto secretary of state. Further, the lieutenant governor oversees state water, transportation, and rural services and plays the role reserved in most states for a secretary of state, being responsible for regulating elections and notary and authentication services. Like many other lieutenant governors, Utah's "second in command" may be responsible for carrying out a number of duties delegated by the governor. Some of these duties can be rather demanding, as Lieutenant Governor Gary Herbert learned when he was recently appointed to serve as chair of the Utah Homeland Security Executive Board by Governor Jon Huntsman. In essence, the lieutenant governor can be as active or passive as the governor deems appropriate along a number of executive dimensions in serving the state; consequently, the actual capacity of the office is determined by the relationship between the governor and his or her lieutenant, as well as the chief executive's personal management style.

Mike Leavitt, former governor of Utah, was appointed as administrator of the U.S. Environmental Protection Agency (2003–2004) and secretary of the U.S. Department of Health and Human Services (2005–). (Department of Health and Human Services)

The attorney general of the state of Utah, like most state attorneys general, serves as the legal adviser for public officials. Additionally, he or she is assigned a number of specific legal duties that expand the providence of the office beyond simply acting as the state's chief legal counsel. Such duties include but are not limited to acting as both prosecuting and defense attorney in all cases involving the state, offering legal opinions to state officials and agencies, purchasing property on behalf of the state, accounting for all funds distributed to the office, and providing service to a variety of state boards.

The Utah state treasurer serves as the chief financial officer of the state. The primary duty is to oversee major Treasury Department officials: the state's investment officer, the administrator of unclaimed property, and the chief deputy officer. These subagents perform various duties, but the most important function is the investment of state revenues so as to generate an increased amount of financial capacity for the state without placing too great a burden on the taxpayers.

On the other side of the state's financial coin is the state auditor. Broken down into three primary divisions (financial, local, and special projects), the office of the state auditor provides a complete accounting and reporting of state fiscal activities. This duty requires not only recording financial intakes and outputs but also maintaining oversight over local governments to ensure that their practices conform to the budgetary regulations of the state.

The tenuous relationship between the state of Utah and the federal government, rooted in historical mistrust and lack of understanding, continues to this day. The feelings of hostility and cynicism toward the national government that are held by a majority of the citizens in Utah means that the governor often must stand up to national policies and mandates in favor of more localized actions and solutions. For example, in a recent campaign for the gubernatorial seat, Republican and Democratic candidates alike argued against federal policies such as the No Child Left Behind program, citing the excessive entanglement of the federal government in state concerns that such policies bring about (KSL News 2004). However, this is not to say that the state of Utah stands apart from national politics. To the contrary, President George W. Bush appointed former Utah governor Mike Leavitt to head the national Environmental Protection Agency because of his conservative but generally effective approach to a number of ecological issues facing his state. Therefore, while a further understanding of the continuing legacy of state-federal tensions in Utah can help to shed light on the actions and leadership efforts of the executive branch, the concomitantly increasing ties between the state and national governments are redefining relations in the twenty-first century.

Joseph J. Foy

References

Arrington, Leonard J., and Davis Bitton. 1992. *The Mormon experience: A history of the Latter-day Saints*, 2nd ed. Champaign and Urbana: University of Illinois Press.

KSL News. 2004. Gubernatorial candidates slam "No Child Left Behind." http://tv.ksl.com/index.php?nid=5&sid=115365.

Poll, Richard D. 2004. Deseret. http://historytogo.utah.gov/deseret.html.

State of Utah, Office of Lieutenant Governor. 2004. Lieutenant governor's duties. http://www.utah.gov/ltgovernor/duties.html.

Utah State Constitution of 1896, Art. 7.

Utah State Department of Community and Economic Development. 2004. Utah state history. http://www.history.utah.gov.

Additional Resources and Recommended Readings

Bagley, Pat, and Will Bagley. 1996. *This is the place: A crossroads of Utah's past.* Carson City, NV: Buckaroo.

May, Dean L. 1987. *Utah: A people's history.* Salt Lake City: University of Utah Press.

The Salt Lake Tribune. http://www.sltrib.com/.

State of Utah, Office of the Executive, governor's official website. 2004. http://www.utah.gov/governor/.

U.S. Politics Today. 2004. Utah political news. http://www.uspoliticstoday.com/utah/.

VERMONT
• • • • • • • • • • • • •

VERMONT ELECTED EXECUTIVE BRANCH OFFICIALS

Governor	Lieutenant Governor
Attorney General	Auditor of Accounts
Secretary of State	Treasurer

http://vermont.gov/

• • • • • • • • • • • • •

Political observers have described Vermont as a contrarian land of "political paradox." And indeed, this is the only state that has both a U.S. senator and a member of the House of Representatives who declare their party status as Independent. While Vermonters can appear to be personally conservative, the state was one of the first to recognize the rights of gays and lesbians in civil unions. Certain characteristics of the Green Mountain State's political makeup identify it as an outlier, including the holdover of two-year gubernatorial terms and its unique status as the only state without a balanced budget requirement. But in the end, the Vermont governor has much the same challenges and opportunities as governors from other states. In the runup to the last presidential election, former governor Howard Dean demonstrated that the state's chief executive can rise to national prominence.

Vermont entered the Union as the fourteenth state in 1791, following a brief period as an independent republic, apart from the thirteen states that signed on to the Articles of Confederation. In 1777, Vermont adopted a constitution based on the Pennsylvania model, but it established its uniqueness by outlawing slavery earlier than any other state and establishing the first American system of public schools. Independent thinking and political action carried forward into Vermont in the last century. In 1936, Vermonters in town meetings and in the state legislature rejected the spending of federal money under President Franklin Delano Roosevelt's New Deal to build a parkway in the state. And in the early 1950s, Vermont senator Ralph Flanders, with other New England Republicans, led the resistance to Joseph McCarthy's anticommunist crusade. The state has a long history of supporting Republican Party candidates; between 1856 and 1963, not a single governor served from another political party (Vermont Republicans were similarly successful in the U.S. Congress). Now, partisanship has been replaced by an independent streak, as the state has a Republican governor (Jim Douglas), a Democratic U.S. senator (Patrick Leahy), and an Independent U.S. senator and Independent House member (James Jeffords and Bernard Sanders, respectively).

The Vermont Constitution has maintained a limitation on the length of time that the governor can serve. Vermont is one of only two states (New Hampshire being the other) where gubernatorial elections are held every two years. The Vermont governor may run for as many terms of office as he or she likes, and in recent years, the chief executive has generally been sufficiently popular to be returned to office multiple times. Madeleine Kunin was elected three times, while Richard Snelling and Howard Dean were both elected five times. It is clear that the Green State's governor can overcome the two-year cycle of elections, but at the same time, he or she needs to spend twice as much time on the campaign trail as a governor elected for the more common four-year term.

The Vermont governor serves along with five other elected officials: the lieutenant governor, the treasurer, the secretary of state, the auditor of accounts, and the attorney general. These different officials develop expertise in various administrative areas, serving, respectively, as the state's chief parliamentarian in the legislature, chief financial officer, clerk of records, watchdog of governmental spending, and legal expert. It should not be surprising that many of the state's executive leaders arise from the political (rather than professional or bureaucratic) ranks.

The state also has a citizen-based legislature, in which state representatives earn a relatively low salary, serve in the state capital of Montpelier for a short time each year, and have little staff support. When all of these political offices come up for reelection every two years, it is possible for outsiders to break into government or for citizens to rise to governmental service for a brief period before returning to private life. The state's current governor, Jim Douglas, served in three other elected roles—as a legislator, secretary of state, and treasurer—before assuming the governorship. His broad experience across Vermont's government has enabled him to understand many facets of the state's political, administrative, and financial operations.

Since the Vermont lieutenant governor is elected separately from the governor, the two highest leaders in the state may come from different parties, and the second-in-command may serve longer than the lead executive. Vermont's lieutenant, in addition to running the state senate, also chairs functional committees in the place of the governor, such as the Homeland Security Advisory Council and the Vermont-Quebec Partnerships, both of which coordinate security and economic relationships with Vermont's neighbors. The Vermont governor sees the importance of a cooperative relationship with the second-in-command and develops it accordingly. The lieutenant governor may have some aspects of the citizen-politician common to other political positions in the state. Former governor Howard Dean was a practicing physician while serving as lieutenant governor; in fact, he heard about the death of Governor Richard Snelling and his own ascendance to the governorship while operating on a patient. The current lieutenant governor, Brian Dubie, served as a military and commercial pilot prior to his election.

The Vermont governor has weaker budgetary powers than most governors, yet the state tends to manage its fiscal affairs effectively. Almost all American governors initiate the budget process by preparing revenue and expenditure plans with the help of their fiscal staff and spending agencies (the exception, in some states, is that the governor must develop the budget in cooperation with a committee of other political actors). Once the budget's revenue and spending figures are complete, the typical governor sends the plan as a document and an appropriations bill to the legislature. Vermont's governor operates like the typical state chief executive to this point. However, the process in Vermont then becomes unique (and weaker for the governor). First, the Vermont Constitution does not require a balanced budget. The governor will typically submit a budget that spends no more than is earned by the state in taxes. But if the legislature wants to fund pet projects or meet other constituent interests with excess expense, it can do so. The governor's recourse to deny funding that he or she does not support is the veto, the denial of bills that the legislature passes. Vermont's governor has one of the weakest veto powers. Most American governors have a line-item veto, with which they can cross out unwanted priorities from legislative bills. But Vermont's veto is limited to turning back entire bills. The governor must decide, when confronted with an unfavorable budget bill, whether it contains more elements that he or she supports than opposes—but the chief executive cannot pick and choose among funding priorities. Even with these constraints on the governor, Vermont budgets for its programs conservatively, and it rarely runs a deficit between tax funding and expenses.

Vermont's governor operates in an environment of shared power, with other elected officials in the cabinet and legislature and even with the state's citizens who have the right to turn the governor out of office every two years. Thus, the governor must walk a fine line to maintain power in the state capital. A prominent policy battle in Vermont underscores the give-and-take that the governor faces. In 1999, the state supreme court decided in *Baker v. Vermont* that denying the right of marriage to gays was inconsistent with the state constitution's "common benefit" clause and the state and U.S. Constitutions' equal protection provisions. The court ordered the state legislature to either legalize gay and lesbian marriage or approve civil unions, so that gays and lesbians could share domestic partnership benefits. Governor Dean used his stature to advocate for civil unions as a middle ground on a highly divisive issue. He made it easier for the legislature to pass the civil unions legislation, the first of its kind in the United States, by announcing from the outset that he would sign it quickly into law. In this case, the Vermont governor was not technically in charge, but he played a leadership role in a policy engagement involving all three branches of state government. Governor Dean did his part to assist in a judicial order and verified that his powers (especially the veto power) would not be used in opposition to the state supreme court. Such is the shared power of the Vermont chief executive and of all effective American governors.

Brendan Burke

References

Beyle, Thad. 2004. The governors. In *Politics in the American states: A comparative analysis*, 8th ed., ed. Virginia Gray and Russell L. Hanson, 194–231. Washington, DC: Congressional Quarterly Press.

Constitution of the State of Vermont. http://www.leg.state.vt.us/statutes/const2.htm.

Kunin, Madeleine M. 1994. *Living a political life: One of America's first woman governors tells her story.* New York: Vintage.

Lockard, Duane. 1959. *New England state politics.* Princeton: Princeton University Press.

Petterson, Paul. 2003. Vermont politics: Consistently contrary. *New England Journal of Political Science* 1(1):224–229.

Additional Resources and Recommended Readings

Bryan, Frank M. 1974. *Yankee politics in rural Vermont.* Hanover, NH: University Press of New England.

Dean, Howard. 2003. *Winning back America.* New York: Simon and Shuster.

Moats, David. 2004. *Civil wars: A battle for gay marriage.* Orlando, FL: Harcourt.

VIRGINIA

● ● ● ● ● ● ● ● ● ● ● ●

VIRGINIA ELECTED EXECUTIVE BRANCH OFFICIALS

Governor   Lieutenant Governor

Attorney General

http://www.virginia.gov/

● ● ● ● ● ● ● ● ● ● ● ●

Virginia, home of the old Confederacy's capital city, made history in the twentieth century when it became the first state to elect an African American as its chief executive. In 1990, L. Douglas Wilder was elected governor of Virginia after serving as the state's lieutenant governor. Wilder has since gone on to further historic service in the state by becoming the first elected African American mayor of the capital city, Richmond.

Prior to 1852, Virginia's governors were elected by the state legislature. Early governors included a group of notable Americans, such as Patrick Henry (the first governor of the commonwealth, as well as being the first to serve two different terms as governor), Thomas Jefferson, and James Monroe. After 1852, the voters of Virginia elected their chief executive.

Virginia's state constitution specifies that candidates for governor must be at least thirty years old, U.S. citizens, and state residents and qualified voters for five years. Virginia governors serve a single,

four-year term, and they cannot run for reelection without sitting out for a term. Only one individual was successful in running for a second term in the commonwealth in the twentieth century: Mills E. Godwin Jr., who served as governor from 1966 to 1970 as a Democrat and from 1974 to 1978 as a Republican. Proposals to allow governors to run for reelection have been introduced in Virginia's general assembly as recently as 2004, but they have died for lack of legislative support. Any revision would have to be approved by two separate sessions of the assembly, with an election to the lower house of delegates in between. The proposal would then be put before the voters for approval.

The governor has the constitutional authority to provide a state of the commonwealth address and to convene a special session of the general assembly when necessary. The governor participates in the lawmaking process as well. First, he or she may sign the bill, automatically making it a law. If the assembly passes a bill and the governor does not act on it within seven days, the bill automatically becomes law. The governor may also veto a bill, and the general assembly may override the veto with a two-thirds majority vote of the members elected in each chamber (the lower chamber, known as the house of delegates, and the upper chamber, known as the senate). The governor may also send the bill back to the legislature with amendments, and the legislature may reconsider the bill with the governor's suggested changes. If the legislature adopts the governor's amendments and the governor then signs the bill, it becomes law. If the legislature rejects the governor's amendments, the governor may sign or veto the legislation. The governor also has the power of the line-item veto for appropriations bills passed by the legislature. Items that are rejected by the governor under this line-item veto can be reconsidered by the legislature, and the chief executive's line-item veto can be overridden by a two-thirds majority of the members elected in both chambers.

The governor is charged with taking care "that the laws be faithfully executed," and serving as commander-in-chief of the commonwealth's armed forces. He or she can also appoint a cabinet, with its members subject to confirmation by both chambers of the general assembly.

Virginia's governor has the power to "grant reprieves and pardons" for convicted individuals, with the exception of when the house of delegates has charged an individual with impeachment. The governor can also commute capital punishment sentences, but in the event of a reprieve, pardon, or commutation, he or she must inform the general assembly as to the reasons for taking such action.

Virginia's lieutenant governor is elected at the same time as the governor and must meet the same requirements for holding office. However, the lieutenant governor is not term limited and can serve as many terms as he or she can win. The lieutenant governor serves as the president of the state senate but can only vote in that body when there is a tie.

The attorney general of Virginia must be a U.S. citizen, at least thirty years old, and have the "qualifications required for a judge of a court of record" or a member of the state bar for at least five years prior to the election. Among many other duties, the attorney general serves as the legal representative for the state, giving advice and representing the state government in court. In addition, he or she is charged with defending the constitutionality of state laws when they are challenged in court. Much like in other states, the attorney general also oversees the protection of consumers in the state.

If the governor is removed from office or cannot continue his or her term, the order of succession runs from the lieutenant governor to the attorney general to the speaker of the house of delegates.

Within the governor's cabinet are several departments that manage various activities of state government—commerce and trade, education, finance, health and human resources, natural resources, public safety, technology, transportation, administration, commonwealth preparedness, and commonwealth. Each of these departments is led by a secretary who is appointed by the governor and approved by the state general assembly.

L. Douglas Wilder was elected governor of Virginia in 1989. He is to date the only African American to be elected to the governorship in any state. After serving the single term allowed by Virginia law, he briefly considered seeking the presidency and the U.S. Senate. In 2004 he was elected mayor of Richmond. (Office of Mayor L. Douglas Wilder)

sees the area of planning and budget, while the secretary of health and human resources oversees programs for the aged, the deaf, and people with disabilities.

The secretary of natural resources is responsible for such areas as environmental quality, game and fisheries, historical resources, and the Virginia Museum of Natural History. The secretary of public safety oversees the Alcohol Beverage Control Department, the Department of Corrections, fire programs, juvenile justice, and the state police. The secretary of transportation is responsible for areas such as aviation, motor vehicles, rail, and the ports of the commonwealth. Finally, the secretary of the commonwealth serves duties akin to secretaries of state and is responsible for the great seal of the commonwealth, as well as aiding the governor in making the 4,000 appointments to various boards and commissions within the commonwealth.

J. Michael Bitzer

The secretary of administration is responsible for a variety of activities, including overseeing the State Board of Elections as well as the Department of Veterans' Services. The secretary of commerce and trade is responsible for leading the Department of Forestry; the Department of Mines, Minerals, and Energy; the Department of Labor and Industry; and the Virginia Racing Commission. The education secretary oversees not only the secondary education system but also the higher education system within the state, as well as the Frontier Culture Museum of Virginia and the Virginia Museum of Fine Arts. The secretary of finance over-

References
Constitution of Virginia, Art. 5.

Additional Resources and Recommended Readings
Heinemann, Ronald L. 1996. *Harry Byrd of Virginia.* Charlottesville: University of Virginia Press.

Jeffries, Judson L. 2000. *Virginia's native son: The election and administration of Governor L. Douglas Wilder.* West Lafayette, IN: Purdue University Press.

Porter, William Earl. 1993. *Virginia state government: Fun, frustrating, and frightening.* Lanham, MD: University Press of America.

Yancey, Dwayne. 1990. *When hell froze over: The story of Doug Wilder—A black politician's rise to power in the South.* Roanoke, VA: Taylor.

WASHINGTON
• • • • • • • • • • • •

Governor   Lieutenant Governor
Attorney General   Auditor
Commissioner of Public Lands
Insurance Commissioner   Secretary of State
Superintendent of Public Instruction
Treasurer
http://access.wa.gov/

• • • • • • • • • • • •

In November 1996, the people of the state of Washington made history by electing Gary Locke as the first Asian American governor in the continental United States. A highly active and popular governor, Locke was later elected to serve as the head of the Democratic Governors Association. With his commitment to education and job development throughout the state, Locke has made quite an impression on Washington since his election. He joins a number of other great Washington governors, such as Daniel Jackson Evans, who helped pioneer the creation of a number of environmental protection bills and the formation of the first state ecology department in the 1970s, and Booth Gardner, who served as chairman of a number of regional and national governmental associations and received an international appointment following his service to the people of Washington. In the state named after George Washington—the man who defined the role of chief executive in the United States—it is clear that a number of officials have risen to the challenge of this legacy in leading the nation's forty-second state.

The nine elected officials who comprise Washington's executive branch are the governor, lieutenant governor, secretary of state, treasurer, auditor, attorney general, superintendent of public instruction, insurance commissioner, and commissioner of public lands. Each of these officials is elected to serve terms of four years, and none is term limited. The line of succession calls for the duties of governor to fall first to the lieutenant governor and then the secretary of state, followed by the treasurer, auditor, attorney general, superintendent of public instruction, and commissioner of public lands. Interestingly enough, the state legislature is constitutionally empowered to abolish, at any point in time, the offices of lieutenant governor, auditor, and commissioner of public lands. However, constitutional tradition dictates that this is not likely to happen except in some extreme, unforeseen circumstance.

In general terms, the governor is charged with overseeing the public agencies that serve the state. At any time, the governor may call on state officials to provide information relating to their duties of office. These reports can assist the governor in better understanding what is happening around the state so that he or she can meet the responsibility of faithfully executing public laws. The governor acts as the commander-in-chief of the state's military forces when they are not already under the direct control of the federal government. The governor of Washington also enjoys exclusive pardoning power, within the limits prescribed by law, but is required to report to the legislature during its next session as to the specific details of and reasoning behind any remissions of fines or forfeitures.

Additionally, the governor has a number of constitutionally defined powers and responsibilities that assist in interactions with the legislative branch. For example, the governor plays an important role in setting the legislative agenda at the start of each session. As the chief executive, he or she is constitutionally obliged to deliver a message on the affairs of the state and offer any recommendations deemed necessary to help the people and state of Washington. The governor may also call special sessions of the legislature to consider extraordinary or unforeseen issues and circumstances. In terms of veto power, the governor of Washington has a combined package and item veto power, depending on the nature and contents of a particular piece of legislation. When presented with items of appropriation, the governor may use an item veto to strike down particular elements of a bill or legislative act. However, in all other cases, the governor must

either sign a bill into law or send it back to the originating legislative house with reasons for its rejection. If, after reconsidering these objections, the originating house votes with a two-thirds majority to override the veto, the bill is then submitted to the second legislative chamber. If two-thirds of this second house also votes in favor of the override, the bill (or items of appropriation being reconsidered) becomes law over the governor's veto. Finally, at times when the legislature is in recess and there are vacancies in public offices, the governor may appoint qualified individuals to fill those spots.

The lieutenant governor is also the presiding officer of the state senate. He or she serves on a number of committees around the state, covering issues from women's health to state finance. The primary responsibility of the lieutenant governor is, however, to fill in for the governor if the chief executive is unable to perform his or her assigned duties. This responsibility is especially significant given that the governor and lieutenant governor are elected separately and not as members of the same ticket. Not surprisingly, conflicts within the executive branch can result if the two officials have different visions for the state. The separate election of the governor and lieutenant governor led to a situation that produced perhaps the most well-known lieutenant governor in the state, John Cherberg. Cherberg, a Democrat who served eight consecutive terms (thirty-two straight years) as lieutenant governor of the state, held his office for longer than any other lieutenant governor in U.S.

history. He was lieutenant governor of Washington from 1957 to 1989. In addition to Cherberg, fourteen other individuals have served as lieutenant governor of the state, and three of them have ascended to the governorship after the passing of the elected chief executive.

The secretary of state is responsible for maintaining an official record of governmental activities in a variety of forms and is legally required to report a number of records and activities to both the legislative and executive branches as necessary. The state treasurer and auditor are in charge of a number of the state's economic records and activities, with the auditor being given the special responsibility of reviewing all public accounts. The attorney general acts as the state's legal adviser, and the superintendent of schools oversees all activities related to public education in the state. The insurance commissioner of Washington has, among other things, the primary responsibility for guaranteeing consumer protection on transactions throughout the state. Finally, the commissioner of public lands acts as the head of the Washington Department of Natural Resources, one of the largest of its kind in the United States. The commissioner has been assigned four primary duties: land manager, regulator, firefighter, and conservator. Because Washington is often seen as one of the nation's most progressive states in terms of environmental policy and ecological protection, this unique elected office is an extremely important one for the executive branch of the state.

One of the most significant and challenging political factors confronting the executive of Washington involves establishing mutually beneficial relationships with the thirty federally recognized, sovereign Native American tribes that occupy a substantial part of the state. Among the ways in which the governor can work to build strong relations is through economic partnerships. In 2000, Governor Gary Locke and his Office of Indian Affairs worked with tribes from around the state to diversify their economies and provide fiscal opportunities apart from the gaming (gambling) industry. Not only would these efforts benefit the tribes by enabling them to develop a stronger and more prosperous infrastructure, they would also continue to benefit the state of Washington, which already had approximately $1 billion of tribal money flowing into its economy (NCSL 2000). Therefore, maintaining and improving state-tribal relations is always extremely important for Washington's chief executive.

Another crucial element of executive politics in Washington is the extreme importance that has been placed on environmental issues since the 1960s and 1970s. Balancing the development of industries and maintaining a sound ecosystem have been a major part of the governor's responsibilities since the administration of Governor Daniel Jackson Evans. In the 1990s, the attempts to satisfy both environmentalists and industrialists came to a head when logging efforts threatened the existence of the endangered spotted owl. Governors Booth

Gary Locke served as governor of Washington from 1997 to 2005. (Office of Governor Gary Locke)

the habitat. Such a measure did not resolve the controversies, but it certainly showed how the governor can help alleviate tensions by working as a mediator among important state interests.

Joseph J. Foy

References

National Conference of State Legislatures (NCSL). 2000. *State Legislatures Magazine.* Native American tribes contribute to state economies. http://www.ncsl.org/programs/pubs/500ofr4.htm.

Nice, David C., John C. Pierce, and Charles H. Seldon. 1992. *Government and politics in the Evergreen State.* Seattle and Tacoma: Washington State University Press.

State of Washington, Public Access System. 2000. Washington State elected officials. http://www.leg.wa.gov/legis/stateinfo/elected.htm.

Washington State Constitution of 1889, Art. 3.

Washington State Department of Natural Resources. 2003. State DNR, WDFW agree on significant step to provide owl habitat in SW Washington. http://www.dnr.wa.gov/htdocs/adm/comm/nr03–007.htm.

———. 2004. DNR's Habitat Convention. http://www.dnr.wa.gov/htdocs/adm/comm/fs04_172.htm.

Additional Resources and Recommended Readings

Seattle Post-Intelligencer Online. http://seattlepi.nwsource.com/.

Seeberger, Edward D. 1997. *Sine Die: A guide to the Washington state legislative process,* 2nd ed. Seattle and Tacoma: University of Washington Press.

State of Washington, Office of the Executive, governor's official website. http://www.governor.wa.gov/.

Tribnet.com, the *Tacoma News Tribune Online.* http://www.tribnet.com/.

Gardner and Mike Lowry both had to deal with the often-explosive controversies between these two groups, and such controversies continue even today. One way that the executive branch under Governor Lowry sought to resolve this issue was through the development of the Habitat Conservation Plan of 1996, which was designed to implement a more comprehensive strategy for dealing with the spotted owl habitats. This plan would rectify the more piecemeal efforts made in the past and would help establish clear standards and approaches to

WEST VIRGINIA

• • • • • • • • • • • • •

WEST VIRGINIA ELECTED EXECUTIVE BRANCH OFFICIALS

Governor	Attorney General
Auditor	Commissioner of Agriculture
Secretary of State	Treasurer

http://www.wv.gov/

• • • • • • • • • • • • •

Since West Virginia broke off from its sister state at the beginning of the Civil War over the issue of secession, it has shared similarities with other states in many aspects of its politics and government. Yet there is a distinctiveness to West Virginia, for the state has enjoyed the richness of coal while suffering the burden of Appalachian poverty. Indeed, it is a state filled with differences. Only 24,000 square miles in size (the ninth-smallest state in the Union), it has seven distinct regions within its borders. And it is one of only thirteen states in the country where a majority of the population lives in nonmetropolitan areas. Clearly, individuals elected to serve as West Virginia's chief executive must oversee a diverse state.

The executive branch for the state of West Virginia is composed of a governor, secretary of state, auditor, treasurer, commissioner of agriculture, and attorney general, all of whom are popularly elected in presidential election years. Only the governor is limited to two consecutive terms (of four years each), but he or she may seek the office after sitting out one term. West Virginia is unusual in that it has no lieutenant governor. If the governor is incapacitated or must leave the office, the president of the state senate is next in the line of succession, followed by the speaker of the house of delegates. If the governor dies, is impeached and convicted, resigns, or is disabled in the first three years of his or her term of office, a new election is held to fill the position. Unlike other states, there are no constitutional requirements regarding age or residency for statewide executive offices.

The governor holds the "chief executive power" of the state and may give a message "of the condition of the state," typically called the state of the state address. In addition, he or she can present the legislature with a budget message for programs and policies. Originally, the governor shared this power of preparing the budget with a Board of Public Works, which consisted of all the statewide executive officers and a superintendent of schools. However, in 1968, West Virginians approved a constitutional amendment that gave the governor sole power to prepare the state's budget. The governor can also call a special session of the legislature, which can only consider the matters outlined by the chief executive.

The governor has the power of appointment, with the advice and consent of a majority of the state senate. West Virginia's governor has appointment power over seven "supersecretaries," which comprise the governor's cabinet. The cabinet oversees policy areas such as commerce, education and the arts, health and human services, public safety, tax and revenue, transportation, and administration. The governor can also make a recess appointment, much like the U.S. president; however, if the appointee is rejected by the state senate, the governor can name that same individual as a recess appointment when the senate goes into recess.

Like other governors, the West Virginia chief executive has the constitutional power of commuting sentences of capital punishment and pardoning other sentences, but he or she must communicate to the legislature the reasons behind the granting of a pardon or commuting of a death sentence.

Also like his or her peers in other states, the governor of West Virginia has the power to veto legislation; the legislature may override that veto with a two-thirds majority of elected members in both chambers. Like the nation's chief executive, the governor must take action within five days or it will automatically become law. The governor also has the power to exercise a line-item veto over appropriations bills, and unlike many other state chief executives, the West Virginia governor can "reduce veto" an appropriations item. In other words, the governor can reduce the amount of appropriations in a budget bill, and the legislature can reconsider that reduction and override the governor's action if it chooses to do so.

In 1970, the voters of West Virginia approved the governor's succession amendment to the state constitution, thereby allowing the chief executive to run for two consecutive terms of four years each. This move reduced the likelihood that one-term governors would be automatically labeled lame ducks once they assumed office. West Virginia governors can serve for two terms, sit out a term, and then run for reelection if they desire. Surprisingly, West Virginia's sister state continues to limit its governor to one term.

The office of secretary of state is regarded as a potential stepping stone to the governor's office. The secretary of state is responsible for overseeing elections and voter registration in the state, as well as maintaining state records and regulations. The attorney general of West Virginia provides legal counsel to all state agencies and defends the state in lawsuits. He or she is also responsible for administering consumer protection programs and prosecuting those charged with consumer fraud.

The two state financial officers are the state treasurer and state auditor. The treasurer oversees all financial transactions for the state, including deposits and payments. The treasurer also maintains a record of all appropriations made by the legislature, in addition to overseeing the investment of state funds. The state auditor, by contrast, is responsible for ensuring that all financial transactions are proper, as well as administering Social Security payments. The state auditor receives tax revenues from sheriffs and public utility taxes for the state and counties. The West Virginia commissioner of agriculture is responsible for inspecting agricultural products in the state; regulating pesticides; and collecting and publishing data regarding the state's climate, soils, and natural resources.

In the event of a vacancy in the other executive offices, the governor may fill the office with an appointee until the next election. Beyond the formal, or constitutional, powers, West Virginia governors, like other chief executives, have informal powers at their disposal. Most recent governors have had a background in either the state legislature or other political office. Often, like other governors, West Virginia's chief executive must rely on the power of persuasion to achieve his or her policy goals. This tool is a particularly useful one, especially since the governor's office is located in the state capitol building: the chief executive can interact with legislative leaders on a daily basis when the legislature is in session.

The legislature can impeach officials, including the governor, based on "maladministration, corruption, incompetency, gross immorality, neglect of duty, or any high crime or misdemeanor." The state house of delegates impeaches the official, while the state senate serves as the venue for his or her trial and conviction. The president of the state supreme court of appeals sits as the presiding officer in the senate while the trial is conducted. To convict and remove an official, the state senate must vote to do so by a two-thirds majority of the members. Most recently, State Treasurer A. James Manchin was impeached by the house of delegates in 1989 when the state's investment fund lost $279 million in junk bond investments. Manchin resigned his office prior to the trial in the state senate.

J. Michael Bitzer

References
Brisbin, Richard A., Jr., Robert Jay Dilger, Allan S. Hammock, and Christopher J. Mooney. 1996. *West Virginia politics and government.* Lincoln: University of Nebraska Press.
West Virginia Constitution of 1872, Art. 7.

Additional Resources and Recommended Readings
Morgan, John C. 1980. *West Virginia governors, 1863–1980*, 2nd ed. Charleston, WV: Charleston Newspapers.

WISCONSIN
• • • • • • • • • • • •

WISCONSIN ELECTED EXECUTIVE BRANCH OFFICIALS

Governor	Lieutenant Governor
Attorney General	Superintendent of Public Instruction
Secretary of State	Treasurer

http://www.wisconsin.gov/

• • • • • • • • • • • •

Wisconsin has been predominantly Republican for most of its history, which befits a state credited, along with Michigan, with establishing the Republican Party. Although Wisconsin voters chose two Democrats and a Whig in the first eight years of statehood after entering the Union in 1848, they became devoutly Republican after the new party competed for the first time in 1856. Like voters in many northern states following the Civil War, Wisconsin voters "equated Republicanism with patriotism and respectability" (Epstein 1958, 35). This approach continued well into the twentieth century as electors picked twenty-six Republicans, three Democrats, and one Progressive as governors through 1958. In this 102-year period, Republicans served as the state's chief executive in all but twelve years (Democrats, 1875–1877, 1891–1895, and 1933–1935; the Progressive, 1935–1939).

Conservative Republicans, backed by lumber interests and railroads, controlled the state through the nineteenth century. But their exploitive policies "left a legacy of land denuded of its forest cover and a people embittered at the excesses of the business community" and led to the election of reform-oriented Republican Robert La Follette as governor in 1900 (Fenton 1966, 72). For the next three decades, Wisconsin politics became a factional battle between progressive Republican reformers and conservative or stalwart Republican regulars, with Democrats a distinct and largely ineffective minority. Wisconsin Democrats achieved rare and modest successes only on those occasions when stalwart Republican voters defected to their side rather than support La Follette-backed candidates.

For his part, La Follette attempted to institute "no-party politics," apparently believing that political parties served to "pervert the real will of the voters" (Epstein 1958, 35). La Follette achieved not only the introduction of the open primary but also the enactment of legislation banning the nomination of candidates by organized parties. As late as the 1960s, Wisconsin political parties had no statutory structure but instead functioned as extralegal organizations. La Follette's influ-

Reformist governor Robert La Follette of Wisconsin garnered 17 percent of the popular vote in his 1924 bid for president under the Progressive Party label. (Library of Congress)

ence over Wisconsin Republican politics continued after he moved to the national scene, first as a U.S. senator in 1905 and later as a Progressive candidate for president in 1924. In that election, La Follette carried only his home state's electoral votes but gained 17 percent of the popular vote, the best showing for a minor party candidate between 1912 (Theodore Roosevelt) and 1992 (H. Ross Perot). Following La Follette's death in 1925, Robert Jr., succeeded his father in the U.S. Senate and was elected in his own right in 1928. La Follette's other son, Philip, took up his interest in state politics. Philip was elected governor as a Republican in 1930 but lost his renomination bid in 1932, a victim of his ambitious social program. Governor La Follette's defeat ushered in a transitional period in Wisconsin politics, which ran from 1932 to 1946.

A conservative resurgence in Republican ranks threatened the political careers of both La Follettes in 1934, and each sought election successfully under a reconstituted Progressive organization that had the tacit support of President Franklin Roosevelt. Governor Philip La Follette won another term in 1936 but suffered a career-ending defeat two years later when the Democratic candidate withdrew to support the Republican nominee. After the successful Progressive gubernatorial candidate in 1942 died before taking office and the party could not field a viable candidate in 1944, organization leaders decided to abandon their separate movement and rejoin the Republicans in 1946. Also in that year, Senator Robert La Follette Jr. lost the Republican primary to Joseph McCarthy. The particular brand of extreme conservatism symbolized by McCarthy caused many progressive and liberal voters to gravitate to the Democrats.

Wisconsin Democrats emerged as a viable political entity in 1958, moving the state from a modified one-party Republican categorization to a competitive two-party status. Democrats perhaps even became the new majority party, winning five of the next seven gubernatorial elections and eight of the next ten presidential races. Through the governor's term ending with the election of 2006, six Democrats served as chief executive for a total of twenty-two years, and three Republicans held the office for twenty-six years. The Republican edge in length of service is attributable to Governor Tommy Thompson, who served fourteen years of his four terms before accepting a cabinet position in Washington, D.C., in 2001. Governor James Doyle,

elected in 2002, is the twelfth Democrat chief executive; his other predecessors consisted of thirty-four Republicans, one Whig, and one Progressive.

These governors possessed partisan and philosophical differences, but all operated under virtually the same state charter. Wisconsin continues to function under its constitution of 1848, which is the sixth oldest in the country, surpassed in longevity only by the constitutions of five New England states. While the Wisconsin document has been amended more than 130 times, few of these amendments have affected the executive branch. The Wisconsin governor remains restricted by the Jacksonian democratic tradition of electing many administrative positions, creating a number of governing commissions, and limiting appointment authority.

Operating under constitutional directives drafted more than 150 years ago, the Wisconsin governor transacts all necessary business; takes care that the laws are faithfully executed; serves as commander-in-chief of the state's military and naval forces; and grants reprieves, commutations, and pardons for all offenses except treason and cases of impeachment. The governor must communicate the condition of the state to lawmakers at each session and recommend measures for their consideration as he or she deems expedient. The governor may call the legislature into special session and convene the lawmakers at any suitable place in the case of invasion or "danger from the prevalence of contagious disease at the seat of government."

Candidates for governor and lieutenant governor must be U.S. citizens and qualified voters. Since 1970, they are elected on a joint ballot and may serve an unlimited number of four-year terms. Prior to the constitutional change, voters elected these two officials separately for two-year terms. The other significant constitutional change involves the extent of the governor's veto power. Wisconsin's constitution originally provided that the governor had to act within six days (excepting Sundays) after receiving a bill by signing the measure into law or vetoing it or exercising an item veto that was intended to apply to appropriations bills. To the surprise of the Democratic-controlled legislature in 1987, conservative Republican governor Thompson creatively employed the item veto over nonappropriations bills by striking out individual letters and numbers to create new words and meanings and alter legislative intent. And to the further surprise of the Democratic legislature, the state supreme court in 1988 upheld his action (Beyle 2004). The governor continues to have the power to strike individual words from legislation.

The legislature responded by proposing a constitutional amendment prohibiting such vetoes. Approved in 1990 by a 62 percent vote, the amendment specifically states that "in approving an appropriation bill in part, the governor may not create a new word by rejecting individual letters in the words of the enrolled bill." Accordingly, the governor now may sign or veto any bill in its entirety and approve appropriations bills "in whole or in part," with the vetoed bills or portions subject to override by a two-thirds vote of the members present in both legislative houses. Any bill not returned by the governor within the six-day time frame becomes law without his or her signature unless the legislature has adjourned.

The governor and all civil officers may be impeached for "corrupt conduct in office, or for crimes and misdemeanors" by a majority of all members elected to the lower house. A vote of two-thirds of members present in the upper house is necessary for conviction. The lieutenant governor becomes governor on the governor's death, resignation, or removal from office. Further, the lieutenant governor serves as acting governor whenever the governor is absent from the state, is incapable of performing the duties of the office due to "mental or physical disease," or is impeached. This officer continues to serve "until the governor returns, the disability ceases or the impeachment is vacated." The secretary of state serves as acting governor if there is a vacancy in the office of lieutenant governor. Significantly, there is no constitutional provision for any outside agency to determine whether a governor is mentally or physically disabled.

Recent constitutional changes only slightly improved the rating of Wisconsin governors among their peers in terms of their formal powers. Before extending the term to four years and clarifying the veto power, Wisconsin's chief executive ranked in the lower half of the nation's governors; following these changes, the governor ranked just above the midpoint as a "moderately strong" chief executive. However, history shows that Wisconsin governors across the political spectrum, from the progressive Robert La Follette Sr. to the conservative Tommy Thompson, can combine their personal abilities with constitutional language to impose their will on the state. The rise of competitive politics and increased national-state conflict in recent years indicates that future Wisconsin chief executives will need to take a strong leadership role.

James McDowell

References

Beyle, Thad. 2004. The governors. In *Politics in the American states: A comparative analysis,* 8th ed., ed. Virginia Gray and Russell L. Hanson, 194–231. Washington, DC: Congressional Quarterly Press.

Epstein, Leon D. 1958. *Politics in Wisconsin.* Madison: University of Wisconsin Press.

Fenton, John H. 1966. *Midwest politics.* New York: Holt, Rinehart and Winston.

Key, V. O., Jr. 1956. *American state politics: An introduction.* New York: Knopf.

Philip, Emanuel L. 1973. *Political reform in Wisconsin.* Madison: State Historical Society of Wisconsin.

Schlesinger, Arthur M., Jr. 1960. *The politics of upheaval.* Boston: Houghton Mifflin.

Wisconsin Constitution of 1848.

Additional Resources and Recommended Readings

Loftus, Tom. 1994. *The art of legislative politics.* Washington, DC: Congressional Quarterly Press.

Miller, John E. 1982. *Governor Philip F. La Follette, the Wisconsin progressives, and the New Deal.* Columbia: University of Missouri Press.

WYOMING

• • • • • • • • • • • •

WYOMING ELECTED EXECUTIVE BRANCH OFFICIALS

Governor   Auditor
Secretary of State
Superintendent of Public Instruction
Treasurer
http://wyoming.gov/

• • • • • • • • • • • •

Is Wyoming the Equality State or the Cowboy State? These nicknames reflect the two different political identities the state has had throughout its history. On one hand, Wyoming has a progressive history, leading the nation in a number of efforts to bring about gender equality. It was the first state to grant women the right to vote and hold elected office, in 1869. And on January 5, 1925, Nellie Tayloe Ross was sworn in as the first female governor in the United States. Governor Ross was convinced to run for office after her husband, William B. Ross, died while serving as governor on October 2, 1924. Although she was defeated in her bid for reelection in 1926, her historic legacy helped to advance the movement for gender equality by leaps and bounds throughout the rest of the nation. On the other hand, the traditional, rugged image of the Wyoming cowboy in the frontier West persists and continues to draw tourists from all over the world (tourism is one of the state's largest industries). However, while attempting to maintain this Old West image, the government of Wyoming has had to take numerous steps to support an agricultural industry that has been on the decline since 1919, for it clings to a number of outdated policies and programs that threaten the economic stability and future of the state.

The tension between progressivism and traditionalism is just one of the unique elements of Wyoming's political environment that help to explain the challenges facing the state's executive. Additionally, although it is the tenth-largest state in terms of area, Wyoming continues to be the least populous state in the Union. In 2003, its estimated population was only around 500,000 people. And because the federal government owns nearly half of the roughly 98,000 square miles that comprise the state, Wyoming often finds itself dependent on and at the mercy of various federal policies that greatly affect it and a number of its western neighbors. The historical and political contexts are, therefore, crucial to understanding the role of the state executive branch in the state that is "what the West was."

The supreme power of the state executive branch is vested in the office of the governor. To qualify for this office, a person must be at least thirty years old, have resided in the state for five years prior to the election, and be a qualified state elector. The governor is not eligible to hold any other offices during his or her elected term. The chief executive is elected by simple majority, and in the event of a tie, both houses of the state legislature decide who will hold the office at the start of their regular session.

A number of the governor's responsibilities, just like the standards and qualifications for election, mirror those in any typical U.S. state. The governor is

Nellie Tayloe Ross served Wyoming from 1925 to 1927 as the nation's first elected female governor. (Library of Congress)

charged with upholding and executing state law and is commander-in-chief of the state's military forces, except when they are under direct orders from the federal government. The governor is also responsible for delivering a state of the state message before both legislative houses prior to the start of each session. Further, he or she has the ability to appoint officials to vacant offices in which there is no means for filling the office prescribed by law. In these ways, the Wyoming governor's power is much the same as that of a chief executive in any other state. However, in regard to the governor's pardoning powers, the state legislature has the right to determine how pardons, reprieves, commutations, and remissions may be applied for, which does limit the governor's ability to exercise these powers to some extent. Additionally, during each regular session, the governor is required by law to report any use of the pardoning power to the legislature, along with his or her reasons for issuing the pardon.

The governor of Wyoming has two forms of veto power, depending on the type of legislative action that is under consideration. For matters of state law, he or she will either approve a bill or send it back to the originating house for reconsideration. If, after reviewing the governor's recommendations, two-thirds of the originating house votes to override the veto, the bill is sent to the second house. If the second house also votes to override with a two-thirds majority, the bill is submitted into law. Thus, for issues of law, the governor has a blanket, "yes-or-no" type of veto power. For issues of appropriation (either money or property), however, the governor is granted line-item veto powers. Accordingly, he or she can choose a part or parts of a bill to remove, rather than being required to either accept or reject the bill in its entirety. In cases where the governor uses the line-item powers, the state legislature is required to follow the same process of review for each item separately if it wishes to overturn the governor's veto.

The issue of bribery and coercion by the state's supreme executive is given a full, detailed treatment in the state's constitution. According to Article 4, Section 10, if a governor is found guilty of any form of bribery (including receiving compensation of any form in exchange for an appointment or the use of the chief executive's power to further some end) or coercion against members of the legislature or other state officials, he or she is stripped of the right to hold "any office of trust or honor" in the state of Wyoming.

Four other executive officials—the secretary of state, state auditor, treasurer, and superintendent of public instruction—are elected to serve the people of Wyoming. Each of these officials must be at least twenty-five years of age and a citizen of the United States, and he or she must meet all the same qualifications as state electors. The term of office for these officials, like the governor's, is four years, and they are not term limited. Like only a few other states, Wyoming has no lieutenant governor. Therefore, the secretary of state is next in the line of succession behind the governor.

The Wyoming secretary of state also plays a number of important roles in determining and reporting the rules and regulations of the state. The secretary is charged with overseeing various administrative divisions, including the corporations, elections, notaries, securities, and rules divisions of the state.

As a gubernatorial appointee, the attorney general of the state of Wyoming is responsible for performing a variety of public services. Although confined by law to offering legal advice and rulings to public officials only, the attorney general plays an important role in the lives of average citizens by overseeing a number of legal administrative divisions (ranging from general civil law to criminal law and more specific tort issues and consumer protection) and law enforcement divisions. Following national reforms and security efforts in response to the September 11, 2001, terrorist attacks, the attorney general also oversees state implementation of homeland security regulations and efforts to inform the people of security issues in the event of an emergency. This responsibility is of particular importance in a state that houses major missile technology at F. E. Warren Air Force Base in Cheyenne. Finally, the attorney general is responsible for dealing with the legal issues behind controversies such as wolf reintroduction, electronic gambling and lottery proposals, and the permissibility and -regulation of snowmobiles in Yellowstone National Park.

The primary function of the state auditor of Wyoming is to perform statewide accounting services and to record and report financial records. Further, the auditor has bureaucratic duties in managing the state's payroll and records. Such services place a large amount of budgetary responsibility with this elected official.

Similar to the state auditor, the state treasurer provides statewide financial and budgetary services. However, the treasurer's primary responsibility is to reinvest state revenues so as to increase the return on moneys generated through taxes and other sources. In 2005, state treasurer Cynthia Lummis's office reported that the treasury had, over the course of the previous biennium, generated an additional $5 billion for the state through investments—approximately $1,000 per worker per year (http://treasurer.state.wy.us/). This investment helps to alleviate some of the tax burdens shouldered by citizens of the state and increase the financial capacities of the government.

An additional item of note in regard to the legislative oversight of the executive branch is the ability of the legislature to review all of the accounts under the control of all of the state's public treasurers, as well as the clerks of the state court system at all levels. This function provides an additional form of legislative check on executive action and a degree of transparency to spending and fiscal allocation.

One of the most important roles the governor must play is as that of mediator and advocate for the state in relation to the federal government. Because there is so much federal control over land in Wyoming, much of the state's economic and resource base is linked to Washington. For example, F. E. Warren Air Force Base, located in the capital city, is a major employer and resource generator for the state. Warren became the first home for the Atlas intercontinental ballistic missiles in 1958, and it continues to be of significance in terms of the national defense. The state in turn relies on the operations at Warren to preserve the economic activities of its capital city. Additionally, Teddy Roosevelt laid the foundation for the state's tourist industry when he proclaimed Yellowstone to be the country's first national park. However, despite the economic benefits the state receives from the federal government, the highly conservative political outlook of the citizens of the Wyoming makes them leery of governmental mandates and regulations. As a consequence, the governor must perform a delicate balancing act to keep the citizens satisfied by standing up to the federal government while being careful not to bite the hand that continues to feed much of the state.

Finally, because so much of the state's political power rests in the hands of agriculture producers, the governor must maintain strong relations with members of that industry. Ultimately, though, the economic future of the state may well lie elsewhere. For example, the Powder River Basin in northeastern Wyoming has a vast coal bed that produces methane gas. In time, this area of the state could end up being the site of North America's largest natural gas operation, which suggests the wealth that could be generated by concentrating more development in the state's rich, natural resources. The key for the governor is to strike a balance with these industries in order to solidify his or her own base of support, while furthering the state's economic hopes for the future. So, as in the past, Wyoming's governor must mediate between the often-competing streams of progressivism and traditionalism in the nation's "cowboy-equality" state.

Joseph J. Foy

References

Larson, T. A. 1978. *History of Wyoming,* 2nd ed. rev. Lincoln: University of Nebraska Press.

Powder River Basin Resource Council. 2004. *Powder River Basin Resource Council on the World Wide Web.* http://www.powderriverbasin.org/.

U.S. Census Bureau. 2004. *State and county QuickFacts: Wyoming.* http://quickfacts.census.gov/qfd/states/56000.html.

Western, Samuel. 2002. *Pushed off the mountain, sold down the river: Wyoming's search for its soul.* Moose, WY, Denver, and San Francisco: Homestead.

Wyoming State Constitution of 1889, Art. 4.

Additional Resources and Recommended Readings

Cawley, Gregg, Michael Horan, Larry Hubbell, James King, and Robert Schuhmann. 2000. *The equality state: Government and politics in Wyoming,* 4th ed. Dubuque, IA: Eddie Bowers.

Hendrickson, Gordon O. 1983. *Living Wyoming's past.* Boulder, CO: Pruett.

Roberts, Philip J., David L. Roberts, and Steven L. Roberts. 1990. *Wyoming almanac.* Laramie, WY, and Seattle: Skyline West.

State of Wyoming, Governor's Office, official web page of the governor of Wyoming. 2004. http://wyoming.gov/governor/governor_home.asp.

Wyoming Recreation Commission. 1976. *Wyoming: A guide to historic sites.* Basin, WY: Big Horn.

GLOSSARY OF COMMON EXECUTIVE TERMS

Agenda setting: Placing issues onto the public agenda for consideration by lawmakers. While any number of issues could be brought forward for government action, only a limited number actually make it to the agenda. Governors are sometimes considered the chief agenda setters because they are better able than any other actors to bring issues forward for consideration.

Amendatory veto: A type of veto that allows the governor to return a bill to the legislature with recommended amendments. If the legislature agrees to the changes, the governor signs the bill into law. A governor sometimes uses this veto to bring together different parts of multiple bills to formulate a single, unified law. If the legislature accepts the proposed amendments, the governor has effectively shaped the legislation after the legislature had completed the lawmaking process. Also referred to as an executive amendment.

Appointment power: The power of the governor to name officials to the executive branch or to the courts. Often, appointments must be approved by some other governmental actor, such as the state senate. This power is particularly useful for governors as they attempt to manage the executive branch.

Apportionment: The drawing of the lines that demarcate state legislative districts, U.S. House of Representative districts, and so forth. This process is performed by state legislatures. Though lines should be drawn to create districts that are roughly equal in population and to keep communities intact, legislators often consider political goals, such as creating districts to protect incumbents or a political party. Various court decisions outline how districts must be created. States can no longer take race into consideration when drawing the lines (except to draw districts with a majority of minority group members). Districts must also encompass as equal as possible a number of people; this rule, brought about by the U.S. Supreme Court decision in *Baker v. Carr,* caused state legislative districts to more fairly represent urban areas.

Articles of Confederation: The first constitution of the United States, ratified in March 1781. Under this constitution, the United States was a confederacy, or a "loose association of states." The states retained nearly all power; the central government had very little. The Articles did not create an environment in which the new country could thrive, especially since the central government had no power to regulate interstate commerce. Because of the shortcomings of the

Articles, a new constitution, the current U.S. Constitution, was drafted to replace it. The Articles were important in that they reflected the early nation's desire to limit central power and vest most power in the states.

Attorney general: The chief legal officer and crime fighter of the state. The powers and activities of the office vary across the states but often include representing the state in court appearances, issuing legal opinions, protecting consumers, and, more recently, creating no-call lists to ban telemarketing calls.

Auditor: The state official responsible for assuring that state dollars have been spent or invested in accordance with state law.

Blanket primary: A variation of the open primary that allows voters to participate in the primaries of both parties (though not for the same office). In a blanket primary, a voter might, for example, participate in the Democratic primary for governor, in the Republican primary for U.S. senator, and in the Democratic primary for U.S. House member.

Brown v. Board of Education of Topeka, KS: A landmark Supreme Court decision handed down in 1954. As a result of this decision, the separate-but-equal rule that was established in *Plessy v. Ferguson* was rejected. Separate but equal was the legal standard that had been used to justify the separation of the races and the treatment of African Americans as second-class citizens under the law. *Brown* required that public schools be integrated with "all deliberate speed." Though the process took many years, separate but equal was no longer the law of the land, and no state could claim it was a legitimate policy.

Bully pulpit: An executive office, especially the presidency, is sometimes referred to as a bully pulpit, a phrase attributed to President Theodore Roosevelt. The term suggests that the executive office is a platform from which to promote an agenda. Executives have access to the public and the media and can capitalize on this access to advocate for their goals.

Bureaucracy: In the generic sense, this is a type of organization marked by a hierarchical arrangement of people and offices and a division of labor. The phrase *the bureaucracy* is often employed to refer to the many employees and offices of the executive branch that are charged with implementing the law. Though the idea of bureaucracy is often disliked by citizens, research has shown that bureaucracy is usually a good way to accomplish a great many repetitive tasks in a timely and fair manner.

Cabinet: The group of high-level executive branch officials who surround the chief executive—the president or the governor. The cabinet traditionally serves as an advisory body to the chief executive. In some states, the cabinet exercises independent power; and the governor must get approval of the cabinet for certain decisions.

Chief executive: One of the roles of the governor, involving overseeing the execution or implementation of state law.

Chief judge: Another role played by many governors, which entails the power to grant clemency to convicted offenders (lessening their sentences) or, in extraordinary situations, to overturn the convictions of those believed to be wrongfully convicted. Governors also often participate in parole decisions, related to releasing certain prisoners before their sentences are completed.

Chief legislator: Among the most important roles of a governor, whereby he or she works to establish the agenda that the legislature will consider and helps to construct policy solutions to problems facing the states.

Chief of party: A role played by the governor as the highest elected official in the state. As head of the party organization in his or her state, the governor attends party functions and raises money for the party's candidates. The governor may also serve an internal leadership role, working out disputes among factions within the party that might weaken the organization if not addressed.

Chief of state (head of state):   A largely symbolic role of the governor, whereby he or she serves as a symbol of the state, embodying the state to those outside the state's boundaries.

Closed primary: A type of primary in which states tightly control which voters are allowed to participate. States with closed primaries typically require that only voters who have previously registered as members of a party may vote in that party's primaries.

Colonial governors: Leaders of states during the colonial period. These officials were appointed by the king of England, and they exercised substantial legal authority. Due to the experience of the states with such powerful governors, early state constitutions established weak governorships with little formal power.

Comptroller (controller):   The executive branch official responsible for ensuring that planned departmental expenditures are in accordance with state law and do not exceed appropriations made by the legislature.

Congressional delegation: The members of Congress who represent a particular state. Governors often attempt to work with their delegations to influence national policy for the benefit of their states.

Contracting out: As a means of saving money, states sometimes accept bids for the provision of public services and enter into contracts with the lowest bidders. Contracting out is believed to deliver services in a more efficient and less costly way, though the actual success of the practice is not fully established.

Crisis manager: One of the key roles of the governor, which entails taking charge of events when crises such as hurricanes, droughts, or riots occur.

Depression (the Great Depression):   A worldwide economic slump that began in 1929 and continued into the 1930s. In the United States, it led to high levels of unemployment, plummeting stock prices, and massive numbers of business failures. This period also included an extreme drought that most significantly affected the middle and western parts of the United States. In the midst of the Depression, President Herbert Hoover was defeated for reelection and Franklin Roosevelt was elected largely in the hope that he could pull the country out of the worst depression the world had ever experienced.

Devolution: The process of devolving, or moving, responsibility for certain governmental services from the national government to the states. Devolution is believed to improve services because the states (and localities) are closer to the populations, better aware of their needs, and therefore better able to provide for them. Devolution has been a popular concept in the late twentieth and early twenty-first centuries, though some argue that little devolution of power has actually taken place.

Divided government: Divided party control of government, wherein the governor's party is in a minority in one or both chambers of the state legislature.

Enabling powers: The support services provided to governors to help them carry out the many duties of the office. Enabling powers include access to staff and other office and administrative support.

Endorsements: The nominations process for choosing nominees gives voters who identify with a party the power to choose its nominee. As part of this nominations process, endorsements are used in some states to give party leaders a chance to designate their preferred candidates before the party voters go to the polls. The power of these endorsements to influence which nominees are chosen varies across the states.

Executive amendment: See *Amendatory veto*

Executive budget: A budget document prepared by the governor's office (often with the help of other executive branch officials). The executive budget gives the governor the opportunity to present a unified statement of his or her spending priorities. State legislatures typically have nearly unlimited power to alter the budget once they receive it.

Executive orders: The power of an executive such as a governor to single-handedly make changes in how laws are executed. This power typically applies to decisions being made by executive branch officials.

Federal government: The national government in Washington, D.C., including the president, the U.S. Congress, and the U.S. Supreme Court.

Federalism: A system of government in which there are multiple sovereign governments. In the United States, federalism refers to the fact that the national government in Washington, D.C., and the governments of the fifty states all have the power to make law as defined by the U.S. Constitution. This form of government replaced the confederation created in the first constitution, the Articles of Confederation.

Formal powers index: A method of categorizing the powers of the governors, created by Joseph Schlesinger and modified and updated by various other scholars. The index includes four elements: tenure potential, the veto, appointment power, and budget power.

Going negative: The use of negative campaigning, or running ads focusing on supposed negative traits of the opponent rather than the positive traits of the candidate creating the ads. Though citizens often complain about the prevalence of negative campaigning, research shows they respond to it. However, excessive levels of negative ads may suppress turnout.

Good-Time Charlies: A term employed to refer to early governors who had little ambition, few formal powers, and questionable credentials for office.

Governor's office staff: The people who surround the governor and help to run the office. Staffs have grown significantly, though they vary from state to state. While early governors had only one or two secretaries, modern governors have large, professional staffs that assist with public relations, legislative relations, the media, and the flow of correspondence into the governor's office.

Great seal: A symbol used by states to give the official stamp of legitimacy to state documents. The power to affix the seal to official state documents is often held by the secretary of state.

Homeland security: A term associated with the period following the terrorist bombings of September 11, 2001. It refers to the governmental responsibility to keep the country safe from external or internal attacks. States hold much of the responsibility for homeland security.

Ideology: Broadly speaking, the way in which a person views the world or, in the present context, whether they are more liberal or more conservative. Liberals more commonly associate with the Democratic Party, and conservatives more often associate with the Republican Party. Ideology is a good predictor of how a person will vote; voters choose the candidate they believe to be closer to them ideologically.

Impeachment: A method of removing a public official before his or her term is completed. One body (typically a lower house of the legislature) has the power to impeach, or bring charges against, the official. This body conducts an investigation and drafts the charges, much like a grand jury in a criminal case. Another body has the power to try the official on the impeachment charges. Punishment is removal from office. Impeachment is typically reserved for extreme cases involving abuse of the office or other illegal activity, since legislators usually defer to the decision of the voters who chose the official.

Incumbent: One who holds an office. Incumbency is beneficial in the electoral process because incumbents typically have a host of benefits that their challengers lack, such as experience, name recognition, and the ability to raise large amounts of campaign funds. Incumbents are therefore usually hard to defeat.

Interest group: An association of individuals or organizations that share a common concern and attempt to influence public policy in that regard. An interest group may also be a public or private institution.

Intergovernmental liaison: One of the responsibilities of the governor, which entails monitoring the actions of the national government and representing the interests of the state and state government to national government decision makers.

Intergovernmental relations: Interactions occurring between governmental units of all types and levels within the U.S. federal system.

Iron triangle: The idea that interest groups, legislative committee members, and agency officials concerned with the same policy area can work together to determine policy in their area. Given this established set of relationships, it is very difficult for others, including the governor, to influence policy in this area.

Issue network: Similar to iron triangles, but instead of including only three sets of actors, issue networks recognize a broader collection of multiple actors concerned with a particular policy area.

Jacksonian democracy: A variant of democracy that evolved during a period in U.S. history when the "common man" first came to participate in government. The name comes from the presidency of Andrew Jackson. Various reforms intended to increase participation by the masses (rather than the elite) were adopted by the states and the national government during this period.

Ku Klux Klan: Originally an organization started by former Confederate soldiers to oppose the reforms forced on the South by federal troops after the Civil War. Since that time, the name has been adopted by various organizations that have taught racism and white supremacy. These groups were particularly active during the 1960s in opposition to changes brought about by the civil rights movement. They used violence and threats of violence in attemtps to maintain the status quo.

Legislative liaison: An official designated within an executive agency to facilitate interaction with the state legislature.

Legislative override: The ability of a legislature to overturn a governor's veto. A successful override typically requires a supermajority of legislators rather than a simple majority of 50 percent plus one.

Legislative professionalism: A term that refers to the capacity of state legislatures. Professionalized legislatures meet in session more days than their amateur counterparts, pay their members enough so that they can make this work their full-time job, and provide members with other resources needed to support them as they perform their duties. Professional legislatures are expected to be able to produce better law. However, some critics worry that professional legislators become too removed from their constituents at home; these observers often advocate for term limits, which are expected to result in greater turnover of membership.

Legislative-executive relations: The interactions between legislators or legislatures and the governor of the state. Since each state has a separation-of-powers arrangement with checks and balances, governors and legislatures must work together to pass law. However, relations are often complex and conflictual because governors and legislators often have different goals and priorities. Conflict is even more likely when the governor and the majority of the legislature do not share a party affiliation.

Legislature: The lawmaking body in the state. In all states but one (Nebraska), the legislature is bicameral, meaning it is divided into two chambers. The names of the legislature and the chambers vary across the states.

Lieutenant governor: The state official who is typically next in line to the governor and is sometimes, but not always, elected on a ticket with the governor. The duties of this official vary. In some states, the only real responsibility is to become governor if the chief executive can no longer serve or to cast a vote in the state senate in the case of a tie. In other states, the lieutenant governor has substantial legislative power.

Line-item veto: A type of veto that allows a governor to strike portions of a bill that he or she opposes while leaving the rest of the bill intact to become law on his or her signature.

Little Rock Central High School: The scene of intense racial unrest in 1957 when attempts were made to integrate this all-white school. A showdown ensued between segregationist governor Orval Faubus and President Dwight Eisenhower. Members of the army's 101st Airborne Division, deployed by the president, finally escorted nine black children into the school.

Lobbyists: Individuals, often working for interest groups, who attempt to influence the decision making of public officials. Lobbying is most often associated with efforts to influence the legislature, but lobbyists often target executive branch officials as well.

Long ballot: A lengthy ballot that results from the tendency in some states to elect multiple statewide executive officers, rather than allowing the governor to appoint them.

Long dynasty, Louisiana: The political dynasty associated with Governors Huey and Earl Long of Louisiana. Politics in Louisiana continued to be divided into pro- and anti-Long factions into the twentieth century.

Mandate: A claim by an elected official, especially a governor, that the election granted him or her the right to pursue some policy goal. When elected by a large margin, a governor will claim the public is clearly behind his or her policy goals and that the legislature should follow their lead.

Merit system: A method of filling offices in the executive branch based on skills and credentials rather than political connections. Often referred to as the civil service plan, the merit system replaced the spoils systems that had given out government jobs as patronage (political rewards).

Military chief: One of the roles of the governor, associated with being the commander-in-chief and head of the National Guard or militia of the state. Governors are responsible for the health and safety of the state citizens. Under certain extreme circumstances, they may use the military chief power to suspend local authority, seize personal property, direct evacuations, and authorize emergency funds.

Missouri Plan: A method of appointing state judges that involves a combination of appointment and election. Though the specifics of the method vary from state to state, the governor usually selects a judge from among a list of names generated by a nominating committee. After some defined interval, the judge faces the public in a retention election, where the voters choose to retain or remove the judge. This plan is a compromise designed to assure both that qualified judges are chosen and that the public has a say in keeping or removing judges from the bench.

Name recognition: The tendency of the public to be familiar with a candidate by name. Voters must recognize a candidate's name before they are willing to vote for that person. Incumbents typically have much better name recognition than challengers.

National Conference of State Legislatures: A bipartisan organization that serves the legislators and staffs of the states, commonwealths, and territories by providing research, technical assistance, and opportunities for policymakers to exchange ideas on the pressing state issues.

National government: The central government in Washington, D.C., including the U.S. president, the Congress, the Supreme Court, and the bureaucracy.

National Governors Association (NGA):   An organization of the nation's governors that provides the governors' offices with a variety of services, such as representing states on Capitol Hill and before the administration on key federal issues, developing policy reports on innovative state programs, and hosting networking seminars for the states' executive branch officials. The NGA is a powerful lobbying group in Washington, D.C.

Neutral competence: The idea that officials in the executive branch should make decisions based on their expertise and skill rather than political or ideological considerations. Merit systems are expected to produce neutral competence, unlike spoils systems, which produce political decisionmaking.

Open primary: A type of primary in which voters can typically choose on primary day which party's primary they wish to participate in. In some open-primary states, voters must publicly state which primary they wish to participate in; in other open-primary states, voters receive both ballots and privately choose which primary to take part in.

Open-seat race: A race in which no incumbent is running. Since incumbents are difficult to defeat, those who aspire to public office often wait for an open-seat race so that they have a better chance of winning. Such races, therefore, tend to attract numerous, high-quality candidates. They also tend to result in high levels of campaign spending.

Package veto: The basic veto that all governors possess. This veto allows the governor to strike a piece of legislation in its entirety. It can be overridden by a vote in both houses of the state legislature.

Pardon power: The authority possessed by some governors to overturn convictions, thereby pardoning those convicted of a crime. The pardon power, or clemency, may give the governors the power to release people from prison, stay their executions, or otherwise lessen their sentences. Advocates for this power view it as a check on miscarriages of justice that sometimes happen in the courts.

Parole: The early release of prisoners, before they have served their complete sentences. Governors often participate in the process of granting parole. Parole is sometimes controversial, as it as seen by some as treating prisoners too leniently. However, prisons in many states are badly overcrowded, and paroling some prisoners is necessary to make room for new prisoners.

Partisanship: Acting in the interest of one's political party. Governors who are steadfast in supporting the position of their own party and unwilling to compromise with the other party are said to be acting in a partisan manner. Such behavior is typically viewed in a negative light, as the governors seem stubborn and unwilling to work with others. However, partisanship can also be viewed positively as standing by one's principles.

Party machine: A tightly disciplined party organization held together and motivated by a desire for tangible benefits rather than by principle or ideology. The party machine is most often associated with major U.S. cities in the nineteenth century. Party bosses involved with these machines sometimes competed with governors for dominance in key parts of the states.

Patronage: The power of the political parties or elected officials to distribute government jobs to their political supporters. Patronage often resulted in having employees who were not well qualified for their jobs.

Pendleton Act: An act that established the civil service system of the national government, doing away with the spoils system that had filled government jobs by patronage.

Plural executive: A situation in many states where executive power is shared between multiple officials, such as the governor, lieutenant governor, secretary of state, attorney general, and treasurer, rather than being held exclusively by the governor. Advocates of the plural executive believe it gives the public a greater voice, since the voters often choose many of these officials. However, reformers assert that governors in a plural executive are hamstrung by having to share their power with so many other officials, some or all of whom may not be loyal to the chief executive.

Pocket veto: A passive means of vetoing bills that allows the governor in a few states to reject a bill by refusing to sign it after the legislature has adjourned. Pocket vetoes typically cannot be overridden by the legislature, since that body has already adjourned.

Policy process: The long and complicated set of procedures employed by the states to make law. It includes five stages: agenda setting, policy formulation, adoption, implementation, and evaluation. Multiple actors, both inside and outside government, participate at each stage.

Political action committee (PAC):   The financial arm of an interest group. Groups typically must form PACs in order to give money to political campaigns.

Politics-administration dichotomy: The idea that the administration or implementation of law should be above politics: the carrying out of law should be done in a neutral fashion by professionals with skill and expertise who are not swayed by political goals.

Popularity: Measured by public opinion polls, popularity is considered one of the informal powers of the office of governor, since a more popular governor is believed to be better able to convince the legislature to support his or her initiatives.

Primary: A method of giving a political party's voters the power to choose the party's nominee for political office. Unlike earlier methods, which allowed party elites to choose candidates, primaries permit voters to go to the polls to choose among candidates seeking the party's designation on the general election ballot.

Privatization: A means of providing certain state services by contracting with private or nonprofit organizations for delivery of those services.

Progressive reform movement: A reform effort in the United States in the early 1900s that focused on encouraging citizen participation and ending corruption and the power of party bosses. Progressives hoped to reduce the influence of wealth in American government and redistribute economic, social, and political power and benefits.

Recall election: A procedure available to voters in some states to remove a public official before the end of his or her term. The details of the process vary across the states but generally require that advocates for a recall gather a certain number of signatures requesting the recall election. Then, an election is held in which voters decide whether to remove (recall) the official or retain him or her in office. If the official is removed, he or she is replaced either by the voters on the same ballot, by a replacement election held at a later date, or by appointment by the governor.

Reinventing government: A set of governmental reform ideas promoting a more competitive form of government in which governments decide what services should be provided and how they should be funded. Under this strategy, governments do not necessarily provide those services. Instead, they might draw on private entities for service delivery. Such reforms are thought to make government more cost effective and provide better-quality services.

Reorganization: A process of rearranging divisions of the bureaucracy, usually into fewer agencies so that the governor has greater power to manage the bureaucracy.

Representative bureaucracy: The idea that employees of the executive branch should reflect, by race and gender, the diversity of the citizens they represent.

Retrospective voting: A means of deciding how to vote based on an assessment of how a candidate (or a party) has performed in the past. If the voter feels the incumbent governor has done a good job, the idea of retrospective voting would predict that the voter would vote for the incumbent.

Scientific management movement: A movement in the early 1900s that encouraged efficiency by identifying the "one best way" to perform specific tasks. Advocates ultimately advocated applying the principles of this approach to organizations, arguing that using organizational principles of managerial efficiency would maximize profits. Others expanded the idea, asserting that reforming governmental organizational structures would produce more economical and efficient governments and help to overcome the power and corruption of party bosses.

Secretary of state: An official of the executive branch, typically elected by the public. The secretary of state often has high name recognition, since driver's licenses and election notices often bear his or her name. The secretary of state often oversees elections and the flow of public information in the states.

Separation of powers: In the national, state, and local governments of the United States, power is divided into three branches with separate but overlapping responsibilities. The legislative branch is chiefly responsible for making the laws, the executive for implementing or executing the laws, and the judiciary for interpreting the laws. This arrangement is designed to limit the power of each of the branches by causing them to jealously guard their areas of authority. It tends to result in greater difficulty in making governmental decisions and perhaps less efficiency, but it also means that government does not become too powerful and destructive to the freedoms of the citizenry.

Speaker of the house: The leader of the house of representatives. Though the job description varies across the states, the speaker often has the power to assign members to committees, refer bills to committees, and recognize members who wish to speak on the floor of the legislative chamber.

Special sessions: In many states, the legislature does not meet year-round. Special sessions may be called by the governor in most states (and sometimes by the legislature itself) to reconvene the legislature in order to address pressing problems. A governor typically uses special sessions to encourage the legislature to focus on policy priorities, though this sometimes backfires and results in outcomes the governor does not favor.

Spoils system: A method of filling government positions based on political considerations—to the victor go the spoils. Spoils systems have been largely replaced by merit systems in most states.

State courts: The branch of the state government charged with interpreting the laws of the state.

State of the state: A speech delivered by governors in which they outline their key legislative goals. Most governors are required by their state constitutions to make these addresses, which have the effect of giving the governors a legitimate role in state lawmaking and particularly in the agenda setting phase of the policy process.

Tenure potential: One of the elements of the formal powers index. It refers to the length of a governor's term and the opportunity to seek reelection. Longer tenure is believed to give the governor greater power, especially in the role of chief legislator.

Term limits: In the 1990s, a movement swept many states that set limits on the number of terms public officials, especially lawmakers, are allowed to serve. Most states have long set term limits for governors and some other elected statewide officials.

Treasurer: The state executive branch official who typically acts as custodian of state funds; his or her duties include collecting taxes, paying state employees, and managing the investment of state money.

Turnout: The number of people who cast their votes on election day. Turnout tends to be highest in presidential elections and lower for other offices down the ballot. Some states traditionally have higher turnouts, while others typically see lower percentages of people voting. Turnout is affected by laws such as registration rules, by party attachment, and by short-term factors such as how close a race appears to be.

Unfunded mandates: Laws that are passed by the U.S. Congress requiring the states to provide a service but that do not provide funding to pay for it. These are supposedly outlawed by federal law, but the difficulty of enforcing this law means that unfunded mandates still occur.

Unicameral legislature: A legislative body that is made up of only one chamber. Unlike the other forty-nine legislatures, Nebraska's legislature is made up of a single chamber, the senate.

Unified government: Unified party control, the situation that occurs when the same party holds the governor's office and a majority of the seats in both chambers of the legislature.

Urban sprawl: The growth of a metropolitan area, particularly when that growth appears uncontrolled. Many states have taken steps to manage growth so that sprawl is reined in, but such moves are difficult because business leaders often see sprawl as a sign of positive economic growth.

Veto: The ability of a governor to reject legislation presented by the legislature. In some states, the governor must accept or reject an entire piece of legislation; in others, governors have the ability to reject portions of a bill while accepting the rest.

Voter registration: All states, empowered under the U.S. Constitution to manage elections, require voters to take the initiative to register to vote. In the past, registration rules were designed to limit participation by making registration cumbersome. The burdens were greatest for the poor and minorities, especially African Americans. Today, most states have made registration easier. All have shortened the residency requirements to thirty days or less in response to U.S. Supreme Court decisions. Some states allow mail-in registration, some allow election day registration, and all allow registration at the bureau of motor vehicles and welfare agencies due to passage of the federal Motor Voter bill. Voting advocates believe that burdensome registration requirements are one reason for the relatively low turnout in American elections.

Washington offices: Given the need to lobby the national government, many governors have established offices in Washington, D.C. Such offices monitor the activities of the federal government, both the Congress and the executive branch, and attempt to influence decision making in the interests of the state government.

ANNOTATED BIBLIOGRAPHY

BIOGRAPHIES

Bridges, Tyler. 2002. *Bad Bet on the Bayou: The Rise of Gambling in Louisiana and the Fall of Governor Edwin Edwards.* New York: Farrar, Straus and Giroux.

Written by a newspaper reporter, this book examines the introduction of gambling in Louisiana and the corruption that came with it, ultimately resulting in the indictment and conviction of Governor Edwards.

Cannon, Lou. 2003. *Governor Reagan: His Rise to Power.* New York: Public Affairs.

An examination of the gubernatorial administrations of Ronald Reagan and his policy successes, such as reforming welfare in California.

Carter, Dan T. 2000. *The Politics of Rage: George Wallace, the Origins of the New Conservatism and the Transformation of American Politics.* Baton Rouge: Louisiana University Press.

A well-regarded biography of Alabama governor George Wallace that emphasizes the influence of his political ideas on Republicans in the decades after his term in office.

Maginnis, John. 1985. *The Last Hayride.* Baton Rouge, LA: Gris Gris.

A lively biography of controversial Louisiana governor Edwin Edwards.

Warren, Robert Penn. 1946. *All the King's Men.* Orlando, FL: Harvest Books, Harcourt Brace.

A fictional account of Huey Long's rule as Louisiana governor.

BUDGETING

Clynch, Edward J., and Thomas P. Lauth. 1991. *Governors, Legislatures and Budgets.* New York: Greenwood.

In addition to an overview of the process of budgeting in the states, this volume includes chapters on the budget process in thirteen states and offers important insights into the varied and complex realm of budgeting in state governments.

Forsythe, Dall W. 1997. *Memos to the Governor: An Introduction to State Budgeting.* Washington, DC: Georgetown University Press.

An introduction to the state budget process written in the form of memos to the governor.

THE BUREAUCRACY

Buck, A. E. 1938. *The Reorganization of State Governments in the United States.* New York: Columbia University Press.

An early but very thorough examination of the development of the executive branch in the states.

Wright, Deil. 1967. "Executive Leadership in State Administration: Interplay of Gubernatorial, Legislative and Administrative Power." *Midwest Journal of Political Science* 11:1–26.

A seminal article on how state executive branch officials view the executive branch. This article draws on data from the American State Administrators Project, which has continued to gather survey data twice a decade. The most recent data collection took place in 2004. The surveys across the years are highly consistent, so comparisons across nearly fifty years can be drawn.

ELECTIONS

Carsey, Thomas. 2000. *Campaign Dynamics: The Race for Governor.* Ann Arbor: University of Michigan Press.

An excellent examination of how the issues raised by campaigns influence vote choice.

Morehouse, Sarah McCally. 1998. *The Governor as Party Leader: Campaigning for Governor.* Ann Arbor: University of Michigan Press.

Written by one of the most distinguished state politics scholars, this book explores the roles played by governors as campaigners and as policy leaders.

Formal Powers

Schlesinger, Joseph A. 1965. "The Politics of the Executive." In *Politics in the American States.* Henry Jacob and Kenneth N. Vines, eds. Boston: Little, Brown.

Schlesinger created the formal index of gubernatorial powers that has been employed (in somewhat modified forms) since the 1960s to characterize and compare the institutional powers of the governors.

Governors: General

Andrisani, Paul J., Simon Hakim, and Eva Leeds. 2000. *Making Government Work: Lessons from America's Governors and Mayors.* Lanham, MD: Rowman and Littlefield.

A bipartisan collection of American governors and mayors discuss how they work to make government more efficient and effective.

Beyle, Thad. 1992. "New Governors in Hard Economic and Political Times." In *Governors and Hard Times.* Thad Beyle, ed. Washington, DC: Congressional Quarterly Press.

An edited volume including chapters on ten governors experiencing difficult leadership challenges, with insights on how they went about addressing them. This volume also includes a chapter that presents a very useful framework for understanding gubernatorial behavior.

Beyle, Thad, and Lynn Muchmore. 1983. *Being Governor: The View from the Office.* Durham, NC: Duke Policy Studies Press.

This volume makes use of extensive surveys of current and former governors to explain the governorship from the perspective of those holding the office.

Council of State Governments. 2004. *The Book of the States,* vol. 30. Lexington, KY: Council of State Governments.

This reference work, published regularly by the Council of State Governments, presents a wealth of information about every aspect of state government. It includes a great deal of data about the governor and the executive branch. Comparing across multiple years is rather easy, since the volumes typically present similar types of content. This book is also published in CD-ROM form.

Gray, Virginia, and Russell L. Hanson, eds. 2004. *Politics in the American States: A Comparative Analysis,* 8th ed. Boston: Little, Brown.

This book comes out in frequent new editions and includes good introductory chapters on each of the key features of state government, including actors both inside and outside government. Examining multiple editions also offers an opportunity to look at the changes that have occurred over time, as each volume covers essentially the same topics.

Hamilton, Gary C., and Nicole Woolsey Biggart. 1984. *Governor Reagan, Governor Brown: A Sociology of Executive Power.* New York: Columbia University Press.

Written by two sociologists, this work presents an examination of the success and leadership style of two California governors.

Hedge, David M. 1998. *Governance and the Changing American States.* Boulder, CO: Westview.

An examination of the changing political and institutional features of state government and how these changes are improving governance in the states.

Herzik, Eric, and Brent Brown. 1991. *Gubernatorial Leadership and State Policy.* New York: Greenwood.

An edited volume including chapters from key state politics researchers examining the role of the governor in the states in general as well as in specific areas of decision making.

Keating, Cathy. 1997. *Our Governors' Mansions.* New York: Harry N. Abrams.

Architectural and historical consideration of the governors' residences in all fifty states.

Marshall, Brenda DeVore, and Molly A. Mayhead, eds. 2000. *Navigating Boundaries: The Rhetoric of Women Governors.* Westport, CT: Praeger.

This edited volume examines the rhetoric of female governors and finds that the introduction of women into the governor's office has had a significant influence on the political landscape of the states.

Masztal, Jaci Jarrett, and Diane M. Salamon. 2002. *Journey to the Top: Life Stories and Insights from Fifty Governors.* Tucson, AZ: Hats Off.

This book presents the life stories of fifty governors, describing their challenges and the goals that led them to the highest office in state government.

Neustadt, Richard. 1980. *Presidential Power: The Politics of Leadership from FDR to Carter.* New York: Wiley.

Though this volume addresses presidential power, rather than the power of governors, it is among the most important examinations of executive power. Neustadt argues that executive power in the United States requires persuasion and bargaining rather than dictating outcomes. The argument is very relevant to understanding the power of American governors.

Rosenthal, Alan. 1990. *Governors and Legislatures: Contending Powers.* Washington, DC: Congressional Quarterly Press.

Rosenthal, a prominent observer of state politics (especially legislatures), examines the interactions between the governors and their legislatures, highlighting the sources of conflict and the possibilities for working in concert.

Sabato, Larry. 1983. *Goodbye to Good-time Charlie,* 2nd ed. Washington, DC: Congressional Quarterly Press.

Using demographic and professional data on the governors, Sabato makes the case that modern governors are finally truly worthy of the title.

Sanford, Terry. 1967. *Storm over the States.* New York: McGraw-Hill.

A book about the governorship by a former governor and member of Congress. Though it was written many years ago, the insights continue to be relevant today.

Van Assendelft, Laura A. 1997. *Governors, Agenda Setting, and Divided Government.* Lanham, MD: University Press of America.

Unlike most studies of divided government, this work examines the effects of partisan divisions during the earliest phase of lawmaking, setting the state political agenda.

GOVERNORS: HISTORY

Lipson, Leslie. 1939. *The American Governor from Figurehead to Leader.* Chicago: University of Chicago Press.

In this book, among the earliest systematic studies of the governorship, Lipson points to improvements that were taking place in the office as early as the 1930s.

Ransone, Coleman B. 1956. *The Office of Governor in the United States.* Tuscaloosa: University of Alabama Press.
———. 1985. *The American Governorship.* Westport, CT: Greenwood.

Ransone is among the earliest and most respected scholars of the office of governor. The first volume presents an exhaustive examination of the office of the governor at mid-century; the second returns to the subject and explains the changes that occurred in the interim.

Schlesinger, Joseph A. 1966. *Ambition and Politics: Political Careers in the United States.* Chicago: Rand McNally.

This is the seminal work examining the paths that governors follow before reaching the governorship.

STATE POLITICS

Bowman, Ann O'M., and Richard C. Kearney. 1986. *The Resurgence of the States.* Englewood Cliffs, NJ: Prentice-Hall.

A solid assessment of the improved capacity of state government in the 1980s, includes a chapter on the executive branch.

Gray, Virginia, and Russell L. Hanson, eds. 2004. *Politics in the American States: A Comparative Analysis,* 8th ed. Boston: Little, Brown.

Please see description under "Governors: General."

Van Horn, Carl E., ed. 1996. *The State of the States,* 3rd ed. Washington, DC: Congressional Quarterly Press.

An edited volume including a chapter on the governor as well as other important topics of state politics.

Weber, Ron E., and Paul Brace, eds. 1999. *American State and Local Politics: Directions for the 21st Century.* New York: Chatham House.

A solid text on state and local politics, this book presents a good overview of information on many topics as well as on the research in the field. The editors and the authors of each chapter are all prominent researchers in the fields on which they write.

USEFUL WEBSITES

Democratic Governors' Association: http://www.democraticgovernors.org/
Governing Magazine: http://www.governing.com/
National Association of Attorneys General: http://www.naag.org/
National Association of Secretaries of State: http://www.nass.org/sos/duties_survey/
National Association of State Auditors, Comptrollers, and Treasurers:
    http://www.nasact.org/
National Association of State Budget Officers: http://www.nasbo.org/
National Association of State Treasurers: http://www.nast.net/
National Conference of State Legislatures: http://www.ncsl.org/
National Governors Association: http://www.nga.org/
National Lieutenant Governors Association: http://www.nlga.us/
Republican Governors Association: http://www.rga.org/
Southern Governors Association: http://www.southerngovernors.org/
Stateline Online Magazine: http://www.stateline.org/live/ViewPage.action
Western Governors' Association: http://www.westgov.org/

INDEX